A History of Psychology

About the Editor

Ludy T. Benjamin, Jr., is Professor of Psychology and Presidential Professor of Teaching Excellence at Texas A&M University, where he teaches graduate and undergraduate courses in the history of psychology. His published works include 21 books and more than 150 journal articles and book chapters. His historical research has included works on popular psychology and psychology's public image; the development of the first American psychology laboratories; applied psychology, including educational, clinical, and industrial-organizational psychology; the psychology of women; and the early organizations of American psychologists. His recent books on the history of psychology include *From Séance to Science: A History of the Profession of Psychology in America* (2004, with David Baker), *A History of Psychology in Letters* (2nd edn. 2006, Wiley-Blackwell), and *A Brief History of Modern Psychology* (2007, Wiley-Blackwell).

Benjamin was elected a Fellow of the American Psychological Association (APA) in 1981 and has served as president of two of APA's divisions, including the Division on the History of Psychology and the Division on the Teaching of Psychology. He serves as a member of the Board of Advisors of the Archives of the History of American Psychology.

In 1986 Benjamin received the prestigious Distinguished Teaching Award from the American Psychological Foundation, and in 2001 he was awarded the Distinguished Contributions to Education and Training Award from the American Psychological Association. In 2007 he received the Lifetime Achievement Award for his research on the history of psychology from the Society for the History of Psychology of the American Psychological Association. He is author and editor of several books on teaching psychology, including a book on teaching the history of psychology. Benjamin's interest in the history of psychology grows from a broader interest in American and world history, and he admits that much of his reading for pleasure is on historical subjects. When not engaged as a professor of psychology he enjoys traveling, baseball, theater, and fishing.

A History of Psychology
Original Sources and
Contemporary Research

Third Edition

Edited by
Ludy T. Benjamin, Jr.

BLACKWELL PUBLISHING
350 Main Street, Malden, MA 02148-5020, USA
9600 Garsington Road, Oxford OX4 2DQ, UK
550 Swanston Street, Carlton, Victoria 3053, Australia

The right of Ludy T. Benjamin, Jr. to be identified as the author of the editorial material in this work has been asserted in accordance with the UK Copyright, Designs, and Patents Act 1988.

Designations used by companies to distinguish their products are often claimed as trademarks. All brand names and product names used in this book are trade names, service marks, trademarks, or registered trademarks of their respective owners. The publisher is not associated with any product or vendor mentioned in this book.

This publication is designed to provide accurate and authoritative information in regard to the subject matter covered. It is sold on the understanding that the publisher is not engaged in rendering professional services. If professional advice or other expert assistance is required, the services of a competent professional should be sought.

First published 2009 by Blackwell Publishing Ltd

1   2009

Library of Congress Cataloging-in-Publication Data

A History of psychology : original sources and contemporary research / edited by Ludy T. Benjamin. – 3rd ed.
      p. cm.
   Includes bibliographical references and index.
      ISBN 978-1-4051-7711-5 (hardcover : alk. paper) – ISBN 978-1-4051-7710-8 (pbk : alk. paper)   1. Psychology–History.   I. Benjamin, Ludy T., 1945–

BF81.H58 2008
150.9–dc22

                                                                2008004441

A catalogue record for this title is available from the British Library.

Set in 9.5 on 11.5 pt Minion
by SNP Best-set Typesetter Ltd., Hong Kong
Printed and bound in Singapore
by Markono Print Media Pte Ltd.

The publisher's policy is to use permanent paper from mills that operate a sustainable forestry policy, and which has been manufactured from pulp processed using acid-free and elementary chlorine-free practices. Furthermore, the publisher ensures that the text paper and cover board used have met acceptable environmental accreditation standards.

For further information on
Blackwell Publishing, visit our website at
www.blackwellpublishing.com

This book is dedicated to the memory of

J. Gilbert McAllister
1904–1983

*who taught his students many things,
especially the importance of thinking for themselves*

Brief Contents

Contents

Preface

This book is a reader in the history of psychology that covers the field from John Locke and the beginnings of modern science through the cognitive psychology of the 1960s. It is unlike any other reader treating the history of psychology in that it combines primary and secondary sources. In this book, primary sources are original material written by the people whose work is the subject matter of a history of psychology course, individuals such as Locke, Mill, Broca, Wundt, James, Titchener, Freud, Watson, Skinner, and Leta Hollingworth. Works by each of those individuals and by others – a total of 20 primary selections – are included in this book. Secondary sources are the articles and books written by historians of psychology and others about the individuals and ideas that are the primary sources. In short, primary source material was written by historical figures such as Freud or James, whereas secondary source material was written about such primary work. There are 24 secondary source articles included in this reader.

The idea for this book grew out of my own classes in the history of psychology, both undergraduate and graduate, which I have been teaching for more than 35 years. Like most faculty, I have used a textbook in teaching those courses because of the integration provided by such books. However, I have two important goals for my classes that cannot be met by the standard textbooks. First, I want my students to read some of the actual primary sources that make up the historical works of psychology. I want them to know what Wundt said and how he said it. It is not enough that they read *about* the marvelous way William James had with words; I want them to read James. Second, I want my students to understand that the history of psychology is an active research specialty in psychology, that the information they are reading in their textbook is the result of some historian's painstaking efforts to reconstruct the past, and that those efforts go on every day. They will not learn that by reading about the work of Michael Sokal or Gail Hornstein or Franz Samelson or Katharine Milar in their textbook; they need to read the actual words of those historians.

Those two goals represent the principal rationale for this book, that is, a collection of both primary source literature in the history of psychology and historical research in psychology done within the past 30 years. There are, however, other objectives that

I wish to accomplish with this book. These objectives can best be introduced historically by reviewing the development of the research specialty of the history of psychology.

History of psychology as a research specialty has been around only for a little more than 40 years, dating to around 1965. That year is especially important because it marks the beginning of the American Psychological Association's Division on the History of Psychology (Division 26, now incorporated as the Society for the History of Psychology); the founding of the Archives of the History of American Psychology at the University of Akron, now the largest assemblage of manuscript collections in psychology in the world; and the establishment of the *Journal of the History of the Behavioral Sciences*, the first journal devoted largely to research in the history of psychology, as well as other fields in the social sciences. With the special interest group, the increased archival collections, and the journal has come improved historical scholarship, showing a sophistication not common prior to 1960. Since the establishment of the first history of psychology journal in 1965, other English-language journals have been founded as well. Furthermore, the history of psychology as a research specialty has been growing internationally, with journals and specialty societies having been founded in many countries including, for example, Canada, the United Kingdom, Italy, Spain, Germany, Japan, China, and Colombia.

Another principal goal of this book is to make the reader aware of the issues one deals with in doing historical research, the sources available for this research, and the techniques historians of psychology use to research and write their histories. This goal is partially accomplished in the opening chapter on *historiography*, meaning the philosophies and methods of doing history. Knowing something about how historians do their work should enhance the understanding and enjoyment of the secondary source articles in this book. Moreover, the historiography lessons introduced in the first chapter are reinforced throughout the book in the introductions to each chapter and especially in the secondary source articles themselves.

Another objective of the book is to provide some coverage, where possible, of material that is often omitted from the standard history of psychology textbooks, or at least not covered in much depth. Most noteworthy in this regard are the two chapters that treat the growth of applied psychology and the development of clinical psychology as the chief professional specialty in American psychology (Chapters 6 and 9), and the chapter on the psychology of race and gender (Chapter 10).

The final objective of this book, and one of the most important, was to assemble some of the most significant literature in the history of psychology. Thus the primary source readings are taken, for example, from Locke's *Essay Concerning Human Understanding* (1690), Mill's *A System of Logic* (1843), James's *Principles of Psychology* (1890), Witmer's founding article on clinical psychology (1907), Freud's first lecture at the Clark conference (1909), Watson's behaviorist manifesto (1913), Bartlett's *Remembering* (1932), Skinner's *Behavior of Organisms* (1938), and the social science brief (1952) written by Kenneth B. Clark and others for the Supreme Court in the *Brown v. Board* decision. These selections are lengthy enough that the reader should get a good flavor of the style and substance of the work. Further, the secondary source articles are selected to represent some of the most important historical scholarship in the field. These studies have radically changed our views, for example, of Wundt's psychology, of the development of psychoanalysis, and of the evolution of behaviorism.

Each chapter (other than the opening chapter) contains both primary source readings and readings from contemporary historians of psychology. The primary source readings were selected, as noted above, for their importance to the evolution of psychology. The secondary source readings were selected, in part, because of the quality of the historical work, but also because of the story they tell when integrated with the primary source material. For example, in the chapter on psychoanalysis the primary source reading is by Freud and is the first of the lectures he gave in 1909 on his only visit to America. The other two readings in that chapter are by contemporary historians who tell the story of that historic visit and its impact on Freud, American psychology, and the spread of psychoanalytic ideas in America. The chapter on behaviorism pairs John Watson's behaviorist manifesto with an article by historian and psychologist Franz Samelson that examines the subsequent reaction in American psychology to Watson's call to arms. In another example, the readings in the chapter on Wundt open with an excerpt from his textbook describing what can be perceived as a mental chemistry approach to psychology. That is followed by two contemporary readings that argue differently about the influence of a chemistry model in Wundt's psychology. The introductory material in each chapter is written to provide the vocabulary and the context needed to understand the readings in that chapter.

This book is intended for use in history of psychology classes at the upper undergraduate and graduate levels. It is designed to be used as a supplement to one of the existing textbooks in the history of psychology and is broad enough in its coverage so that it can be used with any of a number of leading textbooks. In this third edition, I have matched the chapter organization of this reader to my own textbook, *A Brief History of Modern Psychology* (Benjamin, 2007). It is possible to use this book without an accompanying textbook. Nevertheless, I remind the instructor that this book is conceived and designed as a supplement.

New to the Third Edition

This third edition of the book is shorter than the previous two. Instead of 16 chapters, there are 11. The reduction was intended to produce a volume more appropriately sized to fit with a textbook. The initial chapter on historiography has been retained and slightly revised. Thus the readings occupy 10 chapters. Starting with Chapter 2, each chapter begins with an introduction that provides a historical context for the selections included in that chapter, and some information about the importance of the selections for the topic at hand. These introductions are not meant to be comprehensive historical treatments of the subject. Rather, they are intended to provide minimal coverage of vocabulary and context that sets the stage for the reader being able to appreciate the content and importance of the readings.

Approximately half of the selections are adapted in some way, and that is especially true of the primary source material because a number of those selections are excerpts from books. The source note for each selection indicates whether it has been reprinted in full or adapted. In some selections where portions have been omitted, the footnotes in the remaining portions have been renumbered for clarity. The numbers for those footnotes have been placed in parentheses indicating their renumbering.

Of the 44 readings in this book, exactly half are new to this edition. Those changes are due, principally, to two factors: the continued high quality of scholarship in the history of psychology, which has added a number of important articles and books to the field since the second edition was compiled 11 years ago, and feedback from my own students and from other instructors using the second edition of this book about which selections proved troublesome or less useful. Changes in this new edition have resulted in a more readable set of selections, a better-integrated set of readings in each chapter, better coverage of applied psychology and professional psychology, better coverage of the psychology of race and gender, and new coverage of cognitive psychology.

Acknowledgments

The organization of topics in this book and the selection of some of the readings have benefited from the capable advice of my colleagues in the history of psychology and from my students. I want to acknowledge the very helpful assistance of David Baker, Wolfgang Bringmann, Darryl Bruce, William Bryant, Donald Dewsbury, Raymond Fancher, William Hillix, Deborah Johnson, Alfred Kornfeld, David Leary, Katharine Milar, Alfred Raphelson, Elizabeth Scarborough, Stephanie Shields, Michael Sokal, Arlene Stillwell, and George Windholz in reviewing drafts of the previous editions and/or the new edition. Because I have not always followed the advice of these scholars, they cannot be held responsible for any faults in the final product. I am certain, however, that this book is significantly better because of their counsel.

At Blackwell I owe a great debt to the psychology team – production supervisor Jenny Philips and editorial assistants Kelly Basner and Sarah Coleman. Particularly I am grateful for the continued support of my editor Chris Cardone, who has championed my efforts for more than 20 years of collaboration.

Of course, I owe a very special debt to the many authors and publishers who have allowed me to reprint their work in this book.

As always I owe a debt of thanks to my wife, Priscilla Benjamin, for her help in a variety of assignments associated with the writing and production of this book.

Finally, I want to thank the many students from my history of psychology classes whose enthusiasm for the subject has made this project, and my involvement in the field, a labor of love. This new edition is significantly improved because of the many helpful suggestions they provided. I hope that this new collection of readings will both instruct and inspire other students with the fascination and intrigue that are part of psychology's history.

Ludy T. Benjamin, Jr.

Chapter 1

Historiography – Asking and Answering Historical Questions

Who would want to read a chapter about historiography? What a strange word! And when was the last time you heard anyone use it in a sentence?

We begin this book with a discussion of historiography because an understanding of it is critical to an understanding and greater enjoyment of history. Here is why. *History is not what happened in the past. It is what historians tell us happened in the past.* Thus to evaluate the history that you read, you need to know something about how historians do their work, that is, about how they do their research and the written accounts that follow from that research.

You can enjoy listening to music with no knowledge of music theory, but knowing something about music theory can add much richness to your appreciation of music. You can gaze into the Grand Canyon and marvel at this incredible sight carved by the Colorado River, but your appreciation for its structure and spectacular beauty can be magnified by even an elementary understanding of geology. In the same way, your understanding of history will be enhanced when you have some appreciation for the philosophies and methods that underlie historical research. Those philosophies and research methods are the defining elements of *historiography*.

History of Psychology as a Research Specialty

As noted in the preface to this book, the history of psychology as a research specialty is a little more than 40 years old. In those 40 years, history of psychology interest groups have formed, such as Division 26 of the American Psychological Association, a group of psychologists interested in the history of their field, and Cheiron – The International Society for the History of the Behavioral and Social Sciences – a group of historians, including psychologist-historians, of the social and behavioral sciences. Cheiron has a European counterpart that is one of a number of such organizations to emerge abroad in the past 30 years, including history of psychology societies in Spain, Italy, Germany, and Japan.

As a venue for publishing the new scholarship in the history of psychology, specialty journals have been created in the past 40 years, such as the *Journal of the History of the*

Behavioral Sciences (founded in 1965) and *History of Psychology* (begun in 1997), both of which are published in North America. Similar journals can be found in Spain, Italy, England, and Germany. Historians of psychology also publish their work in a variety of historical journals of longer standing such as *Isis* (the quarterly publication of the History of Science Society), the *Journal of the History of Ideas*, and the *American Historical Review*, as well as in related area journals such as the *History of Psychiatry*, *History of the Human Sciences*, *Journal of the History of the Neurosciences*, and the *Bulletin of the History of Medicine*.

Graduate programs have been established to train students in the theory, methods, and content of the history of psychology. The best known of these programs in North America are located at York University in Canada and the University of New Hampshire. Other traditional programs in the history of science, for example, at Indiana University, Harvard University, and the universities of Chicago and Pennsylvania, also train doctoral students who specialize in the history of behavioral sciences.

Archival sources in psychology have grown enormously, led by the Archives of the History of American Psychology, the single largest collection of unpublished materials in psychology in the world, located at the University of Akron in Ohio (see Benjamin, 1980; Popplestone & McPherson, 1976). Historians of psychology make extensive use of archival collections all over the world today. And as interest in the history of psychology has grown, so too has interest in preserving the documents and manuscript collections of psychologists and psychological organizations. Today the manuscript collections of individual psychologists are more frequently being systematically preserved, as are the collections of organizations such as the American Psychological Association (whose archives are in the Library of Congress and at the APA Building in Washington, DC) and the Psychonomic Society and the Association for Psychological Science (whose archives are in the collections at Akron).

With the formation of special groups drawing individuals together with common research interests, the establishment of new journal outlets to publish their research, the formation of new doctoral programs to train students in the new research specialty, and the rapid growth of archival collections providing a rich database for the new research, the history of psychology has emerged as a recognized research specialty in the fields of psychology and the history of science. It is a research field that has been created jointly by psychologists shifting from their original fields of training (for example, cognition, development, personality) to historical research, and by historians of science shifting to psychology from the more traditional research areas of natural sciences and medicine.

Psychology's Interest in its History

As a field, psychology has a long-standing interest in its history. History of psychology courses have been taught since the 1920s and today such courses are commonly part of the undergraduate and graduate curricula in psychology. Indeed, the history of psychology course is frequently a required course for psychology majors and for doctoral students as well. For example, the American Psychological Association requires all graduates of accredited doctoral programs in professional psychology to have had some instruction in the history of psychology. So why are psychologists so interested in their own history? Such interest does not appear to be nearly so active in the other sciences.

In trying to answer this question, consider the following quotations from two eminent British historians. One, Robin Collingwood (1946), wrote that the "proper object of historical study . . . is the human mind, or more properly the activities of the human mind" (p. 215). And the other, Edward H. Carr (1961), proposed that "the historian is not really interested in the unique, but what is general in the unique" and that "the study of history is a study of causes . . . the historian . . . continuously asks the question: Why?" (pp. 80, 113). Thus, according to these historians, to study history is to study the human mind, to be able to generalize beyond the characteristics of a single individual or single event to other individuals and other events, and to be able to answer the "why" of human behavior in terms of motivation, personality, past experience, expectations, and so forth. Historians are not satisfied, for example, with a mere description of the events of May 4, 1970, in which National Guard troops killed four unarmed students on a college campus in Ohio. Description is useful, but it is not the scholarly end-product that is sought. By itself, description is unlikely to answer the questions that historians want to answer. They want to understand an event, like the shootings at Kent State University, so completely that they can explain *why* it happened.

Collingwood (1946) has described history as "the science of human nature" (p. 206). In defining history in that way, Collingwood has usurped psychology's definition for itself. History is not a science in the sense that almost all sciences are experimental. Historians do not do experimental work (except on rare occasions), but they are engaged in empirical work. And they approach their questions in much the same way that psychologists do, by generating hypotheses and then seeking evidence that will confirm or disconfirm those hypotheses. Thus the intellectual pursuits of the historian and the psychologist are not really very different. And so, as psychologists or students of psychology, we are not moving very far from our own field of interest when we study the history of psychology.

In this book you will be reading selections from the scholarly works of the individuals working as historians of psychology today. Among other things, you will learn why James McKeen Cattell's intelligence tests failed, why Watsonian behaviorism was not the immediate revolution that many histories have touted it to be, and why the incorporation of evolutionary theory into psychology was the impetus to the scientific study of claims about sex differences that promoted the belief in the biological inferiority of women. But it is important that you learn more than just what historians discovered in their research. You should also learn something about the nature of the questions they asked and the methods they used to answer their questions. These are issues of historiography, which is the principal subject of this chapter.

Historiography Defined

As noted earlier, historiography refers to the philosophy and methods of doing history. Psychology is certainly guided by underlying philosophies and a diversity of research methods. A behaviorist, for example, has certain assumptions about the influence of previous experience, in terms of a history of punishment and reinforcement, on current behavior. And the methods of study take those assumptions into account in the design and conduct of experiments. A psychoanalytic psychologist, on the other hand, has a very different philosophy and methodology in investigating the questions of interest, for example, believing in the influence of unconscious motives and using techniques such as free association or analysis of latent dream content to understand those motives. Historical research is guided in the same way. So in the same way that it helps you to understand psychology by knowing about the philosophies and methods that underlie psychological research, it will help you to understand history by knowing something about its philosophy and methods as well.

One of the principal questions in historiography is "What is history?" That question was mentioned earlier, but more will be said about it in the next section. In answering that question there are related questions to ponder as well, such as: What are historical facts, and who or what determines if a fact has historical significance? Is objectivity possible in history? What is the nature of historical inquiry, and what are the different goals of historians? Finally, what are the resources and methods of research that historians use? Each of these questions will be addressed in the discussion that follows. Concluding this chapter is a brief section on what has been called the "new history" of psychology. Such an introduction to historiography should help you evaluate more fully the content of this book and other histories that you may read.

What is History?

You have read that historians have defined their field variously as the study of the human mind, as the study of causes, as the study of behavior, and as the science of human nature, definitions that make history seem indistinguishable from psychology. Whereas these fields have many commonalities, they are not indistinguishable. As noted earlier, both use empirical methods to answer their respective questions. However, psychology, as a science, makes use of the experimental method. That means the psychologist can select variables for manipulation and then study the effects of that manipulation. The experiment is a powerful tool that allows the psychologist to determine cause-and-effect relationships. The historian is also interested in such relationships, but must infer them from a reconstruction of past events where all of the relevant variables have already been manipulated, in some cases centuries ago. Gilderhus (2007) has written: "For historians, the identification of cause-and-effect relationships establishes meaning and comprehensibility but can never be proven as literally true" (p. 6). History is not a science; however, as Commager (1965) notes, it is "clear that history uses or aspires to use the scientific method. That is, it tests all things which can be tested" (p. 12).

Psychologists typically study contemporary events (behaviors and mental processes), whereas historians study events of the distant past. Both might be interested in the same behavior, but the time frame and the methods are usually distinct. Psychologists are interested in marriage, for example, and they might study marriage using surveys, ex post facto methods, or quasi-experimental designs using a sample of married couples (or perhaps divorced couples). Historians, on the other hand, would be likely to look at marriage, for example, as an institution in Victorian England, and they would be unable to use any of the methods listed above as part of the arsenal of the psychologist. The questions on marriage that would interest psychologists and historians might be similar – how are mates selected in marriage, at what age do people marry, what roles do wives and husbands play in these marriages, what causes marriages to end? But again, the methods of research and the time frame for the events would be different.

History, then, is the branch of knowledge that attempts to analyze and explain events of the past. The explanatory product is a narrative of those events, a story. Henry Steele Commager (1965), one of America's most eminent historians, put it this way: "history is a story. That was its original character, and that has continued to be its most distinctive character. If history forgets or neglects to tell a story, it will inevitably forfeit much of its appeal and much of its authority as well" (p. 3). History is about telling stories, and about the search for information that allows those stories to be told with considerable accuracy (see Butterfield, 1981). And the building blocks for those stories are facts; they are the information historians seek to be able to tell their stories. Facts are not the whole story, but they are the foundation of all good history. Just what is a fact, and who or what determines which facts have historical significance?

Historical Facts and their Selectivity

In *Dragnet*, a popular television police drama of the 1950s and 1960s, Detective Joe Friday frequently reminded the witnesses he was interviewing that he was only interested in the facts – "Just the facts, Ma'am," he would say. Detective Friday, like most people, used the word "fact" to mean some kind of demonstrable truth, some real event whose occurrence cannot be disputed. Yet facts are more elusive, as evidenced in the typical dictionary definition which notes that a fact is information that is "presented" as objectively real. Historians present as fact, for example, that an atomic bomb was dropped on the Japanese city of Hiroshima on August 6, 1945. And because of detailed records of that event, as well as many eyewitness accounts, that fact seems indisputable. It is the kind of fact that Carr (1961) has called the "backbone" of history, facts on which virtually all historians would agree. But there are other kinds of facts.

In addition to the date of the bombing of Hiroshima, historians have also presented a number of facts relevant to the decision made by the United States government to drop that bomb. Not surprisingly, those facts are more debatable. Thus facts differ in terms of their certainty. Sometimes that is because evidence is incomplete and much inference has to be made, sometimes it is because evidence is contradictory, and sometimes it is because of bias introduced in the observation or in the interpretation of these events. Flawed though they may be, facts are the basis of history. It is the job of the historian to uncover these items of the past and to piece them together in an account that is as accurate as can be constructed.

Not all facts are created equal; a few are of great interest to historians, whereas most are considered to have no historical significance at all. Carr (1961) has expressed it this way: "It is the historian who has decided for his own reasons that Caesar's crossing of that petty stream, the Rubicon, is a fact of history, whereas the crossing of the Rubicon by millions of other people before or since interests nobody at all" (p. 9). He notes that the fact that you crossed the street yesterday is as much a fact as Caesar's crossing the Rubicon, but it is unlikely that anyone will consider your street-crossing as a historically significant fact. So who determines what historical facts are important? Sometimes monarchs do. Sometimes governments do. Sometimes cultures do. And many times historians do. Thus, historians are selective.

Historians determine which facts they will look for and which facts they will not search out. Of the facts they find, they decide which ones they will use and how they will use them. Consider what we know about ancient Greece in the fifth century B.C. Carr (1961) has argued that our picture of Greece in that time is:

> defective, not primarily because so many of the bits have been accidentally lost, but because it is, by and large, the picture formed by a tiny group of people in the city of Athens. We know a lot about what fifth-century Greece looked like to an Athenian citizen; but hardly anything about what it looked like to a Spartan, a Corinthian, or a Theban, not to mention a Persian, or a slave or other non-citizen resident in Athens. Our picture has been preselected and predetermined for us, not so much by accident as by people who were consciously or unconsciously imbued with a particular view and thought the facts which supported that view worth preserving. (p. 12)

Selectivity of facts is a part of contemporary history as well, and it is one of the factors inherent in the historian's concern with objectivity.

Objectivity in History

Psychology was a late arrival in the house of sciences. Partly that was because there were many who agreed with philosopher Auguste Comte that the mind was capable of observing all phenomena but its own. A science of the mind would require that the mind study itself, and philosophers like Comte wondered how that could be possible. Surely, they thought, psychology could not achieve the objectivity that is required of the other sciences. Whereas psychology is not without its share of subjectivity and bias, it has grown as a science, and its methodologies, particularly ways for controlling confounding variables, have matured in ways that have greatly increased objectivity. History too has had to face these issues.

Objectivity is a critical goal for the historian. It has been referred to as "that noble dream" and has functioned as the guiding force for history since professional historians arrived on the scene in the nineteenth century (Novick, 1988). Carr (1961) has argued that objectivity is indeed only a dream: "The emphasis on the role of the historian in the making of history tends, if pressed to its logical conclusion, to rule out any objective history at all: history is what the historian makes" (p. 29).

Like psychologists, historians are human too, and they bring to their task a bundle of prejudices, preconceptions, penchants, predispositions, premises, and predilections. Such baggage does not mean that they abandon their hope for objectivity, nor does it mean that their histories are hopelessly flawed. Good historians know their biases. They use their understanding of them to search for evidence in places where they might not otherwise look or to ask questions that they would not ordinarily ask. And when this searching and questioning causes them to confront facts contrary to their own views, they must deal with those facts as they would with facts that are more consistent with their biases.

Bias in history begins at the beginning: "The historian displays a bias through the mere choice of a subject" (Gilderhus, 2007, p. 80). There are an infinite number of historical subjects to pursue. The historian selects from among those, often selecting one of paramount personal interest. The search within that subject begins with a question or questions that the historian hopes to answer, and likely the historian starts with some definite ideas about the answers to those questions.

Bias is manifested in numerous other ways as well. Already noted are the selectivity of facts – a selection controlled to some degree by the historian – and the bias of nationalistic perspective illustrated by the Athenian view of Grecian history as opposed to that history as it might have been told by a Spartan.

Bias is evident too in the data of history. It can occur in primary source material, for example, census records or other government documents, even though such sources are often regarded as quite accurate. Yet such sources are inherently biased by the philosophies underlying the construction of the instruments themselves and the ways in which those instruments are used. Secondary sources too are flawed. Their errors occur in transcription, translation, selection, and interpretation.

Oral histories are filled with biases of the interviewer and the interviewee. Some questions are asked, others are not. Some are answered, and others avoided. And memories of events long past are often unreliable. Manuscript collections, the substance of modern archives, are selective and incomplete. They contain the documents that someone decided were worth saving, and they are devoid of those documents that were discarded or lost for a host of reasons, perhaps known only to the discarder.

Biases are indigenous to the historian's high art of interpretation. Some historians have based their interpretations of the past on the context of the present, an error called *presentism* or "Whig history" by Butterfield (1931) or "present-mindedness" by Commager (1965). Not only do presentists seek to interpret the past in terms of the attitudes and values of the present, but they seek to interpret the past in a way that emphasizes "certain principles of progress in the past and to produce a story which is the ratification if not the glorification of the present" (Butterfield, 1931, p. v). To avoid this error of interpretation calls for a different approach that Stocking (1965) has labeled *historicism*: an understanding of the past in its own context and for its own sake. Such an approach requires historians to immerse themselves in the context of the times they are studying.

These are just some of the hurdles that the historian faces in striving for objectivity. They are not described here to suggest that the historian's task is a hopeless one; instead, they are meant to show the forces against which historians must struggle in attempts at accuracy and objectivity. Daniels (1981) wrote: "The requirements of reasonable objectivity do not rule out individual interpretation and judgment . . . there is no final truth in matters of historical interpretation and explanation" (p. 92). There is only the expectation that the story will be as objective as is possible. Carr (1961) has characterized the striving for this ideal as follows:

> When we call a historian objective, we mean, I think, two things. First of all, we mean that he has the capacity to rise above the limited vision of his own situation in society and in history . . . Secondly, we mean that he has the capacity to project his vision into the future in such a way as to give him a more profound and lasting insight into the past than can be attained by those historians whose outlook is entirely bounded by their own immediate situation. (p. 163)

In summary, history is a product of selection and interpretation. Knowing that helps us understand why books are usually titled "A History" and not "The History." There are many histories of psychology, and it would be surprising to find any historians so arrogant to presume that their individual narratives constituted "*The* History of Psychology."

The Nature of Historical Inquiry

Historians are clearly interested in the past, and for them to do their work there must be some remnants of the past to be found. If no such traces exist, then there can be no history. History begins, as noted earlier, with the collecting of facts. These facts are then placed into some organized whole that allows for a description of the events in question. In this initial phase of historical research the historian is seeking to answer questions like "What happened?", "When did it happen?", and "Who was involved?" In the history of psychology we know that Wilhelm Wundt began laboratory research in psychology at the University of Leipzig in the 1870s. What was the nature of that laboratory? What was the space like? What kind of equipment did he have? Did students work with him in his research? What kind of studies were done in the lab? Who were the subjects (usually called observers) in these experiments? These questions are largely descriptive in nature and are typically where the historian would begin in piecing together the story of Wundt's psychology laboratory. As noted earlier, historians, however, want to go beyond description. They want to say more than just what happened and who was involved. They want to be able to say "why." Why did Wundt take up this new line of work at age 47? How did he get the financial support from the university for this new venture? Why were students attracted to this new field?

This second phase is the riskier part of historical inquiry, but it is essential for the telling of the story. Just as the psychologist wants to go beyond merely describing behavior to offering some explanation for why the behavior occurred, the historian has a similar goal. And like psychological explanations of behavior, historical explanations are riskier because they are more speculative. They often are based on assumptions that exceed the data and on rationales that may or may not be accurate. They draw on the biases discussed earlier, including the historian's underlying assumptions about human motives. The historian is placed in the role of interpreter, trying to make sense of the assembled facts. Hard work and persistence can uncover the facts, but higher skills are needed to excel in interpretation. The great historians, according to Commager (1965), have been the interpreters. And among those, the greatest have been those with exceptional "judgment, originality, imagination, and art" (p. 6). Historian Arthur Schlesinger, Jr. (1963) has argued that it is in interpretation that history as art is evidenced:

> all the elements of artistic form are as organic in historical as in any other kind of literary composition. There are limits on the historian's capacity for invention, but there need be none on his capacity for insight. Written history, after all, is the application of an aesthetic vision to a welter of facts; and both the weight and the vitality of a historical work depend on the quality of the vision. (p. 36)

It was noted earlier that history is about telling stories. Facts and a striving for accuracy of reconstruction of the past place limits on those stories. But history is a literary form, and in interpretation the literary art is manifested.

Gilderhus (2007) has argued that historical inquiry often proceeds to a third phase in which the historian evaluates the consequences of events. For example, ultimately the war between the United States and Iraq will be put to such historical judgments. Did things turn out well? Ultimately, who benefited from what happened? Would a better result have occurred if the events had happened at a different time or place, or maybe had never happened? Such evaluations, not surprisingly, have led to many disagreements among historians. Still, these evaluations are part of the intellectual and artistic goals of historical writing.

Contemporary Historical Research

Historical writing is said to have begun in the fifth century B.C. in the works of Herodotus and Thucydides. These earliest of historians sought to learn the facts of past events, albeit the recent past, that would allow them to render accounts of truth. They wrote of great wars, a subject that has remained a principal theme of many subsequent histories. Indeed, until the twentieth century much of the focus of history was on war and governments, that is, on events that were largely political in nature. Individuals, who were the subjects described in these histories, were kings and generals, individuals who were presumed to be historically important because of the ways in which their actions changed their world. Painters painted these same subjects, composers honored them in their ballads and symphonies, playwrights made them the subjects of the stage, and historians wrote books about them.

Today history is very different; both the subject matter of histories and the individuals portrayed in those histories are far more diverse than anything the early historians would have ever imagined. Historians today still write about the subjects of old, but they also write about common people, people who had no significant impact on a society, but whose common lives reveal something important about the nature of life in that society. In the same way that Pieter Bruegel (the elder) transformed painting in the sixteenth century from portraits of the rich and famous to paintings of the lives of ordinary people, historians of the twentieth century recognized that the standard historical accounts were incomplete. A change in historical philosophy emphasizing social history greatly broadened the definition of history's subject matter. Although much of contemporary historical writing is about politics, wars, and governments, it is also about peoples whose histories were often unreported, for example, women and African Americans, and about subjects that were rarely covered, such as art, marriage, agricultural methods, childrearing, and the care of the mentally ill.

One of the subjects of importance in twentieth-century history is the history of science. Although the typical survey courses in American history still give little attention to the history of science and the incredibly important role played by science and technology in shaping history in the past hundred years, the history of science scholarship is thriving. And the history of psychology and related behavioral sciences is an important part of the contemporary scene. As noted earlier, a number of the articles reprinted in the subsequent chapters of this book are indicative of today's scholarship in the history of psychology. As background for a better appreciation of those articles, the next two sections discuss the resources and research methods used by these historians.

Resources in History

The facts of history can be found in a multitude of places. They are in the books and articles written by historians and others. Those facts come pre-selected and pre-interpreted by the authors, a reality of using secondary sources as previously noted.

The primary sources, although closer to the events in question, are not without their biases. The primary source material ranges widely in kind and includes books, articles, government documents, business sales records, personal correspondence, patent records, taped or transcribed interviews, diaries, court documents, laboratory notes, patient records, association records, and school documents. And the locations too are many: archives, libraries, schools, corporations, small businesses, courthouses, newspaper files, attics, basements, and garages. In the course of a research project, the historian may search a number of these locations, looking at a variety of records. Let me give you an example from my own research, an investigation of the Coca-Cola court trials in the early 1900s that resulted from a federal government suit against Coca-Cola for marketing a beverage with a deleterious ingredient, namely caffeine (Benjamin, Rogers, & Rosenbaum, 1991). (This study is reprinted in Chapter 6 of this book.)

I was interested in this case because it marked one of the earliest instances of a psychologist being hired by a large corporation to do psychological research to be used in court. The case began when Harvey Wiley, a chemist and important administrator for the U.S. Department of Agriculture, directed federal agents to seize a shipment of Coca-Cola syrup as it crossed state lines from Georgia into Tennessee. The trial was scheduled to begin in the spring of 1911, and as the Coca-Cola Company prepared for its defense, it realized that it had no behavioral data on the effects of caffeine on humans. So it hired a recently graduated psychologist, Harry Hollingworth, to do that research. The case progressed through three trials, starting in Chattanooga, followed by another trial before the Appeals Court in Cincinnati, and finally in 1916 before the U.S. Supreme Court.

The search for the information needed to tell that story led to a number of places. The papers of Harry Hollingworth were found at the Archives of the History of American Psychology at the University of Akron in Ohio. Other relevant Hollingworth materials were found at the Nebraska State Historical Society in Lincoln, whose collection included a 600-page unpublished autobiography that Hollingworth had written in 1940. Harvey Wiley's papers were found at the Library of Congress in Washington, DC. Also there were the papers of James McKeen Cattell, a psychologist who had been contacted by Coca-Cola about doing the research, but who declined the offer.

The court records from the three trials were found in National Archives repositories in Atlanta, Chicago, and Washington, DC. The court record from the Chattanooga trial alone was more than 3,000 pages. Other important documents were found at the Coca-Cola Archives located in Atlanta and in the Coca-Cola Papers located at Emory University, also in Atlanta.

Published sources included the scientific literature on caffeine prior to 1911; biographies of Wiley, including an autobiography; books and articles on the Pure Food and Drug Act of 1906, which was the law used to seize the shipment; histories of the Coca-Cola Company; magazine articles written by Wiley on the dangers of caffeine; the daily local newspaper coverage of the three trials (from microfilm records); Coca-Cola advertisements in magazines from 1906 to 1915; and Hollingworth's own published account of his caffeine studies, and the subsequent reviews of those studies and citations of that research in later books and journal articles.

History research is often like detective work; the search for one piece of evidence leads to the search for another and another. One has to follow all leads, some of which produce no useful information. When all of the leads have been exhausted then you can analyze the facts to see if they are sufficient for telling the story. In the case of the Coca-Cola trials, that search required almost 15 years. It was not a full-time effort, but it is indicative of the time typically required in historical studies, particularly those that have produced landmark books.

Archival Research

Contemporary research in the history of psychology makes great use of archival collections. Archival research does not constitute a methodology *per se*; rather, it is related to research goals, the nature of the archival materials, the finding aids that exist, and the search strategies employed. Undoubtedly the most comprehensive guide to locating a particular manuscript collection is the *National Union Catalog of Manuscript Collections*, a reference guide to collections throughout the United States. Although this reference work contains listings of thousands of collections, it is certainly not complete. Its accuracy depends on archives sending in descriptions of their collections to the *Catalog*'s editor. Many archives do not do that for their smaller collections, so often those go unlisted.

A number of guides to archival collections exist (see Larsen, 1988), many of them organized by disciplinary field. For example, there is a guide to manuscript collections in psychology and related areas, compiled by Michael Sokal and Patrice Rafail (1982), that describes more than 500 collections in North America. This book is an excellent place to begin searching for archives and manuscript collections; its date, however, means that a number of psychology collections deposited since it was published will not be listed. A typical listing from that book is as follows for Robert M. Yerkes, who was the psychologist who led the development of the intelligence testing program for World War I and was one of the principal comparative psychologists of his time, known especially for his work with primates.

> **Yerkes, Robert Mearns, 1876–1956**
> Papers, 1898–1956, 1275 folders.
> In Yale University Library (New Haven, Connecticut)
> Correspondence from professional colleagues and incidental writers totaling 1,787 correspondents. Files cover Yerkes's service to three universities: Harvard (1901–1917), Minnesota (1917–1919), and Yale (1924–1958). Records cover service in two World Wars, including the organization of Army Mental Testing, service to the American Psychological Association, and his work with the National Research Council. Correspondence includes matters of editing the *Journal of Comparative Neurology and Psychology* and the *Journal of Animal Behavior*, and the founding and development of the Yale Laboratory of Primate Biology. Major correspondents include James R. Angell, Edwin G. Boring, Mary W. Calkins, G. Stanley Hall, Alfred Kinsey, Zing Yang Kuo, Edward B. Titchener, Margaret F. Washburn, John B. Watson, and others.

These papers were crucial for the research and writing of Donald Dewsbury's (2006) book, *Monkey Farm: A History of the Yerkes Laboratories of Primate Biology, Orange Park, Florida, 1930–1965*, that tells the fascinating story of the researchers and research that comprised America's most important primate research center. Although the research for that book involved many sources other than the Yerkes Papers, it is doubtful that the book could have been written had those papers not been preserved.

Typically, the descriptions of manuscript collections indicate the size of the collection, the range of years covered by the materials, the principal subject matter of the collection, the names of major correspondents, the location of the collection, and whether or not there are any special restrictions in using the collection. The listings in the *National Union Catalog of Manuscript Collections* use a similar format and can be found online at <http:www.loc.gov/coll/nucmc>.

All archives have a set of finding aids to help the researcher locate relevant materials. Some finding aids are more comprehensive than others. They include inventories of the various collections, indexes to correspondents, and name and subject indexes that cut across collections in the archives. Many of these finding aids are now in electronic form on the websites of the institutions where the particular manuscript collection is located. Thus, in many cases, contemporary historians can use the Web to see what is in an individual's personal papers, but they will most likely have to visit the archives in person to see the papers themselves. Still, despite the best of research strategies, good luck is often as important as diligence. As Brozek (1975) has described it, "In comparison with a history based on already published materials, archival research is apt to be a 'higher risk, higher gain' operation" (p. 15). Hill (1993) also has acknowledged the riskiness of archival work: "Investigations in archives simply cannot be predicted . . . That for me is an attraction, but to others it may seem too indeterminate, too risky" (p. 6). Despite its high-risk nature, archival research provides us with unique value in historical research because the material is itself unique.

Cadwallader (1975) listed the following as the special values of archival labors: unsuspected aspects of history may be discovered, unsuspected personal influences may be revealed, professional politics can be seen to influence personal careers and thus the shape of history, and a more balanced picture of an individual's personality is often revealed through her or his personal correspondence and diaries.

In archival research, one typically begins in one archival collection and then pursues related material through other archives, following wherever the leads suggest one goes. Collections are rarely, if ever, complete. Some documents relating to important questions are almost always missing. Occasionally, documents that were once part of the collection are missing, sometimes stolen by an unscrupulous "scholar." Some materials may be inaccessible, sealed until a certain time because of donor restrictions. Other problems include finding only one side of a correspondence, a problem partially alleviated by the invention of carbon paper in the 1920s, and sometimes solved by finding the other side in another archive.

Perhaps the greatest "problem" in archival research is one of its joys; it is the continual distraction presented by materials not related to the research purposes at hand. I refer to this disorder as *Documentus distractus*, a condition that produces disorientation and distortions in time perception. The affected researcher begins to read documents that are wholly irrelevant to the research effort. In its acute form, this disease greatly prolongs the time required for completion of the intended project. The more serious chronic form typically causes the researcher to abandon one project for a new one that is subsequently abandoned, and so forth, and so forth. Although this problem uses up valuable time in the archives intended for use on the target project, the experienced archival researcher learns to accept it. These distractions often produce discoveries that are quite informative. In my own research, for example, I once pulled two folders from an archival box, when I had meant to look only at the first folder. The second was marked "PRT," and reading the few letters it contained led me to discover a secret psychological society founded in 1936 which was called the Psychological Round Table, a by-invitation-only organization of young, male experimental psychologists, run by a group known as the Secret

Six. This secret society still exists today (women were admitted beginning in 1971), meeting annually, and kicking out attendees once they have turned 40 years of age (see Benjamin, 1977).

Sometimes these serendipitous events refuse to be ignored. Gloria Urch (1992) was searching the records in a county historical society when she discovered Rachel Harris, whom she described as perhaps the only African American nurse during the United States Civil War era:

> I was looking for something else when I found her photo. . . . I held it for a moment and studied it. . . . I put her photo aside and continued my research. A few minutes later the photo – which I thought I had placed securely on the shelf above me – fell into my lap, and those same eyes were gazing up into mine again. Before I left that day I made a copy of Rachel's photo and obituary and tucked it away. (p. 8)

And that discovery started Urch on her quest to learn about the life and career of this unknown nurse.

Note that the discovery of Rachel Harris began with perhaps a casual interest in finding out a bit more about this nineteenth-century nurse. Intellectual curiosity usually begins the search; the excitement over discovery often comes later. Archival work is a source of great pleasure to historians, a point that is typically difficult for others to realize. The hours spent in these collections go by all too quickly. Often the researcher is waiting at the door when the archive opens in the morning and has to be told to leave at closing time. The hours in between are arguably the most enjoyable for the historical worker. Michael Hill (1993) has described the joys of archival research in this way:

> Archival work appears bookish and commonplace to the uninitiated, but this mundane simplicity is deceptive. It bears repeating that events and materials in archives are not always what they seem on the surface. There are perpetual surprises, intrigues, and apprehensions. . . . Suffice it to say that it is a rare treat to visit an archive, to hold in one's hand the priceless and irreplaceable documents of our unfolding human drama. Each new box of archival material presents opportunities for discovery as well as obliga- tions to treat the subjects of your . . . research with candor, theoretical sophistication, and a sense of fair play. Each archival visit is a journey into an unknown realm that rewards its visitors with challenging puzzles and unexpected revelations. (pp. 6–7)

The papers of important psychologists are spread among archives and libraries all over the world. In the United States you will find the papers of William James and B. F. Skinner in the collections at Harvard University. The papers of Hugo Münsterberg, a pioneer in the application of psychology to business, can be found at the Boston Public Library. The papers of Mary Whiton Calkins and Christine Ladd-Franklin, important early contributors to experimental psychology, can be found at Wellesley College, and Vassar College and Columbia University respectively. The Library of Congress includes the papers of James McKeen Cattell and Kenneth B. Clark. Cattell was one of the founders of American psychology and a leader among American sci- entists in general, and Clark, an African American psychologist, earned fame when his research on self-esteem in black children was cited prominently in the U.S. Supreme Court decision that made school segregation illegal (*Brown v. the Board of Education*, 1954).

As noted earlier, the single largest collection of archival materials on psychology anywhere in the world is the Archives of the History of American Psychology (AHAP), located at the University of Akron. This archive opened in 1965 and has grown enormously in the size and importance of its collection. Today it contains the papers of more than 800 individuals and organizations. In addition to the extensive manuscript collections of unpublished materials, AHAP also contains more than 1,000 pieces of early psychological apparatus, a collection of more than 8,000 psychological tests, 15,000 photographs, 6,000 reels of movie film, and a large collection of rare books in the history of psychology. The collection includes the papers of such psychologists as Abraham Maslow, Mary Ainsworth, Henry H. Goddard, Harry and Leta Hollingworth, Kurt Koffka, Walter Miles, and Carolyn Sherif, and of such organizations as the American Group Psychotherapy Association, the Association for Humanistic Psychology, and the Midwestern Psychological Association.

The archive at Akron, although unique as a central repository for American psychology, is one of many archival collections available to researchers interested in psychology's past. As you read the articles in this book written by researchers in the history of psychology you will see the pervasive influence of archival materials on contemporary scholarship.

Oral History

When the events of interest are historically recent, that is within the last 75 years or so, a source of information for the historian is the oral history. The oral history is an autobiographical account, a personal history, usually in response to an interviewer and recorded on audio or video tape. Oral history research:

> is a test of other people, of the accuracy of their memories, of their ability to assess their own lives realistically, and of their ability to profit from experience. In a sense it is a test of other people as historians, a test of how well they can deal with their personal histories. But oral history research is also a test of ourselves, of our ability to deserve and win the confidence of other people, of our ability to deal sympathetically but honestly and imaginatively with their memories, and of our ability to deal honestly with ourselves. (Hoopes, 1979, p. 5)

The oral historian, who is the person who will serve as the interviewer, must prepare carefully for the oral history. Following contact with the person to be interviewed, the oral historian collects relevant documents, perhaps including unpublished materials such as correspondence, and asks for names of persons (colleagues, friends, students) who might be contacted prior to the interview. The interviewer should read whatever books and articles are relevant to the subject, including any written by the interviewee and those written about that individual's life or work. At the end of the preparation, the oral historian should be *very familiar* with the facts surrounding the content of the history to be taken. Typically an outline is prepared that lists the topics and subtopics to be covered in the interview.

The rules for the conduct of the interview can be quite specific (see Hoopes, 1979; Lummis, 1987; Ritchie, 2003). They describe acceptable limits for socializing, the balance that must be struck between leading the interview and dominating it, and procedures for following up on questions to complete the record, and backing off when the interviewee does not wish to pursue discussion in a particular area. Usually a transcript is typed from the tape, in part to protect preservation of the taped material. Often the transcript is sent to the interviewee for editing to promote accuracy (see Baum, 1981).

In short, an oral history is not a casual chat between interviewer and interviewee, although some "histories" are taken in that way. An oral history will be as valuable as the preparation that goes into it. Professional oral historians know that and prepare, often for months, for an encounter that may last only a day or two, or even a few hours. They are knowledgeable about both the method and the content of the interview. As a result, the quality of their product is significantly better than that of interviewers who are more casual in their approach.

Some archives, recognizing the unique value of oral histories, have collected these personal accounts. The Archives at the University of Akron has a large collection of these histories in psychology. Two collections of approximately 175 oral histories on the subjects of child development and child guidance are housed in the National Library of Medicine in Bethesda, Maryland. Another large collection of more than 140 oral histories of American psychologists can be found in the American Psychological Association Archives. And a similar collection of tapes and transcripts of more than 100 Canadian psychologists is housed in the Public Archives of Canada in Ottawa, Ontario.

Often oral history data are criticized on the basis of poor reliability. Because the oral history may involve recall of events many years in the past, that recall is suspect. Further, the interviewee is not always forthright in answering questions and may slant answers, even unintentionally, in a self-serving way. That is, the person being interviewed may respond "truthfully" but it will be the truth as they wish to remember it. These problems with oral history data are both significant and controversial. Some historians have argued that both problems – problems of recall and bias – should be addressed in order to reduce the error in oral histories. They suggest that to deal with errors of recall, one should try to corroborate the testimony with written records or with the testimony from other individuals who would have knowledge of the same events. In terms of the personal bias of the subject, they suggest interviewing other persons who would have reason to hold different biases, thus broadening the perspective on the content in question. Of course, sometimes those cross-checks are not possible.

Trevor Lummis (1987) has questioned the critics who have labeled oral history data as unreliable. He has argued that "The value of oral evidence as a historical source must ultimately be established within its own authenticity. If it is accepted as authentic only when confirmed by documentary sources then one might as well use the documents" (p. 155). He reminds the critics that documentary evidence is not without its own bias, as we have noted earlier, and that "history does not happen in documents. Human activity happens" (p. 13) before being recorded by someone. And clearly there is opportunity for biases being introduced in that recording. For Lummis and his colleagues in oral history, oral histories provide historical evidence of independent value. These proponents of oral history do not deny the flaws of this method, and they take steps in the evaluation of oral history data to minimize errors of fact and interpretation. Still, they argue for the special value of oral histories as sources for personal feelings and motives, information that may be impossible to recover from any other kind of historical evidence.

In summary, oral history data are valuable in their own right and as a complement to other data sources in history. In some cases they may be the only data, for example, in situations where no written records were made. They are particularly valuable in revealing personal information about emotions and motives, about self-awareness, and about personality. These important records can significantly enhance the historian's role in the telling of stories.

Quantitative Methods

Although quantitative methods have enjoyed popularity in a number of historical fields (see Jarausch & Hardy, 1991), they have become part of the historiography of psychology only in the past 35 years, and then only marginally so. Content analysis and citation analysis are two of the more frequently used quantitative approaches in psychology, and in recent years both have benefited considerably from the convenience of computer analysis and online sources.

Content analysis is a method that converts verbal, written, or other kinds of symbolic material into categories and numbers in order that statistical operations might be performed on the material (see Holsti, 1969). The method is typically used to quantify material that is largely qualitative in nature. Although the method is not without its critics, its use has brought some degree of objectivity and meaning to subject areas that were often in great disarray. One begins by formulating a system of classification, that is, a system of categories that are usually mutually exclusive. Those categories should be clearly defined so that there will be good interjudge reliability in determining what material should be included in what categories. Further, the unit of analysis must be specified: words, phrases, sentences, headings, pages, or chapters.

Some examples of historical questions and materials that could be subjected to content analysis are: What were the intellectual themes expressed in William James's letters? How did research methodologies change over time in the articles of the *American Journal of Psychology* between 1887 and 1930? What common themes can be found in the presidential addresses for the American Psychological Association from 1892 to 1940? Virtually any written materials can be subjected to content analysis, for example, psychology department catalogs, oral history transcripts, laboratory notes, and introductory psychology textbooks. For an example of its use in psychology see Cardno's (1965) analysis of Victorian psychology.

In short, the strategy in using content analysis is to choose a content domain of interest, develop appropriate categories for the analysis, decide on the unit of analysis, and then analyze the content domain. Often the analysis will reveal features of the material that were not apparent in merely reading that material.

Citation analysis, or citation indexing as it is sometimes called, is the study of relationships of published material through an analysis of citation networks (see Garfield, 1964, 1979). As it is used in history, the purpose is often to find the influence of a particular publication or publications on subsequent writing in the field, or to trace the evolution of ideas through a quantitative analysis of citations.

A major development in this field has been the work of the Institute for Scientific Information, which publishes the *Science Citation Index* (begun in 1963) and the *Social Sciences Citation Index* (begun in 1973). Both indexes are now online (see ISI Web of Knowledge, available through many library computers). These indexes provide one measure of the importance of a particular publication, that is, how frequently that publication is cited. Other questions that could be answered using citation analysis include: In what subfields of psychology is the publication cited? Does the frequency of citations increase or decrease over the years? Thus, from the point of view of the historian, one can get answers to questions about the influence of a particular theory and the evolution of ideas, that is, the issues of intellectual history in psychology. By examining who is doing the citing, one can trace the influence of a particular publication.

If you would like to see some examples of how this technique is used in history of psychology research, see Elizabeth Scarborough's (1971) analysis of the influence on contemporary psychology of an 1868 paper on mental reaction time written by F. C. Donders, Josef Brozek's (1980) study of the decay of Wilhelm Wundt's influence in American psychology, Franz Samelson's (1981) analysis of the influence of John Watson's 1913 behaviorist manifesto (included in Chapter 8 of this book), Darryl Bruce and Gene Winograd's (1998) study of the differential reception of James Deese's memory research, and Lydia Lange's (2005) analysis of publications in psychology that were cited immediately as opposed to others that were only discovered years later.

Other quantitative methods have also been used in historical research in psychology, such as a hypothesis-testing procedure known as *historiometry*. This method is actually more than 100 years old, but has been applied to historical questions in psychology in recent years largely through the work of Dean Keith Simonton (1990). He defines historiometry as the use of quantitative techniques to test hypotheses about the behavior of historical individuals. The ultimate goal of historiometry is the discovery of general principles that are descriptive of a certain class of individuals, for example, Nobel Prize winners, generals, composers, and presidents of the American Psychological Association. The method begins with defining a hypothesis in components that are quantifiable, and then testing that hypothesis. In Simonton's own work he has used this technique to investigate the causal relationship between war and scientific discovery, the relationship of creative productivity and age, the factors associated with greatness in American presidents, and the genius and creativity of individuals important in the history of psychology.

The New History of Psychology

In the middle of the 1970s, as the history of psychology specialty began its second decade, it underwent a change that many would argue reflected an important maturational step for the field (Furumoto, 1989). Research and writing in the history of psychology progressed from ceremonial history to critical history, a change that mirrors historical evolution in other fields as well. The "new history" movement came from both psychologist historians and from historians of science who were working in the history of psychology. They called for a number of changes in the way the history of psychology was being done; most of those changes were conceptual rather than methodological.

First, advocates of the new history called for a more critical history that examined the givens that form the myths of psychology. They cautioned against the fictions that were often created in moments of celebration and ceremony (for example, the hundredth anniversary of Wundt's laboratory). They asked for a more objective evaluation of individuals and events, and called for histories that adopted new perspectives in looking at familiar subjects. The celebration of the centennial of the American

Psychological Association in 1992 is a case in point. As part of the celebration of that event, historian Michael Sokal (1992) wrote an article on the origins of the APA, providing a somewhat unflattering portrait of G. Stanley Hall, APA's founder and first president. Likely that article, critical of Hall, would not have been written 20 years earlier in the history of psychology. Critical history does not mean character assassination of the idols of psychology's past. Rather it is a thorough and objective examination of the record, published and unpublished, that allows the chips to fall where they may.

In terms of resources, the new history of psychology has made greater use of archival sources and primary documents, understanding the importance of those as the raw data of history. And in terms of philosophy, there has been greater attention to the dangers of interpretive errors, such as presentism. There has also been a much greater interest in *intellectual history*, that is, focusing on the developmental history of ideas rather than on the great personalities of psychology.

Perhaps of greatest importance, the new history of psychology has adopted what is often called an externalist approach, contrasted with the internalist work of the old history of psychology (Hilgard, Leary, & McGuire, 1991). *External histories* are those that move outside of the narrow confines of the discipline to recognize the broader socio-cultural context in which psychology has emerged. For example, one could write a history of business psychology that focused entirely on the early psychologists who did contract research for various businesses. That is, the story would be told by staying solely within that segment of the discipline of psychology. But such an internalist history would be an impoverished one. It would not only misrepresent the history of business psychology in terms of errors of omission, but it would distort that history by ignoring a potential host of external variables that shaped what was happening within psychology. Clearly psychology does not exist in a vacuum. What happens in psychology influences events outside of psychology, and, of greater importance, events outside of psychology shape the field considerably. An external history means that the history of psychology is told in the context of the social, cultural, political, economic, and geographic factors that affect it.

Another part of the new history of psychology comes from a philosophy that is variously described as *postmodernism* or *deconstructionism*, a philosophy of history that emphasizes context and evidences a critical attitude toward the aims of science (Anderson, 1998). These historians presuppose science as an enterprise guided by political or social or economic agendas, rather than an objective and honest search for the truth. Such a deconstructionist approach has not been without criticism from other historians, who see it as historical bias at its worst (see Bruce, 2000; Popplestone, 2004; Zammito, 2004). This controversy is indicative of the ongoing historiographic debates in psychology, and more broadly in the history of science.

The impact of the new history of psychology has been a richer product for both the scholar and the student of history. It has encouraged scholarship in new fields, particularly in social history, and especially so with regard to the psychology of racism, prejudice, discrimination, and racial identity (see, as examples, Guthrie, 1998; Philogène, 2004; Pickren, 2004; Winston, 2004). That work, like the rest of the new history, has reminded us of the critical importance of painting history with the broad brush of context.

The contemporary selections reprinted in this book are representative of this new history. As you read these selections, I encourage you to keep in mind the lessons of this chapter. See if you can identify the questions that led the authors to their research.

What methods did they use? What are the facts of their stories and where did they uncover those facts? What archival records were used? What conclusions did they draw, and do those conclusions seem supported by the evidence? Would you draw different conclusions from the evidence and arguments presented, and why? With your know-ledge of historiography you should have a greater appreciation of the important stories that these historians tell.

Chapter 2

Philosophical and Physiological
Roots of Modern Psychology

This chapter examines 200 years of intellectual history that set the stage for the founding of a science of psychology toward the end of the nineteenth century. It is a very selective and obviously compressed view of ideas from philosophy, principally mechanism and empiricism, and physiology, emphasizing nerve, brain, and sensory functions, that proved important for the beginnings of laboratory psychology.

The Renaissance, which began in the fourteenth century and lasted through the early part of the seventeenth century, started in Italy and spread to the rest of Europe. It represented a revival of interest in, and new approaches to, art, literature, and knowledge, including science. It was the era of Michelangelo and Leonardo da Vinci, of Shakespeare and Chaucer, and of Copernicus and Galileo. Its importance for science, including the science of psychology, is that the late Renaissance marked an end to the dominance of *rationalism*, a philosophy that sought knowledge through reason and common sense. In opposition to rationalism was *empiricism*, a philosophical viewpoint whose chief tenet was that knowledge should be acquired through observation and experimentation, a philosophy that signaled the beginning of the *scientific method*. Psychology, as an experimental science, would grow from the post-Renaissance developments in philosophy and from eighteenth- and nineteenth-century physiological studies of the nervous system and sensory mechanisms.

A new world view emerged from the Renaissance, most significantly due to the work of Galileo Galilei (1564–1642). For Galileo, the universe was composed of matter in motion; minute particles of one object would come into contact with particles of another object, causing movement or a change in the second object. This view of the world was known as *mechanism*, and because it conceived of the universe as a giant machine, it implied that lawful explanations of the universe were possible. Like any machine, the universe would operate in an orderly way, and its operation could thus be understood by discovering the laws that governed it. The order and lawfulness meant that actions in the universe could be predicted by understanding the causal relationships within the world. Such a view was an especially important advance for science.

But if humans were part of the universe, could they also be viewed as machines? The answer was "Yes" according to French philosopher and mathematician René

Descartes (1596–1650), who extended the mechanistic view to human behavior. Descartes viewed the human body as a material entity that functioned as a machine, whereas the mind was nonmaterial and free to carry out the functions of consciousness. According to Descartes, however, the mind and body interacted with one another in such a way that not only did the mind influence the body but also the body influenced the mind, a view now referred to as interactive dualism. This idea, radical at the time, provided an excellent explanation for involuntary (reflexive) behavior and voluntary behavior. In adding human actions to the mechanistic world view, Descartes was arguing that human behavior was lawful and that its causes could be understood. He also localized the functions of the mind in the brain, whereas some earlier views had assigned certain mental processes, for example emotion, to such organs as the liver and heart.

Descartes was interested in the nature of the human mind. He proposed that mind consisted of two kinds of ideas: *innate ideas*, such as self and God, and *derived ideas*, which are acquired through experience in the world. Descartes studied the mind through a technique that he called meditation, an introspective approach, that is, an inward looking at the contents of the mind. In his meditative studies he stressed reason over perception and innate ideas over experience. He was thus both a rationalist and a mechanist, a philosophical combination that some historians (for example, Leahey, 1992a) have labeled paradoxical. (Such unlikely philosophical partners have coexisted in other great thinkers such as Isaac Newton [1642–1727], who developed a mechanistic view of the world using rationalist methods in his *Philosophiae Naturalis Principia Mathematica*, published in 1687.) Yet, for Descartes, it was his mechanistic views that ultimately contributed to an empirical psychology.

In contrast to Descartes' notion of innate ideas and knowledge by reason stood the *British empiricists*, a group of philosophers who spanned a period of approximately 200 years, beginning with John Locke (1632–1704). Locke rejected the notion of innate ideas and argued forcefully that all ideas were derived from experience. Resurrecting Aristotle's idea of *tabula rasa*, Locke described how experience would write on the blank slate of the mind, thus filling the mind with the sum total of its ideas. Although all ideas were derived from experience, they were not all derived from direct sensory experience; some were the products of the mind from the processes of reflection, or what Locke called the internal operations of the mind. Thus one could know a rose from direct sensory experience, sensing its aroma, color, and texture. But it was also possible to experience the rose when it was not present by reflecting on these earlier experiences. These ideas of reflection were thus derived wholly from the mind and were not the product of any sensory contact of the moment.

Unlike Descartes, Locke was more interested in how the mind works, that is, how it acquires knowledge, than in what it actually knows. He studied that question for 20 years, writing and rewriting his most important work for psychology, *An Essay Concerning Human Understanding*, which was finally published in 1690. Many historians use the publication of that book to mark the formal beginning of British empiricism.

In this classic work, Locke discussed the origin and nature of ideas, drawing distinctions between *simple* and *complex ideas* and *primary* and *secondary qualities*. Simple ideas are derived from either sensory experience or reflection, but complex ideas are the product only of reflection. Primary and secondary qualities he distinguished as follows. Primary qualities are sensory qualities that exist in an object, such as the thorny shape of a rose stem or the whiteness of a feather. Secondary qualities exist in the experiencing individual and are not a part of the object itself, for example, the pain experienced from the rose thorn or the tickle from the feather. That is, the pain is not part of the rose thorn, nor is the tickle part of the feather. Instead, these qualities of sensory experience are part of the individual. Locke's distinction between primary and secondary qualities was especially important for the science of psychology because it recognized experience that was independent of physical objects of the world. In essence, these secondary qualities were products of the mind, and as such they were the very basis of psychological study.

Empiricism continued its development through the work of George Berkeley (1685–1753), David Hume (1711–1776), and John Stuart Mill (1806–1873), each of whom wrote important treatises on cognitive processes such as sensation, perception, and learning. Mill published his most important book for psychology, *A System of Logic*, in 1843, a little more than 150 years after Locke's critically important book. In this book, Mill argued for the feasibility of a science of psychology, a hotly debated topic in Mill's time. Many agreed with positivist philosopher Auguste Comte (1798–1857) that there could be no science of the mind because the mind was not capable of studying its own processes. Although Mill acknowledged that psychology was, in his time, an inexact science, he believed it was as precise as some sciences, such as astronomy, and worthy of study. He called for an empirical, but not experimental, science of psychology. He drew on the success of chemistry in his time, arguing that a science of psychology should begin with an analysis of the mental elements. In what has been labeled *Mill's mental chemistry*, he called for a breaking down of the complex of mind into its component elements. Although he acknowledged that such a mental analysis would not deliver the full truths of a science of psychology, he believed that it was "an indefensible first step" in establishing the causal relationships of specific antecedents and consequents. Wilhelm Wundt was one of many individuals influenced by Mill's book. He later acknowledged that it contributed to his decision to found an experimental science of psychology, a subject covered in the next chapter.

From Descartes and Locke to John Stuart Mill, the philosophical approaches to studying the mind enjoyed an evolution that deepened the emphases of mechanism and empiricism. The British empiricists stressed the role of sensations, the nature of ideas, how those ideas were acquired, and how more complex ideas were formed through associations. These areas of philosophical inquiry would form the basis for the study of consciousness in the experimental psychology that was about to take shape in Germany.

Also of crucial importance to a science of psychology was the progress in studying the brain and nervous system, including the various senses. The brain had long been recognized as important for mental and motor functioning and the nineteenth century proved to be a century of enormous progress in understanding its anatomy and physiology. In the early 1800s it was discovered that the nerves in the spinal cord served different functions. Those in the dorsal region of the cord carried information from the senses to the brain (thus afferent processes), whereas those in the ventral section of the cord carried information from the brain to the motor effectors (efferent processes). This spinal nerve specificity was named the *Bell–Magendie law* after the two scientists who had independently discovered this anatomical and functional division.

The idea of nerve specificity was further delineated by a German physiologist, Johannes Müller (1801–1858), who discovered that the nerves of the five different sensory systems carried only the information specific to a single sensory system, regardless of the nature of stimulation of the sensory nerve. Thus visual nerves carried only visual information, whether the stimulation came from light or from physical pressure exerted on the eyeball. In each case the end product would be the subject reporting seeing something. Müller's discovery is usually referred to as the *law of specific nerve energies*.

Scientists were interested in neural questions other than nerve specificity, such as the speed at which information traveled in the nerves. Writing in 1840, Müller espoused the view, shared by most physiologists of his time, that the *speed of nerve conduction* was essentially instantaneous, and thus nerve impulses could not be measured. It was one of his students, Hermann von Helmholtz (1821–1894), who would prove him wrong. Studying a motor nerve in a frog's leg, Helmholtz calculated the speed of the impulse traveling at about 90 feet per second. Clearly nerve impulses were measurable, a fact that gave rise to studies of reaction time – motor responses to sensory stimuli – that would become one of the starting points for the science of psychology, as psychologists used the technique to study the speed of mental processing.

If nerves had demonstrated specificity of function, it seemed likely that the brain was divided on some functional basis as well. By the middle of the nineteenth century there was clear evidence of anatomical differences within the brain. Might those cortical differences be associated with different functions? Such beliefs had been around for many years, associated, for example, with the pseudoscience of phrenology. Evidence was presented on both sides of this question. Arguably the turning point in favor of what was known as the *cortical localization of function* came from the work of a French surgeon, Paul Broca (1824–1880). In 1861, Broca performed an autopsy on the brain of a man who, 20 years earlier, had lost his ability to speak (expressive aphasia), although he could understand what was said to him. The man also suffered paralysis on the right side of his body. Because contralateral projection of the nervous system was already understood, Broca suspected the right-side paralysis would indicate brain damage in the left hemisphere. The location of a large lesion in the left frontal lobe convinced Broca that that area was the location for speech production. But he needed more evidence to be sure. Over the next several years he examined the brains of another dozen cases of expressive aphasia, finding a left frontal lobe lesion in each case, virtually in the identical cortical area. Today that area of the brain is known as *Broca's area*.

In addition to the studies of nerve function and cortical function, there were a great many physiological investigations in the realm of sensation and perception that proved to be important for the science of psychology. If, as the empiricists had emphasized, all knowledge comes by way of the senses, then understanding the senses was critical for an understanding of mental functioning. Physiologists focused on identifying the specific receptors in each sensory system and identifying the range of stimuli to which those receptors responded. There were studies of color vision, of visual acuity, of depth perception, of pitch perception, of the basic tastes, of the perception of cold and warmth, and of pain. Understanding the functioning of the senses was thought to be important as a window into understanding how information was acquired and used. Of all the topics of investigation in the early psychology laboratories, none received more attention than sensation and perception.

The Readings

Five readings are presented in this chapter. The first selection is from John Locke's *Essay*. He begins by asking and answering perhaps the most important of psychological questions – where do the contents of the mind come from? Denying the existence of any innate ideas, he wrote, "Let us then suppose the mind to be, as we say, white paper, void of all characters, without any ideas; how comes it to be furnished? ... To this I answer, in one word, From experience; in that all our knowledge is founded and from that it ultimately derives itself" (Locke, 1905/1690, p. 25). As noted earlier, this notion of the blank slate, of white paper void of all writing, we know as *tabula rasa*. It was clearly one of the cornerstones of British empiricism, and a basis for psychology's early view of the mind. Also in this selection, Locke discusses his concepts of simple and complex ideas, focusing on the processes of perception, reflection, and association. The ideas expressed in this excerpt were crucial in defining the course of empiricist thought and ultimately the new science of psychology.

The second reading is by sociologist Nicholas Petryszak, who provides a most interesting interpretation of Locke's concept of tabula rasa. Remember that the idea of mind as a blank slate was a bold, if not dangerous, concept in Locke's time. In denying the existence of innate ideas, Locke was removing God from the inherent makeup of human beings, at least with regard to the notion of ideas. He did not deny a role for God in creating inherent faculties that allowed humans to know and investigate their world. Petryszak (1981) argues that Locke introduced the concept of tabula rasa in order "to resolve two conflicting world views towards which he was equally sympathetic" (p. 16): a belief in divine determination and a belief in individualism. In our exploration of the issues of historiography in Chapter 1, the importance of context was emphasized as crucial for accurate historical interpretation. In this reading, Petryszak skillfully illustrates that point by exploring Locke's ideas as they were shaped by the social and intellectual milieu of the Enlightenment of the late seventeenth and eighteenth centuries.

The third reading is an excerpt from John Stuart Mill's *A System of Logic*. The focus of the excerpt is on Mill's mental chemistry, his description of what a science of psychology would look like, and his belief in the legitimacy of a science of psychology. In this excerpt he leaves no doubt about his beliefs of the lawfulness of human behavior: "if we knew the person thoroughly, and know all the inducements which are acting upon him, we could foretell his conduct with as much certainty as we can predict any physical event" (Mill, 1843, p. 81). We have included this excerpt, in part, because of its continuity with the earlier excerpt from Locke, showing the progression of thought in British empiricism. It is also included, however, because of its importance to the psychology of Wundt, and its ties specifically to a reading in the next chapter (by Schmidgen) that portrays the influence of Mill's mental chemistry on Wundt's mode of experimentation.

The fourth selection, originally published in 1861, is Paul Broca's classic account of his famous patient Leborgne (also known as Tan). Broca presented his important finding at a meeting of the Paris Anthropological Society, during which he allowed members to see Leborgne's brain, preserved in a jar. This article is, without a doubt, the most significant piece of scientific literature on the subject of cortical localization of function, and thus marks a watershed event in our understanding of the organization and functioning of the brain.

The final selection is a contemporary historical work that treats the issues of cortical localization in the nineteenth century. The author is biopsychologist and historian Stanley Finger, whose many works in the history of science include an outstanding book on the history of neuroscience (Finger, 1994), from which this selection is taken. Finger discusses the importance of Broca's work and why, in the midst of considerable controversy over the specificity of brain function, it had such a significant impact on the acceptance of cortical localization and on notions of cerebral dominance.

Altogether, these five readings convey some of the most central ideas from philosophy and physiology that prepared the way for Wundt to open his pioneering psychology laboratory at the University of Leipzig in 1879. That is the subject of our next chapter.

On Simple and Complex Ideas
John Locke

Of Ideas in General, and their Original

1. *Idea is the object of thinking.* – Every man being conscious to himself, that he thinks, and that which his mind is applied about, whilst thinking, being the ideas that are there, it is past doubt that men have in their mind several ideas, such as are those expressed by the words, "whiteness, hardness, sweetness, thinking, motion, man, elephant, army, drunkenness," and others: it is in the first place then to be inquired, How he comes by them? I know it is a received doctrine, that men have native ideas and original characters stamped upon their minds in their very first being. This opinion I have at large examined already; and, I suppose, what I have said in the foregoing book will be much more easily admitted, when I have shown whence the understanding may get all the ideas it has, and by what ways and degrees they may come into the mind; for which I shall appeal to every one's own observation and experience.

2. *All ideas come from sensation or reflection.* – Let us then suppose the mind to be, as we say, white paper, void of all characters, without any ideas; how comes it to be furnished? Whence comes it by that vast store, which the busy and boundless fancy of man has painted on it with an almost endless variety? Whence has it all the materials of reason and knowledge? To this I answer, in one word, From experience; in that all our knowledge is founded, and from that it ultimately derives itself. Our observation, employed either about external sensible objects, or about the internal operations of our minds, perceived

From J. Locke (1690). *An essay concerning human understanding.* Adapted from edition published by the Open Court Publishing Company, Chicago, 1905. pp. 25–30, 33–36, 90–94.

and reflected on by ourselves, is that which supplies our understandings with all the materials of thinking. These two are the fountains of knowledge, from whence all the ideas we have, or can naturally have, do spring.

3. *The object of sensation one source of ideas.* – First. Our senses, conversant about particular sensible objects, do convey into the mind several distinct perceptions of things, according to those various ways wherein those objects do affect them; and thus we come by those ideas we have of yellow, white, heat, cold, soft, hard, bitter, sweet, and all those which we call sensible qualities; which when I say the senses convey into the mind, I mean, they from external objects convey into the mind what produces there those perceptions. This great source of most of the ideas we have, depending wholly upon our senses, and derived by them to the understanding, I call, "sensation."

4. *The operations of our minds the other source of them.* – Secondly. The other fountain, from which experience furnisheth the understanding with ideas, is the perception of the operations of our own minds within us, as it is employed about the ideas it has got; which operations when the soul comes to reflect on and consider, do furnish the understanding with another set of ideas which could not be had from things without; and such are perception, thinking, doubting, believing, reasoning, knowing, willing, and all the different actings of our own minds; which we, being conscious of, and observing in ourselves, do from these receive into our understandings as distinct ideas, as we do from bodies affecting our senses. This source of ideas every man has wholly in himself; and though it be not sense as having nothing to do with external objects, yet it is very like it, and might properly

enough be called "internal sense." But as I call the other "sensation," so I call this "reflection," the ideas it affords being such only as the mind gets by reflecting on its own operations within itself. By reflection, then, in the following part of this discourse, I would be understood to mean that notice which the mind takes of its own operations, and the manner of them, by reason whereof there come to be ideas of these operations in the understanding. These two, I say, viz., external material things as the objects of sensation, and the operations of our own minds within as the objects of reflection, are, to me, the only originals from whence all our ideas take their beginnings. The term "operations" here, I use in a large sense, as comprehending not barely the actions of the mind about its ideas, but some sort of passions arising sometimes from them, such as is the satisfaction or uneasiness arising from any thought.

5.   *All our ideas are of the one or the other of these.* – The understanding seems to me not to have the least glimmering of any ideas which it doth not receive from one of these two. External objects furnish the mind with the ideas of sensible qualities, which are all those different perceptions they produce in us; and the mind furnishes the understanding with ideas of its own operations.

These, when we have taken a full survey of them, and their several modes, [combinations, and relations,] we shall find to contain all our whole stock of ideas; and that we have nothing in our minds which did not come in one of these two ways. Let any one examine his own thoughts, and thoroughly search into his understanding, and then let him tell me, whether all the original ideas he has there, are any other than of the objects of his senses, or of the operations of his mind considered as objects of his reflection; and how great a mass of knowledge soever he imagines to be lodged there, he will, upon taking a strict view, see that he has not any idea in his mind but what one of these two have imprinted, though perhaps with infinite variety compounded and enlarged by the understanding, as we shall see hereafter.

6.   *Observable in children.* – He that attentively considers the state of a child at his first coming into the world, will have little reason to think him stored with plenty of ideas that are to be the matter of his future knowledge. It is by degrees he comes to be furnished with them; and though the ideas of obvious and familiar qualities imprint themselves before the memory begins to keep a register of time or order, yet it is often so late before some unusual qualities come in the way, that there are few men that cannot recollect the beginning of their acquaintance with them: and, if it were worth while, no doubt a child might be so ordered as to have but a very few even of the ordinary ideas till he were grown up to a man. But all that are born into the world being surrounded with bodies that perpetually and diversely affect them, variety of ideas, whether care be taken about it or not, are imprinted on the minds of children. Light and colours are busy at hand every where when the eye is but open; sounds and some tangible qualities fail not to solicit their proper senses, and force an entrance to the mind; but yet I think it will be granted easily, that if a child were kept in a place where he never saw any other but black and white till he were a man, he would have no more ideas of scarlet or green than he that from his childhood never tasted an oyster or a pine-apple has of those particular relishes.

7.   *Men are differently furnished with these according to the different objects they converse with.* – Men then come to be furnished with fewer or more simple ideas from without, according as the objects they converse with afford greater or less variety; and from the operations of their minds within, according as they more or less reflect on them. For, though he that contemplates the operations of his mind cannot but have plain and clear ideas of them; yet, unless he turn his thoughts that way, and considers them attentively, he will no more have clear and distinct ideas of all the operations of his mind, and all that may be observed therein, than he will have all the particular ideas of any landscape, or of the parts and motions of a clock, who will not turn his eyes to it, and with attention heed all the parts of it. The picture or clock may be so placed, that they may come in his way every day; but yet he will have but a confused idea of all the parts they are made of, till he applies himself with attention to consider them each in particular.

8. *Ideas of reflection later, because they need attention.* – And hence we see the reason why it is pretty late before most children get ideas of the operations of their own minds; and some have not any very clear or perfect ideas of the greatest part of them all their lives: – because, though they pass there continually, yet like floating visions, they make not deep impressions enough to leave in the mind, clear, distinct, lasting ideas, till the understanding turns inwards upon itself, reflects on its own operations, and makes them the objects of its own contemplation. Children, when they come first into it, are surrounded with a world of new things, which, by a constant solicitation of their senses, draw the mind constantly to them, forward to take notice of new, and apt to be delighted with the variety of changing objects. Thus the first years are usually employed and diverted in looking abroad. Men's business in them is to acquaint themselves with what is to be found without; and so, growing up in a constant attention to outward sensations, seldom make any considerable reflection on what passes within them till they come to be of riper years; and some scarce ever at all.

9. *The soul begins to have ideas when it begins to perceive.* – To ask, at what time a man has first any ideas, is to ask when he begins to perceive; having ideas, and perception, being the same thing. I know it is an opinion, that the soul always thinks; and that it has the actual perception of ideas in itself constantly, as long as it exists; and that actual thinking is as inseparable from the soul, as actual extension is from the body: which if true, to inquire after the beginning of a man's ideas is the same as to inquire after the beginning of his soul. For by this account, soul and its ideas, as body and its extension, will begin to exist both at the same time.

Of Simple Ideas

1. *Uncompounded appearances.* – The better to understand the nature, manner, and extent of our knowledge, one thing is carefully to be observed concerning the ideas we have; and that is, that some of them are simple, and some complex.

Though the qualities that affect our senses are, in the things themselves, so united and blended that there is no separation, no distance between them; yet it is plain the ideas they produce in the mind enter by the senses simple and unmixed. For though the sight and touch often take in from the same object, at the same time, different ideas – as a man sees at once motion and colour, the hand feels softness and warmth in the same piece of wax – yet the simple ideas thus united in the same subject are as perfectly distinct as those that come in by different senses; the coldness and hardness which a man feels in a piece of ice being as distinct ideas in the mind as the smell and whiteness of a lily, or as the taste of sugar and smell of a rose: and there is nothing can be plainer to a man than the clear and distinct perception he has of those simple ideas; which, being each in itself uncompounded, contains in it nothing but one uniform appearance or conception in the mind, and is not distinguishable into different ideas.

2. *The mind can neither make nor destroy them.* – These simple ideas, the materials of all our knowledge, are suggested and furnished to the mind only by those two ways above mentioned, viz., sensation and reflection. When the understanding is once stored with these simple ideas, it has the power to repeat, compare, and unite them, even to an almost infinite variety, and so can make at pleasure new complex ideas. But it is not in the power of the most exalted wit or enlarged understanding, by any quickness or variety of thought, to invent or frame one new simple idea in the mind, not taken in by the ways before mentioned; nor can any force of the understanding destroy those that are there: the dominion of man in this little world of his own understanding, being much-what the same as it is in the great world of visible things, wherein his power, however managed by art and skill, reaches no farther than to compound and divide the materials that are made to his hand but can do nothing towards the making the least particle of new matter, or destroying one atom of what is already in being. The same inability will every one find in himself, who shall go about to fashion in his understanding any simple idea not received in by his senses from external objects, or by reflection from the operations of his own mind about

them. I would have any one try to fancy any taste which had never affected his palate, or frame the idea of a scent he had never smelt; and when he can do this, I will also conclude, that a blind man hath *ideas* of colours, and a deaf man true, distinct notions of sounds.

3.   This is the reason why, though we cannot believe it impossible to God to make a creature with other organs, and more ways to convey into the understanding the notice of corporeal things than those five as they are usually counted, which he has given to man; yet I think it is not possible for any one to imagine any other qualities in bodies, howsoever constituted, whereby they can be taken notice of, besides sounds, tastes, smells, visible and tangible qualities. And had mankind been made with but four senses, the qualities then which are the objects of the fifth sense had been as far from our notice, imagination, and conception, as now any belonging to a sixth, seventh, or eighth sense can possibly be; which, whether yet some other creatures, in some other parts of this vast and stupendous universe, may not have, will be a great presumption to deny. He that will not set himself proudly at the top of all things, but will consider the immensity of this fabric, and the great variety that is to be found in this little and inconsiderable part of it which he has to do with, may be apt to think, that in other mansions of it there may be other and different intelligible beings, of whose faculties he has as little knowledge or apprehension, as a worm shut up in one drawer of a cabinet hath of the senses or understanding of a man; such variety and excellency being suitable to the wisdom and power of the Maker. I have here followed the common opinion of man's having but five senses, though perhaps there may be justly counted more; but either supposition serves equally to my present purpose.

Of Complex Ideas

1.   *Made by the mind out of simple ones.* – We have hitherto considered those ideas, in the reception whereof the mind is only passive, which are those simple ones received from sensation and reflection before mentioned, whereof the mind cannot make one to itself, nor have any idea

which does not wholly consist of them. [But as the mind is wholly passive in the reception of all its simple ideas, so it exerts several acts of its own, whereby out of its simple ideas, as the materials and foundations of the rest, the other are framed. The acts of the mind wherein it exerts in power over its simple ideas are chiefly these three: (1) Combining several simple ideas into one compound one; and thus all complex ideas are made. (2) The second is bringing two ideas, whether simple or complex, together, and setting them by one another, so as to take a view of them at once, without uniting them into one; by which way it gets all its ideas of relations. (3) The third is separating them from all other ideas that accompany them in their real existence; this is called "abstraction:" and thus all its general ideas are made. This shows man's power and its way of operation to be much the same in the material and intellectual world. For, the materials in both being such as he has no power over, either to make or destroy, all that man can do is either to unite them together, or to set them by one another, or wholly separate them. I shall here begin with the first of these in the consideration of complex ideas, and come to the other two in their due places.] As simple ideas are observed to exist in several combinations united together, so the mind has a power to consider several of them united together as one idea; and that not only as they are united in external objects, but as itself has joined them. Ideas thus made up of several simple ones put together I call "complex;" such as are beauty, gratitude, a man, an army, the universe; which, though complicated of various simple ideas or complex ideas made up of simple ones, yet are, when the mind pleases, considered each by itself as one entire thing, and signified by one name.

2.   *Made voluntarily.* – In this faculty of repeating and joining together its ideas, the mind has great power in varying and multiplying the objects of its thoughts infinitely beyond what sensation or reflection furnished it with; but all this still confined to those simple ideas which it received from those two sources, and which are the ultimate materials of all its compositions. For, simple ideas are all from things themselves; and of these the mind can have no more nor other than what are suggested to it. It can have no other ideas of sensible qualities than what come from

without by the senses, nor any ideas of other kind of operations of a thinking substance than what it finds in itself: but when it has once got these simple ideas, it is not confined barely to observation, and what offers itself from without; it can, by its own power, put together those ideas it has, and make new complex ones which it never received so united.

3.   *Are either modes, substances, or relations.* – Complex ideas, however compounded and decompounded, though their number be infinite, and the variety endless wherewith they fill and entertain the thoughts of men, yet I think they may be all reduced under these three heads: 1. *Modes.* 2. *Substances.* 3. *Relations.*

4.   *Modes.* – First. "Modes" I call such complex ideas which, however compounded, contain not in them the supposition of subsisting by themselves, but are considered as dependences on, or affections of, substances; such are the ideas signified by the words, "triangle, gratitude, murder," &c. And if in this I use the word "mode" in somewhat a different sense from its ordinary signification, I beg pardon; it being unavoidable in discourses differing from the ordinary received notions, either to make new words or to use old words in somewhat a new signification: the latter whereof, in our present case, is perhaps the more tolerable of the two.

5.   *Simple and mixed modes.* – Of these modes there are two sorts which deserve distinct consideration. First. There are some which are only variations or different combinations of the same simple idea, without the mixture of any other, as a dozen, or score; which are nothing but the ideas

of so many distinct units added together: and these I call "simple modes," as being contained within the bounds of one simple idea. Secondly. There are others compounded of simple ideas, of several kinds, put together to make one complex one; *v.g.*, beauty, consisting of a certain composition of colour and figure, causing delight in the beholder; theft, which, being the concealed change of the possession of any thing, without the consent of the proprietor, contains, as is visible, a combination of several ideas of several kinds; and these "I call mixed modes."

6.   *Substances single or collective.* – Secondly. The ideas substances are such combinations of simple ideas as are taken to represent distinct particular things subsisting by themselves, in which the supposed or confused idea of substance, such as it is, is always the first and chief. Thus, if to substance be joined the simple idea of a certain dull, whitish colour, with certain degrees of weight, hardness, ductility, and fusibility, we have the idea of lead; and a combination of the ideas of a certain sort of figure, with the powers of motion, thought, and reasoning, joined to substance, make the ordinary idea of a man. Now of substances also there are two sorts of ideas, one of single substances, as they exist separately, as of a man or a sheep; the other of several of those put together, as an army of men or flock of sheep; which collective ideas of several substances thus put together, are as much each of them one single idea as that of a man or an unit.

7.   *Relation.* – Thirdly. The last sort of complex ideas is that we call "Relation," which consists in the consideration and comparing one idea with another.

Tabula Rasa – Its Origins and Implications
Nicholas G. Petryszak

There is no doubt that the Enlightenment held significant implications for the development of intellectual thought in the Western world. To this end a number of contemporary social historians and scientists contend that social theory as we know it today first emerged during this time.[1] While some students and critics of the Enlightenment have been willing to attribute the origins of social theory to this period in general, others have been more specific and argued that the initial impetus for the emergence of social theory originated in the writings of one theorist in particular, John Locke.[2]

In this regard it has been pointed out that Locke's notion of *tabula rasa* contributed the necessary conceptual framework for the development of a science of society. Marvin Harris, for example, has emphatically argued that "Locke's *An Essay Concerning Human Understanding* was the midwife of all those modern behavioral disciplines, including psychology, sociology, and cultural anthropology, which stress the relationship between conditioning, environment and human thought and actions.... What Locke attempted to prove was that the human mind at birth was an 'empty cabinet' [tabula rasa]. The knowledge or the ideas which the mind later come to be filled are all acquired during the process of ... enculturation."[3]

The concept of tabula rasa plays a conspicuous role in modern social theory. Undoubtedly, the most pervasive and widespread opinion shared by social scientists today is that man is essentially "a social animal."[4] Most social scientists understand that human behavior is largely

formed through social relationships between individuals acting together as members of larger groups.[5] In short, contemporary social theorists emphasize that mans's inner nature is a tabula rasa which is fully dependent for its development on the processes of social interaction and socialization.[6]

It is apparent that at present a significant number of social theorists and historians are content in believing that it was John Locke's original intention to demonstrate that human nature is a product of society and the dynamics of socialization.[7] Most, it seems, are also satisfied with the idea that it was Locke's purpose, in developing the concept of tabula rasa, to explain the universe in general, and nature and man in particular, in secular and rational terms. In addition, they are willing to attribute to the concept of tabula rasa the important consequence of undermining Christian mysticism and the belief in Original Sin.[8] Likewise, it is uncritically accepted that Locke built his system of thought, especially his concept of tabula rasa, upon the combined bases of rationalism and experience in order to demonstrate that although man was imperfect, he was nevertheless susceptible to definite improvement through the application of the laws of science to the dimensions of human psychology and socialization as well as through the instituting of programs of social reform. For this reason, it is felt that Locke's emphasis on environmental influences rather than on the inner will in the shaping of the self places him in the modern line. Furthermore, his writings are interpreted as having set the task of education in ensuring that the mind "receives the right impressions, under the right circumstances." On the basis of these particular interpretations Locke is enthusiastically designated by many as the founder of modern pedagogical theory. His concept of tabula rasa is seen as the essential means for rationalizing various social and envi-

Adapted from N. G. Petryszak (1981). Tabula rasa – Its origins and implications. *Journal of the History of the Behavioral Sciences. 17*, 15–27. Copyright © by Wiley-Blackwell. Reprinted by permission of the publisher.

ronmental deterministic solutions to the ills of society.

Despite these prevailing beliefs, it is readily evident when the concept of tabula rasa is examined in terms of the social, religious, and ideological circumstances within which it was written, that Locke's purposes were quite different from those which are commonly assumed today. In fact, it will be argued that Locke formulated the concept of tabula rasa and its related theoretical framework to resolve two conflicting world views towards which he was equally sympathetic. These world views consisted of the belief in divine determination, on the one hand, and the liberal belief in individualism, on the other. Furthermore, on the basis of a critical exegesis of Locke's original writings it is apparent that he did not wish to deny the possibility of the existence of certain biologically innate aspects of human nature, at least as he understood it from a theological nativistic point of view.

These various long-neglected features of Locke's theory of tabula rasa will be explored in the attempt to gain a better understanding of its original meanings and purposes as well as the implications which it holds for certain beliefs, assumptions, and theories popular within the social sciences at the present time. In this respect, this analysis provides the opportunity of determining whether existing theories dealing with concept and theory formation in the social sciences are entirely adequate for explaining the origins of such important and key concepts as tabula rasa. In addition, the question will be dealt with of whether it was Locke's goal to utilize this concept as a means to realize the ideals of rationalism and to provide the groundwork for the development of a science of society. Finally, close attention shall be given to the problem of whether or not the tabula rasa doctrine can be considered as the original impetus to the development of the theory of the social determination of human behavior.

Locke and the Enlightenment

In order to come to terms with the intentions and purposes of Locke's theoretical arguments as related to the concept of tabula rasa, it is first necessary to review the social and ideological context within which he wrote. Locke with other intellectuals in the early period of the Enlightenment of the late seventeenth and eighteenth centuries came to question the traditional, legal, moral, and religious foundations of Western European culture. The Enlightenment is of course older than the eighteenth century and wider than the territory of France. Its overall orientation towards skepticism and science was already widespread in England during the latter half of the seventeenth century and it is in this sense that Locke may be understood as one of its earliest contributors.

While generalizations about the common beliefs shared among theorists of the Enlightenment will be made here, it is nevertheless important to keep in mind that there existed a wide disparity of opinion among them. In many respects it would be difficult to relate such thinkers among others as Locke, David Hume, Adam Ferguson, Baron de Montesquieu, and Jean-Jacques Rousseau to one another, or to the philosophes. As a consequence, it is necessary to qualify any generalization about this body of theorists in a careful and tentative fashion.[9] However, what can be argued is that all of these theorists shared "the spirit of the Enlightenment" which, even in its earliest stages, was expressive of varying levels of inquisitive skepticism towards many traditional beliefs and institutions. The underlying assumption maintained by the Enlightenment thinkers was that the world of reason and the world of phenomena formed a single, unitary structure.[10] It was the articulation of this assumption which initiated the post-Newtonian phase of science by making far-reaching changes in the West's concept of scientific method and its view of nature.[11] The overall revolutionary significance of the Enlightenment consisted of the promotion of the ideal of reason and a secular naturalism which represented a complete reversal of the medieval distrust of the phenomenal world.[12]

One of the chief figures responsible for shifting the general orientation of social thought away from the theories of Descartes and the belief in divine determination was John Locke. Locke's theoretical perspective was directed against metaphysical speculation and the complete reliance on ideas of Divine Will to explain the origins of human thought and action. This does not mean, however, that Locke was intent on undermining the whole credibility of the Christian religion. He set himself the task of understanding how human knowledge was gained without having to rely on the notions of innate ideas implanted by God. The intention of his social theories was to demonstrate that man himself played an important part in the development of human knowledge, moral law, and the law of nature which Locke felt to be synonymous with God's will.[13] Locke sought to solve the rather different problem of combining the traditional belief in the divine determination of behavior with the liberal belief in individual freedom and independent initiative of action.

Locke, like the later philosophes, felt it necessary to demonstrate that the natural as well as the human social world conformed to the dictates of human reason; at the same time, he encouraged the reconstruction of European society according to these dictates. The belief of many of the Enlightenment thinkers in a natural science of society was also intimately related to the liberal orientation of their values. To some extent, Locke as well as others shared the idea that society was ruled by predictable, mechanistically determined processes in the form of natural laws. The affirmative belief in natural law was closely linked with their support of the leading liberal ideas of individual freedom and the exemption of man from all forms of arbitrary authority. One of the most striking accomplishments of the Enlightenment theorists was that, in maintaining their liberal ideals of individuality, they seemed to have discovered a concept of social freedom that could reconcile a faith in the orderly, predictable, mechanistically determined operation of society with a commitment to individual liberty.[14] Ideally, the liberal definition of freedom exempted the individual from human authority by subjecting him to the impersonal authority of mechanistic social forces. It was believed that perception and definition of natural law required no aid other than the rational forces of knowledge, which communicated its findings to scientists through sense perception and its supplementary process of logical judgment and inference.[15] This idea was expressed in the famous empirical adage, "*Nihil est in intellectu guod non prius fuit in sensu*" (nothing is in the mind which is not first perceived by the senses.) For this reason it was believed that the realm of nature was opposed, to a greater or lesser degree, to the realm of divine grace and that it was the application of the methods of science which ultimately gave the individual control over the environment. In this sense, the writings of Locke and later intellectuals of the Enlightenment constituted "the intellectual climax to the gradual emancipation of economic and political structures from the framework of feudal Christendom."

Locke's liberal values have been interpreted by many social historians as a leading element in all his theoretical discussions. Theodore Artz and others have emphasized that in Locke's writings there existed a close association between his political ideas and the scientific movement. While he approached social and political questions from the point of view of a seventeenth-century physicist, his emphasis was always on "the liberal side of things.[16] The content of Locke's theories bear the characterizing and distinguishing features of liberal society: individualism, private property, the primacy of economic motives and market relations, utilitarianism, and a separate and supreme realm of positive law."[17]

Also implicit within the social critiques formulated by Locke and other Enlightenment thinkers was the assumption that the prevailing institutions in society were contrary to human nature and thus inhibitive of human growth and development.[18] Human nature was assumed to be innately good and it was the social environment which was responsible for man's aggressive and unjust actions, as well as for the inequalities which could be observed between men.[19] As Lord Morly said, it was believed "that human nature is good, and that the world is capable of being a desirable place and that the evil of the world is the fruit of bad education and bad institutions."[20] Such views about human nature were antithetical to clerical and aristocratic assumptions about human nature of the early- and mid-seventeenth century.[21] It is clear from this that there existed a strong interdependent relationship between the liberal ideals of Locke and other thinkers of the Enlightenment, their theories of man, society, social reform, and their explicit assumptions about man's innate nature.

The question of religion must also be dealt with in the consideration of the overall intellectual orientation of John Locke and the other Enlightenment thinkers. One of the most intense intellectual debates which began in the early period of the Enlightenment was over the question of religion. The "crisis of religious consciousness" in the late seventeenth and early eighteenth centuries would never have developed its distinctive anti-Christian tone if the Church had not been in some sense a political as well as an intellectual force.[22] While some theorists directly criticized the structure and power relationships of the Church, the earlier theorists inclusive of John Locke addressed themselves to the problem of the role which God played in the determination of human thought and action. As a consequence, Locke, as well as others, was faced with the problem of criticizing the then-popular Cartesian world view.

By the mid-seventeenth century, Cartesianism had come to dominate philosophical thought in Western Europe. As a form of methodological inquiry, Cartesianism was applied to a wide range of subjects including history, ethics, and religion. Descartes' method was one of cautious and systematic inquiry aimed at the reductive analysis of complex phenomena into their simplest constituent parts which were explained in terms of truths which are derived from the will of the "Divine Spirit of God."[23] Descartes' discourse of methodological reasoning, given in his famous *Discourse on the Method For Rightly Conducting One's Reason and Seeking Truth in the Sciences* (1637), denied the validity of the axiomatic truths and syllogisms of the scholastics.

Descartes sought to establish a system of rationalism deduced from clear and innate intuitions. His support of the validity of scientific research was complemented by his belief in the existence of fixed and immutable laws of nature, inertia, and the conservation of energy. The material universe, according to Descartes, was ordered by the laws of motion which were determined once and for all by the divine intelligence.[24] In his opinion, man was unique insofar as his nature was characterized by the union of soul and body. Mind, which Descartes saw

as equal in importance to man's soul, contained a number of innate ideas. He admitted that ultimately the existence of these innate ideas could be attributed to the hand of God. As he stated, "the whole force of the argument lies in this – that I now would not exist, and possess the nature I have, that nature which puts me in possession of the idea of God, unless God did really exist, the God, the idea of whom is found in me."[25] The laws of nature, man's innate nature, and human ideas were ascribed to the workings of a divine intelligence. He felt that the "idea of God" was innate to the human consciousness. By showing the interrelationship between natural law on the one hand and God on the other, Descartes was able to reconcile to some extent the interests of science and the Church.

Descartes' ideas were subjected to severe criticisms by many social theorists in the late-seventeenth century. The criticism of Descartes originated in the growing discontent of early Enlightenment thinkers with all forms of metaphysical idealism, especially that type of idealism which legitimated the authority of the Church in acting as a mediator between man, the laws of nature, and the ideas which were believed to be innate in human consciousness.[26] Many intellectuals in the initial stages of the Enlightenment increasingly came to believe, contrary to the opinions of Descartes, that man was an individual who played an active role in determining his own behavior and thoughts.

It is within this intellectual climate of liberal individualism, the belief in certain innate features of human nature, and the rejection of the Cartesian paradigm that Locke's theory of tabula rasa must be specifically understood and evaluated.

Locke's Theory of Tabula Rasa

John Locke's major theoretical contributions were formulated in his well-known *An Essay on Human Understanding* (1689). In this essay he explained that the mind of a child at birth, rather than being characterized by a number of innate ideas attributable to divine will, was in fact a tabula rasa – a blank slate upon which experience and reflection, derived from senses, wrote their effects. The creation of human knowledge was attributed not completely to divine will, but to experience and its individual interpretation by man. Locke's rejection of the Cartesian notion of innate ideas was in one respect indicative of his liberal world view by which he sought to establish man as a relatively independent actor, able to determine his own affairs and actions although to some extent subject to the influence of God's will. The question nevertheless remains, to what degree might Locke have made use of specific assumptions about the innate features of human nature in order to confirm and legitimize his liberal belief in the autonomy of the individual in the creation of human knowledge on the one hand and on the other, his belief as a Christian that God was the ultimate arbiter of human affairs?

The purpose of Locke's *Essay on Human Understanding* was to inquire into "the origin, certainty, and extent of human knowledge, together with the grounds and degrees of belief, opinion and assent."[27] In rejecting the notion of innate ideas, he argued that "to say, that there are truths imprinted on the soul, which it perceives or understands most; imprinting, if it signify any thing, being nothing else but the making of certain truths to be perceived. For to imprint any thing on the mind, without the mind's perceiving it, seems to me hardly intelligible."[28] Locke added that while there are no innate ideas, there are also no innate moral principles insofar as "the ignorance wherein many men are of them, and the slowness of assent wherewith others receive them, are manifest proofs that they are not innate and such as offer themselves to their view without searching."[29] It was further maintained that knowledge, rather than being based on innate ideas, comes instead from experience. As Locke argues, "our observation employed either about external sensible objects, or about the internal operations of our minds, perceived and reflected on by ourselves, is that which supplies our understandings with all the materials of thinking. These two are the fountains of knowledge, from whence all the ideas we have, or can naturally have do spring."[30] The "human soul" accordingly, "begins to have ideas, when it begins to perceive."[31]

The development of ideas was defined by Locke as a dynamic process in that "in time

the mind comes to reflect on its own operations about the ideas got by sensation, and thereby stores itself with a new set of ideas, which I call ideas of reflection. These are the impressions that are made on our senses by outward objects that are intrinsical to the mind, and its own operations, proceeding from powers intrinsical and proper to itself; which when reflected on by itself, becoming also objects of its contemplation."[32]

Despite denying the existence of ideas in the human consciousness since birth, Locke nevertheless admitted that the human mind was characterized by a number of innate faculties which enabled the individual to retain "those simple ideas which from sensation and reflection it hath received."[33] These faculties included perception, contemplation, memory, attention, repetition, pleasure and pain, discerning, comparing, and abstraction."[34] He also believed that the sensing of pleasure and pain played a significant role in the development of the passions which all men share insofar as ". . . we love, desire, rejoice, and hope, only in respect to pleasure; we hate, fear and grieve, only in respect to pain . . . all these passions are moved by things only as they appear to be causes of pleasure and pain . . ."[35] In direct conjunction with this idea of pleasure was the understanding that the "necessity of perceiving true happiness is the foundation of liberty" and is "the greatest good" of intellectual beings.[36] In this fashion Locke purported almost a classical Epicurean view of human nature which maintained that man is motivated by the search for pleasure and the avoidance of pain.[37]

In explaining the origins of man's various faculties, Locke was quite emphatic in pointing out that they were ultimately provided by God in ensuring that man would have the ability to gain knowledge about His good works. He contended that God "furnished man with those faculties, which will serve for the sufficient discerning of all things requisite to the end of such a being. And I doubt not but to show that a man, by the right use of his natural abilities, may, without any innate principles, attain a knowledge of a God, and other things that concern him. God having endowed man with those faculties of knowing which he hath, was no more obliged by his goodness to plant those innate notions in his mind, than that, having given him reasons, hands, and materials, he should build him bridges or houses."[38]

While Locke disclaimed the existence of innate ideas in man as elementary features of human nature, he was at the same time willing to argue that human nature was characterized by certain innate faculties of perception and experience which were given to man, as aspects of his nature by God. It is important to point out from this that Locke in the development of the tabula rasa doctrine was not aloof from using assumptions about the nature of human nature. Nor was he exempt from ascribing the ultimate origins of those innate faculties to the will of God. On the basis of these observations we may justifiably ask the question, already articulated by a number of prominent social historians, whether it is correct to consider Locke's tabula rasa theory as a denial of the role which certain features of man's innate nature may play in the determination of human knowledge and behavior as well as a denial of God's evident intervention in human affairs?[39]

In other major works, Locke also relied on a number of assumptions about the innate features of human nature as well as making overt references to the role which God played in directing human action. His *Essays on the Law of Nature* (1663) was an attempt to define the degree of obligation which the individual had towards natural law. By natural law he meant a "law promulgated by God in a natural way." The binding force of natural law according to this argument was predicated on the interdependent relationship between God, natural law, and human nature. It was assumed that the individual had a moral as well as a natural obligation to natural law. On the one hand, it was felt that there are moral obligations which are binding because they arise from the commands of a superior will, which according to Locke is the final source of all obligation. Conversely, there are also natural obligations which are binding because they arise from man's innate nature.[40] The essential character of natural law was defined as being "implanted in man's heart by God so that reason can only discover and interpret it."[41] In addition, he asserted that all men are compelled to search out and discover natural laws ". . . since man is very much urged on this part of his duty by an

inward instinct."[42] Moreover, man is driven by his own innate nature to seek out the existence of natural law and is compelled by his own nature to obey it. As he explained this point, "For in the first place, it cannot be said that some men are born so free that they are not in the least subject to this law, for this is not a private or positive law created according to circumstances . . . rather it is a fixed and permanent rule of morals, which reason itself pronounces, and which persists being a fact so firmly rooted in the soul of human nature."

Locke, in his discussion of natural law, was again able to reconcile the belief in individual freedom of action with the Christian idea of divine determination by emphasizing that obedience to natural law is dictated by man's individual reason, which is in turn an element of human nature given to man by God. In this instance we see the specific interrelationships which existed between Locke's use of assumptions about human nature, his adamant belief in the liberal ideals of individual freedom, and his determination to avoid overt conflict with the more traditional Church doctrines which asserted that human action, at least to some degree, was ultimately influenced by divine will.

The popular belief maintained today by Marvin Harris and others that Locke's theory of tabula rasa was meant to demonstrate the social determination of human action and the denial of an innate human nature which may affect human behavior is a serious misinterpretation of Locke's actual intentions. The fact is that Locke utilized a whole number of assumptions about man's innate nature to justify his theories about man's ability to reason, his willingness to obey natural law, his right to individual liberty, and the role which God played in human affairs. In general, his social theories exemplify a basic interrelationship between his liberal views on individual liberty and his Christian background. Locke made use of assumptions about human nature to objectify, manifest, and legitimize both his liberal ideals and his Christian beliefs. His rejection of the Cartesian theory of innate ideas did not, in itself, mean that Locke accepted the idea that man is without any form of an innate human nature or that the individual is completely determined by social experience . . .

Notes

1 See John H. Abraham, *Origins and Growth of Sociology* (Middlesex, England: Penguin, 1973).

2 John W. Yolton, *John Locke and the Theory of Ideas* (Oxford: Clarendon Press, 1968).

3 Marvin Harris, *The Rise of Anthropological Theory* (New York: Crowell, 1968), p. 18.

4 Dennis Forcese and Stephen Richer, *Issues In Canadian Society* (Scarborough, Ontario: Prentice-Hall, 1975), p. 7.

5 Leonard Broom and Philip Selznick, *Sociology* (New York: Harper & Row, 1963), p. 15.

6 Robert Nisbet, *The Social Bond* (New York: Knopf, 1950), p. 46.

7 See: James Gibson, *Locke's Theory of Knowledge and Its Historical Relations* (Cambridge, England: University Press, 1960); Ernest L. Tuueson, *The Imagination As A Means of Grace – Locke and the Aesthetics of Romanticism* (Berkeley: University of California, 1960); Emile Brehier, *The Seventeenth Century* (Chicago: University of Chicago, 1966); Marvin Harris, *The Rise of Anthropological Theory* (New York: Crowell, 1968); John L. Kraus, *John Locke: Empiricist, Atomist, Conceptualist and Agnostic* (New York: Philosophical Library, 1968); and John W. Yolton, *Locke and the Compass of Human Understanding* (Cambridge, England: University Press, 1970).

8 Kraus, *John Locke*, pp. 26–27.

9 Daniel W. Rossides, *The History and Nature of Sociological Theory* (Boston: Houghton Mifflin, 1978), p. 47.

10 Ernst Cassirer, *The Philosophy of the Enlightenment* (Boston: Beacon, 1962), p. 29.

11 Peter Gay, *Age of Enlightenment* (NY: Time, 1969).

12 Rossides, *Sociological Theory*, p. 29.

13 See Gordon Hefelbower, *The Relation of John Locke to English Deism* (Chicago: University of Chicago, 1919).

14 Ellen M. Wood, *Mind and Politics* (Berkeley, Calif.: University of California, 1972), p. 177.

15 Cassirer, *The Enlightenment*, p. 39.

16 Frederick B. Artz, *The Enlightenment in France* (Kent, Ohio: Kent University, 1968), p. 12.

17 Crawford B. Macpherson, *The Political Theory of Possessive Individualism* (London: Oxford University, 1962), p. 3.

18 Irving M. Zeitlin, *Ideology and the Development of Sociological Theory* (New Jersey: Prentice-Hall, 1968), p. 3.

19 Shirley Gruner, *Economic Materialism and Social Moralism* (The Hague: Mouton, 1973), pp. 14–15.

20 John R. White, *The Anti-Philosophes* (London: Martin Press, 1970), p. 5.

21 William J. Brandt, *The Shape of Medieval History – Studies in Modes and Perception* (New York: Schoken, 1977).

2 John H. Brumfitt, *The French Enlightenment* (Cambridge, Mass.: Schenkman, 1972), p. 44.

23 Ibid.

24 Norman L. Torrey, *Les Philosophes* (New York: Capricorn, 1960), pp. 12–13.

25 René Descartes, *Objections and Replies*, ed. Margaret Wilson (New York: Mentor, 1969), p. 260.

26 Lionel Gossman, *French Society and Culture* (Englewood Cliffs, N.J.: Prentice-Hall, 1972), pp. 76–77.

27 John Locke, *Essay On Human Understanding* (Germany: Scientia Verlage Aalen, 1968), p. 1.

28 Ibid., p. 15.

29 Ibid., p. 35.

30 Ibid., pp. 82–83.

31 Ibid., p. 86.

32 Ibid., pp. 97–98.

33 Ibid., p. 137.

34 Ibid., pp. 137–138.

35 Ibid., p. 234.

36 Ibid., pp. 270–271.

37 Norman W. DeWitt, *Epicurus and His Philosophy* (New York: Paulist Press, 1964), pp. 216–248.

38 Locke, *Essay On Human Understanding*, p. 67.

39 Roland N. Stromberg, *An Intellectual History of Modern Europe* (New York: Prentice-Hall, 1975), p. 113.

40 John Locke, *Essays On the Law of Nature*, ed. William Von Leyden (Oxford: Clarendon, 1954), p. 50.

41 Ibid., p. 95.

42 Ibid., p. 159.

A System of Logic
John Stuart Mill

From Book I, Chapter 3: Feelings, or States of Consciousness

§3. A Feeling and a State of Consciousness are, in the language of philosophy, equivalent expressions everything is a feeling of which the mind is conscious; everything which it *feels*, or, in other words, which forms a part of its own sentient existence. In popular language Feeling is not always synonymous with State of Consciousness; being often taken more peculiarly for those states which are conceived as belonging to the sensitive, or to the emotional, phasis of our nature, and sometimes, with a still narrower restriction, to the emotional alone, as distinguished from what are conceived as belonging to the percipient or to the intellectual phasis. But this is an admitted departure from correctness of language; just as, by a popular perversion the exact converse of this, the word Mind is withdrawn from its rightful generality of signification, and restricted to the intellect. The still greater perversion by which Feeling is sometimes confined not only to bodily sensations, but to the sensations of a single sense, that of touch, needs not to be more particularly adverted to.

Feeling, in the proper sense of the term, is a genus, of which Sensation, Emotion, and Thought, are subordinate species. Under the word Thought is here to be included whatever we are internally conscious of when we are said to think; from the consciousness we have when we think of a red colour without having it before our eyes, to the most recondite thoughts of a philosopher or poet. Be it remembered, however, that by a thought is to be understood what passes

From J. S. Mill (1843). *A system of logic, ratiocinative and inductive, being a connected view of the principles of evidence, and the methods of scientific investigation.* London: John W. Parker.

in the mind itself, and not any object external to the mind, which the person is commonly said to be thinking of. He may be thinking of the sun, or of God, but the sun and God are not thoughts; his mental image, however, of the sun, and his idea of God, are thoughts; states of his mind, not of the objects themselves; and so also is his belief of the existence of the sun, or of God; or his disbelief, if the case be so. Even imaginary objects (which are said to exist only in our ideas) are to be distinguished from our ideas of them. I may think of a hobgoblin, as I may think of the loaf which was eaten yesterday, or of the flower which will bloom tomorrow. But the hobgoblin which never existed is not the same thing with my idea of a hobgoblin, any more than the loaf which once existed is the same thing with my idea of a loaf, or the flower which does not yet exist, but which will exist, is the same with my idea of a flower. They are all, not thoughts, but objects of thought; though at the present time all the objects are alike non-existent.

In like manner, a Sensation is to be carefully distinguished from the object which causes the sensation; our sensation of white from a white object: nor is it less to be distinguished from the attribute whiteness, which we ascribe to the object in consequence of its exciting the sensation. Unfortunately for clearness and due discrimination in considering these subjects, our sensations seldom receive separate names. We have a name for the objects which produce in us a certain sensation: the word *white*. We have a name for the quality in those objects, to which we ascribe the sensation: the name *whiteness*. But when we speak of the sensation itself (as we have not occasion to do this often except in our scientific speculations), language, which adapts itself for the most part only to the common uses of life, has provided us with no single-worded or immediate designation; we must employ a circumlocution, and say, The sensation of white, or The sensation of whiteness; we must denominate the sensation either from the object, or from the attribute, by which it is excited. Yet the sensation, though it never *does*, might very well be *conceived* to exist, without anything whatever to excite it. We can conceive it as arising spontaneously in the mind. But if it so arose, we should have no name to denote it which would not be a misnomer. In the case of our sensations of hearing we are better provided; we have the word Sound, and a whole vocabulary of words to denote the various kinds of sounds. For as we are often conscious of these sensations in the absence of any perceptible object, we can more easily conceive having them in the absence of any object whatever. We need only shut our eyes and listen to music, to have a conception of an universe with nothing in it except sounds, and ourselves hearing them: and what is easily conceived separately, easily obtains a separate name. But in general our names of sensations denote indiscriminately the sensation and the attribute. Thus, *colour* stands for the sensations of white, red, &c., but also for the quality in the coloured object. We talk of the colours of things as among their *properties*.

§4. In the case of sensations, another distinction has also to be kept in view, which is often confounded, and never without mischievous consequences. This is, the distinction between the sensation itself, and the state of the bodily organs which precedes the sensation, and which constitutes the physical agency by which it is produced. One of the sources of confusion on this subject is the division commonly made of feelings into Bodily and Mental. Philosophically speaking, there is no foundation at all for this distinction: even sensations are states of the sentient mind, not states of the body, as distinguished from it. What I am conscious of when I see the colour blue, is a feeling of blue colour, which is one thing; the picture on my retina, or the phenomenon of hitherto mysterious nature which takes place in my optic nerve or in my brain, another thing, of which I am not at all conscious, and which scientific investigation alone could have apprised me of. These are states of my body: but the sensation of blue, which is the consequence of these states of body, is not a state of body: that

which perceives and is conscious is called Mind. When sensations are called bodily feelings, it is only being the class of feelings which are immediately occasioned by bodily states; whereas the other kinds of feelings, thoughts, for instance, or emotions, are immediately excited not by anything acting upon the bodily organs, but by sensations, or by previous thoughts. This, however is a distinction not in our feelings, but in the agency which produces our feelings: all of them when actually produced are states of mind.

From Book III, Chapter 7: Of Observation and Experiment

§1. It results from the preceding exposition, that the process of ascertaining what consequents in nature are invariably connected with what antecedents, or, in other words, what phenomena are related to each other as causes and effects, is in some sort a process of analysis. That every fact which begins to exist has cause, and that this cause must be found in some fact or concourse of facts which immediately preceded the occurrence, may be taken for certain. The whole of the present facts are the infallible result of all past facts, and more immediately of all the facts which existed at the moment previous. Here, then, is a great sequence, which we know to be uniform. If the whole prior state of the entire universe could again recur, it would again be followed by the present state. The question is, how to resolve this complex uniformity into the simpler uniformities which compose it, and assign to each portion of the vast antecedent the portion of the consequent which is attendant on it.

This operation, which we have called analytical, inasmuch as it is the resolution of a complex whole into the component elements, is more than a merely mental analysis. No mere contemplation of the phenomena, and partition of them by the intellect alone, will of itself accomplish the end we have now in view. Nevertheless, such a mental partition is an indispensable first step. The order of nature, as perceived at a first glance, presents at every instant a chaos followed by another chaos. We must decompose each chaos into single facts. We must learn to see in the chaotic antecedent a multitude of distinct antecedents, in the chaotic consequent a multitude of distinct consequents. This, supposing it done, will not of itself tell us on which of the antecedents each consequent is invariably attendant. To determine that point, we must endeavour to effect a separation of the facts from one another, not in our minds only, but in nature. The mental analysis, however, must take place first. And every one knows that in the mode of performing it, one intellect differs immensely from another. It is the essence of the act of observing, for the observer is not he who merely sees the thing which is before his eyes, but he who sees what parts that thing is composed of. To do this well is rare talent. One person, from inattention, or attending only in the wrong place, overlooks half of what he sees; another sets down much more than he sees, confounding it with what he imagines, or with what he infers; another takes note of the *kind* of all the circumstances, but being inexpert in estimating their degree, leaves the quantity of each vague and uncertain; another sees indeed the whole, but makes such an awkward division of it into parts, throwing things into one mass which require to be separated, and separating others which might more conveniently be considered as one, that the result is much the same, sometimes even worse, than if no analysis had been attempted at all. It would be possible to point out what qualities of mind, and modes of mental culture fit a person for being a good observer: that, however, is a question not of Logic, but of the Theory of Education, in the most enlarged sense of the term. There is not properly an Art of Observing. There may be rules for observing. But these, like rules for inventing, are properly instructions for the preparation of one's own mind; for putting it into the state in which it will be most fitted to observe, or most likely to invent. They are, therefore, essentially rules of self-education, which is a different thing from Logic. They do not teach how to do the thing, but how to make ourselves capable of doing it. They are an art of strengthening the limbs, not an art of using them.

The extent and minuteness of observation which may be requisite, and the degree of decomposition to which it may be necessary to carry the mental analysis, depend on the particular purpose in view. To ascertain the state of the whole universe at any particular moment is impossible, but would also be useless. In making chemical experiments, we do not think it necessary to note the position of the planets; because experience has shown, as a very superficial experience is sufficient to show, that in such cases that circumstance is not material to the result: and accordingly, in the ages when men believed in the occult influences of the heavenly bodies, it might have been unphilosophical to omit ascertaining the precise condition of those bodies at the moment of the experiment. As to the degree of minuteness of the mental subdivision, if we were obliged to break down what we observe into its very simplest elements, that is, literally into single facts, it would be difficult to say where we should find them: we can hardly ever affirm that our divisions of any kind have reached the ultimate unit. But this, too, is fortunately unnecessary. The only object of the mental separation is to suggest the requisite physical separation, so that we may either accomplish it ourselves, or seek for it in nature; and we have done enough when we have carried the subdivision as far as the point at which we are able to see what observations or experiments we require. It is only essential, at whatever point our mental decomposition of facts may for the present have stopped, that we should hold ourselves ready and able to carry it farther as occasion requires, and should not allow the freedom of our discriminating faculty to be imprisoned by the swathes and bands of ordinary classification, as was the case with all early speculative inquirers, not excepting the Greeks, to whom it seldom occurred that what was called by one abstract name might, in reality, be several phenomena, or that there was possibility of decomposing the facts of the universe into any elements but those which ordinary language already recognised.

§2. The different antecedents and consequents being, then, supposed to be, so far as the case requires, ascertained and discriminated from one another, we are to inquire which is connected with which. In every instance which comes under our observation, there are many antecedents and many consequents. If those antecedents could not be severed from one another except in thought, or if those consequents never were found apart, it would be impossible for us to distinguish (*à posteriori* at least) the real laws, or to assign to any cause its effect, or to any effect its cause. To do so, we must be able to meet with some of the antecedents apart from the rest, and observe what follows from them; or some of the consequents, and observe by what they are preceded. We must, in short, follow the Baconian rule of *varying the circumstances*. This is, indeed, only the first rule of physical inquiry, and not, as some have thought, the sole rule; but it is the foundation of all the rest.

For the purpose of varying the circumstances, we may have recourse (according to a distinction commonly made) either to observation or to experiment; we may either *find* an instance in nature suited to our purposes, or, by an artificial arrangement of circumstances, *make* one. The value of the instance depends on what it is in itself, not on the mode in which it is obtained: its employment for the purposes of induction depends on the same principles in the one case and in the other, as the uses of money are the same whether it is inherited or acquired. There is, in short, no difference in kind, no real logical distinction, between the two processes of investigation. There are, however, practical distinctions to which it is of considerable importance to advert.

§3. The first and most obvious distinction between Observation and Experiment is, that the latter is an immense extension of the former. It not only enables us to produce a much greater number of variations in the circumstances than nature spontaneously offers, but, also, in thousands of cases, to produce the precise *sort* of variation which we are in want of for discovering the law of the phenomenon, – a service which nature, being constructed on a quite different scheme from that of facilitating our studies, is seldom so friendly as to bestow upon us. For example, in order to ascertain what principle in the atmosphere enables it to sustain life, the variation we require is that a living animal should be immersed in each component element of the atmosphere separately. But nature does not supply either oxygen or azote in a separate state. We are indebted to artificial experiment for our knowledge that it is the former, and not the latter, which supports respiration; and for our knowledge of the very existence of the two ingredients.

Thus far the advantage of experimentation over simple observation is universally recognised:

all are aware that it enables us to obtain innumerable combinations of circumstances which are not to be found in nature, and so add to nature's experiments a multitude of experiments of our own. But there is another superiority (or, as Bacon would have expressed it, another prerogative) of instances artificially obtained over spontaneous instances, – of our own experiments over even the same experiments when made by nature, – which is not of less importance, and which is far from being felt and acknowledged in the same degree.

When we can produce a phenomenon artificially, we can take it, as it were, home with us, and observe it in the midst of circumstances with which in all other respects we are accurately acquainted. If we desire to know what are effects of the cause A, and are able to produce A by means at our disposal, we can generally determine at our own discretion, so far as is compatible with the nature of the phenomenon A, the whole of the circumstances which shall be present along with it: and thus, knowing exactly the simultaneous state of everything else which is within the reach of A's influence, we have only to observe what alteration is made in that state by the presence of A.

From Book VI, Chapter 2:
Of Liberty and Necessity

§1. The question whether the law of causality applies in the same strict sense to human actions as to other phenomena, is the celebrated controversy concerning the freedom of the will, which, from at least as far back as the time of Pelagius, has divided both the philosophical and the religious world. The affirmative opinion is commonly called the doctrine of Necessity, as asserting human volitions and actions to be necessary and inevitable. The negative maintains that the will is not determined, like other phenomena, by antecedents, but determines itself; that our volitions are not, properly speaking, the effects of causes, or at least have no causes which they uniformly and implicitly obey.

I have already made it sufficiently apparent that the former of these opinions is that which I consider the true one; but the misleading terms in which it is often expressed, and the indistinct manner in which it is usually apprehended, have both obstructed its reception and perverted its influence when received. The metaphysical theory of free will, as held by philosophers, (for the practical feeling of it, common in a greater or less degree to all mankind, is in no way inconsistent with the contrary theory), was invented because the supposed alternative of admitting human actions to be *necessary* was deemed inconsistent with every one's instinctive consciousness, as well as humiliating to the pride, and even degrading to the moral nature, of man. Nor do I deny that the doctrine, as sometimes held, is open to these imputations; for the misapprehension in which I shall be able to show that they originate unfortunately is not confined to the opponents of the doctrine, but is participated in by many, perhaps we might say by most, of its supporters.

§2. Correctly conceived, the doctrine called Philosophical Necessity is simply this: that, given the motives which are present to an individual's mind, and given likewise the character and disposition of the individual, the manner in which he will act might be unerringly inferred; that if we knew the person thoroughly, and knew all the inducements which are acting upon him, we could foretell his conduct with as much certainty as we can predict any physical event. This proposition I take to be a mere interpretation of universal experience, a statement in words of what every one is internally convinced of. No one who believed that he know thoroughly the circumstances of any case, and the characters of the different persons concerned, would hesitate to foretell how all of them would act. Whatever degree of doubt he may in fact feel arises from the uncertainty whether he really knows the circumstances, or the character of some one or other of the persons, with the degree of accuracy required; but by no means from thinking that if he did know these things, there could be any uncertainty what the conduct would be. Nor does this full assurance conflict in the smallest degree with what is called our feeling of freedom. We do not feel ourselves the less free because those to whom we are intimately known are well assured how we shall will to act in a particular case. We often, on the contrary, regard the doubt what our conduct will be as a mark of ignorance of our character, and sometimes even resent it as in imputation. The religious metaphysicians who have asserted the freedom of the will have always maintained it to be consistent with divine foreknowledge of our actions; and if with divine, then with any other foreknowledge. We may be free, and yet another may have reason to be perfectly certain what use we shall make of our freedom. It is not, therefore, the doctrine that our volitions and actions are invariable consequents of our antecedent states of mind, that is either contradicted by our consciousness or felt to be degrading.

From Book VI, Chapter 4:
Of the Laws of Mind

§1. What the Mind is, as well as, what Matter is, or any other question respecting Things in themselves, as distinguished from their sensible manifestations, it would be foreign to the purposes of this treatise to consider. Here, as throughout our inquiry, we shall keep clear of all speculations respecting the mind's own nature, and shall understand by the laws of mind those of mental phenomena – of the various feelings or states of consciousness of sentient beings. These, according to the classification we have uniformly followed, consist of Thoughts, Emotions, Volitions, and Sensations; the last being as truly States of Mind as the three former. It is usual, indeed, to speak of sensations as states of body, not of mind. But this is the common confusion of giving one and the same name to a phenomenon and to the proximate cause or conditions of the phenomenon. The immediate antecedent of a sensation is a state of body, but the sensation itself is a state of mind. If the word mind means anything, it means that which feels.

Whatever opinion we hold respecting the fundamental identity or diversity of matter and mind, in any case the distinction between mental and physical facts, between the internal and the external world, will always remain as a matter of classification; and in that classification, sensations, like all other feelings, must be ranked as mental phenomena. The mechanism of their production, both in the body itself and in what is called outward nature, is all that can with any propriety be classed as physical.

The phenomena of mind, then, are the various feelings of our nature, both those improperly called physical and those peculiarly designated as mental; and by the laws of mind I mean the laws according to which those feelings generate one another.

§2. All states of mind are immediately caused either by other states of mind or by states of body. When a state of mind is produced by a state of mind, I call the law concerned in the ease a law of Mind. When a state of mind is produced directly by a state body, the law is a law of Body, and belongs to physical science.

With regard to those states of mind which are called sensations, all are agreed that these have for their immediate antecedents states of body. Every sensation has for its proximate cause some affection of the portion of our frame called the nervous system, whether this affection originate in the action of some external object, or in some pathological condition of the nervous organisation itself. The laws of this portion of our nature – the varieties of our sensations and the physical conditions on which they proximately depend – manifestly belong to the province of Physiology.

Whether the remainder of our mental states are similarly dependent on physical conditions, is one of the *vexatæ questiones* in the science of human nature. It is still disputed whether our thoughts, emotions, and volitions are generated through the intervention of material mechanism; whether we have organs of thought and of emotion in the same sense in which we have organs of sensation. Many eminent physiologists hold the affirmative. These contend that a thought (for example) is as much the result of nervous agency as a sensation; that some particular state of our nervous system, in particular of that central portion of it called the brain, invariably precedes, and is presupposed by, every state of our consciousness. According to this theory, one state of mind is never really produced by another; all are produced by states of body. When one thought seems to call up another by association, it is not really a thought which recalls a thought; the association did not exist between the two thoughts, but between the two states of

the brain or nerves which preceded the thoughts: one of those states recalls the other, each being attended, in its passage, by the particular state of consciousness which is consequent on it. On this theory the uniformities of succession among states of mind would be mere derivative uniformities, resulting from the laws of succession of the bodily states which cause them. There would be no original mental laws, no Laws of Mind in the sense in which I use the term, at all; and mental science would be a mere branch, though the highest and most recondite branch, of the science of Physiology. M. Comte, accordingly, claims the scientific cognisance of moral and intellectual phenomena exclusively for physiologists; and not only denies to Psychology, or Mental Philosophy properly so called, the character of a science, but places it, in the chimerical nature of its objects and pretensions, almost on a par with astrology.

But, after all has been said which can be said, it remains incontestable that there exist uniformities of succession among states of mind, and that these can be ascertained by observation and experiment. Further, that every mental state has a nervous state for its immediate antecedent and proximate cause, though extremely probable, cannot hitherto be said to be proved, in the conclusive manner in which this can be proved of sensations; and even were it certain, yet every one must admit that we are wholly ignorant of the characteristics of these nervous states; we know not, and at present have no means of knowing, in what respect one of them differs from another; and our only mode of studying their successions or co-existences must be by observing the successions and co-existences of the mental states of which they are supposed to be the generators or causes. The successions, therefore, which obtain among mental phenomena do not admit of being deduced from the physiological laws of our nervous organisation; and all real knowledge of them must continue, for a long time at least, if not always, to be sought in the direct study, by observation and experiment, of the mental successions themselves. Since, therefore, the order of our mental phenomena must be studied in those phenomena, and not inferred from the laws of any phenomena more general, there is a distinct and separate Science of Mind.

On the Speech Center
Paul Broca

A twenty-one-year case of aphemia produced by the chronic and progressive softening of the second and third convolutions of the superior portion of the left frontal lobe

On 11 April 1861 there was brought to the surgery of the general infirmary of the hospice at Bicêtre a man named Leborgne, fifty-one years old, suffering from a diffused gangrenous cellulitis of his whole right leg, extending from the foot to the buttocks. When questioned the next day as to the origin of his disease, he replied only with the monosyllable *tan*, repeated twice in succession and accompanied by a gesture of his left hand. I tried to find out more about the antecedents of this man, who had been at Bicêtre for twenty-one years. I questioned his attendants, his comrades on the ward, and those of his relatives who came to see him, and here is the result of this inquiry.

Since youth he had been subject to epileptic attacks, yet he was able to become a maker of lasts, a trade at which he worked until he was thirty years old. It was then that he lost his ability to speak and that is why he was admitted to the hospice at Bicêtre. It was not possible to discover whether his loss of speech came on slowly or rapidly or whether some other symptom accompanied the onset of this affliction.

When he arrived at Bicêtre he had already been unable to speak for two or three months. He was then quite healthy and intelligent and differed from a normal person only in his loss of articulate language. He came and went in the hospice, where he was known by the name of "Tan." He understood all that was said to him. His hearing was actually very good, but whenever one questioned him he always answered, "Tan,

tan," accompanying his utterance with varied gestures by which he succeeded in expressing most of his ideas. If one did not understand his gestures, he was apt to get irate and added to his vocabulary a gross oath ["Sacré nom de Dieu!"] . . . Tan was considered an egoist, vindictive and objectionable, and his associates, who detested him, even accused him of stealing. These defects could have been due largely to his cerebral lesion. They were not pronounced enough to be considered pathological, and, although this patient was at Bicêtre, no one ever thought of transferring him to the insane ward. On the contrary, he was considered to be completely responsible for his acts.

Ten years after he lost his speech a new symptom appeared. The muscles of his right arm began to get weak, and in the end they became completely paralyzed. Tan continued to walk without difficulty, but the paralysis gradually extended to his right leg; after having dragged the leg for some time, he resigned himself to staying in bed. About four years had elapsed from the beginning of the paralysis of the arm to the time when paralysis of the leg was sufficiently advanced to make standing absolutely impossible. Before he was brought to the infirmary, Tan had been in bed for almost seven years. This last period of his life is the one for which we have the least information. Since he was incapable of doing harm, his associates had nothing to do with him anymore, except to amuse themselves at his expense. This made him angry, and he had by now lost the little celebrity which the peculiarity of his disease had given him at the hospice. It was also noticed that his vision had become notably weaker during the last two years. Because he kept to his bed this was the only aggravation one could notice. As he was not incontinent, they changed

Adapted from P. Broca (1861). Remarques sur le siège de la faculté du langage articulé, suivies d'une observation d'aphémie. *Bulletin de la Société Anatomiaque de Paris*, 6, 343–357.

his linen only once a week; thus the diffused cellulitis for which he was brought to the hospital on 11 April 1861 was not recognized by the attendants until it had made considerable progress and had infected the whole leg. . . .

The study of this unfortunate person, who could not speak and who, being paralyzed in his right hand, could not write, offered some difficulty. His general state, moreover, was so grave that it would have been cruel to torment him by long interviews.

I found, in any case, that general sensitivity was present everywhere, although it was unequal. The right half of his body was less sensitive than the left, and that undoubtedly contributed to the diminished pain at the site of the diffuse cellulitis. As long as one did not touch him, the patient did not suffer much, but palpation was painful and the incisions that I had to make provoked agitation and cries.

The two right limbs were completely paralyzed. The left ones could be moved voluntarily and, though weak, could without hesitation execute all movements. Emission of urine and fecal matter was normal, but swallowing was difficult. Mastication, on the other hand, was executed very well. The face did not deviate from normal. When he whistled, however, his left cheek appeared a little less inflated than his right, indicating that the muscles on this side of the face were a little weak. There was no tendency to strabismus. The tongue was completely free and normal; the patient could move it anywhere and stretch it out of his mouth. Both of its sides were of the same thickness. The difficulty in swallowing . . . was due to incipient paralysis of the pharynx and not to a paralysis of the tongue, for it was only the third stage of swallowing that appeared labored. The muscles of the larynx did not seem to be altered. The timbre of the voice was natural, and the sounds that the patient uttered to produce his monosyllable were quite pure.

Tan's hearing remained acute. He heard well the ticking of a watch but his vision was weak. When he wanted to see the time, he had to take the watch in his left hand and place it in a peculiar position about twenty centimeters from his right eye, which seemed better than his left.

The state of Tan's intelligence could not be exactly determined. Certainly, he understood almost all that was said to him, but, since he could express his ideas or desires only by movements of his left hand, this moribund patient could not make himself understood as well as he understood others. His numerical responses, made by opening or closing his fingers, were best. Several times I asked him for how many days had he been ill. Sometimes he answered five, sometimes six days. How many years had he been in Bicêtre? He opened his hand four times and then added one finger. That made 21 years, the correct answer. The next day I repeated the question and received the same answer, but, when I tried to come back to the question a third time, Tan realized that I wanted to make an exercise out of the questioning. He became irate and uttered the oath, which only this one time did I hear from him. Two days in succession I showed him my watch. Since the second hand did not move, he could distinguish the three hands only by their shape and length. Still, after having looked at the watch for a few seconds, he could each time indicate the hour correctly. It cannot be doubted, therefore, that the man was intelligent, that he could think, that he had to a certain extent retained the memory of old habits. He could understand even quite complicated ideas. For instance, I asked him about the order in which his paralyses had developed. First he made a short horizontal gesture with his left index finger, meaning that he had understood; then he showed successively his tongue, his right arm and his right leg. That was perfectly correct, for quite naturally he attributed his loss of language to paralysis of his tongue.

Nevertheless there were several questions to which he did not respond, questions that a man of ordinary intelligence would have managed to answer even with only one hand. At other times he seemed quite annoyed when the sense of his answers was not understood. Sometimes his answer was clear but wrong – as when he pretended to have children when actually he had none. Doubtless the intelligence of this man was seriously impaired as an effect either of his cerebral lesion or of his devouring fever, but obviously he had much more intelligence than was necessary for him to talk.

From the anamnesis and from the state of the patient it was clear that he had a cerebral lesion that was progressive, had at the start and for the first ten years remained limited to a fairly well circumscribed region, and during this first period had attacked neither the organs of motility nor of sensitivity; that after ten years the lesion had spread to one or more organs of motion, still leaving unaffected the organs of sensitivity; and that still more recently sensitivity had become dulled as well as vision, particularly the vision of the left eye. Complete paralysis affected the two right limbs; moreover, the sensitivity of these two limbs was slightly less than normal. Therefore, the principal cerebral lesion should lie in the left hemisphere. This opinion was reinforced by the incomplete paralysis of the left cheek and of the left retina, for, needless to say, paralyses of cerebral origin are crossed for the trunk and the extremities but are direct for the face. . . .

The patient died on 17 April [1861]. The autopsy was performed as soon as possible – that is to say, after 24 hours. The weather was warm but the cadaver showed no signs of putrefaction. The brain was shown a few hours later to the Société d'Anthropologie and was then put immediately into alcohol. It was so altered that great care was necessary to preserve it. It was only after two months and several changes of the fluid that it began to harden. Today it is in perfect condition and has been deposited in the Musée Depuytren. . . .

The organs destroyed are the following: the small inferior marginal convolution of the temporal lobe, the small convolutions of the insula, and the underlying part of the striate body, and, finally, in the frontal lobe, the inferior part of the transverse frontal convolution and the posterior part of those two great convolutions designated as the second and third frontal convolutions. Of the four convolutions that form the superior part of the frontal lobe, only one, the superior and most medial one, has been preserved, although not in its entirety, for it is softened and atrophied, but nevertheless indicates its continuity, for, if one puts back in imagination all that has been lost, one finds that at least three quarters of the cavity has been hollowed out at the expense of the frontal lobe.

Now we have to decide where the lesion started. An examination of the cavity caused by the lack of substance shows at once that the center of the focus corresponds to the frontal lobe. It follows that, if the softening spread out uniformly in all directions, it would have been this lobe in which the disease began. Still we should not be guided solely by a study of the cavity, for we should also keep an eye on the parts that surround it. These parts are very unequally softened and cover an especially variable extent. Thus the second temporal convolution, which bounds the lesion from below, exhibits a smooth surface of firm consistency; yet it is without doubt softened, though not much and only in its superficial parts. On the opposite side on the frontal lobe, the softened material is almost fluid near the focus; still, as one goes away from the focus, the substance of the brain becomes gradually firmer, although the softening extends in reality for a considerable distance and involves almost the whole frontal lobe. It is here that the softening mainly progressed and it is almost certain that the other parts were affected only later.

If one wished to be more precise, he could remark that the third frontal convolution is the one that shows the greatest loss of substance, that not only is it cut transversely at the level of the anterior end of the Sylvian fissure but it is also completely destroyed in its posterior half, and that it alone has undergone a loss of substance equal to about one-half of its total. The second or middle frontal convolution, although deeply affected, still preserves its continuity in its innermost parts; consequently it is most likely that the disease began in the third convolution. . . .

Anatomical inspection shows us that the lesion was still progressing when the patient died. The lesion was therefore progressive, but it progressed very slowly, taking twenty-one years to destroy a quite limited part of the brain. Thus it is reasonable to believe that at the beginning there was a considerable time during which degeneration did not go past the limits of the organ where it started. We have seen that the original focus of the disease was situated in the frontal lobe and very likely in its third frontal convolution. Thus we are compelled to say, from the point of view of pathological anatomy, that there were two periods, one in which only one frontal convolution, probably the third one, was attacked, and another period in which the disease gradually spread toward other convolutions, to the insula, or to the extraventricular nucleus of the corpus striatum.

When we now examine the succession of the symptoms, we also find two periods, the first of which lasted ten years, during which the faculty of speech was destroyed while all other functions of the brain remained intact, and a second period of eleven years, during which paralysis of movement, at first partial and then complete, successively involved the arm and the leg of the right side.

With this in mind it is impossible not to see that there was a correspondence between the anatomical and the symptomological periods. Everyone knows that the cerebral convolutions are not motor organs. Of all the organs attacked, the corpus striatum of the left hemisphere is the only one where one could look for the cause of the paralysis of the two right extremities. The second clinical period, in which the motility changed, corresponds to the second anatomical period, when the softening passed beyond the limit of the frontal lobe and invaded the insula and the corpus striatum.

It follows that the first period of ten years, clinically characterized only by the symptom of aphemia, must correspond to the period during which the lesion was still limited to the frontal lobe.

Cortical Localization and Cerebral Dominance: The Work of Paul Broca
Stanley Finger

Speech and the Frontal Lobe

The first cortical localization that became widely accepted linked fluent, articulate speech to the frontal cortex. The issue of cortical localization of function was being debated in the French learned societies when Paul Broca presented his famous clinical case showing this in 1861. Although many other scientists had previously presented data both for and against the theory, earlier contributions failed to have the impact of Broca's case study.

For example, Jean-Baptiste Bouillaud (1796–1881), a student of Magendie and a respected figure in French science, had long emphasized the use of clinical examinations and autopsy material to support the case for localization of function. In 1825, after examining data from a large number of cases, an approach that clearly distinguished him from his predecessors, he wrote:

> In the brain there are several special organs, each one of which has certain definite movements depending upon it. In particular, the movements of speech are regulated by a special cerebral centre, distinct and independent. Loss of speech depends sometimes on loss of memory for words, sometimes of want of the muscular movements of which speech is composed. . . . Loss of speech does not necessitate want of movements of the tongue, considered as an organ of prehension, mastication, deglutination of food; nor does it necessitate loss of taste. The nerves ani-

mating the muscles, which combine in the production of speech arise from the anterior lobes or at any rate possess the necessary communications with them. (Translated in Head, 1926, 13–14)

Bouillaud cited Claud-François Lallemand (1790–1854) and Léon Louis Rostan (1790–1866) to bolster his case. In 1820 and 1823, respectively, these men had also reported loss of speech after anterior lobe damage. Bouillaud then argued that lesions elsewhere did not affect fluent speech (see Head, 1926; Ombredane, 1951; Stookey, 1963).

Unfortunately, Bouillaud had two negative factors working against him. First, he had been a founding member of the *Société Phrénologique*. Although he soon questioned Gall's cranioscopy procedures and recommended the use of brain-injured patients to study structure-function relationships, the scientific community remained overly cautious about anything or anyone associated in any way with Gall or phrenology.

Second, Bouillaud's descriptions of the causal lesions, like those of his predecessors and contemporaries, were less than satisfactory. As stated by Adolf Kussmaul (1822–1902) in 1878 (p. 721):

> In order to understand how superficially localizations are recorded even in the writings of the best of the older observers, let one cast a glance at the principal works of such men as Bouillaud, Lallemand and Rostan, to whom, notwithstanding, the pathology of the brain owes so much. They are content to indicate the affected lobe with the general designation, "in front," "behind," "in the middle," etc., and with equally indefinite appreciation of the extent of the lesion. One seldom learned whether the cortex or the white

medulla, corpum striatum, centrum, semiovale, etc., was the seat of the lesion.

It should also be noted that not everyone at this time was finding impairments in speech after frontal lobe lesions. For instance, Gabried Andral (1797–1846) discussed 37 cases of frontal lobe lesions collected at the Charité hospital between 1820 and 1831 and found speech to be seriously impaired in only 21 of these cases. Andral (1840) did not say anything about the side of damage, but he did mention that he also had 14 cases of speech loss who had sustained brain damage posterior to the frontal lobes. These findings left him cautious at best about accepting localization.

Even more disconcerting was the response from Jean Cruveilhier (1791–1874) to Bouillaud's assertions. Cruveilhier stated:

> If it is pathologically demonstrated that a lesion of the anterior lobes is constantly accompanied by a corresponding alteration of speech; on the other hand, if lesions of all parts of the brain other than the anterior lobes never entail speech alterations, the question is solved, and I immediately become a phrenologist. . . . In fact, the loss of the faculty of sound articulation is not always the result of a lesion of the anterior lobes of the brain; moreover, I am able to prove that the loss of the faculty of sound articulation can accompany a lesion of any other part of the brain. (Translated in Riese, 1977, 59)

Thus, rather than being a time of calm, this was a time of controversy and debate, especially in the halls of the French scientific academies. On the whole, the conservatives were on Flourens' side, while the liberals were the localizers (Head, 1926). It was in this far from tranquil environment, with men like Simon Alexandre Ernest Aubertin (1825–1893) arguing for localization and Pierre Gratiolet (1815–1865) taking the opposing position, that an enfeebled Monsieur Leborgne was transferred to Broca's surgical ward. This dying man had been hospitalized for 21 years, and he now showed epilepsy, loss of speech, and right hemiplegia. Broca took it upon himself to examine Leborgne as a test of Bouillaud's and Aubertin's contention that speech loss will always be associated with a large lesion of the anterior lobes.

Six days after Broca saw him, Leborgne died. His brain, which proved to be in poor condition due to infarctions, was removed and presented to the Société d'Anthropologie the next day. Broca issued a weak statement about localization at this time, but at a decidedly more animated meeting of the Société d'Anatomie later that year, he boldly proclaimed that his case study of Leborgne placed him in firm agreement with the localizationists. Broca was especially careful to emphasize that his localization of a faculty for articulate language in the frontal lobe differed from that proposed by Gall, although both he and the phrenologists believed that articulate speech was an anterior lobe function.

Broca's "conversion" was a true landmark event, and many people who were vacillating about localization accepted the localizationist doctrine after Broca took his stand. As for Monsieur Leborgne, because he had often uttered a word that sounded like "tan," Broca's first and most famous case became known as Tan to the scientific community.

Just why did the case of Tan have so much impact relative to the material presented by Bouillaud, Aubertin, and others who favored localization? The answer to this question probably rests on four important factors that converged in Broca's report (Sondhaus and Finger, 1988). First, Broca's paper contained detail: detail in the case history, detail in its emphasis on articulate speech as opposed to any defect in speech, and detail in trying to find a more circumscribed locus to account for the symptoms. Second, the findings did not support the site of the faculty proposed by the phrenologists. Third, there was a willingness on the part of the scientific community to listen to these ideas at this time; the Zeitgeist was right. And fourth, it was Paul Broca, the highly respected scientist, physician, and esteemed head of academic societies, who was now willing to lead the fight for cortical localization of function.

It is worth noting that two more years would pass before Broca would note that the lesion affecting speech was usually on the left side. But even in his 1863 statements, Broca seemed uncomfortable about dealing with the issue of dominance. Perhaps it was because the two sides of the brain looked so similar to him and because, as a scientist, he felt it best always to proceed cautiously. Hence, it was not until 1865 that he addressed this issue in a more direct and meaningful way. Further, while Broca might at first have believed that he was observing an invariant principle when he argued that the center for articulate language resided in the third left frontal convolution, he soon found himself discussing and trying to account for exceptions to this "rule" (Berker, Berker, and Smith, 1986; Finger and Wolf, 1988).

Broca's Case for Dominance

In his note, in the *Bulletins de la Société d' Anthropologie,* published in May 1863, Paul Broca described eight cases of aphasia, all with lesions on the left side. At the time, this seemed surprising to him. Unlike Marc Dax, Broca could only say that whereas this caught his attention, he could not draw firm conclusions until he had accumulated more facts.

Later that year, Jules Parrott (1829–1883) presented the case of a patient who had a lesion of the right frontal lobe without an articulate language disturbance. Broca recognized that this finding also pointed to the special role of the left hemisphere in speech. Nevertheless, Broca seemed to realize that given how hard it was for the conservative scientific establishment to accept a frontal lobe localization for articulate speech, it was going to be even more difficult to present the novel idea that only the left frontal lobe was essential for this function.

In 1864, Broca described two more patients who had traumatic head injuries on the left side (cited in Duval, 1864). Here he referred to the mounting evidence for left side involvement.

> Numerous observations gathered during the last three years have a tendency to indicate that lesions of the left hemisphere are solely susceptible for causing aphemie. This proposition is no doubt strange, but however perplexing it may be for physiology, it must be accepted if subsequent findings continue to indicate the same view point. (Translated in Berker, Berker, & Smith, 1986, p. 1066)

In contrast to this relative conservatism, and perhaps now stirred by his knowledge of the Dax findings, Broca's 1865 paper dealt directly and extensively with the issue of left hemispheric dominance for language. This extraordinary paper appeared in the June 15 issue of the *Gazette Hebdomadaire de Médecine et de Chirurgie,* the same journal that published the Marc and Gustave Dax paper less than two months earlier. Broca now took a firm position about left hemispheric dominance for articulate speech, but was careful to add that language was not the exclusive function of the left hemisphere.

> This does not mean to say that the left hemisphere is the exclusive center of the general capacity of language, which consists of establishing a determined relationship between an idea and a sign, nor even of the special capacity of articulate speech, which consists of establishing a determined relationship between an idea and an articulate word. The right hemisphere is not more a stranger than the left hemisphere to this special faculty, and the proof is that the person rendered speech disabled through a deep and extensive lesion of the left hemisphere is, in general, deprived only of the faculty to reproduce the sounds of articulate speech; he understands perfectly the connection between ideas and words. In other words, the capacity to conceive these connections belongs to both hemispheres, and these can, in the case of a malady, reciprocally substitute for each other; however, the faculty to express them by means of coordinated movements in which the practice requires a very long period of training, appears to belong to but one hemisphere, which is almost always the left hemisphere. (Translated in Berker, Berker, & Smith, 1986, p. 1068)

Armand Trousseau (1864), like Bouillaud, felt that the statistics offered good support for the statements made by Marc Dax and Paul Broca about the significance of the left side of the brain for speech. He thought the data were also relevant to the question of the seat of the intellect. This view stemmed from his observations of many aphasic patients who showed impairments in general intelligence that went well beyond their language difficulties. Trousseau speculated that the cause of these functional asymmetries might be different blood supplies and other anatomical differences between the hemispheres.

These ideas were acknowledged positively by Jules Gabriel François Baillarger, who postulated that the more rapid growth of the left hemisphere could also explain handedness. In addition, Pierre Gratiolet and François Leuret (1797–1851) had claimed some years earlier that there were differences of a few grams between the two hemispheres during development, with the left hemisphere being the heavier (Gratiolet and Leuret, 1839–1857).

Broca himself accepted these ideas. Hence, in 1865, he made a strong case for the two hemispheres not being innately different from each other, but for the left being more precocious. The implication was that the left hemisphere would be educated first and would take the lead in the acquisition of speech and handedness.

In his 1865 paper, Broca wrote that he believed speech was mediated by the right hemisphere in left-handed people. The concept of reversed dominance was readily accepted, as seen in this quotation from William Gowers 20 years later:

In left-handed persons the "speech-centre" is usually on the right, and not on the left side of the brain, and the association just mentioned was well exemplified by a left-handed man, who, at the age of thirty-one, became liable to fits

which commenced by spasms in the left side of the face, spreading thence to the left arm, without loss of consciousness. Inability to speak preceded each attack for ten minutes, and persisted afterwards for the same time. (1885, 38)

Only in the twentieth century did scientists begin to wonder whether Broca might have been wrong about dominance in left-handed people. In his 1914 review of cerebral functions, Shepherd Ivory Franz stated that the general belief that aphasias in left-handed people are produced by lesions in the right hemisphere was not borne out by case studies. Franz specifically discussed one case in which the author found that a left-handed person developed an aphasia after a lesion of the left frontal lobe. With more time, it was recognized that a majority of left-handed people still have speech localized on the left side of the brain or exhibit more of a "mixed" dominance.

References

Andral, G. (1840). *Clinique medicale* (4th edn.) Paris: Fortin, Massonet Cie.

Berker, E. A., Berker, A. H., & Smith, A. (1986). Translation of Broca's 1865 report: Localization of speech in the third frontal convolution. *Archives of Neurology, 43*, 1065–1072.

Duval, A. (1864). Deux cas d'aphémie traumatique, produite par des lesions de la troisième circonvolution frontale gauche: Diagnostique chirurgical. *Société de Chirurgerie de Paris Bulletin, 5*, 51–63.

Finger, S., & Wolf, C. (1988). The "Kennard effect" before Kennard: The early history of age and brain lesion effects. *Archives of Neurology, 45*, 1136–1142.

Franz, S. I. (1914). The functions of the cerebrum. *Psychological Bulletin, 11*, 131–140.

Gowers, W. R. (1885). *Epilepsy.* London: William Woods & Co.

Gratiolet, P., & Leuret, F. (1839–1857). *Anatomie comparée du système nerveux, considerée dans ses rapports avec l'intelligence* (2 vols; Vol. 2). Paris: J. B. Balliere.

Head, H (1926). *Aphasia and kindred disorders of speech.* New York: Macmillan.

Kussmaul, A. (1878). Disturbances of speech: An attempt in the pathology of speech. In H. V. Ziemssen (Ed.), *Cyclopedia in the practice of medicine*, Vol. 14. New York: Wood.

Ombredane, A. (1951). *L'aphasie et l'elaboration de la pensée explicite.* Paris: Presses Universitaires de France.

Riese, W. (1977). Discussions about cerebral localization in the learned societies of the nineteenth century. In K. Hoops, Y. Lebrun, & E. Buyssens (Eds.), *Selected papers on the history of aphasia*, Vol. 7. Amsterdam: Swets and Zeitling.

Sondhaus, E., & Finger, S. (1988). Aphasia and the C. N. S. from Imhotep to Broca. *Neuropsychology, 2*, 87–110.

Stookey, B. (1963). Jean Baptiste-Bouillaud and Ernest Aubertin: Early studies on cerebral localization and the speech center. *Journal of the American Medical Association, 184*, 1024–1029.

Trousseau, A. (1864). De l'aphasie, maladie décrite recemment sous le nom impropre d'aphémie. *Gazette des Hopitaux, Paris, 37*, 13–14, 25–26, 37–39, 48–50.

Chapter 3

Wilhelm Wundt and the Founding of Scientific Psychology

Recall, from Chapter 2, John Locke's distinction between primary and secondary qualities. That distinction acknowledged the existence of experience that was independent of the physical objects of the world. As psychology sought to establish itself as a scientific discipline, it was important that human perception and physical stimulation not be perfectly correlated. If such a relationship existed, meaning that changes in physical stimuli always resulted in similar changes in the perception of those stimuli, then it meant that perception (and, more broadly, psychology) and physical stimuli were the same. Under those circumstances there would be no need for psychology; human perception would be wholly explained by the laws of the discipline of physics.

But how was it possible to compare the physical world with the psychological world? (The reader should recognize that question as a version of the centuries-old mind–body problem.) One answer to that question came to Gustav Theodor Fechner (1801–1887) on the morning of October 22, 1850, while he was lying in bed. He reasoned that mind could be studied by recording an individual's reactions to known changes in physical stimulation. This approach, which Fechner labeled *psychophysics*, allowed the comparison of the psychological world and the physical world. Fechner made two other important discoveries. First, he demonstrated that there was not a one-to-one correspondence between changes in the physical world (stimuli) and changes in the psychological world (the perception of those stimuli). Second, he demonstrated that although the relationship between stimuli and perceptions was not linear, it was predictable; that is, the psychological and physical worlds are lawfully related.

In 1860, Fechner published one of the most important books in the history of psychology, *Elements of Psychophysics*, a treatise of such consequence that it has led some historians of psychology to name Fechner as the founder of scientific psychology (for example, Adler, 1977; Boring, 1950). Fechner's book laid out the conceptual issues in measuring the physical and psychological worlds, described a set of methods for undertaking that measurement, and reported his own psychophysical work, including his derivation of a logarithmic law that predicted stimulus–perception relationships better than an earlier law proposed by Ernst Weber. Fechner's 1860 book proved of great influence in psychology, both conceptually and methodologically, as evidenced by the late nineteenth-century work of Wilhelm Wundt and Hermann Ebbinghaus in Germany, and Charles S. Peirce and George Trumbull Ladd in the United States.

Although Fechner's role in the science of psychology is an important one, he is not the popular favorite for "founder of the new science." That honor is typically accorded to Wilhelm Wundt (1832–1920), who established what most scholars agree was the earliest psychology laboratory in the world in Leipzig, Germany, in 1879. But the laboratory founding, albeit important, is not the reason most historians acknowledge Wundt as founder. According to historian Thomas Leahey (1991), "Wundt is the founder because he wedded physiology to philosophy and made the resulting offspring independent. He brought the empirical methods of physiology to the questions of philosophy and also created a new, identifiable role – that of the psychologist, separate from the roles of philosopher, physiologist, or physician" (p. 55). Another historian, John O'Donnell (1985), has referred to Leipzig as the place where psychology was initially manufactured, and argues that Wundt's central role in the development of psychology "derives not from any scientific discovery that bears his name eponymously but rather from his heroic propagandizing for experimentalism" (p. 16). Wundt's plans for psychology gestated for more than 20 years before the Leipzig laboratory was founded.

Wundt graduated from the University of Heidelberg in 1855, finishing at the top of his medical school class. After a short time in Berlin, where he worked with the famous physiologist Johannes Müller, Wundt returned to Heidelberg to work as Helmholtz's assistant (recall the work of Müller and Helmholtz discussed in the previous chapter). There he published his first book, on muscular movements and sensations, in 1858. A second book followed in 1862, entitled *Contributions to the Theory of Sense Perception*. It was in this book that Wundt laid out his plans for psychology, an experimental science that would uncover the facts of consciousness. At this time he was teaching a course on experimental physiology that included some psychological material. By 1867 the title of Wundt's course had become "Physiological Psychology," and out of these lectures emerged his most important work for the founding of psychology, the *Principles of Physiological Psychology* (1874). This work went through six editions in Wundt's lifetime and is clearly among the most important publications in the history of psychology. It was a compendium of all the research to that date related to Wundt's vision of an experimental psychology. In the preface to that work he made his vision clear, noting that it was his intention to establish psychology as a new domain of science.

In 1874 Wundt took a faculty position at Zurich University, but he stayed there only a year before accepting a newly established professorship in philosophy at the University of Leipzig. There he would remain for the rest of his life, establishing the laboratory in 1879 and the first psychological journal, *Philosophische Studien*, two years later in 1881. It was the beginning of an academic Mecca for psychology that would draw students from all over Europe, particularly Germany and Austria, and from the United States and Canada. In his career, Wundt directed the doctoral theses of 66 students in psychology. That number included such famous individuals as Hugo Münsterberg, Edward Bradford Titchener, and Emil Kraepelin.

In the latter half of the nineteenth century, it was not uncommon for American students to go abroad for their graduate education (see Sokal, 1981). Of Wundt's psychology students, 16 came from Canada and the United States (see Benjamin, Durkin, Link, Vestal, & Acord, 1992). That number included Lightner Witmer, who founded the first psychological clinic in the United States at the University of Pennsylvania (see Baker, 1988; O'Donnell, 1979); Walter Dill Scott, who was one of the pioneers of industrial psychology (see Ferguson, 1976); Edward Wheeler Scripture, who would distinguish himself in speech pathology; Charles H. Judd, whom many consider to be the founder of educational psychology; and James McKeen Cattell, who founded the psychology laboratories at the University of Pennsylvania and Columbia University and pioneered the use of mental tests (see Sokal, 1981, 1982).

Wundt's psychology was actually two psychologies. One he labeled *voluntarism* and the other he called *Völkerpsychologie*. The former was his experimental psychology, the psychology of his laboratory studies; the latter was an empirical but nonexperimental psychology whose scope included art, religion, language, law, morality, and culture. *Völkerpsychologie* doesn't translate well into English. It has been variously termed ethnic psychology or social psychology or cultural psychology or folk psychology. None of those labels does justice to this version of his psychology. He spent the last 20 years of his life working on this psychology, producing 10 lengthy volumes, most of which have never been translated into English. While immersed in this work, he continued his experimental studies, supervising doctoral students into his eighties. Our focus in this chapter will be on voluntarism. For more on Wundt's *Völkerpsychologie*, see Cahan & White (1992) and Danziger (1980).

For Wundt, the goal of psychology was to discover the facts of consciousness and the relationships among these facts, including the combinations that were produced. Influenced by the mental chemistry of Mill, he called for an analysis of consciousness into its psychical elements and compounds, to identify those elements and to understand how they combined to produce more complex mental experiences. As Mill had suggested, this was a logical beginning. But it was just that, a beginning. Wundt recognized that the human mind was more than a summary of its elements and compounds. The mind was an active entity that organized, analyzed, and altered the psychical elements and compounds of consciousness, creating experiences, feelings, and ideas that would not be evident from any analysis of just the components. Wundt's selection of the label voluntarism was to indicate the voluntary, active, and willful nature of the mind. Key to understanding his voluntaristic psychology is the concept of *apperception*. Apperception is the process that gives clarity to consciousness. It is an active, willful process by which the individual brings a mental focus to the complexity of conscious experience. Apperception had another role, however, beyond that of clarifying, and that was to synthesize psychical elements and compounds into new conscious experiences.

Another crucial part of Wundt's voluntaristic psychology was his distinction between *mediate experience* and *immediate experience* and his insistence that the latter constituted the subject matter of scientific psychology. Mediate experience was the domain of the physical sciences such as physics and chemistry, where physical events (for example, the intensity of a sound) might be measured by a device such as a sound-level meter. But the psychologist, according to Wundt, was interested in another kind of experience, and that was the conscious experience of that sound by a human listener. The human listener would make judgments about sounds based on how loud or how soft the sounds appeared to that individual. This is immediate experience. It is experience as felt by the individual and not as mediated through some external measuring device (thus mediate experience). In making this important distinction, Wundt was reflecting the beliefs about human experience identified in the works of Locke, Mill, and Fechner.

Eventually, Wundt's psychology, and that of his contemporaries, was replaced by newer psychological approaches. Although parts of his psychological system exist in modern psychology (see Blumenthal, 1975, in this chapter), we continue to remember him primarily for his vision in seeing the promise of a science of psychology and then taking the truly giant steps required in the nineteenth century to establish the discipline. It is true that Wundt built on the work of those philosophers and physiologists who came before him, just as a mason mixes gravel and cement, but it was Wundt who fashioned those elements into the concrete blocks of psychology and laid them in place to form a new scientific structure.

The Readings

The first selection is from Wundt's *Outlines of Psychology*, which he published in 1896, and which is one of the many books of Wundt that have been translated into English. It begins with a discussion of psychical elements, distinguishing between sensations and feelings. (Compare these ideas with the opening of the Mill excerpt in the previous chapter on consciousness and feelings.) Overlaying this section is an explanation of immediate experience as related to sensations and feelings. The excerpt finishes with a brief treatment of psychical compounds. It is in this section that the seeds of a voluntaristic psychology are made most evident. Wundt talks about psychical compounds as processes, not things (a point noted in Blumenthal's article which appears as the second reading in this chapter). Wundt (1896) wrote that "the attributes of psychical compounds are never limited to those of the elements that enter into them . . . that new attributes, peculiar to the compounds themselves, always arise as a result of the combination of these elements" (p. 40). This was the process of synthesis, sometimes called creative synthesis, that was the willful, active part of the mind.

Knowledge of Wundt has increased considerably in the past several decades. Partly this new vision was facilitated by the attention given to the celebration, in 1979, of the centennial of Wundt's laboratory, but it is also the result of at least two other factors. First, historians of psychology have begun to read Wundt in the original German, rather than the English translations. Not only has this scholarship resulted in a new image of Wundt's theoretical system in psychology, but it has portrayed a breadth of interest (for example, his *Völkerpsychologie*) that has been missing from biographical and theoretical accounts of Wundt. Second, these historians have made much use of archival material in Germany associated with Wundt and his contemporaries.

These recent studies that have redefined Wundt are often referred to as the "new Wundt scholarship," meaning that they have led to a reinterpretation of Wundt as scientist and of the nature of his psychology. Primary in this new scholarship was an article by Arthur Blumenthal published in 1975 and entitled "A reappraisal of Wilhelm Wundt." This author set out to "examine the fundamentals of Wundt's psychology that have, for better or worse, been disguised or lost in the course of history's machinations" (p. 1081). It is the second of the readings in this chapter and is acknowledged to have initiated this reexamination. Blumenthal begins with a discussion of Wundt's theoretical system and the methods of Wundt's laboratory. He points to a number of contemporary trends in psychology that bear relevance to Wundt's work, particularly in cognitive psychology, a relevance that has been missing in contemporary accounts. He also addresses the issue of Wundt's debt to Mill in terms of mental chemistry, arguing that such influence was important for Wundt at the beginning of his work, but that Wundt later rejected the chemical analogy as too limiting.

This article served as a springboard for much of the historical research on Wundt that would follow. One of those studies is the final reading of this chapter, an article by Henning Schmidgen (2003) that reexamines the question of Wundt's mental chemistry. Schmidgen, a historian of science, disagrees with Blumenthal's interpretation of the influence of chemistry on Wundt. He cites Wundt's claim that the lectures of Robert Bunsen (of Bunsen burner fame) were so compelling that he considered switching from medicine to chemistry. Schmidgen argues that it was neither medicine nor physiology that stimulated Wundt's interest in experimentation, but Bunsen's classroom demonstrations that led him to pursue life as a scientist. Wundt had wanted to work in Bunsen's lab but was a novice, and Bunsen wouldn't take a beginner. Instead, Wundt got a position working in the private chemistry laboratory of Gustav Herth. There he conducted his first experiment, a chemical analysis of his own urine which was published in 1853 as his first article. Schmidgen states that this initial experiment had a profound impact in shaping Wundt's views of how to proceed in psychological science. The importance of this study is discussed in detail, as is the influence of Mill's *System of Logic*.

We will get one more look at the new Wundt scholarship in Chapter 5 in an article by Thomas Leahey (1981) that compares the psychologies of Wundt and one of his most famous students, E. B. Titchener. Together these articles by contemporary historians and the excerpt from Wundt provide a provocative look at Wundt's experimental psychology and the varied interpretations of historical evidence.

Psychical Elements and Compounds
Wilhelm Wundt

I. Psychical Elements

1. All the contents of psychical experience are of a composite character. It follows, therefore, that *psychical elements*, or the absolutely simple and irreducible components of psychical phenomena are the products of analysis and abstraction. This abstraction is rendered possible by the fact that the elements are in reality united in different ways. If an element, *a*, is connected in one case with the elements *b*, *c*, *d*, . . . and in another case with *b'*, *c'*, *d'*, . . . it is possible to abstract it from all the other elements, because none of them is always united with it. If, for example, we hear a simple tone of a certain pitch and intensity, it may be located now in this direction, now in that, and may be heard at different times in connection with various other tones. But since the direction is not constant, or the accompanying tone in all cases the same, it is possible to abstract from these variable elements, and we have the single tone as a psychical element.

2. As a result of psychical analysis, we find that there are *psychical elements of two kinds,* corresponding to the *two factors* contained in immediate experience, namely, to the objective contents of experience and to the experiencing subject. The elements of the objective contents we call *sensational elements,* or simply *sensations:* such are a tone, or a particular sensation of heat, cold, or light, if in each case we neglect for the moment all the connections of these sensations with others, and also all their spacial and temporal relations. The subjective elements, on the other hand, are designated as *effective elements,* or *simple feelings.* We may mention as examples, the

feelings accompanying sensations of light, sound, taste, smell, heat, cold, or pain, the feelings aroused by the sight of an agreeable or disagreeable object, and the feelings arising in a state of attention or at the moment of a volitional act. Such simple feelings are in a double sense products of abstraction: every such feeling is connected in reality with an ideational element, and is furthermore a component of a psychical process which occurs in time, during which the feeling itself is continually changing.

3. The actual contents of psychical experience always consist of various combinations of sensational and affective elements, so that the specific character of a given psychical process depends for the most part, not on the nature of its elements, so much as on their union into a composite psychical compound. Thus, the idea of an extended body or of a rhythm, an emotion, and a volition, are all *specific* forms of psychical experience. But their character as such is as little determined by their sensational and affective elements as are the chemical properties of a compound body by the properties of its chemical elements. *Specific* character and *elementary* nature of psychical processes are, accordingly, two entirely different concepts. Every psychical element is a specific content of experience, but not every specific content is at the same time a psychical element. Thus, spacial and temporal ideas, emotions, and volitional acts, are specific, but not elementary processes.

4. Sensations and simple feelings exhibit certain common attributes and also certain characteristic differences. They have in common *two determinants,* namely, *quality* and *intensity.* Every simple sensation and every simple feeling has a definite *qualitative* character that marks it off from all other sensations and feelings; and this quality must always have some degree of *intensity*.

From W. Wundt (1896). *Grundriss der Psychologie.* Leipzig: Engelmann. From C. H. Judd (Trans.), *Outlines of psychology.* New York: Gustav Sechert, 1902, pp. 32–41, 100–103.

Our *designations* of psychical elements are based entirely upon their qualities; thus, we distinguish such sensations as blue, grey, yellow, warmth and cold, or such feelings as grave, cheerful, sad, gloomy, and sorrowful. On the other hand, we always express the differences in the intensity of psychical elements by the same quantitative designations, as weak, strong, medium strong, and very strong. These expressions are in both cases class-concepts which serve for a first superficial arrangement of the elements, and each expression embraces an unlimitedly large number of concrete elements. Language has developed a relatively complete stock of names for the qualities of simple sensations, especially for colors and tones. Names for the qualities of feelings and for degrees of intensity are far behind in number and precision. Certain attributes other than quality and intensity, such as distinctness and indistinctness, are sometimes classed with quality and intensity as fundamental attributes. But since clearness, obscurity, etc., . . . always arise from the interconnection of psychical compounds, they can not be regarded as determinants of psychical elements.

5.   Made up, as it is, of the *two* determinants, quality and intensity, every psychical element must have a certain *degree of intensity* from which it is possible to pass, by continual gradations, to every other degree of intensity in the same quality. Such gradations can be made in only *two* directions: one we call *increase* in intensity, the other *decrease*. The degrees of intensity of every qualitative element, form in this way a single dimension, in which, from a given point, we may move in two opposite directions, just as from any point in a straight line. This fact in regard to intensity may be expressed in the general statement: *The various intensities of every psychical element form a continuity of one dimension.* The extremities of such a continuity we call the *minimal* and *maximal sensations,* or the *minimal* or *maximal feelings,* as the case may be.

In contrast with this uniformity in intensities, *qualities* have more variable attributes. Every quality may, indeed, be assigned a place in a definite continuity of similar qualities in such a way that it is possible to pass uninterruptedly from a given point in this continuous series to any other point. But the various continuities of different

qualities, which we may call *systems of quality,* exhibit differences both in the variety of possible gradations and in the number of directions of gradation. With reference to these two kinds of variations in systems of quality, we may distinguish, on the one hand, *homogeneous* and *complex systems,* and on the other hand, *one-dimensional, two-dimensional,* and *many-dimensional* systems of quality. Within a homogeneous system, only such small differences are possible, that generally there has never arisen any practical need of distinguishing them by different names. Thus, we distinguish only *one* quality of pressure, of heat, of cold, or of pain, only *one* feeling of pleasure or of excitement, although, in intensity, each of these qualities may have many different grades. It is not to be inferred from this fact that in each of these systems there is really only *one* quality. The truth is that in these cases the number of different qualities is merely very limited; if we were to represent the system geometrically, we should probably never reduce it to a *single* point. Thus, for example, sensations of pressure from different regions of the skin show, beyond question, small qualitative differences which are great enough to make it possible for us to distinguish clearly any point of the skin from others at some distance from it. Such differences, however, as arise from contact with a sharp or dull point, or from a rough or smooth body, are not to be regarded as different qualities. They always depend on a large number of simultaneous sensations, and without the various combinations of these sensations into composite psychical compounds, the impressions mentioned would be impossible.

Complex systems of quality differ from those we have been discussing, in that they embrace a large number of clearly distinguishable elements between which all possible intermediate forms exist. In this class we must include the tonal system and color system, the systems of smells and tastes; and among the complex feeling systems we must include those which form the subjective complements of these sensational systems, such as the systems of tonal feelings, color feelings, etc. It is probable also that many systems of feelings belong here, which are objectively connected with composite impressions, but are as feelings, simple in character; such are the various feelings of harmony or discord which correspond to various combinations of tones. The differences in the *number of dimensions* have been determined with certainty only in the case of two or three sensational systems. Thus, the tonal system is one-dimensional. The ordinary color system, which includes the colors and their transitional qualities to white, is two-dimensional; while the complete system of light sensations, which includes also the dark color-tones and the transitional qualities to black, is three-dimensional.

6. In regard to the relations discussed thus far, sensational elements and affective elements agree in general. They differ, on the other hand, in certain essential attributes which are connected with the fact that sensations are immediately related to objects, while feelings are immediately related to the subject.

(1) When varied in a single dimension, sensational elements exhibit *pure qualitative differences,* which are always in the *same direction* until they reach the possible limits of variation, where they become *maximal differences.* Thus, in the color system, red and green, blue and yellow, or in the tonal system, the lowest and highest audible tones, are the maximal differences and are at the same time purely qualitative differences. Every affective element, on the contrary, when continuously varied in the proper direction of quality, passes gradually into a feeling of *opposite quality.* This is most obvious in the case of those affective elements which are regularly connected with certain sensational elements, as for example, tonal feelings or color feelings. As sensations, a high and low tone present differences that approach more or less the maximal differences of tonal sensation; the corresponding tonal feelings are opposites. In general, then, *series of sensational qualities are bounded at their extremes by maximal differences; series of affective qualities are bounded by maximal opposites.* Between affective opposites is a middle-zone, where the feeling is not noticeable at all. It is, however, frequently impossible to demonstrate this indifference-zone, because, while certain simple feelings disappear, other affective qualities remain, or new ones may arise. The latter case appears most commonly when the passing of the feeling into the indifference-zone depends on a change in sensations. Thus, in the middle of the musical scale, those feelings disappear which correspond to the high and low tones, but the middle tones have independent affective qualities of their

own which appear clearly only when the other complicating factors are eliminated. This is to be explained by the fact that a feeling which corresponds to a certain sensational quality is, as a rule, a component of a complex affective system, in which it belongs at the same time to various dimensions. Thus, the affective quality of a tone of given pitch belongs not only to the dimension of pitch feelings, but also to that of feelings of intensity, and finally to the different dimensions in which the clang character of tones may be arranged. A tone of middle pitch and intensity may, in this way, lie in the indifference-zone so far as feelings of pitch and intensity are concerned, and yet have a very marked clang feeling. The passage of affective elements through the indifference-zone can be directly observed only when care is taken to abstract from other accompanying affective elements. The cases most favorable for this observation are those in which the accompanying elements disappear entirely or almost entirely. Wherever such an indifference-zone appears without complication with other effective elements, we speak of the state as *free from feelings,* and of the sensations and ideas present in such a state, as *indifferent.*

(2) Feelings which have specific, and at the same time simple and irreducible quality, appear not only as the subjective complements of simple sensations, but also as the characteristic attendants of composite ideas or even of complex ideational processes. Thus, there is a simple tonal feeling which varies with the pitch and intensity of tones, and there is also a feeling of harmony which, regarded as a feeling, is just as irreducible as the tonal feeling, but varies with the character of compound clangs. Still other feelings, which may in turn be of the most various kinds, arise from melodious series of clangs. Here, again, each single feeling taken by itself at a given moment, appears as an irreducible unit. Simple feelings are, then, much more various and numerous than simple sensations.

(3) The various pure sensations may be arranged in a number of separate systems, between the elements of which there is no qualitative relation whatever. Sensations belonging to different systems are called *disparate.* Thus, a tone and a color, a sensation of heat and one of pressure, or, in general, any two sensations between which there are no intermediate qualities, are dis-

parate. According to this criterion, each of the four special senses (smell, taste, hearing, and sight) has a closed, complex sensational system, disparate from that of the other senses; while the general sense (touch) contains four homogeneous sensational systems (sensations of pressure, heat, cold, and pain). All simple feelings, on the other hand, form a single interconnected manifold, for there is no feeling from which it is not possible to pass to any other, through intermediate forms or through indifference-zones. But here too we may distinguish certain systems the elements of which are more closely related, as, for example, feelings from colors, tones, harmonies and rhythms. These are, however, not absolutely closed systems, for there are everywhere relations either of likeness or of opposition to other systems. Thus, feelings such as those from sensations of moderate warmth, from tonal harmony, and from satisfied expectation, however great their qualitative differences may be, are all related in that they belong to the general class of "pleasurable feelings." Even closer relations exist between certain single affective systems, as for example, between tonal feelings and color feelings, where the feelings from deep tones seem to be related to those from dark colors, and feelings from bright colors to those from high tones. When in such cases a certain relationship ascribed to the sensations themselves, it is probably due entirely to a confusion of the accompanying feelings with the sensations.

This third distinguishing characteristic shows conclusively that the source of the feelings is *unitary* while that of the sensations, which depend on a number of different, and in part distinguishable, conditions, is not unitary. Probably this difference in the character of the sources of feeling and sensations is directly connected, on the one hand, with the relation of the feelings to the unitary subject, and, on the other hand, with the relation of sensations of the great variety of *objects*.

6a. It is only in modern psychology that the terms "sensation" and "feeling" have gained the meanings assigned to them in the definitions above given. In older psychological literature these terms were sometimes used indiscriminatingly, sometimes interchanged. Even yet sensations of touch and sensations from the internal organs are called feelings by physiologists, and the sense of touch itself is known as the "sense of feeling." This corresponds, it is true, to the original significance of the word, where feeling is the same as touching, and yet, after the differentiation has once been made, a confusion of the two terms should be avoided. Then again, the word "sensation" is used even by psychologists to mean not only simple, but also composite qualities, such as compound clangs and spacial and temporal ideas. But since we have the entirely adequate word "idea" for such compounds, it is more advantageous to limit the word sensation to sense qualities which are psychologically simple. Finally the term "sensation" has sometimes been restricted so as to mean only those impressions which come directly from external sense stimuli. For the psychological attributes of a sensation, however, this circumstance is entirely indifferent, and therefore, such a definition of the term is unjustifiable.

The discrimination between sensational elements and affective elements in any concrete case is very much facilitated by the existence of indifference-zones in the feelings. Then again it follows from the fact that feelings range between opposites rather than mere differences, that feelings are much the more variable elements of our immediate experience. This changeable character, which renders it almost impossible to hold an effective state constant in quality and intensity, is the cause of the great difficulties that stand in the way of the exact investigation of feelings.

Sensations are present in all immediate experiences, but feelings may disappear in certain special cases, because of their oscillation through an indifference-zone. Obviously, then, we can, in the case of sensations, abstract from the accompanying feelings, but we can never abstract from sensations in the case of feelings. In this way two false views may easily arise, either that sensations are the *causes* of feelings, or that feelings are a particular species of sensations. The first of these opinions is false because affective elements can never be derived from sensations as such, but only from the attitude of the subject, so that under different subjective conditions the same sensation may be accompanied by different feelings. The second view, that feelings are a particular species of sensations, is untenable because the two classes of elements are distinguished, on the one hand by the immediate relation of sensations to objects and of feelings to the subject, and on the other hand, by the fact that the former range between maximal differences, the latter between maximal opposites. Because of the objective and subjective factors belonging to all psychical experience, sensations and feelings are to be looked upon as real and equally essential, though everywhere interrelated, elements of psychical phenomena. In the interrelation of the two groups of elements, the sensational elements appear as the more constant; they alone can be isolated through abstraction, by referring them to external objects. It follows, therefore, of necessity that in investigating the attributes of both kinds of elements, we must start with the sensations. Simple sensations, in the consideration of which we abstract from the accompanying affective elements, are called *pure sensations*. . . .

II. Psychical Compounds

1.   By "psychical compound" we mean any composite component of our immediate experience which is marked off from other contents of this experience by characteristics peculiarly its own, in such a way that it is recognized as a relatively independent unity and is, when practical necessity demands it, designated by a special name. In developing such a name, language has followed the general rule that only *classes* and the most important *species* into which phenomena may be grouped shall have special designations. Thus such terms as idea, emotion, volitional act, etc., designate general classes of psychical compounds, such terms as visual idea, joy, anger, hope, etc., designate special species included in these classes. So far as these designations are based upon actual, distinguishing characteristics, they have a certain value for psychological analysis. But in granting this, we must avoid from the first, *two* presuppositions to which the existence of these names might easily mislead us. The first is, that a psychical compound is an absolutely independent content of immediate experience. The second is, that certain compounds, as for example, ideas, have the *nature of things*. The truth is that compounds are only *relatively* independent units. Just as they are made up of various elements, so they themselves unite to form a complete interconnection in which relatively simple compounds may

continually combine to form more composite ones. Then, again, compounds, like the psychical elements contained in them, are never things, but *processes* which change from moment to moment, so that it is only through deliberate abstraction, which is, indeed, indispensable for the investigation in many cases, that they can be thought of as constant at any given moment. . . .

2.   All psychical compounds may be resolved into psychical elements, that is, into pure sensations and simple feelings. The two kinds of elements behave, however, in an essentially different manner, in keeping with the special properties of simple feelings. . . . The sensational elements found by such a resolution, always belong to one of the sensational systems already considered. The effective elements, on the other hand, include not only those which correspond to the pure sensations contained in the compounds, but also those due to the interconnection of the elements into a compound. The systems of sensational qualities, accordingly, remain the same, no matter how many varieties of compounds arise, while the systems of simple affective qualities continually increase. Furthermore, it is a general principle valid for all psychical compounds, whether they are composed of sensations only, of feelings only, or of combinations of both sensations and feelings, that *the attributes of psychical compounds are never limited to those of the elements that enter into them*. It is true rather that *new* attributes, peculiar to the compounds themselves, always arise as a result of the combination of these elements. Thus, a visual idea has not only the attributes of the light sensations and sensations of ocular position and movements contained in it, but it has also the attribute of spacial arrangement of the sensations, a factor not present in the elements themselves. Again a volition is made up not only of the ideas and feelings into which its single acts may be resolved, but there result also from the combination of these single acts, new affective elements which are specifically characteristic of the complex volition. Here, again, the combinations of sensational and affective elements are different. In the first case, on account of the constancy of the sensational systems, no new sensations can arise, but only peculiar *forms of their arrangement*. These forms are the *extensive spacial* and *temporal manifotds*. When, on the other hand,

affective elements combine, *new simple feelings* arise, which unite with those originally present to make *intensive* affective units of composite character.

3. The classification of psychical compounds is naturally based upon the character of the elements that enter into them. Those composed entirely or chiefly of sensations are called *ideas*, those consisting mainly of affective elements, *affective processes*. The same limitations hold here as in the case of the corresponding elements. Although compounds are more the products of immediate discrimination among actual psychical processes than are the elements, still, there is in all exactness no pure ideational process and

no pure affective process, but in both cases we can only abstract to a certain extent from one or the other component. As in the case of the two kinds of elements, so here, we can neglect the accompanying subjective states when dealing with ideas, but we must always presuppose some idea when giving an account of the affective processes.

We distinguish, accordingly, three chief forms of *ideas*: (1) intensive ideas, (2) spacial ideas, (3) temporal ideas; and three forms of *affective processes*: (1) intensive affective combinations, (2) emotions, (3) volitions. Temporal ideas constitute a sort of link between the two kinds of compounds, for certain feelings play an important part in their formation.

References

Kant, *Anthropologie*, 2nd. Bk. Herbart, *Textbook of Psychology*, §68 and 95. (Differentiation of the concepts sensation and feeling in the present-day sense.)

Horwicz, *Psychologische Analysen auf physiolog Grundlage*, 2 vols., 1872–1878.

Wundt, *Ueber das Verhältniss der Gefühle zu den Vorstellungen*, Vierteljahrsschr. f. wiss. Philos., III, 1879. (Also in *Essays*, 1885).

A Reappraisal of Wilhelm Wundt
Arthur L. Blumenthal

Approximately 100 years ago, in an era of intellectual ferment, events of marked consequence took place in the history of psychology. It was in the decade of the 1870s that the first handbook of experimental psychology appeared, followed soon by the founding of the first formal laboratory of experimental psychology. Both were the achievements of Wilhelm Wundt, ever since recognized as experimental psychology's great patron, though later barred from any role that might remotely resemble sainthood. Soon after the wave of "new" psychologists spread out from Wundt's laboratory, a series of intellectual revolutions largely erased from memory the content of Wundtian psychological theory.

Now that the movement set in motion by Wundt has come through its first century, it would seem fitting to mark the centenary by briefly turning back, reexamining psychology's historical foundations, and paying homage to the founding father. There is, however, another reason for review, being less ceremonial and clearly more interesting. To put it simply, the few current Wundt-scholars (and some do exist) are in fair agreement that Wundt as portrayed today in many texts and courses is largely fictional and often bears little resemblance to the actual historical figure (cf. Blumenthal, 1970; Bringmann, Balance, & Evans, 1975; Mischel, 1970).

Naturally, it might be suspected that the above radical statement is only the nit-picking of a few antiquarians obsessed with minor matters of interpretation. But alas, such is not the case. These are claims about the very fundamentals of

A. L. Blumenthal (1975). A reappraisal of Wilhelm Wundt. *American Psychologist, 30,* 1081–1088. Copyright © 1975 by the American Psychological Association. Reprinted by permission of the publisher and the author.

Wundt's work, often asserting the opposite of what has been a standard description prevailing over much of the past century. Yet, if popular historical accounts of Wundt are in need of serious correction, then one might again ask whether Wundt still turns out to be irrelevant and of little interest. This article is addressed to that question, and its answers will, I suspect, contain some surprises for many readers.

There is another question that immediately follows upon these claims. It is, How could such historical misinterpretations have arisen? This is surely a fascinating question but one requiring separate treatment. For the moment merely take note that Wundtian anecdotes have long been passed down from author to author without worthy recourse to original sources, and, also, that it is common in intellectual history for later schools of thought to foster distortions and misinterpretations of earlier ones – psychology of course, offering numerous opportunities. For now, let us examine the fundamentals of Wundt's psychology that have, for better or worse, been disguised or lost in the course of history's machinations.

Wundt's Method

The basic premise in Wundtian psychology is that the only certain reality is immediate experience. Proceeding from this premise. Wundt had accepted the following goals for all science: the construction of explanations of experience and the development of techniques for objectifying experience. By the latter, he meant that the scientist attempts to communicate and reproduce his experiences in others in standardized ways; thus it becomes possible to perform tests that lead to public agreement about phenomena and to agreement about their explanation. This was commonplace for Wundt and is found at the outset of many of his texts.

In the natural sciences, as Wundt continues, it is the attributes of experience derived from external objects and energies that are subjected to tests, explanations, and public agreement. But in the case of psychology, it is the attributes of experience derived from the processes of the experiencing subject that are made the object of tests, explanations, and public agreement. These psychological entities include experienced memory and perceptual capacities, fluctuations of attention or alertness, ranges of our sensitivities, etc. In the jargon of today, we would without hesitation say "human information-processing capacities."

Yet it is this subtle division between the physical and the psychological sciences that has led to innumerable textbook treatments of Wundt as a mind-body dualist, and that is one of history's glaring distortions. For if you read Wundt, in almost any of his texts, you will discover that his rejection of mind-body dualism is as emphatic a statement on the matter as you are likely ever to encounter. He often said that psychology cannot be defined as the science of the mind because there are no objects called "minds" that are distinct from objects called "bodies," a scenario that appears repeatedly in his works.

Although physiologists and psychologists study one and the same organism, Wundt viewed them as analyzing and objectifying different experiences derived from different vantage points. This is now usually called the "double-aspect" resolution of the mind-body problem. And Wundt's use of the phrase "psychophysical parallelism" referred to this same view, though again it unfortunately led many later reviewers to the mind–body-dualism interpretation. Rather, it referred to the separate orientations of physiology and psychology where it is separate *methodologies*, in the sense of separate types of observations, that here run in parallel.

Another serious problem of misinterpretation concerns Wundt and *introspection*. Contrary to frequent descriptions, Wundt was not an introspectionist as that term is popularly applied today. The thrust behind his entire experimental program was the claim that progress in psychology had been slow because of reliance on casual, unsystematic introspection, which had led invari-

ably to unresolvable debates. In several books and monographs (in particular, 1888 and 1907) Wundt argued that armchair introspection could in principle, never succeed, being a logical impossibility as a scientific technique. The 1907 monograph was a severe critique of the Würzburg psychologists for their return to an earlier style of unverifiable introspection.

Wundt promoted the cause of experimental psychology more through accomplishments in his laboratory than through polemics. From its outset, the Wundtian program followed the general conceptions of experimental science and the requirement that private experience be made public and replicable, in this case for the study of perception, attention, memory, etc. To be sure, there were some disagreements, conflicting data, and unsupported speculations in those days, just as there are today.

Wundt's adherence to the canons of experimental procedure was so strict that, in fact, it sharply limited his use of experiments in psychology. Thus, in the case of most "higher" mental processes such as language or concept formation, he felt that true experiments were not feasible. Instead, these topics must, he argued, be studied through techniques of historical and naturalistic observation and also of logical analysis. This Wundt did by examining the social-cultural products of human mental activity, making logical inferences about the underlying processes. In the case of language, for example, he went deeply into the technical study of linguistics (Blumenthal, 1970). So in these ways, a large part of Wundt's psychological work is not experimental.

Wundt's Theoretical System

But so far these are methodological matters and do not speak to the essence of Wundt's psychological theory. What emerged as the paradigm psychological phenomenon in his theoretical system would now be described as selective volitional attention. It is why he identified his psychology as "voluntaristic" to distinguish it from other schools (see especially Wundt, 1896b). He did not use the label "structuralist" which was proffered and perpetuated by Titchener and James.

Mischel (1970) has recently surveyed Wundt's writings, detailing Wundt's grounding in volitional-motivational processes. Yet it was with apparent forceful impact on later historical interpretation that Titchener (1908) had given short shrift to this theme, at the very heart of Wundtian psychology, because of the overtones of continental idealist philosophy in notions of volition. Titchener's longest period of formal education came at Oxford, and not surprisingly he maintained certain biases toward the British empiricist-sensationist tradition, even though that tradition was anathema to Wundt's views, and more than any other topic the brunt of Wundt's polemical writings.

Without giving supportive citation, Boring (1950) states that Wundt had opposed the implication of an active volitional agent in psychology. But now Mischel (1970) with extensive citation has shown, on the contrary, that volition-motivation is a central, primary theme in Wundt's psychology. Briefly, that theme runs as follows: To explain a volitional act on the basis of its motives is different from the explanation of occurrences in the physical sciences, and "volitional activities are the type in terms of which all other psychological phenomena are to be construed" (Wundt, 1908, Vol. 3, p. 162).

Wundt's studies of volition, in turn, amounted to an elaborate analysis of selective and constructive attentional processes (often summarized under the term *apperception),* which he localized in the brain's frontal lobes. Other psychological processes (perceptions, thoughts, memories) are, according to Wundt, generally under the control of the central attentional process.

It is on this basis that Wundt claimed another point of separation between psychology and physics – a difference between psychological and physical causality (see especially, Wundt, 1894). In the case of physics, actions and events obey inviolable laws; but in the case of psychosocial phenomena, actions are *made* by an active agent with reference to rule systems.

Wundt acknowledged the principle of the conservation of energy and, consequently, the theoretical possibility of reducing psychological observations to physiological or physical descriptions. Still, he argued, these physical sciences would then describe the act of greeting a friend, eating an apple, or writing a poem in terms of the laws of mechanics or in terms of physiology. And no matter how fine-grained and complicated we make such descriptions, they are not useful as descriptions of psychological events. Those events need be described in terms of intentions and goals, according to Wundt, because the actions, or physical forces, for a given psychological event may take an infinite variety of physical forms. In one notable example, he argued that human language cannot be described adequately in terms of its physical shape or of the segmentation of utterances, but rather must be described as well in terms of the rules and intentions underlying speech. For the ways of expressing a thought in language are infinitely variable, and language is governed by creative rules rather than fixed laws (Wundt, 1900–1920).

Mechanism or Organism?

These distinctions lead to a related and consistent theme in Wundt's writings concerning what he called "the false materialization of mental processes," which he found prevalent in other schools of psychology, especially associationism. His reactions against associationism were directed mostly at the form it had assumed in mid-19th-century Germany in Herbart's psychology.

Herbart, you may recall, had atomized mental processes into elemental ideas that became associated into compounds according to classical associationist descriptions. Wundt considered that approach to be a mere primitive analogy to systems of physical mechanics, and he argued at length that those systems teach little about the interrelations of psychological processes (Wundt, 1894). For those systems were oblivious to what he felt was the essential distinction between psychological and physical causality; they portrayed mental processes as if they were a "mere field of billiard balls" colliding and interacting with each other, where central control processes are lacking.

Boring's widely repeated assertion that Wundt turned to chemistry for his model seems clearly inaccurate to the serious reader of Wundt.

However, the Wundtian mental-chemistry cliché did become popular among later textbook writers. Wundt did in his early years make brief, passing reference to J. S. Mill's use of a chemical analogy to describe certain perceptual processes, namely, that one cannot determine the quality of water (i.e., "wetness") from the separate qualities of oxygen and hydrogen. Similarly, the qualities of a perception are not directly given in its underlying elements.

But Wundt points out that this analogy does not go far enough, and by the end of the century he is describing it as a false analogy because the chemical synthesis is, in the final analysis, wholly determined by its elements while the psychological synthesis is "truly a new formation, not merely the result of a chemical-like formation." And, "J. S. Mill's discussion in which the mental formation is conceived as a 'psychic chemistry' leaves out its most significant aspect – the special creative character of psychic syntheses" (Wundt, 1902, p. 684). What the chemical analogy lacks is the independent, constructive, attentional process which in the psychological case is the source of the synthesis.

Wundt did, of course, write chapters on elementary sensory-perceptual processes and elemental affective processes, but with the emphasis on *process*. And he acknowledged that a major part of any scientific methodology involved analysis of a system into component processes. Further, he stressed that these elements were to be taken as hypothetical constructs. Such elemental processes would never actually be observed, he thought, in pure isolation but would always be aspects or features of larger images or configurations.

Here Wundt used the German word *Gebilde.* For a translation, the dictionary (*Cassell's*) gives us the following choices: either "creation," "product," "structure," "formation," "system," "organization," "image," "form," or "figure." But in the few English translations of Wundt, we find the word "compound," unfortunately again suggesting analogy to chemistry. "Compound" is a conceivable choice, but in the context of Wundt's configurational system it seems not the best term. Another example: Wundt's "whole or unified mental impression" (*Gesamtvorstellung*) is unfortunately translated as "aggregate ideas."

In the following note in an obscure book, published in 1944, Wundt's own son, Max Wundt, rebutted the caricature of his father's work as a psychology of mental elements:

> One may follow the methodologically obvious principle of advancing from the simple to the complicated, indeed even employing the approach that would construct the mind from primitive mechanical elements (the so-called psychology of mental elements). In this case, however, method and phenomena can become grossly confused. . . . Whoever in particular ascribes to my father such a conception could not have read his books. In fact, he had formed his scientific views of mental processes in reaction against a true elementistic psychology, namely against that of Herbart, which was dominant in those days. (p. 15)

To confound matters further the later movement toward holism in Gestalt psychology placed Wundt in a contrastive position and again portrayed him as an elementalist and associationist in ways not characteristic of his intentions. True, there is always a chapter titled "Associations" in Wundt's texts – but it is a far cry from the serial linkages of atomistic ideas found among many associationists. Wundt's "associations" are "structural integrations," "creative syntheses," "fusions," and "perceptual patternings."

Wundt's later students, including Sander, Krueger, and Volkelt, renamed their school *Ganzheit* psychology or roughly "holistic psychology," and throughout the 1920s and 1930s the old Wundtian institute at Leipzig was a center for theorists with a holistic bent. Wundt's journal, the *Psychologische Studien,* which had ceased publication upon his retirement, was then reactivated with the title, *Neue Psychologische Studién.* It was the central organ of the *Ganzheit* psychologists; however, its articles primarily followed Wundt's interests in the "higher" mental processes and hence were mostly nonexperimental investigations.

Werner (1948) has written that Wundt represented the halfway mark in the transition from Herbart's atomism to the Gestaltists' holism. But from the point of view of Wundt's voluntaristic psychology, the essential central control processes were of no more primacy to the Gestaltists than to Herbart – both conceived a rather passive organism, one that is controlled by external or independent forces such as the a priori self-organizing qualities of sensory fields. Both, in sharp contrast to Wundt, appealed to physics for models and theories.

Modern Reconstructions

Now to describe Wundt's psychology in more detail, and to consider its present relevance, I want to outline some six current trends that could be viewed as reconstructions of Wundt's psychology in modern clothing:

First, Wundt's central emphasis on volitional processes bears noteworthy resemblance to the modern work on "cognitive control" as found, for example, in extensive research by Gardner, Klein, Holzman, and their associates (cf. Gardner, Holzman, Klein, Linton, & Spence, 1959). Both traditions used notions of different styles of attention deployment to explain a variety of perceptual and thought processes (sometimes even involving the same materials, e.g., the Müller–Lyer illusion).

The recent research, employing factor analyses of a variety of performance tasks, has determined two independent variables of cognitive control, which Gardner et al. call "field-articulation" and "scanning." These can be defined, as well, simply by substituting a similar description found in Wundt's psychology texts, as follows: First, in corresponding order, is Wundt's mental "clearness" process that concerns the focusing or emphasizing of a single item of experience. Wundt described this as "apperceptive synthesis" where variations from broad to narrow syntheses may occur. The second variable is a mental "distinctiveness" process which is the marking off of an item of experience from all others. Wundt described this as "apperceptive analysis," a relating and comparing function. The discovery and testing of nearly identical attention deployment factors in recent times occurred independently of the old Wundtian psychology. And too, the recent studies make frequent use of elaborate personality theories that were unavailable to Wundt.

Second, detailed comparisons have been made recently between the development of psycholin-

guistics in the 1960s and that of Wundtian psycholinguistics at the turn of the century (Blumenthal, 1970). Both the modern transformational grammarians after Chomsky and the Wundtian psycholinguists at the turn of the century trace their notions of language back to the same historical sources (e.g., to Humboldt). The psycholinguistic issues debated in the 1960s often parallel those debated at the turn of the century, such as the opposition between taxonomic and generative descriptions of language. Very briefly, Wundt's analysis of language usage depicts the transformation of simultaneous configurations of thought into sequential representations in language symbols by means of the scanning activities of attention (Wundt, 1900–1920, Vol. 1).

A *third* reconstruction concerns abnormal psychology. Among his students, the one who maintained the longest intellectual association with Wundt was the psychiatrist Emil Kraepelin (see Fischel, 1959). Kraepelin's (1919) attentional theory of schizophrenia is an application of Wundtian psychology, an explanation of schizophrenias as abnormalities of the attention deployment (apperception) process. It conceives certain abnormalities of behavior as resulting from flaws in the central control process that may take the form of either highly reduced attentional scanning, or highly erratic scanning, or extremes of attentional focusing. Kraepelin proposed that abnormalities in simple perceptual tests should show up in schizophrenic individuals corresponding to these particular control-process distortions.

The modern attentional theory of schizophrenia is a direct revival of the Kraepelinian analysis, as noted, for example, in an extensive review by Silverman (1964). As in the Kraepelinian descriptions, abnormalities of behavior result from disruptions of the central attentional processes where there is either highly reduced or highly erratic attentional scanning and focusing. And these mental changes, again, are indicated by divergent performances in simple perceptual tests.

Fourth is Wundt's three-factor theory of affect, which was developed by analogy to his formulations of multidimensional descriptions of certain areas of sensory experience. For the description of emotional experience, he used these three bipolar affective dimensions: *pleasant versus unpleasant, high arousal versus low arousal,* and *concentrated attention versus relaxed attention.* Wundt had adopted the first two dimensions from earlier writers on the topic of emotion. The third dimension reflects his characteristic emphasis on the process of attention.

Around the turn of the century, an intensive sequence of investigations to relate these dimensions to unique bodily response patterns did not meet with popular success. However, years later, when factor analysis became available, statistical studies of affective and attitudinal behavior again yielded factors that parallel those of Wundt rather closely (cf. Burt, 1950; Osgood, Suci, & Tannenbaum, 1957; Schlosberg, 1954; and several others reviewed by Strongman, 1973). Osgood's three dimensions are described as "good-bad," "active-passive," and "strong-weak." Schlosberg's dimensions are "pleasantness-unpleasantness," "high-low activation," and "attention-rejection."

Emotions and affects held an important place in Wundt's system because they were postulated as the constituents of volition. Further, Wundt suggested that almost every experience (perception, thought, or memory) has an affective component. Thus, affect became the basis for his explanation of pattern recognition: a melody, for instance, produces a very similar emotional configuration as it is transformed to other keys or played on other instruments. Wundt speculated that affect was the by-product of the act of apperceptive synthesis, and as such it was always on the periphery of consciousness. That is, we can never focus our attention upon an emotion, but can only focus on objects or memories that produce an emotional aura in immediate experience.

Fifth, the study of selective attention has been at the core of much of the recent work on human information processing (e.g., Broadbent, 1958; Kahneman, 1973; Moray, 1970; Neisser, 1967). It is impossible here to relate this highly complex field to the early Wundtian psychology other than to note the prominence of attention in both and that the time variable is central to both. Space permits mention of only two examples:

The seminal investigations of Sperling (1960) concerning perceptual masking are one example. Sperling took direct inspiration from Wundt's 1899 monograph on the use of tachistoscopes in psychological research in which Wundt came to

the following three conclusions about the perception of extremely brief stimuli: (1) the effective duration of a percept is not identical with the duration of the stimulus – but rather reflects the duration of a psychological process; (2) the relation between accuracy of a perception and stimulus duration depends on pre- and post-exposure fields (which may induce what we now call masking); and (3) central processes, rather than peripheral sense organ aftereffects, determine these critical times. Wundt's observations spurred a body of early research, and those early data are now relevant to a large body of similar modern investigations.

Perhaps the most frequently employed technique in Wundt's laboratory was that of reaction-time measurement. This was the direct adoption of a program suggested earlier by Donders (1868–1869). Essentially, inferences were made about human information-processing capacities on the basis of measured performance times under systematically varied performance conditions. This program has now, in post-mid-20th century, been widely and successfully revived. It is well illustrated, for instance, in the seminal studies of Sternberg (1970) on the attentional scanning of immediate-memory images, in which Sternberg draws the relation between his work and the earlier Donders program.

For a *sixth* and final comparison, I must refer to what Wundt called his deepest interest, which resulted in a 10-volume work titled *Völkerpsychologie: Eine Untersuchung der Entwicklungsgestze von Sprache, Mythus, und Sitte.* An English version of this title could be *Cultural Psychology: An Investigation of the Developmental Laws of Language, Myth, and Morality.** Appearing from 1900 through 1920, this series contains two books

---

* *Völkerpsychologie* has also been translated as "folk psychology," "psychology of peoples," and "ethnic psychology." Wundt quite deliberately avoided the terms *sociology* and *anthropology* because they were then heavily identified with the mid-19th-century positivism of Auguste Comte and related Anglo-French trends, which Wundt opposed. Some later writers on the history of psychology erroneously stated that the *Völkerpsychologie* is available in English translation. They apparently mistook a different and simpler one-volume work that E. Schaub (1916) translated as *Elements of Folk Psychology.*

on language, three on myth and religion, one on art, two on society, one on law, and one on culture and history. If there is a current work by another author that is conceptually close to these volumes, it is Werner's (1948) *Comparative Psychology of Mental Development*, today read in some circles of developmental psychologists.

Following Wundt, Werner described an *organismic* psychology that is in opposition to *mechanistic* psychologies. He also drew parallels, as did Wundt, between the development of individuals and of societies. And Werner acknowledged indebtedness to Wundt. But in Wundt's *Völkerpsychologie* there is, again, greater emphasis on volitional and attentional processes in the analysis of the development of human culture; he theorized that those central mental processes had emerged as the highest evolutionary development, and that they are the capacities that set men above other animals. It is the highly developed selective-attention capacities that, as he claimed, enabled mankind to make a consistent mental advance and to develop human culture. For without these capacities, men would forever be at the mercy of sporadic thoughts, memories, and perceptions.

Wundt's Historical Contexts

Wundt was not a mere encyclopedist or compiler of volumes, contrary to many descriptions. It was typical of him, however, always to compare and to contrast his system with other schools of thought, ancient and modern. Perhaps in that sense he could be considered an encyclopedist. True, most of his works begin with a long recital of his antecedents and the antecedents of rival positions.

Wundt's motivation for scholarly productivity should not be surprising, considering the strong family traditions that lay behind him (and that went unrecognized by most historical writers). Recent researchers (Bringmann et al., 1975) claim that no other German intellectual has a family tree containing as many ancestors engaged in intellectual pursuits. On his father's side were historians, theologians, economists, and geographers. On his mother's side were natural scientists and physicians. Two of his ancestors had been rectors of the University of Heidelberg.

To conclude, I wish to draw an outline of the streams of history in which Wundt lived and worked. Historians have often defined a few broad, alternating cultural epochs in the 19th century. At some risk in using a much-abused word, one might call each a "zeitgeist" – a time that favored a particular cultural style. These periods begin with the dominant romanticism and idealism early in the century, largely a German-inspired ethos shared by Kant, Humboldt, Schopenhauer, Goethe, Hegel, and Fichte, to mention a few. In that era, philosophy, science, religion, and art were often combined into something called "nature-philosophy." Such an integration was exemplified in the pantheistic writings of Gustav Fechner, an exotic latecomer to the romantic movement and an important source of inspiration for Wundt. (In several ways, Wundt's 10-volume *Völkerpsychologie* reflects the spirit of the old nature-philosophy.)

Around the mid-19th century, a positivist and materialist movement grew dominant by vigorously rejecting the previous idealism. There then appeared the influential Berlin Physical Society, the mechanistic psychology of Herbart, the behavioristic linguistics of the so-called *Junggrammatiker* linguists, and Comtean positivist sociology, among other examples across the disciplines. At the peak of this movement, academicians became methodology conscious to the extreme. The taxonomic methods of biology were imported into the social sciences. There was often a downgrading of "mentalism" in favor of "physicalism" and "environmentalism."

Then, toward the end of the 19th century came a resurgence of the romanticist-idealist outlook, particularly in continental Europe. It has been described either as neoromanticism, neoidealism, or neo-Kantianism. H. Stuart Hughes (1958) has provided summarization in his influential book, *Consciousness and Society: The Reorientation of European Social Thought, 1890–1930*. At around the time of World War I, this movement went into sharp decline, being displaced by a rebirth and rise in popularity of positivism and behaviorism which subsequently dominated many intellectual circles well into the 20th century.

Wundt's psychology rose and fell with the late-19th-century neoidealism. His core emphasis on volition and apperception comes straight from the earlier German idealist philosophy. It is not surprising that this should be so, for as a youth he was deeply inspired by the romanticist-idealist literature and nature-philosophy (Wundt, 1920). Certainly his intellectual development also included the influence of mid-19th-century positivism, especially in his promotion of experimental psychology. Yet, during that positivist period, he had remained largely unrecognized as a psychological theorist. The popular success of his theoretical system seems coordinated with the beginnings of neoidealist reorientations, and his system became fully formed in the *Grundriss* of 1896 (and later editions; Wundt, 1896a).

But unfortunately for Wundt, zeitgeist support disappeared rapidly in the early 20th century; definitions of psychology were then changing, and his works were soon meaningless to a newer generation. Few, especially outside Germany, understood any more what the old term *apperception* had once referred to.

Strange as it may seem, Wundt may be more easily understood today than he could have been just a few years ago. This is because of the current milieu of modern cognitive psychology and of the recent research on human information processing. Yet this new understanding does require serious study of Wundt in the original German. Most current textbook summaries of Wundt grew out of a time when early behaviorist and positivist movements were eager to encourage a break with the past, hence giving understandably little effort to careful description of the enormous body of writings they were discarding. Simplistic historical accounts resulted.

Today much of the history of Wundt remains to be told, both of his personal development and of his psychological system. It is well worth telling.

References

Blumenthal, A. L. *Language and psychology: Historical aspects of psycholinguistics.* New York: Wiley, 1970.

Boring, E. G. *A history of experimental psychology.* New York: Appleton-Century-Crofts, 1950.

Bringmann, W. G., Balance, W., & Evans, R. B. Wilhelm Wundt 1832–1920: A biographical sketch. *Journal of the History of the Behavioral Sciences,* 1975, *11,* 287–297.

Broadbent, D. *Perception and communication.* New York: Pergamon, 1958.

Burt, C. The factorial study of emotions. In M. Reymert (Ed.), *Feelings and emotions.* New York: McGraw-Hill, 1950.

Donders, F. Over de snelheid van psychische processen. *Tweede Reeks,* 1868–1869, II, 92–120. (Trans. by W. Koster as On the speed of mental processes, In *Acta Psychologica,* 1969, *30,* 412–431.)

Fischel, W. Wilhelm Wundt und Emil Kraepelin. *Karl Marx Universität Leipzig, Beiträge zur Universität Geschichte,* 1959, *1.*

Gardner, R. W., Holzman, P. S., Klein, G. S., Linton, H., & Spence, D. P. Cognitive control: A study of individual consistencies in cognitive behavior. *Psychological Issues,* 1959, Monograph 4.

Hughes, H. S. *Consciousness and society: The reorientation of European social thought,* 1890–1930. New York: Knopf, 1958.

Kahneman, D. *Attention and effort.* Englewood Cliffs, N.J.: Prentice Hall, 1973.

Kraepelin, E. *Dementia praecox and paraphrenia* (Trans. by M. Barclay from selected writings of Kraepelin). Chicago: Chicago Medical Book, 1919.

Mischel, T. Wundt and the conceptual foundations of psychology. *Philosophical and Phenomenological Research,* 1970, *31,* 1–26.

Moray, N. *Attention.* New York: Academic Press, 1970.

Neisser, U. *Cognitive psychology.* New York: Appleton-Century-Crofts, 1967.

Osgood, C., Suci, G., & Tannenbaum, P. *The measurement of meaning.* Urbana: University of Illinois Press, 1957.

Schlosberg, H. Three dimensions of emotion. *Psychological Review,* 1954, *61,* 81–88.

Silverman, J. The problem of attention in research and theory in schizophrenia. *Psychological Review,* 1964, *71,* 352–379.

Sperling, G. The information available in brief visual presentations. *Psychological Monographs,* 1960, *74* (11, Whole No. 498).

Sternberg, S. Memory-scanning: Mental processes revealed by reaction-time experiments. In J. Antrobus (Ed.), *Cognition and affect.* Boston: Little, Brown, 1970.

Strongman, K. T. *The psychology of emotion.* New York: Wiley, 1973.

Titchener, E. B. *The psychology of feeling and attention.* New York: Macmillan, 1908.

Werner, H. *The comparative psychology of mental development.* New York: Science Editions, 1948.

Wundt, M. *Die Wurzeln der deutschen Philosphie in Stamm und Rasse.* Berlin: Junker & Dunnhaupt, 1944.

Wundt, W. Selbstbeobachtung und innere Wahrnehmung. *Philosophische Studien,* 1888, *4,* 292–309.

Wundt, W. Ueber psychische Kausalität und das Prinzip des psychophysichen Parallelismus. *Philosophische Studien,* 1894, *10,* 1–124.

Wundt, W. *Grundriss der Psychologie.* Leipzig: Engelmann, 1896 (10th edn., 1911). (Trans. by C. Judd of 1896 and 1907 editions as *Outlines of psychology.*) (a).

Wundt, W. Ueber die Definition der Psychologie. *Philosophische Studien,* 1896, *12,* 1–66 (b).

Wundt, W. Zur Kritik tachistokopischer Versuche. *Philosophische Studien,* 1899, *15,* 287–317.

Wundt, W. *Völkerpsychologie: Eine Untersuchung der Entwicklungsgesetze von Sprache, Mythus, und Sitte* (10 vols.). Leipzig: Engelmann, 1900–1920.

Wundt, W. *Grundzüge der physiologischen Psychologie* (Vol. 2). Leipzig: Engelman, 1902 (5th edn.).

Wundt, W. Ueber Ausfrageexperimente und ueber Methoden zur Psychologie des Denkens. *Psychologische Studien,* 1907, *3,* 301–360.

Wundt, W. *Logik* (3 vols.). Leipzig: Engelmann, 1908.

Wundt, W. *Erlebtes und Erkanntes.* Stuttgart: Krohner, 1920.

Wundt as Chemist? A Fresh Look at his Practice and Theory of Experimentation

Henning Schmidgen

Mid-19th-century chemistry constituted a practically and theoretically important resource for experimental psychology as conceived by Wilhelm Wundt (1832–1920). In the early 1850s, Wundt began working in Gustav Herth's private chemical laboratory in Heidelberg. The experimental work Wundt conducted under Herth's direction provided the practical model for the psychological methods advocated in Wundt's pioneering publication on visual perception in 1862. With respect to theory, Wundt relied on John Stuart Mill's *System of Logic*, a book often referring to the chemical writings by Justus Liebig. Wundt not only read and quoted Mill's logic but also was personally acquainted with its German translator, the former Liebig student Jacob Schiel. Thus, in various ways, chemistry influenced Wundt's early theory and practice of experiment.

Recent studies in the history of science have recalled attention to a basic aspect of scientific activity: experimentation. Taking Ian Hacking's (1983, p. 150) statement that "experimentation has a life of its own" as a leitmotiv, scholars such as Frederic Holmes (1991–1993), Robert Kohler (1994), and Hans-Joerg Rheinberger (1994, 1995, 1997) have turned away from institutions, paradigms, and ideas. Instead they have begun to tell the history of modern life sciences focusing on "experimental systems," that is, concrete setups or arrangements combining technological, biological, architectural and graphic components in locally specific circumstances.

However, the resulting studies (e.g., on the synthesis of protein in the test tube) do not result in a neglect of external aspects of scientific activ-

ity. On the contrary, the "new experimentalism," as it is sometimes called, provides rich insight into the connectedness of experimental science to cultural and social contexts. The works of Rheinberger (1997) and Peter Galison (1997) amply demonstrate how the tools of scientists (i.e., the instruments, apparatus, and machines scientists use in their laboratories) participate in a larger material culture that also concerns technology, urbanism, and the military. Furthermore, these studies show that scientists sometimes acquired their laboratory skills in nonscientific contexts. Thus, H. O. Sibum (1995) has shown that James P. Joule's experimental work on the mechanical equivalent of heat would hardly have been possible to Joule if he had not acquired "tacit knowledge" on how to handle heat in his father's brewery.

Reconsidering the experimental practices of psychologists certainly is a promising endeavor. Following psychologists to the sites where they actually produced their knowledge (be it the lab, the field station, or the clinic) and looking closely at the instruments and model organisms they assembled on their workbenches contributes significantly to contextualize psychological research practices, often in surprising ways. Thus, the history of the reaction time experiment takes one back to the Leipzig laboratory of Wilhelm Wundt (1832–1920) and the Hipp chronoscope. It also leads to the observatory of Neuchâtel in Switzerland, to the clock industry in the nearby Jura mountains and the production of telegraphic systems. As I try to show in another article (Schmidgen, 2003), the psychological reaction time experiment with chronoscope was part of a large technical system devoted to the cultural work on time or, more precisely, to the coordination and distribution of time by means of telegraphy.

American Journal of Psychology, 2003, 116(3), 469–476.

This article deals with the various contexts in which Wundt acquired his experimental skills. It is a first step of an attempt to site the experimental knowledge Wundt acquired in his early years. Between 1851 and 1858, before he was appointed as a *Privatdozent* of physiology at Heidelberg University, Wundt moved through at least three contexts in which he learned how to carry out experiments:

The private chemical laboratory of Gustav Herth in Heidelberg, the place where Wundt elaborated his first publication

The medical clinic of Carl Ewald Hasse, the often-neglected director of Wundt's doctoral thesis

The Berlin laboratory of electrophysiologist Emil Du Bois-Reymond, where Wundt spent some 6 months after having received his doctoral degree in 1856[1]

In this article I will limit myself to the first context. Contrary to other studies on Wundt (see Blumenthal, 1975), I will argue that chemistry was a field of scientific practice and theory with which Wundt was well acquainted, which influenced psychological experimentation as it was practiced by the later Wundt. The importance of chemistry is indicated by the fact that Wundt, when starting to carry out experiments, was directed by a chemist. In contrast physiological experimentation was something that Wundt learned by himself. Before going to Berlin to do research in the physiological laboratory of Du Bois-Reymond, Wundt derived his "practical" knowledge in physiology from the textbooks of the well-known pathological anatomist Carl Rokitansky (Wundt, 1922, p. 81).

Indicative of the important role of chemistry is also the fact that Wundt's first project for a scientific psychology, the Heidelberg program of 1862, was inspired by John Stuart Mill's *System of Logic* (Graumann, 1980),[2] an epistemological work that takes many of its concrete examples from chemistry. Mill's "mental chemistry" provided an important resource for Wundt's conception of experimentation and psychology. Following the model of chemistry, Wundt saw the principal aim of experimental psychology as "a complete decomposition [*Zergliederung*] of con-

scious phenomena into their elements" (Wundt, 1882, p. 399). Psychological research in that sense was nothing but "psychological analysis" by means of experimentation.

Wundt's Chemical Experiments

As Wundt wrote in his autobiography, he seriously considered shifting his studies from medicine to chemistry in the early 1850s. In fact, it was neither medicine nor physiology that got Wundt interested in experimentation, but chemistry. As was the case with many of his contemporaries, the lectures of the Heidelberg chemist Robert Bunsen made an "unforgettable impression" on Wundt. As Wundt explained, Bunsen accompanied his lectures on general experimental chemistry "with experimental demonstrations of wonderful perfection":

> [In Bunsen,] every chemical element formed an independent whole that he then brought to intuition [*Anschauung*] in treating all its qualities and in presenting all its relations. Thus he placed the listener so much in the middle of the research on an object as if he, the listener, was carrying it out by himself. Since the old auditorium where the lecture took place hardly could hold the listeners, the first bench, where I could conquer a seat, stood so close to the experimentation table that the idea to carry out the experiment nearly became an illusion. (Wundt, 1922, p. 76)

Bunsen's performance had a powerful impact on the young Wundt. His lectures stimulated Wundt's desire to work experimentally on his own (see Wundt, 1922, p. 77). As a consequence, Wundt tried to get himself a place in Bunsen's new laboratory, which was under construction. However, this attempt failed: "Bunsen had no time to take care of beginners" (Wundt, 1922, p. 77). Instead, Wundt entered the private laboratory of Gustav Herth. Under Herth's direction he elaborated his first experimental investigation, a chemical analysis of urine, which was published in 1853 in the *Journal für Praktische Chemie*.

The aim of Wundt's study was to find out whether the addition of table salt to food is necessary for human beings or is only a cultural convention. Thus, Wundt's study was meant to contribute to the field of "physiological chemistry" as it was promoted in the 1850s by Justus Liebig, Jacob Moleschott, Carl G. Lehmann, and others (Glas, 1979; Holmes, 1975, 1988; Lieben, 1970). Wundt tackled the question by means of a self-experiment. He tried to eliminate table salt from his diet and to observe the amount of salt in his own urine (Wundt, 1853, p. 355). He was aware that the amount of salt in urine differs with the individual, so he first determined the amount of salt in his urine "while keeping a completely normal way of living." For 6 days he made measurements: in the morning (with an empty stomach), at noon (before eating), and in the evening. Over the following 5 days, he determined the amount of salt in the urine and its specific weight while eating "without any consummation of table salt." Finally he made comparative measurements after having begun to eat salted food again. Wundt then made comparisons between the daily amount of urine and the daily amount of table salt in the urine and presented his results in tables.

However, the values he obtained did not show any pattern. Between "the intake and the output of the organism" there was no "determined relation that could be expressed mathematically" (Wundt, 1853, p. 357). Still, with his investigation Wundt established a way of experimenting that remained important to him in the years that followed. In a deliberately anachronistic move one can even show that Wundt's first study already fulfills the criteria of good experimentation that he devised in the 1880s and later for the emerging field of experimental psychology (see Wundt, 1882, 1907, 1910). Thus, Wundt himself could determine the beginning of the process or the phenomena to be observed. It was he who decided when to begin reducing his salt intake. Then, the conditions under which the observed phenomena appeared were systematically varied (i.e., by excluding salt). Repetition to confirm the results was practiced because Wundt conducted the experiment over the course of 6 days and made comparative measurements before and after the experiment. Finally, one might say that Wundt observed the phenomena under investigation "in a state of heightened attention" and followed them in their succession, which was all the more easy because the experiment in question was not a psychological but a chemico-physiological one (Wundt, 1907, pp. 307–308).

Wundt's Mental Chemistry

The importance of Wundt's chemical experience is reflected in the first program of scientific psychology that he presented in the early 1860s. In the introduction to his *Beiträge zur Theorie der Sinneswahrnehmung*, titled "Ueber die Methoden in der Psychologie," chemistry functioned as an important model for the "science of the facts of consciousness." To Wundt, *Zergliederung*, that is, decomposition or analysis, was the central strategy for investigating psychological phenomena. He explained that like the other sciences, psychology deals with complex phenomena whose simplicity is at first hidden when they present themselves to the observer. For Wundt, *Entwickelungslehre*, statistics, and experimentation were the methods that could uncover the basic elements of consciousness remaining unseen at first glance (Wundt, 1862, p. XIV; Graumann, 1980).

In this context, Wundt defended himself against a possible objection, dictating that an experiment allows one only to shed light on the relationships between psychological elements and does not allow one to illuminate these elements as such. Invoking the example of chemistry, he argued,

> When the chemist wants to determine the constitution of a substance [*Stoff*] he has found, he investigates the way it behaves in comparison to various other stuffs; but what he wants to find through his experiments and what he really finds is not only the behavior in comparison to the other substances, but the chemical nature of that very substance. (Wundt, 1862, p. XXIX)

In the same way, the psychological experiment explores, by means of variations, not only the behavior of the soul toward effects coming from outside but also the very laws of psychological life. As examples of such investigations, Wundt pointed to Fechner's *Elemente der Psychophysik* and to his own analysis of visual perception in the *Beiträge*.

Wundt's reference to chemistry resulted not only from the concrete knowledge Wundt had acquired in chemical experimentation. It also reflected the epistemological positions that he assimilated in his Heidelberg days. As Boring (1935, pp. 216–223) showed, John Stuart Mill's *System of Logic, Ratiocinative and Inductive* (1843/1996a, 1843/1996b) played a crucial role in stimulating experimental research on psychological phenomena. In his *System*, Mill presented observation and experiment as central aspects of scientific activity. At the same time, he used examples from chemistry, especially from the works of Liebig, to explain epistemological issues. Mill also provided a general theory of inductive knowledge and a tentative application of this theory to the moral sciences, including psychology, offering an outline of psychological science similar to Wundt's later conceptions (Mill, 1843/1996b, pp. 849–860).

In addition, chemistry played an important role in the German reception of Mill's philosophy. In 1849, the *System of Logic* became available in a first, highly abridged German translation. The translator of Mill's book was Jacob Schiel, a former student of Liebig and, as the title page of Mill's German *Logik* reads, a *Privatdozent* in chemistry at the University of Heidelberg. It was Liebig himself who sent the English version of Mill's book to Schiel. Liebig encouraged his former student to translate the book, and he recommended that his friend, editor Eduard Vieweg at Braunschweig, publish the translated version. The fact that a chemist and not a philosopher made the first German translation of Mill must be seen, as Pat Munday (1998) has shown, against the background of Liebig's activities as a scientist and politician. For Schiel, the involvement in this context apparently had harsh consequences. Schiel seems to have been involved in the democratic movement and had to flee Germany after the so-called revolution of 1848. Schiel went to

America, where he stayed until 1857. Upon his return to Heidelberg, he undertook a second, more extended translation of Mill's *Logic* that was published in 1862–1863.

Wundt read Mill after Schiel's return to Heidelberg. Apparently, Wundt was personally acquainted with Schiel; in a short remark in his autobiography he said he entertained "a friendly intercourse with the first translator of Mill's logic" (Wundt, 1922, p. 57). That translator recommended the logic of Mill to Wundt as "a philosophy at the height of its time." And although Wundt had some "severe objections" to Mill's theory of mathematics, it is quite probable that the *System of Logic* as a whole affected Wundt as much as the lectures by Bunsen.

Conclusion

It should be emphasized that chemistry constituted, both practically and theoretically, an important resource for Wundt's experimental psychology. John Stuart Mill's reflections on the logic of the moral sciences and his conception of a "mental chemistry" stressed the independence of the "laws of mind" from bodily processes, and Wundt later spoke of a specifically "psychological causality" that cannot be reduced to the laws of physiology (Wundt, 1894). Furthermore, chemistry, as Wundt had practiced it, provided an important key to the experimental study of psychological phenomena. Investigating the relationship between the "intake and the output of an organism" as Wundt had done in his study on salt provided a concrete model for studying psychological reactions of laboratory subjects. In both cases, a comprehensive knowledge of the interior of the organism was not needed. The very term *reaction* indicates that Wundtian psychology was looking only for relationships between intakes and outputs, that is, relationships that could be expressed mathematically. That proved to be a highly productive endeavor.

Notes

This article was written in conjunction with "The Experimentalization of Life: Configurations between Science, Art, and Technology (1830–1930)," a project based at the Max-Planck Institute for the History of Science, Berlin, which receives funding from the Volkswagen Stiftung (Hannover).

1 On Wundt's formative years, see also Bringmann, Bringmann, & Cottrell (1976); Diamond (1980); and Robinson (1987, pp. 22–63).

2 Ungerer (1980) claimed that Wundt also read an apocryphal text by Auguste Comte dealing

with the "chemistry of the soul" that functioned as a starting point for his psychological research. Unfortunately, Ungerer did not give any more details.

References

Blumenthal, A. L. (1975). A reappraisal of Wilhelm Wundt. *American Psychologist, 30,* 1081–1088.

Boring, E. G. (1935). *A history of experimental psychology.* New York: Century.

Bringmann, W. G., Bringmann, G., & Cottrell, D. (1976). Helmholtz und Wundt an der Heidelberger Universität 1858–1871 [Helmholtz and Wundt at Heidelberg University, 1858–1871]. *Heidelberger Jahrbücher, 20,* 78–88.

Diamond, S. (1980). Wundt before Leipzig. In R. W. Rieber (Ed.), *Wilhelm Wundt and the making of a scientific psychology* (pp. 3–70). New York: Plenum.

Galison, P. (1997). *Image and logic: The material culture of microphysics.* Chicago: University of Chicago Press.

Glas, E. (1979). *Chemistry and physiology in their historical and philosophical relations.* Delft: Delft University Press.

Graumann, C. F. (1980). Experiment, statistics, history. In W. G. Bringmann & R. D. Tweney (Eds.), *Wundt studies. A centennial collection* (pp. 33–41). Toronto: Hofgrefe.

Hacking, I. (1983). *Representing and intervening.* Cambridge: Cambridge University Press.

Holmes, F. L. (1975). The transformation of the science of nutrition. *Journal of the History of Biology, 8,* 135–144.

Holmes, F. L. (1988). The formation of the Munich school of metabolism. In W. Coleman & F. L. Holmes (Eds.), *The investigative enterprise: Experimental physiology in nineteenth-century medicine* (pp. 179–210). Berkeley: University of California Press.

Holmes, F. L. (1991–1993). *Hans Krebs: Architect of intermediary metabolism, 1933–1937.* New York: Oxford University Press.

Kohler, R. E. (1994). *Lords of the fly:* Drosophila *genetics and the experimental life.* Chicago: University of Chicago Press.

Lieben, F. (1970). *Geschichte der physiologischsen Chemie* [History of physiological chemistry]. Hildesheim: Olms. Original work published 1935.

Mill, J. S. (1996a). *A system of logic, ratiocinative and inductive: Being a connected view of the principles of evidence and the methods of scientific investigation* (Books I–III). London: Routledge. Original work published 1843.

Mill, J. S. (1996b). *A system of logic, ratiocinative and inductive: Being a connected view of the principles of evidence and the methods of scientific investigation* (Books IV–VI and appendices). London: Routledge. Original work published 1843.

Mill, J. S. (1849). *Die inductive Logik: Eine Darlegung der philosophischen Principien wissenschaftlicher Forschung, insbesondere der Naturforschung.* Nach dem Engl. des John Stuart Mill in's Dt. übertr. von J. Schiel [Inductive logic: A depiction of the philosophical principles of scientific research, in particular natural research. Translated into German by J. Schiel according to the English version by John Stuart Mill]. Braunschweig: Vieweg.

Munday, P. (1998). Politics by other means: Justus von Liebig and the German translation of John Stuart Mill's Logic. *British Journal for the History of Science, 31,* 403–418.

Rheinberger, H.-J. (1994). Experimental systems: Historiality, narration, and deconstruction. *Science in Context, 7*(1), 65–81.

Rheinberger, H.-J. (1995). Beyond nature and culture: A note on medicine in the age of molecular biology. *Science in Context, 8*(1), 249–263.

Rheinberger, H.-J. (1997). *Toward a history of epistemic things: Synthesizing proteins in the test tube.* Stanford, CA: Stanford University Press.

Robinson, D. K. (1987). *Wilhelm Wundt and the establishment of experimental psychology: The context of a new field of scientific research.* PhD dissertation, University of California.

Schmidgen, H. (2003). Time and noise: On the stable surroundings of reaction experiments, 1860–1890. *Studies in History and Philosophy of Biological and Biomedical Sciences 34*(2), 237–275.

Sibum, H. O. (1995). Reworking the mechanical value of heat: Instruments of precision and gestures of accuracy in early Victorian England. *Studies in the History and Philosophy of Science, 26*(1), 73–106.

Ungerer, G. A. (1980). Wilhelm Wundt als Psychologe und Politiker. Anmerkungen zur Biographie

[Wilhelm Wundt as psychologist and politician. Biographical notes]. *Psychologische Rundschau, 31*, 99–110.

Wundt, W. (1853). Ueber den Kochsalzgehalt des Hams [On the amount of table salt in urine]. *Journal für Praktische Chemie, 59*, 354–359.

Wundt, W. (1862). Ueber die Methoden in der Psychologie [On the methods of psychology]. In *Beiträge zur Theorie der Sinneswahrnehmung* [Contributions to the theory of sensory perception] (pp. XI–XXXII). Leipzig: Wintersche Verlagsbuchhandlung.

Wundt, W. (1882). Die Aufgaben der experimentellen Psychologie [The problems of experimental psychology]. *Unsere Zeit, 3*, 389–406.

Wundt, W. (1894). Ueber psychische Causalität und das Princip des psychophysischen Parallelismus [On psychological causality and the principles of psychophysiological parallelism]. *Philosophische Studien, 10*, 1–124.

Wundt, W. (1907). Über Ausfrageexperimente und über die Methoden zur Psychologie des Denkens [On question experiments and the methods of the psychology of thought]. *Psychologische Studien, 3*, 301–360.

Wundt, W. (1910). Über reine und angewandte Psychologie [On psychology, pure and applied]. *Psychologische Studien, 5*(1910), 1–47.

Wundt, W. (1922). *Erlebtes und Erkanntes* [Experience and recognition] (2nd edn.) Stuttgart: Kröner.

Chapter 4

Origins of Scientific Psychology in America

The establishment of psychology laboratories in North America followed closely those founded by Wundt and his contemporaries in Germany. Most of the earliest of these American labs were founded by students who had trained with Wundt in Germany or students who had trained with American psychologist G. Stanley Hall (1844–1924) in the United States. Hall is often credited with founding the first American psychology laboratory at Johns Hopkins University in 1883. He had earned his doctoral degree with William James (1842–1910) at Harvard University in 1878 and had traveled to the University of Leipzig for additional study in 1879, visiting Wundt at the time of the opening of his laboratory. Hall's students founded psychology laboratories at Indiana University in 1887, the University of Wisconsin in 1888, Clark University in 1889 (where Hall was president), the University of Iowa in 1890, and Bryn Mawr College in 1898. Wundt's students began laboratories at the universities of Pennsylvania and Nebraska in 1889; Catholic University, Cornell University, and Columbia University in 1891; Harvard and Yale universities in 1892; Stanford University in 1893; and others still later.

Although there are many players in the beginnings of American scientific psychology, this chapter will discuss three – G. Stanley Hall, William James, and James McKeen Cattell (1860–1944) – with the readings focusing on the last of those two. All three are related in an academic lineage. As we have noted, Hall took his doctorate with James. When Hall opened his laboratory at Johns Hopkins, Cattell was one of his first graduate students. A disagreement between the two caused Cattell to leave Hopkins and go to Leipzig, where he earned his degree in psychology from Wundt in 1886, the first American to finish there with a degree in psychology. Although it might seem that these three individuals represent three generations, they in fact were all active forces in psychology from the 1880s through the span of their lives. Each of them contributed to the development of American psychology in profoundly important, albeit different, ways.

Hall's role was that of an organizer, editor, and publisher. He had been at Hopkins for only a few years when he was given the opportunity to be president of a new university in Worcester, Massachusetts – Clark University, which opened in 1889 with Hall as its president, a position he held until his retirement in 1920. Hall was responsible for many "firsts" in American psychology. In addition to founding the first psychology laboratory, he began the first American psychology journal in 1887, appropriately named the *American Journal of Psychology*. He later founded other journals, including ones on applied psychology, religious psychology, and child study. The last of those was associated with the *Child Study Movement*, a national movement begun by Hall in the 1890s to apply scientific psychology to education and parenting by learning everything that could be known about children and adolescents (see Davidson & Benjamin, 1987; Ross, 1972). Hall also founded the American Psychological Association in 1892, which he served as its initial president. Further, he was responsible for bringing Sigmund Freud to America in 1909, his only American visit (see Rosenzweig, 1994). We will have more to say about Freud and Hall in Chapter 7.

As a researcher, Hall is best characterized in modern terms as a developmental psychologist, whose principal research tool was the questionnaire (Hogan, 2003). His involvement in the Child Study Movement is evidence of those interests, as were his published volumes on adolescence and the psychology of aging. Indeed, his two-volume work on *adolescence* (Hall, 1904) was of considerable importance, albeit controversial, in bringing the concept of adolescence as a definable stage of development into public consciousness. Although Hall published a large number of books and articles, his influence was in his journal and organizational efforts and in the large number of doctoral graduates that he produced who went on to make important contributions in psychology.

It may seem odd to discuss William James at this point in our story because he was Hall's mentor. But James's placement here is meant to make sense chronologically. Although James's many contributions to psychology and philosophy are paramount, there is one that stands above the rest. This accomplishment, a book, took him 12 years to write, and when it finally appeared it dominated psychology in a way that few books, if any, can claim. The book is the *Principles of Psychology*. It was published in the fall of 1890 in two volumes, and it has been in print continuously ever since. It has been acknowledged as a work of literature, reflecting James's skills as a writer (after all he and his novelist brother, Henry James, shared similar genes). This book became a popular text in colleges of the time and served as a recruiting tool for a generation of psychologists, drawn to the field because of James's vision of psychology as a natural science and the contributions it could make to understanding the human condition in the twentieth century.

James's *Principles* was a compendium of all that was known about the fledgling science of psychology. Its content reflected the psychological work of his times, bolstered by many trips to the European laboratories to learn the latest developments in perception, memory, learning, and so forth. The book has been recognized as a great work in part because of its thoroughness, but more so because of the accessibility of the content. Whereas Hall could be flowery yet obtuse in his prose, James was an artist who painted psychological pictures of exceptional clarity, relying greatly on the power of metaphors. Consider this excerpt in which James (1890) was explaining the role of consciousness in selectivity that has adaptive significance for each unique individual.

> The mind, in short, works on the data it receives very much as a sculptor works on his block of stone. In a sense the statue stood there from eternity. But there were a thousand different ones beside it, and the sculptor alone is to thank for having extricated this one from the rest. Just so the world of each of us, howsoever different our several views of it may be, all lay embedded in the primordial chaos of sensations. . . . By all the world we

feel and live in will be that which our ancestors and we, by slowly cumulative strokes of choice, have extracted out of this, like sculptors, by simply rejecting certain portions of the given stuff. Other sculptors, other statues from the same stone! Other minds, other worlds from the same monotonous and inexpressive chaos! My world is but one in a million alike embedded, alike real to those who may abstract them. How different must be the worlds in the consciousness of ant, cuttle-fish, or crab? (Vol. 1, pp. 288–289)

James was not much interested in involvement in a psychology laboratory. He recognized the value of laboratory work and recruited Hugo Münsterberg (1863–1916) from Germany to head the psychology laboratory at Harvard. In addition to the *Principles of Psychology*, James made other contributions to psychology, for example, his books on the psychology of religion and on psychology as related to teaching. Yet the bulk of his published work was in philosophy, earning him a place as one of the two or three most distinguished philosophers in American history. He did very little research in psychology and, instead, focused what research he did on the subject of paranormal phenomena, such as the possibility of communication with the spirits of deceased individuals. It is easy to understand why his contemporaries in American psychology, who were trying diligently to establish psychology as a legitimate science, would have been particularly displeased with his occult pursuits (see Bjork, 1983; Murphy & Ballou, 1961).

James McKeen Cattell, the last of our triumvirate, was roughly 20 years younger than Hall and James. Upon completing his degree with Wundt, Cattell spent some time in England, where he was greatly influenced by the work of Francis Galton (1822–1911), a first cousin of Charles Darwin (1809–1882). Galton had developed a program of testing that he referred to as *anthropometric testing*, a combination of measures of physical characteristics, motor performance, and sensory functioning. These tests measured the circumference of the skull, reaction time to sound, breathing capacity, color vision, auditory range, visual acuity, and several other measures. Galton was seeking a way to measure genius, and he had devised these tests in that pursuit. Head size was related to brain size, reaction-time was believed to be a measure of the speed of information processing in the brain, and sensory acuity – drawing on the empiricists' emphases on the key role of the senses in acquiring all knowledge – was also believed to signal the degree of intelligence, that is, those with the most acute senses might be expected to be the most intelligent.

Cattell brought this model of intelligence testing to the United States, modified the tests to include more cognitive measures and fewer physical measurements, and called his test battery *mental tests*, coining that term in an article he published in 1890. He was involved with this testing program for a decade, assessing all incoming students at Columbia University where he was a faculty member beginning in 1891. When the correlation coefficient was invented at the beginning of the twentieth century (by Galton and his student Karl Pearson), Cattell was finally able to measure the validity of his tests. He assigned the task to one of his graduate students to measure the relationship between his mental tests and the performance of students in their classes. To Cattell's dismay the correlation coefficients were essentially zero, indicating no relationship. This stark reality ended his work in mental testing and essentially ended his research career.

Cattell was already heavily involved in other activities when his mental testing program was shown to be a failure. In addition to his faculty duties at Columbia University, he was editor of several journals, including the journal *Science*, which he had purchased in 1894. Under Cattell's editorship, this journal soon become the most influential publication on science in the world. As a weekly journal it carried up-to-date coverage of the latest scientific discoveries. While its prestige grew, scientists from all fields sought to publish their most important work there. It became indispensable reading for anyone who wanted to keep abreast of the latest key research. Although the coverage of the journal focused more on the fields of the physical sciences, such as chemistry and physics, it also included work from the social sciences, especially psychology. Indeed, Cattell's position as editor guaranteed psychology a forum for its best work in this the best journal, and it proved to be a godsend for psychology as it sought to gain a place of respectability among the more established sciences. Cattell edited this journal for 50 years until his death in 1944 (Sokal, 1980b).

For a science to exist it needs doctoral programs to train the scientists, places for the scientists to work, journals where they can publish their work, and organizations where they can meet to exchange ideas. These three pioneering American psychologists – Hall, James, and Cattell – provided all of those components for the new science. They founded doctoral programs and laboratories, established journals, founded organizations, and wrote seminal books, launching psychology in the United States at the end of the nineteenth century.

The Readings

There are six readings in this chapter. The first two relate to William James, the next two to James McKeen Cattell, and the final two to the nature of the beginning psychology laboratories and the instrumentation and research typical of those early labs.

The first reading is an excerpt entitled "The Stream of Thought," taken from James's *Principles of Psychology*. The focus of this excerpt is on selective attention and in it James addresses the question, given that we encounter a vast array of sensory information in our daily experience, why is it that we pay attention to some information while ignoring most of the rest? It will give you a sense of James's prose and will perhaps stimulate you to read more from his works.

The second reading is by historian of psychology David Leary. Leary (1992) briefly describes James's early career aspirations as an artist. In preparation for life as an artist, James, at the age of 18, studied with the famous American painter William Morris Hunt. Although James would not take up art as a career, Leary shows how James's artistic sensibilities forever shaped his philosophical and psychological ideas and how those ideas were manifested in his writing. James was especially skilled in the use of metaphor, as noted earlier (recall the sculptor and the statue). Leary draws on a number of metaphors from James's *Principles* to show how the arts impacted his psychology. Be sure to read the footnotes, something that is very important to do in reading history. There you will find much additional explanatory material that adds to the richness of this account and your understanding of it. For example, it is in the footnotes that Leary tells you how James's views on art led him to organize the chapters of the *Principles* in a very unusual way.

The third and fourth readings deal with Cattell's program of anthropometric mental testing. The first of this pair is an article published by Cattell in 1893 and written for school teachers, in which he described the many valuable uses of mental tests. The claims that Cattell makes in this article for the value of psychological testing are quite extraordinary. For example, he suggests that these tests can answer career questions.

He writes that in testing a child, "[s]pecial aptitudes will not be lost through unsuitable surroundings and uncongenial work, but the child may be led to the course of life in which he will be most happy and most useful" (p. 259). The second of the readings in this pair shows the ultimate failure of these tests. The article is by a distinguished historian of science, Michael Sokal, and it provides a detailed history of Cattell's mental testing program from 1890 until its demise in 1901. Included in this account are the beginnings of the Binet testing method in France, a testing method that would become the defining paradigm of American intelligence testing for more than half a century, replacing the failed intelligence tests of Cattell.

The last pair of articles focuses on the establishment of the North American psychology laboratories between 1883 and 1900 and the "brass instrumentation" that was integral to the work of the early psychologists. The first article (Benjamin, 2000) describes the development of the laboratories and their importance for establishing psychology as a science. As James Capshew (1992) has written, the laboratory has proven to be the "enduring motif in the story of modern psychology" (p. 132).

The final reading is by historian of psychology Rand Evans, the foremost authority on early psychological instrumentation. Evans (2000) describes the uses of some of the more common instruments in the early psychology laboratories such as the Hipp chronoscope, that could measure time in thousandths of a second, and the Stern variator, an important device for studies of the psychology of pitch (in audition). As Evans makes clear, in establishing their experimental laboratories, psychologists were trying to emulate the successes in experimental physiology and physics that had occurred earlier in the nineteenth century.

These readings are meant to give you a flavor of the "new psychology" in America at the end of the nineteenth century as psychologists sought to put in place the markers of their discipline. These beginnings would lay the groundwork not only for the science of psychology but, as we shall soon see, for the psychological profession as well.

The Stream of Thought
William James

We now begin our study of the mind from within. Most books start with sensations, as the simplest mental facts, and proceed synthetically, constructing each higher stage from those below it. But this is abandoning the empirical method of investigation. No one ever had a simple sensation by itself. Consciousness, from our natal day, is of a teeming multiplicity of objects and relations, and what we call simple sensations, are results of discriminative attention, pushed often to a very high degree. It is astonishing what havoc is wrought in psychology by admitting at the outset apparently innocent suppositions, that nevertheless contain a flaw. The bad consequences develop themselves later on, and are irremediable, being woven through the whole texture of the work. The notion that sensations, being the simplest things, are the first things to take up in psychology is one of these suppositions. The only thing which psychology has a right to postulate at the outset is the fact of thinking itself, and that must first be taken up and analyzed. If sensations then prove to be amongst the elements of the thinking, we shall be no worse off as respects them than if we had taken them for granted at the start.

The first fact for us, then, as psychologists, is that thinking of some sort goes on. I use the word thinking . . . , for every form of consciousness indiscriminately. If we could say in English "it thinks," as we say "it rains" or "it blows," we should be stating the fact most simply and with the minimum of assumption. As we cannot, we must simply say that *thought goes on.*

Adapted from W. James (1890). *Principles of psychology.* New York: Henry Holt & Co., pp. 224–225, 283–290.

Five Characters in Thought

How does it go on? We notice immediately five important characters in the process, of which it shall be the duty of the present chapter to treat in a general way:

1 Every thought tends to be part of a personal consciousness.
2 Within each personal consciousness thought is always changing.
3 Within each personal consciousness thought is sensibly continuous.
4 It always appears to deal with objects independent of itself.
5 It is interested in some parts of these objects to the exclusion of others, and welcomes or rejects – *chooses* from among them, in a word – all the while. . . .

The last peculiarity of consciousness to which attention is to be drawn is this first rough description of its stream in that *It is always interested more in one part of its object than in another, and welcomes and rejects, or chooses, all the while it thinks.*

The phenomena of selective attention and of deliberative will are of course patent examples of this choosing activity. But few of us are aware how incessantly it is at work in operations not ordinarily called by these names. Accentuation and Emphasis are present in every perception we have. We find it quite impossible to disperse our attention impartially over a number of impressions. A monotonous succession of sonorous strokes is broken up into rhythms, now of one sort, now of another, by the different accent which we place on different strokes. The simplest of these rhythms is the double one, tick-tóck, tick-tóck, tick-tóck. Dots dispersed on a surface are perceived in rows and groups. Lines separate into diverse figures. The ubiquity of the distinctions, *this* and *that, here* and *there, now* and *then,* in our minds is the result of our laying the same selective emphasis on parts of place and time.

But we do far more than emphasize things, and unite some, and keep others apart. We actually *ignore* most of the things before us. Let me briefly show how this goes on.

To begin at the bottom, what are our very senses themselves but organs of selection? Out of the infinite chaos of movements, of which physics teaches us that the outer world consists, each sense-organ picks out those which fall within certain limits of velocity. To these it responds, but ignores the rest as completely as if they did not exist. It thus accentuates particular movements in a manner for which objectively there seems no valid ground; for, as Lange says, there is no reason whatever to think that the gap in Nature between the highest sound-waves and the lowest heat-waves is an abrupt break like that of our sensations; or that the difference between violet and ultra violet rays has anything like the objective importance subjectively represented by that between light and darkness. Out of what is in itself an undistinguishable, swarming *continuum,* devoid of distinction or emphasis, our senses make for us, by attending to this motion and ignoring that, a world full of contrasts, of sharp accents, of abrupt changes, of picturesque light and shade.

If the sensations we receive from a given organ have their causes thus picked out for us by the conformation of the organ's termination, Attention, on the other hand, out of all the sensations yielded, picks out certain ones as worthy of its notice and suppresses all the rest. Helmholtz's work on Optics is little more than a study of those visual sensations of which common men never become aware – blind spots, *muscæ volitantes,* after-images, irradiation, chromatic fringes, marginal changes of color, double images, astigmatism, movements of accommodation and convergence, retinal rivalry, and more besides. We do not even know without special training on which of our eyes an image falls. So habitually ignorant are most men of this that one may be blind for years of a single eye and never know the fact.

Helmholtz says that we notice only those sensations which are signs to us of *things.* But what are things? Nothing, as we shall abundantly see, but special groups of sensible qualities, which happen practically or æsthetically to interest us, to which we therefore give substantive names, and which we exalt to this exclusive status of independence and dignity. But in itself, apart from my interest, a particular dust-wreath on a windy day is just as much of an individual thing, and just as much or as little deserves an individual name, as my own body does.

And then, among the sensations we get from each separate thing, what happens? The mind selects again. It chooses certain of the sensations to represent the thing most *truly,* and considers the rest as its appearances, modified by the conditions of the moment. Thus my table-top is named *square,* after but one of an infinite number of retinal sensations which it yields, the rest of them being sensations of two acute and two obtuse angles; but I call the latter *perspective* views, and the four right angles the *true* form of the table, and erect the attribute squareness into the table's essence, for æsthetic reasons of my own. In like manner, the real form of the circle is deemed to be the sensation it gives when the line of vision is perpendicular to its centre – all its other sensations are signs of this sensation. The real sound of the cannon is the sensation it makes when the ear is close by. The real color of the brick is the sensation it gives when the eye looks squarely at it from a near point, out of the sunshine and yet not in the gloom; under other circumstances it gives us other color-sensations which are but signs of this – we then see it looks pinker or blacker than it really is. The reader knows no object which he does not represent to himself by preference as in some typical attitude, of some normal size, at some characteristic distance, of some standard tint, etc., etc. But all these essential characteristics, which together form for us the genuine objectivity of the thing and are contrasted with what we call the subjective sensations it may yield us at a given moment, are mere sensations like the latter. The mind chooses to suit itself, and decides what particular sensation shall be held more real and valid than all the rest.

Thus perception involves a twofold choice. Out of all present sensations, we notice mainly such as are significant of absent ones; and out of all the absent associates which these suggest, we again pick out a very few to stand for the objective reality *par excellence*. We could have no more exquisite example of selective industry.

That industry goes on to deal with the things thus given in perception. A man's empirical thought depends on the things he has experienced, but what these shall be is to a large extent determined by his habits of attention. A thing may be present to him a thousand times, but if he persistently fails to notice it, it cannot be said to enter into his experience. We are all seeing flies, moths, and beetles by the thousand, but to whom, save an entomologist, do they say anything distinct? On the other hand, a thing met only once in a lifetime may leave an indelible experience in the memory. Let four men make a tour in Europe. One will bring home only picturesque impressions – costumes and colors, parks and views and works of architecture, pictures and statues. To another all this will be non-existent; and distances and prices, populations and drainage-arrangements, door- and window-fastenings, and other useful statistics will take their place. A third will give a rich account of the theatres, restaurants, and public balls, and naught beside; whilst the fourth will perhaps have been so wrapped in his own subjective broodings as to tell little more than a few names of places through which he passed. Each has selected, out of the same mass of presented objects, those which suited his private interest and has made his experience thereby.

If, now, leaving the empirical combination of objects, we ask how the mind proceeds *rationally* to connect them, we find selection again to be omnipotent. We shall see that all Reasoning depends on the ability of the mind to break up the totality of the phenomenon reasoned about, into parts, and to pick out from among these the particular one which, in our given emergency, may lead to the proper conclusion. Another predicament will need another conclusion, and require another element to be picked out. The man of genius is he who will always stick in his bill at the right point, and bring it out with the right element – "reason" if the emergency be theoretical, "means" if it be practical – transfixed upon it. I here confine myself to this brief statement, but it may suffice to show that Reasoning

is but another form of the selective activity of the mind.

If now we pass to its æsthetic department, our law is still more obvious. The artist notoriously selects his items, rejecting all tones, colors, shapes, which do not harmonize with each other and with the main purpose of his work. That unity, harmony, "convergence of characters," as M. Taine calls it, which gives to works of art their superiority over works of nature, is wholly due to *elimination*. Any natural subject will do, if the artist has wit enough to pounce upon some one feature of it as characteristic, and suppress all merely accidental items which do not harmonize with this.

Ascending still higher, we reach the plane of Ethics, where choice reigns notoriously supreme. An act has no ethical quality whatever unless it be chosen out of several all equally possible. To sustain the arguments for the good course and keep them ever before us, to stifle our longing for more flowery ways, to keep the foot unflinchingly on the arduous path, these are characteristic ethical energies. But more than these; for these but deal with the means of compassing interests already felt by the man to be supreme. The ethical energy *par excellence* has to go farther and choose which *interest* out of several, equally coercive, shall become supreme. The issue here is of the utmost pregnancy, for it decides a man's entire career. When he debates, Shall I commit this crime? choose that profession? accept that office, or marry this fortune? – his choice really lies between one of several equally possible future Characters. What he shall *become* is fixed by the conduct of this moment. Schopenhauer, who enforces his determinism by the argument that with a given fixed character only one reaction is possible under given circumstances, forgets that, in these critical ethical moments, what consciously *seems* to be in question is the complexion of the character itself. The problem with the man is less what act he shall now choose to do, than what being he shall now resolve to become.

Looking back, then, over this review, we see that the mind is at every stage a theatre of simultaneous possibilities. Consciousness consists in the comparison of these with each other, the selection of some, and the suppression of the rest by the reinforcing and inhibiting agency of attention. The highest and most elaborated mental products are filtered from the data chosen by the faculty next beneath, out of the mass offered by the faculty below that, which mass in turn was sifted from a still larger amount of yet simpler material, and so on. The mind, in short, works on the data it receives very much as a sculptor works on his block of stone. In a sense the statue stood there from eternity. But there were a thousand different ones beside it, and the sculptor alone is to thank for having extricated this one from the rest. Just so the world of each of us, howsoever different our several views of it may be, all lay embedded in the primordial chaos of sensations, which gave the mere *matter* to the thought of all of us indifferently. We may, if we like, by our reasonings unwind things back to that black and jointless continuity of space and moving clouds of swarming atoms which science calls the only real world. By all the while the world *we* feel and live in will be that which our ancestors and we, by slowly cumulative strokes of choice, have extricated out of this, like sculptors, by simply rejecting certain portions of the given stuff. Other sculptors, other statues from the same stone! Other minds, other worlds from the same monotonous and inexpressive chaos! My world is but one in a million alike embedded, alike real to those who may abstract them. How different must be the worlds in the consciousness of ant, cuttle-fish, or crab!

But in my mind and your mind the rejected portions and the selected portions of the original world-stuff are to a great extent the same. The human race as a whole largely agrees as to what it shall notice and name, and what not. And among the noticed parts we select in much the same way for accentuation and preference or subordination and dislike. There is, however, one entirely extraordinary case in which no two men ever are known to choose alike. One great splitting of the whole universe into two halves is made by each of us; and for each of us almost all of the interest attaches to one of the halves; but we all draw the line of division between them in a different place. When I say that we all call the two halves by the same names, and that those names are "*me*" and "*not-me*" respectively, it will at once be seen what I mean. The altogether unique kind of interest which each human mind feels in those parts of creation which it can call *me* or *mine* may be a moral riddle, but it is a fundamental psychological fact. No mind can take the same interest in his neighbor's *me* as in his own. The neighbor's me falls together with all the rest of things in one foreign mass, against which his own *me* stands out in startling relief. Even the trodden worm, as Lotze somewhere says, contrasts his own suffering self with the whole remaining universe, though he have no clear conception either of himself or of what the universe may be. He is for me a mere part of the world; for him it is I who am the mere part. Each of us dichotomizes the Kosmos in a different place.

William James and the Art of Human Understanding
David E. Leary

It has long been noted that William James, one of the founders of philosophical pragmatism as well as psychological science, had the sensibility of an artist. It has also been suggested that his artistic sensibility made a tangible difference in the crafting of his thought, both in philosophy and in psychology. G. Stanley Hall (1891), for instance, said that James was "an impressionist in psychology" whose "portfolio" (*The Principles of Psychology*, W. James, 1890/1983c) contained many stimulating and even brilliant "sketches" (Hall, 1891, p. 585). Later, James Jackson Putnam (1910) averred that James was "through and through an artist" (p. 842), and John Dewey (1910) stated that he was "an artist who gave philosophical expression to the artist's sense of the unique" (p. 507). Still later, George Santayana (1930) referred to James's "pictorial cosmology" (p. 252), and Ralph Barton Perry (1935) wrote about his "pictorial manner of philosophizing" (Vol. 2, p. 684).

It may surprise some to learn that James not only had the sensibility of an artist, but that his first vocation (as he himself called it) was to be an artist. This was no whimsical aspiration. From a young age, James drew very capably and persistently, he studied art in American and European museums with great avidity and insight, and at the age of 18, he committed himself to an apprenticeship with William Morris Hunt, one of the major painters in America. As testimony to his ability, the well-known artist John La Farge, who had been an apprentice to Hunt at the same time as James, asserted that James "had the promise of being a remarkable, perhaps a great, painter" (La Farge, 1910, p. 8).

D. E. Leary (1992). William James and the art of human understanding. *American Psychologist, 47,* 152–160. Copyright © 1992 by the American Psychological Association. Reprinted by permission of the publisher and the author.

Recently, Jacques Barzun (1983, 1985), Daniel Bjork (1983, 1988), and Howard Feinstein (1984) have suggested some of the possible consequences of James's artistic ability, aesthetic interests, and abbreviated artistic career for his subsequent work in psychology and philosophy. Their scholarship is extremely valuable, but it has left many unresolved questions and issues to be explored. For instance, Barzun (1985) argued that "the Jamesian mind is artist first and last" (p. 909) but he did not articulate in concrete detail what this meant, nor did he relate his thesis to James's own particular artistic experiences. Feinstein (1984), whose detailed and fascinating research has provided grist for many mills (including my own), was primarily concerned with the emotional antecedents and consequences of James's turn away from his early artistic vocation and with the effects of these emotional factors (rather than artistic factors per se) on the development of James's thought. Even Bjork, who has examined the extent to which James, the psychologist, was a "compromised artist" (Bjork, 1983, pp. 15–36) and has portrayed the center of James's subsequent vision (Bjork, 1988), has not analyzed many of the tangible ways in which James's artistic background and sensitivities affected the development of his specific premises and doctrines. Nor has he pursued his insight that James often articulated his thought in terms of metaphors drawn from the arts.

Through the aid of such metaphors, drawn by James from the realm of the arts, I will introduce and illustrate my thesis in the next section. This thesis is simply that James's artistic sensibility and experience were critically important in the development of his psychological and philosophical thought and, more particularly, in the articulation of a view of human understanding that was fundamental to his psychology and philosophy. This view of human understanding, I will argue, underlay how James characterized all thought, ranging from the philosophical and psychological through the common-sensical and scientific. It also influenced the way in which he thought about and formulated his own specific psychological and philosophical doctrines. To underscore its centrality as a fundamental motif throughout all his work, I shall begin by reviewing the ways in which – and the artistic metaphors through which – James characterized philosophy and philosophizing over the course of his career. Subsequently, I shall turn my attention to James's view of human understanding, its development, and its further articulation and application in his psychology.

James's Portrait of Philosophy

The heuristic goal of philosophy, according to James, is to achieve the most all-encompassing view, or perspective, possible. In practice, however, "no philosophy can ever be anything but a summary sketch, a picture of the world in abridgment, a foreshortened bird's-eye view of the perspective of events" (James, 1909/1977, p. 9). Because no single person or group can achieve a view that is all-inclusive, James (1876/1978b) defined philosophical study as "the habit of always seeing an alternative," of gaining and changing "mental perspective," like a connoisseur walking around a three-dimensional statue (p. 4).

Just as Plato once described science as the search for likely stories, James (1905/1978a) said that the philosopher searches for "more or less plausible pictures" (p. 143). Concepts are "views taken on reality," he suggested (James, 1910/1979, p. 200), and "philosophies are only pictures of the world which have grown up in the minds of different individuals" (quoted in Myers, 1986, p. 570). If you want to understand anyone's philosophical system, James argued, you should "place yourself . . . at the centre of [that person's] philosophic vision." When you do, "you understand at once all the different things it makes [that person] write or say. But keep outside [that vision] . . . and of course you fail" (James, 1909/1977. p. 117) For "philosophy is more a matter of passionate vision than of logic. . . . Logic only find[s] reasons for the vision afterwards" (p. 81). Given this conviction, it is not surprising that James felt that "a man's vision is the great fact about him" (p. 14).

Although James had a special affinity for the notion that philosophers "paint" their views (see, e.g., James 1907/1975b, p. 275; 1903–1904/1988), he was not indelibly wedded to the painting metaphor. On occasion he characterized his system of thought, instead, as a "mosaic philosophy" in which the picture of reality was composed of myriad little pieces or aspects of reality (James, 1912/1976, pp. 22, 42). The mosaic, James said, would never be completed, for "every hour of human life" can add a new aspect, achieved from a novel perspective, guided by a distinctive interest, thus enlarging the "picture gallery" of human life (p. 83). Because "of no concrete bit of experience was an exact duplicate ever framed" (James, 1910/1979, p. 76), he insisted that truth should be conceptualized "to mean everywhere, not duplication, but addition" (James, 1909/1975a, p. 41). The full truth about the universe, which includes the experiences and conceptual constructions of humans within it, cannot possibly be known – it will not even exist – until all its aspects have been created.

James's Portrait of Human Understanding

The preceding review of James's metaphorical descriptions of philosophy and philosophizing should serve as an apt introduction to his view of human understanding in general. This view was solidly grounded in the analyses presented in his masterpiece, *The Principles of Psychology* (1890/1983c), and these psychological analyses were based, in turn, on insights gained or corroborated through his experiences as a fledgling artist and artist's apprentice and through his reading of Ralph Waldo Emerson, William Wordsworth, and others.

Before discussing these experiences, I want to provide a "charcoal sketch" (to use a Jamesian term) of two major features in James's portrait of human understanding. Stated most simply, these features (or claims) are (a) that all knowledge, including science, is ultimately based on the finding of analogy, which is to say, on the finding of an appropriate, enlightening comparison or metaphor; and (b) that the analogies or metaphors in any field of knowledge, including science, are (or should be) always changing rather than fixed. In the words of his much-beloved Emerson, they should be "fluxional" rather than "frozen" (Emerson, 1837/1983a, p. 55; 1844/1983c, p. 463; on these important points, see James, 1890/1983c, pp. 500, 753–754; 984; Leary, 1987, pp. 326–327; 1988; 1990a, pp. 19–20, 45–47). In other words, James felt that the analogies, comparisons, or metaphors that provide the means of human understanding are partial and temporary in their utility, and that they should be changed as newer aspects of reality come to the fore in the stream of experience. For James, a staunch empiricist, there was always a new way to experience any reality and a new way to categorize any experience. Although a given analogy may provide useful insight into experience and reality, it can never provide a truly definitive and final view of it. His convictions in this regard pertained perforce to his philosophy of science. "Any bit of scientific research," he wrote, "becomes an angle and place of vantage from which arguments are brought to bear" (James, 1885/1987b, pp. 383–384). Whenever a scientific theory is taken as "definitive," it cuts off other vantage points and hence becomes "perspectiveless and short" (James, 1896/1986a, p. 136).

For example, if one wishes to understand the nature of the mind, it might be helpful to note that the mind is like a machine in a number of regards, and it may prove fruitful to explicate the ways in which, and the degrees to which, this is the case. But James would insist that the mind is not identical, structurally or functionally, with any known machine, including the most sophisticated computer of our own day. The use of other analogies will be necessary to elucidate the mind's other, perhaps neglected aspects.

Another way to express James's belief – a belief that he began to articulate in the 1870s – is to say that we humans can understand things, events, and experiences only from and through the viewpoint of other things, events, and experiences. This belief or thesis by no means rules out valid and reliable human understanding. On the contrary, if in addition to noting parallels among a variety of phenomena, we abstract and name the specific similarities that account for these parallels, we can develop reasonable and coherent arguments regarding the aptness of particular analogies and of the theories based on them. Such arguments will sometimes result in quite reliable inferences. Crafting such arguments, James pointed out, is something that occupies both scientists and philosophers: Disconfirming or verifying them is something at which scientists excel, and leaving analogical or metaphorical insights in their more complex, "unresolved," but highly suggestive form accounts for the genius and fertile works of poets, artists, and others (see James, 1890/1983c, pp. 984–988). Whatever the various uses to which analogies and metaphors can be put, James emphasized that the offering of what he called "similar instances," far from being "a perverse act of thought," is "the necessary first step" in any type of human understanding, whether scientific or nonscientific (p. 987).

It should also be noted, because it will underscore the *art* involved (according to James) in creative cognition, that the conjuring of "similar instances" was, for him, a very subtle affair. Some individuals, and not others, are unusually adept at this task. As he stated in *The Principles of Psychology*, "*some people are far more sensitive to resemblances, and far more ready to point out wherein they consist, than others are*" (James, 1890/1983c, p. 500). Indeed, he was convinced that "*a native talent for perceiving analogies is . . . the leading fact in genius of every order*" (p. 500). For whereas most people "have no eyes but for those aspects of things which [they] have already been taught to discern," creative individuals are precisely those who further human understanding by noting analogies that others "could never cogitate alone," although they may recognize and appreciate them once they are pointed out, whether by Shakespeare, Newton, Darwin, Tolstoy, or some other genius (p. 420). (The persons I have just named were some of James's favorite examples of genius. See James, 1890/1983c, pp. 984–988.)

Development of James's Portrait of Human Understanding

James's theory of what I shall call the *art of human understanding* – the art of grasping similarities among phenomena and of thus forging perceptual patterns and conceptual categories out of the flux or chaos of experience – evolved in the 1870s from a very rich mixture of his own reading and experience. The reading, as I have argued elsewhere (Leary, 1988), included especially the work and thought of Ralph Waldo Emerson and William Wordsworth – for instance, Emerson's essays on "The American Scholar" (1837/1983a), "Art" (1841/1983b), and "The Poet" (1844/1983c), and Wordsworth's long poem, "The Excursion" (1814/1977). It also included works by Robert Browning, Johann Wolfgang von Goethe, and Nathaniel Hawthorne. The experience, as opposed to the reading, that formed the basis for James's insight and belief had more to do with his efforts and encounters with art, and it started long before his time as a painter and artist's apprentice. Here is the way that his brother, the novelist Henry James (1913/1983b), subsequently described the youthful William: "As I catch W. J.'s image, from far back, at its most characteristic, he sits drawing and drawing, always drawing . . . and not as with a plodding patience . . . but easily, freely and . . . infallibly" (p. 118). This image is repeated in Henry's various reminiscences, and it is a picture that emerges from other sources as well, not least from William's own drawing notebooks (many fine examples of James's drawings are reproduced in Feinstein, 1984). From early in life, James showed a remarkable aptitude with a pencil and a strong inclination to give free rein to it. In addition, first in New York City, then in Europe, and finally in Newport, Rhode Island, James took lessons and developed the obvious abilities that he had. Supplementing the exercise and development of his own talent, he also showed a distinctive interest and an unusual sensitivity as an observer of art. Throughout his life he was a curious and omnivorous museum visitor, often attracted to what was new and experimental.[1]

In this context, James was persuaded at the age of 18 to become an artist, and he committed himself wholeheartedly to an apprenticeship in Newport, Rhode Island, with the highly regarded painter, William Morris Hunt (on this period of James's life, see Bjork, 1988, pp. 22–36; Feinstein, 1984, pp. 103–145; Perry, 1935, Vol. 1, pp. 190–201). Significantly, this was James's first commitment to any field of study or potential career.

In explaining his decision to his father, he said that he continually received from his "intercourse with art . . . spiritual impressions the intensest and purest I know." Not only was he inclined toward art, he said, but life "would be embittered if I were kept from it." With foresight he added, "That is the way I feel *at present*. Of course I may change" (quoted in Perry, 1935, Vol. 1, pp. 199–200).

The following year was full of the explorations, discoveries, and trials of apprenticeship, enhanced in significant ways by the friendship and ideas of his fellow apprentice, John La Farge. La Farge was seven years older than William and much more experienced than either William or William's younger brother Henry, who often accompanied him to Hunt's studio. As Henry (1914/1983a) later recalled, La Farge quickly became "quite the most interesting person we knew" (p. 287). Although Hunt was clearly "a figure unmistakable" (p. 279) from whom William learned a great deal, La Farge became "the figure of figures" for both William and Henry (p. 289). "An embodiment of the gospel of aesthetics" (p. 290), La Farge "opened up . . . prospects and possibilities that made the future flush and swarm" (p. 287). Besides introducing them to Browning and Balzac, who were to influence William and Henry respectively, he represented for William a continuation of the visual and intellectual challenges presented earlier by Delacroix. He also encouraged Henry to turn from dabbling in art to committing himself seriously to writing. As La Farge's Newport paintings show, he was already guided by his later-renowned proposition that, in human consciousness or experience, subjectivity is intertwined with the supposedly objective, material world. One critic who has speculated on La Farge's influence on William and Henry (Adams, 1985) expressed it this way:

La Farge's paintings created a new relation between the artist and his subject. His paintings unite the external world with subjective inner experience to the point where subject and object, the viewer and the thing seen, merge into one. Perception ceases to lead to solid, substantive qualities but culminates instead in feelings of transition and relation – in ever-changing gradations of light, focus, interest, and emotion, in continually fluctuating perceptual nuances, which never become fixed or solid. (Adams, 1987, p. 30)

William was so struck by the technical and conceptual issues with which La Farge was struggling at that time that he remembered and discussed them with La Farge – to La Farge's amazement – almost 50 years later (La Farge, 1910). Although James's subsequent "psychology of consciousness" was no doubt multiply determined, Gay Wilson Allen (1967) had good reason to suggest that La Farge was among those who influenced its development (p. 69).[2]

Despite the creative energy and growth produced during this apprenticeship, by the fall of 1861 James had left Hunt's studio, given up his aspiration to an artistic career, and moved with his family to Cambridge, Massachusetts. He entered Lawrence Scientific School at Harvard University, thus starting down the path that led to his accomplishments and renown in psychology and philosophy.

Much has been written about James's one-year apprenticeship. In particular, there has been a great deal of speculation about James's motives for giving up his calling to become an artist, despite plentiful evidence of his interest and ability; but in fact, little is known for certain. That his father was not happy about his choice of vocation is abundantly clear, and this almost certainly played a role in James's decision (see especially Feinstein, 1984, pp. 140–145). However, it is also plausible, as Perry (1935, Vol. 1, p. 200), and Bjork (1988, pp. 30–31) have suggested, that James simply concluded that he could not become a painter of the very first rank, and hence turned to science, another of his (and his father's) many interests. In any case, as his brother Henry (1914/1983a) put it, "nothing . . . could have been less logical, yet at the same time more natural, than that William's interest in the practice of painting should have suddenly and abruptly ceased" (p. 300). There was in the event "no repining at proved waste" on William's part (pp. 300–301), perhaps because on a deeper level there was no waste. As Henry (1913/1983b) had noted earlier, William "flowered in every [seeming] waste" (p. 117). And indeed, with hindsight, I would argue that his year-long stay in Newport was a tutorial for his later philosophical and scientific work, not a detour on the way to it.

Whatever factors were involved, the motives and rationale for James's turn from art to science are less important than the fact that he had such a formative exposure to art and painting.[3] This experience, building on his native artistic aptitude, prepared him to be sympathetic and responsive, in the 1860s and 1870s, to Emerson's and Wordsworth's ideas regarding the nature of human thought. In James's own rendition, as in Emerson's and Wordsworth's, the notion that human understanding is basically analogical or metaphorical was often expressed with visual imagery. It wasn't simply that humans can apply different analogies or metaphors; rather, humans can assume different viewpoints and achieve new perspectives. As a former artist, James felt the rightness of Emerson's and Wordsworth's claims. He was deeply and intimately aware that one can come to see things anew, to notice fresh aspects, and to create novel possibilities in reality. As Wordsworth put it in "The Excursion," which James read and reread in the early 1870s much as Charles Darwin had done to similar effect in the early 1840s (see Perry, 1935, Vol. 1, pp. 338–339, 355), the mind has an "excursive power" to "wander about" the world, viewing it from this and now that vantage point, thus shaping its "prospects" (Wordsworth, 1814/1977, pp. 155, 173). Even what is taken to be normal reality needs to be learned, as James came to realize. As he put it quite tellingly in *The Principles of Psychology* (1890/1983c), just as "in poetry and the arts, someone has to come and tell us what aspects we may single out" (p. 420), so too all humans "must go through a long education of the eye and ear before they can perceive the realities which adults perceive" (p. 724). Ideally, the labels for reality that are thus stamped in our mind through this long education will be fluxional rather than frozen. Unfortunately, this proves often not to be the case, so that we become all too conventional or literal in our mentality. As a result, James said, "if we lost our stock of labels we should be intellectually lost in the midst of the world" (p. 420). Human understanding, he realized, depends on such labels, whose meanings are derived (or were derived long ago) from their analogical relations. It can be advanced, however, only with the exchange of these labels for new concepts and terms, grounded in new views of reality.

Further Articulation and Application of James's View of Human Understanding in Psychology

James's belief in the analogical or metaphorical foundations of knowledge is richly illustrated in his psychological writings. His treatment of thought or consciousness as a stream instead of a chain or train is well-known (see James, 1890/1983c, chap. 9), and his discussion of other psychological topics is similarly informed by underlying analogies and metaphors. The ultimate metaphors that founded and framed his psychological thinking, and that came to undergird his philosophical pragmatism, pluralism, and radical empiricism, were the Darwinian metaphors of variation, selection, and function. All psychological states and actions, according to James, are products of spontaneous variation or selection in terms of their consequential utility. This functionalist orientation has influenced many other American psychologists and has structured much of the theoretical argumentation in modern psychology. Unfortunately, it has in some respects become frozen, despite James's advocacy of a fluxional approach to human and scientific understanding and it is often taken (in one or another of its contemporary versions) as a definitively authoritative portrait of human nature.

I have discussed this elsewhere (Leary, 1990a, pp. 20–21, 47–49). The point here is that James's own psychology (not to mention his philosophy) reflected and reinforced his view of human understanding. James used analogies and metaphors throughout his works, not simply as ways of expressing his ideas, but as ways of constructing them. He often drew on his artistic experiences in his attempt to understand and explain psychological phenomena as well as in his attempt to pursue philosophical reflection. In fact, the frequency with which he drew on his artistic experience in important, often critical, passages is noteworthy. Insofar as these passages often have to do with the nature of human cognition and understanding, which he conceived from the start on the model of artistic experience, this is not surprising. But his use of artistic experience as a source of metaphorical referents suggests a basic principle of human cognition – that humans tend, naturally enough, to draw their most telling analogies from their own experience. In other words, they use what is familiar to understand the less familiar.

In this section I quote at length from various passages in *The Principles of Psychology* (1890/1983c) to demonstrate sufficiently how James often used a transparently artistic analogy to reach, explicate, and defend a point. In these passages, note how often the notion of *perspective*, of seeing from a different angle or within a different context, was crucial for James, and attend to his frequent references to what he had learned as an artist. For instance, looking forward to his chapter on perception, James wrote,

> We shall see how inveterate is our habit of not attending to sensations as subjective facts, but of simply using them as stepping-stones to pass over to the recognition of the realities whose presence they reveal. The grass out of the window now looks to me of the same green in the sun as in the shade, and yet a painter would have to paint one part of it dark brown, another part bright yellow, to give its real sensational effect. We take no heed, as a rule, of the different way in which the same things look and sound and smell at different distances and under different circumstances. The sameness of the *things* is what we are concerned to ascertain; and any sensations that assure us of that will probably be considered in a rough way to be the same with each other. . . . What appeals to our attention far more than the absolute quality or quantity of a given sensation is its *ratio* to whatever other sensations we may have at the same time, When everything is dark a somewhat less dark sensation makes us see an object white. (pp. 225–226)

Further on:

> If the assumption of "simple ideas of sensation" recurring in immutable shape is so easily shown to be baseless, how much more baseless is the assumption of immutability in the larger masses of our thought! For there it is obvious and palpable that our state of mind is never precisely the same. Every thought we have of a given fact is, strictly speaking, unique, and only bears a resemblance of kind with our other thoughts of the same fact. When the identical fact recurs, we

must think of it in a fresh manner, see it under a somewhat different angle, apprehend it in different relations from those in which it last appeared . . . From one year to another we see things in new lights. What was unreal has grown real, and what was exciting is insipid. (p. 227)

In summing up at the end of his critical "Stream of Thought" chapter, in a famous passage that articulated his view of human understanding as well as anything he ever wrote, James wrote,

> Looking back, then, over this review, we see that the mind is at every stage a theatre of simultaneous possibilities. Consciousness consists in the comparison of these with each other, the selection of some, and the suppression of the rest by the reinforcing and inhibiting agency of attention. . . . The mind, in short, works on the data it receives very much as a sculptor works on his block of stone. In a sense the statue stood there from eternity. But there were a thousand different ones beside it [within the same block of stone], and the sculptor alone is to thank for having extricated this one from the rest. Just so the world of each of us, howsoever different our several views of it may be, all lay embedded in the primordial chaos of sensations, which gave the mere *matter* to the thought of all of us indifferently. . . . Other sculptors, other statues from the same stone! Other minds, other worlds from the same monotonous and inexpressive chaos! My world is but one in a million alike embedded, alike real to those who may abstract them. How different must be the worlds in the consciousness of ant, cuttle-fish, or crab! (p. 277)

The selection of one possible statue, of one possible view of the world, rather than another was intricately and deeply related, for James, to the interests of each person. The concept of *interest* is thus fundamental to James's psychology and philosophy, and in particular to his view of human understanding. The next passage provides James's definition of interest. It should be clear that the artistic analogies that he used in this passage are not secondary; rather, they reflect the most fundamental way in which he conceived this important concept.

Millions of items of the outward order are present to my senses which never properly enter into my experience. Why? Because they have no *interest* for me. *My experience is what I agree to attend to.* Only those items which I *notice* shape my mind – without selective interest, experience is an utter chaos. Interest alone gives accent and emphasis, light and shade, background and foreground – intelligible perspective, in a word. It varies in every creature, but without it the consciousness of every creature would be a gray chaotic indiscriminateness, impossible for us even to conceive. . . . The interest itself, though its genesis is doubtless perfectly *natural, makes* experience more than it is made by it. (pp. 380–381)

To underscore how fundamental this concept of interest is, recall that in James's psychology, interest directs attention, attention directs selection, and selection confers coherence on each level of psychological functioning – the perceptual, the conceptual, the practical, the aesthetic, and the moral (see James, 1890/1983c, pp. 273–278).[4] Interest, then, defined as "intelligible perspective," underlies the art of human understanding.

James supplied a nice example of the application of this art:

> Let four men make a tour in Europe. One will bring home only picturesque impressions – costumes and colors, parks and views and works of architecture, pictures and statues. To another all this will be non-existent; and distances and prices, populations and drainage-arrangements, door- and window-fastenings, and other useful statistics will take their place. A third will give a rich account of the theatres, restaurants, and public balls, and naught beside; whilst the fourth will perhaps have been so wrapped in his own subjective broodings as to tell little more than a few names of places through which he passed. Each has selected, out of the same mass of presented objects, those which suited his private interest and has made his experience thereby. (pp. 275–276)

Many other passages could be cited, making the same point. For instance, in a passage already quoted in part, James wrote,

Men have no eyes but for those aspects of things which they have already been taught to discern. Any one of us can notice a phenomenon after it has once been pointed out, which not one in ten thousand could ever have discovered for himself. . . . *The only things which we commonly see are those which we preperceive* [those for which we are on the lookout], and the only things which we preperceive are those which have been labelled for us, and the labels stamped into our mind. (p. 420)[5]

After discussing the perception of likeness, which is to say, the perception of analogies or metaphors, James said,

If the reader feels that this faculty [of perceiving similarities] is having small justice done it. . . . I think I emphasize it enough when I call it one of the ultimate foundation-pillars of the intellectual life. (p. 500)

Not surprisingly, James drew on his sensibilities and experience as an artist and artist's apprentice throughout his chapter on perception, pointing out (for instance) that the "eye-picture" created by stimuli impinging on the optic nerve is quite different from the mind-picture that is produced, the mind somehow correcting for the angle of vision and substituting a concept of the object as it would appear from a hypothetically ideal vantage point (James, 1890/1983c, p. 724). Similarly, in the chapter on space perception, James discussed what is now called brightness and size constancy. In one passage he explicitly referred to the training that underlay his psychological insights:

Usually we see a sheet of paper as uniformly white, although a part of it may be in shadow. But we can in an instant, if we please, notice the shadow as local color. A man walking towards us does not usually seem to alter his size; but we can, by setting our attention in a peculiar way, make him appear to do so. The whole education of the artist consists in his learning to see the presented signs as well as the represented things. No matter what the field of view *means*, he seeks it also as it *feels* – that is, as a collection of patches of color bounded by lines – the whole forming an optical diagram of whose intrinsic proportions one who is not an artist has hardly a con-

scious inkling. The ordinary man's attention passes *over* them to their import; the artist's turns back and dwells *upon* them for their own sake. "Don't draw the thing as it *is*, but as it *looks!*" is the endless advice of every [art] teacher to his pupil; forgetting that what "is" is what it would also "look," provided it were placed in what we have called the "normal" [that is, the ideal] situation for vision. (pp. 874–875)[6]

In his chapter on the perception of reality, in which the psychology of belief was his central concern, James went beyond the usual focus on things and distinguished very effectively among a number of different worlds – the world of sensory things, the world of scientific qualities and forces, the world of ideal relations and abstract truths, the world of "idols of the tribe," the various supernatural worlds of religious belief, the innumerable worlds of individual opinion, and the worlds of "sheer madness and vagary" (pp. 920–922). *"Every object we think of gets at last referred to one world or another of this or of some similar list,"* he wrote (p. 922).

Propositions concerning the different worlds are made from "different points of view"; and in this more or less chaotic state the consciousness of most thinkers remains to the end. Each world *whilst it is attended to* is real after its own fashion; [but] the reality lapses with the attention. (p. 923)

I need not remind you that attention is directed by interest, which for James is a natural, individuating factor. Thus, he said,

The fons et origo [that starting point and foundation] of all reality, whether from the absolute or the practical point of view, is . . . subjective, is ourselves . . . Reality, starting from our Ego, thus sheds itself from point to point. . . . It only fails when the connecting thread is lost. A whole system may be real, if it only hang to our Ego by one immediately stinging term. (pp. 925–926)

What is felt and understood to be real, then, is what is of "stinging" interest, which according to James's definition of interest is whatever is linked to a compelling intelligible perspective.[7]

As the fundamental role of perspective in James's thought becomes clearer, his later reduction of the self or ego to a point of view or field of vision, in the years after the publication of *The Principles of Psychology*, begins to make increasing sense (see Leary, 1990b, pp. 116–117).[8] In this little-known development of his thought, James came to depict the individual ego, not human understanding alone, in terms of the fundamental artistic concept of perspective. From the present historical vantage point, one can see how this largely unexplored extension of his thought was consistent with his career-long reliance on the concept of perspective. Starting from his earliest definition of philosophy as "the possession of mental perspective" (James, 1876/1978b, p. 4), James had infused his principles of psychology with his perspectivalist vision, and he went on subsequently to develop versions of philosophical pragmatism, pluralism, and radical empiricism that were equally premised on the assumption that there is always another view to be had. Together with many other artistic insights and metaphors, this belief in the fundamental reality of alternative and supplemental perspectives permeated James's entire system of thought.

Conclusion

I have argued that William James's portrait of human understanding was influenced, as he put it, by "the whole drift of my education" (James, 1902/1985, p. 408). In particular, it was influenced in a deep and lasting way by his artistic sensitivity, experience, and training. On the basis of this view of human understanding, James felt that it was perfectly legitimate – even necessary – to use analogies and metaphors, often from the realm of the arts, in the development of his psychological and philosophical doctrines. It also led him to organize his major psychological work in a very distinctive manner.[9]

Given this background and orientation, it is not surprising that James came to understand the place and type of his psychology and philosophy, in relation to previous and alternative modes of thought, in explicitly artistic terminology. His

system of thought, he said, was "romantic" rather than "classic" (James, 1901/1986b, pp. 193–194). His views, he explained, were concrete, uncouth, complex, overflowing, open-ended, and incomplete. On the one hand, they lacked the "clean pure lines and noble simplicity" typical of the abstract constructions of the "classic-academic" approach, but on the other, they were consonant with the art of human understanding as he comprehended it (see James, 1907/1975b, pp. 16–17; 1910/1979, pp. 76–79).

The fact that his view of human understanding was based on his experience as an artist may help explain why James's psychology and philosophy grounded as they are on this view of human understanding, have attracted the attention and respect of so many artists and humanists – not to mention scientists and psychologists – to the present day.[10] As James (1897/1987a) once said of someone else's work, his own works do not "violate" the "deepest instincts" of artists (p. 536).

Perhaps the leading artist in James's life was his brother Henry James, Jr., the novelist. It is interesting to note that Henry published a novel, *The Tragic Muse* (1890/1988), in the same year that William published *The Principles of Psychology*. William himself suggested that this concurrence made 1890 a banner year for American literature (James, 1920, p. 299). Not purely by chance, Henry's novel dealt with the world of art.[11] In his own inimitable language (H. James, 1906–1908/1934), the "pictorial fusion" of the novel brings together a "multiplication of aspects" (p. 85) that denies any "usurping [specially privileged] consciousness" (p. 90). The overlap of Henry's and William's motifs has often been noted. I use Henry's quotation here simply to provide a context for saying that I do not intend my view of William James's art of human understanding, and of its impact on his system of thought, to have any undue privilege over other perspectives on the development of his thought. Both James and his work are incredibly rich and overdetermined. But I do believe that the particular aspect of William James's life and work that I have pointed out in this article is important and needs to be fused into our picture of this remarkable and influential person.

Notes

1 James's fascination with, and close study of, the paintings of Eugène Delacroix in Paris – at thirteen years of age – is a relevant example (see Bjork, 1988, pp. 14–19). There is good reason to suppose that his ruminations on the works of Delacroix stimulated his thinking about the lack of any clear distinction between the subjective and objective poles in experience. This was an important concern of his later work. At the other end of his life, perhaps the best example of his continuing openness to novelty in art was his joyful astonishment at the work of Matisse and Picasso (see Stein, 1933/1960, p. 80). Clearly, his awareness that modes of representation and understanding are liable to change was nurtured and sustained by his familiarity with art. If he sometimes expressed regret about his lack of formal education, he could nonetheless have agreed with his brother Henry that, for them, "the great rooms of the Louvre" were "educative, formative, fertilizing, in a degree which no other 'intellectual experience' . . . could pretend . . . to rival" (H. James, 1913/1983b, p. 197). My argument here is that James's shortcomings in terms of mathematics and logic, which formal education would have corrected, were more than counterbalanced by the insights he gained from art. As his "master" William Morris Hunt (1875–1883/1976) said with considerable foresight, at least as regards James, "mathematics . . . don't develop a person like painting" (p. 86).

2 Allen (1967) also claimed that "it would be futile to attempt to trace any lasting influence of William Hunt on his life," although Hunt's school of painting was consonant with James's later insights (p. 69). Without asserting any singularity of influence, I think that Allen's claim is exaggerated. Hunt's (1875–1883/1976) repeated admonishments to his students contained many hints of James's later doctrines (e.g., regarding the centrality of experience and the primacy of action), and James himself suggested how sensitive and retentive he was with regard to these hints by periodically referring to "the endless advice of every [art] teacher to his pupil" (James, 1890/1983c, p. 875). Indeed, James's portrait of philosophy echoed his teacher's dictum that painting is "the *only universal language!* All nature is creation's picture-book!" (Hunt, 1875–1883/1976, p. 73).

3 After leaving Newport, James kept his drawing alive for another decade before he claimed to have let it "die out" (quoted in Perry, 1935, Vol. 1, p. 330). He regretted this loss of serious drawing, but he main-tained his interest in art, with some fluctuations, throughout his life. As he told his brother in 1872, he envied Henry's belonging to "the world of art" because "away from it, as we live, we sink into a flatter, blanker kind of consciousness, and indulge in an ostrich-like forgetfulness of all our richest potentialities." These potentialities, he said, "startle us now and then when by accident some rich human product, pictorial, literary, or architectural slaps us with its tail" (quoted in Perry, 1935, Vol. 1, p. 327). At critical points in 1868, 1873–1874, 1882, and 1892, art "slapped" him into important meditations. This remains a largely untold story.

4 James's critical concept of selection was not drawn solely from Darwinian thought. Rather, his artistic experience prepared the way for his acceptance of this Darwinian principle and its application on all levels of psychological phenomena. As he wrote in an unpublished manuscript on the psychology of aesthetics, there is an "analogy between art and life in that by both, results are reached only by selection & elimination." Quoting Robert Louis Stevenson, he went on to say that "there is but one art – to omit" (James, ca. 1894). The importance of selection in James's psychology was unambiguously expressed when he asserted that "selection is the very keel on which our mental ship is built" (James, 1890/1983c, p. 640).

5 James articulated a version of this principle in his first psychological essay, in which he pointed out that "a layman present at a shipwreck, a battle, or a fire is helpless. . . . But the sailor, the fireman, and the general know directly at what point to take up the business. They 'see into the situation' . . . with their first glance" (James, 1878/1983a, p. 15).

6 This "endless advice" about drawing a thing as it looks was obviously given to James by his art teacher. In the very first of his published talks on painting and drawing, Hunt (1875–1883/1976) proclaimed, "You are to draw *not reality, but the appearance of reality!*" (p. 3).

7 Not only reality, but also its meaning and worth are a matter of perspective. As James (1899/1983b) wrote in an essay that expressed the heart of his thought: "Some years ago, whilst journeying in the mountains of North Carolina, I passed by a large number of 'coves'. . . . The impression on my mind was one of unmitigated squalor. . . . I said to the mountaineer who was driving me: 'What sort of people are they who have to make these new clearings?' 'All of us,' he replied; 'why, we ain't happy here unless we are getting one of these coves under cul-

tivation.' I instantly felt that I had been losing the whole inward significance of the situation. . . . When *they* looked on the hideous stumps, what they thought of was personal victory. . . . I had been as blind to the peculiar ideality of their conditions as they certainly would also have been to the ideality of mine, had they had a peep at my strange indoor academic ways of life at Cambridge" (pp. 133–134). "Neither the whole of truth, nor the whole of good, is revealed to any single observer, although each observer gains a partial superiority of insight from the peculiar position in which he stands" (p. 149).

8 Having extended perspectivism to his treatment of the self or ego, James came to understand personal identity and religious conversion as involving, respectively, a centering or changing of one's perspective (James, 1902/1985, pp. 161–162). Beyond that, he came to understand "the Absolute" as the sum of all actual perspectives, nonhuman as well as human, and thus to suggest that even the Absolute is open to continual development, as more pictures of reality are created by its constituent points of view (1909/1977, pp. 130–131, 139–144; 1899/1983d, p. 4; 1902/1985, pp. 409–414). This led Santayana (1913/1940) to comment, with perhaps more justification than he knew, that James's God was "a sort of . . . struggling artist" (p. 210).

9 The organization of *The Principles of Psychology* (James, 1890/1983c) has baffled many psychologists and critics. In fact, this organization makes reasonably good sense if one assumes James's artistic point of view. After getting preliminary discussions out of the way in the first eight chapters, James provided an overview of his psychology of consciousness (or "our study of the mind from within," as he called it on p. 219) in the "Stream of Thought" chapter. This chapter, James said, is "like a painter's first charcoal sketch upon his canvas, in which no niceties appear" (p. 220). Then, after reviewing the various levels of psychological functioning in this chapter, James went on in subsequent chapters to fill in his charcoal sketch with more detailed treatments of the various aspects of his system, proceeding from the most general (consciousness of self) to the most circumscribed (the will) of the mind's experiences. Although his scheme does not account completely for the placement of each chapter, it makes sense of the book's overall organization.

10 Besides the various roles that he played in establishing the physiological, behavioral, cognitive, and therapeutic traditions in contemporary psychology, James profoundly influenced individuals all across the cultural landscape – individuals as disparate as Bernard Berenson, Niels Bohr, Jorge Luis Borges, John Dewey. W. E. B. DuBois, Nelson Goodman, Helen Keller, Walter Lippmann, Stephen Pepper, Oliver Sacks, Gertrude Stein, and Wallace Stevens. Another such person, Alfred North Whitehead, the great mathematician, philosopher, and historian of science, considered James to be one of the four major thinkers in the entire Western tradition, along with Plato, Aristotle, and Leibniz (see Whitehead, 1938, pp. 3–4). Whitehead (1956) noted that when the foundations of the modern worldview were blown apart by various discoveries at the turn of this century, William James was one of the few intellectuals prepared and able to withstand the blow (p. 272), and James withstood it without having to change his way of thinking.

11 Art and artists in modern society – especially painting and painters – provided frequent topics, themes, motifs, and devices in Henry's work (e.g. H. James, 1868–1897/1956; 1874–1909/1984; see also Bowden, 1956; Holland, 1964; Hopkins, 1961; Ward, 1965; Winner, 1967, 1970). The importance of art, particularly painting, in Henry's conceptual scheme is strongly suggested by his assertion that "the analogy between the art of the painter and the art of the novelist is, so far as I am able to see, complete" (H. James, 1884/1987, p. 188).

References

Adams, H. (1985). William James, John La Farge, and the foundations of radical empiricism. *American Art Journal, 17,* 60–67.

Adams, H. (1987). The mind of John La Farge. In H. Adams (Ed.), *John La Farge* (pp. 11–77). New York: Abbeville Press.

Allen, G. W. (1967). *William James: A biography.* New York: Viking Press.

Barzun, J. (1983). *A stroll with William James.* New York: Harper & Row.

Barzun, J. (1985). William James: The mind as artist. In S. Koch & D. E. Leary (Eds.), *A century of psychol-*ogy as science (pp. 904–910). New York: McGraw-Hill.

Bjork, D. W. (1983). *The compromised scientist: William James in the development of American psychology.* New York: Columbia University Press.

Bjork, D. W. (1988). *William James: The center of his vision.* New York: Columbia University Press.

Bowden, E. T. (1956). *The themes of Henry James: A system of observation through the visual arts.* New Haven, CT: Yale University Press.

Dewey, J. (1910). William James. *Journal of Philosophy, Psychology and Scientific Methods, 7,* 505–508.

Emerson, R. W. (1983a). The American scholar. In J. Porte (Ed.), *Essays and lectures* (pp. 51–71). New York: Library of America. (Original work published 1837)

Emerson, R. W. (1983b). Art. In J. Porte (Ed.), *Essays and lectures* (pp. 429–440). New York: Library of America. (Original work published 1841)

Emerson, R. W. (1983c). The poet. In J. Porte (Ed.), *Essays and lectures* (pp. 445–468). New York: Library of America. (Original work published 1844)

Feinstein, H. M. (1984). *Becoming William James.* Ithaca, NY: Cornell University Press.

Hall, G. S. (1891). Review of William James's *Principles of psychology. American Journal of Psychology, 3,* 578–591.

Holland, L. B. (1964). *The expense of vision: Essays on the craft of Henry James.* Princeton, NJ: Princeton University Press.

Hopkins, V. (1961). Visual art devices and parallels in the fiction of Henry James. *Modern Language Association Publications, 76,* 561–574.

Hunt, W. M. (1976). *On painting and drawing* (H. M. Knowlton, Ed.). New York: Dover. (Original two-volume work published 1875–1883)

James, H., Jr. (1934). *The art of the novel: Critical prefaces* (R. P. Blackmur, Ed.). New York: Scribner. (Original works published 1906–1908)

James, H., Jr. (1956). *The painter's eye* (J. L. Sweeney, Ed.). Cambridge, MA: Harvard University Press (Original works published 1868–1897)

James, H., Jr. (1983a). Notes of a son and brother. In F. W. Dupee (Ed.), *Autobiography* (pp. 237–544). Princeton, NJ: Princeton University Press. (Original work published 1914)

James, H., Jr. (1983b). A small boy and others. In F. W. Dupee (Ed.), *Autobiography* (pp. 1–236). Princeton, NJ: Princeton University Press. (Original work published 1913)

James, H., Jr. (1984). *Tales of art and life* (H. Terrie, Ed.). Schenectady, NY: Union College Press. (Original works published 1874–1909)

James, H., Jr. (1987). The art of fiction, In R. Gard (Ed.). *The critical muse: Selected literary criticism* (pp. 186–206). London: Penguin Books. (Original work published 1884)

James, H., Jr. (1988). *The tragic muse.* New York: Viking Penguin. (Original work published 1890)

James, W. (ca. 1894). *Manuscript on psychology of aesthetics.* In William James Papers, File 4393. Houghton Library, Harvard University, Cambridge, MA.

James, W. (1920). *The letters of William James* (Vol. 1; Henry James III, Ed.). Boston: Atlantic Monthly Press.

James, W. (1975a). *The meaning of truth: A sequel to "pragmatism."* Cambridge, MA: Harvard University Press. (Original work published 1909)

James, W. (1975b). *Pragmatism: A new name for some old ways of thinking.* Cambridge, MA: Harvard University Press. (Original work published 1907)

James, W. (1976). *Essays in radical empiricism.* Cambridge, MA: Harvard University Press. (Original work published 1912)

James, W. (1977). *A pluralistic universe.* Cambridge, MA: Harvard University Press. (Original work published 1909)

James, W. (1978a). Preface to Harald Höffding's *Problems of philosophy.* In *Essays in philosophy* (pp. 140–143). Cambridge, MA: Harvard University Press. (Original work published 1905)

James, W. (1978b). The teaching of philosophy in our colleges. In *Essays in philosophy* (pp. 3–6). Cambridge, MA: Harvard University Press. (Original work published 1876)

James, W. (1979). *Some problems of philosophy.* Cambridge, MA: Harvard University Press. (Original manuscript incomplete and unpublished at James's death in 1910)

James, W. (1983a). Brute and human intellect. In *Essays in psychology* (pp. 1–37). Cambridge, MA: Harvard University Press. (Original work published 1878)

James, W. (1983b). On a certain blindness in human beings. In *Talks to teachers on psychology and to students on some of life's ideals* (pp. 132–149). Cambridge, MA: Harvard University Press. (Original work published 1899)

James, W. (1983c). *The principles of psychology.* Cambridge, MA: Harvard University Press. (Original work published 1890)

James, W. (1983d). *Talks to teachers on psychology and to students on some of life's ideals.* (Cambridge, MA: Harvard University Press. (Original work published 1899)

James, W. (1985). *The varieties of religious experience.* Cambridge, MA: Harvard University Press. (Original work published 1902)

James, W. (1986a). Address of the president before the Society for Psychical Research. In *Essays in psychical research* (pp. 127–137). Cambridge, MA: Harvard University Press. (Original work presented 1896).

James, W. (1986b). Frederic Myers's service to psychology. In *Essays in psychical research* (pp. 192–202). Cambridge, MA: Harvard University Press. (Original work published 1901)

James, W. (1987a). Review of George Santayana's *The sense of beauty.* In *Essays, comments, and reviews* (pp. 536–539). Cambridge, MA: Harvard University Press. (Original work published 1897)

James, W. (1987b). Review of Josiah Royce's *The religious aspect of philosophy.* In *Essays, comments, and reviews* (pp. 383–388). Cambridge, MA: Harvard University Press. (Original work published 1885)

James, W. (1988). Introduction: Philosophies paint pictures. In *Manuscript essays and notes* (pp. 3–6). Cambridge, MA: Harvard University Press. (Original work written 1903–1904)

La Farge, J. (1910, September 2). A new side of Prof. James. *The New York Times*, p. 8.

Leary, D. E. (1987). Telling likely stories: The rhetoric of the New Psychology, 1880–1920. *Journal of the History of the Behavioral Sciences. 23,* 315–331.

Leary, D. E. (1988, August). *Poetry and science: Wordsworth's influence on Darwin and James.* Paper presented at the 96th Annual Convention of the American Psychological Association, Atlanta, GA.

Leary, D. E. (1990a). Psyche's muse: The role of metaphor in the history of psychology. In D. E. Leary (Ed.), *Metaphors in the history of psychology* (pp. 1–78). New York: Cambridge University Press.

Leary, D. E. (1990b). William James on the self and personality: Clearing the ground for subsequent theorists, researchers, and practitioners. In M. G. Johnson & T. B. Henley (Eds.), *Reflections on The Principles of Psychology: William James after a century* (pp. 101–137). Hillsdale, NJ: Erlbaum.

Myers, G. E. (1986). *William James: His life and thought.* New Haven, CT: Yale University Press.

Perry, R. B. (1935). *The thought and character of William James* (Vols. 1 and 2). Boston: Little, Brown.

Putnam, J. J. (1910). William James. *Atlantic Monthly, 106,* 835–848.

Santayana, G. (1930), Brief history of my opinions. In G. P. Adams & W. P. Montague (Eds.), *Contemporary American philosophy* (Vol. 2, pp. 239–257). New York: Scribner.

Santayana, G. (1940). The genteel tradition in American philosophy. In *Winds of doctrine: Studies in contemporary opinion* (pp. 186–215). New York: Scribner. (Original work published 1913)

Stein, G. (1960). *The autobiography of Alice B. Toklas.* New York: Vintage Books. (Original work published 1933)

Ward, J. A. (1965). Picture and action; The problem of narration in James's fiction. *Rice University Studies. 51,* 109–123.

Whitehead, A. N. (1938). *Modes of thought.* New York: Macmillan.

Whitehead, A. N. (1956). *Dialogues of Alfred North Whitehead.* (L. Price, Ed.), New York: New American Library.

Winner, V. H. (1967). Pictorialism in Henry James's theory of the novel. *Criticism, 9,* 1–21.

Winner, V. H. (1970). *Henry James and the visual arts.* Charlottesville: University Press of Virginia.

Wordsworth, W. (1977). The excursion. In J. O. Hayden (Ed.), *The poems* (Vol. 2, pp. 35–289). Harmondsworth, Middlesex, England: Penguin. (Original work published 1814)

Tests of the Senses and Faculties
James McKeen Cattell

Tests of the senses and faculties concern the teacher from three points of view. In the first place, those who wish to contribute to the advancement of psychology will find here a convenient opening. In the second place, such tests give a useful indication of the progress, condition, and aptitudes of the pupil. In the third place, the carrying out of the tests might serve as a means of training and education.

The senses and faculties have been studied hitherto by men of science, who have mostly made the determinations upon themselves. This is a necessary beginning, but now that methods have been elaborated, it is very desirable that the measurements should be extended so as to include different classes of persons. There are no individuals better suited for such experiments than the pupils in our schools. They are classified according to age, acquirements, and sex, and the teacher has considerable knowledge of their ability, character, and heredity. A careful investigation of the variation in the senses and faculties under such conditions would at the present time be an important contribution to science. In so far as experiment can be used in the study of mind, scientific progress is assured. The traditional psychology is vague and inexact, and cannot rank as co-ordinate with physical science. But when we regard the history of the several physical sciences, we see that they too at one time consisted of inexact descriptions, artificial classifications, dubious anecdotes, and verbal explanations. With the introduction of experiment and measurement astrology has become astronomy, allchemy has become chemistry, and natural history has become natural science. Physical sciences, such as astronomy, in which measurements could be readily undertaken were the first to be developed, while those, such as electricity, in which it is difficult to make measurements, are still backward. Matter in motion is more readily subject to experiment when passive than when organic and living. Physics has consequently preceded biology in its development. But the progress of biology has recently been rapid, and it will be found that nearly all advances have been due to the application of experiment and measurement. As the living organism is more complex and changeable than inert matter, so the mind is more complicated, protean, and inaccessible than the body. It is natural, therefore, that psychology should be the last science to be weaned by philosophy and to begin an independent growth. Those who have followed the recent development of psychology know that this has been the result of experiment and measurement. Each new application of experimental methods subserves the advancement of psychology, and the very backwardness of the science gives the teacher an opportunity to contribute to its progress.

When our knowledge of the normal variation of mental processes has been somewhat further increased, its determination will give useful indications of individual condition, progress, and ability. In conjunction with the ordinary school examination such tests would show whether the course of study is improving or blunting the fundamental processes of perception and mental life. Tests made at the beginning and end of the day, week, and session would show whether the student is exhausted by the required curriculum. They could be used in comparing different systems of education, different schools, the advantages of city and country, etc. They would show whether girls are able, without injury to health, to follow the same courses of study as boys. Careful tests must almost of necessity be introduced into the public schools. If attendance be made compulsory, the state is undoubtedly responsible for any bad consequences which

From J. McK. Cattell (1893). Tests of the senses and faculties. *Educational Review*, 5, 257–265.

could be avoided. Thus if the eyesight of a student be injured, so as to involve a loss of ability to earn a living, the state would, under our present laws, probably be liable for damages. In many cases tests which could readily be made would indicate disease, especially of the nervous system, long before it becomes apparent to common observation. The tendency to certain diseases counterindicate certain employments. Thus a very large percentage of women teachers become insane; consequently those having neuropathic tendencies should not enter on this profession. One boy in twenty is color blind, and this defect, which is never discovered by the individual himself, but may be determined by the teacher in one minute, unfits him for work so far separated as that of the railway signal man or of the artist. As our knowledge increases we shall, on the one band, be able to indicate very early in the life of the child tendencies to insanity and other diseases, to dipsomania and other vices, and to crime, and precautions may be taken which will limit the range of these abnormal tendencies in the individual, and prevent their spreading in the race. On the other hand, valuable qualities may be early discovered and developed. Special aptitudes will not be lost through unsuitable surroundings and uncongenial work, but the child may be led to the course of life in which he will be most happy and most useful. Many tendencies are likely to be eliminated or increased in offspring according to the marriage of the parents. While instinct is probably a better guide to suitable marriage than scientific principles, it cannot be denied that parents and the conventions of society have much to do with the conditions under which choice is made. Somewhat of the backwardness of the dark ages may be due to the fact that many of the best men were celibates. If a code of honor (such as obtains in some aristocracies, and prevents its members from marrying below their rank) could be developed, and directed toward eliminating degenerative tendencies, and developing valuable traits, the race would be greatly strengthened and perfected.

Such experiments on the senses and faculties would not only advance our knowledge of the mind, and serve as a useful criterion in many ways, but they would also be a valuable training for the pupil. The senses and faculties would be developed as well as measured. In the child and

savage every sensation from without is apt to distract the attention and lead to some movement. In the language of physiology, afferent impulses are immediately converted into efferent, and nothing is stored up within. Education seeks to prevent such dispersion, and the importance of manual training and laboratory work for this purpose is now universally admitted. The senses and faculties are trained wherever the student makes special movements and independent observations, but the direction in which these should be undertaken remains an open question. It should be remembered that a laboratory course, as in chemistry, is intended rather for training the pupil than for learning about the combinations of elements, etc. It is, in fact, a course in experimental psychology as much as a course in experimental physics. It can only be decided after practical trial whether a laboratory course expressly directed to studying the senses and faculties would serve better or worse than a physical or biological science as a means of training. Such tests certainly require the most complete abstraction and concentration, and every wandering of the attention is at once betrayed by the experiments themselves. The stimulus of competition and of the effort to improve will certainly secure the interest of the student. It may be found that the experiments will become too much of a "game." But they require a steady hand, undimmed senses, and a clear mind, and any effort to secure these cannot but benefit the student. Those who have marked the improvement in health of students in the English universities as they train for a boat race must wish that some such healthy competition could be more widespread in schools and colleges.

In this paper suitable tests can be indicated only; the teacher who wishes to study methods and results must work over special books and papers.* Experiments can be made in an hour which would leave a record of permanent value

---

* We are fortunate in having the recent psychologies of Professor James and Professor Ladd. Those who know German should also read Professor Wundt's *Physiologische Psychologie*. Mr. Galton's *Inquiries into Human Faculty* and other writings are of special interest. Professor Jastrow has given in the *Educational Review* (II:442) an excellent example of tests on memory and association.

both to science and to the individual student. If the experiments be regarded as a means of training and made part of the school curriculum, and an hour a week throughout the year be devoted to them, much more can be accomplished. In this case the senses may be taken up in order, beginning, say, with vision. The sharpness of sight may be easily measured by determining the distance at which a printed page can be read. If the sharpness be defective an oculist should be consulted, as the difficulty is usually mechanical and may be readily corrected. Each eye should be tested separately, as one eye is often defective, and an excess of strain is needlessly thrown on the better eye. Color blindness may be detected by letting the student select all the green shades from a heap of colored wools, and more exactly determined by matching colors on revolving wheels. The size of the field of vision may be mapped out by letting the observer look at a fixed point and determining how far in every direction letters can be read and colors seen.

The error in perceiving size may be tested by drawing a line as nearly as possible the length of a standard line, and in perceiving intensity by matching shadows or revolving wheels. The perception of size, distance, and solidity with one and with two eyes may be studied, and its exactness measured. If time permit contrast and after-images may be observed, and the individual variation determined. Useful training in subjective observation may be obtained by noticing that things not looked at directly are seen double, and by observing entoptic phenomena. These are various images due to the structure of the eye. They are often discovered by the individual, and lead him to think that his eyes are failing.

The sharpness of hearing may be tested by determining the distance at which the ticking of a watch can be heard. The test should be made for each ear separately. The range of pitch which can be heard varies considerably with different individuals, and this may be determined. The accuracy with which small differences in pitch can be distinguished and with which intervals can be adjusted should be measured. Time is often misspent by girls who learn to play the piano mechanically with no ear for music. The exactness with which distance and direction can be recognized with the ear may be measured. Learn-ing to distinguish the simple tones in a complex sound is a useful training.

Touch may be tested and trained by determining how far apart two points must be in order that they may be recognized as two when they touch the skin. This distance differs greatly in different parts of the body. Taste and smell are neglected senses, and ones peculiarly open to education. Considering its importance to comfort and health, cooking is a backward art, and our housewives should be trained to distinguish and value small differences. If good water could be distinguished from bad by the average individual as well as it is by the horse, many cases of typhoid fever and diphtheria would be avoided. The same holds for smells, which are invaluable criteria of unhygienic surroundings. The sense of temperature could also be trained so that one may know when a room becomes overheated, and may distinguish subjective from objective causes. The organic changes within the body are obscure and not easy to observe and study, but they are of enormous importance. To recognize correctly the need for fresh air, food, sleep, rest, and exercise would be an acquirement whose value cannot be overstated. If the causes leading to *malaise* and *bien être*, tedium and comfort, could be learned and the mode of living adjusted accordingly, the value of life and all the institutions of society would be affected.

Movement and its perception offer a valuable series of tests. The strength of the grasp of the hand and the rate at which a blow can be struck should be measured. These are convenient tests of bodily condition, and a difference between two hands is often characteristic. The tremor of the hand and the sway of the body give early and important indications of overstrain. The way we judge movements by their extent, their force, and their time should be studied, and the accuracy of discrimination measured. It is easy to find how much difference there must be between two weights, in order that their difference may be noticed.

Feelings of pleasure and pain may be tested in such a course, and possibly elementary aesthetic perceptions trained. It would be a great gain if students could learn to appreciate simplicity and taste in dress and surroundings. The colors and their combinations liked best and least may be determined, as also shapes, relative sizes, etc. A corresponding experiment may be made for the combinations of tones used in speech and music. The pressure or temperature which just hurts may be determined.

Leaving the senses and turning to the faculties we find that imagination, memory, and the association of ideas may be tested. Thus a series of questions can be framed the answers to which will throw light on the mental imagery of the pupil. The thoughts of some are accompanied by vivid pictures, others think more in sounds or movements. Some can call up a scene so as to see all the details before them, others only remember the relations. Such differences are highly characteristic, and indicate special aptitudes which should not be disregarded. The accuracy of ordinary observation may be tested by requiring the student to draw the plan of the hall of the schoolhouse; or to give an account of some event, say something that happened in the school the day before. Casual observation will be found very defective, and the student will learn that but little reliance can be placed on stories of extraordinary events, or even on the testimony in a court of justice. He may also learn to distinguish clearly what he in fact knows, and what he surmises and invents. If so he will have acquired nothing more valuable in his whole school course. Memory may be tested by reading a passage aloud, and requiring the student to write down afterward as much as he can remember. It can be measured more exactly by reading a series of numerals, and determining how many can be remembered. The experiment may be varied by choosing a series of numerals greater than can be remembered on hearing once and determining how often it must be repeated in order that it may be learned. The same series may be used a day or a week afterward; the greater rapidity with which it is learned indicates unconscious memory, and the experiment may be arranged to measure the rate of forgetting. The rate at which a simple sensation fades from the memory may also be determined. The range of consciousness may be measured by uncovering objects for a very short time and determining how much the student can perceive simultaneously. The association of ideas may be studied by giving a word to the class, and letting them write down what idea or other word is suggested by it. The train of ideas for twenty seconds may

be recorded. Questions may also be arranged in such a manner that the answers will throw light on the acquirements and interests of the student.

The time of mental processes is a useful text. The accuracy with which an interval of time can be judged is a somewhat different matter; it may be tested readily by giving the student an interval, say one minute, and letting him note when an equal period has elapsed. The time passing before a movement can be made in answer to a stimulus may be measured, but it is so short that delicate apparatus is required. The time needed to see and name series of colors, letters, and words should be found. An educated man can read words making sentences in about half the time that he can read disconnected words. The absolute and relative times are consequently a good test of progress in learning to read. The rate of reading foreign languages measures familiarity with the language. The time of mental processes, such as translating words from one language to another, adding or multiplying digits, remembering the country in which a city is situated, or the author of a book, may be measured readily by letting the student make ten trials in succession. The time in coming to a decision or in making a judgment may also be measured. In normal mental life the attention waxes and wanes and the duration of this rhythm may be measured.

In conjunction with these mental tests certain anthropometric data should be secured. Such are the height, weight, breathing capacity, the color of eyes and hair, etc. Age and sex and the nationality and position of the parents should always be noted. If possible it will be well to record what diseases the student has suffered, as also the age, state of health, etc., of his brothers and sisters, his parents, and other near relatives.

This series of tests of the senses and faculties by no means exhausts such as may be made to advantage. Those wishing to undertake more advanced work will seek to study and measure mental time, intensity and extensity, and the correlation of these magnitudes. But all the tests enumerated here may be made by an intelligent teacher on even the youngest school children, and without expensive or complicated apparatus. It may seem surprising that, with the exception of a few isolated tests, this has not as yet been attempted anywhere; but it must be remembered that experimental psychology is a recent study even in our universities. The first laboratory for research work was established by Professor Wundt at Leipzig in 1879, and the second by Dr. G. Stanley Hall at Baltimore in 1882. The first course in which students carried out a series of experiments in the laboratory was given by the writer in 1888. Now, however, the teacher can prepare himself for such work in most of the leading universities – at Harvard, Yale, Columbia, Pennsylvania, Cornell, Clark, Brown, Washington, Chicago, Wisconsin, Michigan, Indiana, Nebraska, Stanford, and Toronto. The rapid extension of the study of experimental psychology in American universities leads to the expectation that tests of the senses and faculties will soon be undertaken in many schools, and will perhaps be made part of the regular curriculum.

James McKeen Cattell and the Failure of Anthropometric Mental Testing, 1890–1901
Michael M. Sokal

Cattell's Program for Anthropometric Mental Testing

On January 1, 1889, Cattell was appointed to a professorship of psychology at the University of Pennsylvania that he later claimed (erroneously) to be the world's first. His father's advocacy and his European scientific pedigree played a part in this high honor to a twenty-nine-year-old youth. Within a year, he had established a laboratory, begun to train students, and sketched out a research program on "mental tests and measurements," which coined the term now in common use.[1] He explicitly ignored the simple measurements of bodily dimensions that had been so much a part of Galton's program; instead, he concentrated on procedures to examine both physiological and psychological characteristics. These tests, carried out sporadically on his students at the University, were dynamometer pressure, rate of movement, sensation areas, pressure causing pain, least noticeable difference in weight, reaction time to sound, time for naming colors, bisection of a 50 cm line, judgment of 10 seconds' time, and number of letters remembered on one hearing.

Cattell was clearly skillful in parlaying this simple program into a major institutional and eventually public commitment. He effectively alluded to Helmholtzian science with the term "mental energy," flimsily applied to the tasks mea-suring strength of squeeze and rate of arm movement in the first two tests above. The ideology of evolution was also invoked by his claim that the tests "would be of considerable value in discovering the constancy of mental processes, their interdependence, and their variation under different circumstances." Galton himself amplified this point in a series of comments, comparing Cattell's testing to "sinking shafts . . . at a few critical points." He admitted that one goal of Cattell's procedures was exploratory, to determine "which of the measures are the most instructive."[2] Cattell also hinted at a public need when he commented that the tests might "perhaps [be] useful in regard to training, mode of life or indication of disease."

Cattell was not the only American to sense a public need to be tapped by mental testing in the 1890s. By that decade, scientists working in physical anthropometry began to claim that they could measure "The Physical Basis of Precocity and Dullness," and though their claim was disputed,[3] their studies continued throughout the decade. Within the discipline just beginning to identify itself as psychology, testing boomed. At Clark University, for example, Edmund C. Sanford extended his colleague Franz Boas's anthropometric studies of school children.[4] At the University of Nebraska, Harry K. Wolfe, the second American doctoral student of Wundt in experimental psychology, urged the adoption of mental tests in the local public schools. Like Cattell, he admitted that he was not sure what he was studying, and he reminded teachers "not [to] be uneasy because the meaning of any peculiarities is obscure."[5] At Yale, another of Wundt's students, Edward Wheeler Scripture, tried out various mental testing procedures and even published a paper on fencing as an indication of mental ability.[6]

Adapted from M. M. Sokal (1982). James McKeen Cattell and the failure of anthropometric mental testing, 1890–1901. In W. R. Woodward & M. G. Ash (Eds.), *The problematic science: Psychology in nineteenth-century thought.* New York: Praeger, pp. 322–345. Copyright © 1982. Reproduced with permission of Greenwood Publishing Group, Inc., Westport, CT.

Most important from the viewpoint of legitimating the new discipline in the public eye was the work of Joseph Jastrow. He had earned a Ph.D. with G. Stanley Hall at Johns Hopkins in 1886. He began corresponding with Francis Galton about his anthropometric interest in 1887, and he became professor of psychology at the University of Wisconsin in 1888. By 1890, his concern with mental testing paralleled Cattell's; early in 1892 he published a proposal for "Some Anthropological and Psychological Tests on College Students" based almost completely on Galton's program.[7] He also used tests to investigate sex differences and clashed with Mary Whiton Calkins, the distinguished Wellesley psychologist, as to the meaning of the differences his tests revealed.[8]

Under Jastrow's direction in 1893, the two streams of interest in anthropometric mental testing converged at the World's Columbian Exposition in Chicago. At this World's Fair, Frederic Ward Putnam, Curator of the Peabody Museum of American Archaeology and Ethnology at Harvard University, planned a Department of Ethnology to include a Section on Physical Anthropology under the direction of Franz Boas. Part of Boas's plan was to carry out a program of anthropometric measurements on the visitors to the Fair, including as many foreign visitors as possible, and the members of the Indian tribes brought to Chicago for the occasion. Jastrow, Boas, and Putnam saw no reason why the program should be limited to physical anthropometry and extended it to include mental tests.[9] The result was to be an outgrowth of Galton's Anthropometric Laboratory, and Jastrow wrote to Galton in 1892, asking for suggestions as to procedures and apparatus. He even went before the preliminary meeting of the American Psychological Association and "asked the cooperation of all members for the Section of Psychology at the World's Fair and invited correspondence on the matter."[10] Using a schedule of tests that resembled Galton's and Cattell's, Jastrow tested thousands of individuals with the help of the army of graduate student volunteers he had assembled for the occasion.

Despite this flurry of interest in testing that he had in large part set off, Cattell was unable to devote much time to this work between 1891 and 1894. About the time he published his "Mental Tests and Measurements" paper, he began to commute to New York from Philadelphia to lecture a day or so a week at Columbia College. In 1891, Cattell moved to Columbia and so had to give up his program of testing at Pennsylvania. He devoted the next three years to establishing the psychological laboratory at Columbia, completing two major experimental studies[11] and planning the *Psychological Review.* He did find time to review books on anthropometry of interest to psychologists and to prepare a popular article on mental testing at the invitation of the editor of the *Educational Review.*[12]

In January, 1893, Cattell wrote to the President of Columbia "concerning the possibility of using tests of the senses and faculties in order to determine the condition and progress of students, the relative value of different courses of study, etc." Beneath his rationale for educational efficiency, he had to admit that he did not have specific tests designed for specific purposes; he compared his program of testing with the work of researchers in electricity 50 years earlier: "they believed that practical applications would be made, but knew that their first duty was to obtain more exact knowledge." He carried this argument to its Baconian conclusion: "The best way to obtain the knowledge we need is to make the tests, and determine from the results what value they have."[13]

It was not, however, until September 1894 that Cattell finally received authorization for the testing program he wanted. He was granted permission to examine every student on entering Columbia College and the Columbia School of Mines for the next four years, and in fact he tested students throughout the 1890s and into the twentieth century. Cattell, his junior colleague Livingston Farrand, and all their graduate students were deeply involved in the testing program, which soon began to attract national attention. The scope of their reputation may be appreciated from the diversity of their audiences. Cattell and Farrand described their work in papers presented at meetings of the New York Schoolmasters' Association, The New York Academy of Sciences, the American Psychological Association, and the American Association for the Advancement of Science.[14] The day had yet to come when errors in the Scholastic Aptitude Test were front-page news, but the clipping service to which Cattell subscribed certainly kept busy.

The schedule of tests that Cattell prepared at Columbia was explicitly concerned with both physical and mental measurements. Cattell stressed again that he did not "wish to draw any definite conclusions from the results of the tests made so far" because they were "mere facts." However, like the positivist he was, he noted that "they are quantitative facts and the basis of science." He concluded with the pragmatic resolution that "there is no scientific problem more important than the study of the development of man, and no practical problem more urgent than the application of our knowledge to guide this development." The questions he hoped to answer were:

> To what extent are the several traits of body, of the senses and of mind interdependent? How far can we predict one thing from our knowledge of another? What can we learn from the tests of elementary traits regarding the higher intellectual and emotional life?[15]

Within a few years, Cattell's testing program provided answers to at least the last two of these questions, but these were to be extremely disappointing to him.

Perhaps the weakness of his testing program stemmed from the ad hoc manner in which Cattell adapted Wundt's reaction-time experiment into a testing instrument. The technical details are of interest in appreciating just what he was offering to society. The experimenter, now called a tester, sits at the left in front of a Hipp chronoscope, which measures time intervals accurately to milliseconds.... The subject or person being tested sits... in front of a Cattell gravity chronograph, with a Cattell lip key in his mouth. The experiment or test begins when the experimenter, or tester, pulls the string... to start the mechanism of the chronoscope and then closes the switch.... The closing of the switch completes an electric circuit that starts the hands of the chronoscope revolving and allows the screen of the chronograph to fall, thus revealing a card to the subject, on which is printed a stimulus. He then responds verbally in a previously agreed-upon way, thus opening the lip key and breaking the electric circuit, which stops the hands of the chronoscope. The experimenter, or tester, then reads the reaction time directly from the chronoscope dials.[16]

The transformation of an experimental situation into a testing one brought with it several major innovations. Wundt required that his subjects introspect while carrying out the reaction, while Cattell arranged his tests so that those being tested did not have to introspect at all. To be sure, Wundt's use of this technique did not resemble the systematic introspection developed by Edward B. Titchener, and both he and Cattell were concerned primarily with the reaction time itself as self-contained datum, rather than as an adjunct to a subject's mental observations. Titchener, in fact, complained in print when Jastrow adopted Cattell's approach to the reaction-time experiment at the Chicago World's Fair.[17] In any event, by adopting only the mechanics of Wundt's procedures while ignoring his broader concerns, Cattell was acting no differently with respect to his German teacher than did the American historians who studied with Ranke or the American chemists who studied with Liebig.[18] Paradoxically, what they lost by over-simplifying their European models the Americans gained back in social usefulness.

Professional Judgments about Mental Testing

Interest in mental testing in the United States reached a peak in December 1895, when the American Psychological Association, meeting under Cattell's presidency, appointed a committee "to consider the feasibility of cooperation among the various psychological laboratories in the collection of mental and physical characteristics." The committee took upon itself the task to "draw up a series of physical and mental tests which are regarded as especially appropriate for college students."[19] It consisted of Cattell, Jastrow, Sanford, and two other psychologists: James Mark Baldwin of Princeton University and Lightner Witmer of the University of Pennsylvania. Witmer had been Cattell's student at Pennsylvania and had earned a Ph.D. with Wundt, at Cattell's insistence. He then succeeded Cattell to the chair of psychology at Pennsylvania, and in many ways his approach to psychology was similar to Cattell's.[20] Baldwin, by contrast, was broadly educated in philosophy and, though he had experimented, was not convinced that the laboratory provided the best approach to an understanding of individuals. Instead, he worked on broader questions and in 1895 had published his *Mental Development in the Child and the Race*.[21] As such, he was the only member of the committee to come to the problem of testing without a commitment to an anthropometric approach to the study of human differences.

The committee presented a preliminary report in December 1896 and a detailed report in December 1897, and both accounts stressed mental anthropometry as a preferred method. Sanford, for example, wrote that he "approved the Columbia schedule as it stands." Jastrow did recognize that at least three categories of tests could be developed, namely, those of "(a) the senses, (b) the motor capacities, and (c) the more complex mental processes." But he argued that the last category should be ignored and that "it is better to select, even if in part arbitrarily, on part of a certain sense capacity" than a broader aspect of mental life.[22]

But the report of the committee was not unanimous. Baldwin presented a minority report in which he agreed that tests of the senses and motor abilities were important, but he argued that such essentially physiological tests had received too great a place in a schedule developed by a committee of the American Psychological Association. He asked for additional tests of the higher mental processes and discussed several possible approaches that could be used in testing memory. He concluded by arguing for giving the tests as psychological a character as possible.[23]

Baldwin's criticisms of the anthropometric tests were the first, but not the last. Some of the critiques took the form of attacks on the assumptions made by the testers. Hugo Münsterberg, for example, director of the psychological laboratory at Harvard, wrote about the "danger" of believing that psychology could never help educators. More directly, he attacked Scripture's work and the scientific assumptions that underlay much of the test, claiming that "I have never measured a psychical fact, I have never heard that anyone has measured a psychical fact, I do not believe that in centuries to come a psychical fact will ever be measured."[24] To be sure, there were other reasons for Münsterberg's attack,[25] and it went beyond the criticisms that most psychologists would make of what the testers were doing. Furthermore, it was not directed at Scripture solely as a tester and, if Baldwin's criticisms were taken seriously, it was not clear that the testers were trying to measure psychological quantities. But to deny that psychological processes were in principle measurable was to undercut the positivistic assumption of Cattell that quantifiable data was the only type worthy of scientific attention.

Other critics were to compare Cattell's tests to others then being developed in France by Alfred Binet and his collaborators, which were explicitly concerned with the higher mental processes.[26] Cattell knew of Binet – who was a cooperating editor of the *Psychological Review* – and of his work. He even cited Binet's work in his major paper on anthropometric tests. There he noted that he and his coauthor "fully appreciate the arguments urged by ... M. M. Binet and Henri in favor of making tests of a strictly psychological character, "but he stressed that 'measurements of the body and of the senses come as completely within our scope as the higher mental processes." They went even further, noting that "if we undertake to study attention or suggestibility we find it difficult to measure definitely a definite thing."[27] In other words, Cattell's stress on quantification led him to avoid investigating that which was difficult to quantify and to concentrate on what he could measure. His positivistic Baconianism therefore had him avoid what he knew was more important, or at least what his colleagues told him was more important, to focus on that which he could work with easily. He was like a man who lost a quarter one night in the middle of the block, but who looked for it at the corner, because that was where the light was better.

One psychologist who compared Cattell's work with Binet's was Stella Emily Sharp, a graduate student of Edward Bradford Titchener at Cornell. In 1898, she published her doctoral dissertation in which she compared the theories of "individual psychology" – the phrase is Binet's – of the American and French testers. In it, she stressed that "the American view is founded upon no explicit theory," a conclusion with which

Cattell would have agreed entirely, and presented Binet's view as the belief that "the complex mental processes . . . are those the variations of which give most important information in regard to those mental characteristics whereby individuals are commonly classed." She did not describe her classification scheme but informally tried out some of Binet's suggested procedures on several of her graduate student classmates. For example, she asked them to remember sentences (rather than Cattell's series of letters) and to describe a picture that they had seen sometime before (rather than reproduce the length of a line seen earlier). Her results for some tests seemed to form "a basis of a general classification of the individuals," but she also found that "a lack of correspondences in the individual differences observed in the various tests was quite as noticeable as their presence." She therefore concluded that she had demonstrated the "relative independence of the particular mental activities under investigation" and hence the uselessness of Binet's procedures. But she went further. If Binet's tests did not give a good picture of the variations among individuals, she argued, then "mental anthropometry," which lacked any theoretical superstructure, could not yield results of any value either.[28]

Sharp's results are still quoted today,[29] but other events of the late 1890s had more to do with the failure of anthropometric mental testing. At least two were personal. At Yale, Scripture's personality had led him into conflicts with most of his colleagues and in the last years of the decade he was too busy fighting for his academic life to continue testing. Jastrow, meanwhile, had given up his struggle to publish the results of his testing program; this effort had led to conflicts with the officials at the Exposition and contributed to his nervous breakdown in the mid-1890s.[30] Scripture's and Jastrow's abandonment of anthropometric mental testing left Cattell and Witmer the only prominent psychologists working in the area, and Witmer's attention was soon focused on narrow applications of tests in his clinical psychology. Cattell was therefore left alone with his tests, which he continued throughout the decade, and by the late 1890s he was able to subject the data he collected to a new form of analysis. And this analysis, carried out by one of his graduate

students, led most directly to the failure of his testing program.

Clark Wissler was an 1897 graduate of Indiana University who had come to Columbia as a graduate student primarily to work with Cattell on his anthropometric testing program. At Columbia, he was especially impressed by Franz Boas, the distinguished anthropologist whom Cattell had brought to the University, and soon grew interested in the anthropological implications of Cattell's work. He later had an important career as an anthropologist, but his studies with Boas in the late 1890s had a more immediate effect. Cattell was mathematically illiterate – his addition and subtraction were often inaccurate – but Boas, with a Ph.D. in physics, was mathematically sophisticated. Cattell knew that Galton had developed mathematical techniques to measure how closely two sets of data were related, or were correlated, and he made sure that Wissler learned these procedures from Boas. He then had Wissler apply these techniques to the data collected during his decade-long testing program at Columbia.[31]

Wissler calculated the correlation between the results of any one of Cattell's tests and the grades the students tested earned in their classes; and between the grades earned in any class and those earned in any other. His results showed that there was almost no correlation among the results of the various tests. For example, in calculating the correlation between the results of the reaction-time test and the marking-out-A's test,[32] Wissler found that 252 students took both tests, and he measured the correlation between the results of the two tests as − 0.05. Consequently, despite the fact that the two tests might appear to be closely related "an individual with a quick reaction-time [was] no more likely to be quick in marking out the A's than one with a slow reaction-time." Furthermore, Wissler's analysis showed that there was no correlation between the results of any of Cattell's tests and the academic standing of any of the students tested. In contrast, Wissler found that academic performance in most subjects correlated very well with that in other subjects. Even "the gymnasium grade, which [was] based chiefly on faithfulness in attendance, correlated with the average class standing to about the same degree as one course with another."[33] In all, Wissler's analysis struck most psychologists as definitive and, with it, anthropometric mental testing, as a movement, died.

Cattell, of course, abandoned his career as an experimental psychologist, but he continued his activity within the American psychological community. For example, in the 1920s he founded The Psychological Corporation. From about 1900 on, he was better known as an editor and as an entrepreneur of science than he was as a psychologist. In many ways, his later career is more interesting than his earlier one, though as his experience with The Psychological Corporation shows, it may not have been any more successful.[34]

The Influence of the Mental Testing Movement

But despite the death of the anthropometric movement as such, anthropometric testing itself – in many ways a product of nineteenth-century philosophy of science – continued into the first years of the twentieth century. America at that time was engaged in what has been called "The Search for Order."[35] Millions of new immigrants – most with cultural backgrounds totally different from those of the early nineteenth century – were flocking to the New World. The rapid industrialization of the period and the rise of the new professions placed a heavy premium on a standardized work style and on the development of formalized criteria for judging applicants for universities and jobs. Many citizens looked to education as an ordering, and Americanizing, process, and compulsory education laws were enacted by 1900. The rising concern for the welfare, and evil influence, of the delinquent, dependent, and defective classes led to the rapid growth of institutions to serve their needs and to protect the public from them.[36]

In such an atmosphere of social concern, mental testing was seen to be too valuable a tool to be completely abandoned, even if anthropometric mental testing was shown to have extreme limitations. On one level, specialized anthropometric tests, designed for specialized uses, were found to be useful. Even one of Titchener's students, who was studying the sense of hearing and techniques for evaluating it, had to admit

that they served "practical purposes" when designed carefully. In many ways, the clinical psychology developed by Witmer in the late 1890s illustrates the point perfectly. After all, in diagnosing what are today called sensory disorders and learning disabilities, Witmer applied the tests developed by Cattell and others in particularly appropriate ways. Similarly, Scripture's best-known student – Carl E. Seashore – merely developed a set of specialized tests relating to the sense of hearing when he constructed his widely used tests of musical talent.[37] In these ways anthropometric mental tests, especially designed to focus on specific sensory problems, played (and continue to play) a major role in bringing order to American society and, especially to American education.

On another level, however, the continued use of anthropometric tests in the early twentieth century was much less successful. Though testing worked when applied narrowly, it yielded essentially useless results when the testers set larger goals. One can readily see eugenical implications in Cattell's goals for his early tests. Similarly, Jastrow believed that his tests demonstrated the proper spheres of activity for each of the sexes. Others used anthropometric tests to justify, and argue for, their own ideas as to the proper relations between the races.[38] More prosaically, though still on a large scale, Frank Parsons in the early 1900s established a vocational guidance bureau in Boston with a goal of helping young men find the profession for which they were best suited. Here he used tests of the "delicacy of touch, nerve, sight and hearing reactions, association time, etc." And as late as 1908, Parsons argued that reaction-time tests had a great value for judging an "individual's probable aptitudes and capacities."[39]

More important for psychology was the work of Henry H. Goddard, a Clark Ph.D. and student of G. Stanley Hall. In 1906, after several years of teaching psychology at a small state college, he became director of the psychological laboratory at the Vineland, New Jersey, Training School for the Feeble-Minded. There he worked with children who would today be called retarded or developmentally disabled. To obtain some estimate of the children's abilities, he used various anthropometric techniques – more than five years after Wissler's analysis was published.

Although he did not find this approach very helpful, he continued to employ it for lack of another. Finally, in the last years of the decade, he traveled to France and there discovered in detail the full range of the work of Binet and his colleagues. When he brought this knowledge back to America, his English version of Binet's tests finally supplanted anthropometric mental testing, at least outside its narrower applications.[40] Thereby, Goddard introduced a new testing movement, which has done much to shape modern America. But that is another story . . .

Notes

(1) James McKeen Cattell, "Mental Tests and Measurements," *Mind 15* (1890): 373–81.

(2) Ibid., pp. 373, 379–81.

(3) William T. Porter, "The Physical Basis of Precocity and Dullness," *Transactions of the Academy of Science of St. Louis* 6 (1893): 161–81; Franz Boas, "On Dr. William Townsend Porter's Investigation of the Growth of School Children of St. Louis," *Science* 1 (1895): 225–30.

(4) For example, Arthur MacDonald, "Mental Ability in Relation to Head Circumference, Cephalic Index, Sociological Conditions, Sex, Age, and Nationality," unpublished paper, Arthur MacDonald files, U.S. Office of Education papers, U.S. National Archives, Washington, D.C. See also Michael M. Sokal, "Anthropometric Mental Testing in Nineteenth-Century America"; James Allen Young, "Height, Weight, and Health: Anthropometric Study of Human Growth in Nineteenth-Century American Medicine," *Bulletin of the History of Medicine* 53 (1979): 214–43; Elizabeth Lomax, "Late Nineteenth-Century American Growth Studies: Objectives, Methods and Outcomes," unpublished paper, Fifteenth International Congress of the History of Science, Edinburgh, Scotland, August 1977.

(5) Sokal, M. M., "Anthropometric Mental Testing in Nineteenth-Century America," unpublished Sigma Xi national, Lecture, 1979–81; Harry K. Wolfe, "Simple Observations and Experiments: Mental Tests and Their Purposes," *North Western Journal of Education* 7 (1896): 36–37.

(6) Edward W. Scripture, "Tests of Mental Ability as Exhibited in Fencing," *Studies from the Yale Psychological Laboratory* 2 (1894): 114–19; Michael M. Sokal, "The Psychological Career of Edward Wheeler Scripture," *Historiography of Modern Psychology: Aims, Resources, Approaches,* ed. Josef Brožek and Ludwig J. Pongratz (Toronto: C. J. Hogrefe, 1980), pp. 255–78.

(7) For example, Joseph Jastrow to Galton, August 19, 1887, Galton papers; Joseph Jastrow, "Some Anthropometric and Psychologic Tests on College Students; A Preliminary Survey," *American Journal of Psychology* 4 (1892): 420–28.

(8) Joseph Jastrow, "A Study in Mental Statistics," *New Review* 5 (1891): 559–68; Mary Whiton Calkins, "Community of Ideas of Men and Women," *Psychological Review* 3 (1896): 426–30. Cf. Laurel Furumoto, "Mary Whiton Calkins (1863–1930)," *Psychology of Women Quarterly* 5 (1980): 55–68.

(9) World's Columbian Exposition, *Official Catalogue, Department M Ethnology: Archaeology, Physical Anthropology, History, Natural History, Isolated and Collective Exhibits* (Chicago: W. B. Conkey, 1893).

(10) Jastrow to Galton, July 17, 1892. Galton papers; Michael M. Sokal (ed.), "APA's First Publication: Proceedings of the American Psychological Association, 1892–1893," *American Psychologist 28* (1973): 277–92.

(11) James McKeen Cattell and George S. Fullerton, *On the Perception of Small Differences, with Special Reference to the Extent, Force and Time of Movement,* Publications of the University of Pennsylvania, Philosophical Series, no. 2 (Philadelphia: University of Pennsylvania, 1892): James McKeen Cattell and Charles S. Dolley, "On Reaction-Times and the Velocity of the Nervous Impulse," *Proceeding of the National Academy of Sciences* 7 (1896): 393–415.

(12) James McKeen Cattell, "Psychological Literature: Anthropometry," *Psychological Review* 2 (1895): 510–11; James McKeen Cattell, "Tests of he Senses and Faculties," *Education Review* 5 (1893): 257–65.

(13) Cattell to Seth Low, January 30, 1893. James McKeen Cattell collection, Columbia University Archives, New York.

(14) Sokal, "Anthropometric Mental Testing."

(15) James McKeen Cattell and Livingston Farrand, "Physical and Mental Measurements of the Students of Columbia University," *Psychological Review* 3 (1896): 618–48.

(16) Michael M. Sokal, Audrey B. Davis, and Uta C. Merzbach, "Laboratory Instruments in the History of Psychology," *Journal of the History of the Behavioral Sciences* 12 (1976): 59–64.

(17) Edward B. Titchener, "Anthropometry and Experimental Psychology," *Philosophical Review* 2 (1893): 187–92.

(18) George G. Iggers, "The Image of Ranke in American and German Historical Thought," *History and Theory* 2 (1962): 17–33; Margaret W. Rossiter, *The Emergence of Agricultural Science: Justus Liebig and the Americans, 1840–1880* (New Haven, Conn.: Yale University Press, 1975). Cf. Sokal, "Foreign Study before Fulbright: American Students at European Universities in the Nineteenth Century," unpublished Sigma Xi National Lecture, 1979–81.

(19) Edmund C. Sanford, "The Philadelphia Meeting of the American Psychological Association" *Science* 3 (1896): 119–21.

(20) John O'Donnell, "The Clinical Psychology of Lightner Witmer: A Case Study of Institutional Innovation and Intellectual Change," *Journal of the History of the Behavioral Sciences* 15 (1979): 3–17.

(21) James Mark Baldwin, *Mental Development in the Child and the Race: Methods and Processes* (New York: Macmillan, 1895).

(22) Sanford to Baldwin, December 7, 1896, Cattell papers; James Mark Baldwin, James McKeen Cattell, and Joseph Jastrow, "Physical and Mental Tests," *Psychological Review* 5 (1898): 172–79.

(23) Baldwin et al., "Physical and Mental Tests."

(24) Hugo Münsterberg, "The Danger from Experimental Psychology," *Atlantic Monthly* 81 (1898): 159–67.

(25) Matthew Hale, Jr., *Human Science and Social Order: Hugo Münsterberg and the Origins of Applied Psychology* (Philadelphia: Temple University Press, 1980); Sokal, "The Psychological Career of Edward Wheeler Scripture."

(26) Alfred Binet and Victor Henri, "La psychologie individuelle," *L'Annee psychologique* 2 (1895): 411–15.

(27) Cattell and Farrand, "Physical and Mental Measurements."

(28) Stella Emily Sharp, "Individual Psychology: A Study in Psychological Method," *American Journal of Psychology* 10 (1898): 329–91.

(29) See Richard J. Herrnstein and Edwin G. Boring (ed.), *A Source Book in the History of Psychology* (Cambridge: Harvard University Press, 1965), pp. 438–42.

(30) Sokal, "The Psychological Career of Edward Wheeler Scripture," Joseph Jastrow, autobiography, *A History of Psychology in Autobiography*, vol. 1, edited by Carl Murchison (Worcester: Clark University Press, 1930), pp. 135–62. Cf. Jastrow, correspondence with Frederic Ward Putnam, 1891–1900, Frederic Ward Putnam papers, Harvard University Archives, Cambridge, Massachusetts.

(31) Clark Wissler, "The Contribution of James McKeen Cattell to American Anthropology," *Science* 99 (1944): 232–33; James McKeen Cattell, "Memorandum for Miss Helen M. Walker," undated note, Cattell papers.

(32) Individuals were presented with a ten-by-ten array of one hundred letters in which were scattered ten A's. The time required to strike out all A's was measured.

(33) Clark Wissler, "The Correlation of Mental and Physical Tests," *Psychological Review Monograph Supplements* 3, no. 6 (1901).

(34) Sokal, M. M. "The Origins of the Psychological Corporation." *Journal of the History of the Behavioral Science* 17 (1981): 54–67.

(35) Robert H. Wiebe, *The Search for Order, 1877–1920* (New York: Hill and Wang, 1967).

(36) This paragraph summarizes many years of scholarship in the social history of American ideas. See Wiebe, *The Search for Order*; Henrika Kuklick, "The Organization of Social Science in the United States," *American Quarterly* 28 (1976): 124–41; Burton J. Bledstein, *The Culture of Professionalism: The Middle Class and the Development of Higher Education in America* (New York: Norton, 1978).

(37) Benjamin Richard Andrews, "Auditory Tests," *American Journal of Psychology* 15 (1904): 14–56; O'Donnell, "The Clinical Psychology of Lightner Witmer," Audrey B. Davis and Uta C. Merzbach, *Early Auditory Studies: Activities in the Psychology Laboratories of American Universities*, Smithsonian Studies in History and Technology, no. 31 (Washington: Smithsonian Institute Press, 1975).

(38) R. Meade Bache, "Reaction Time with Reference to Race," *Psychological Review* 2 (1895): 475–86; Anna Tolman Smith, "A Study of Race Psychology," *Popular Science Monthly* 50 (1896): 354–60, Arthur MacDonald, "Colored Children – A Psycho-Physical Study," *Journal of the American Medical Association* 32 (1899): 1140–44. Cf. Charles S. Johnson and Horace M. Bond, "The Investigation of Racial Difference Prior to 1910," *Journal of Negro History* 3 (1934): 328–39.

(39) Frank Parson, "The Vocation Bureau: First Report to Executive Committee and Trustees, May 1st, 1908," as reprinted in John M. Brewer, *History of Vocational Guidance: Origins and Early Development* (New York: Harper and Brothers, 1942), pp. 303–8.

(40) Henry H. Goddard, *The Research Department: What It Is, What It Is Doing, What It Hopes to Do* (Vineland, New Jersey: The Training School 1914).

The Psychology Laboratory at the Turn of the 20th Century
Ludy T. Benjamin, Jr.

The dating of modern psychology begins not with the sensory physiology of Hermann von Helmholtz or Johannes Müller, nor with Gustav Fechner's crucial insight on October 22, 1850, about how the physical and psychological worlds could be compared quantitatively, nor with the 1874 publication of Wilhelm Wundt's *Grundzüge der Physiologischen Psychologie*, the book that offered the first compendium of the 19th-century work that was the basis for the science of psychology. Instead, we date the new psychology from the establishment of the research laboratory at the University of Leipzig. It is the establishment of the laboratory that marks the transition of psychology from philosophy to science.

The middle of the 19th century witnessed the birth of American science laboratories – initially in chemistry – and the start of a 100-year American love affair with science and technology (Bruce, 1987). American psychology laboratories joined their natural science counterparts in the 1880s, bringing the experimental method to the investigation of mind, an event that E. G. Boring (1929) declared had no equal in the history of the study of the mind. Indeed, both editions of Boring's classic textbook defined the history of psychology almost exclusively in terms of the laboratory. One could argue that such an emphasis could be expected because his textbook was, as the title indicated, a history of experimental psychology; yet for Boring that *was* psychology.

By the 1880s, the laboratory was, arguably, the public's icon for natural science, but the same cannot be said of psychology's version. Psychologists were aware of the common public percep-

American Psychologist, 2000, *55*(3), 318–321. Copyright 2000 by the American Psychological Association, Inc. Reprinted by permission of the publisher and author.

tions that associated psychology with spiritism, the occult, and other paranormal subjects. They sought to change those views with articles in newspapers and popular magazines, public exhibitions, and popular speeches, all touting the new science of psychology.

Shortly after Hugo Münsterberg arrived at Harvard University in 1892 to direct the psychology laboratory there, his assistant announced in *McClure's Magazine* that the psychology laboratory resembled any other science laboratory. "Around the rooms run glass-cases filled with fine instruments. Shelves line up, row after row, of specimen jars and bottles. Charts cover the remainder of the walls. The tables and floors are crowded with working apparatus" (Nichols, 1893, p. 399). However, he continued, the laboratory is more than jars, charts, and apparatus: "the spirit that reigns in these rooms is the same that is found in other laboratories of exact science" (Nichols, 1893, p. 399).

The importance of the laboratory for the beginnings of the new psychology would be difficult to overstate. Historian James Capshew (1992) has written that "the enduring motif in the story of modern psychology is neither a person nor an event but a place – the experimental laboratory" (p. 132). As such, this snapshot in the history of psychology begins in Leipzig, Germany, where in 1879 Wundt and his graduate students began conducting original research as a "community of investigators" (Danziger, 1990, p. 18). Danziger (1990) has argued that "the strongest grounds for locating the beginnings of experimental psychology in Wundt's laboratory ... [were that it was in this laboratory] that scientific psychology was first practiced as the organized and self-conscious activity of a community of investigators" (p. 18).

Thus, the laboratory was more than specimen bottles, charts, and apparatus, and it was more than the presence of a scientific spirit; it was, in addition, and perhaps of greatest importance, a community of scholars who conducted collaborative research in pursuit of scientific explanations of mind. They shared not only the physical space of the laboratory but an interest in common questions. As students graduated, others came to the laboratory to work on the same questions or to extend the research to new questions. This community approach stood in stark contrast to the solitary investigations of Wundt's predecessors, such as Helmholtz and Fechner, and even some of his contemporaries, for example, Hermann Ebbinghaus.

Wundt's laboratory attracted many American students, particularly as fame of the laboratory spread in the United States. G. Stanley Hall arrived in Leipzig in the fall of 1879 for postdoctoral study, having just finished his doctoral degree with William James at Harvard. Hall spent some time with Wundt but worked principally in the physiological laboratory of Carl Ludwig. In 1883, Hall founded what is usually recognized as the first psychology laboratory in America at Johns Hopkins University. Many of the American laboratories that followed in the last two decades of the 19th century were founded by individuals who had studied with Wundt or Hall (Table 1 lists the 41 psychology laboratories founded in the United States by 1900 and their founders, and indicates which ones studied with Wundt or Hall). Popplestone and McPherson (1984) have observed that there were fewer than 50 psychology laboratories worldwide by 1900, making the United States home to the great majority of them.

James McKeen Cattell was the founder of two of those early American laboratories, those at the University of Pennsylvania and Columbia University. He was the first American student to earn his doctorate with Wundt in the new experimental psychology, finishing in 1886. As a 24-year-old graduate student, Cattell wrote to his parents, giving them and us an image of what life was like in the initial laboratory of this new science:

I spend four mornings and two afternoon's [sic] working in Wundt's laboratory. . . . Our work is interesting. If I should explain it to you you might not find it of vast importance, but we discover new facts and must ourselves invent the methods we use. We work in a new field, where others will follow us, who must use or correct our results. We are trying to measure the time it takes to perform the simplest mental acts – as for example to distinguish whether a color is blue or red. As this time seems to be not more than one hundredth of a second, you can imagine this is no easy task. (Sokal, 1981, p. 89)

The early psychologists, like Cattell, received their training in philosophy departments of which the new experimental psychology was a part. When they looked for academic jobs, those jobs were in philosophy, a discipline that was, of course, not a laboratory discipline. It is not surprising that many university administrators were reluctant to provide the financial resources necessary to establish, equip, and maintain these laboratories. No doubt many agreed with philosopher August Comte that a science of mind was not possible. Thus, the new psychologists found themselves defending the scientific nature of their discipline and arguing that their laboratories needed more space and equipment. These activities, sadly, may seem more traditional than historical to many psychologists today.

Typical of these academic struggles was the effort of Harry Kirke Wolfe to establish his laboratory at the University of Nebraska in 1889 (see Benjamin, 1991). Wolfe, like Cattell, had received his doctorate with Wundt in 1886. He began laboratory work at Nebraska with his students using minimal equipment that he built, borrowed from other departments, or purchased using funds from his library book budget. In his first annual report to the regents, Wolfe asked for $500 to equip the laboratory at a minimal level. First he stressed the low start-up costs, "I cannot emphasize too strongly the necessity of providing some facilities for experimental work. . . . It is possible to build up an experimental dept. in Psychology with little outlay" (Benjamin, 1993, p. 58). Then he argued for the promise of the discipline, "No field of scientific research offers such excellent opportunities for original work; chiefly because the *soil is new*" (Benjamin, 1993, p. 58).

Wolfe didn't get any money for his laboratory, so he spent even more of his book budget for

Table 1 The Founding of American Psychology Laboratories: 1883–1900

Year	Laboratory	Founder
1883	Johns Hopkins University	Granville Stanley Hall
1887	Indiana University	William Lowe Bryan[a]
1887	University of Pennsylvania	James McKeen Cattell[b]
1888	University of Wisconsin	Joseph Jastrow[a]
1889	Clark University	Edmund Clark Sanford[a]
1889	University of Kansas	Olin Templin
1889	University of Nebraska	Harry Kirke Wolfe[b]
1890	Columbia University	James McKeen Cattell[b]
1890	University of Iowa	George T. W. Partick[a]
1890	University of Michigan	James Hayden Tufts
1891	Catholic University	Edward Aloyius Pace[b]
1891	Cornell University	Frank Angell[b]
1891	Wellesley College	Mary Whiton Calkins
1892	Brown University	Edmund Burke Delabarre
1892	Harvard University	Hugo Münsterberg[b]
1892	University of Illinois	William Otterbein Krohn
1892	Trenton State Normal College	Lillie A. Williams
1892	Yale University	Edward Wheeler Scripture[b]
1893	University of Chicago	Charles Augustus Strong
1893	Princeton University	James Mark Baldwin
1893	Randolph-Macon College	Celestia S. Parrish
1893	Stanford University	Frank Angell[b]
1894	Amherst College	Charles Edward Garman
1894	Denison University	Clarence Luther Herrick
1894	University of Minnesota	Harlow Stearns Gale
1894	University of the City of New York	Charles Bemis Bliss
1894	Pennsylvania State University	Erwin W. Runkle
1894	Wesleyan University	Andrew C. Armstrong, Jr.
1894	Western Reserve University	Herbert Austin Aikins
1895	Smith College	William George Smith
1896	University of California	George Malcolm Stratton[b]
1896	Wilson College	Anna Jane McKeag
1897	Ohio State University	Clark Wissler
1898	Bryn Mawr College	James Henry Leuba[a]
1898	University of Texas	Not identified
1899	University of Oregon	Benjamin J. Hawthorne
1900	University of Maine	M. C. Fernald
1900	University of Missouri	Max Frederick Meyer
1900	New York University	Charles Hubbard Judd[b]
1900	Northwestern University	Walter Dill Scott[b]
1900	University of Wyoming	June Etta Downey

Note: This information was compiled principally from Garvey (1929) and Murray and Rowe (1979).
[a] Studied with G. Stanley Hall. [b] Studied with Wilhelm Wundt.

equipment and then appealed to the regents once more in his second annual report:

> The scientific nature of Psychology is not so generally recognized. . . . The advantages offered by experimental Psychology, as a discipline in scientific methods, are not inferior to those offered by other experimental sciences. The measurement of the Quality, Quantity, and Time Relations of mental states is as inspiring and as good discipline as the determination of, say the percent of sugar in a beet or the variation of an electric current. (Benjamin, 1993, p. 59)

You may have noticed that Wolfe's appeals used agricultural metaphors and examples, devices that he perhaps believed would influence the administrators of a largely agricultural university. He should have tried some other strategy; the university gave him no more money for his laboratory, and he received a written warning about spending book money for other purposes.

Not all laboratory founders faced the resistance experienced by Wolfe. By the 1890s, the founding pace accelerated (see Table 1), and many of the new laboratories touted the excellence of their facilities in the pages of journals such as the *American Journal of Psychology* and *Science*. It even became commonplace for the psychology laboratories to be described in the university catalogs, as was the case for the natural science laboratories. These brief published accounts usually named the person in charge of the laboratory and included descriptions of the physical facilities, the apparatus, and sometimes the type of work done in the laboratory. For psychologists, this marketing of the laboratory was important for student recruitment, but it was also a public statement of the scientific legitimacy of the discipline. Psychologists could be said to be engaged in "the flaunting of the laboratory as evidence of worthy membership in the fraternity of science" (Popplestone & McPherson, 1984, p. 197).

The proliferation of American laboratories at the turn of the century changed the nature of graduate education for American psychology students. Whereas before 1900 the majority had journeyed to one of the European universities for their doctoral degrees, in the 25 years after 1904

less than 15% of American psychologists had earned degrees from foreign universities. These new American laboratories, however, did not long remain the exclusive province of graduate student training and research.

In a practice that spawned some controversy (see French, 1898; Wolfe, 1895), laboratory training was extended to undergraduate students in psychology. By the first decade of the 20th century, a year-long laboratory course in experimental psychology had become a standard part of the curriculum for undergraduates studying psychology. To meet the needs of undergraduate laboratory work, a number of prominent psychologists, such as Carl Seashore, Edmund Sanford, Lightner Witmer, and most notably Edward B. Titchener, published textbooks for laboratory training of undergraduates. Titchener's four volumes (1901–1905) – two for the instructor and two for the student – described nearly 100 qualitative and quantitative experiments that could be conducted by undergraduate students in a laboratory setting. Thus, the psychology laboratory, in its first 25 years, became fully integrated into the university, housing its community of investigators for original research and serving as a training ground for students at all levels.

In the course of the 20th century, psychology departments have changed much, and the discipline of psychology has changed in ways psychologists 100 years ago could never have imagined. The psychology laboratory is still a fixture in most colleges and universities (and in many nonacademic settings), although the diverse brass instruments and specimen jars that filled the laboratory shelves have been replaced largely by a single instrument, the computer. Psychology faculty and students (both graduate and undergraduate) continue to be involved in laboratory training, and laboratory investigators remain plentiful in psychology today.

Still, among psychologists at the beginning of the new millennium, the laboratory no longer serves as an enduring motif. Within the discipline, the icon of the laboratory and its attendant community of scholars has been replaced by an image of clinical psychologist and client, an image, ironically that has been the public's perception of psychology since the rise of psychoanalysis in America in the 1920s (Hornstein, 1992).

References

Benjamin, L. T., Jr. (1991). *Harry Kirke Wolfe: Pioneer in psychology.* Lincoln: University of Nebraska Press.

Benjamin, L. T., Jr. (1993). *A history of psychology in letters.* Dubuque, IA: Brown & Benchmark.

Boring, E. G. (1929). *A history of experimental psychology.* New York: Century Company.

Bruce, R. V. (1987). *The launching of modern American science, 1846–1876.* Ithaca, NY: Cornell University Press.

Capshew, J. H. (1992). Psychologists on site: A reconnaissance of the historiography of the laboratory. *American Psychologist, 47,* 132–142.

Danziger, K. (1990). *Constructing the subject: Historical origins of psychological research.* New York: Cambridge University Press.

French, F. C. (1898). The place of experimental psychology in the undergraduate course. *Psychological Review, 5,* 510–512.

Garvey, C. R. (1929). List of American psychology laboratories. *Psychological Bulletin, 26,* 652–660.

Hornstein, G. A. (1992). The return of the repressed: Psychology's problematic relations with psycho-analysis, 1909–1960. *American Psychologist, 47,* 254–263.

Murray, F. S., & Rowe, F. B. (1979). Psychology laboratories in the United States prior to 1900. *Teaching of Psychology, 6,* 19–21.

Nichols, H. (1893, October). The psychological laboratory at Harvard. *McClure's Magazine, 1,* 399–409.

Popplestone, J. A., & McPherson, M. W. (1984). Pioneer psychology laboratories in clinical settings. In J. Brozek (Ed.), *Explorations in the history of psychology in the United States* (pp. 196–272). Lewisburg, PA: Bucknell University Press.

Sokal, M. M. (1981). *An education in psychology: James McKeen Cattell's journal and letters from Germany and England, 1880–1888.* Cambridge, MA: MIT Press.

Titchener, E. B. (1901–1905). *Experimental psychology: A manual of laboratory practice* (Vols. 1–4). New York: Macmillan.

Wolfe, H. K. (1895). The new psychology in undergraduate work. *Psychological Review, 2,* 382–387.

Psychological Instruments at the Turn of the Century
Rand B. Evans

Just 100 years ago the devices that came to be called "brass instruments" pervaded psychological research. (For turn-of-the-century descriptions of instruments current at the time and their use, see Titchener, 1901–1905.) Such instruments were not necessarily made of brass but often were. These were typically mechanical, clockwork-driven, or electromagnetic devices that produced stimuli for experiments or demonstrations and recorded or timed responses. There were no electronic devices in 1900, of course, and except for electromagnets and some electrical lights and batteries, only a few electrical devices were being used in mainstream psychological research.

The "new psychology" was the psychology of the laboratory, and the laboratory meant instruments because psychologists were attempting to duplicate in their own field the success of experimental physiology and physics earlier in the century. James lamented in his *Principles of Psychology* the change that instruments had brought about in the field: "There is little of the grand style about these prism, pendulum, and chronograph philosophers. They mean business, not chivalry" (1890, Vol. 1, p. 193). James's concerns about the dominance of laboratory science over philosophical inquiry in psychology were realized by 1900.

By 1900 scientific instruments were definitely in vogue in psychology for laboratory research and in classroom lecture demonstrations for introductory psychology courses. The psychological lecture hall in many universities and colleges was hard to distinguish from the hall for physics. It was around 1900 that courses in "experimental psychology" became more common and typically involved a student laboratory. William James had initiated a laboratory course as early as the 1880s at Harvard, and E. B. Titchener conducted undergraduate experimental psychology laboratory courses at Cornell soon after his coming to America in 1892. However, it was the publication of Edmund C. Sanford's *A Course in Experimental Psychology* (1894), based on a series of articles in the *American Journal of Psychology*, that seems to have spurred the creation of student laboratories. Sanford's little book was quite popular but would be eclipsed not long after the turn of the century by E. B. Titchener's massive four-volume *Experimental Psychology: A Manual of Laboratory Practice* (1901–1905). Titchener's "manuals" would become the standard for laboratory instruction well into the 1930s, and they inspired a number of briefer competitors.

The three uses of psychological instruments – in scientific research, in classroom demonstrations, and in undergraduate instructional laboratories – often required quite different types of devices for the same subject matters. For instance, for the study of human reaction times, a faculty researcher or dissertation student might have used a Hipp chronoscope (see Figure 1A), which was an electromechanically controlled clockwork timer accurate to 1/1000th of a second. Because of its expense and both physical and electrical fragility, a Hipp chronoscope would not be trusted to the undergraduate experimental course laboratory. Undergraduates would use a far simpler, more rugged, and less expensive device, such as Sanford's completely mechanical vernier chronoscope (see Figure 1B), in their student laboratory work. It worked on the principle of a

American Psychologist, 2000, *53*(3), 322–325. Copyright 2000 by the American Psychological Association, Inc. Reprinted by permission of the publisher and author.

vernier. It had two pendulums, one set longer than the other but both set at known lengths. When the stimulus appeared, the longer pendulum was released mechanically. When the participant pressed the key in response, the shorter pendulum was similarly released. By counting the number of swings it took the shorter pendulum to catch up with the longer, experimenters could use a mathematical formula to calculate the difference in time between the two events. Accurate only to 1/100th of a second, Sanford's vernier chronoscope cost only about $15, so most laboratories could afford several of them. For demonstrations in a lecture hall, a larger timer would be used, such as Wundt's demonstrational chronoscope (see Figure 1C). This device made use of a Hipp chronoscope mechanism with the dial shafts brought out to turn very large clock indicator hands on a 43-cm-diameter dial. The dial could be illuminated from the rear and so read in the largest lecture hall.

Most of the instruments used in psychology a century ago were derived from instruments devised for other disciplines. The connection between psychology, physiology, and physics remained quite close, with people in the separate disciplines often working on similar problems, although from different perspectives. This was particularly true in the areas of audition, vision, touch, and reaction time. Psychology and physiology also shared research interests as well as instruments in the measurement of emotion and fatigue. During this era in psychology researchers made primary use of one form or another of introspection, the description of an individual's experiences in a stimulus situation. Instruments were essential for producing and controlling those stimulus conditions. Often introspective descriptions were considered along with objective records, particularly in the study of emotions making use of the "method of expression."

By the late 1890s, many original instruments created by psychologists began to appear to compete with those derived earlier from physics and physiology. William Stern, better known for his formulation of IQ, devised his tone variator, which was based on the principle of blowing a stream of air across the a mouth of a bottle. As the depth of the "bottle" changed, the pitch would vary as well. Stern's variators (see Figure 2) produced a continuous change in tone, much as would be done later with electronic variable audio frequency oscillators. This device became a standard laboratory piece in experimental, demonstrational, and student laboratories in psychology and was used by physicists as well in their demonstrational courses.

New classes of instruments that originated from psychological research programs began to appear around the turn of the century. One of

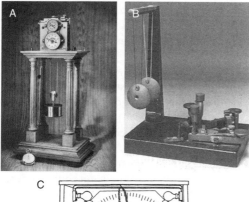

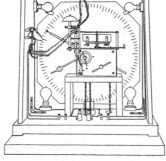

Figure 1 *Examples of early chronoscopes. Note:* A. Hipp's chronoscope. B. Sanford's vernier chronoscope. C. Wundt's demonstrational chronoscope

Figure 2 *Stern's variator*

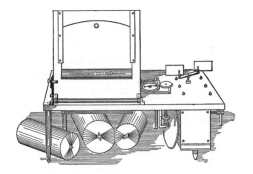

Figure 3 *G. E. Müller's memory drum*

great importance was the memory drum. Based on the principle of a rotating kymograph drum, the memory drum allowed lists of words or other verbal or figural stimuli to appear for fixed periods of time so they could be viewed individually. The designs of G. E. Müller, Otto Lipmann, and others would add this family of instruments to the collection of standard psychological instruments (see Figure 3).

Most of the instruments used in psychology by 1900 had to do with human sensation, perception, action, and emotion. Except for physiology or physiological psychology, there was little research being done with animals. However, just at the turn the century, E. L. Thorndike's research on trial-and-error learning (1898), Robert M. Yerkes's work on habits in turtles (1901), Willard S. Small's research on maze learning using a maze copied from the Hampton Court maze (1901), and the work of a few others began to introduce animals into the psychology laboratory. James Rowland Angell's laboratory at the University of Chicago, where John B. Watson and Walter Hunter both received their training, allowed the use of animals in research. Most of the instruments used in animal research around the turn of the century were homemade or at best made in departmental shops.

If experimental psychology began as a German science, so its instruments were still largely German made in 1900. Makers such as Zimmermann in Leipzig had been producing instruments for the psychological market and for the laboratory of Wilhelm Wundt for years. The various European makers were each identified with one or more major research laboratories in the field: Zimmermann with Wilhelm Wundt, Rothe with

Ewald Hering, and Spindler and Hoyer, who had succeeded Carl Diederichs, with G. E. Müller, just to name a few. There were major manufacturers in France and England as well, notably Rudolf Koenig in Paris for Helmholtz's instruments, but for psychology Germany was still the center of research and demonstration instruments.

In the late 1890s, however, some American firms began making their own instruments for the American market. Some were shop men for departments of psychology, who made pieces for the laboratory in their university of employment and made duplicates for others in other universities to supplement their income. The "mechanicians" at Titchener's Cornell, Cattell's Columbia, and Sanford's Clark University all provided this service, and a few branched out to form instrument companies and make a range of instruments. Most such firms were short-lived.

Perhaps the first dedicated psychological instrument maker not connected with a department of psychology was Elmer Willyoung of Philadelphia, who began making instruments in the mid-1890s under the patronage of E. C. Scripture of Yale and a few others. Willyoung's enterprise died out around the turn of the century, however, as did others such as the Michigan Apparatus Company and the Garden City Model Works.

The most significant American instrument maker at the turn of the century was the Chicago Laboratory Supply and Scale Company, which began importing and making instruments for psychological and physiological laboratories in the late 1890s. Its president, C. H. Stoelting, would change the name of the company before 1905 to C. H. Stoelting Co., a name that would be well-known to every American experimental psychologist throughout most of the 20th century. Stoelting would come to dominate the sale of instruments to most departments of psychology after the outbreak of World War I, when acquiring German instruments became impractical.

E. B. Titchener had privately published a pamphlet in 1900 titled "The Psychological Laboratory of Cornell University," which was distributed widely across America. This pamphlet listed all the instruments used at Cornell with floor plans of the laboratories and photographs of the major instrument rooms. Titchener's *Experimental Psychology* and the description of his laboratory in his pamphlet did much to set the standard for instruments for the experimental laboratories in the newly emerging departments of psychology. Stoelting was a great promoter and had the astuteness to latch on to E. B. Titchener's rising star. In 1902 Stoelting issued a pamphlet of his own listing every instrument in the first volume of Titchener's *Experimental Psychology* and advertising its price and availability through his company. Stoelting not only produced Titchener's instruments and improvements on other instruments, but either manufactured or imported virtually every standard instrument used in the laboratories of the period (Stoelting Co., 1997).

This was the era of standard instruments. *Standard* is meant here in two ways. A standard instrument was one that was found in most laboratories and was considered an essential part of a quality laboratory. Standard instruments included such devices as the Hipp chronoscope, Ludwig kymograph, string galvanometer, Stern variators, Helmholtz/Titchener telestereoscope, Helmholtz resonators, tuning forks, stereoscopes, and many other similar devices. Another way for an instrument to be standard was if it was used in experiments in which there were no absolute physical standards, usually for stimuli. For this reason the stimulus value was often expressed in terms of the instrument itself. For example, there was no way to measure the intensity of a sound except in terms of the sound made by the fall of an object, such as a small metal shot of a certain diameter and metal, over a certain distance onto a given material surface. The height of fall for this shot in this situation would then become the measure of intensity. To guarantee that the stimulus would be the same from place to place, it was thought better to use the identical instrument, preferably made by the same maker, from laboratory to laboratory.

In 1900 psychology was very much a natural science with the attitudes and values of natural science. It was only much later that researchers in fields such as social psychology, abnormal psychology, and developmental psychology would begin to apply experimental methods to their observations and inject their own values and approaches into the field. But in 1900, it was the laboratory that made the new psychology new. The careful use of instruments to measure and control experimental situations showed it was possible for psychology to take its seat with its more established cousins, physics and physiology, at the table of the experimental sciences.

References

James, W. (1890). *Principles of psychology* (Vols. 1–2). New York: Macmillan.

Sanford, E. C. (1894). *A course in experimental psychology*. Boston: Heath.

Small, W. S. (1901). Experimental study of the mental processes of the rat, II. *American Journal of Psychology*, *12*, 206–240.

Stoelting Co., C. H. (1997). *The great catalog of the C. H. Stoelting Company, 1930–1937*. New York: Scholars Facsimiles & Reprints. (Original work published as *Psychological and physiological apparatus and supplies* in 1930)

Thorndike, E. L. (1898). Animal intelligence: An experimental study of the associative processes in animals. *Psychological Monographs*, *2*(4), 1–109.

Titchener, E. B. (1900). *The psychological laboratory of Cornell University* [Pamphlet]. Worcester, MA: Oliver B. Wood.

Titchener, E. B. (1901–1905). *Experimental psychology: A manual of laboratory practice* (Vols. 1–4). New York: Macmillan.

Yerkes, R. M. (1901). The formation of habits in the turtle. *Popular Science Monthly*, *58*, 519–525.

Chapter 5

Structuralism and Functionalism

In the summer of 1892, G. Stanley Hall hosted a meeting of American psychologists in his study at his home in Worcester, Massachusetts, to discuss the need for a national organization of psychologists. The outcome was the formation of the American Psychological Association. The group would hold its first meeting in the chapel of the University of Pennsylvania in December of that year, with Hall serving as president of the new organization.

Laboratory psychology in America was now roughly a decade old, dating from Hall's laboratory at Johns Hopkins University in 1883. By 1892 there were laboratories at 19 North American universities, including James Mark Baldwin's laboratory, founded at the University of Toronto in 1891. The laboratory at Cornell University was also begun in 1891 by Frank Angell, who had studied with Wundt. Angell left Cornell in 1892, after only one year, to start the first psychology laboratory on the West Coast at Stanford University.

Angell's replacement at Cornell was another of Wundt's students, an Englishman who would soon become a prominent figure in American psychology. His name was Edward Bradford Titchener (1867–1927), and he would spend the rest of his life at Cornell, promoting his psychology program as the one true scientific psychology and criticizing his American colleagues for an approach to psychology that was misguided at best and unscientific at worst. Titchener labeled his psychology *structuralism*, and he contrasted it with the extant American psychology he saw at other universities, which he labeled *functionalism*.

Titchener was only one of several new laboratory directors beginning their tenure in the United States in 1892. Three other graduates of Wundt's doctoral program would begin their work in the same year. Edward Wheeler Scripture (1864–1945) would start the laboratory at Yale University. Lightner Witmer (1867–1956), who had been an undergraduate student with Cattell at the University of Pennsylvania, returned to Penn to head the laboratory there after Cattell had moved on to Columbia University in 1891. In addition, Hugo Münsterberg, recruited heavily by William James, arrived to head the Harvard laboratory. You encountered each of these individuals in Michael Sokal's article on anthropometric mental testing in the previous chapter.

American psychology of the 1890s was defined as the scientific study of consciousness. For Titchener, consciousness was the sum total of mental processes that occurred at any given moment. Titchener approached the science of psychology in the way that he believed all sciences proceeded. The initial task in understanding consciousness was to discover its structure, that is, what are its basic *elements*. The second task was to discover *how these elements combined*. And the third task was to understand *why the combinations occurred as they did*, which Titchener believed could be explained by making connections to underlying physiological processes. These were the *what, how,* and *why* questions basic to scientific investigation.

Whereas Titchener was interested in discovering the structure of consciousness, that is, what consciousness is, many of his contemporaries were more interested in discovering the functions of consciousness, that is, what consciousness does for the organism. It was this basic difference in scientific goals that led Titchener to label his own approach structuralism and that of the other approach as functionalism.

Titchener discerned three kinds of elements that made up consciousness: *sensations, images, and feelings*. Although he studied all three, the focus of his research was on sensations, the subject that had dominated research in Wundt's laboratory. Whereas Wundt had delineated sensations according to two characteristics – *quality* and *intensity* (recall that discussion from the Wundt excerpt in Chapter 3) – Titchener would add two more: *duration* and *clearness* (Titchener, 1910a). Indeed, sensations and images could be described in terms of all four dimensions, yet feelings could be described only in regard to the first three. For example a light (a sensation) could be described in terms of quality (red), intensity (dim), duration (present for five seconds), and clarity (distinct as opposed to indistinct). By 1896, Titchener's quest to identify all the separate elements of consciousness had led him to discover more than 44,000 separately identifiable visual and auditory sensations.

How did Titchener identify these elements? What scientific methods did he use? He relied on observation, more accurately self-observation. He labeled his method *introspection*, meaning looking within. His students were rigorously trained in how to render proper scientific introspections, introspections that would produce reliable results. In an experiment, the subject would be exposed to a stimulus event, perhaps the tactile presence of a cold piece of metal applied gently to the skin of the subject's forearm. The subject would be asked to report the initial sensation. Was it one of cold? Did it feel like a burn? Was there any pain? How did the sensation change over time? Did the cold sensation diminish? Did the pain increase? What about when the piece of metal was applied to another part of the person's body, say the back of the neck or the heel of the foot? Titchener's introspective method allowed for frequent interruptions of the conscious experience at any time, to obtain an introspective report. Moreover, replications of the stimulus presentation allowed for multiple introspections and thus reliability checks.

Functionalism or functional psychology was a much more diverse approach, both conceptually and methodologically. Influenced by the evolutionary ideas of Charles Darwin, the functionalists sought to discover the adaptive significance of consciousness. Surely consciousness had evolved and, if it evolved, it must have done so because it offered the organism some adaptive advantage. William James, G. Stanley Hall, and James McKeen Cattell had all been influenced by Darwin and it showed in their psychologies. For example, in the section you read from James's *Principles* in the previous chapter, James described the evolutionary advantage of consciousness in allowing the organism to make choices. James, Hall, and Cattell are not typically labeled functional psychologists, and they did not characterize themselves as such, but their psychologies gave rise to a functional psychology that asked what it is that consciousness does for the organism.

Whereas structural psychology under Titchener focused on defining the "what" of consciousness and doing so mostly exclusively with the method of introspection, those psychologists identified in the functional camp were seeking answers to the functions of consciousness, using a variety of methods such as mental testing, questionnaires, psychophysical methods, animal studies, experiments, and even introspection. They were involved in studying children, developing psychological tests, opening psychological clinics, working with businesses to determine the varied effectiveness of advertisements, and using animal studies to generalize to explanations of human consciousness. As noted earlier, structural psychology focused mostly on the study of sensations. Functional psychologists, however, spent more time on studies of learning and motivation. Learning was particularly important from a Darwinian point of view. If consciousness served to help the organism better adapt to the environment, then that adaptation would come about through learning.

The psychologist most identified with the functional position was James Rowland Angell (1869–1949). Angell, a cousin of Frank Angell mentioned earlier, was head of the psychology laboratory at the University of Chicago. It was a new university, having opened in 1892, largely with the financial support of oil baron John D. Rockefeller. Angell arrived at Chicago in 1894 and would build one of the best-known psychology programs in the country, producing many distinguished graduates, including John B. Watson, the founder of behaviorism, who will be discussed in Chapter 8. In 1906, Angell was elected president of the American Psychological Association, and he used the occasion of his presidential address to define functional psychology and to argue against the exclusivity of structuralism that Titchener had proposed. In a clear rebuke of Titchener he wrote:

> the moment [functionalism] takes unto itself the pretense of scientific finality its doom will be sealed. It means to-day a broad and flexible and organic point of view in psychology. The moment it becomes dogmatic and narrow its spirit will have passed and undoubtedly some worthier successor will fill its place. (Angell, 1907, p. 91)

To get an idea of the dogmatism Angell was describing, consider the following words from Titchener:

> It cannot be said that this functional psychology . . . has been worked out either with as much patient enthusiasm or with as much scientific accuracy as has the psychology of mind structure . . . the methods of [functional] psychology cannot . . . lead to results of scientific finality. (Titchener, 1898, p. 450)

For Titchener, the distinction between his psychology and the other was obvious: structuralism was a science, functionalism was nothing more than technology (Evans, 1985). Titchener was particularly critical of the applied (practical) psychological work that was a major part of functional psychology. He wrote, "the diversion into practical channels of energy which would otherwise have been expended in the service of the laboratory must be regarded as a definite loss to pure science" (Titchener, 1910b, p. 407).

For functional psychologists the applied work in education, business, and clinical areas was crucial if they were to be able to answer their questions about the functions of consciousness. They found Titchener's psychology too constraining, and they wondered ultimately what could be gained in understanding the mind by an exhaustive delineation of the elements of consciousness.

The story of these two early approaches to psychology is far more complex than its description in the brief coverage here. Suffice it to say that both systems contributed positively to psychology. Likely no other American psychologist did more than Titchener to promote the importance of the well-controlled laboratory study in psychology (see Evans, 1985, 1991). The four volumes of Titchener's manuals of experimental psychology (1901–1905) were used for more than 30 years to train students in the laboratory methods of psychology, and they likely were most responsible for establishing the year-long sequence of a laboratory course in experimental psychology as a standard feature of most undergraduate and graduate curricula in psychology. Functional psychology greatly expanded the methodological choices for psychologists. Furthermore, their pioneering efforts in applied psychology led to the establishment of a profession of psychology which will be discussed in Chapter 9.

The Readings

There are four readings in this chapter, two on the subject of structuralism and two on functionalism. The first reading is an excerpt from Titchener's 1910 textbook of psychology, a section entitled "The Method and Scope of Psychology." He begins with a distinction between mind and consciousness, continues with a discussion of his method of introspection, and concludes with a brief treatment of the scope of psychology. This section will indicate that Titchener is not as narrow in his interests as he has been portrayed to this point. Indeed, Titchener was not opposed to practical work in psychology. His objection was that the studies of function should not be done until the requisite work on structure had been accomplished.

The second reading is by historian of psychology Thomas Leahey. It compares the psychological systems of Wundt and Titchener, thus drawing on some material covered in Chapter 3 of this book. When this article was written in 1981, it was not uncommon to see textbooks in psychology treat Wundt and Titchener as though their psychologies were identical. Many books referred to Wundt as a structuralist, a label that is wholly inappropriate for his psychology, as Leahey's article shows. Today, textbooks tend to be more accurate, drawing on the more recent scholarship to correct this error. Still, this article continues to be an important contribution because of the comparisons between the two psychologies, in terms of both their similarities and differences.

The third selection is by James Rowland Angell and is the APA presidential address that we mentioned earlier in this chapter, an address given in 1906 and published the following year. This article is arguably the defining statement of the functional psychology position. In it Angell stresses three identifying features of functional psychology: (a) it is concerned with mental operations and not mental elements; (b) it seeks to identify the ways in which consciousness helps the organism adapt to the environment; and (c) it is a psychophysical psychology that recognizes the role of mind and body in adaptation.

The final reading is by psychologist Stephanie Shields, who describes the emerging field of the psychology of women in the social and scientific context of a functional psychology. Shields (1975) discusses why psychological studies of sex differences came about at the beginning of the twentieth century:

> It was the functionalist movement in the United States that fostered academic psychology's study of sex differences and, by extension, a prototypic psychology of women. The incorporation of evolutionary theory into the practice of psychology made the study of the female legitimate, if not imperative. (p. 739)

This article is an exceptionally good example of the role of a broader social context impacting developments within psychology. Shields discusses the work of Helen Thompson Woolley (one of James Angell's doctoral students) and Leta Hollingworth, pioneers in the psychology of women. Their work is discussed in more detail in Chapter 10, where you will find articles by and about both of these important researchers.

These readings set the stage for several chapters yet to come. The treatment of functionalism provides an introduction to the beginnings of applied psychology in America, the subject of the next chapter, which will cover the origins of clinical, school, and business psychology.

The Method and Scope of Psychology
Edward Bradford Titchener

§5. Mental Process, Consciousness and Mind

The most striking fact about the world of human experience is the fact of change. Nothing stands still; everything goes on. The sun will someday lose its heat; the eternal hills are, little by little, breaking up and wearing away. Whatever we observe, and from whatever standpoint we observe it, we find process, occurrence; nowhere is there permanence or stability. Mankind, it is true, has sought to arrest this flux, and to give stability to the world of experience, by assuming two permanent substances, matter and mind: the occurrences of the physical world are then supposed to be manifestations of matter, and the occurrences of the mental world to be manifestations of mind. Such an hypothesis may be of value at a certain stage of human thought; but every hypothesis that does not accord with the facts must, sooner or later, be given up. Physicists are therefore giving up the hypothesis of an unchanging, substantial matter, and psychologists are giving up the hypothesis of an unchanging, substantial mind. Stable objects and substantial things belong, not to the world of science, physical or psychological, but only to the world of common sense.

We have defined mind as the sum-total of human experience considered as dependent upon the experiencing person. We have said, further, that the phrase "experiencing person" means the living body, the organised individual; and we have hinted that, for psychological purposes, the living body may be reduced to the nervous system and its attachments. Mind thus becomes the sum-total of human experience considered as depen-

dent upon a nervous system. And since human experience always process, occurrence, and the dependent aspect of human experience is its mental aspect, we may say, more shortly, that mind is the sum-total of mental processes. All these words are significant. "Sum total" implies that we are concerned with the whole world of experience, not with a limited portion of it; "mental" implies that we are concerned with experience under its dependent aspect, as conditioned by a nervous system; and "processes" implies that our subject-matter is a stream, a perpetual flux, and not a collection of unchanging objects.

It is not easy, even with the best will possible, to shift from the common-sense to the scientific view of mind; the change cannot be made all in a moment. We are to regard mind as a stream of processes? But mind is personal, my mind; and my personality continues throughout my life. The experiencing person is only the bodily organism? But, again, experience is personal, the experience of a permanent self. Mind is spatial, just as matter is? But mind is invisible, intangible; it is not here or there, square or round.

These objections cannot be finally met until we have gone some distance into psychology, and can see how the scientific view of mind works out. Even now, however, they will weaken as you look at them. Face that question of personality. Is your life, matter of fact, always personal? Do you not, time and again, forget yourself, lose yourself, disregard yourself, neglect yourself, contradict yourself, in a very literal sense? Surely, the mental life is only intermittently personal. And is your personality, when it is realised, unchanging? Are you the same self in childhood and manhood, in your working and in your playing moods, when you are on your best behaviour and when you are freed from restraint?

From E. B. Titchener (1910). *A textbook of psychology.* New York: Macmillan, pp. 15–30.

Surely, the self-experience is not only intermittent, but also composed, at different times, of very different factors. As to the other question: mind is, of course, invisible, because sight is mind, and mind is intangible, because touch is mind. Sight-experience and touch-experience are dependent upon the experiencing person. But common sense itself bears witness, against its own belief, to the fact that mind is spatial: we speak, and speak correctly, of an idea in our head, a pain in our foot. And if the idea is the idea of a circle seen in the mind's eye, it is round; and if it is the visual idea of a square, it is square.

Consciousness, as reference to any dictionary will show, is a term that has many meanings. Here it is, perhaps, enough to distinguish two principal uses of the word.

In its first sense, consciousness means the mind's awareness of its own processes. Just as, from the common-sense point of view, mind is that inner self which thinks, remembers, chooses, reasons, directs the movements of the body, so is consciousness the inner knowledge of this thought and government. You are conscious of the correctness of your answer to an examination question, of the awkwardness of your movements, of the purity of your motives. Consciousness is thus something more than mind; it is "the perception of what passes in a man's own mind";[1] it is "the immediate knowledge which the mind has of its sensations and thoughts."[2]

In its second sense, consciousness is identified with mind and "conscious" with "mental." So long as mental processes are going on, consciousness is present; as soon as mental processes are in abeyance, unconsciousness sets in. "To say I am conscious of a feeling, is merely to say that I feel it. To have a feeling is to be conscious; and to be conscious is to have a feeling. To be conscious of the prick of the pin, is merely to have the sensation. And though I have these various modes of naming my sensation, by saying, I feel the prick of a pin, I feel the pain of a prick, I have the sensation of a prick, I have the feeling of a prick, I am conscious of the feeling; the thing named in all these various ways is one and the same."[3]

The first of these definitions we must reject. It is not only unnecessary, but it is also misleading, to speak of consciousness as the mind's awareness of itself. The usage is unnecessary, because, as we shall see later, this awareness is a matter of observation of the same general kind as observation of the external world; it is misleading, because it suggests that mind is a personal being, instead of a stream of processes. We shall therefore take mind and consciousness to mean the same thing. But as we have the two different words, and it is convenient to make some distinction between them, we shall speak of mind when we mean the sum-total of mental processes occurring in the life-time of an individual, and we shall speak of consciousness when we mean the sum-total of mental processes occurring *now*, at any given "present" time. Consciousness will thus be a section, a division, of the mind-stream. This distinction is, indeed, already made in common speech: when we say that a man has "lost consciousness," we mean that the lapse is temporary, that the mental life will shortly be resumed; when we say that a man has "lost his mind," we mean – not, it is true, that mind has altogether disappeared, but certainly that the derangement is permanent and chronic.

While, therefore, the subject-matter of psychology is mind, the direct object of psychological study is always a consciousness. In strictness, we can never observe the same consciousness twice over; the stream of mind flows on, never to return. Practically, we can observe a particular consciousness as often as we wish, since mental processes group themselves in the same way, show the same pattern of arrangement, whenever the organism is placed under the same circumstances. Yesterday's high tide will never recur, and yesterday's consciousness will never recur; but we have a science of psychology, as we have a science of oceanography.

§6. The Method of Psychology

Scientific method may be summed up in the single word "observation"; the only way to work in science is to observe those phenomena which form the subject-matter of science. And observation implies two things: attention to the phenomena, and record of the phenomena; that is, clear and vivid experience, and an account of the experience in words or formulas.

In order to secure clear experience and accurate report, science has recourse to experiment. An experiment is an observation that can be repeated, isolated and varied. The more frequently you can *repeat* an observation, the more likely are you to see clearly what is there and to describe accurately what you have seen. The more strictly you can *isolate* an observation, the easier does your task of observation become, and the less danger is there of your being led astray by irrelevant circumstances, or of placing emphasis on the wrong point. The more widely you can *vary* an observation, the more clearly will the uniformity of experience stand out, and the better is your chance of discovering laws. All experimental appliances, all laboratories and instruments, are provided and devised with this one end in view: that the student shall be able to repeat, isolate and vary his observations.

The method of psychology, then, is observation. To distinguish it from the observation of physical science, which is inspection, a looking-at, psychological observation has been termed introspection, a looking-within. But this difference of name must not blind us to the essential likeness of the methods. Let us take some typical instances.

We may begin with two very simple cases. (1) Suppose that you are shown two paper discs: the one of an uniform violet, the other composed half of red and half of blue. If this second disc is rapidly rotated, the red and blue will mix, as we say, and you will see a certain blue-red, that is, a kind of violet. Your problem is, so to adjust the proportions of red and blue in the second disc that the resulting violet exactly matches the violet of the first disc. You may repeat this set of observations as often as you like; you may isolate the observations by working in a room that is free from other, possibly disturbing colours; you may vary the observations by working to equality of the violets first from a two-colour disc that is distinctly too blue, and secondly from a disc that is distinctly too red. (2) Suppose, again, that the chord *c-e-g* is struck, and that you are asked to say how many tones it contains. You may repeat this observation; you may isolate it, by working in a quiet room; you may vary it, by having the chord struck at different parts of the scale, in different octaves.

It is clear that, in these instances, there is practically no difference between introspection and inspection. You are using the same method that you would use for counting the swings of a pendulum, or taking readings from a galvanometer scale, in the physical laboratory. There is a difference in subject-matter: the colours and the tones are dependent, not independent experiences: but the method is essentially the same.

Now let us take some cases in which the material of introspection is more complex. (1) Suppose that a word is called out to you, and that you are asked to observe the effect which this stimulus produces upon consciousness: how the word affects you, what ideas it calls up, and so forth. The observation may be repeated; it may be isolated, – you may be seated in a dark and silent room, free from disturbances; and it may be varied, – different words may be called out, the word may be flashed upon a screen instead of spoken, etc. Here, however, there seems to be a difference between introspection and inspection. The observer who is watching the course of a chemical reaction, or the movements of some microscopical creature, can jot down from moment to moment the different phases of the observed phenomenon. But if you try to report the changes in consciousness, while these changes are in progress, you interfere with consciousness; your translation of the mental experience into words introduces new factors into that experience itself. (2) Suppose, again, that you are observing a feeling or an emotion: a feeling of disappointment or annoyance, an emotion of anger or chagrin. Experimental control is still possible; situations may be arranged, in the psychological laboratory, such that these feelings may be repeated, isolated and varied. But your observation of them interferes, even more seriously than before, with the course of consciousness. Cool consideration of an emotion is fatal to its very existence; your anger disappears, your disappointment evaporates, as you examine it.

To overcome this difficulty of the introspective method, students of psychology are usually recommended to delay their observation until the process to be described has run its course, and then to call it back and describe it from memory. Introspection thus becomes retrospection; introspective examination becomes *post mortem* examination. The rule is, no doubt, a good one for the beginner; and there are cases in which even the experienced psychologist will be wise to follow it. But it is by no means universal. For we must remember (*a*) that the observations in question may be repeated. There is, then, no reason why the observer to whom the word is called out, or in whom the emotion is set up, should not report at once upon the first stage of his experience: upon the immediate effect of the word, upon the beginnings of the emotive process. It is true that this report interrupts the observation. But, after the first stage has been accurately described, further observations may be taken, and the second, third and following stages similarly described; so that presently a complete report upon the whole experience is obtained. There is, in theory, some danger that the stages become artificially separated; consciousness is a flow, a process, and if we divide it up we run the risk of missing certain intermediate links. In practice, however, this danger has proved to be very small; and we may always have recourse to retrospection, and compare our partial results with our memory of the unbroken experience. Moreover, (*b*) the practised observer get into an introspective habit, has the introspective attitude ingrained in his system; so that it is possible for him, not only to take mental notes while the observation is in progress, without interfering with consciousness, but even to jot down written notes, as the histologist does while his eye is still held to the ocular of the microscope.

In principle, then, introspection is very like inspection. The objects of observation are different; they are objects of dependent, not of independent experience; they are likely to be transient, elusive, slippery. Sometimes they refuse to be observed while they are in passage; they must be preserved in memory, as a delicate tissue is preserved in hardening fluid, before they can be examined. And the standpoint of the observer is different; it is the standpoint of human life and of human interest, not of detachment and aloofness. But, in general, the method of psychology is much the same as the method of physics.

It must not be forgotten that, while the method of the physical and the psychological sciences is substantially the same, the subject-matter of these sciences is as different as it can well be. Ultimately, as we have seen, the subject-matter

of all the sciences is the world of human experience; but we have also seen that the aspect of experience treated by physics is radically different from the aspect treated by psychology. The likeness of method may tempt us to slip from the one aspect to the other, as when a textbook of physics contains a chapter on vision and the sense of colour, or a text-book of physiology contains paragraphs on delusions of judgement; but this confusion of subject-matter must inevitably lead to confusion of thought. Since all the sciences are concerned with the one world of human experience, it is natural that scientific method, to whatever aspect of experience it is applied, should be in principle the same. On the other hand, when we have decided to examine some particular aspect of experience, it is necessary that we hold fast to that aspect, and do not shift our point of view as the enquiry proceeds. Hence it is a great advantage that we have the two terms, introspection and inspection, to denote observation taken from the different standpoints of psychology and of physics. The use of the word introspection is a constant reminder that we are working in psychology, that we are observing the dependent aspect of the world of experience.

Observation, as we said above, implies two things: attention to the phenomena, and record of the phenomena. The attention must be held at the highest possible degree of concentration; the record must be photographically accurate. Observation is, therefore, both difficult and fatiguing; and introspection is, on the whole, more difficult and more fatiguing than inspection. To secure reliable results, we must be strictly impartial and unprejudiced, facing the facts as they come, ready to accept them as they are, not trying to fit them to any preconceived theory; and we must work only when our general disposition is favourable, when we are fresh and in good health, at ease in our surroundings, free from outside worry and anxiety. If these rules are not followed, no amount of experimenting will help us. The observer in the psychological laboratory is placed under the best possible external conditions; the room in which he works is fitted up and arranged in such a way that the observation may be repeated, that the process to be observed may stand out clearly upon the background of consciousness, and that the factors in the process may be separately varied. But all this care is of no avail, unless the observer himself comes to the work in an even frame of mind, gives it his full attention, and is able adequately to translate his experience into words.

§7. The Scope of Psychology

If mind is the sum-total of human experience considered as dependent upon the experiencing person, it follows that each one of us can have direct acquaintance only with a single mind, namely, with his own. We are concerned in psychology with the whole world of human experience; but we are concerned with it solely under its dependent aspect, as conditioned by a nervous system; and a nervous system is a particular thing, possessed by a particular individual. In strictness, therefore, it is only his own mind, the experience dependent upon his own nervous system, that each of us knows at first-hand; it is only to this limited and individual subject-matter that the method of experimental introspection can be directly applied. How, then, is a scientific psychology possible? How can psychology be anything more than a body of personal beliefs and individual opinions?

The difficulty is more apparent than real. We have every reason to believe, not only in general that our neighbours have minds like our own, that is, are able like ourselves to view experience in its dependent aspect, but also in detail that human minds resemble one another precisely as human bodies do. Within a given race there is much apparent diversity of outward form: differences in height and figure, in colour of hair and eyes, in shape of nose and mouth. We notice these differences, because we are obliged in everyday life to distinguish the persons with whom we come in contact. But the resemblances are more fundamental than the differences. If we have recourse to exact measurements, we find that there is in every case a certain standard or type to which the individual more or less closely conforms and about which all the individuals are more or less closely grouped. And even without measurement we have evidence to the same effect: strangers see family likenesses which the members of the family cannot themselves detect, and the units in a crowd of aliens, Chinese or Negroes, look bewilderingly alike.

Now all of our main social institutions rest upon the assumption that the individuals of whom society is composed possess minds, and possess minds that are of the same sort. Language, religion, law and custom, – they one and all rest upon this assumption, and they one and all bear testimony that the assumption is well grounded. Would a man invent language in order to talk to himself? Language implies that there are more minds than one. And would the use of a common speech be possible if minds were not essentially alike? Men differ in their command of language, as they differ in complexion, or in liability to disease; but the general use of language testifies to a fundamental likeness of mental constitution in us all.

Hence the psychologist is fully justified in believing that other men have minds of the same kind as his own, and in basing psychology upon the introspective reports furnished by a number of different observers. These reports show, in point of fact, just what we should expect them to show: a fundamental agreement, and a great variety of detail, – the mental differences grouping themselves, as we have seen that physical differences group themselves, about a central type or standard.

If, however, we attribute minds to other human beings, we have no right to deny them to the higher animals. These animals are provided with a nervous system of the same pattern as ours, and their conduct or behaviour, under circumstances that would arouse certain feelings in us, often seems to express, quite definitely, similar feelings in them. Surely we must grant that the highest vertebrates, mammals and birds, have minds. But the lower vertebrates, fishes and reptiles and amphibia, possess a nervous system of the same order, although of simpler construction. And many of the invertebrates, insects and spiders and crustaceans, show a fairly high degree of nervous development. Indeed, it is difficult to limit mind to the animals that possess even a rudimentary nervous system; for the creatures that rank still lower in the scale of life manage to do, without a nervous system, practically everything that their superiors do by its assistance. The range of mind thus appears to be as wide as the range of animal life.

The plants, on the other hand, appear to be mindless. Many of them are endowed with what we may term sense-organs, that is, organs differentiated to receive certain forms of stimulus, pressure, impact, light, etc. These organs are analogous in structure to the sense-organs of the lower animal organisms: thus, plant "eyes" have been found, which closely resemble rudimentary animal eyes, and which – if they belonged to animals – might mediate the perception of light: so that the development of the plant-world has evidently been governed by the same general laws of adaptation to environment that have been at work in the animal kingdom. But we nave no evidence of plant-consciousness.

Just as the scope of psychology extends beyond man to the animals, so does it extend from the individual man to groups of men, to societies. The subject-matter of psychology is human experience considered as dependent upon the individual. But since the individuals of the same race and epoch are organised in much the same way, and since they live together in a society where their conduct affects and is affected by the conduct of others, their view of experience under its dependent aspect naturally becomes, in certain main features, a common or general view; and this common view is embodied in those social institutions to which we have referred above, – in language, religion, law and custom. There is no such thing as a collective mind, or a national mind, or a social mind, if we mean by mind some immaterial being; but there is a collective mind, if we mean by it the sum-total of human experience considered as dependent upon a social group of similar individuals. The study of the collective mind gives us a psychology of language, a psychology of myth, a psychology of custom, etc.; it also gives us a differential psychology of the Latin mind, of the Anglo-Saxon mind, of the Oriental mind, etc.

And this is not all: the scope of psychology extends, still further, from the normal to the abnormal mind. Life, as we know, need not be either complete or completely healthy life. The living organism may show defect, the lack of a limb or of a sense-organ; and it may show disorder and disease, a temporary or a permanent lapse from health. So it is with mind. The consciousnesses of those who are born deaf or blind are defective; they lack certain sensations and images that are normally present. In dreaming and the hypnotic state, during intoxication, after

prolonged sleeplessness or severe strain of any kind, we have illustrations of temporary mental derangement. And the various forms of insanity – mania, melancholia, dementia – are forms of permanent mental disorder.

Derangement of the social mind may be studied in the various panics, fads, epidemics of speculation, of false belief, etc., which occur from time to time even in the most highly civilised societies. The mob consciousness stands to a healthy social consciousness very much as dreaming to the waking life. Permanent disorder of the social mind means the downfall of society.

All these various fields of psychology may be cultivated for their own sake, on account of their intrinsic interest and value; they must, indeed, be so cultivated, if psychology is to progress. At the same time, their facts and laws often throw light upon the problems of normal human psychology. Suppose, for instance, that a man, blind from his birth, is rendered able to see by a surgical operation. He must learn to use his eyes, as a child learns to walk. And the gradual perfecting of his vision, the mistakes and confusions to which he is liable, all the details of his visual education, form a storehouse of facts upon which the psychologist can draw when he seeks to illustrate the development of the perception of space in the normal mind, – the manner in which we come to judge of the distance of objects from ourselves and from one another, of their direction, and of their size and shape. Instructive, also, are those forms of mental unsoundness which consist in the derangement of single group of processes. The various types of morbid fear – agoraphobia, the fear of being alone in open spaces; neophobia, the fear of everything that is new; phobophobia, the nervous dread of being afraid – are only exaggerated forms of experiences that most of us have had. The sanest man will feel lost when he passes, suddenly, from a quiet country life to the bustle of a large town; we are all a little timid when we enter a strange community; we have all been afraid that on such-and-such an occasion we shall show our nervousness. Similarly, the self-importance of paranoia is merely an exaggeration of the pleased self-consciousness, the self-complacency, that we often observe in others and, if we are honest, must often detect in ourselves. In all these instances, the strong lines of the caricature may help us to a more correct picture of the normal consciousness.

Notes

1 John Locke, *An Essay Concerning Human Understanding*, [1690] Bk. II., Ch. i., §19.

2 Dugald Stewart, *Outlines of Moral Philosophy*, [1793]. Pt. I., Section i., §7.

3 James Mill, *Analysis of the Phenomena of the Human Mind*, [1829] Vol. I., Ch. v. Mill uses the word "feeling" to denote what we have called "mental process."

The Mistaken Mirror: On Wundt's and Titchener's Psychologies

Thomas H. Leahey

It is widely believed by American psychologists that Edward Bradford Titchener was a loyal pupil of Wilhelm Wundt who acted as a kind of English-speaking double for the founder of psychology. Only recently have historians of psychology begun to cast doubt on this belief,[1] but no one has as yet explored the systematic differences between the psychologies of Wundt and Titchener. The present paper has a twofold purpose. The first is historical, to demonstrate that Titchener was not Wundt's double, and to explore some of the sources of the modern misconception. The second is systematic, for Titchener and Wundt represent two different metatheoretical orientations that transcend commonly recognized psychological, and even scientific systems. We will then find that Titchener does have a mirror image in a most surprising place.

A Sketch of Wundtian Psychology

Wundt's psychology was produced by a wide-ranging mind and developed over a long lifetime, and so cannot be briefly summarized. Most important for present purposes, however, was Wundt's division of mental phenomena into inner and outer phenomena. The distinction is most easily grasped today in the study of language, since it resembles Chomsky's distinction of deep and surface structure. According to Wundt, a sentence consists of a set of visual or auditory sensations given in consciousness.

T. H. Leahey (1981). The mistaken mirror: On Wundt's and Titchener's psychologies. *Journal of the History of the Behavioral Sciences*, 17, 273–282. Copyright © 1981 by John Wiley and Sons. Reprinted by permission of the publisher and the author.

However, underlying the sentence are certain cognitive processes whose operations in the speaker produce the sentence, or analyze it and extract the meaning for the hearer. These processes are the inner phenomena of language.[2] We may note in passing that although there is some similarity between Wundt's distinction of inner phenomena and outer phenomena and Chomsky's deep and surface structures, Wundt's formulation is more psychological. Wundt treats a sentence as a consciously given experience produced by general cognitive processes; Chomsky treats a sentence as embodying abstract and specifically linguistic structures.

For Wundt the distinction of inner and outer phenomena was not limited to language, however. In all its aspects, the mind could be viewed as a set of conscious experiences produced jointly by external stimuli and various higher mental processes. The most important of those processes was apperception, which served a number of mental functions according to Wundt. It was responsible for attention: we apperceive those stimuli we want to attend to, but only incompletely apprehend others. It was responsible for perceptual grouping: "word" is more than a collection of letters because apperception synthesizes them into a more meaningful whole. It was also responsible, reciprocally, for analysis: "word" can be analyzed into four letters because we can focus our attention on each of its elements. Apperception played a similar role in sentence production and comprehension.

A complete understanding of the mind required study of both outer and inner mental phenomena, and Wundt adopted two methods appropriate to each study. The first method, applicable to outer phenomena, is the better known to modern psychologists. It is Wundt's so-called physiological psychology. For Wundt, physiological psychology was the study of individual human consciousness by means of self-observation. I avoid the more widely used term *introspection*, for as Blumenthal has pointed out, Wundt did not ask his subjects to introspect in the commonly used Cartesian sense, in which introspection is an intensely analytical reflection on a remembered event experienced without experimental control.[3] Wundt harshly criticized his student Külpe for adopting such a procedure.[4] Self-observation as used by Wundt was a simple report of an experience not too different from procedures used by modern, thoroughly "objective" anti-introspective, cognitive psychologists.[5]

The second method, appropriate to inner mental phenomena, is much less well known. It is Wundt's *Völkerpsychologie*.[6] Wundt believed that "(we) cannot experiment upon mind itself, but only upon its outworks, the organs of sense and movement . . ."[7] However, ". . . fortunately for science there are other sources of objective psychological knowledge which become accessible at the very point where the experimental method fails us. These are certain products of the common mental life," especially language, myth, and custom, which form the subject matter of *Völkerpsychologie*, "our chief source of information regarding the general psychology of the complex mental processes."[8] These phenomena expand the range of human experience by including historical experience, and Wundt thought that by comparing primitive and complex societies we could trace the development of mind. A complete psychology thus had to include physiological psychology as a direct study of outer mental phenomena given in consciousness, and *Völkerpsychologie* as an indirect study of the inner phenomena of mind.

The most important goal of psychology, given Wundt's framework, was an explanation of human consciousness. Self-observation produced a descriptive classification of conscious experience, or outer phenomena, but this is only the first stage for psychological science. The second stage would be an explanation of the facts of immediate experience by reference to indirectly known, voluntarily controlled cognitive processes, such as attention.[9] Furthermore, psychological explanation was to resemble historical explanation. Wundt believed that the mind was

creative, which meant that reported experience could not be predicted from initial conditions, as in physics. Instead, a psychologist could show that an experience, once reported, was an orderly product of sensation and the operation of cognitive processes, as the historian shows an event to be an orderly product of a situation and human action.[10] We may note that Sigmund Freud shared this same historical orientation.[11]

Titchener's System Contrasted with Wundt's

We may let Titchener speak for himself:

> Wundt . . . accepts . . . a whole array of explanatory terms: consciousness, attention, association – perception, emotion, memory, imagination. If only he had the insight to throw them all away! Wundt possessed, in fact, just one clear concept, the concept of sensation. . . . All the rest were foggy from much argument . . . we ourselves are getting rid of the theory-ridden terms piecemeal . . . and it will be long before experimental psychology is finally free of them.[12]

We find that Titchener was not afraid to criticize his teacher in the broadest and harshest terms. It is clear from this passage that Titchener viewed much of Wundt's system as unnecessary, overspeculative, and even unscientific.

The most obvious of Titchener's excisions is the entire *Völkerpsychologie*; Titchener had nothing like it, and did little to bring it to the attention of others. He himself, like another of Wundt's students, Oswald Külpe, essayed a direct experimental attack on the higher mental processes.[13] However, and herein lies the crucial difference between Titchener and Wundt, Titchener did not view cognitive processes as underlying and giving rise to conscious experience, but as completely analyzable complexes of conscious sensations to be reduced to their elemental constituents.

Titchener acknowledged his own system to be a kind of sensationism, a meaning-free description of the elements of consciousness, in contrast to Wundt's voluntarism. Wundt emphasized the voluntary activity of mind, especially in the process of apperception, but Titchener preferred pure sensationism. To define sensationism, he quoted, and appeared to accept, Baldwin's definition: "the theory that all knowledge originates in sensations; that all cognitions, even reflective ideas and so-called intuitions, can be traced back to the elementary sensations."[14]

The three original tasks expected of this sensationistic psychology were: to discover and catalogue the simplest sensations given in consciousness; to discover how these sensations were connected; and to discover, for both sensations and connections, their underlying physiological processes. The method by which the first two tasks were to be accomplished may best be termed analytical or anatomical introspection. Unlike Wundt's, Titchener's subjects did not just briefly report an experimentally controlled experience, they had to dissect it, attempting to discover the sensation-elements given at that moment in consciousness. Titchener's analytic introspection was similar to the methods adopted by Külpe at Würzburg, which Wundt himself criticized as a return to the philosophical introspection he had abandoned. Titchener also discarded Wundt's goal of a psychological explanation of mind in favor of a physiological one.

Let us consider an example – attention. For Wundt, attention was one aspect of the cognitive process of apperception, whose operation gave rise to various conscious phenomena. Titchener, however, pleads for a "simplification of the psychology of attention." He would rather have "a psychology of clearness – considering clearness as an attribute of sensation."[15] Titchener's key move is this: It is not that some sensations are clear *because* they are attended to, but that we say we have attended to some sensations *because* we find them clear in our consciousness. Where Wundt had explained sensory clarity by appealing to the process of attention, Titchener argued that "attention" is just a descriptive label given to what we experience with clarity. Titchener's analysis also applies to the feeling of effort that Wundt held accompanied active attention. Titchener writes: "When I am trying to attend I . . . find myself frowning, wrinkling my forehead etc. All such . . . bodily sets and movements give rise to characteristic sensations. Why should not these sensations be what we call 'attention'."[16]

Attention for Titchener is something of a rationalization after the fact of an experience, in that it is only a label we apply to clear sensations accompanied by certain bodily sets that indicate effort.

Titchener did away with Wundt's distinction between inner and outer aspects of mind. Titchener attempted to turn Wundt's inner cognitive processes into descriptive attributes of the outer, conscious, region of mind as bundles of sensations. In short, Titchener wanted psychology primarily to describe conscious facts, not explain them. Explanation of mental events Titchener referred to physiology, by linking conscious experience to its substrate in the material processes of the brain. In any event, terms such as apperception were given no explanatory role.

In his latest work, Titchener's descriptive emphasis was sharpened. He abandoned the search for elements and their connections in consciousness in favor of phenomenological description, and he abandoned the goal of explanation altogether, be it physiological or psychological. In a letter to Adolf Meyer written in 1918, Titchener declares, "I don't *explain* or *causally relate* at all at all! . . . Causality I regard as mythological, – if you mean by it anything more than correlation."[17] Titchener thus departed even further from Wundt, but the change only strengthened existing differences.

Given Titchener's background, that Titchener is not Wundt's double should not surprise us. After all, he was an Englishman, and Fritz Ringer has shown how great was the intellectual gulf between English and German intellectual Zeitgeiste. Although Titchener studied with Wundt, Titchener's earlier grounding in philosophy in England undoubtedly kept him from absorbing the Wundtian paradigm, and predisposed him to accept the Machian positivism espoused by some, but not all, young German psychologists such as Külpe and Ebbinghaus. The founding Gestalt psychologists, on the other hand, rejected positivism.[18] So when he set out on his own, he reverted to what he knew. In his *An Outline of Psychology*, Titchener wrote that "the general standpoint of the book is that of the traditional English psychology."[19] The differences between Titchener and Wundt are more than a matter of historical accident, however. Titchener sought a descriptive psychology and Wundt an explanatory psychology. This brings us to the systematic side of our problem.

Descriptive and Explanatory Science

In his recent study of behaviorism, Brian Mackenzie argues that the behaviorist's acceptance of positivism created an excessive commitment to experimental method as the savior of psychology.[20] For example, John B. Watson in his famous 1913 paper urged that psychologists should temporarily avoid studies of complex mental processes, but that "As our methods become better developed it will be possible to undertake investigations of more and more complex forms of behavior."[21] There is no mention of better theory, only "refined" method. Titchener wrote on the same topic: "We may have absolute confidence in our method . . . there is not the slightest doubt that the patient application of the experimental method will presently solve the problems of feeling and attention."[22] Titchener and Watson were equally committed to good experimental method, although to different methods, as the surety of scientific progress. If Mackenzie's analysis of behaviorism can be applied to Titchener, we should find evidence of positivism in Titchener as well as Watson.

Titchener's most extended treatment of his philosophy of science is given in the posthumously published *Systematic Psychology: Prolegomena.* Titchener here affirmed his descriptive orientation: "Institutional science . . . is descriptive and not explanatory; it stops short of the 'why' of things." Titchener "denies that science has anything to do with explanation, with Why and Because." He seems to reduce natural law to simple correlation "expressing" "covariation among phenomena" which cannot be sharply distinguished from a "law of facts."[23] This attitude is further confirmed by the letter to Meyer printed in the 1972 edition of *Systematic Psychology,* quoted above. The synthesis of laws into a theory "never transcends description, a shorthand description which . . . brackets together a multitude of related facts."[24] Just as terms such as "force" and "cause" are retained by physics because they are convenient, while protesting "against [their] mythical power of explanation," psychology may still use "memory" and "imagination"

while disavowing "common sense ideas as both superfluous and misleading. . . . "[25]

In saying all this, Titchener advocated the radical positivism of Ernst Mach and other nineteenth-century positivist philosophers, a tradition of which Titchener was well aware. He cited Mach, for example, to the effect that " 'the grand universal laws of physics . . . are not essentially different from descriptions'."[26] Mach advocated a completely descriptive approach to physics, and rejected the use of any purely theoretical terms, such as "atom," on the grounds of unobservability. Mach's positivism is more radical than later logical positivism, which admitted theoretical terms to science as long as they were empirically defined.

Wundt, on the other hand, was one of those German academic mandarins described by Ringer for whom the word "positivism" was a term of opprobrium. Titchener himself noted that Wundt was a voluntarist, not a sensationist. Wundt believed descriptive psychology to be incomplete and felt that explanation was the proper goal of science. In the explanatory psychology he sought "the chief emphasis is laid on the way in which immediate experience arises in the subject, so that a variety of explanatory psychology results which attributes to those subjective activities not referred to external objects, a position as independent as that assigned to ideas. This variety has been called *Voluntaristic psychology,* because of the importance that must be conceded to volitional processes . . . "[27] Furthermore, in contrast to Titchener, Wundt believed in "an *independent psychical causality,*" compatible with, but "different from" the physical causality of physiology. Alongside "*laws of nature*" there exist "*laws of psychical phenomena.*"[28] Titchener did not "causally relate at all" beyond mere correlation, while Wundt listed six causal laws of the mind in his *Outlines of Psychology.*[29]

The issue between Wundt and Titchener was what to do with the data of psychology. They agreed that psychology's data were the facts of conscious experience, but they completely disagreed on what needed to be explained. For Wundt, what we experience in consciousness is the outcome of deeper mental processes not directly subject to self-observation. The goal of psychology, therefore, was to use the data of individual (physiological psychology) and collective (*Völkerpsychologie*) experience to discover the hidden cognitive processes. These processes could be used to scientifically explain the facts of experience, which in turn provide evidence for the existence and operation of the cognitive processes.

Titchener, on the other hand, as a positivist, believed that what was not observable was not admissable in science, including the so-called cognitive processes for which Titchener rebuked Wundt in the passage quoted [earlier]. . . . As purely theoretical, nonobservable terms, apperception, memory, attention, and so on were for Titchener essentially mythical. Titchener began, like Wundt, with the facts of experience, but instead of seeing them as evidence of the workings of mental processes, as in need of explanation, he saw them as the rock bottom bed of science. The facts of experience were not to be explained, held Titchener, but were to be used to explain the supposed processes of apperception and attention. As we have seen, Wundt said a sensation is clear because we attended to its source; the clear sensation is evidence of the process of attention. According to Titchener, however, people have learned to say they attended to something because the sensation was clear. In Titchener's view, the myth of attention is a sort of rationalization or label attached to clear sensation. The explanation of sensory clarity for Titchener would come from revealing the physiology of clarity. And then, in good positivist fashion, one observable fact, sensory clarity, would be explained by another observable fact, a brain-process; nowhere would one need to introduce an unobservable cognitive process of apperception or attention.

We may conclude, then, that underlying the distinct psychological systems of Wundt and Titchener are two different philosophies of science. For Wundt, scientific psychology should be causal and explanatory, accounting for the facts of immediate experience by showing how they depend on the operation of complex, inner mental processes. For Titchener, on the other hand, scientific psychology should be correlational and descriptive, accounting for the facts of immediate experience by showing how they depend on (nonpsychological) nerve processes, or, later, by simply describing regularities in experience. Titchener is not Wundt's double, in

method, theory, or philosophy of science. Why then, is he so often believed to be Wundt's double?

Mistaking Titchener for Wundt

As Henry Veatch has remarked, scientists are a very present-minded group,[30] and psychologists are no exception. A useful example of modern psychologists' misunderstanding of their own past may be found in Ulric Neisser's recent *Cognition and Reality*.[31] Neisser is an interesting case, for although he did much to found contemporary information-processing cognitive psychology with his 1967 *Cognitive Psychology*,[32] he now opposes much of what the movement has become. He is familiar with a fair amount of very early psychological research,[33] and in some respects his current orientation resembles Wundt's.[34] Nevertheless, in his recounting of the failures of introspective psychology, he makes a number of erroneous charges. He attributes much of the failure of early mentalistic psychology to its employment of "a special form of introspection," in which the mind's activities are observed. He has in mind the analytic introspection of Külpe or Titchener, not Wundt's self-report. He also writes that "the introspectionists had no theory of cognitive development."[35] This is essentially true of Wundt's physiological psychology and Titchener's system, but Neisser seems unaware of *Völkerpsychologie*, Wundt's tool for studying cognitive development. Such conflating of Wundt and Titchener into a single "introspective psychology" is typical of the beliefs of psychologists today.

As is typical of the present-minded scientist, Neisser cites neither Titchener nor Wundt, but seems to draw his information from unnamed "(t)extbooks in the history of psychology."[36] Blumenthal has already pointed to textbooks as a source of ignorance about the true Wundt: "American textbook accounts of Wundt now present highly inaccurate and mythological accounts of the man and his work."[37] The classic history is, of course, E. G. Boring's *History of Experimental Psychology*.[38] Boring treats Wundt as something of a British associationist. Association is given more space than apperception. Creative synthesis is said to be "not too different" from J. S. Mill's mental chemistry, a passive process of association determined by the elements themselves. The *Völkerpsychologie* is given no more than a mention. Titchener is described as "an Englishman who represented the German psychological tradition in America."[39]

More recent texts have done little to correct, and much to further distort, Boring's description of Wundt. Duane Schultz, for example, in his popular work, explicitly equates Wundt and Titchener, which at least Boring did not do: "The orthodox Wundtian brand of . . . psychology was transplanted to the United States by Wundt's most devoted pupil, E. B. Titchener, and underwent its fullest development at his hands." Schultz's presentation of Wundt closely follows Boring, and he writes that "A knowledge of Wundt's psychology provides a reasonably accurate picture of Titchener's system"[40] although the two are not identical. In his text, William Sahakian titles his section on Titchener, "Titchener: Wundt in America."[41] He fails to go beyond Boring in his brief consideration of Wundt's system, and describes the *Völkerpsychologie* only on the basis of the *Elements of Folk Psychology*[42] which has little in common with the developed *Völkerpsychologie*. Daniel Robinson gives neither Wundt nor Titchener their own sections in his text. His presentation of Wundt is sketchy, not even mentioning the *Völkerpsychologie*, while his treatment of Titchener is almost nonexistent. He does say that Titchener's system was "not far removed from" Wundt's. Both are criticized for having "no theory worth the name."[43] This is true of Titchener, though given his descriptive orientation he would not find it troubling, but it is certainly untrue of Wundt. His theory of attention, for example, is a worthy rival to any modern account, as I have argued earlier.[44] Watson's *Great Psychologists* treats Wundt at some length, unlike other texts after Boring, but it shares the same difficulties as the others.[45] The most extreme equation of Wundt and Titchener is found in Fred Keller's *Definition of Psychology*: "Titchener's system was so close to Wundt's and so much easier to describe, that we shall not here dwell on . . . Wundt. . . . "[46] The thinking reader should be left wondering how two things can be identical but one be "much simpler" than the other.

To the extent that working psychologists know Wundt only through textbook accounts, as

Neisser seems to, they will confuse Titchener with Wundt, as the texts do. With Blumenthal, I believe that textual distortions of Wundt's psychology are the major reason for Wundt's low status today. A contributing factor is the lack of translations of Wundt's volumes on *Völkerpsychologie*. Enough of his works on individual psychology are available in English that Americans can get an accurate picture of that side of Wundt's work, but until Blumenthal's *Language and Psychology* none of the important *Völkerpsychologie* was available. Finally, the rise of American behaviorism made unacceptable any form of mentalistic psychology, to the point where differences among mentalists became blurred. This blurring has been continued by behaviorism's antihistorical bias. Behaviorism was launched in a fervor of optimism that the past could be forgotten in pursuit of the utopian future, so that accurate historical scholarship was deemed irrelevant:[47] history was not taught at Walden Two.[48]

Strange Bedfellows in Description

Titchener is not Wundt's mirror-image: he does not accurately reflect Wundt's psychology. However, we should bear in mind that a mirror image has a peculiar characteristic: every detail of the original is faithfully reflected, but the whole scene is reversed. If we look, we may find a living psychologist who *is* Titchener's mirror double.

This psychologist espouses a system which, unlike methodological behaviorism, does not rule mental events out of psychology, but like Titchener on attention, writes that "what one feels or introspectively observes are conditions of one's own body," not explanatory cognitive processes. As Titchener optimistically and directly studied the higher mental processes, so today this writer's psychology "does . . . not reject any . . . 'higher mental processes';" but it has taken the lead in investigating their conditions. Like Titchener, he cites Ernst Mach favorably, writing that science is a search for "lawful relations among the events in nature." Like Titchener, he reduces cause to correlation between independent and dependent variables: "The old 'cause-and-effect connection' becomes a 'functional relation'." In short, although this psychologist admits that we can talk about attention, memory, and other mental processes, he considers them myths that explain nothing, and adopts an essentially descriptive stance.

Space limitations preclude further exposition of the similarities between Titchener's system and this new one. Some readers may have guessed Titchener's double, B. F. Skinner, the father of radical behaviorism.[49] I believe that Titchener and Skinner do stand in a true mirror-image relation: both adopt the same descriptive, Machian, philosophy of science and both adopt the same view of conscious phenomena, as sensations which we learn to label in different ways. The emphases in each system, however, are entirely different. Skinner cannot deny the possibility of a mentalistic psychology like Titchener's, but he certainly denies its scientific status, since it cannot predict and control behavior.[50] Titchener did not want psychology to be useful; Skinner does. Nevertheless, each adopts a radically positivist approach to science, as something that has as little to do with theory as possible.[51] On the contrary, both think that psychology should deal in exact objective description. It is an attitude equally applicable to mentalism or behaviorism.

Finally, we may note a personal similarity between the two. In 1914, Titchener, whose system was shortly to be erased by behaviorism, wrote at the end of his reply to Watson: ". . . introspective psychology . . . will go quietly about its task . . . declining, with the mild persistence natural to

matters of fact – either to be eliminated or ignored."[52] In 1963, after hearing the death-knell of behaviorism pronounced by Sigmund Koch,[53] Skinner said that he finds trends in psychology "still running away from me," but that nevertheless his "science of behavior is moving very rapidly and powerfully . . . it justifies itself by its success in dealing with the subject matter."[54] Whether Skinner's dogged optimism will prove any more justified than Titchener's remains to be seen.

Positivism, however, is a philosophy of science that has been tried and found wanting. Mach's radical positivism, which motivated both Titchener's and Skinner's descriptive psychologies, was long ago superseded by logical positivism, which in turn has been rejected by contemporary philosophers of science.[55] Studies by N. R. Hanson and Thomas Kuhn have shown that no scientific system can be theory-free even if the effort is made,[56] and Edwin Burtt has observed that "there is an exceedingly subtle and insidious danger in positivism," for in trying to avoid theoretical "metaphysics," which is impossible, the positivist's "metaphysics will be held uncritically because it is unconscious."[57] Secret theory replaces explicit theory. Titchener and Skinner both accepted positivism and sought theory-free descriptive psychologies. Titchener's failed, and it is now only an historical curiosity. The cognitive revolt against behaviorism may give radical behaviorism the same fate.[58]

Notes

1 Arthur Blumenthal, "A Reappraisal of Wilhelm Wundt," *American Psychologist* 30 (1975): 1081–1088.

2 See the fragment of Wundt's *Völkerpsychologie* translated by Arthur Blumenthal in his *Language and Psychology* (New York: Wiley, 1970), pp. 20–31, and Blumenthal's preceding commentary.

3 Blumenthal, speaking in a discussion session on "European Influence Upon American Psychology," in *The Roots of American Psychology*, ed. R. W. Rieber and K. Salzinger (*Annals of the New York Academy of Sciences* 291 [1977]: 1–394), pp. 66–73. The best English discussion of Wundt's strictures on proper experimental method is Wilhelm Wundt, *Principles of Physiological Psychology* Vol. I, trans. E. B. Titchener (London: Swan Sonnenschein; New York: Macmillan, 1910). pp. 4–6. Wundt's views on method, description, and explanation have been

discussed by Theodore Mischel, "Wundt and the Conceptual Foundations of Psychology," *Philosophy and Phenomenological Research* 31 (1900): 1–26. But Mischel persists in identifying, incorrectly, Wundt's and Titchener's views on introspection (p. 13); for a corrective, see Kurt Danziger, "The Positivist Repudiation of Wundt," *Journal of the History of the Behavioral Sciences* 15 (1979): 205–230.

4 Good English accounts of Wundt's criticisms of Külpe may be found in the first edition of Robert S. Woodworth, *Experimental Psychology* (New York: Holt, 1938), pp. 784–786 and in George Humphrey, *Thinking* (New York: Science Editions, 1963), pp. 106–132.

5 See, for example, George Sperling, "The Information Available in Brief Visual Presentation," *Psychological Monographs* 74, whole number 498 (1960)

which uses one of Wundt's own visual apperception tasks; or E. Colin Cherry, "Some Experiments on the Recognition of Speech, with One and Two Ears," *Journal of the Acoustic Society of America* 26 (1953): 554–559, which asks subjects to attend and describe auditory information.

6 Wilhelm Wundt, *Völkerpsychologie*, 10 vols. (Leipzig: Englemann, 1900–1920).

7 Wundt, *Lectures on Human and Animal Psychology* (London: Swan Sonnenschein; New York: Macmillan, 1894), p. 10.

8 Wundt, *Principles of Physiological Psychology*, p. 4.

9 Wundt, *Outlines of Psychology*, trans. Charles Judd (Leipzig: Englemann; London: Williams and Norgate; New York: Gustav E. Stechert, 1897; repr. St. Clair Shores, Mich.: Scholarly Press), pp. 11–15.

10 Wundt, *Introduction to Psychology*, trans. Rudolph Pintner (London: Allen, 1912; repr. New York: Arno, 1973), pp. 166–167.

11 Sigmund Freud, "The Psychogenesis of a Case of Homosexuality in a Woman," in *Collected Papers* (London: Hogarth Press, 1953), pp. 202–231; see pp. 226–227.

12 Edward Bradford Titchener, "Experimental Psychology: A Retrospect," *American Journal of Psychology* 36 (1925): 313–323, p. 318.

13 Titchener, *Lectures on the Elementary Psychology of the Thought Processes* (New York: Macmillan, 1909; repr. New York: Arno, 1973).

14 Ibid., p. 23.

15 Titchener, *Lectures on the Elementary Psychology of Feeling and Attention* (New York: Macmillan; repr. New York: Arno, 1973), p. 209.

16 Titchener, *Experimental Psychology*, vol. I (New York: Macmillan, 1901), p. 109.

17 Titchener, in Appendix to reprint edition of *Systematic Psychology: Prolegomena* (New York: Macmillan, 1929; repr. Ithaca and London: Cornell University Press, 1972), p. 273. See also Rand B. Evans, "E. B. Titchener and His Lost System," *Journal of the History of the Behavioral Sciences* 11 (1972): 334–341.

18 For the comparison of English and German intellectual environments, see Fritz K. Ringer, *The Decline of the German Mandarins* (Cambridge, Mass.: Harvard University Press, 1969); for the appeal of positivism to Titchener and others, see Danziger, "The Positivist Repudiation of Wundt;" on the Gestalt psychologists, see Michael Wertheimer, "Max Wertheimer: Gestalt Prophet." Presidential address to Division 26, annual meeting of the American Psychological Association, Toronto, Ontario, August 31, 1978.

19 Edward Bradford Titchener, *An Outline of Psychology* (New York: Macmillan, 1897), p. vi.

20 Brian Mackenzie, *Behaviorism and the Limits of Scientific Method* (London: Routledge and Kegan Paul, 1977).

21 John B. Watson, "Psychology as the Behaviorist Views It," *Psychological Review* 20 (1913): 158–176, p. 175.

22 Titchener, *Lectures on Feeling and Attention*, p. 317.

23 Titchener, *Prolegomena*, pp. 65, 56, and 61.

24 Ibid., p. 63

25 Ibid., pp. 57–58.

26 Ibid., p. 63.

27 Wundt, *Outlines*, p. 12.

28 Ibid., p. 320.

29 Ibid., pp. 321–328. A shorter list is given in his *Introduction*, pp. 154–198.

30 Henry B. Veatch, "Science and Humanism" in *Theories in Contemporary Psychology*, 2nd edn., ed. Melvin Marx and Felix Goodson (New York: Macmillan, 1976), pp. 61–66.

31 Ulric Neisser, *Cognition and Reality* (San Francisco: Freeman, 1976).

32 Neisser, *Cognitive Psychology* (New York: Appleton-Century-Crofts, 1967).

33 Elizabeth Spelke, William Hirst, and Neisser, "Skills of Divided Attention," *Cognition* 4 (1976): 215–230.

34 Thomas H. Leahey, "Something Old, Something New: Wundt and Contemporary Theories of Attention," *Journal of the History of the Behavioral Sciences* 15 (1979): 242–252.

35 Neisser, *Cognition and Reality*, pp. 1–3.

36 Ibid., p. 2.

37 Blumenthal, *Language and Psychology*, p. 11.

38 Edwin G. Boring, *History of Experimental Psychology*, 2nd edn. (New York: Appleton-Century-Crofts, 1950).

39 Ibid., p. 410.

40 Duane Schultz, *A History of Modern Psychology*, 2nd edn. (New York: Academic Press, 1975), both quotes p. 83.

41 William Sahakian, *History and Systems of Psychology* (New York: Schenkman, 1975), p. 352.

42 Wilhelm Wundt, *Elements of Folk Psychology* (London: George Allen, 1916).

43 Daniel Robinson, *An Intellectual History of Psychology* (New York: Macmillan, 1976), pp. 329–333.

44 Leahey, "Something Old, Something New."

45 Robert Watson, *The Great Psychologists*, 3rd edn. (New York: Lippincott, 1971). The most recent, fourth, edition (1978) contains an improved presentation of Wundt's psychology, but still calls Titchener "Wundt's most faithful pupil," who "in most respects . . . held to the tradition of Wundt," giving his "master's" ideas "a systematic explictness" (pp. 413–414).

46 Fred S. Keller, *The Definition of Psychology*, 2nd edn. (Englewood Cliffs, N.J.: Prentice-Hall, 1973), p. 19.

47 Joseph R. Royce, "Pebble Picking vs. Boulder Building," *Psychological Reports* 16 (1965): 447–450.

48 Reinforcement history is not the same as history as usually understood. Reinforcement creates a certain present state in the organism that disposes it to respond in a certain way. Ideally, this state could be known without knowing the actual reinforcement history (i.e., through neurophysiological state-description or behavioral testing). In this context, history is not seen as a developmental process but only as a means of changing an organism's (or a society's) momentary state.

49 The first two quotes came from Burrhus F. Skinner, *About Behaviorism* (New York: Knopf, 1974), pp. 216 and 223; the second two came from Skinner, *Science and Human Behavior* (New York: Macmillan, 1953), pp. 13 and 23.

50 Skinner, *About Behaviorism*, p. 165.

51 Compare Skinner's "Are Theories of Learning Necessary?" *Psychological Review* 57 (1950): 193–216, to Titchener's comments on Wundt's "theory ridden terms" quoted above (see note 12).

52 Titchener, "On Psychology as the Behaviorist Views It," *Proceedings of the American Philosophical Society* 53 (1914): 1–17, p. 17.

53 Sigmund Koch, "Psychology and Emerging Conceptions of Knowledge as Unitary," in *Behaviorism and Phenomenology*, ed. T. W. Wann (Chicago: University of Chicago Press, 1964).

54 Skinner, Speaking in the "Discussion of Koch" (note 53), in *Behaviorism and Phenomenology, p. 42*.

55 Frederick Suppe, "The Search for Philosophic Understanding of Scientific Theories," in *The Structure of Scientific Theories*, ed. F. Suppe (Urbana: University of Illinois Press, 1974), pp. 3–254. See also Peter Achinstein, *Concepts of Science* (Baltimore: Johns Hopkins Press, 1968) for a rigorous analysis of positivism.

56 Norwood Russell Hanson, *Patterns of Discovery* (Cambridge: Cambridge University Press, 1958) and *Observation and Explanation* (New York: Harper Torchbooks, 1971). Thomas S. Kuhn, *The Structure of Scientific Revolutions*, enl. edn. (Chicago: University of Chicago Press, 1970).

57 Edwin A. Burtt, *The Metaphysical Foundations of Modern Science*, rev. edn. (1932; repr. Garden City, N.Y.: Doubleday Anchor, 1954), p. 229.

58 An extended analysis of the effects of positivism on psychology will be given in my "The Myth of Operationism," *Journal of Mind and Behavior*, in press. The question of whether cognitive psychology represents a real revolt against behaviorism and positivism is explored at length in my *A History of Psychology* (Englewood Cliffs, N.J.: Prentice Hall, 1980), chap. 13, esp. pp. 371–376 and chap. 15, esp. pp. 392–394.

The Province of Functional Psychology
James Rowland Angell

Functional psychology is at the present moment little more than a point of view, a program, an ambition. It gains its vitality primarily perhaps as a protest against the exclusive excellence of another starting point for the study of the mind, and it enjoys for the time being at least the peculiar vigor which commonly attaches to Protestantism of any sort in its early stages before it has become respectable and orthodox. The time seems ripe to attempt a somewhat more precise characterization of the field of functional psychology than has as yet been offered. What we seek is not the arid and merely verbal definition which to many of us is so justly anathema, but rather an informing appreciation of the motives and ideals which animate the psychologist who pursues this path. His status in the eye of the psychological public is unnecessarily precarious. The conceptions of his purposes prevalent in non-functionalist circles range from positive and dogmatic misapprehension, through frank mystification and suspicion up to moderate comprehension. Nor is this fact an expression of anything peculiarly abstruse and recondite in his intentions. It is due in part to his own ill-defined plans, in part to his failure to explain lucidly exactly what he is about. Moreover, he is fairly numerous and it is not certain that in all important particulars he and his confrères are at one in their beliefs. The considerations which are here-with offered suffer inevitably from this personal limitation. No psychological council of Trent has as yet pronounced upon the true faith. But in spite of probable failure it seems worth while to hazard an attempt at delineating the scope of functionalist principles. I formally renounce any intention to strike out new plans; I am engaged in what is meant as a dispassionate summary of actual conditions.

Whatever else it may be, functional psychology is nothing wholly new. In certain of its phases it is plainly discernible in the psychology of Aristotle and in its more modern garb it has been increasingly in evidence since Spencer wrote his *Psychology* and Darwin his *Origin of Species*. Indeed, as we shall soon see, its crucial problems are inevitably incidental to any serious attempt at understanding mental life. All that is peculiar to its present circumstances is a higher degree of self-consciousness than it possessed before, a more articulate and persistent purpose to organize its vague intentions into tangible methods and principles.

A survey of contemporary psychological writing indicates, as was intimated in the preceding paragraph, that the task of functional psychology is interpreted in several different ways. Moreover, it seems to be possible to advocate one or more of these conceptions while cherishing abhorrence for the others. I distinguish three principal forms of the functional problem with sundry subordinate variants. It will contribute to the clarification of the general situation to dwell upon these for a moment, after which I propose to maintain that they are substantially but modifications of a single problem.

I

There is to be mentioned first the notion which derives most immediately from contrast with the ideals and purposes of structural psychology so-called. This involves the identification of functional psychology with the effort to discern and portray the typical *operations* of consciousness under actual life conditions, as over against the attempt to analyze and describe its elementary

From J. R. Angell (1907). The province of functional psychology. *Psychological Review*, 14, 61–91.

and complex *contents*. The structural psychology of sensation, *e.g.*, undertakes to determine the number and character of the various unanalyzable sensory materials, such as the varieties of color, tone, taste, etc. The functional psychology of sensation would on the other hand find its appropriate sphere of interest in the determination of the character of the various sense activities as differing in their *modus operandi* from one another and from other mental processes such as judging, conceiving, willing and the like.

In this its older and more pervasive form functional psychology has until very recent times had no independent existence. No more has structural psychology for that matter. It is only lately that any motive for the differentiation of the two has existed and structural psychology – granting its claims and pretensions of which more anon – is the first, be it said, to isolate itself. But in so far as functional psychology is synonymous with descriptions and theories of mental action as distinct from the materials of mental constitution, so far it is everywhere conspicuous in psychological literature from the earliest times down.

When the structural psychologists define their field as that of mental *process*, they really preëmpt under a fictitious name the field of function, so that I should be disposed to allege fearlessly and with a clear conscience that a large part of the doctrine of psychologists of nominally structural proclivities is in point of fact precisely what I mean by one essential part of functional psychology, *i.e.*, an account of psychical operations. Certain of the official exponents of structuralism explicitly lay claim to this as their field and do so with a flourish of scientific rectitude. There is therefore after all a small but nutritious core of agreement in the structure-function apple of discord. For this reason, as well as because I consider extremely useful the analysis of mental life into its elementary forms, I regard much of the actual work of my structuralist friends with highest respect and confidence. I feel, however, that when they use the term structural as opposed to the term functional to designate their scientific creed they often come perilously near to using the enemy's colors.

Substantially identical with this first conception of functional psychology, but phrasing itself somewhat differently, is the view which regards the functional problem as concerned with discovering how and why conscious processes are what they are, instead of dwelling as the structuralist is supposed to do upon the problem of determining the irreducible elements of consciousness and their characteristic modes of combination. I have elsewhere defended the view that however it may be in other sciences dealing with life phenomena, in psychology at least the answer to the question "what" implicates the answer to the questions "how" and "why."

Stated briefly the ground on which this position rests is as follows: In so far as you attempt to analyze any particular state of consciousness you find that the mental elements presented to your notice are dependent upon the particular exigencies and conditions which call them forth. Not only does the affective coloring of such a psychical moment depend upon one's temporary condition, mood and aims, but the very sensations themselves are determined in their qualitative texture by the totality of circumstances subjective and objective within which they arise. You cannot get a fixed and definite color sensation for example, without keeping perfectly constant the external and internal conditions in which it appears. The particular sense quality is in short functionally determined by the necessities of the existing situation which it emerges to meet. If you inquire then deeply enough what particular sensation you have in a given case, you always find it necessary to take account of the manner in which, and the reasons why, it was experienced at all. You may of course, if you will, abstract from these considerations, but in so far as you do so, your analysis and description is manifestly partial and incomplete. Moreover, even when you do so abstract and attempt to describe certain isolable sense qualities, your descriptions arc of necessity couched in terms not of the experienced quality itself, but in terms of the conditions which produced it, in terms of some other quality with which it is compared, or in terms of some more overt act to which the sense stimulation led. That is to say, the very description itself is functionalistic and must be so. The truth of this assertion can be illustrated and tested by appeal to any situation in which one is trying to reduce sensory complexes, e.g., colors or sounds, to their rudimentary components.

II

A broader outlook and one more frequently characteristic of contemporary writers meets us in the next conception of the task of functional psychology. This conception is in part a reflex of the prevailing interest in the larger formulae of biology and particularly the evolutionary hypotheses within whose majestic sweep is nowadays included the history of the whole stellar universe; in part it echoes the same philosophical call to new life which has been heard as pragmatism, as humanism, even as functionalism itself. I should not wish to commit either party by asserting that functional psychology and pragmatism are ultimately one. Indeed, as a psychologist I should hesitate to bring down on myself the avalanche of metaphysical invective which has been loosened by pragmatic writers. To be sure pragmatism has slain its thousands, but I should cherish scepticism as to whether functional psychology would the more speedily slay its tens of thousands by announcing an offensive and defensive alliance with pragmatism. In any case I only hold that the two movements spring from similar logical motivation and rely for their vitality and propagation upon forces closely germane to one another.

The functional psychologist then in his modern attire is interested not alone in the operations of mental process considered merely of and by and for itself, but also and more vigorously in mental activity as part of a larger stream of biological forces which are daily and hourly at work before our eyes and which are constitutive of the most important and most absorbing part of our world. The psychologist of this stripe is wont to take his cue from the basal conception of the evolutionary movement, i.e., that for the most part organic structures and functions possess their present characteristics by virtue of the efficiency with which they fit into the extant conditions of life broadly designated the environment. With this conception in mind he proceeds to attempt some understanding of the manner in which the psychical contributes to the furtherance of the sum total of organic activities, not alone the psychical in its entirety, but especially the psychical in its particularities – mind as judging, mind as feeling, etc.

This is the point of view which instantly brings the psychologist cheek by jowl with the general biologist. It is the presupposition of every philosophy save that of outright ontological materialism that mind plays the stellar rôle in all the environmental adaptations of animals which possess it. But this persuasion has generally occupied the position of an innocuous truism or at best a jejune postulate, rather than that of a problem requiring, or permitting, serious scientific treatment. At all events, this was formerly true.

It is not unnatural perhaps that the frequent disposition of the functional psychologist to sigh after the flesh-pots of biology should kindle the fire of those consecrated to the cause of a pure psychology and philosophy freed from the contaminating influence of natural science. As a matter of fact, alarms have been repeatedly sounded and the faithful called to subdue mutiny. But the purpose of the functional psychologist has never been, so far as I am aware, to scuttle the psychological craft for the benefit of biology. Quite the contrary. Psychology is still for a time at least to steer her own untroubled course. She is at most borrowing a well-tested compass which biology is willing to lend and she hopes by its aid to make her ports more speedily and more surely. If in use it prove treacherous and unreliable, it will of course go overboard.

This broad biological ideal of functional psychology of which we have been speaking may be phrased with a slight shift to emphasis by connecting it with the problem of discovering the fundamental utilities of consciousness. If mental process is of real value to its possessor in the life and world which we know, it must perforce be by virtue of something which it does that otherwise is not accomplished. Now life and world are complex and it seems altogether improbable that consciousness should express its utility in one and only one way. As a matter of fact, every surface indication points in the other direction. It may be possible merely as a matter of expression to speak of mind as in general contributing to organic adjustment to environment. But the actual contributions will take place in many ways and by multitudinous varieties of conscious process. The functionalist's problem then is to determine if possible the great types of these processes in so far as the utilities which they present lend themselves to classification.

The search after the various utilitarian aspects of mental process is at once suggestive and disappointing. It is on the one hand illuminating by virtue of the strong relief into which it throws the fundamental resemblances of processes often unduly severed in psychological analysis. Memory and imagination, for example, are often treated in a way designed to emphasize their divergences almost to the exclusion of their functional similarities. They are of course functionally but variants on a single and basal type of control. An austere structuralism in particular is inevitably disposed to magnify differences and in consequence under its hands mental life tends to fall apart; and when put together again it generally seems to have lost something of its verve and vivacity. It appears stiff and rigid and corpse-like. It lacks the vital spark. Functionalism tends just as inevitably to bring mental phenomena together, to show them focalized in actual vital service. The professional psychologist, calloused by long apprenticeship, may not feel this distinction to be scientifically important. But to the young student the functionalistic stress upon community of service is of immense value in clarifying the intricacies of mental organization. On the other hand the search of which we were speaking is disappointing perhaps in the paucity of the basic modes in which these conscious utilities are realized.

III

The third conception which I distinguish is often in practice merged with the second, but it involves stress upon a problem logically prior perhaps to the problem raised there and so warrants separate mention. Functional psychology, it is often alleged, is in reality a form of psychophysics. To be sure, its aims and ideals are not explicitly quantitative in the manner characteristic of that science as commonly understood. But it finds its major interest in determining the relations to one another of the physical and mental portions of the organism.

It is undoubtedly true that many of those who write under functional prepossessions are wont to introduce frequent references to the physiological processes which accompany or condition mental life. Moreover, certain followers of this faith are prone to declare forthwith that psychology is simply a branch of biology and that we are in consequence entitled, if not indeed obliged, to make use where possible of biological materials. But without committing ourselves to so extreme a position as this, a mere glance at one familiar region of psychological procedure will disclose the leanings of psychology in this direction.

The psychology of volition affords an excellent illustration of the necessity with which descriptions of mental process eventuate in physiological or biological considerations. If one take the conventional analysis of a voluntary act drawn from some one or other of the experiences of adult life, the descriptions offered generally portray ideational activities of an anticipatory and deliberative character which serve to initiate immediately or remotely certain relevant expressive movements. Without the execution of the movements the ideational performances would be as futile as the tinkling cymbals of Scripture. To be sure, many of our psychologists protest themselves wholly unable to suggest why or how such muscular movements are brought to pass. But the fact of their occurrence or of their fundamental import for any theory of mental life in which consciousness is other than an epiphenomenon, is not questioned.

Moreover, if one considers the usual accounts of the ontogenesis of human volitional acts one is again confronted with intrinsically physiological data in which reflexes, automatic and instinctive acts, are much in evidence. Whatever the possibilities, then, of an expurgated edition of the psychology of volition from which should be blotted out all reference to contaminating physiological factors, the actual practice of our representative psychologists is quite otherwise, and upon their showing volition cannot be understood either as regards its origin or its outcome without constant and overt reference to these factors. It would be a labor of supererogation to go on and make clear the same doctrine as it applies to the psychology of the more recondite of the cognitive processes; so intimate is the relation between cognition and volition in modern psychological theory that we may well stand excused from carrying out in detail the obvious inferences from the situation we have just described.

Now if someone could but devise a method for handling the mind-body relationships which would not when published immediately create cyclonic disturbances in the philosophical atmosphere, it seems improbable that this disposition of the functional psychologist to inject physiology into his cosmos would cause comment and much less criticism. But even parallelism, that most insipid, pale and passionless of all the inventions begotten by the mind of man to accomplish this end, has largely failed of its pacific purpose. It is no wonder, therefore, that the more rugged creeds with positive programs to offer and a stock of red corpuscles to invest in their propagation should also have failed of universal favor.

This disposition to go over into the physiological for certain portions of psychological doctrine is represented in an interesting way by the frequent tendency of structural psychologists to find explanation in psychology substantially equivalent to physiological explanation. Professor Titchener's recent work on *Quantitative Psychology* represents this position very frankly. It is cited here with no intent to comment disparagingly upon the consistency of the structuralist position, but simply to indicate the wide-spread feeling of necessity at certain stages of psychological development for resort to physiological considerations.

Such a functional psychology as I have been presenting would be entirely reconcilable with Miss Calkins' "Psychology of selves" (so ably set forth by her in her presidential address last year) were it not for her extreme scientific conservatism in refusing to allow the self to have a body, save as a kind of conventional biological ornament. The real psychological self, as I understand her, is pure disembodied spirit – an admirable thing of good religious and philosophic ancestry, but surely not the thing with which we actually get through this vale of tears and not a thing, before which psychology is under any obligation to kowtow.

It is not clear that the functional psychologist because of his disposition to magnify the significance in practice of the mind-body relationships is thereby committed to any special theory of the character of these relationships, save as was said

a moment since, that negatively he must seemingly of necessity set his face against any epiphenomenalist view. He might conceivably be an interactionist, or a parallelist or even an advocate of some wholly outworn creed. As a matter of fact certain of our most ardent functionalists not only cherish highly definite articles of faith as regards this issue, they would even go so far as to test functional orthodoxy by the acceptance of these tenets. This is to them the most momentous part of their functionalism, their holy of holies. It would display needless temerity to attempt within the limitations of this occasion a formulation of doctrine wholly acceptable to all concerned. But I shall venture a brief reference to such doctrine in the effort to bring out certain of its essentials.

The position to which I refer regards the mind-body relation as capable of treatment in psychology as a methodological distinction rather than a metaphysically existential one. Certain of its expounders arrive at their view by means of an analysis of the genetic conditions under which the mind-body differentiation first makes itself felt in the experience of the individual. This procedure clearly involves a direct frontal attack on the problem.

Others attain the position by flank movement, emphasizing to begin with the insoluble contradictions with which one is met when the distinction is treated as resting on existential differences in the primordial elements of the cosmos. Both methods of approach lead to the same goal, however, i.e., the conviction that the distinction has no existence on the genetically lower and more naif stages of experience. It only comes to light on a relatively reflective level and it must then be treated as instrumental if one would avoid paralogisms, antinomies and a host of other metaphysical nightmares. Moreover, in dealing with psychological problems this view entitles one to reject as at least temporarily irrelevant the question whether mind *causes* changes in neural action and conversely. The previous question is raised by defenders of this type of doctrine if one insists on having such a query answered. They invite you to trace the lineage of your idea of causality, insisting that such a searching of one's intellectual reins will always disclose the inappropriateness of the inquiry as formulated above. They urge further that the profitable and significant thing is to seek for a more exact appreciation of the precise conditions under which consciousness is in evidence and the conditions under which it retires in favor of the more exclusively physiological. Such knowledge so far as it can be obtained is on a level with all scientific and practical information. It states the circumstances under which certain sorts of results will appear.

One's view of this functionalistic metaphysics is almost inevitably colored by current philosophical discussion as to the essential nature of consciousness. David Hume has been accused of destroying the reality of mind chiefly because he exorcised from it relationships of various kinds. If it be urged, as has so often been done, that Hume was guilty of pouring out the baby with the bath, the modern philosopher makes good the disaster not only by pouring in again both baby and bath, but by maintaining that baby and bath, mind and relations, are substantially one. Nor is this unity secured after the manner prescribed by the good Bishop Berkeley. At all events the metaphysicians to whom I refer are not fond of being called idealists. But the psychological functionalist who emphasizes the instrumental nature of the mind-body distinction and the metaphysician who regards mind as a relation are following roads which are at least parallel to one another if not actually convergent.

Whether or not one sympathizes with the views of that wing of the functionalist party to which our attention has just been directed it certainly seems a trifle unfair to cast up the mind-body difficulty in the teeth of the functionalist as such when on logical grounds he is no more guilty than any of his psychological neighbors. No courageous psychology of volition is possible which does not squarely face the mind-body problem, and in point of fact every important description of mental life contains doctrine of one kind or another upon this matter. A literally pure psychology of volition would be a sort of hanging-garden of Babylon, marvelous but inaccessible to psychologists of terrestrial habit. The functionalist is a greater sinner than others only in so far as he finds necessary and profitable a more constant insistence upon the translation of mental process into physiological process and conversely.

IV

If we now bring together the several conceptions of which mention has been made it will be easy to show them converging upon a common point. We have to consider (1) functionalism conceived as the psychology of mental operations in contrast to the psychology of mental elements; or, expressed otherwise, the psychology of the how and why of consciousness as distinguished from the psychology of the what of consciousness. We have (2) the functionalism which deals with the problem of mind conceived as primarily engaged in mediating between the environment and the needs of the organism. This is the psychology of the fundamental utilities of consciousness; (3) and lastly we have functionalism described as psychophysical psychology, that is the psychology which constantly recognizes and insists upon the essential significance of the mind-body relationship for any just and comprehensive appreciation of mental life itself.

The second and third delineations of functional psychology are rather obviously correlated with each other. No description of the actual circumstances attending the participation of mind in the accommodatory activities of the organism could be other than a mere empty schematism without making reference to the manner in which mental processes eventuate in motor phenomena of the physiological organism. The overt accommodatory act is, I take it, always sooner or later a muscular movement. But this fact being admitted, there is nothing for it, if one will describe accommodatory processes, but to recognize the mind-body relations and in some way give expression to their practical significance. It is only in this regard, as was indicated a few lines above, that the functionalist departs a trifle in his practice and a trifle more in his theory from the rank and file of his colleagues.

The effort to follow the lead of the natural sciences and delimit somewhat rigorously – albeit artificially – a field of inquiry, in this case consciousness conceived as an independent realm, has led in psychology to a deal of excellent work and to the uncovering of much hidden truth. So far as this procedure has resulted in a focusing of scientific attention and endeavor on a relatively narrow range of problems the result has more than justified the means. And the functionalist by no means holds that the limit of profitable research has been reached along these lines. But he is disposed to urge in season and out that we must not forget the arbitrary and self-imposed nature of the boundaries within which we toil when we try to eschew all explicit reference to the physical and physiological. To overlook this fact is to substitute a psychology under injunction for a psychology under free jurisdiction. He also urges with vigor and enthusiasm that a new illumination of this preëmpted field can be gained by envisaging it more broadly, looking at it as it appears when taken in perspective with its neighboring territory. And if it be objected that such an inquiry however interesting and advantageous is at least not psychology, he can only reply; psychology is what we make it, and if the correct understanding of mental phenomena involves our delving in regions which are not at first glance properly mental, what recks it, provided only that we are nowhere guilty of untrustworthy and unverifiable procedure, and that we return loaded with the booty for which we set out, and by means of which we can the better solve our problem?

In its more basal philosophy this last conception is of course intimately allied to those appraisals of mind which emphasize its dominantly social characteristics, its rise out of social circumstances and the pervasively social nature of its constitutive principles. In our previous intimations of this standpoint we have not distinguished sharply between the physical and the social aspect of environment. The adaptive activities of mind are very largely of the distinctly social type. But this does not in any way jeopardize the genuineness of the connection upon which we have been insisting between the psychophysical aspects of a functional psychology and its environmental adaptive aspects.

It remains then to point out in what manner the conception of functionalism as concerned with the basal operations of mind is to be correlated with the other two conceptions just under discussion. The simplest view to take of the relations involved would apparently be such as would regard the first as an essential propaedeutic to the other two. Certainly if we are intent upon discerning the exact manner in which mental process contributes to accommodatory efficiency, it is natural to begin our undertaking by determining

what are the primordial forms of expression peculiar to mind. However plausible in theory this conception of the intrinsic logical relations of these several forms of functional psychology, in practice it is extremely difficult wholly to sever them from one another.

Again like the biological accommodatory view the psychophysical view of functional psychology involves as a rational presupposition some acquaintance with mental processes as these appear to reflective consciousness. The intelligent correlation in a practical way of physiological and mental operations evidently involves a preliminary knowledge of the conspicuous differentiations both on the side of conscious function and on the side of physiological function.

In view of the considerations of the last few paragraphs it does not seem fanciful nor forced to urge that these various theories of the problem of functional psychology really converge upon one another, however divergent may be the introductory investigations peculiar to each of the several ideals. Possibly the conception that the fundamental problem of the functionalist is one of determining just how mind participates in accommodatory reactions, is more nearly inclusive than either of the others, and so may be chosen to stand for the group. But if this vicarious duty is assigned to it, it must be on clear terms of remembrance that the other phases of the problem are equally real and equally necessary. Indeed the three things hang together as integral parts of a common program.

The functionalist's most intimate persuasion leads him to regard consciousness as primarily and intrinsically a control phenomenon. Just as behavior may be regarded as the most distinctly basic category of general biology in its functional phase so control would perhaps serve as the most fundamental category in functional psychology, the special forms and differentiations of consciousness simply constituting particular phases of the general process of control. At this point the omnipresent captious critic will perhaps arise to urge that the knowledge process is no more truly to be explained in terms of control than is control to be explained in terms of knowledge. Unquestionably there is from the point of view of the critic a measure of truth in this contention. The mechanism of control undoubtedly depends on the cognitive processes, to say nothing of other factors. But if one assumes the vitalistic point of view for one's more final interpretations, if one regards the furtherance of life in breadth and depth and permanence as an end in itself, and if one derives his scale of values from a contemplation of the several contributions toward this end represented by the great types of vital phenomena, with their apex in the moral, scientific and aesthetic realms, one must certainly find control a category more fundamental than the others offered by psychology. Moreover, it may be urged against the critic's attitude that even knowledge itself is built up under the control mechanism represented by selective attention and apperception. The basic character of control seems therefore hardly open to challenge.

One incidental merit of the functionalist program deserves a passing mention. This is the one method of approach to the problem with which I am acquainted that offers a reasonable and cogent account of the rise of reflective consciousness and its significance as manifested in the various philosophical disciplines. From the vantage point of the functionalist position logic and ethics, for instance, are no longer mere disconnected items in the world of mind. They take their place with all the inevitableness of organic organization in the general system of control, which requires for the expression of its immanent meaning *as psychic* a theoretical vindication of its own inner principles, its modes of procedure and their results. From any other point of view, so far as I am aware, the several divisions of philosophical inquiry sustain to one another relations which are almost purely external and accidental. To the functionalist on the other hand they are and must be in the nature of the case consanguineous and vitally connected. It is at the point, for example, where the good, the beautiful and the true have bearing on the efficacy of accommodatory activity that the issues of the normative philosophical sciences become relevant. If good action has no significance for the enriching and enlarging of life, the contention I urge is futile, and similarly as regards beauty and truth. But it is not at present usually maintained that such is the fact.

These and other similar tendencies of functionalism may serve to reassure those who fear that in lending itself to biological influences psychology may lose contact with philosophy and so sacrifice the poise and balance and sanity of outlook which philosophy undertakes to furnish. The particular brand of philosophy which is predestined to functionalist favor cannot of course be confidently predicted in advance. But anything approaching a complete and permanent divorce of psychology from philosophy is surely improbable so long as one cultivates the functionalist faith. Philosophy cannot dictate scientific method here any more than elsewhere, nor foreordain the special facts to be discovered. But as an interpreter of the psychologist's achievements she will always stand higher in the functionalist's favor than in that of his colleagues of other persuasions, for she is a more integral and significant part of his scheme of the cosmos. She may even outgrow under his tutelage that "valiant inconclusiveness" of which the last of her long line of lay critics has just accused her.

A sketch of the kind we have offered is unhappily likely to leave on the mind an impression of functional psychology as a name for a group of genial but vaguer ambitions and good intentions. This, however, is a fault which must be charged to the artist and to the limitations of time and space under which he is here working. There is nothing vaguer in the program of the functionalist when he goes to his work than there is in the purposes of the psychologist wearing any other livery. He goes to his laboratory, for example, with just the same resolute interest to discover new facts and new relationships, with just the same determination to verify and confirm his previous observations, as does his colleague who calls himself perhaps a structuralist. But he looks out upon the surroundings of his science with a possibly greater sensitiveness to its continuity with other ranges of human interest and with certainly a more articulate purpose to see the mind which he analyzes as it actually is when engaged in the discharge of its vital functions. If his method tempts him now and then to sacrifice something of petty exactitude, he is under no obligation to yield, and in any case he has for his compensation the power which comes from breadth and sweep of outlook.

So far as he may be expected to develop methods peculiar to himself – so far, indeed, as in genetic and comparative psychology, for example, he has already developed such – they will not necessarily be iconoclastic and revolutionary, nor such as flout the methods already devised and established on a slightly different foundation. They will be distinctly complementary to all that is solid in these. Nor is it in any way essential that the term functionalism should cling to this new-old movement. It seems at present a convenient term, but there is nothing sacrosanct about it, and the moment it takes unto itself the pretense of scientific finality its doom will be sealed. It means to-day a broad and flexible and organic point of view in psychology. The moment it becomes dogmatic and narrow its spirit will have passed and undoubtedly some worthier successor will fill its place.

Functionalism, Darwinism, and the Psychology of Women:
A Study in Social Myth
Stephanie A. Shields

The psychology of women is acquiring the character of an academic entity as witnessed by the proliferation of research on sex differences, the appearance of textbooks devoted to the psychology of women, and the formation of a separate APA division, Psychology of Women. Nevertheless, there is almost universal ignorance of the psychology of women as it existed prior to its incorporation into psychoanalytic theory. If the maxim "A nation without a history is like a man without a memory" can be applied, then it would behoove the amnesiacs interested in female psychology to investigate its pre-Freudian past.

This article focuses on one period of that past (from the latter half of the 19th century to the first third of the 20th) in order to clarify the important issues of the time and trace their development to the position they occupy in current psychological theory. Even a limited overview leads the reader to appreciate Helen Thompson Woolley's (1910) early appraisal of the quality of the research on sex differences:

> There is perhaps no field aspiring to be scientific where flagrant personal bias, logic martyred in the cause of supporting a prejudice, unfounded assertions, and even sentimental rot and drivel, have run riot to such an extent as here. (p. 340).

Adapted from S. A. Shields (1975). Functionalism, Darwinism, and the psychology of women: A study in social myth. *American Psychologist, 30,* 739–754. Copyright © 1975 by the American Psychological Association. Adapted and reprinted by permission of the publisher and the author.

The Functionalist Milieu

Although the nature of woman had been an academic and social concern of philosopher psychologists throughout the ages, formal psychology (its inception usually dated 1879) was relatively slow to take up the topic of female psychology. The "woman question" was a social one, and social problems did not fall within the sharply defined limits of Wundt's "new" psychology. The business of psychology was the description of the "generalized adult mind," and it is not at all clear whether "adult" was meant to include both sexes. When the students of German psychology did venture outside of the laboratory, however, there is no evidence that they were sympathetic to those defending the equality of male and female ability (cf. Wundt, 1901).

It was the functionalist movement in the United States that fostered academic psychology's study of sex differences and, by extension, a prototypic psychology of women. The incorporation of evolutionary theory into the practice of psychology made the study of the female legitimate, if not imperative. It would be incorrect to assume that the psychology of women existed as a separate specialty within the discipline. The female was discussed only in relation to the male, and the function of the female was thought to be distinctly different from and complementary to the function of the male. The leitmotiv of evolutionary theory as it came to be applied to the social sciences was the evolutionary supremacy of the Caucasian male. The notion of the supplementary, subordinate role of the female was ancillary to the development of that theme.

The influence of evolutionary theory on the psychology of women can be traced along two major conceptual lines: (a) by emphasizing the biological foundations of temperament, evolutionary theory led to serious academic discussion of maternal instinct (as one facet of the general topic of instinct); and (b) by providing a theoretical justification of the study of individual differences, evolutionary theory opened the door to the study of sex differences in sensory, motor, and intellectual abilities. As a whole, the concept of evolution with its concomitant emphasis on biological determinism provided ample "scientific" reason for cataloging the "innate" differences in male and female nature.

This article examines three topics that were of special significance to the psychology of women during the functionalist era: (a) structural differences in the brains of males and females and the implications of these differences for intelligence and temperament, (b) the hypothesis of greater male variability and its relation to social and educational issues, and (c) maternal instinct and its meaning for a psychology of female "nature." As the functionalist paradigm gave way to behaviorism and psychoanalytic theory, the definition and "meaning" of each of these issues changed to fit the times. When issues faded in importance, it was not because they were resolved but because they ceased to serve as viable scientific "myths" in the changing social and scientific milieu. As the times change, so must the myths change.

The Female Brain

The topic of female intelligence came to 19th-century psychology via phrenology and the neuroanatomists. Philosophers of the time (e.g., Hegel, Kant, Schopenhauer) had demonstrated, to their satisfaction, the justice of woman's subordinate social position, and it was left to the men of science to discover the particular physiological determinants of female inadequacy. In earlier periods, woman's inferiority had been defined as a general "state" intimately related to the absence of qualities that would have rendered her a male and to the presence of reproductive equipment that destined her to be female. For centuries the mode of Eve's creation and her greater guilt for the fall from grace had been credited as the cause of woman's imperfect nature, but this was not an

adequate explanation in a scientific age. Thus, science sought explanations for female inferiority that were more in keeping with contemporary scientific philosophy.

Although it had long been believed that the brain was the chief organ of the mind, the comparison of male and female mental powers traditionally included only allusions to vague "imperfections" of the female brain. More precise definition of the sites of these imperfections awaited the advancement of the concept of cortical localization of function. Then, as finer distinctions of functional areas were noted, there was a parallel recognition of the differences between those sites as they appeared in each sex.

At the beginning of the 19th century, the slowly increasing interest in the cerebral gyri rapidly gathered momentum with the popularization of phrenology. Introduced by Franz Joseph Gall, "cranioscopy," as he preferred to call it, postulated that the seat of various mental and moral faculties was located in specific areas of the brain's surface such that a surfeit or deficiency could be detected by an external examination of the cranium. Phrenology provided the first objective method for determining the neurological foundation of sex differences in intelligence and temperament that had long been promulgated. Once investigation of brain structure had begun, it was fully anticipated that visible sex differences would be found: Did not the difference between the sexes pervade every other aspect of physique and physiological function? Because physical differences were so obvious in every other organ of the body, it was unthinkable that the brain could have escaped the stamp of sex.

Gall was convinced that he could, from gross anatomical observation, discriminate between male and female brains, claiming that "if there had been presented to him in water, the fresh brains of two adult animals of any species, one male and the other female, he could have distinguished the two sexes" (Walker, 1850, p. 317). Gall's student and colleague, Johann Spurzheim, elaborated on this basic distinction by noting that the frontal lobes were less developed in females, "the organs of the perceptive faculties being commonly larger than those of the reflective powers." Gall also observed sex differences in the nervous tissue itself, "confirming" Malebranche's belief that the female "cerebral fibre" is softer than that of the male, and that it is also "slender and long rather than thick" (Walker, 1850, p. 318). Spurzheim also listed the cerebral "organs" whose appearance differed commonly in males and females: females tended to have the areas devoted to philoprogenetiveness and other "tender" traits most prominent, while in males, areas of aggressiveness and constructiveness dominated. Even though cranioscopy did not survive as a valid system of describing cortical function, the practice of comparing the appearance of all or part of the brain for anatomical evidence of quality of function remained one of the most popular means of providing proof of female mental inferiority. Most comparisons used adult human brains, but with the rise of evolutionary theory, increasing emphasis was placed on the value of developmental and cross-species comparisons. The argument for female mental inferiority took two forms: some argued that quality of intellect was proportional to absolute or relative brain size; others, more in the tradition of cortical localization, contended that the presence of certain mental qualities was dependent upon the development of corresponding brain centers.

The measurement of cranial capacity had long been in vogue as one method of determining intellectual ability. That women had smaller heads than men was taken by some as clear proof of a real disparity between male and female intelligence. The consistently smaller brain size of the female was cited as another anatomical indicator of its functional inferiority. More brain necessarily meant better brain; the exception only proved this rule. Alexander Bain (1875) was among those who believed that the smaller absolute brain size of females accounted for a lesser mental ability. George Romanes (1887) enumerated the "secondary sex characteristics" of mental abilities attributable to brain size. The smaller brain of women was directly responsible for their mental inferiority, which "displays itself most conspicuously in a comparative absence of originality, and this more especially in the higher levels of intellectual work" (p. 655). He, like many, allowed that women were to some degree compensated for intellectual inferiority by a superiority of instinct and perceptual ability. These advantages carried with them the germ of female failure, however, by making women more subject to emotionality.

Proof of the male's absolute brain-size superiority was not enough to secure his position of intellectual superiority, since greater height and weight tended to offset the brain-size advantage. Reams of paper were, therefore, dedicated to the search for the most "appropriate" relative measures, but results were equivocal: if the ratio of brain weight to body weight is considered, it is found that women possess a proportionately larger brain than men; if the ratio of brain surface to body surface is computed, it is found to favor men. That some of the ratios "favored" males while others "favored" females led some canny souls to conclude that there was no legitimate solution to the problem. That they had ever hoped for a solution seems remarkable; estimates of brain size from cranial capacity involve a large margin of error because brains differing as much as 15 percent have been found in heads of the same size (Elliott, 1969, p. 316).

Hughlings Jackson has been credited as the first to regard the frontal cortex a the repository of the highest mental capacities, but the notion must have held popular credence as early as the 1850s because that period saw sporadic references to the comparative development of the frontal lobes in men and women. Once the function of the frontal lobes had been established, many researchers reported finding that the male possessed noticeably larger and more well-developed frontal lobes than females. The neuroanatomist Hischke came to the conclusion in 1854 that woman is *homo parietalis* while man is *homo frontalis* (Ellis, 1934). Likewise, Rudinger in 1877 found the frontal lobes of man in every way more extensive than those of women, and reported that these sex differences were evident even in the unborn fetus (Mobius, 1901).

At the turn of the century, the parietal lobes (rather than the frontal lobes) came to be regarded by some as the seat of intellect, and the necessary sex difference in parietal development was duly corroborated by the neuroanatomists. The change in cerebral hierarchy involved a bit of revisionism:

the frontal region is not, as has been supposed smaller in woman, but rather larger relatively. . . . But the parietal lobe is somewhat smaller, [furthermore,] a preponderance of the frontal region does not imply intellectual superiority . . . the parietal region is really the more important. (Patrick, 1895, p. 212)

Once beliefs regarding the relative importance of the frontal and parietal lobes had shifted, it became critical to reestablish congruence between neuroanatomical findings and accepted sex differences. Among those finding parietal predominance in men were Paul Broca, Theodore Meynert, and the German Rudinger (see Ellis, 1934, p. 217).

Other neuroanatomical "deficiencies" of the female were found in (a) the area of the corpus callosum, (b) the complexity of the gyri and sulci, (c) the conformation of gyri and sulci, and (d) the rate of development of the cortex of the fetus (Woolley, 1910, p. 335). Franklin Mall (1909) objected to the use of faulty research methods that gave spurious differences the appearance of being real. Among the most serious errors he noted was the practice of making observations with a knowledge of the sex of the brain under consideration.

The debate concerning the importance of brain size and anatomy as indicators of intelligence diminished somewhat with the development of mental tests; nevertheless, the brain-size difference was a phenomenon that many felt obligated to interpret. Max Meyer (1921) attempted to settle the matter by examining the various measures of relative difference that had been employed. After finding these methods far too equivocal, he concluded, in the best behavioristic terms, that sex differences in intelligence were simply "accidents of habits acquired."

Characteristics of the female brain were thought not simply to render women less intelligent but also to allow more "primitive" parts of human nature to be expressed in her personality. Instinct was thought to dominate woman, as did her emotions, and the resulting "affectability" was considered woman's greatest weakness, the reason for her inevitable failure. Affectability was typically defined as a general state, the manifestation of instinctive and emotional predispositions that in men were kept in cheek by a superior intellect.

One of the most virulent critics of woman was the German physiologist Paul Mobius (1901), who argued that her mental incapacity

was a necessary condition for the survival of the race. Instinct rendered her easily led and easily pleased, so much the better for her to give her all to bearing and rearing children. The dependence of woman also extracted a high price from man:

> All progress is due to man. Therefore the woman is like a dead weight on him, she prevents much restlessness and meddlesome inquisitiveness, but she also restrains him from noble actions, for she is unable to distinguish good from evil. (p. 629)

Mobius observed that woman was essentially unable to think independently, had strong inclinations to be mean and untrustworthy, and spent a good deal of her time in an emotionally unbalanced state. From this he was forced to conclude that: "If woman was not physically and mentally weak, if she was not as a rule rendered harmless by circumstances, she would be extremely dangerous" (Mobius, 1901, p. 630). Diatribes of this nature were relatively common German importations; woman's severest critics in this country seldom achieved a similar level of acerbity. Mobius and his ilk (e.g., Weininger, 1906) were highly publicized and widely read in the United States, and not a little of their vituperation crept into serious scientific discussions of woman's nature. For example, Porteus and Babcock (1926) resurrected the brain-size issue, discounting the importance of size to intelligence and instead associating it with the "maturing of other powers." Males, because of their larger brains, would be more highly endowed with these "other powers," and so more competent and achieving. Proposals such as these, which were less obviously biased than those of Mobius, Weininger, and others, fit more easily into the current social value system and so were more easily assimilated as "good science" (cf. Allen, 1927, p. 294).

The Variability Hypothesis

The first systematic treatment of individual differences in intelligence appeared in 1575. Juan Huarte attributed sex differences in intelligence to the different humoral qualities that characterized each sex, a notion that had been popular in Western thought since ancient Greece. Heat and dryness were characteristic of the male principle, while moisture and coolness were female attributes. Because dryness of spirit was necessary for intelligence, males naturally possessed greater "wit." The maintenance of dryness and heat was the function of the testicles, and Huarte (1959) noted that if a man were castrated the effects were the same "as if he had received some notable dammage in his very braine" (p. 279). Because the principles necessary for cleverness were only possessed by males, it behooved parents to conduct their life-style, diet, and sexual intercourse in such a manner as to insure the conception of a male. The humoral theory of sex differences was widely accepted through the 17th century, but with the advent of more sophisticated notions of anatomy and physiology, it was replaced by other, more specific, theories of female mental defect: the lesser size and hypothesized simpleness of the female brain, affectability as the source of inferiority, and complementarity of abilities in male and female. It was the developing evolutionary theory that provided an overall explanation for why these sex differences existed and why they were necessary for the survival of the race.

The theory of evolution as proposed by Darwin had little to say regarding the intellectual capacity of either sex. It was in Francis Galton's (Charles Darwin's cousin) anthropometric laboratory that the investigation of intellectual differences took an empirical form (Galton, 1907). The major conclusion to come from Galton's research was that women tend in all their capacities to be inferior to men. He looked to common experience for confirmation, reasoning that:

If the sensitivity of women were superior to that of men, the self interest of merchants would lead to their being always employed; but as the reverse is the case, the opposite supposition is likely to be the true one. (pp. 20–21)

This form of logic – women have not excelled, therefore they cannot excel – was often used to support arguments denigrating female intellectual ability. The fact of the comparative rarity of female social achievement was also used as "evidence" in what was later to become a widely debated issue concerning the range of female ability.

Prior to the formulation of evolutionary theory, there had been little concern with whether deviation from the average or "normal" occurred more frequently in either sex. One of the first serious discussions of the topic appeared in the early 19th century when the anatomist Meckel concluded on pathological grounds that the human female showed greater variability than the human male. He reasoned that because man is the superior animal and variability a sign of inferiority, this conclusion was justified (in Ellis, 1903, p. 237). The matter was left at that until 1871. At that time Darwin took up the question of variability in *The Descent of Man* while attempting to explain how it could be that in many species males had developed greatly modified secondary sexual characteristics while females of the same species had not. He determined that this was originally caused by the males' greater activity and "stronger passions" that were in turn more likely (he believed) to be transmitted to male offspring. Because the females would prefer to mate with the strong and passionate, sexual selection would insure the survival of those traits. A tendency toward greater variation per se was not thought to be responsible for the appearance of unusual characteristics, but "development of such characters would be much aided, if the males were more liable to vary than the females" (Darwin, 1922, p. 344). To support this hypothesis of greater male variability, he cited recent data obtained by anatomists and biologists that seemed to confirm the relatively more frequent occurrence of physical anomaly among males.

Because variation from the norm was already accepted as the mechanism of evolutionary progress (survival and transmission of adaptive variations) and because it seemed that the male was the more variable sex, it soon was universally concluded that the male is the progressive element in the species. Variation for its own sake took on a positive value because greatness, whether of an individual or a society, could not be achieved without variation. Once deviation from the norm became legitimized by evolutionary theory, the hypothesis of greater male variability became a convenient explanation for a number of observed sex differences, among them the greater frequency with which men achieved "eminence." By the 1890s it was popularly believed that greater male variability was a principle that held true, not only for physical traits but for mental abilities as well:

> That men should have greater cerebral variability and therefore more originality, while women have greater stability and therefore more "common sense," are facts both consistent with the general theory of sex and verifiable in common experience. (Geddes & Thomson, 1890, p. 271)

Havelock Ellis (1894), an influential sexologist and social philosopher, brought the variability hypothesis to the attention of psychologists in the first edition of *Man and Woman*. After examining anatomical and pathological data that indicated a greater male *variational tendency* (Ellis felt this term was less ambiguous than *variability*), he examined the evidence germane to a discussion of range of intellectual ability. After noting that there were more men than women in homes for the mentally deficient, which indicated a higher incidence of retardation among males, and that there were more men than women on the roles of the eminent, which indicated a higher incidence of genius among males, he concluded that greater male variability probably held for all qualities of character and ability. Ellis (1903) particularly emphasized the wide social and educational significance of the phenomenon, claiming that greater male variability was "a fact which has affected the whole of our human civilization" (p. 238), particularly through the production of men of genius. Ellis (1934) was also adamant that the female's tendency toward the average did not necessarily imply inferiority of talent; rather, it simply limited her expertise to "the sphere of concrete practical life" (p. 436).

The variability hypothesis was almost immediately challenged as a "pseudo-scientific superstition" by the statistician Karl Pearson (1897). Though not a feminist, Pearson firmly believed that the "woman question" deserved impartial, scientific study. He challenged the idea of greater male variability primarily because he thought it contrary to the fact and theory of evolution and natural selection. According to evolutionary theory (Pearson, 1897), "the more intense the struggle the less is the variability, the more nearly are individuals forced to approach the type fittest

to their surroundings, if they are to survive" (p. 258). In a "civilized" community one would expect that because men have a "harder battle for life," any difference in variation should favor women. He took Ellis to task by arguing it was (a) meaningless to consider secondary sex characteristics (as Ellis had done) and, likewise, (b) foolish to contrast the sexes on the basis of abnormalities (as Ellis had done). By redefining the problem and the means for its solution, he was able to dismiss the entire corpus of data that had been amassed: "the whole trend of investigations concerning the relative variability of men and women up to the present seems to be erroneous" (Pearson, 1897, p. 261). Confining his measurements to "normal variations in organs or characteristics not of a secondary sexual character," he assembled anthropometric data on various races, from Neolithic skeletons to modern French peasants. He also challenged the adequacy of statistical comparison of only the extremes of the distribution, preferring to base his contrasts on the dispersion of measures around the mean. Finding a slight tendency toward greater female variability, he concluded that the variability hypothesis as stated remained a "quite unproven principle."

Ellis countered Pearson in a lengthy article, one more vicious than that ordinarily due an intellectual affront. Pearson's greatest sins (according to Ellis) were his failure to define "variability" and his measurement of characteristics that were highly subject to environmental influence. Ellis, of course, overlooked his own failure to define variability and his inclusion of environmentally altered evidence.

In the United States the variability hypothesis naturally found expression in the new testing movement, its proponents borrowing liberally from the theory of Ellis and the statistical technique of Pearson. The favor that was typically afforded the hypothesis did not stem from intellectual commitment to the scientific validity of the proposal as much as it did from personal commitment to the social desirability of its acceptance. The variability hypothesis was most often thought of in terms of its several corollaries: (a) genius (seldom, and then poorly, defined) is a peculiarly male trait; (b) men of genius naturally gravitate to positions of power and prestige (i.e., achieve eminence) by virtue of their talent; (c) an equally high ability level should not be expected of females; and (d) the education of women should, therefore, be consonant with their special talents and special place in society as wives and mothers.

Woman's education

The "appropriate" education for women had been at issue since the Renaissance, and the implications of the variability hypothesis favored those who had been arguing for a separate female education. Late in the 18th century, Mary Wollstonecraft Godwin (1759–1797) questioned the "natural" roles of each sex, contending that for both the ultimate goal was the same: "the first object of laudable ambition is to obtain a character as a human being, regardless of the distinction of sex" (Wollstonecraft, 1955, p. 5). Without education, she felt, women could not contribute to social progress as mature individuals, and this would be a tragic loss to the community. Though not the first to recognize the social restrictions arbitrarily placed on women, she was the first to hold those restrictions as directly responsible for the purported "defective nature" of women. She emphasized that women had never truly been given an equal chance to prove or disprove their merits. Seventy years later, John Stuart Mill (1955) also took up the cause of women's education, seeing it as one positive action to be taken in the direction of correcting the unjust social subordination of women. He felt that what appeared as woman's intellectual inferiority was actually no more than the effort to maintain the passive-dependent role relationship with man, her means of support:

> When we put together three things – first, the natural attraction between the sexes; secondly, the wife's entire dependence on the husband . . . and lastly, that the principal object of human pursuit, consideration, and all objects of social ambition, can in general be sought or obtained by her only through him, it would be a miracle if the object of being attractive to men had not become the polar star of feminine education and formation of character. (pp. 232–233)

Although Mill objected to fostering passivity and dependency in girls, other educators felt that this was precisely their duty. One of the more influential of the 19th century, Hannah More, rejected outright the proposal that women should share the same type of education as men, because "the chief end to be proposed in cultivating the understanding of women" was "to qualify them for the practical purposes of life" (see Smith, 1970, p. 101). To set one's sights on other than harmonious domesticity was to defy the natural order. Her readers were advised to be excellent women rather than indifferent men; to follow the "plain path which Providence has obviously marked out to the sex . . . rather than . . . stray awkwardly, unbecomingly, and unsuccessfully, in a forbidden road" (Smith, 1970, pp. 100–101). Her values were constant with those held by most of the middle class, and so her *Strictures on the Modern System of Female Education* (More, 1800) enjoyed widespread popularity for some time.

By the latter part of the century, the question had turned from whether girls should be educated like boys to how much they should be educated like boys. With the shift in emphasis came the question of coeducation. One of the strongest objections to coeducation in adolescence was the threat it posed to the "normalization" of the menstrual period. G. Stanley Hall (1906) waxed poetic on the issue:

> At a time when her whole future life depends upon normalizing the lunar month, is there not something not only unnatural and unhygienic, but a little monstrous, in daily school associations with boys, where she must suppress and conceal her instincts and feelings, at those times when her own promptings suggest withdrawal or stepping a little aside to let Lord Nature do his magnificent work of efflorescence. (p. 590)

Edward Clarke (see Sinclair, 1965, p. 123) had earlier elucidated the physiological reason for the restraint of girls from exertion in their studies: by forcing their brains to do work at puberty, they would use up blood later needed for menstruation.

Hall proposed an educational system for girls that would not only take into consideration their delicate physical nature but would also be tailored to prepare them for their special role in society. He feared that women's competition with men "in the world" would cause them to neglect their instinctive maternal urges and so bring about "race suicide." Because the glory of the female lay in motherhood, Hall believed that all educational and social institutions should be structured with that end in mind. Domestic arts would therefore be emphasized in special schools for adolescent girls, and disciplines such as philosophy, chemistry, and mathematics would be treated only superficially. If a girl had a notion to stay in the "male" system, she should be able to, but, Hall warned, such a woman selfishly interested in self-fulfillment would also be less likely to bear children and so be confined to an "agamic" life, thus failing to reproduce those very qualities that made her strong (Hall, 1918).

Throughout Hall's panegyric upon the beauties of female domestic education, there runs an undercurrent of the *real* threat that he perceived in coeducation, and that was the "feminization" of the American male. David Starr Jordan (1902) shared this objection but felt that coeducation would nevertheless make young men more "civilized" and young women less frivolous, tempering their natural pubescent inclinations. He was no champion of female ability though, stressing that women "on the whole, lack originality" (p. 100). The educated woman, he said, "is likely to master technic rather than art; method, rather than substance. She may know a good deal, but she can do nothing" (p. 101). In spite of this, he did assert that their training is just as serious and important as that of men. His position strongly favored the notion that the smaller range of female ability was the cause of lackluster female academic performance.

The issue of coeducation was not easily settled, and even as late as 1935, one finds debates over its relative merits (*Encyclopedia of the Social Sciences*, 1935, pp. 614–617).

The biological bases of sex differences

The variability hypothesis was compatible not only with prevailing attitudes concerning the appropriate form of female education but also with a highly popular theory of the biological complementarity of the sexes. The main tenet of Geddes and Thomson's (1890) theory was that males are primarily "catabolic," females "anabolic." From this difference in metabolism, all other sex differences in physical, intellectual, and emotional makeup were derived. The male was more agile, creative, and variable: the female was truer to the species type and therefore, in all respects, less variable. The conservatism of the female insured the continuity of the species. The author stressed the metabolic antecedents of female conservatism and male differentiation rather than variational tendency per se, and also put emphasis on the complementarity of the two natures:

> The feminine passivity is expressed in greater patience, more open-mindedness, greater appreciation of subtle details, and consequently what we call more rapid intuition. The masculine activity lends a greater power of maximum effort, of scientific insight, or cerebral experiment with impressions, and is associated with an unobservant or impatient disregard of minute details, but with a more stronger grasp of generalities. (p. 271)

The presentation of evolutionary theory anchored in yin-yang concepts of function represents the most positive evaluation of the female sex offered by 19th-century science. Whatever woman's shortcomings, they were necessary to complete her nature, which itself was necessary to complete man's: "Man thinks more, woman feels more. He discovers more, but remembers less; she is more receptive, and less forgetful" (Geddes & Thomson, 1890, p. 271).

Variability and the testing movement

Helen Thompson (later Woolley) put Geddes and Thompson's and other theories of sex differences in ability to what she felt was a crucial experimental test (see Thompson, 1903). Twenty-five men and 25 women participated in nearly 20 hours of individual testing of their intellectual, motor, and sensory abilities. Of more importance than her experimental results (whether men or women can tap a telegraph key more times per minute has lost its significance to psychology) was her discussion of the implications of the resulting negligible differences for current theories of sex differences. She was especially critical of the mass of inconsistencies inherent in contemporary biological theories:

Women are said to represent concentration, patience, and stability in emotional life. One might logically conclude that prolonged concentration of attention and unbiased generalization would be their intellectual characteristics, but these are the very characteristics assigned to men. (p. 173)

In the face of such contradictions, she was forced to conclude that "if the author's views as to the mental differences of sex had been different, they might as easily have derived a very different set of characteristics" (pp. 173–174). Thompson singled out the variability hypothesis for special criticism, objecting not only to the use of physical variation as evidence for intellectual variation but also to the tendency to minimize environmental influences. She held that training was responsible for sex differences in variation, and to those who countered that it is really a fundamental difference of instincts and characteristics that determines the differences in training, she replied that if this were true, "it would not be necessary to spend so much time and effort in making boys and girls follow the lines of conduct proper to their sex" (p. 181).

Thompson's recommendation to look at environmental factors went unheeded, as more and more evidence of woman's incapability of attaining eminence was amassed. In the surveys of eminent persons that were popular at the turn of the century, more credence was given to nature (à la Hall) than nurture (à la Thompson) for the near absence of eminent women (Cattell, 1903; Ellis, 1904). Cattell (1903) found a ready-made explanation in the variability hypothesis: "Women depart less from the normal than man," ergo "the distribution of women is represented by a narrower bell-shaped curve" (p. 375). Cora Castle's (1913) survey of eminent women was no less critical of woman's failure to achieve at the top levels of power and prestige.

One of the most significant individuals to take up the cause of the variability hypothesis was Edward Thorndike. Much of the early work in the testing movement was done at Columbia University, which provided the perfect milieu for Thorndike's forays into the variability problem as applied to mental testing and educational philosophy. Thorndike based his case for the accep-

tance of the variability hypothesis on the reevaluation of the results of two studies (Thompson, 1903; Wissler, 1901) that had not themselves been directed toward the issue. Thorndike insisted that greater male variability only became meaningful when one examined the distribution of ability at the highest levels of giftedness. Measurement of more general sex differences could only "prove that the sexes are closely alike and that sex can account for only a very small fraction of human mental differences in the abilities listed" (Thorndike, 1910, p. 185). Since the range of female ability was narrower, he reasoned, the talents of women should be channeled into fields in which they would be most needed and most successful because "this one fundamental difference in variability is more important than all the difference between the average male and female capacities" (Thorndike, 1906):

> Not only the probability and the desirability of marriage and the training of children as an essential feature of woman's career, but also the restriction of women to the mediocre grades of ability and achievement should be reckoned with by our educational systems. The education of women for . . . professions . . . where a very few gifted individuals are what society requires, is far less needed than for such professions as nursing, teaching, medicine, or architecture, where the average level is the essential. (p 213)

He felt perfectly justified in this recommendation because of "the patent fact that in the great achievements of the world in science, as, invention, and management, women have been far excelled by men" (Thorndike 1910, p. 35). In Thorndike's view, environmental factors scarcely mattered.

Others, like Joseph Jastrow (1915), seemed to recognize the tremendous influence that societal pressure had upon achievement. He noted that even when women had been admitted to employment from which they had previously been excluded, new prejudices arose; "allowances and considerations for sex intrude, favorably or unfavorably; the avenues of preferment, though ostensibly open are really barred by invisible barriers of social prejudice" (pp. 567–568). This was little more than lip service because he was even more committed to the importance of variational tendency and its predominance over any possible extenuating factors the effects of the variability of the male and the biological conservatism of the female "radiates to every distinctive aspect of their contrasted natures and expressions" (p. 568).

A small but persistent minority challenged the validity of the variability hypothesis, and it is not surprising that this minority was composed mainly of women. Although the "woman question" was, to some degree, at issue, the larger dispute was between those who stressed "nature" as the major determinant of ability (and therefore success) and those who rejected nature and its corollary, instead emphasizing the importance of environmental factors. Helen Thompson Woolley, while remaining firmly committed to the investigation of the differential effects of social factors of each sex, did not directly involve herself in the variability controversy. Leta Stetter Hollingworth, first a student and then a colleague of Thorndike's at Teachers College of Columbia University, actively investigated the validity of the hypothesis and presented sound objections to it. She argued that there was no real basis for assuming that the distribution of "mental traits" in the population conforms without exception to the Gaussian distribution. The assumption of normality was extremely important to the validity of the variability hypothesis, because only in a normal distribution would a difference in variability indicate a difference in range. It was the greater range of male ability that was used to "prove" the ultimate superiority of male ability. Greater range of male ability was usually verified by citing lists of eminent persons (dominated by men) and the numbers and sex of those in institutions for the feebleminded (also dominated by men). Hollingworth (1914) saw no reason to resort to biological theory for an explanation of the phenomenon when a more parsimonious one was available in social fact. Statistics reporting a larger number of males among the feebleminded could be explained by the fact that the supporting data had been gathered in institutions, where men were more likely to be admitted than women of an equal degree of retardation. That better ability of feebleminded women to survive outside the institutional setting was simply a function of female social role:

Women have been made and are a dependent and non-competitive class, and when defective can more easily survive outside of institutions, since they do not have to compete *mentally* with normal individuals, as men do, to maintain themselves in the social *milieu*. (Hollingworth, 1914 p. 515)

Women would therefore be more likely to be institutionalized at an older age than men, after they had become too old to be "useful" or self-supporting. A survey of age and sex ratios in New York institutions supported her hypothesis; the ratio of females to males increased with the age of the inmates (Hollingworth, 1913). As for the rarity of eminence among women, Hollingworth (1914) argued that because of the social role of women was defined in terms of housekeeping and child-rearing functions, "a field where eminence is not possible," and because of concomitant constraints placed on the education and employment of women by law, custom, and the demands of the role, one could not possibly validly compare the achievements of women with those of men who "have followed the greatest possible range of occupations, and have at the same time procreated unhindered" (p. 528). She repeatedly emphasized (Hollingworth, 1914, 1916) that the true potential of woman could only be known when she began to receive social acceptance of her right to choose career, maternity, or both.

Hollingworth's argument that unrecognized differences in social training had misdirected the search for *inherent* sex differences had earlier been voiced by Mary Calkins (1896). Just as Hollingworth directed her response particularly at Thorndike's formulation of the variability hypothesis, Calkins objected to Jastrow's (1896) intimations that one finds "greater uniformity amongst women than amongst men" (p. 431).

Hollingworth's work was instrumental in bringing the variability issue to a crisis point, not only because she presented persuasive empirical data to support her contentions but also because this was simply the first major opposition that the variability hypothesis had encountered. Real resolution of this crisis had to await the development of more sophisticated testing and statistical techniques. With the United States' involvement in World War I, most testing efforts were redirected to wartime uses. This redirection effectively terminated the variability debate, and although it resumed during the postwar years, the renewed controversy never attained the force of conviction that had characterized the earlier period. "Variational tendency" became a statistical issue, and the pedagogic implications that had earlier colored the debate were either minimized or disguised in more egalitarian terms.

After its revival in the mid-1920s, investigation of the variability hypothesis was often undertaken as part of larger intelligence testing projects. Evidence in its favor began to look more convincing than it ever had. The use of larger samples, standardized tests, and newer methods of computing variation gave an appearance of increased accuracy, but conclusions were still based on insubstantial evidence of questionable character. Most discussions of the topic concluded that there were not enough valid data to resolve the issue and that even if those data were available, variation within each sex is so much greater than the difference in variation between sexes that the "meaning" of the variability hypothesis was trivial.[1]

Maternal Instinct

The concept of maternal instinct was firmly entrenched in American psychology before American psychology itself existed as an entity. The first book to appear in the United States with "psychology" in its title outlined the psychological sex differences arising from the physical differences between men and women. Differences in structure were assumed to imply differences in function, and therefore differences in abilities, temperament, and intelligence. In each sex a different set of physical systems was thought to predominate; "In man the arterial and cerebral system prevail, and with them irritability; in women the venous and ganglion systems and with them plasticity and sensibility" (Rausch, 1841, p. 81). The systems dominant in woman caused her greatest attributes to lie in the moral sphere in the form of love, patience, and chastity. In the intellectual sphere, she was not equally blessed, "and this is not accidental, not because no opportunity has offered itself to their productive genius . . . but because it is their

highest happiness to be mothers" (Rausch, 1841, p. 83).

Although there was popular acceptance of a maternal instinct in this country, the primary impetus for its incorporation into psychology came by way of British discussion of social evolution. While the variability hypothesis gained attention because of an argument, the concept of maternal instinct evolved without conflict. There was consistent agreement as to its existence, if not its precise nature or form. Typical of the evolutionary point of view was the notion that woman's emotional nature (including her tendency to nurturance) was a direct consequence of her reproductive physiology. As Herbert Spencer (1891) explained it, the female's energies were directed toward preparation for pregnancy and lactation, reducing the energy available for the development of other qualities. This resulted in a "rather earlier cessation of individual evolution" in the female. Woman was, in essence, a stunted man. Her lower stage of development was evident not only in her inferior mental and emotional powers but also in the resulting expression of the parental instinct. Whereas the objectivity of the male caused his concern to be extended "to all the relatively weak who are dependent upon him" (p. 375), the female's propensity to "dwell on the concrete and proximate rather than on the abstract and remote" made her incapable of the generalized protective attitude assumed by the male. Instead, she was primarily responsive to "infantile helplessness."

Alexander Sutherland (1898) also described a parental instinct whose major characteristic (concern for the weak) was "the basis of all other sympathy," which is itself "the ultimate basis of all moral feeling" (p. 156). Like his contemporaries (e.g., McDougall, 1913, 1923; Shand, 1920; Spencer, 1891), Sutherland revered maternal sentiment but thought the expression of parental instinct in the male, that is, a protective attitude, was a much more significant factor in social evolution, an attitude of benevolent paternalism more in keeping with Victorian social ethic than biological reality. The expression of the parental instinct in men, Sutherland thought, must necessarily lead to deference toward women out of "sympathetic regard for women's weakness." He noted that male protectiveness had indeed wrought a change in the relations between the sexes, evident in a trend away from sexual motivations and toward a general improvement in moral tone, witness the "large number of men who lead perfectly chaste lives for ten or twenty years after puberty before they marry," which demonstrated that the "sensuous side of man's nature is slowly passing under the control of sympathetic sentiments" (p. 288).

Whatever facet of the activity that was emphasized, there was common agreement that the maternal (or parental) instinct was truly an instinct. A. F. Shand (1920) argued that the maternal instinct is actually composed of an ordered "system" of instincts and characterized by a number of emotions. Despite its complexity, "maternal love" was considered to be a hereditary trait "in respect not only of its instincts, but also of the bond connecting its primary emotions, and of the end which the whole system pursues, namely, the preservation of the offspring" (p. 42). The sociologist L. T. Hobhouse (1916) agreed that maternal instinct was a "true" instinct, "not only in the drive but in some of the detail." He doubted the existence of a corresponding paternal instinct, however, since he had observed that few men have a natural aptitude with babies.

The unquestioning acceptance of the maternal instinct concept was just as prevalent in this country as it was in Britain. William James (1950) listed parental love among the instincts of humans and emphasized the strength with which it was expressed in women. He was particularly impressed with the mother-infant relationship and quoted at length from a German psychologist concerning the changes wrought in a woman at the birth of her child: "She has, in one word, transferred her entire egoism to the child, and lives only in it" (p. 439). Even among those who employed a much narrower definition of instinct than James, maternal behavior was thought to be mediated by inherent neural connections. R. P. Halleck (1895) argued that comparatively few instincts are fully developed in humans, because reason intervenes and modifies their expression to fit the circumstances. Maternal instinct qualified as a clear exception, and its expression seemed as primitive and unrefined as that of infants' reflexive behavior.

Others (e.g., Jastrow, 1915; Thorndike, 1914a, 1914b) treated instinct more as a quality of character than of biology. Edward Thorndike (1911)

considered the instincts peculiar to each sex to be the primary source of sex differences: "it appears that if the primary sex characters – the instincts directly related to courtship, love, childbearing, and nursing – are left out of account, the average man differs from the average woman far less than many men differ from one another" (p. 30). Thorndike taught that the tendency to display maternal concern was universal among women, although social pressures could "complicate or deform" it. He conceded that males share in an instinctive "good will toward children," but other instincts, such as the "hunting instinct," predominated (Thorndike, 1914b). He was so sure of the innate instinctual differences between men and women that it was his contention (Thorndike, 1914b) that even "if we should keep the environment of boys and girls absolutely similar these instincts would produce sure and important differences between the mental and moral activities of boys and girls" (p. 203). The expression of instincts therefore was thought to have far-reaching effects on seemingly unrelated areas of ability and conduct. For example, woman's "nursing instinct," which was most often exhibited in "unreasoning tendencies to pet, coddle, and 'do for' others," was also "the chief source of woman's superiorities in the moral life" (Thorndike, 1914a, p. 203). Another of the female's instinctive tendencies was described as "submission to mastery":

> Women in general are thus by original nature submissive to men in general. Submissive behavior is apparently not annoying when assumed as the instinctive response to its natural stimulus. Indeed, it is perhaps a common satisfier. (Thorndike, 1914b, p. 34)

The existence of such an "instinct" would, of course, validate the social norm of female subservience and dependence. An assertive woman would be acting contrary to instinct and therefore contrary to *nature*. There is a striking similarity between Thorndike's description of female nature and that of the Freudians with their mutual emphasis on woman's passivity, dependency, and masochism. For Thorndike, however, the *cause* of such a female attitude was thought to be something quite different from mutilation fears and penis envy.

The most vocal proponent of instinct, first in England and later in this country, was William McDougall (1923). Unlike Shand, he regarded "parental sentiment" as a primary instinct and did not hesitate to be highly critical of those who disagreed with him. When his position was maligned by the behaviorists, his counterattack was especially strong:

> And, when we notice how in so many ways the behavior of the human mother most closely resembles that of the animal-mother, can we doubt that . . . if the animal-mother is moved by the impulse of a maternal instinct, so also is the woman? To repudiate this view as baseless would seem to me the height of blindness and folly, yet it is the folly of a number of psychologists who pride themselves on being strictly "scientific" (p. 136)

In McDougall's system of instincts, each of the primary instincts in humans was accompanied by a particular emotional quality. The parental instinct had as its primary emotional quality the "tender emotion" vaguely defined as love, tenderness, and tender feeling. Another of the primary instincts was that of "pairing," its primary emotional quality that of sexual emotion or excitement, "sometimes called love – an unfortunate and confusing usage" (p. 234). Highly critical of what he called the "Freudian dogma that all love is sexual," McDougall proposed that it was the interaction of the parental and pairing instincts that was the basis of heterosexual "love," "Female coyness," which initiated the courtship ritual, was simply the reproductively oriented manifestation of the instincts of self-display and self-abasement. The appearance of a suitable male would elicit coyness from the female, and at that point the male's parental instinct would come into play:

> A certain physical weakness and delicacy (probably moral also) about the normal young woman or girl constitute in her a resemblance to a child. This resemblance . . . throws the man habitually into the protective attitude, evokes the impulse and emotion of the parental instinct. He feels that he wants to protect and shield and help her in every way. (p. 425)

Once the "sexual impulse" had added its energy to the relationship, the young man was surely

trapped, and the survival of the species was insured. McDougall, while firmly committed to the importance of instinct all the way up the evolutionary ladder, never lost his sense of Victorian delicacy: while pairing simply meant reproduction in lower animals, in humans it was accorded a tone of gallantry and concern.

The fate of instinct at the hands of the radical behaviorists is a well-known tale. Perhaps the most adamant, as well as notorious, critic of the instinct concept was J. B. Watson (1926). Like those before him who had relied upon observation to prove the existence of maternal instinct, he used observation to confirm its nonexistence:

> We have observed the nursing, handling, bathing, etc. of the first baby of a good many mothers. Certainly there are no new ready-made activities appearing except nursing. The mother is usually as awkward about that as she can well be. The instinctive factors are practically nil. (p. 54)

Watson attributed the appearance of instinctive behavior to the mother's effort to conform to societal expectations of her successful role performance. He, like the 19th-century British associationist Alexander Bain, speculated that not a little of the mother's pleasure in nursing and caring for the infant was due to the sexually stimulating effect of those activities.

Even the most dedicated behaviorists hedged a bit when it came to discarding the idea of instinct altogether. Although the teleology and redundancy of the concept of instinct were sharply criticized, some belief in "instinctive activity" was typically retained (cf. Dunlap, 1919–1920). W. B. Pillsbury (1926), for example, believed that the parental instinct was a "secondary" instinct. Physical attraction to the infant guided the mother's first positive movements toward the infant, but trial and error guided her subsequent care. Instinct was thought of as that quality which set the entire pattern of maternal behavior in motion.

In time instinct was translated into *drive* and *motivation*, refined concepts more in keeping with behavioristic theory. Concomitantly, interest in the maternal instinct of human females gave way to the study of mothering behavior in rodents. The concept of maternal instinct did find a place in psychoanalytic theory, but its definition bore little resemblance to that previously popular. Not only did maternal instinct lose the connotation of protectiveness and gentility that an earlier generation of psychologists had ascribed to it, but it was regarded as basically sexual, masochistic and even destructive in nature (cf. Rheingold, 1964).

The Ascendancy of Psychoanalytic Theory

The functionalists, because of their emphasis on "nature," were predictably indifferent to the study of social sex roles and cultural concepts of masculine and feminine. The behaviorists, despite their emphasis on "nurture," were slow to recognize those same social forces. During the early 1930s, there was little meaningful ongoing research in female psychology: the point of view taken by the functionalists was no longer a viable one, and the behaviorists with their emphasis on nonsocial topics (i.e., learning and motivation) had no time for serious consideration of sex differences. While the functionalists had defined laws of behavior that mirrored the society of the times, behaviorists concentrated their efforts on defining universal laws that operated in any time, place, or organism. Individual differences in nature were expected during the functionalist era because they were the sine qua non of a Darwinian view of the world and of science. The same individual differences were anathema to early learning-centered psychology because, no longer necessary or expedient they were a threat to the formulation of universal laws of behavior.

In the hiatus created by the capitulation of functionalism to behaviorism, the study of sex differences and female nature fell within the domain of psychoanalytic theory – the theory purported to have all the answers. Freudian theory (or some form of it) had for some years already served as the basis for a psychology of female physiological function (cf. Benedek & Rubenstein, 1939). The application of principles popular in psychiatry and medicine (and their inescapable identification with pathology) to academic psychology was easily accomplished. Psychoanalytic theory provided psychology with the first comprehensive theoretical explanation of sex differences. Its novelty in that respect aided its assimilation.

Psychology proper, as well as the general public, had been well-prepared for a biological, and frankly sexual, theory of male and female nature. Havelock Ellis, although himself ambivalent and even hostile toward Freudian teachings, had done much through his writing to encourage openness in the discussion of sexuality. He brought a number of hitherto unmentionable issues to open discussion, couching them in the commonly accepted notion of the complementarity of the sexes, thus insuring their popular acceptance. Emphasis on masculinity and femininity as real dimensions of personality appeared in the mid-1930s in the form of the Terman Masculinity-Femininity Scale (Terman & Miles, 1968). Although Lewis Terman himself avoided discussion of whether masculinity and femininity were products of nature or nurture, social determinants of masculinity and femininity were commonly deemphasized in favor of the notion that they were a type of psychological secondary sexual characteristic. Acceptance of social sex role soon came to be perceived as an indicator of one's mental health.

The traps inherent in a purely psychoanalytic concept of female nature were seldom recognized. John Dewey's (1957) observation, made in 1922, merits attention, not only for its accuracy but because its substance can be found in present-day refutations of the adequacy of psychoanalytic theory as an explanation of woman's behavior and "nature":

> The treatment of sex by psycho-analysts is most instructive, for it flagrantly exhibits both the consequences of artificial simplification and the transformation of social results into psychic causes. Writers, usually male, hold forth on the psychology of women, as if they were dealing with a Platonic universal entity, although they habitually treat men as individuals, varying with structure and environment. They treat phenomena which are peculiarly symptoms of civilization of the West at the present time as if they were the necessary effects of fixed nature impulses of human nature. (pp. 143–144)

The identification of the psychology of women with psychoanalytic theory was nearly complete by the mid-1930s and was so successful that many psychologists today, even those most deeply involved in the current movement for a psychology of women, are not aware that there was a psychology of women long before there was a Sigmund Freud. This article has dealt only with a brief period in that history, and then only with the most significant topics of that period. Lesser issues were often just as hotly debated, for example, whether there is an innate difference in the style of handwriting of men and women (cf. Allen, 1927; Downey, 1910).

And what has happened to the issues of brain size, variability, and maternal instinct since the 1930s? Where they are politically and socially useful, they have an uncanny knack of reappearing, albeit in an altered form. For example, the search for central nervous system differences between males and females has continued. Perhaps the most popular form this search has taken is the theory of prenatal hormonal "organization" of the hypothalamus into exclusively male or female patterns of function (Harris & Levine, 1965). The proponents of this theory maintain an Aristotelian view of woman as an incomplete man:

> In the development of the embryo, nature's first choice or primal impulse is to differentiate a female. . . . The principle of differentiation is always that to obtain a male, something must be added. Subtract that something, and the result will be a female. (Money, 1970, p. 428)

The concept of maternal instinct, on the other hand, has recently been taken up and refashioned by a segment of the woman's movement. Pregnancy and childbirth are acclaimed as important expressions of womanliness whose satisfactions cannot be truly appreciated by males. The idea that women are burdened with "unreasoning tendencies to pet, coddle, and 'do for' others" has been disposed of by others and replaced by the semiserious proposal that if any "instinctive" component of parental concern exists, it is a peculiarly male attribute (Stannard, 1970). The variability hypothesis is all but absent from contemporary psychological work, but if it ever again promises a viable justification for existing social values, it will be back as strongly as ever. Conditions which would favor its revival include the renaissance of rugged individualism or the "need" to suppress some segment of society, for example, women's aspirations to positions of power. In the first case the hypothesis would serve to reaffirm that there are those "born to lead," and in the latter that there are those "destined to follow."

Of more importance than the issues themselves or their fate in contemporary psychology is the recognition of the role that they have played historically in the psychology of women: the role of social myth. Graves (1968, p. v) included among the functions of mythologizing that of justification of existing social systems. This function was clearly operative throughout the evolutionist-functionalist treatment of the psychology of women: the "discovery" of sex differences in brain structure to correspond to "appropriate" sex differences in brain function; the biological justification (via the variability hypothesis) for the enforcement of woman's subordinate social status; the Victorian weakness and gentility associated with maternity; and pervading each of these themes, the assumption of an innate emotional, sexless, unimaginative female character that played the perfect foil to the Darwinian male. That science played handmaiden to social values cannot be denied. Whether a parallel situation exists in today's study of sex differences is open to question.

Note

1 Shields, S. A. *The variability hypothesis and sex differences in intelligence.* Unpublished manuscript, 1974. (Available from Department of Psychology, Pennsylvania State University.)

References

Allen, C. N. Studies in sex differences. *Psychological Bulletin*, 1927, *24*, 294–304.

Bain, A. *Mental science*. New York: Appleton, 1875.

Benedek, T., & Rubenstein, B. B. The correlations between ovarian activity and psychodynamic processes II. The menstrual phase. *Psychosomatic Medicine*, 1939, *1*, 461–485.

Calkins, M. W. Community of ideas of men and women. *Psychological Review*, 1896, *3*, 426–430.

Castle, C. A. A statistical study of eminent women. *Columbia Contributions to Philosophy and Psychology*, 1913, *22*(27).

Cattell, J. McK. A statistical study of eminent men. *Popular Science Monthly*, 1903, *62*, 359–377.

Darwin, C. *The descent of man* (2nd edn.). London: John Murray, 1922. (Originally published 1871; 2nd edition originally published, 1874.)

Dewey, J. *Human nature and conduct*. New York: Random House, 1957.

Downey, J. E. Judgment on the sex of handwriting. *Psychological Review*, 1910, *17*, 205–216.

Dunlap, J. Are there any instincts? *Journal of Abnormal and Social Psychology*, 1919–1920, *14*, 307–311.

Elliott, H. C. *Textbook of neuroanatomy* (2nd edn.). Philadelphia: Lippincott, 1969.

Ellis, H. *Man and woman: A study of human secondary sexual characters*. London: Walter Scott; New York: Scribner's, 1894.

Ellis, H. Variation in man and woman. *Popular Science Monthly*, 1903, *62*, 237–253.

Ellis, H. *A study of British genius*. London: Hurst & Blackett, 1904.

Ellis, H. *Man and woman, a study of secondary and tertiary sexual characteristics* (8th rev. edn.). London: Heinemann, 1934.

Encyclopedia of the Social Sciences. New York: Macmillan, 1935.

Galton, F. *Inquiries into the human faculty and its development*. London: Dent, 1907.

Geddes, P., & Thomson, J. A. *The evolution of sex*. New York: Scribner & Welford, 1890.

Graves, R. Introduction. In *New Larousse encyclopedia of mythology* (rev. edn.). London: Paul Hamlyn, 1968.

Hall, G. S. The question of coeducation. *Munsey's Magazine*, 1906, *34*, 588–592.

Hall, G. S. *Youth, its education, regimen and hygiene*. New York: Appleton, 1918.

Halleck, R. *Psychology and psychic culture*. New York: American Book, 1895.

Harris, G. W., & Levine, S. Sexual differentiation of the brain and its experimental control. *Journal of Physiology*, 1965, *181*, 379–400.

Hobhouse, L. *Morals in evolution*. New York: Holt, 1916.

Hollingworth, L. S. The frequency of amentia as related to sex. *Medical Record*, 1913, *84*, 753–756.

Hollingworth, L. S. Variability as related to sex differences in achievement. *American Journal of Sociology*, 1914, *19*, 510–530.

Holiingworth, L. S. Social devices for impelling women to bear and rear children. *American Journal of Sociology*, 1916, *22*, 19–29.

Huarte, J. *The examination of mens wits* (trans. from Spanish to Italian by M. Camilli; trans. from Italian to English by R. Carew). Gainesville, Fla.: Scholars' Facsimiles and Reprints, 1959.

James, W. *The principles of psychology*. New York: Dover, 1950.

Jastrow, J. Note on Calkins' "Community of ideas of men and women." *Psychological Review*, 1896, *3*, 430–431.

Jastrow, J. *Character and temperament*. New York: Appleton, 1915.

Jordan, D. S. The higher education of women. *Popular Science Monthly*, 1902, *62*, 97–107.

Mall, F. P. On several anatomical characters of the human brain, said to vary according to race and sex, with especial reference to the weight of the frontal lobe. *American Journal of Anatomy*, 1909, *9*, 1–32.

McDougall, W. *An introduction to social psychology* (7th edn.). London: Methuen, 1913.

McDougall, W. *Outline of psychology*. New York: Scribner's, 1923.

Meyer, M. *Psychology of the other-one*. Columbia: Missouri Book, 1921.

Mill, J. S. *The subjection of women*. London: Dent, 1955.

Mobius, P. J. The physiological mental weakness of woman (A. McCorn, Trans.) *Alienist and Neurologist*, 1901, *22*, 624–642.

Money, J. Sexual dimorphism and homosexual gender identity. *Psychological Bulletin*, 1970, *74*, 425–440.

More, H. *Strictures on the modern system of female education. With a view of the principles and conduct prevalent among women of rank and fortune*. Philadelphia, Pa.: Printed by Budd and Bertram for Thomas Dobson, 1800.

Patrick, G. T. W. The psychology of women. *Popular Science Monthly*, 1895, *47*, 209–225.

Pearson, K. Variation in man and woman. In *The chances of death* (Vol. 1). London: Edward Arnold, 1897.

Pillsbury, W. B. *Education as the psychologist sees it*. New York: Macmillan, 1926.

Porteus, S., & Babcock, M. E. *Temperament and race.* Boston: Gorham Press 1926.

Rausch, F. A. *Psychology; Or, a view of the human soul including anthropology* (2nd rev. edn.). New York: Dodd, 1841.

Rheingold, J. *The fear of being a woman.* New York: Grune & Stratton, 1964.

Romanes, G. J. Mental differences between men and women. *Nineteenth Century*, 1887, *21*, 654–672.

Shand, A. F. *The foundations of character.* London: Macmillan, 1920.

Sinclair, A. *The better half: The emancipation of the American woman.* New York: Harper & Row, 1965.

Smith, P. *Daughters of the promised land.* Boston: Little, Brown, 1970.

Spencer, H. *The study of sociology.* New York: Appleton, 1891.

Stannard, U. *Adam's rib, or the woman within. Trans Action*, 1970, *8*, 24–35.

Sutherland, A. *The origin and growth of the moral instinct* (Vol. 1). London: Longmans, Green, 1898.

Terman, L., & Miles, C. C. *Sex and personality.* New York: Russell and Russell, 1968.

Thompson, H. B. *The mental traits of sex.* Chicago: University of Chicago Press, 1903.

Thorndike, E. L. Sex in education. *The Bookman*, 1906, *23*, 211–214.

Thorndike, E. L. *Educational psychology.* (2nd edn.). New York: Teachers College, Columbia University, 1910.

Thorndike, E. L. *Individuality.* Boston: Houghton Mifflin, 1911.

Thorndike, E. L. *Educational psychology* (Vol. 3). New York: Teachers College, Columbia University, 1914. (a)

Thorndike, E. L. *Educational psychology briefer course.* New York: Teachers College, Columbia University, 1914. (b)

Walker, A. *Woman physiologically considered.* New York: J. & H. G. Langley, 1850.

Watson, J. B. Studies on the growth of the emotions. In *Psychologies of 1925.* Worcester, Mass.: Clark University Press, 1926.

Weininger, O. *Sex and character* (trans.). London. Heinemann, 1906.

Wissler, C. The correlation of mental and physical tests. *Psychological Review Monograph Supplements*, 1899–1901. *3* (6, Whole No. 16).

Wollstonecraft, M. *A vindication of the rights of woman.* New York: Dutton, 1955.

Woolley, H. T. Psychological literature: A review of the recent literature on the psychology of sex. *Psychological Bulletin*, 1910, *7*, 335–342.

Wundt, W. *Ethics.* Vol. 3: *The principles of morality, and the departments of the moral life* (M. F. Washburn, Trans.). London: Sonnenschein, 1901.

Chapter 6

Birth of the New Applied Psychology

G. Stanley Hall's founding of the Child Study Movement in the early 1890s can be seen as the initial application of the new scientific psychology in America. In describing the new psychology, Hall (1893) wrote, "The one chief and immediate field of application for all this work is its application to education" (p. 441). It was a first step to demonstrate the value of the new science, and other applications would follow close behind.

Before there was a science of psychology toward the end of the nineteenth century, there was a popular psychology, and it had existed for hundreds, likely thousands, of years. This popular psychology, or public psychology, was manifested in the many ways in which individuals offered their services in activities that would be similar to the psychological services provided today by the modern profession of licensed psychologists. These "psychologists" practiced under a variety of names such as shaman, seer, medicine man, sorcerer, and enchanter, and later, in the nineteenth century, as phrenologist, physiognomist, mesmerist, mental healer, spiritualist, and even psychologist. In most cases, training of these practitioners was minimal, but they used their expertise and position of authority to offer vocational counseling, marital counseling, cures for depression, parenting advice, and all kinds of psychological advice. Thus a phrenologist practicing in the nineteenth century would measure the bumps and indentations on the skull of the client and from that analysis might advise the client about career possibilities that were in line with the client's talents as indicated by the phrenological examination. Indeed, businesses in the nineteenth century often used the services of a phrenological clinic as a kind of personnel office to help the business make hiring or promotion decisions. Thus when scientific psychology arrived on the scene, there was already a role in society for the application of psychology for the public good. It should be no surprise, then, that the new scientific psychologists would be eager to apply their science to the problems being addressed by individuals whom the psychologists considered to be charlatans.

Application of the new science was one way to demonstrate its validity as a science. If education was about development, perception, learning, memory, thinking, and motivation, then surely psychology as a science that investigated those topics would have something to say about improving education. If advertising was about perception, persuasion, emotion, and suggestibility, again, psychology as the science of those topics ought to have something to offer the advertising world. If various business positions required different behavioral skills, for example, aggressiveness in a salesperson versus tactfulness and empathy in a customer relations employee, then psychologists, who were developing all sorts of mental tests intended to measure such traits, ought to be able to assist businesses in their employee selection work.

The turn of the twentieth century witnessed great technological changes in American society via inventions such as the automobile, the telephone, and motion pictures. Cities were undergoing unprecedented growth, mass production was creating product surpluses leading to national advertising as a way to dispose of such surpluses, new technologies and new factory practices meant hundreds of new job titles and the need for people to be trained for these new jobs. Child labor laws were being passed to eliminate children from the labor force, and mandatory school attendance laws were passed to keep children in school longer. These changes, and issues of urbanization and immigration, meant changes in the dynamics of the American family, creating stresses that many families had never known. These changes in America's way of life offered the new psychologists a great opportunity to demonstrate the worth of their science.

These early psychologists were college professors, housed typically in departments of philosophy. College teaching wages were often meager, and consequently some of these professors, especially the younger ones, looked for ways beyond the university to supplement their incomes. Some got involved with businesses, some with public schools, and some with special institutions such as insane asylums and schools for the feebleminded (as they were known at that time).

In March of 1896, a schoolteacher visited Lightner Witmer at the University of Pennsylvania. She brought with her a 14-year-old boy who had difficulty spelling. The teacher had decided that the boy's problem was a mental one, and that because psychology was the science of the mind, psychology should be able to help him. Witmer treated the case successfully and soon saw additional cases, as word of his accomplishments spread within the Philadelphia educational community. As a result of this need and Witmer's apparent successes, he founded a *psychological clinic* at Penn that year, very likely the first psychological clinic in the world. Witmer was so taken with the prospects of his applied work that he sought to recruit his colleagues at other universities to get involved in similar work. At the meeting of the American Psychological Association in 1896, Witmer issued a call for the application of psychology, urging his colleagues to use psychology "to throw light upon the problems that confront humanity" (Witmer, 1897, p. 117).

In the beginning, Witmer handled all of the clinic cases himself. But as the numbers grew he was forced to add staff to the clinic, including some of his own doctoral students. Believing that descriptions of the cases and their successful (and sometimes unsuccessful) treatment could be useful to others, Witmer founded a journal, *The Psychological Clinic*, in 1907, to publish the work of his clinic. Eventually specialty clinics were added at Penn, including one for speech defects and another for vocational guidance. Because of his applied work in this field, Witmer is usually acknowledged as the founder of clinical psychology and school psychology.

One of the first American psychologists to venture into the field of business was Walter Dill Scott (1869–1955), like Witmer, one of Wundt's doctoral graduates. Scott was a faculty member at Northwestern University in 1901, when he gave a public lecture on psychology in Chicago. In the audience was John Mahin, head of the leading advertising agency in Chicago. Mahin approached Scott about writing a series of articles on the psychology of advertising for a magazine that Mahin proposed to found. Scott agreed and thus launched himself into a career in business psychology that proved most successful. Scott wrote 12 articles for the magazine in 1902, which were collectively published in 1903 as Scott's first book, *The Theory of Advertising*. Another 21 articles were written for the magazine, and those appeared in Scott's second book in 1908, *The Psychology of Advertising*. These articles led to Scott being recognized as the leading psychological expert on advertising by the advertising community (Kuna, 1976).

One of the controversies in the field of advertising was speculation about how to influence the consumer. One side argued that humans were basically rational creatures and that advertisements that appealed to reason would be most successful. The other side argued that humans were highly suggestible and could be manipulated by advertisements that appealed to that suggestibility. Scott's Leipzig dissertation was on the psychology of impulses, and he strongly believed in the power of suggestion in advertisements, emphasizing that effective advertisements should, in effect, tell the consumer what to do, for example, "Use Ipana Toothpaste," that is, direct the consumer to a particular action (Benjamin, 2004).

Scott's advertising work led to other work in the psychology of business. In 1916 he accepted a position at Carnegie Institute of Technology in Pittsburgh as director of the Bureau of Salesmanship Research, part of the Division of Applied Psychology. There Scott developed a number of selection tests for people in sales as well as other occupations. When the United States entered World War I in 1917, Scott was pressed into government service as head of the Committee on the Classification of Personnel in the Army. In a matter of months his committee developed selection tests for more than 80 military jobs, based in part on the tests he had developed at Carnegie Tech. By the war's end those tests had been administered to 3.5 million soldiers and recruits. That work won him the Distinguished Service Medal in 1919 from the United States government, the only psychologist to be so decorated as a result of war work. After the war, Scott returned to Carnegie Tech briefly, but left in 1919 to form the Scott Company, the first private consulting firm of psychologists to provide services to businesses and governments.

Scott's success in the field of advertising opened doors for other psychologists to follow. One of those was Harry Levi Hollingworth (1880–1956), who earned his PhD in psychology with Cattell at Columbia in 1909. After graduation, Hollingworth got a job teaching at Barnard College, Columbia University's women's college. He was married, living in a small apartment in Manhattan, trying to survive on his salary of $1,000 a year. His activities to expand his income included offering an evening course through Columbia University's extension division. The course was on the psychology of advertising, and many of those in attendance were part of the New York City advertising community. The lectures for that course would eventually be published in Hollingworth's book, *Advertising and Selling* (1913).

Hollingworth's big break, in terms of business opportunities, came in 1911. You may recall a brief discussion of this story in Chapter 1. The Coca-Cola Company was about to go to trial in Chattanooga having been sued by the federal government under the authority of the Pure Food and Drug Act for marketing a beverage containing a deleterious ingredient – caffeine. As the Coca-Cola attorneys were preparing for trial, they realized that there was virtually no existing research on the effects of caffeine on mental processes in humans. Cattell was approached about doing the research but was not interested. Likely he recommended his former student, whom he knew had experience in the business world. The Hollingworths were in need of money, and the Coca-Cola Company was willing to pay handsomely because it needed the research results in less than two months. Harry Hollingworth agreed to do the research. We will return to this story later.

In Chapter 4 we described the origins of scientific psychology in North America and continued that story in Chapter 5 with a discussion of the first "schools" of psychology known as structuralism and functionalism. We noted that the ventures into applied psychology came from the functionalists, who viewed the application of psychology to problems outside the laboratory as another way to investigate the functions of consciousness. In the introductory material for this chapter we have focused on the origins of psychological involvement in the clinical, school, and business domains. Each of these would spawn a separate professional specialty known as clinical psychology, school psychology, and industrial-organizational psychology. More will be said about the modern profession of psychology, especially clinical psychology, in Chapter 9.

The Readings

The six readings in this chapter focus on clinical, school, and business psychology. The first reading is by Lightner Witmer (1907) and is entitled "Clinical Psychology." It was the lead article in the first issue of Witmer's journal, *The Psychological Clinic*. Witmer begins the article with a discussion of his early cases in his clinic, including the problematic speller. About that case he wrote: "here was a simple developmental defect of memory; and memory is a mental process of which the science of psychology is supposed to furnish the only authoritative knowledge" (p. 4). The remainder of the article is Witmer's vision for a field of practice called clinical psychology, and his recommended model for how clinical psychologists should be trained. For obvious reasons this article is considered one of the foundational treatises for the modern profession of clinical psychology.

The second reading is by historian of science John O'Donnell, and it tells the story of the origins and development of Witmer's clinical psychology. A principal focus of the article addresses the fact of the relative neglect of Witmer in most histories of psychology, and the reasons for that neglect. O'Donnell (1979) notes that Witmer is often credited with some role in the history of clinical psychology but little, if anything, is said about him other than the fact that Witmer established his clinic in 1896. Witmer has actually received a lot more attention in the 30 years since O'Donnell wrote his article; there is even a full-length biography (McReynolds, 1997). Some of this recent scholarship has, no doubt, been stimulated by O'Donnell's article. Still, this article is the best source for understanding Witmer's passion for his clinical work, the way in which that work affected his relations with his psychological contemporaries, and the way in which he is regarded today for his role in clinical and school psychology.

The third article is by Leta Hollingworth (1886–1939). She was discussed in the previous chapter in the article by Stephanie Shields with regard to her work on the psychology of women (and more of her work will be covered in Chapter 10). She was the wife of Harry Hollingworth, who was able to use the money from the Coca-Cola Company to fund her graduate studies, finishing her PhD in psychology in 1916. Prior to that time she had worked for several years in New York City agencies dealing with issues relevant to clinical psychology. She was one of the co-founders, in 1917, of the American Association of Clinical Psychologists, a small group of psychologists, employed mostly outside of university settings, who were largely engaged in psychological testing. This brief article deals with her suggestions for the certification of practicing psychologists. It was published at a time (1918) when applied psychologists outside of universities were seeking a way to identify themselves as legitimate psychologists in contrast to the pseudopsychologists who continued to market their dubious practices to the public. It would be almost another 30 years before the first certification law would be passed for psychologists (in Connecticut in 1945), and it was not until the late 1970s that all 50 states and all Canadian provinces had passed licensing laws (see Benjamin & Baker, 2004). You will also note in Hollingworth's article that she proposed a new professional degree – the Doctor of Psychology. That degree (the PsyD) became a reality 50 years later in 1968, when it was first offered by the Illinois School of Professional Psychology.

The fourth reading is by historian of psychology Thomas Fagan, who is the leading authority on the history of school psychology. This article draws on the work of Lightner Witmer and J. E. Wallace Wallin to describe the origins of the profession of school psychology at the turn of the twentieth century.

The final two readings deal with the caffeine studies of Harry Hollingworth. The first of those is an excerpt from Hollingworth's 166-page report of the studies, published in 1912. You will read the preface to the studies, the chapter that deals with the methodology of the several research studies, and the brief conclusion section. The focus of this excerpt is on the research methods for reasons that will become obvious in the last reading in this chapter.

The final reading is a history of the caffeine studies and the Coca-Cola trials. It tells the fascinating story of the involvement of a young psychologist engaged in a hurried research project being sponsored by a major corporation that has a clear idea of how it wants the research to turn out. How can Hollingworth ensure his integrity in this arrangement? What if the results of his research show that caffeine is indeed harmful to mental activity? Will he be able to report the results anyway? This study could have marked the end of Harry Hollingworth's career as an industrial psychologist. Instead it earned him a reputation in the business world that allowed him to prosper financially with many more contract projects, and a reputation for integrity among his colleagues that led to his election to the presidency of the American Psychological Association.

Collectively, these six readings should give you insight into and understanding of what it was like for these early psychologists as they ventured beyond the security of the walls of the academy where their science had begun only a few short years earlier, and into the public arena, where they sought to apply their fledgling science to the difficult problems of their society. We will continue the story of the development of the psychological profession in Chapter 9.

Clinical Psychology
Lightner Witmer

During the last ten years the laboratory of psychology at the University of Pennsylvania has conducted, under my direction, what I have called "a psychological clinic." Children from the public schools of Philadelphia and adjacent cities have been brought to the laboratory by parents or teachers; these children had made themselves conspicuous because of an inability to progress in school work as rapidly as other children, or because of moral defects which rendered them difficult to manage under ordinary discipline.

When brought to the psychological clinic, such children are given a physical and mental examination; if the result of this examination shows it to be desirable, they are then sent to specialists for the eye or ear, for the nose and throat, and for nervous diseases, one or all, as each case may require. The result of this conjoint medical and psychological examination is a diagnosis of the child's mental and physical condition and the recommendation of appropriate medical and pedagogical treatment. The progress of some of these children has been followed for a term of years.

To illustrate the operation of the psychological clinic, take a recent case sent to the laboratory from a city of Pennsylvania, not far from Philadelphia. The child was brought by his parents, on the recommendation of the Superintendent of Schools. Examination revealed a boy ten years of age, without apparent physical defect, who had spent four years at school, but had made so little progress that his ignorance of the printed symbols of the alphabet made it necessary to use the illiterate card to test his vision. Nothing in the child's heredity or early history revealed any ground for the suspicion of degeneracy, nor did the child's physical appearance warrant this diagnosis. The boy appeared to be of normal intelligence, except for the retardation in school work. The examination of the neurologist to whom he was sent, Dr. William G, Spiller, confirmed the absence of conspicuous mental degeneracy and of physical defect. The oculist, Dr. William C. Posey, found nothing more serious than a slight far-sighted astigmatism, and the examination of Dr. George C. Stout for adenoids, gave the child a clean bill of health, so far as the nose and pharynx were concerned. On the conclusion of this examination he was, necessarily, returned to the school from which he came, with the recommendation to the teacher of a course of treatment to develop the child's intelligence. It will require at least three months' observation to determine whether his present pedagogical retardation is based upon a arrest of cerebral development or is merely the result of inadequate methods of education. This case is unequivocally one for the psychologist.

My attention was first drawn to the phenomena of retardation in the year 1889. At that time, while a student of psychology at the University of Pennsylvania, I had charge of the English branches in a college preparatory school of Philadelphia. In my classes at this academy I was called upon to give instruction in English to a boy preparing for entrance to college, who showed a remarkable deficiency in the English language. His compositions seldom contained a single sentence that had been correctly formed. For example, there was little or no distinction between the present and the past tenses of verbs; the endings of many words were clipped off, and this was especially noticeable in those words in which a final ending distinguished the plural from the singular, or an adverb from an adjective. As it seemed doubtful whether he would ever be able to enter college without special

L. Witmer (1907). Clinical psychology. *The Psychological Clinic*, *1*, 1–9.

instruction in English, I was engaged to tutor him in the English branches.

I had no sooner undertaken this work than I saw the necessity of beginning with the elements of language and teaching him as one would teach a boy, say, in the third grade. Before long I discovered that I must start still further back. I had found it impossible, through oral and written exercises, to fix in his mind the elementary forms of words as parts of speech in a sentence. This seemed to be owing to the fact that he had verbal deafness. He was quite able to hear even a faint sound, like the ticking of a watch, but he could not hear the difference in the sound of such words as *grasp* and *grasped.* This verbal deafness was associated with, and I now believe was probably caused by, a defect of articulation. Thus the boy's written language was a fairly exact replica of his spoken language; and he probably heard the words that others spoke as he himself spoke them. I therefore undertook to give him an elementary training in articulation to remedy the defects which are ordinarily corrected, through imitation, by the time a child is three or four years old. I gave practically no attention to the subjects required in English for college entrance, spending all my time on the drill in articulation and in perfecting his verbal audition and teaching him the simplest elements of written language. The result was a great improvement in all his written work, and he succeeded in entering the college department of the University of Pennsylvania in the following year.

In 1894–1895, I found him as a college student in my classes at the University of Pennsylvania. His articulation, his written discourse and his verbal audition were very deficient for a boy of his years. In consequence he was unable to acquire the technical terminology of my branch, and I have no doubt that he passed very few examinations excepting through the sympathy of his instructors who overlooked the serious imperfections of his written work, owing to the fact that he was in other respects a fair student. When it came to the final examinations for the bachelor's degree, however, he failed and was compelled to repeat much of the work of his senior year. He subsequently entered and graduated from one of the professional departments of the University. His deficiencies in language I believe, have never been entirely overcome.

I felt very keenly how much this boy was losing through his speech defect. His school work, his college course, and doubtless his professional career were all seriously hampered. I was confident at the time, and this confidence has been justified by subsequent experience with similar cases, that if he had been given adequate instruction in articulation in the early years of childhood, he could have overcome his defect. With the improvement in articulation there would have come an improved power of apprehending spoken and written language. That nothing was done for him in the early years, nor indeed at any time, excepting for the brief period of private instruction in English and some lessons in elocution, is remarkable, for the speech defect was primarily owing to an injury to the head in the second year of life, and his father was a physician who might have been expected to appreciate the necessity of special training in a case of retardation caused by a brain injury.

The second case to attract my interest was a boy fourteen years of age, who was brought to the laboratory of psychology by his grade teacher. He was one of those children of great interest to the teacher, known to the profession as a chronic bad speller. His teacher, Miss Margaret T. Maguire, now the supervising principal of a grammar school of Philadelphia, was at the time a student of psychology at the University of Pennsylvania; she was imbued with the idea that a psychologist should be able, through examination, to ascertain the causes of a deficiency in spelling and to recommend the appropriate pedagogical treatment for its amelioration or cure.

With this case, in March, 1896, the work of the psychological clinic was begun. At that time I could not find that the science of psychology had ever addressed itself to the ascertainment of the causes and treatment of a deficiency in spelling. Yet here was a simple developmental defect of memory; and memory is a mental process of which the science of psychology is supposed to furnish the only authoritative knowledge. It appeared to me that if psychology was worth anything to me or to others it should be able to assist the efforts of a teacher in a retarded case of this kind.

"The final test of the value of what is called science is its applicability" are words quoted from the recent address of the President of the

American Association for the Advancement of Science. With Huxley and President Woodward, I believe that there is no valid distinction between a pure science and an applied science. The practical needs of the astronomer to eliminate the personal equation from his observations led to the invention of the chronograph and the chronoscope. Without these two instruments, modern psychology and physiology could not possibly have achieved the results of the last fifty years. If Helmholtz had not made the chronograph an instrument of precision in physiology and psychology; if Fechner had not lifted a weight to determine the threshold of sensory discrimination, the field of scientific work represented to-day by clinical psychology could never have been developed. The pure and the applied sciences advance in a single front. What retards the progress of one, retards the progress of the other; what fosters one, fosters the other. But in the final analysis the progress of psychology, as of every other science, will be determined by the value and amount of its contributions to the advancement of the human race.

The absence of any principles to guide me made it necessary to apply myself directly to the study of these children, working out my methods as I went along. In the spring of 1896 I saw several other cases of children suffering from the retardation of some special function, like that of spelling, or from general retardation, and I undertook the training of these children for a certain number of hours each week. Since that time the psychological clinic has been regularly conducted in connection with the laboratory of psychology at the University of Pennsylvania. The study of these cases has also formed a regular part of the instruction offered to students in child psychology.

In December, 1896, I outlined in an address delivered before the American Psychological Association a scheme of practical work in psychology. The proposed plan of organization comprised:

1 The investigation of the phenomena of mental development in school children, as manifested more particularly in mental and moral retardation, by means of the statistical and clinical methods.

2 A psychological clinic, supplemented by a training school in the nature of a hospital school, for the treatment of all classes of children suffering from retardation or physical defects interfering with school progress.

3 The offering of practical work to those engaged in the professions of teaching and medicine, and to those interested in social work, in the observation and training of normal and retarded children.

4 The training of students for a new profession – that of the psychological expert, who should find his career in connection with the school system, through the examination and treatment of mentally and morally retarded children, or in connection with the practice of medicine.

In the summer of 1897 the department of psychology in the University of Pennsylvania was able to put the larger part of this plan into operation. A four weeks' course was given under the auspices of the American Society for the Extension of University Teaching. In addition to lecture and laboratory courses in experimental and physiological psychology, a course in child psychology was given to demonstrate the various methods of child psychology, but especially the clinical method. The psychological clinic was conducted daily, and a training school was in operation in which a number of children were under the daily instruction of Miss Mary E. Marvin. At the clinic, cases were presented of children suffering from defects of the eye, the ear, deficiency in motor ability, or in memory and attention; and in the training school, children were taught throughout the session of the Summer School, receiving pedagogical treatment for the cure of stammering and other speech defects, for defects of written language (such as bad spelling), and for motor defects.

From that time until the present I have continued the examination and treatment of children in the psychological clinic. The number of cases seen each week has been limited, because the means were not at hand for satisfactorily treating a large number of cases. I felt, also, that before offering to treat these children on a large scale I needed some years of experience and extensive study, which could only be obtained through the prolonged observation of a few cases.

Above all, I appreciated the great necessity of training a group of students upon whose assistance I could rely. The time has now come for a wider development of this work. To further this object and to provide for the adequate publication of the results that are being obtained in this new field of psychological investigation, it was determined to found this journal, *The Psychological Clinic.*

My own preparation for the work has been facilitated through my connection as consulting psychologist with the Pennsylvania Training School for Feeble-Minded Children at Elwyn, and a similar connection with the Haddonfield Training School and Miss Marvin's Home School in West Philadelphia.

Clinical psychology is naturally very closely related to medicine. At the very beginning of my work I was much encouraged by the appreciation of the late Provost of the University of Pennsylvania, Dr. William Pepper, who at one time proposed to establish a psychological laboratory in connection with the William Pepper Clinical Laboratory of Medicine. At his suggestion, psychology was made an elective branch in what was then the newly organized fourth year of the course in medicine. At a subsequent reorganization of the medical course, however, it was found necessary to drop the subject from the curriculum.

I also desire to acknowledge my obligation to Dr. S. Weir Mitchell for co-operation in the examination of a number of cases and for his constant interest in this line of investigation. I have also enjoyed the similar co-operation of Dr. Charles K. Mills, Dr. William G. Spiller, the late Dr. Harrison Allen, Dr. Alfred Stengel, Dr. William Campbell Posey, Dr. George C. Stout, and Dr. Joseph Collins, of New York. Dr. Collins will continue this co-operation as an associate editor of *The Psychological Clinic.*

The appreciation of the relation of psychology to the practice of medicine in general, and to psychiatry in particular, has been of slow growth. The first intelligent treatment of the insane was accorded by Pinel in the latter part of the eighteenth century, a century that was marked by the rapid development of the science of psychology, and which brought forth the work of Pereire in teaching oral speech to the deaf, and the "Emile" of Rousseau. A few medical men have had a natural aptitude for psychological analysis. From them has come the chief development of the medical aspects of psychology, – from Seguin and Charcot in France, Carpenter and Mandsley in England, and Weir Mitchell in this country. Psychological insight will carry the physician or teacher far on the road to professional achievement, but at the present day the necessity for a more definite acquaintance with psychological method and facts is strongly felt. It is noteworthy that perhaps the most prominent name connected with psychiatry to-day is that of Kraepelin, who was among the first to seek the training in experimental psychology afforded by the newly established laboratory at Leipzig.

Although clinical psychology is closely related to medicine, it is quite as closely related to sociology and to pedagogy. The school room, the juvenile court, and the streets are a larger laboratory of psychology. An abundance of material for scientific study fails to be utilized, because the interest of psychologists is elsewhere engaged, and those in constant touch with the actual phenomena do not possess the training necessary to make their experience and observation of scientific value.

While the field of clinical psychology is to some extent occupied by the physician, especially by the psychiatrist, and while I expect to rely in a great measure upon the educator and social worker for the more important contributions to this branch of psychology, it is nevertheless true that none of these has quite the training necessary for this kind of work. For that matter, neither has the psychologist, unless he has acquired this training from other sources than the usual course of instruction in psychology. In fact, we must look forward to the training of men to a new profession which will be exercised more particularly in connection with educational problems, but for which the training of the psychologist will be prerequisite.

For this reason not a small part of the work of the laboratory of psychology in the University of Pennsylvania for the past ten years has been devoted to the training of students in child psychology, and especially in the clinical method. The greater number of these students have been actively engaged in the profession of teaching. Important contributions to psychology and pedagogy, the publication of which in the form of monographs has already been begun, will serve to demonstrate that original research of value can be carried on by those who are actively engaged in educational or other professional work. There have been associated in this work of the laboratory of psychology, Superintendent Twitmyer, of Wilmington; Superintendent Bryan, of Camden; District Superintendent Cornman, of Philadelphia; Mr. J. M. McCallie, Supervising Principal of the Trenton Schools; Mr. Edward A. Huntington, Principal of a Special School in Philadelphia; Miss Clara H. Town, Resident Psychologist at the Friends' Asylum for the Insane, and a number of special teachers for the blind, the deaf, and mentally deficient children. I did not venture to begin the publication of this journal until I felt assured of the assistance of a number of fellow-workers in clinical psychology as contributors to the journal. As this work has grown up in the neighborhood of Philadelphia, it is probable that a greater number of students, equipped to carry on the work of clinical psychology, may be found in this neighborhood than elsewhere, but it is hoped that this journal will have a wider influence, and that the co-operation of those who are developing clinical psychology throughout the country will be extended by the journal.

The phraseology of "clinical psychology" and "psychological clinic" will doubtless strike many as an odd juxtaposition of terms relating to quite disparate subjects. While the term "clinical" has been borrowed from medicine, clinical psychology is not a medical psychology. I have borrowed the word "clinical" from medicine, because it is the best term I can find to indicate the character of the method which I deem necessary for this work. Words seldom retain their original significance, and clinical medicine, is not what the word implies, – the work of a practicing physician at the bedside of a patient. The term "clinical" implies a method, and not a locality. When the clinical method in medicine was established on a scientific basis, mainly through the efforts of Boerhaave at the University of Leiden, its development came in response to a revolt against the philosophical and didactic methods that more or less dominated medicine up to that time. Clinical psychology likewise is a protestant against a psychology that derives psychological and pedagogi-

cal principles from philosophical speculations and against a psychology that applies the results of laboratory experimentation directly to children in the school room.

The teacher's interest is and should be directed to the subjects which comprise the curriculum, and which he wishes to impress upon the minds of the children assigned to his care. It is not what *the child is*, but *what he should be taught*, that occupies the center of his attention. Pedagogy is primarily devoted to mass instruction, that is, teaching the subjects of the curriculum to classes of children without reference to the individual differences presented by the members of a class. The clinical psychologist is interested primarily in the individual child. As the physician examines his patient and proposes treatment with a definite purpose in view, namely the patient's cure, so the clinical psychologist examines a child with a single definite object in view, – the next step in the child's mental and physical development. It is here that the relation between science and practice becomes worthy of discrimination. The physician *may* have solely in mind the cure of his patient, but if he is to be more than a mere practitioner and to contribute to the advance of medicine, he will look upon his efforts as an experiment, every feature of which must indeed have a definite purpose – the cure of the patient – but he will study every favorable or unfavorable reaction of the patient with reference to the patient's previous condition and the remedial agents he has employed. In the same way the purpose of the clinical psychologist, as a contributor to science, is to discover the relation between cause and effect in applying the various pedagogical remedies to a child who is suffering from general or special retardation.

I would not have it thought that the method of clinical psychology is limited necessarily to mentally and morally retarded children. These children are not, properly speaking, abnormal, nor is the condition of many of them to be designated as in any way pathological. They deviate from the average of children only in being at a lower stage of individual development. Clinical psychology, therefore, does not exclude from consideration other types of children that deviate from the average – for example, the precocious child and the genius. Indeed, the clinical method is applicable even to the so-called normal child. For the methods of clinical psychology are necessarily invoked wherever the status of an individual mind is determined by observation and experiment, and pedagogical treatment applied to effect a change, *i.e.*, the development of such individual mind. Whether the subject be a child or an adult, the examination and treatment may be conducted and their results expressed in the terms of the clinical method.

The Clinical Psychology of Lightner Witmer: A Case Study of Institutional Innovation and Intellectual Change
John M. O'Donnell

In his 1895 presidential address to the American Psychological Association, James McKeen Cattell announced, "In the struggle for existence that obtains among the sciences psychology is continually gaining ground." The purpose of this nascent organization inhered in what Cattell perceived to be its precocious achievement: "This Association demonstrates the organic unity of psychology, while the wide range of our individual interests proves our adjustment to a complex enviroment."[1] Seated in the Philadelphia audience was one of Cattell's former students, Lightner Witmer. "One of the all-but-forgotten names in American psychology,"[2] Witmer was shortly to exhibit one aspect of its wide-ranging interests by founding the world's first psychological clinic. His anonymity reinforces the appropriateness of Cattell's Darwinian rhetoric, and the extinction of Witmer's clinical species provokes inquiry into the complexity of American psychology's intellectual, social, and professional environment.

Unfortunately, such complexity is often oversimplified by evolutionary assumptions implicit in disciplinary history.[3] In historiography as in nature, the fittest seem tautologically to survive and, therefore, to merit recognition. Consequently, Witmer, one of the earliest proponents of utilitarian psychology, has attracted little historical attention because institutionally his efforts were ultimately unsuccessful. His career seems negligible because he remained outside his disciplinary elite, failed to create a role that perpetu-

ated itself, and created no coherent intellectual system.[4]

History usually attends the victor. Hence, psychologist-historians who have attempted to elucidate their field's scientific and theoretical consistency have relegated Witmer to the periphery of psychology's development. And from their perspective rightly so. Opposed to what he considered the sterility of "brass instrument psychology," Witmer emerges in the words of a recent intellectual historian as "a voice crying in the wilderness."[5] Similarly, modern-day clinicians, seeking historical validation for their contemporary scientific procedures and professional styles, have treated Witmer in more breadth but with more disparagement, for the intellectual tributaries that formed clinical psychology in fact did not flow through his terrain.[6] These disciplinary chroniclers have deprecated Witmer for his failure to achieve for psychology professional hegemony over the "problem child." The fact that the original applications of experimental and scientific psychology to the mental and behavioral problems of individuals were eventually subsumed under a more general medical and psychiatric point of view has led to a repudiation of clinical psychology's progenitor. Thus, David Shakow concludes that "Witmer failed to make the contributions which he was in such a strategic position to make, with the result that clinical psychology passed him by."[7]

In fact, Witmer was in no such strategic position and must therefore be excused for not charting the ideal course so apparent to those blessed with 20-20 hindsight. Yet the chief concern of this article is not to restore Witmer to the position of initiator of all that followed. Nor is it my intention to exonerate him of deficiencies of intellectual and professional imagination. What I wish to suggest is that ventures which in Joseph Ben

J. M. O'Donnell (1979). The clinical psychology of Lightner Witmer: A case study of institutional innovation and intellectual change. *Journal of the History of the Behavioral Sciences, 15,* 3–17. Copyright 1979 John Wiley and Sons, Inc. Reprinted by permission of the publisher and author.

David's phrase fail to "take off" constitute extremely illuminating historical indicators of a discipline's shifting ideas, styles, and roles. Witmer's importance is not diminished by his inability to invest present-day psychology with adducible precedent. Failure to sire a fertile lineage, in other words, does not imply lack of contemporary relevance. To the contrary, precocious subgroups of larger disciplines – social manifestations of what Cattell called "our individual interests" – should become loci of investigation for historians seeking to uncover the process of intellectual change. Efforts to explain the decline of evolutionary naturalism or the demise of recapitulation theory within psychology through the explication of textbooks and theoretical tracts describe change rather than explain it.[8] Cross-disciplinary efforts to account for oscillating psychologistic tendencies toward hereditary and environment by invoking innovations in biological theory often overlook the fact that psychologists usually enlisted biology to validate a point of view rather than to inform it. Furthermore, such historical procedure merely shifts the ultimate burden of explanation to a neighboring discipline.

By examining in more detail subgroups of larger disciplines, one often finds that new trends are not created by new ideas but rather by a growing conviction that old ideas can be put to new uses. This depends not so much upon the implementation of new thought as upon the creation of innovative roles – products of social demands, professional opportunities, and economic exigencies.[9] Precisely at this point intellectual history becomes social history. In the case of clinical psychology, the conscription of extant scientific ideas and procedures in behalf of diagnosing and treating children with what we would nowadays label learning disabilities led to the formulation of novel problems, the solutions of which required the development of new viewpoints and the discarding of old theories. This process does not imply that older theories were necessarily disproved; rather they simply became irrelevant to tasks at hand. Paradigms need not be destroyed in order to become defunct.

One final disavowal. This article makes no attempt to deal with the fascinating social aspects of what may be called the "mainstream" of clinical psychology's professional development.

Simultaneously with Witmer's creation there arose a tradition in clinical treatment centered around concepts of mental illness, sponsored by individuals often possessing both medical and psychological training, and located within hospitals, medical schools, and state asylums.[10] Modern clinical and consulting psychology emerged from this latter tradition, whereas Witmer's interests evolved into the comparatively low-status school psychology and remedial education. Much of the historical polemic that surveys the growth of clinical psychology involves criticisms of Witmer for his excessive reliance on psychometrics, his unreceptivity toward dynamic trends in psychiatry, and his consequent failure to treat the conative and affective aspects of the child's personality and behavior.[11] On the positive side, however, Witmer's establishment of a novel social function – the "restoration" of the "retarded" school child – discloses to the historian early tendencies within academic psychology which subsequently informed other areas of pure and applied endeavor: a growing environmentalism, a quest to make psychology serviceable, an increasing skepticism of the value of intelligence tests, the growing disenchantment with genetic psychology, and an emphasis on psychology as the study of behavior.[12] These tendencies became important trends, and Witmer's articulation of them came not so much from theoretical investigations as from two decades of clinical experience.

While a graduate student at the University of Pennsylvania, Lightner Witmer became the assistant of psychologist Cattell, who in Germany in 1883 had himself become Wilhelm Wundt's first assistant.[13] At Leipzig, Cattell applied reaction time experiments to the problem of "mental measurement." Whereas scientific psychology at the time was primarily interested in such experiments in order to provide generalizations about the normal mind, Cattell was interested in them from the point of view of individual differences. In 1888 he lectured at Cambridge, where he came in close contact with Francis Galton and the Gaussian normal distribution curve. A familiar verbalism among psychologist-historians relates Galton's interest to "the central values of this curve" while applauding Cattell's attention to the "tails."[14] In 1890 Cattell coined the term "mental test" in an article dealing with the results of his experiments upon students at Pennsylvania.[15]

The following year he left Pennsylvania for Columbia and historians of psychology have, in a sense, followed him there, leaving behind the laboratory which he developed and its new director, Lightner Witmer, recently returned from Leipzig (1892) with a doctorate in psychology and an interest in individual differences. Four years later Witmer founded the first psychological clinic.

The catalytic event which prompted the birth of the Psychological Clinic came in the form of a challenge. In March 1896, a teacher in the Philadelphia public school system, Margaret Maguire, brought to Witmer's laboratory a fourteen-year-old boy described as a "chronic bad speller." The implication of Miss Maguire's challenge involved the practical assumption that if psychology were worth anything it should be able to diagnose the boy's problems. Happily, the "mental deficiency" retarding the pupil's academic progress was remediated through optometrical prescription.[16] In short, eyeglasses seemed to improve intellect. The ramifications of what might otherwise be recalled as a cute pedagogical success story were not lost upon Witmer. Within months he published an article proposing the establishment both of a practical laboratory capable of examining the physical and mental conditions of school children and also a training school for the remedial treatment of those psychologically or physiologically diagnosed as deviates or defectives.[17] In December 1896, Witmer proposed before the annual meeting of the American Psychological Association (APA) a more detailed program for "The Organization of Practical Work in Psychology."[18] Repeating the call for diagnostic laboratories and training schools, he urged, "the direct application . . . of psychological principles to therapeutics and to education." This plan involved extending instruction in psychology to doctors and teachers and demanded a closer relationship between departments of psychology and public schools, medical schools, and departments of education. The statement of one of Witmer's admirers to the effect that the professional response to his suggestion that the pure science of psychology should engage in utilitarian pursuits was a polite round of apathy underestimates the vitality of certain applied trends in psychology and the strength of various professional pressures and aspirations.[19] Had these tendencies not

been present in 1896 it is doubtful that Maguire would have approached an academic psychologist with her pupil's problem.

The reasons for a growing tendency on the part of many psychologists to define for themselves utilitarian roles can only be hinted at here.[20] Backed by the reform presidents of many of the major universities,[21] reinforced by a growing professional awareness of a crisis in public education and by educators' wishes to enhance their professional status by scientizing their pursuits,[22] and recognizing the growing need to justify their own scientific endeavor in order to secure institutional and financial supports,[23] many psychologists began to see themselves as reformers and looked to the field of education as a legitimating arena and occupational haven for their expertise.[24] Inaugurated by G. Stanley Hall, the child study movement represented an early association of educators and psychologists.[25] One of Hall's foremost students, William Lowe Bryan, warned of the professional dangers of pursuing pure science unresponsive to utilitarian demand when he declared before the National Education Association in 1893, "We promise a science of conscious life. . . . But we shall be false to all our promise, and we shall turn the confidence and sympathy which has endowed chairs and built laboratories, into derision and rejection if we confine our science to a little round of testing in the laboratory."[26] Witmer shared Bryan's sensibilities but not his program. The child study movement was a relatively conservative scientific venture involving a massive empirical compilation of the results of mental tests, questionnaires, and report from teachers and parents aimed at producing a statistical composite of the cognitive and emotional development of the normal child.[27] Upon this basis pedagogy would be reformed to coincide with the developmental sequence of the child's mental growth. Witmer, however, was concerned with children's minds, not the Mind of the Child. His more radical plan met with resistance within the APA because it prescribed to psychologists a therapeutic function which most thought premature and a role not yet legitimated for the academic scientist.[28]

Undeterred, Witmer returned to Philadelphia and established his plan of operation, conducting a summer school for the treatment of "backward children."[29] The success of this program prompted

University officials in 1907, during what has been described as an "era of expansion,"[30] to enlarge the clinic. Monies were procured to inaugurate publication of a specialized journal, *The Psychological Clinic*, partially patterned after Hall's important *Pedagogical Seminary*. In 1909 the University allocated to the clinic an enlarged budget and increased physical plant, and designated it a distinct administrative unit directly responsible to the Trustees.[31]

Though the organization of the clinic expanded with increased funding, the operational format remained basically unchanged throughout its history. Children would be referred to the clinic through the school system. Following medical diagnosis, subjects would undergo anthropometric, optometric, and psychometric examination. The latter testing is particularly interesting because it illustrates ways in which old technology was adapted to new uses. Witmer converted such experimental apparatus as the chronoscope, kymograph, ergograph, and plethysmograph into diagnostic devices merely by substituting the child for the trained introspectionist. Similarly, the Seguin form board – formerly used as a pedagogical tool – was transformed into an instrument for testing a child's powers of memory, visual discrimination, and muscular coordination. Complementing psychologist and physician, the social worker would prepare a case study of the child's background. Clinical records were compiled with the threefold purpose of correlating case histories in order to produce generalizations, of standardizing tests, and of establishing new diagnostic techniques.[32] Testing completed, a final diagnosis would be made, followed by attempts at remedial treatment.

Contrary to the frequently raised charge that the founder of clinical psychology was inordinately preoccupied with narrow concerns narrowly conceived,[33] the hallmark of Witmer's approach was his catholicity. At a time when nascent social sciences and services were busy erecting boundaries about their peculiar specialties, Witmer's liberal ecleticism exhibited in his attitude toward training, organization, research, diagnosis, and remediation enabled him to interact with medical practitioners, educators, school administrators, sociologists, and social workers, and even to advocate a close connection between clinical psychology and psychiatry, psychoanaly-

sis and anthropology.[34] Witmer's new role can be pronounced narrow only in one sense: he focused unremittingly upon the individual child and upon the possibility of his or her educational rehabilitation.[35] From such constriction of focus came breadth of approach, for an ethical element implicit in the clinical goal of effecting a cure involved a pragmatic attitude toward diagnosis and an openness to nonpsychological sources of assistance. Such openness was undoubtably facilitated by the fact that "special" teachers often possessed greater expertise in remedial matters than did the psychologist himself. Eclectic rather than experimental attitudes were required. The clinician confronted children in pedagogical disarray, not chickens in puzzle-boxes. He had neither the time nor the right to relegate some subjects to control groups for purposes of comparative analysis. Witmer's diagnostic data included, as I have mentioned, medical examinations and social case studies as well as mental tests. Often following the surgical removal of sources of physical discomfort such as impacted teeth or adenoids, the restoration of defective vision, or the improvement of the subject's environment by means of proper hygienic and dietary care, the subject would be retested in the various psychological examinations and would show marked improvement. Hence, the eclecticism implicit in Witmer's new role added a new dimension – though not yet a conclusively environmental one – to the diagnosis of the so-called feebleminded.

The implications of that new dimension for a changing psychological theory become more apparent when Witmer's approach is compared with that of his eugenically minded colleague in neighboring Vineland, H. H. Goddard. For Witmer the battery of mental examinations which he employed were, in a way "before-and-after" tests of the child's performance. For the Vineland psychologist, on the other hand, his revisions of the Binet test were strictly post hoc results. His tests were administered to groups of delinquents who, in Witmer's phrase, were already "socially diagnosed."[36] Goddard's task was merely to account for this moral delinquency by correlating criminality with low intelligence; a secondary and practical aspect of this endeavor involved the placement of delinquent individuals within institutions according to their trainability.[37] Goddard's conviction that intelligence was an hereditary unit-character explicable in terms of Mendelian genetics would appear to be substantiated as long as his testing took place – as one of Witmer's students perceptively pointed out[38] – in the relatively unchanging, regimented environment of the detention home. The antipodal social locations and antithetical social functions of their respective clinics continually reinforced Goddard's and Witmer's diametrically opposed intellectual assumptions and social perceptions.

Goddard, the Philadelphia clinician argued, dismissed the influence of environment without examining it. But despite assertions of social and intellectual historians that between 1910 and 1920 hereditarians prevailed,[39] it must be emphasized that they did so over determined opposition. In 1911, shortly before Goddard released the final results of his first testing of delinquents, Witmer, in an article pointedly entitled "Criminals in the Making," unleashed a scathing attack on the dismal implications of Goddard's approach.[40] Confronted with a case of juvenile delinquency, Witmer brought extensive medical, genealogical, and sociological evidence to bear upon and to reinforce his conclusion that his subject, the pseudononymous Harry, was "the product of his environment." Witmer's argument is of special interest since it marks his apparent acceptance of the Weismannian dualism and the consequent repudiation of Neo-Lamarckianism which, as will be later shown, was so much a part of the genetic psychology that formed the basis of his early educational theory. "Feeblemindedness, insanity, moral degeneracy," claimed Witmer,

> . . . these are doubtless in a certain proportion of cases the direct result of an inherited factor. Nevertheless, mental and moral degeneracy are just as frequently the result of the environment. In the absence of the most painstaking investigation, accompanied by a determined effort at remedial treatment, it is usually impossible to decide, when confronted by an individual case, whether heredity or environment has played the chief role. Who can improve a man's inheritance? And what man's environment can not be bettered? In the place of the hopeless fatalism of those who constantly emphasize our impotence in the presence of the hereditary factor, we prefer a hopeful optimism of those who point out the destructive activity of the environment. To

ascribe a condition to the environment, is a challenge to do something for its amelioration; to ascribe it to hereditary too often means that we fold our hands and do nothing.

> Take for instance the belief in human depravity and criminal instincts. Public opinion, even scientific opinion, is clearly fatalistic. In this country the treatment of the criminal is still conducted with a view only to punish and segregate, scarcely ever to educate or cure.[41]

This passage has been quoted at length to illustrate the ideological flavor of Witmer's vision with its typically progressive faith in the efficacy of the environment and in the plasticity of the human being. Regardless of the *ultimate* source of this faith, it was undoubtably invigorated by fifteen years of successful remediation of children who elsewhere and on different scales of intelligence might have been diagnosed as permanently feebleminded. Likewise, it was reinforced by the vast numbers of case studies surrounding Witmer's articles in his journal, *The Psychological Clinic*.[42] Written by psychological examiners and social workers at the exact time when the genre of muckraking journalism was filling the more popular magazines, many of these short pieces were rhetorically identical (if less polished stylistically) with the offerings appearing in *McClure's Magazine*, which began its sensationalist version of literary progressivism the year before Witmer's journal began its scientific one. It is appropriate that Witmer referred to the "destructive activity of the environment" as opposed to its more salutary aspects. Social perception has a way of adjusting scientific focus.

Programmatically, Witmer's focus was still upon the individual as the proper object of psychological study and upon insistence that environmental influences must be observed before they are counted or discounted. More important, the above passage enunciates a second major purpose of clinical practice. It is to fulfill not only a remedial but a research function and so reorient public and scientific opinion away from fatalism. Witmer sought to correct both children's performance and psychological assumptions by bridging the gap between research and clinical activity. A "determined effort at remedial treatment" becomes a way of assessing the relative importance of nature and nurture identified as they seemed to be with organic and nonorganic etiologies of abnormal behavior. Throughout the decade that ostensibly belonged to the Neo-Darwinian determinists in psychology, Witmer would elaborate his empirical results into a theoretical formulation involving modification of current theories of genetic and educational psychology. So long as animals and introspectionists remained the subjects of experimentation such reformulations would not emerge.

In the 1890s psychologists increasingly looked to evolutionary explanations of mental processes. The older physiological psychology of the structuralists, essentially descriptive, could not answer questions of causation and, hence, could never provide the dynamic explanation of behavior which psychologists needed in order to distinguish their experimental programs from those of physiologists. G. Stanley Hall saw in the extension of biological explanations of the evolution of the race to an understanding of the evolution of mental life of the individual the hope for a theoretical reconstruction of the science of mind. The recapitulation theory, explicit in the works of Herbert Spencer and E. H. Haeckel, was given added impetus by the comparative psychology of George John Romanes in England and the philosophical psychology of James Mark Baldwin in America.[43] The study of a child's mental development, thought Hall, would become the basis for a synthetic evolutionary psychology. A comparison of the mental growth of the child with the instinctive development of animals would then provide answers to the central problem of educational psychology; namely, what traits are innate and what characteristics are acquired.

Involving the idea that habits might become organized as instincts, Hall's genetic psychology was distinctly Lamarckian.[44] Hall was au courant with the biological thought of the day and, as George Stocking, Jr., has pointed out, he was gradually forced without ever fully discarding his Lamarckianism toward an accommodation with August Weismann's position.[45] In addition to biological objections to Hall's theories, psychologists enamored with the vogue of experimentalism were increasingly anxious to discredit Hall's unscientific procedures of using analogous records of parallel development to account for mental growth in humans.[46] Such assaults manifestly constituted the preconditions for repudiating the last great systematic articulation of naturalistic psychology. Understandably, such assaults form the investigative locus for historians attempting to explain intellectual change. The fascinating aspect of early twentieth-century psychology, however, is that naturalistic theories were not so much over-whelmed as they were overlooked. Overlooked because a new generation of psychologists was no longer seeking solutions to the problems that had motivated its mentors. The historian who would account for the demise of naturalistic psychology need not look for smoldering ruins but for evidences of new and ongoing construction in areas once considered the outer provinces of psychology. The new psychological clinic was one such structure.

Often the new would resemble the old architecturally. In 1907, for example, Witmer announced a course offering by Herbert Strotesbury of Temple College in genetic psychology. Strotesbury would discuss the inheritance of acquired characteristics.[47] Four years later Witmer offered a summer course in developmental psychology which would attend to "the problem of heredity by tracing the individual growth from the remotest period of its genesis in the germ-cell – the physical basis of heredity, in which are focused all the influences, actual and potential, of remote and immediate ancestry, and from which emerges the future human being."[48] By 1914 he was still insisting that the "whole problem of the mental development of the individual personality belongs to genetic psychology. . . ."[49] This, however, was genetic psychology with a difference. The developmental model to which Witmer adhered was strictly ontogenic. Recapitulation and evolution had dropped out of the picture. And why should they not? The scales with which Witmer was concerned were not phylogenic but pedagogical. Recapitulation, as Dorothy Ross has pointed out, "seemed most plausible for those aspects of child behavior most removed from the central learning experiences of children."[50] Concentrating on these more germane and manifest experiences, Witmer seems also to have obviated Lamarckianism. Strotesbury, for example, was scheduled to discuss inheritance of acquired characteristics through "congenital factors (non-hereditary)."[51] This appears at first to be self-contradictory, but it is safe to conclude that Witmer was here making a distinction between those acquirements of an individual organism in the course of uterine development subsequent to genetic action but prior to delivery (congenital) and genetic endowment (hereditary). In this view, not uncommon among contemporary biologists, the word inheritance assumes the pejorative meaning of the combined endowment of congenital and hereditary factors with which the organism is presented at birth.[52]

"Whether the existence of a congenital ability can be explained as the effect of causes acting through heredity or derived from the environment," quips the pragmatic Witmer, "I leave to philosophers and biologists. The starting point in psychology is the assumption of a number of congenital abilities. . . ."[53] The disclaimer is, of course, rhetorical. By moving the psychologist's frame of reference from the genetic to the congenital in this era of hereditary determinism, Witmer was able to leave open the possibility of environmental influences without having to plead guilty to Lamarckianism. Indeed, it had been his experience that medical examinations and clinical biographies of retarded children often uncovered evidence of intrauterine accidents, maternal disease during pregnancy, attempted abortions, miscarriages, and so forth.[54] Moreover, therapy often succeeded in overcoming these handicaps which affected the child's ability to learn. A pregnant mother's inclination toward alcoholic beverages can surely have an adverse effect upon the fetus. Witmer did not believe, however, that this habit would result in degenerate grandchildren. More to the point, the problem was irrelevant to clinical aims.

Having discarded the evolutionary brand of genetic psychology, Witmer found it easier to downplay the significance of instincts. In his course in developmental psychology he stated that individual inheritance, "as typified in the instincts, will receive the large attention they demand as congenital sources of habits and as primary springs of conduct during much of the child's life."[55] He continued: "Their origin, nature, variableness and transitoriness . . . will be treated in their psychological aspect as impulses to conduct."[56] Transitoriness is the key word.

Nowhere does Witmer suggest that instincts are modified; on the contrary, like old psychological theories, they seem to fade away as the environment assumes command. "By the age of six," concluded Witmer, "the child is more or less affected by his environment. . . . Upon inherited tendencies, habits have been grafted."[57] In a sense the child is continually trading instinct psychology for associationism, and the answer to the question of whether instinct or habit is more influential depends upon either the age of the subject or the tense of the application.

Witmer's genetic psychology embodied an uncomplex version of the familiar and bothersome idea of psychophysical parallelism. The organism is presented at birth with a set of congenital mental givens which develop – that is, become modified and "complexified" – at first through "the genetic process alone," or, in other words, by responding to internal physiological changes in organic structure, size, and function. Later, as we have seen, the mind is sufficiently developed to let the environment take over. As the body grows, so grows the mind. Any obstacle to physiological growth will probably frustrate mental development by depriving mind of the genetic stimulation which normal physical growth supplies.[58] The practical psychology enlisted to remove these obstacles or to reinvigorate retarded mental functions Witmer labelled "orthogenics," "the science of normal development [which] comprehends within its scope all the conditions which facilitate, conserve, or obstruct the normal development of mind and body."[59] Witmer was enough of an hereditarian to realize that people vary in their provisions of innate mental capacities and enough of an egalitarian to insist that everyone had the right to achieve his or her level of normal development. But what constituted a retardate's normal development – the essential question for the clinician – would depend upon a determination of the *extent* of hereditary endowment. Such a determination, however, would have to be based on statistical probability and Witmer had always divided applied psychology into two exclusive approaches according to method: the statistical and the clinical.[60] His attempt to resolve this dilemma by formulating a definition of normality from within the clinical tradition would lead him to downplay the concept of intelligence altogether and to emphasize a behavioral interpretation of test results.

Binet testers in the Goddard mold administered tests to *groups* of children in an attempt to correlate statistically mental with behavioral abnormalities. What Goddard considered the benefits of such compilation Witmer considered its drawbacks. Both found interpretations and methods of administration which coincided with their respective roles. Even the colleague of Witmer most sympathetic to Goddard's work realized that:

> while it may be possible to tabulate statistics of the percentage of moral degenerates that will spring from morally degenerate or imbecile stock, it by no means follows that any particular individual can be pronounced a moral imbecile from heredity alone, nor can it be predicted with any certainty that particular parents like A and B will have particular children like a and b who may be morally deficient.[61]

Unlike Goddard, Witmerians used so-called intelligence tests as structured opportunities to observe the subject perform certain mental tasks. The clinician observed performance and, in the process, those things which inhibited performance. For example, attention was considered a mental ability readily improvable with practice. All things being equal, an inattentive child would not achieve the same results in a testing situation as an attentive child. Raw scores from group tests can not only be deceiving but also damaging to accurate prognosis. Witmer claimed that his "very early experience . . . revealed the necessity for keeping the examination in a fluid state. I acquired a fear of the formalism of the blank. . . ."[62]

Tests were, therefore, clinically useful but statistically dangerous and throughout the period in which clinical psychologists were increasingly coming to be identified with mental tests, Witmer repeatedly sounded the call for skepticism and caution.[63] Once again, it was a caution based upon experience. For example, Witmer had examined a delinquent boy whose father had a record of alcoholism. There was a place on clinical examination forms for such information, but such information, claimed Witmer, would be misleading. In this particular case, five of the boy's brothers and sisters born after his father's drinking became excessive were quite normal. Such findings were the result of individual examinations and they led Witmer to "look with skepticism on family and social statistics reported by physicians or gathered by eugenicists."[64] The clinician's melioristic orientation precluded facile correlations between statistical probability and clinical prognosis. Witmer was preoccupied with assessing the relative importance of nature and nurture. For the clinician, however, the issue was more of practical than theoretical significance. The clinic was a social and educational service and in the interests of efficiency and alumni funds it should not spend time attempting to retrieve the irretrievable or to reform the incorrigible.[65] Witmer's procedure was therefore to work backwards from the most probable proximate cause of defect until remediation produce an improvement. At that point the etiological significance of the ailment might possibly make itself known. Lengthy Galtonian genealogical recording would simply constitute "wasting paper, ink, and my assistant's time," complained Witmer, "besides producing statistics which may be misused, as so many statistics of heredity are misused today, to uphold unsound contentions and to urge legislation of doubtful social value."[66]

Eschewing eugenicist data and turning, therefore, to E. L. Thorndike's educational psychology for an estimation of the role of heredity in mental development, Witmer subscribed to the idea of innate intelligence. The discovery, however, of wide-ranging test scores administered to an individual before and after medical, hygienic, or pedagogical treatment convinced him that intelligence tests do not, in fact, measure intelligence. This conclusion had been reached by a number of clinical investigations between 1912 and 1920 and Witmer was quick to draw upon the results.[67] Herein rests the strongest argument for historical focus upon institutions as catalysts for intellectual change: *the clinic provided an arena in which generalizations were made visible and theory tangible.* As such it quickened the pace of psychology's development in a way that nonapplied branches could never duplicate. When, for example, the eugenicist Lewis Terman retested a group of geniuses in 1927–1928, he discovered a striking downward deviation in the group's I.Q. that led him to conclude that factors of environment, personality, and health played a role in the measurement of intelligence. What is remarkable about this revision is that the original testing of the group occurred in 1921. The earlier conclusions of his *Genetic Studies in Genius* were allowed to stand authoritatively for over six years.[68] Within the clinic, however, where timely retesting was required, results were allowed to stand for only a number of weeks. To be sure, it would take years to produce a significant statistical deviation within a large group; but this justification can also be taken to indicate the remedial drawbacks rather than the benefits of statistical compilations.[69]

It is no coincidence that prior to World War One the two chief attacks upon the hereditarian implications of psychological testing came from William Healy and J. E. Wallace Wallin.[70] In 1906 Wallin visited Witmer's clinic and carried away with him the approach which was to emerge in his own clinic a few years later.[71] Healy likewise explored Witmer's organization and later commented that the creation of his psychiatric clinic in Chicago – which constituted the institutional beginnings of the child guidance movement in the United States – was partially modeled after Witmer's establishment.[72] Thus, it was from the psychological clinics, those supposed centers for eugenicist propaganda, that the earliest complaints about eugenics appeared.[73]

By 1920 the institutional vulnerabilities of Witmer's brand of clinical psychology were becoming apparent. Alliances with medical departments broke down as psychiatry came into closer contact with the universities.[74] Psychiatric clinics were steadily growing and psychiatrists, in a better position to assert their therapeutic claims, began to complain the psychologists were encroaching upon their legitimate territory while ironically adapting the program of clinical psychology to their own operational procedures. Aware of their comparative institutional weaknesses and lacking sufficient support from the American Psychological Association, clinical psychologists tenaciously held onto the one aspect of clinical practice over which they could reasonably claim authority. They insisted that psychiatrists were unqualified to administer psychological tests. Implemented at the highest levels of their respective professional organizations, the resultant compromise was decidedly adverse to clinical psychology's status. Psychologists gained hegemony over testing but little else. Diagnosis is not as prestigious a function as cure and clinical psychologists after 1920, as psychometricians, became subordinate components within psychiatric clinics. By 1935 only seven of the original psychological clinics cited by Wallin in 1911 were

still in existence.[75] In that year there were 87 child clinics directed by psychologists in comparison to 755 psychiatric clinics.[76]

In professional terms, however, psychologists did not suffer. Though they lacked the legitimacy of the therapeutic role neither were their activities circumscribed by that exclusive function. Their clinical training served them well in other areas of applied endeavor. The success of the testers during the war broadened their occupational horizons after the Armistice. In the twenties the business of psychology, like that of the country, was business. Led by Morris Viteles, many of Witmer's students, admirably prepared, went into personnel work or into industrial psychology.[77] Others converted their associations with educators into positions as school administrators. Their individual careers were not unlike those of the Peace Corps volunteers of the sixties – those corporation men of the seventies. Clinical psychology of the educational variety went the way of the Progressive Movement. Its larger concerns were assimilated into increasingly viable departments of education, whose prestige in the first decade of the century psychology had helped enhance.

In many respects, the psychologist-historian Robert I. Watson is correct to have dismissed Witmer as a man "of historical significance only."[78] Yet those of us from whom that verdict holds significance enough should be suspicious of his assertion that Witmer's articles – from which much of the above analysis is drawn – "are chiefly of antiquarian interest today."[79] The nature of Witmer's work and the requirements of his role prompted him to discard the genetic model of recapitulation, to regard intelligence tests as indicators of performance, to adopt environmental explanations of human behavior, and to call for a psychology that takes into account nature and culture as mutually exclusive categories.[80] To assume that Witmer transformed American psychology is to go to the opposite extreme, for in crucial ways his pursuits were parochial. But to assert that his activities were irrelevant to essential changes within American psychology because "his influence did not spread beyond Philadelphia to any considerable degree"[81] likewise misses the point. Such a conception of intellectual change as rooted in patterns of linear influences serves to keep disciplinary history at an essentially descriptive level of analysis. If Witmer's institutional situation, social location, role identification, and social function caused him to alter his intellectual suppositions and if the locations, roles, and functions of clinical (or, for that matter, of any applied) psychologists elsewhere were analogous,[82] then new ideas need not the postal service and the annual meeting to obtain salvation. Similar undertakings will tend to produce similar responses. The cumulative effect upon theory of changing ideas emerging simultaneously in disparate geographical and institutional locations and connected by a novel similarity of roles will go a long way toward explaining a discipline's general susceptibility to new paradigms.

Regardless of the institutional fate of that variety of clinical psychology which Witmer initiated, the intellectual viewpoints of those who participated in that and similar disciplinary episodes remained intact to inform associated endeavors. That Lightner Witmer failed to perpetuate his particular role does not diminish his relevance, for while others called for an applied psychology, Witmer enacted one. His theoretical formulations may have been incomplete and, in retrospect, roughhewn and hidebound, but they were never irrelevant. Although his intellectual contributions may seem imperceptible to us today, we must not forget that he prescribed and performed a social function which remains his legacy.

Notes

1 *Psychological Review 3* (1896): 134.
2 A. A. Roback, *A History of American Psychology*, rev. edn. (New York: Collier, 1964), p. 230.
3 Henrika Kuklick, "The Organization of Social Science in the United States," *American Quarterly* 28 (1976): 129.
4 Employing the sociological surrogate of evolutionary theory, the professionalization model, historians often adduce the creation of viable social roles as proof of a discipline's intellectual legitimacy. If a movement fails to perpetuate itself, we are thereby absolved of the obligation to look at its ideas. I call this assumption "intellectual Darwinism" and attempt in this article to develop an argument for circumventing it.
5 Hamilton Cravens, "American Scientists and the Hereditary-Environment Controversy, 1883–1940" (Ph.D. dissertation, University of Iowa, 1969), p. 266. At the risk of formulating a frontier thesis of disciplinary history, I am suggesting that crucial developments within American psychology have occurred exactly in such "wilderness" areas.
6 C. M. Louttit, "The Nature of Clinical Psychology," *Psychological Bulletin* 36 (1939): 366; Robert I. Watson, "A Brief History of Clinical Psychology," ibid. 50 (1953): 327–328; David Shakow, "Clinical Psychology: An Evaluation," in *Orthopsychiatry, 1923–1948: Retrospect and Prospect*, ed. L. G. Lowrey and Victoria Sloane (New York: American Orthopsychiatric Association, 1948), p. 234; Shakow, "Clinical Psychology," in *International Encyclopedia of the Social Sciences*, ed. David L. Sills, vol. 2 (New York: Macmillan and Free Press, 1968), p. 514.

7 Shakow and David Rapaport, *The Influence of Freud on American Psychology* (*Psychological Issues*, Monograph 13, Vol. 4, No. 1), p. 85, n. 37.
8 See, for example, Charles Everett Strikland, "The Child and the Race: The Doctrines of Recapitulation and Culture Epochs in the Rise of the Child-Centered Ideal in American Educational Thought, 1875–1900" (Ph.D. dissertation, University of Wisconsin, 1963). An excellent study which partially attends to the relationship of psychological thought to psychological practice is John C. Burnham and Hamilton Cravens, "Psychology and Evolutionary Naturalism in American Thought, 1890–1940," *American Quarterly* 23 (1971): 635–657.
9 For a systematic approach to the impact of institutional change upon intellectual innovation, see Thomas C. Cochran, *Social Change in America: The Twentieth Century* (New York: Harper Torchbooks, 1972), pp. 11–29.
10 The instable mixture of psychiatry and psychology which was distilled in such institutional settings required the establishment of novel inter-professional arrangements and the elaboration of consensualized theory. Though the history of this relationship has not yet been written, cursory investigations can be found in Thomas Verner Moore, "A Century of Psychology in its Relationship to American Psychiatry," in *One Hundred Years of American Psychiatry*, ed. J. K. Hall et al. (New York: Columbia University Press, 1944), pp. 443–477. For a general account, see John M. Reisman, *The Development of Clinical Psychology* (New York: Appleton-Century-Crofts, 1966).

11 Shakow, "Clinical Psychology," p. 514 summarizes this critique. Witmer's actual awareness of these trends reinforces this retrospective verdict.

12 John C. Burnham, "On the Origins of Behaviorism," *Journal of The History of the Behavioral Sciences* 4 (1968): 151, reminds us that "the evolution of Watson's thinking, on the one hand, is not necessarily relevant to the origins of behaviorism, on the other hand." As a complementary thesis, I am suggesting that behaviorism, broadly construed, represented the theoretical rationalization of trends within American psychology toward application, service, and social control. Watson seemed to provide intellectual legitimacy for psychologists whose social roles involved them in practical problems of human behavior. Much of his support came from these academically marginal areas. This essay constitutes a case study of one such outpost. The cumulative impact upon psychological thought of "practising" psychologist's engagements with actual social and behavioral problems partially accounts for the widespread acceptance of behaviorism after World War One.

13 Although is usually assumed that Witmer was a student in philosophy, he had actually changed his major from political science under Edmund James to experimental psychology in exchange for an assistantship offered by the philosopher George Fullerton, one of James's academic rivals. Witmer states that later his salary was significantly increased "on condition that I would go to Leipzig and remain there eighteen months." Witmer to Edwin G. Boring, 18 March 1948, Boring Correspondence, Harvard University Archives, Cambridge. Massachusetts. Both incidents are herein related as antidotes (though not, of course, contradictions) to the heroic historiographic portrayals of vocational motivation as a product of altruistic inspiration. See, for example, Edna Heidbreder, *Seven Psychologies* (New York: Appleton-Century-Crofts, 1933), pp, 94–95.

14 Edwin G. Boring, *A History of Experimental Psychology*, 2nd edn. (New York: Appleton-Century-Crofts, 1950), pp. 533–534; Samuel W. Fernberger, "The Training of Mental Hygienists," *Psychological Clinic* 19 (1930): 139.

15 James McKeen Cattell, "Mental Tests and Their Measurements," *Mind* 15 (1890) 373–380.

16 Witmer, "The Psychological Clinic," *Old Penn* 8 (1909): 100; Arthur Holmes, *The Conservation of the Child: A Manual of Clinical Psychology Presenting the Examination and Treatment of Backward Children* (Philadelphia: Lippincott, 1912), pp. 28–29. The title of Holmes's volume is indicative of the progressive rhetoric that informed and inspired turn-of-the-century clinical practice.

17 Witmer, "Practical Work in Psychology," *Pediatrics* 2 (1896): 462–471.

18 *Psychological Review* 4 (1897): 116–117.

19 Joseph Collins, "Lightner Witmer: A Biographical Sketch," in *Clinical Psychology: Studies in Honor of Lightner Witmer*, ed. Robert A. Brotemarkle (Philadelphia: University of Pennsylvania Press, 1931), p. 5; Reisman, *Clinical Psychology*, p. 46.

20 See John M. O'Donnell, "The Transformation of American Psychology 1890–1920" (M.A. thesis, University of Delaware, 1974), esp. chap. 4; John C. Burnham, "Psychiatry, Psychology and the Progressive Movement," *American Quarterly* 12 (1960): 457–465; David Bakan, "Behaviorism and American Urbanization," *Journal of the History of the Behavioral Sciences* 2 (1966): 5–28.

21 Laurence R. Veysey, *The Emergence of the American University* (Chicago: University of Chicago Press, 1965), pp. 57–120, 159, 177.

22 Lawrence A. Cremin, *The Transformation of the School: Progressivism in American Education, 1876–1957* (New York: Knopf, 1961), pp. 168–176; Arthur G. Powell, "Speculations on the Early Impact of Schools of Education on Educational Psychology," *History of Education Quarterly 11* (1971): 406–412.

23 George H. Daniels, "The Process of Professionalization in American Science: The Emergent Period, 1820–1860," *Isis* 58 (1967): 151–166. Daniels regards such justification (legitimation) as an essential step in the institutional growth of new sciences. The dramatic increase in public financial support of education in the United States between 1880 and 1900 surely helped psychologists focus their professional and intellectual attentions; Albert Fishlow, "Levels of Nineteenth-Century American Investment in Education," *Journal of Economic History* 26 (1966): 418–436.

24 Of the 160 individuals who listed psychology as their primary or exclusive field in the second edition of Cattell's *American Men of Science*, 67 or nearly 42% indicated educational concerns and interests. The 1910 edition was selected for its temporal proximity to Watson's 1913 behaviorist manifesto and because it encompasses the period of the Psychological Clinic's most rapid institutional growth.

25 James Dale Hendricks, "The Child-Study Movement in American Education, 1880–1910: A Quest for Educational Reform through a Scientific Study of the Child" (Ph.D. dissertation, Indiana University, 1968): Dorothy Ross, *G. Stanley Hall: The Psychologist as Prophet* (Chicago: University of Chicago Press, 1972), pp. 279–308, 350–367.

26 "A Plea For Special Child Study," *Proceedings of the International Congress of Education, 1883* (New York: Little, 1884), p. 778.

27 Hendricks, "Child-Study Movement," pp. 138–140, 186–198; Jason R. Robarts, "The Quest for a Science of Education in the Nineteenth Century," *History of Education Quarterly* 8 (1968): 431–446.

28 Robert L. Church, "Educational Psychology and Social Reform in the Progressive Era," *History of Education Quarterly* 11 (1971): 390–405, attempts to explain why educational psychologists did not share the reform concerns of educators. Implicitly, Church (esp. pp. 396–397) argues for psychologists' need to create a new role, a role which I maintain was defined by Witmer as the clinical psychologist.

29 Witmer et al., *The Special Class for Backward Children* (Philadelphia: The Psychological Clinic Press, 1911); Holmes, *Manual*, p. 30.

30 Edward Potts Cheyney, *History of the University of Pennsylvania* (Philadelphia: University of Pennsylvania Press, 1940), pp. 353–355, 401.

31 Fernberger, "History of the Psychological Clinic," in Brotemarkle, *Clinical Psychology*, pp. 14, 15.

32 These records have recently been microfilmed and surveyed. See Murray Levine and Julius Wishner, "The Case Records of the Psychological Clinic at the University of Pennsylvania (1896–1961)," *Journal of The History of the Behavioral Sciences* 13 (1977): 59–66.

33 This criticism has been invoked not only retrospectively but contemporaneously as well; R. H. Sylvester, "Clinical Psychology Adversely Criticized," *Psychological Clinic* 7 (1913). 182.

34 Witmer, "Clinical Psychology," *Psychological Clinic* 1 (1907): 6–7; "Courses at the Summer School of the University of Pennsylvania," ibid. 4(1911): 246; "The Scope of Education as a University Department," ibid. 7 (1914): 245. 246; Sylvester, "Clinical Psychology," pp. 182, 186; Holmes, *Manual*, pp. 40–41, 91, 299.

35 Witmer, "Clinical Records," *Psychological Clinic* 9 (1915): 3, "The Exceptional Child at Home and at School," *University Lectures Delivered by Members of the Faculty in the Free Public Lecture Course, 1913–1914* (Philadelphia: University of Pennsylvania Press, 1915), p. 538; "Psychonomic Personeering," *Psychological Clinic* 19 (1930): 73.

36. Quoted in Francis M. Maxfield, "Mental Deficiency," in Brotemarkle, *Clinical Psychology*, p. 44.

37 Mark H. Haller, *Eugenics: Hereditarian Attitudes in American Thought* (New Brunswick: Rutgers University Press, 1963) pp. 95–96.

38 M. S. Viteles, "The Children of a Jewish Orphanage," *Psychological Clinic* 12 (1918): 254.

39 Haller, *Eugenics*, p. 112; Cravens, "American Scientists," p. 265. Witmer's interpretation of Goddard sounds unduly harsh to historians of mental retardation. Such hyperbole, however, constitutes early evidence of polarization of debate between hereditarians and environmentalists.

40 *Psychological Clinic* 4 (1911): 221–238.

41 Ibid., pp. 231–232.

42 While Witmer's articles represented the clinic's viewpoint, his writings largely constituted theoretical generalizations based upon the findings of social workers, educators, and graduate students whose writings formed a large portion of the journal's commentary.

43 Ross, *G. Stanley Hall*, p. 261. My debt to Ross in this passage will be obvious to those familiar with her excellent biography. See also Robert E. Grinder, *A History of Genetic Psychology: The First Science of Human Development* (New York: John Wiley, 1967).

44 Ross, *G. Stanley Hall*, p. 371.

45 George W. Stocking, Jr., *Race, Culture, and Evolution: Essays in the History of Anthropology* (New York: Free Press, 1968), pp. 254–255.

46 Ross, *G. Stanley Hall*, p. 371.

47 Witmer, "University Courses in Psychology," *Psychological Clinic* 1 (1907): 32.

48 Witmer, "Courses in Psychology at the Summer School," pp. 259–260.

49 Witmer, "The Scope of Education," p. 239.

50 Ross, *G. Stanley Hall*, p. 350.

51 Witmer, "University Courses in Psychology," p. 32.

52 Charles E. Rosenberg has stated that after 1900 "the reformist in temperament tended, as their emotional position dictated, to disassociate behavioral characteristics entirely from a possible genetic basis." Rosenberg, *No Other Gods: On Science and American Social Thought* (Baltimore: Johns Hopkins University Press, 1976), p. 10. The clinic's social function likewise required such a dissociation in an era of hereditary determinism.

53 Witmer. "Performance and Success: An Outline of Psychology for Diagnostic Testing and Teaching," *Psychological Clinic* 12 (1919): 150.

54 See, for example, Witmer, "Clinical Records," pp. 5–6.

55 Witmer, "Courses in Psychology at the Summer School," p. 260.

56 Ibid.

57 Ibid.

58 Witmer, "Retardation Through Neglect in Children of the Rich," *Psychological Clinic* 1 (1907): 157.

59 Frontispiece, *Psychological Clinic*; Witmer, "Diagnostic Education – An Education For the Fortunate Few," ibid. 11 (1917): 70.

60 Witmer, "Courses in Psychology at the Summer School," p. 271.

61 Holmes, *Manual*, pp. 273–274.

62 Witmer, "Clinical Records," p. 2.

63 Ibid., p. 5; Witmer, "Performance and Success," p, 155.

64 Witmer, "Clinical Records," p. 6.

65 Witmer, "The Scope of Education," p. 246.

66 Witmer, "Clinical Records," p. 5.

67 Sylvester, "Clinical Psychology," p. 182; Witmer, "Performance and Success"; "On the Relation of Intelligence to Efficiency," *Psychological Clinic* 9 (1915): 61–86; Fernberger, "Statistical and Non-Statistical Interpretations of Test Results," ibid. 14 (1922): 68–72; William Filler Lutz, "The Relation of Mental to Physical Growth," ibid. 15 (1924): 125–129; Witmer, "What's Intelligence and Who Has It?" *Scientific Monthly* 15 (1922): 57–67.

68 Alice M. Jones (Rockwell), "The Superior Child," in Brotemarkle, *Clinical Psychology*, pp. 46–55.

69 I am not, of course, arguing that individualized clinical conclusions are necessarily more scientific or more accurate than longitudinal statistical ones. Nevertheless, for an amusing experimental account of how applied psychologists jump to conclusions often fortuitously correct, see H. J. Eysenck, *Uses and Abuses of Psychology* (Baltimore: Penguin Books, 1953), p. 11.

70 Haller, *Eugenics*, pp. 112–113.

71 J. E. W. Wallin, *The Odyssey of a Psychologist* (Wilmington, Delaware: by the author, 1955), p. 32.

72 William Healy, *Twenty-Five Years of Child Guidance Studies From the Institute For Juvenile Research* (Chicago: Illinois Dept. of Public Welfare, 1934), p. 46.

73 Haller, *Eugenics*, pp. 92, 101. Haller's depiction of psychological clinics as centers of eugenicist preachings is somewhat misleading in that he tends to equate clinical psychology at large with clinical psychology at Vineland. Witmer's clinic was prototypical of developments in the United States. It is hardly surprising that in a period of increasing hereditary determinism those institutions attempting remediation would tend to criticize the pessimistic implications of eugenicist thought. For synopses of the growth (and, more important, of the typology) of psychological clinics, see Theodate L. Smith, "The Development of Psychological Clinics in the United States," *Pedagogical Seminary* 21 (1914): 143–153; Wallin; "The New Clinical Psychology and the Psycho-Clinicist," *Journal of Educational Psychology* 2 (1911); 121–132, 191–210; and the American Psychological Association's Clinical Section's "Guide to the Psychological Clinics in the United States," reprinted in *Psychological Clinic* 23 (1935): 9–140.

74 The literature encompassing the furious debate between psychologists and psychiatrists in the second decade of this century is too vast to be cited here. The nature of the controversy can be apprehended from the psychologists' side in Carl E. Seashore, *Pioneering in Psychology* (Iowa City: University of Iowa Press, 1942), pp. 128–134 and from the psychiatrists' viewpoint in Moore, "A Century of Psychology in its Relationship to American Psychiatry," pp. 468–477. See also William J. Goode, "Encroachment, Charlatanism, and the Emerging Profession: Psychology, Sociology, and Medicine," *American Sociological Review* 25 (1960): 907–913; John C. Burnham, "The Struggle between Physicians and Paramedical Personnel in American Psychiatry, 1917–1941," *Journal of the History of Medical and Allied Sciences* 29 (1974): 93–106.

75 Louttit, "The Nature of Clinical Psychology," p. 372.

76 M. A. Clark, "Directory of Psychiatric Clinics in the United States," *Mental Hygiene* 20 (1936): 66–129.

77 Viteles himself discusses the linkage between clinical and industrial psychology in *Industrial Psychology* (New York: Norton, 1932), pp. 34–36. Industrial psychology has other roots; see Leonard W. Ferguson, *The Heritage of Industrial Psychology* (n. p., 1963–1965) and Loren Baritz, *Servants of Power: A History of the Use of Social Sciences in American Industry* (Middletown, Conn.: Wesleyan University Press, 1960).

78 Watson, "A Brief History of Clinical Psychology," p. 329.

79 Ibid., p. 328.

80 Witmer, "Performance and Success," p. 148.

81 Watson, "A Brief History," p. 328.

82 I have chosen to concentrate in depth on one case study. Nevertheless, even a casual reading of Wallin's descriptions of clinics elsewhere, which he gathered together in *The Mental Health of the School Child* (New Haven: Yale University Press, 1914), reinforces the conviction that many psychologists' experiences were not only analogous but very nearly identical.

Tentative Suggestions for the Certification of Practicing Psychologists
Leta S. Hollingworth

It is with pleasure that I accept the invitation of *The Journal of Applied Psychology* to participate in the symposium on qualifications for psychological experts. Since my own practical experience has been very largely in the so-called clinical field, I do not doubt that what I have to say will be conditioned to a great extent by that experience.

In the first place, there is distinction among the various fields in which psychologists serve, in spite of the fact that there is much overlapping among these fields. We have educational psychology, industrial psychology, clinical (medical) psychology, etc. Not only are these various fields to be distinguished, but upon reflection it becomes clear that they are at the present moment in different stages of development, both in regard to the preparation obtainable in the universities, and in regard to the actual demand for services to be rendered.

It is my impression that so-called clinical psychology is more advanced in many respects than are the others. Educational psychology, though well established, has devoted itself to teacher-training, rather than to the development of the expert educational psychologist; so that the latter (insofar as he can be differentiated from the clinical psychologist) is among the most recent innovations. Industrial psychology can hardly be said to be taught as yet, even in first rate university departments (Carnegie Institute for Technology being a notable exception). On the other hand, preparation for clinical psychology is now being offered in several of the large universities; the demand for psycholo-

gists in this field is steady and increasing; a national association of those already in the field has been formed; and some of the states have even set legal standards for the practice of clinical psychology.

This inequality of development in the various branches of applied psychology complicates the matter of certification of individuals. Certification in the clinical field seems feasible and necessary at this time, whereas certification in the industrial field seems impracticable.

In the present state of affairs, it seems to me that the most workable plan is to certify institutions. Let there be a standing committee of a responsible body, such as The American Psychological Association, to prepare a list of departments of psychology, where prescribed training has been made available. This list should be published annually, and printed in the report of the APA, and in the technical journals, and posted in departments of psychology. Then, for the immediate present, let the certified institutions certify individuals, by conferring upon qualified persons the prescribed diploma.

In this there would, of course, be nothing legally mandatory. Ultimately the legal certification of individuals must be brought about, but in my judgment this will not be practicable until the courses of study have been standardized, and have actually been offered for three or four years at the universities.

As to the various degrees of expertness, and the recognition of each by means of a suitable diploma, Dr. Geissler, in his initial article on the subject, distinguished three possible levels of skill. It seems to me that but one level of fitness should be certified, namely the fitness of an individual who will be an expert psychologist, with all the knowledge necessary (so far as knowledge is available) for the direction and

From L. S. Hollingworth (1918). Tentative suggestions for the certification of practicing psychologists. *Journal of Applied Psychology*, 2, 280–284.

control of human behavior. This person should earn and receive a doctor's degree in psychology, and should be given a professional diploma as Psychologist.

Many will hold that the grade of attainment represented by the master's degree (a college course and one year of specialization beyond), should be distinguished and certified. At times it seems to me that this should be done, and that some such title as Assistant Psychologist should be conferred; yet the more closely I consider the question the more convincing seem to me the arguments against certifying an inferior grade of training. Will not such certification tend to create a supply of certified inferior and hence inexpensive service, the inferiority of which will be condoned in many quarters for the sake of the inexpensiveness? Will not the distinction between Psychologist and Assistant Psychologist be too vague to function, especially since one costs much more than the other? And will not the whole purpose of the attempt at standardization be thus frustrated? For, as I conceive it, the purpose of standardization is twofold, (a) to assure the best possible quality of service to the public, and (b) to protect those who are able and willing to undertake thorough preparation against the competition of those who are unable or unwilling to undergo the same training. The accomplishment of the first purpose is inseparably bound up with the accomplishment of the second.

It may be argued that the doctor's degree in psychology is at present awarded largely on the basis of research, in our most completely equipped universities, and hence requires a higher type of intellectual capacity than is necessary for the average practitioner. To me it seems doubtful whether the average successful candidate for the doctor's degree in psychology has more intellectual ability than should be required of one who aspires to be trusted with the direction and control of human behavior. It is at least doubtful that the average ability of those who have won the doctorate in psychology during the decade just passed is higher than that of the graduates of good professional schools, such as schools of medicine and schools of engineering. As fast as really good prospects are established in applied psychology, really good people will come to qualify, – people who are fully capable of earning a doctor's degree. But prospects in applied psychology will not be good, so long as persons of mediocre qualifications occupy the field.

It has been suggested that the traditional divisions of academic training into that for the MA and that for the PhD are not very fortunate for the present purposes. The PhD is not in a strict sense a professional degree. There exists at present no degree to indicate the completion of a prescribed professional course in psychology, which does not involve intensive research, but which does involve practice in applications. It has occurred to me that perhaps the situation calls for a new departure, the "invention" of a new degree, – Doctor of Psychology, – which would involve six years of training, including college, with an additional apprenticeship year (instead of research). I think this suggestion is worth considering, as the old PhD is scarcely appropriate to many of the modern uses it is made to serve. Sooner or later it ought to fall away from the sciences through sheer weight of its irrelevancy.

As I have often stated, I am convinced by personal experience and by the experience of colleagues in the field, that it will hardly be possible for applied psychologists to succeed (in clinical practice at any rate), without the doctor's degree. The reasons why this is so probably go back, in the last analysis, to the fact that the doctor's degree has come to signify adequate skill in him who presumes to direct human welfare. Thus competing professions can and do play in many subtle ways upon the lack of a professional title, to the detriment of the psychologist's legitimate work and service. Furthermore, the general public is disinclined to accept the advice of one who lacks the title of doctor in his field. Thus the usefulness of the psychologist is materially impaired, in cases where he is not qualified with the doctor's degree. These are phases of social psychology which it is necessary to admit, in considering the matter of certification. To ignore them would be to betray ineptitude as an applied psychologist at the very outset. Either we can fall in with the social habit, or dedicate ourselves to a long and tedious process of reforming it.

This emphasis upon the importance of formal titles, certificates, degrees, etc., does not, I find, impress the academic psychologists, who have not personally experienced the limitations upon usefulness resulting from the lack of a "suitable" title out in the practical field. Thus they are inclined to urge that certification is a relatively insignificant matter, and scarcely worthy of dignified discussion. It seems to them that the only really important consideration is that the instruction shall be of first rate quality. To them it is important that the professional teacher of psychology should have the doctor's degree, but unimportant that the practical psychologist should have it. They feel, somehow, that it probably requires less training and ability actually to direct and control human behavior, than to teach how to direct and control it.

Here we see the difference in viewpoint between the pure scientist and the practitioner. This divergence is inevitable; and it is only to be expected that the majority of psychologists, whose interests are mainly in teaching and research, will not be much moved by the subject which we are here considering, *i.e.,* certificates for practitioners. The adequate solution of the problem is, nevertheless, essential to the progress of practical psychology.

Summary of Suggestions

1.   Legal certification of individuals will ultimately be necessary, but for the immediate present is scarcely feasible, owing to the unstandardized condition of curricula, and the inequality of development in the various branches of applied psychology. Standardization of curricula must *precede* legal certification of individuals.

2.   For the present, institutions should be certified. Lists of certified institutions should be published. These institutions should be charged, for the time being, with the certification of individuals, by conferring upon qualified persons the prescribed diploma.

3.   Only one grade of professional qualifications should be recognized by formal certification: persons who earn the doctor's degree, specializing in psychology as prescribed, should receive a professional diploma carrying the title, Psychologist.

4.   The suggestion is worth considering as to whether the situation does not call for an innovation, – the creation of a new professional degree, Doctor of Psychology.

Practicing School Psychology:
A Turn-of-the-Century Perspective
Thomas K. Fagan

The field of school psychology has achieved the major characteristics of professionalization: a body of knowledge that it shares with other specialties, a separate and identifiable literature, training programs with recognizable student and faculty groups, practitioner credentials, training and practice guidelines promoted through accreditation and credentialing, employment opportunities, professional associations, and codes of ethics. Just 30 years ago, school psychology's identity was much less established than it is today, and some symbols of professionalization were barely discernible. Imagine a time, however, when the practice of psychology in schools was delivered in the absence of most symbols of professional development. Just such a time occurred during the origin of school psychology from 1890 to 1920 (Fagan, 1985, 1992).

The major determinants for the development and practice of school psychology have been the value placed on childhood and the status of children, the development of general and special public education, and the experimental and professional developments in psychology and education. At the turn of the 20th century, a sense of optimism about improving society by improving the quality of its children encouraged several reforms. Historical analyses of that era of child saving reveal the shifting status of children from economic to emotional family assets (Zelizer, 1985), the growth of agencies to protect and promote child development (Cravens, 1985; Levine & Levine, 1992), and the evolution of experts (Fagan & Wise, 2000; Hiner & Hawes, 1985; Wishy, 1968). Among the agencies were

American Psychologist, 2000, 55(7), 754–757. Copyright 2000 by the American Psychological Association, Inc. Reprinted by permission of the publisher and author.

juvenile courts, public schools, and community service agencies including psychological clinics. Among the experts were persons who applied psychological knowledge to the rapidly growing system of American public education. The early practice of these experts was influenced particularly by the contributions of Lightner Witmer and G. Stanley Hall (Fagan, 1992; McReynolds, 1997).

By 1920, all states had enacted compulsory attendance laws, and the subsequent increases in school enrollment were dramatic. During the period from 1890 to 1930, the average number of days in the school year increased from 135 to 173 (a 28% increase), and the average days attended increased from 86 to 143 (an increase from 64% to 83%). Public school enrollment rose from 12.7 to 25.7 million students, including a rise in secondary enrollment from a mere 203,000 to 4,4 million (Snyder, Hoffman, & Geddes, 1997). These changes provided the circumstances under which public education required the expertise of school practitioners in the evolving areas of attendance, guidance, health, psychology, social work, and speech and hearing to facilitate structural changes in the schools, including categorical special education classes.

Early psychological practitioners worked under several titles and practiced a generic form of clinical psychology, the application of psychology to the problems of individuals. The title *school psychologist* was not in use until after 1910. School psychological services were a mix of clinical and educational psychology, both fields emerging at about the same time.[1] Some practitioners worked in community or school-based clinics along the lines of Witmer's idiographic conceptualizations of clinical psychology; others worked in school-based research bureaus along the lines of Hall's nomethetic child study and educational psychology (Fagan, 1985). Services varied considerably from individual case studies intended to alleviate the problems of selected children in their adjustment to the demands of the school, to large-scale research projects aimed at shaping school administrative practices, including the curricular demands placed on children. Both aspects of practice have persisted, although the clinical aspect dominated service delivery throughout the 20th century.

School districts soon developed systems for managing academic, behavioral, and health problem referrals. Witmer's clinic at the University of Pennsylvania served school children, but the first school-based clinic was the Chicago Public Schools' Department of Scientific Pedagogy and Child Study founded in 1899 (Slater, 1980). Clinics spread quickly to many school districts and community agencies mainly in the Northeast, Great Lakes, and West Coast states (Wallin, 1914). By 1910 a child classification scheme had evolved that in several ways resembled contemporary schemes of federal and state regulations (Van Sickle, Witmer, & Ayres, 1911). However, school children in the early part of the century were more likely to evidence speech, sensory, and health impairments (especially respiratory disorders). Thus, many early psychological referrals for academic and behavioral problems were complicated by problems of physical health. Service provision often necessitated consultation with other "experts" in vision, speech and hearing, and medicine, and it was common for large districts to employ a school physician in addition to psychologists. The extent of these mental and physical health problems is described by King (1993), Safford and Safford (1996), and Wallin (1914), and they are evident in the case records of Witmer's clinic (Levine & Wishner, 1977). Many diseases were life-threatening, and some school districts published a necrology identifying the children who had died and the cause of death. Although divorce was less common, single-parent families often resulted from the death of a parent. Perhaps our contemporary interest in the psychological needs of children is related to the comparative absence of concern about life-threatening diseases.

The following two Witmer clinic case summaries reflect the referral problems and the context of school services.[2]

1. The first case example is of a girl who was 14 years old and was in fifth grade; she had poor vision, chorea attacks, and excessive stammering. On the basis that "she will pick up a little here and there," she was advanced to fifth grade despite her problems. She was left "absolutely alone" in a class of 65–68 students. Her mother was deceased. File notes reveal concern by the teacher for having this child in class because she did very poorly and because the teacher's success was evaluated on the basis of the general class average for achievement.

2. The second case example involves a boy who was nine years old and making no progress in second grade. He had a history of accidents and illnesses; for example, he fell from bed at nine months of age and had hemorelagic measles at seven years of age. Following this, he had a discharge from the ear, for which he received treatment. Witmer referred him for medical examination. A letter from the school principal and teacher indicated that he was making no progress at school, that he screamed out in class, and that he was very active and restless. Furthermore, the letter stated that the boy was "disobedient, lies, swears, fights, steals (e.g., he stole three bananas from an old man in the street) and will not attend to his lessons."

The case records also include a comprehensive clinic interview form that investigated family history and living conditions; the child's physical appearance and apparent health; academic, perceptual, and motor status; hearing and vision; and behavioral characteristics. Some items appear in a crude checklist format, such as "Disposition: impulsive, affectionate, trustful, passionate, morose, snappish, snarly, ugly."

Cases were referred by teachers, parents, or both through the channels of the school district and usually were children in the first several years of school for suspected giftedness, mental retardation, or academic failure. Older child referrals often concerned delinquency; truancy and school dropouts were widespread concerns. Referrals of boys exceeded those of girls. Case study methods focused on the child and home and included questionnaires; observations of the child; inspection of school records; teacher, child, and parent interviews; family histories; and psycho-educational tests. The orientation was based on the conceptualizations of child development, including the comparative importance of genetics and a medical model of child disability. Later developments in psychology, including behaviorism, would spur a broader ecological model of child study (Fagan, 1995).

Instrumentation was unsophisticated by contemporary standards. For example, the Chicago school clinic used anthropometric and physical measures including height, weight, endurance, lung capacity, and cranial widths (Slater, 1980). Examinations often included reaction times, hearing, vision, motor skills, academic subjects, judgment, perception, and memory. Puzzles and form boards were in common use, as were some anthropometric instruments such as the dynamometer (to test one's strength of grip). Practitioners were forced to emphasize their skills from clinical experience owing to the general absence of norms, reliability, validity, and standardization (see, e.g., Whipple, 1914, 1915). The technical adequacy of instrumentation was meager in comparison with just a few decades later. Binet-type scales were not widely available until the Stanford revision of 1916.

Although school psychology practice has been closely related to the growth of special education, at the turn of the century, special class development was just getting started, and case study work often provided the basis on which special classes were formed. The introduction of Binet-type scales into practice facilitated the formation of special classes based on measured intelligence, and by 1920 there were several educational tests. The new technology provided a more reliable means of establishing levels of intelligence and academic achievement. Hence the evolution of special classes based on normative severity of one's disabilities became popular.

As important, the new technology was portable. The school psychologist could transport equipment with relative ease from one school to another, managing referrals on a district-wide basis. The technology and model were rapidly accepted by school officials. In what may be the most important aspect of school psychology's history, increasing numbers of psychologically trained personnel began to take full-time positions as employees of school districts. This aspect separated school psychology from other psychological practitioners and appears to have stigmatized the field as essentially public school based, functionally connected to a limited psychometric technology in a symbiotic relationship with the growth of special education. The field has never been that narrow, either in its settings or its practices. School-based employment is also associated with the stronger presence of women in school psychology than in other psychology fields, the development of school psychology as a largely nondoctoral specialty, and, often, lower salaries; a typical salary for a school psychologist in the period 1900–1920 was between $1,000 and $2,000 (Fagan, 1995). In the 1920s, the Cleveland Public Schools reported that "an individual study of a case requires from thirty minutes to over an hour to give, according to the age of the child, with an average cost of about $2.50" (Cleveland Public Schools, n.d., p. 3). The extent of formal preparation for practice in the schools at that time was highly varied (Fagan, 1999).

Despite the rapid growth of interest in school psychological work, the turn-of-the-century period for school psychology was without much formal professional development. Training programs were sparse, and none were identified specifically as school psychology. There were no state or national level organizations to serve the interests of school psychologists, no codes of practice, no training or credentialing guidelines, and no accreditation or credentialing. For all practical purposes, school psychology at the turn of the 20th century was unregulated except for the restrictions placed on it by school policies and by organized medicine (see, e.g., Wallin, 1955).

Notes

1 For historical perspectives on educational psychology, see Berliner (1993). Glover and Ronning (1987), and Walberg and Haertel (1992).

2 The summaries are from personal notes based on the early clinic records (late 1890s) available at the Archives of the History of American Psychology. University of Akron.

References

Berliner, D. C. (1993). The 100-year journey of educational psychology: From interest, to disdain, to respect for practice. In T. K. Fagan & G. R. Vanden-Bos (Eds.), *Exploring applied psychology: Origins and critical analyses* (pp. 41–78). Washington, DC: American Psychological Association.

Cleveland Public Schools. (n.d.), *Psychological clinic: Brief survey.* Cleveland, OH: Author. (Estimated to be produced in 1929).

Cravens, H. (1985). Child saving in the age of professionalism. In J. M. Hawes & N. R. Hiner (Eds.), *American childhood: A research guide and historical handbook* (pp. 415–488). Westport, CT: Greenwood Press.

Fagan, T. K. (1985). Sources for the delivery of school psychological services during 1890–1930. *School Psychology Review 14*, 378–382.

Fagan, T. K. (1992). Compulsory schooling, child study, clinical psychology, and special education: Origins of school psychology. *American Psychologist, 47,* 236–243,

Fagan, T. K. (1995). Trends in the history of school psychology in the United States. In A. Thomas & J. Grimes (Eds.), *Best practices in school psychology – III* (pp. 59–67). Washington, DC: National Association of School Psychologists.

Fagan, T. K. (1999). Training school psychologists before there were school psychologist training programs: A history – 1890–1930. In C. R. Reynolds & T. B. Gutkin (Eds.), *The handbook of school psychology* (pp. 2–33). New York: Wiley.

Fagan, T. K., & Wise, P. S. (2000). *School psychology: Past, present, and future* (2nd edn.). Bethesda, MD: National Association of School Psychologists.

Glover, J. A., & Ronning, R. R. (Eds.). (1987). *Historical foundations of educational psychology.* New York: Plenum Press.

Hiner, N. R., & Hawes, J. M. (Eds.). (1985). *Growing up in America: Children in historical perspective.* Urbana, IL: University of Illinois Press.

King, C. R. (1993). *Children's health in America: A history.* New York: Twayne.

Levine, M., & Levine, A. (1992). *Helping children: A social history.* New York: Oxford University Press.

Levine, M., & Wishner, J. (1977). The case records of the psychological clinic at the University of Pennsylvania. *Journal of the History of the Behavioral Sciences, 13,* 59–66.

McReynolds, P. (1997). *Lightner Witmer: His life and times.* Washington, DC: American Psychological Association.

Safford, P. L., & Safford, E. J. (1996). *A history of childhood and disability.* New York: Teachers College Press.

Slater, R. (1980). The organizational origins of public school psychology. *Educational Studies, 2,* 1–11.

Snyder, T. D., Hoffman, C. M., & Geddes, C. M. (1997). *Digest of educational statistics 1997.* Washington, DC: U.S. Department of Education, Office of Educational Research and Improvement.

Van Sickle, J. H., Witmer, L., & Ayres, L. P. (1911). *Provision for exceptional children in the public schools* (U.S. Bureau of Education Bulletin No. 14). Washington, DC: U.S. Government Printing Office.

Walberg, H. J., & Haertel, G. D. (1992). Educational psychology's first century. *Journal of Educational Psychology, 84,* 6–19.

Wallin, J. E. W. (1914). *The mental health of the school child.* New Haven, CT: Yale University Press.

Wallin, J. E. W. (1955). *The odyssey of a psychologist: Pioneering experiences in special education, clinical psychology, and mental hygiene with a comprehensive bibliography of the author's publications.* Wilmington, DE: Author.

Whipple, G. M. (1914). *Manual of mental and physical tests: Part 1. Simpler processes.* Baltimore: Warwick & York.

Whipple, G. M. (1915). *Manual of mental and physical tests: Part 2. Complex processes.* Baltimore: Warwick & York.

Wishy B. (1968). *The child and the republic: The dawn of modern American child nurture.* Philadelphia: University of Pennsylvania Press.

Zelizer, V. A. (1985). *Pricing the priceless child: The changing social value of children.* New York: Basic Books.

The Influence of Caffein on Mental and Motor Efficiency
Harry S. Hollingworth

Preface

In the spring of 1911 the writer was called on by the Coca-Cola Company, of Atlanta, Ga., for an opinion as to the influence of caffein on mental and motor processes. In the absence of adequate reliable data (see discussion of previous investigations) it seemed necessary to conduct a set of careful experiments before any opinion could be rendered with either fairness or certainty. Such an investigation was made possible by an appropriation by the Coca-Cola Company sufficient to cover all the expenses of the experiments. A later appropriation made possible the publication of this monograph, which presents in full the results of that investigation, a preliminary oral report of which was made by the writer in the U. S. Court at Chattanooga in March, 1911.

The writer is well aware of a popular tendency to discredit the results of investigations financed by commercial firms, especially if such concerns are likely to be either directly or indirectly interested in the outcome of the experiments. He is also aware of a similar human impulse at once to attribute interpretative bias to the investigator whose labors are supported and made possible by the financial aid of a business corporation, and hence do not represent a vicarious sacrifice of time and effort on his own part.

From the point of view of the immediate data any such bias can easily be avoided by having the measurements made and recorded by assistants who know neither the experimental conditions under which the records are being made nor the direction in which the facts may be pointing. If these data are then presented in full they may receive independent interpretation by any one who is inclined to take the pains to examine them. Such conditions were adhered to throughout the experiments to be reported here, and the immediate data are given in full. Thus in no case did any assistant know whether the measurement being made was a caffein record or a control record (see chapter on method), and separate tables are given which present all these records.

But the monograph would be relatively useless were no attempt made to interpret the data. The writer has therefore given the conclusions based on his own careful study of the records, and these conclusions are, to the best of his ability, free from all suggestion of prejudice or bias. While he was compensated for the time given to the experiments themselves and to the preliminary oral report, the considerable labor involved in preparing the results for publication is entirely his own contribution, and was undertaken on his own initiative. The invitation to direct such an investigation provided opportunity for a most valuable addition to scientific knowledge of the effects of the substance specifically studied; for a careful examination into the value of various sorts of tests for the purposes of such a study; and for the accumulation of a great mass of data on a variety of problems of intense psychological interest. To have refused the opportunity to make a useful contribution to knowledge, and to hesitate to interpret the results of the study, simply through fear of the suspicion of bias, would have been nothing less than an evasion of scientific duty.

In the light of these statements the reader must place his own estimate on the ability of the writer to free his interpretation of any suggestion of bias. The complete data are given. They have been compared from several points of view and by various methods of computation. The condi-

From H. L. Hollingworth (1912). The influence of caffein on mental and motor efficiency. *Archives of Psychology*, 22, pp. iii–iv, 6–15, 164–166. New York: Science Press.

tions of each experiment are explicitly stated. Conclusions can thus be checked up without difficulty by reference to the records themselves, or somewhat more inconveniently by a repetition of the experiments reported.

H. L. HOLLINGWORTH
COLUMBIA UNIVERSITY

Chapter II The Purpose and Method of the Experiment

Previous experiments on the influence of caffein on psychological processes have been limited to a few tests of a very limited number of individuals, and have not been carried out under sufficiently rigorous experimental conditions. The processes tested in a given experiment have been few in number, the subjects have not been on a practise level of performance, the size of the dose has not been varied over any considerable range, nor has the drug been administered unmixed with other substances which have in themselves a measurable influence on the processes tested, nor has the caffein influence been traced for any considerable length of time. Hence in making the present elaborate series of experiments the following five chief purposes were held in mind. Of these five topics the first four can be appropriately discussed in the present monograph. The fifth must be left for a future series of papers.

Purposes

1.   To determine both qualitatively and quantitatively the effect of caffein on a wide range of mental and motor processes, by studying the performance of a considerable number of individuals for a long period of time, under controlled conditions.

2.   To study the way in which this influence is modified by such factors as the age, sex, weight, idiosyncrasy and previous caffein habits of the subjects, and the degree to which it depends on the amount of the dose and the time and conditions of its administration.

3.   To investigate the influence of caffein on the general health, on the quality and amount of sleep, and on the food habits of the individuals tested.

4.   To inquire into the value and adaptability of a considerable array of simple tests with a view to their standardization for the purposes of pharmaco-dynamic research.

5.   To accumulate data on the effects of practise, fatigue, diurnal variations in efficiency, the physiological limit, individual and sex differences and various other allied topics growing out of such an extended series of tests on a large number of subjects.

Plan and procedure

In order to reduce to a minimum distractions and disturbances to which such experiments are likely to be subjected, and to provide for the greatest convenience of the experimenters and the comfort of the subjects, a well-lighted and ventilated six-room apartment on the ground floor of a building in a quiet part of the city was rented and equipped as a special Laboratory. An abundance of chairs, tables, recording materials and files was secured, and special lights, batteries and the requisite psychological apparatus installed, including two motor test boards, two Columbia chronoscopes, ten stop watches, a stethoscope, illusion weights (3 sets), test blanks and the special tests to be described later. The tests were assigned to the various rooms and each room placed in charge of a competent assistant.

Sixteen subjects, ten men and six women, were engaged for full time for a period of 40 days, and were required to appear at the laboratory at stated times during the day or to remain there permanently as the case might be, and submit themselves at regular intervals to the series of mental and motor tests. These subjects were to abstain from the use of all forms of caffein (coffee, tea, chocolate, cocoa), alcohol, nicotine and all other drugs, as well as from soda fountain drinks containing patent syrups, except in so far as these drugs were prescribed by the director or by the medical assistant. They were also to observe regular hours of eating and sleeping and to report any unavoidable irregularities in these matters. Before beginning the experiment each subject subscribed to the following agreement:

IT IS HEREBY AGREED

1.   That I will abstain from the use in any form or quantity, of tea, coffee, tobacco, chocolate aud cocoa, soda-fountain drinks containing patent syrups, alcoholic drinks (including beer) and all other such drugs, except at the prescription of the Director, so long as I shall serve as subject in this experiment.

2.   That I will observe regular hours of eating and sleeping during the same period, taking my meals at the hours to be later prescribed by the Director.

3.   That I will exert myself in every trial of every test to make the best and speediest record possible for me.

4.   That I will conscientiously report to the medical adviser the condition of my health from day to day, along with any other items concerning which information may be desired.

5.   That I will serve as subject in this experiment for as many of forty days as my assistance may be desired.

6.   That I will appear regularly and promptly at the test hours.

7.   That I will observe all other reasonable instructions which the Director may from time to time suggest for the good of the experiment.

8.   That the failure to observe these instructions and conditions to the satisfaction of the Director shall be deemed sufficient reason for forfeiting all compensation for any service I may have rendered up to that time and for terminating my connection with the experiment.

9.   That I will if desired, at the close of the experiment, take oath before a notary public that I have lived up to the conditions of this agreement.
Signed,

The experiment as performed consists of three separate sections.

A.   A series of tests covering a period of four weeks, in which all the subjects went through the tests five times a day (each time requiring about one hour) at 7:45 and 10:00 a.m. and at 12:15, 3:10 and 5:30 p.m. This arrangement left about one hour between tests, during which time the subjects were free to go about their own work or to remain in the laboratory reading, sewing, etc. During the first week, in order to allow all subjects to get perfectly adapted to the experiment and to become practised in the tests, sugar of milk doses were given to all individuals daily.

After this week the caffein doses began. The subjects were then divided into four squads. To one squad (I) consisting of four subjects, no caffein was administered throughout the experiment, but the control capsule, containing sugar of milk, was given daily. A second squad (II) consisting of three subjects, alternated throughout the experiment, taking caffein on three days and sugar of milk on the following three days, at 10:30 a.m. This squad lunched between one and two o'clock. The caffein dose varied from one to six grains, the same amount being taken on each of a given set of three caffein days. A third squad (III) consisting of three subjects, took caffein and sugar of milk on alternate days, at the lunch hour, the dose varying from one to six grains. Squad IV consisting of five subjects took caffein and sugar of milk on alternate days from two and half to three hours after lunch, which was, in these cases, at 11:30 a.m. (For details concerning the character of the doses and the methods of administering them, see a later section of this chapter).

B.   The second section, an intensive experiment of three days, was performed in order to study at close range the effect of caffein on the various processes tested, and to determine its time relations in the various cases and with the different subjects and squads. In this experiment the plan was followed of having all the subjects assemble at the laboratory at 10:00 a.m. At this hour the tests were begun and were kept up continuously for about 12 hours, except for two 45-minute periods allowed for lunch and dinner. All subjects ate at the same place at lunch and dinner of these three days, in order to eliminate variations due to differences in diet, condition of stomach, and to exercise going to and from the laboratory. The meals were prepared and eaten in the house in which the laboratory was situated. By this means the action of the doses could be traced at close range, since all subjects returned repeatedly to the same test after having just passed through all the others in immediate succession. Fifteen records for each subject were thus secured to each test on each of the three days.

The same subjects were used as in the first section of the experiment, except that one man and one woman were absent throughout. These subjects were, then, all trained and practically on their practise level in the tests, having perfected themselves by the 140 trials during the preceding four weeks' experiment. In this section the subjects were again divided into four squads. Squad I took caffein along with soda fountain syrup and carbonated water, after the 6th trial on the 1st and 3d days, and a sugar of milk capsule at the same time on the 2d day. Squad II served as a control squad. On the first two days they took only sugar of milk capsules, but on the last day, after the 6th trial, they took 3 gr. of caffein, which was followed by 2 gr. more about an hour and a half after the evening meal, Squad III took 3 gr. of caffein on the 1st day, after the 6th trial. On the two remaining days they took only sugar capsules, the object being to trace the action of the original dose for at least three days after taking. Squad IV took 6 gr. of caffein on the first day, and only sugar capsules on the days following, the object being here, as in Squad III, to trace the action of the first dose during the following two days.

C. The third section of the experiment was designed to determine the effect of caffein when taken along with food substance in the form of syrup such as is commonly contained in soda fountain drinks, and to compare this effect with the action of the syrup when taken with no caffein ingredient. This experiment occupied 7 days. On two of these days no dose was administered to the subjects. These are called blank days, and they show what sort of performance one may expect in the tests employed when thoroughly practised subjects are used and no drug of any kind taken. On two other days all the subjects took doses of any syrup, served with carbonated water so as to enable the effects of simple sensory stimulation to become apparent. On the remaining three days the same syrup was served in the same way, except that 1.2 grains of caffein alkaloid were added to each glass of the drink. On one day 1 glass of the caffeinated syrup was given to all subjects 15 minutes before beginning the tests at the 3:10 period. On another day 3 glasses and on the third day 5 glasses were given, the three amounts thus containing 1.2, 3.6 and 6.0 grains of caffein.

The tests during this third section of the experiment were held five times a day, as in section 1, and at the same time of day. When the one glass dose was taken it was served just before

the 3:10 test. In the other cases a dose was taken before each of the afternoon tests. As subjects in this section, twelve of the persons used in the tests of the previous month were used. They were hence practised in all the tests, thoroughly familiar with the method of procedure and perfectly adjusted to the experimental conditions. The whole group of 12 acted as a single squad, so that all received the same dose at the same time of day. The subjects in no case knew whether they were taking the plain or the caffeinated syrup. In fact they knew nothing about the character of the dose except that the experiment was to determine the effects of soda fountain syrups on mental and motor processes.

Subjects

In going through the tests at the appointed hour the subjects came to the various rooms in squads of three, the identity of the squads being permanent throughout a given section of the experiment. The tests were so distributed in the various rooms and among the various assistants that all the five squads would complete their tests in the respective rooms at approximately the same time. At a whistle signal on the part of the director the squads shifted from room to room, and so on through the five shifts which completed the hour's work. Each subject was given a number by which he or she was known throughout the experiment, and by which reference to individuals will be made in the chapters to follow. The following table gives the number and name of all the subjects, along with their age, sex, weight, occupation, previous caffein habits, and the squad to which each belonged in Section 1 and Section 2 of the experiment. The writer wishes at this point to acknowledge his obligation to these subjects for their faithfulness and zeal throughout the experiment.

Doses and their administration

Many sources of error exist, in such experiments, in the character of the dose and in the way in which it is administered. The principal dangers have been so clearly pointed out by Rivers that I can do no better than quote, at this point, the following important paragraphs from his chapter on the action of drugs.

"I can now pass to a feature of method . . . designed to eliminate the influence of certain psychical factors which have undoubtedly been allowed to affect the results of nearly all who have experimented on the action of drugs. Many of these workers have considered the possibility that their results may have been influenced by suggestion, or of bias towards results which were to be expected theoretically, and some have shown that effects similar to those following the administration of a drug may be the consequence of the administration of a wholly inactive substance which is supposed by the subject to be the drug in question. Few, however, have adopted the obvious precautions which such considerations suggest (that of using a control substance).

"The factor which previous writers have considered under the title of 'suggestion' is far from being the only source of error work on the action of drugs. Feré has shown that the sensory stimulation involved in the act of taking a drug into the mouth and swallowing it may have a very decided effect on the amount of work executed

on the ergograph, but even this knowledge did not lead him to adopt any control in his numerous researches on drugs.

"There is however another factor which is probably more important than either sensory stimulation or suggestion, viz., the interest and excitement produced by taking a substance when the discovery of its effect is the motive of the whole experiment. . . . If such a condition of interest as that arising from its being the first or last day of an experiment, or that resulting from the view of the weight rising as the finger contracts, can have very appreciable effects on the amount of work, it is clear that so interesting an occurrence as the administration of a drug must have a decided influence and the interest so aroused will probably be equally great whether the nature of the drug is unknown, so that there is an element of mystery in the occurrence, or whether its nature is known.

"A difficulty which arises in drug experiments is due to the practise of taking as part of the normal diet substances which have an effect on the capacity for work; and this difficulty becomes

Table 1 The subjects

No.	Name	Age	Weight	M – Male F – Female	Occupation	Caffein Habits	Squad Sec. 1	Squad Sec. 2
1	C. R. A.	39	?	M	Teacher	Regular	I.	II.
2	E. A. B.	38	?	F	Wife of College Instructor	Regular	Worked alone at typewriting	
3	A. E. C.	39	159	F	Wife of Graduate Student	Abstainer	III.	IV.
4	H. W. E.	19	124	M	Student	Moderate	I.	I.
5	R. N. G.	33	105	F	Wife of Teacher	Regular	IV.	—
6	W. A. J.	33	125	F	Wife of College Instructor	Regular	IV.	III.
7	S. A. F.	19	153	M	Student	Moderate	I.	II.
8	C. L. L.	24	144	M	Graduate Student	Regular	II.	III.
9	A. M. McC.	21	130	M	Student	Abstainer	III.	III.
10	C. H. N.	28	157	M	Law Student	Occasional	IV.	IV.
11	F. C. R.	27	110	F	Wife of Graduate Student	Abstainer	IV.	I.
12	K. E. R.	24	160	M	Graduate Student	Regular	II.	III.
13	V. H. R.	22	175	M	Student	Regular	II.	—
14	B. E. S.	27	193	M	Graduate Student	Occasional	III.	IV.
15	S. R. S.	34	108	F	Wife of College Instructor	Occasional	I.	II.
16	T. W. V.	24	174	M	Law Student	Regular	IV.	III.

especially great when it is one of these drugs which is the subject of the experiment.

"If the use of the active substance is only given up shortly before the commencement of the experiments, there is a further danger. Even in those who only take such a substance in moderate amounts, its disuse is probably followed in some degree by the craving which is so pronounced after discontinuance of large amounts, and, slight and hardly noticeable as this craving may be, it may yet be sufficient to produce an obvious effect when the article of which the person has been deprived is administered experimentally. The effect of the substance given experimentally may be the result, not of it normal physiological action, but of the satisfaction of the craving.

"In carrying out an experiment of this kind, extending over a number of days, it is essential that all the conditions of life be kept as constant as possible. The same amount of sleep must be taken every night, the meals must be of the same kind and at the same times every day, the same amount of exercise must be taken, and the same amount of other work done." (Rivers, "The Influence of Alcohol and Other Drugs on Fatigue," pp. 15–21.)

In the present experiment an attempt was made to take account of all the sources of error pointed out in this excellent analysis. The first error was avoided by administering, on days known only to the director, an inactive substance (sugar of milk) in the same manner and at the same time that the caffein doses were given on the remaining days. These days were not the same for all the subjects, and the result was that neither the subjects going through the tests nor the assistants who were making the measurements and records knew at any time whether the record was being made under the influence of caffein or of the inactive control substance.

In order to make the two substances completely indistinguishable and to reduce to a minimum the factor of sensory stimulation, the doses were administered in capsule form (except in a few test cases specified in the text). The caffein and the control substance presented the same appearance and neither substance was ever tasted. In some cases the capsule was taken along with a drink of water, but in most cases no such assistance was required.

The fact that the caffein days were thus unrecognizable helped to reduce the disturbing influence of excitement and interest. These factors were further reduced by running all subjects for one week on control doses only (quite without their knowledge, of course). This procedure not only served to get the subjects adapted to the conditions of the experiment before the drug doses began, but at the same time brought their performance to a more uniform practise level. Since all subjects gave up the use of all drugs three days before the experiments began, this additional week gave an interval of 10 days in which those who had previously used caffein might become adapted to its discontinuance.

It has already been stated that all the subjects conformed to a fixed routine of time of meals, hour of retiring, amount of work, etc., so far as this was possible. And during the intensive experiment, in order to perfect this routine, all the subjects were fed at the same table and spent the whole day in the laboratory.

As a further check on the character and quality of the drug used, two commercial brands of caffein were administered and the records of administration of doses distinguished between these two brands. One of these (Schaeffer's) was identified and prepared in capsule form by the prescription department of Eimer and Amend, wholesale druggists in New York City. The other brand (Mallinckrodt's) was taken directly from the stock of the same firm. No difference was found in the action of the two brands, but the facts are given here simply as a point in the general technique of the experiment.

Supplementary information

Through fixed routine of life on the part of the subjects, by the maintenance of uniform temperature in the laboratory, etc., it was endeavored to keep the conditions of the experiment as constant as possible. But no amount of precaution can perfectly control the conditions to which an organism is subject throughout a period of 40 days. In order to supplement these precautions, and for the personal information of the director and the convenience of the medical adviser, the results coming from the tests were further checked up by daily memoranda recorded by each subject throughout the experiment. Each individual kept a "daily health book," in which record was made of the condition of health and spirits in both forenoon and afternoon. Any unusual indications, symptoms, etc., were noted, the hour of appearance and the continuance of these indications, and their character in detail stated. This account was of course purely introspective. Any outside circumstances of an unusual or disturbing character were also reported. The approximate number of hours sleep was recorded after each night, and the quality of sleep classified as *better than usual, ordinary*, or *worse than usual*. In the case of the female subjects the beginning and end of the menstrual period were also noted. The hearts of these subjects were also examined stethoscopically at the beginning of the experiment by the medical assistant.

At the close of the complete experiment each subject was requested to reply to the following questionnaire:

QUESTIONNAIRE

(To be answered by all subjects in the book provided)

1.   If before the experiment began you were accustomed to the use of coffee, tea, tobacco or any form of alcohol, have you found yourself missing or longing for any of these during the past five weeks, or have you been able to go without them without any desire or discomfort? Specify concerning each of the substances mentioned. Explain as fully as possible with reference to coffee and tea in particular.

2.   On the whole do you find yourself in better or worse general condition of health, spirits and general efficiency, or do you notice any change at all? What was your weight when the experiment began? What is it now?

3.   Have you at any time during the experiment read up in any kind of treatise a discussion of the supposed effects of caffein on mental and physiological processes, or in any other way made such inquiry? If so, do you think that knowledge or suggestion thus acquired has in any way influenced your health reports, or suggested special symptoms which you might otherwise have ignored? Kindly discuss this as fully as possible.

4.   Will you kindly discuss each of the following tests to the best of your ability, giving as much information as possible, from your own observation and self-examination, on the questions which follow the list of tests. All that you can say here with certainty,

and with no attempt at mere guessing will be much appreciated.

Color-naming Test,	Weight Test,
Naming Opposites,	Discrimination Reaction,
Calculation Test,	Tapping Test,
Cancellation Test,	Steadiness Test.
Three-hole Test,	

(*a*)   What particular difficulties did you have with the test in the beginning? Did you overcome these difficulties in any conscious way which you can here describe or did you just happen upon the better method quite unexpectedly and unconsciously?

(*b*)   On days when you did not seem to be able to do the test as well as usual, what seemed to be the difficulty? Were you able to overcome this difficulty in any way on the days in question or did it simply stay and go away later of its own accord?

(*c*)   If in the course of the experiment you came to change your method of doing the test from time to time will you kindly describe these changes, tell in what they consisted, what suggested them, and whether they proved better or worse than the original methods. Did your chief improvement come from simple practise and repetition, from observing the better methods employed by others, by deliberately trying improvements of your own, or by accidentally happening upon better methods? Explain in each case as fully and clearly as you can.

Kindly answer the above questions as fully as you can, for each of the tests.

5.   Have you at any time during the experiment been able to know whether you were taking caffein or not, in your capsules, at the time of taking? This does not mean, of course, after any effect which the substance may have had begun to show itself. If so, kindly state how and when.

6.   Will you kindly state at this point whether or not you have conformed to all the requirements concerning sleep, diet and regular habits which you agreed to observe throughout the experiment.

The tests

The tests employed have been briefly enumerated in the preceding questionnaire. Each will be described in detail in the appropriate chapters of the following discussion of results. Except in the case of the size-weight illusion and in that of the steadiness test, the quality and quantity of the performance remained constant and the measurement was made in terms of the time of performance (speed). A rough record was made at the time of the test and this record was subsequently copied into a final book and a duplicate of this book made. The individual records were then averaged in various ways, and these averages placed in separate books. The averages of the various squads were also computed and recorded separately. These five methods of recording were adhered to in all the tests, by all the assistants. No assistant was aware of the records made at any time by any of the subjects in any test save those of which he was in charge. Except for a weekly announcement of the best five records in each test, the subjects themselves knew nothing concerning the record they were making except in so far as this knowledge was based on their own opinion of their performance.

Assistants

The writer's appreciation of the splendid service rendered by the following corps of assistants is here gladly expressed.

LABORATORY ASSISTANTS

Leta Stetter Hollingworth, A.B., Assistant Director.
Miss L. G. Stevenson, A.B., M.D., Assistant and Medical Adviser.
Miss Margaret Tower Hart, A.B., Assistant Experimental Psychology, Barnard College.
A. E. Chrislip, A.B., M.A., Candidate for Ph.D. in Psychology, Columbia University.
A. J. Culler, A.B., Candidate for Ph.D. in Psychology, Columbia University.
E. K. Strong, Jr., A.B., M.A., Ph.D., Fellow in Psychology, Columbia University.

Chapter XV Conclusion

The results for each test have been briefly summarized at the close of the chapters. No attempt need be made to restate these conclusions here except perhaps by way of a schematic review of all the tests. Such a review is presented in the following tabular summary. Such a summary is of course wholly inadequate to express the significant facts which the various chapters have brought forward. Its chief interest comes from the assemblage of the various tests in groups, the groups being roughly designated by the psychological process or function which is especially prominent in the performance of the tests included in the group. It is clear at once that the caffein influences all the tests in a given group in much the same way. The effect on motor processes comes quickly and is transient. The effect on higher mental processes comes more slowly and is more persistent. Whether this result is due to quicker reaction on the part of motor nerve centers, or whether it is due to a direct peripheral effect on the muscle tissue, the pure psychologist can hardly be expected to know. Physiological experiment, however, seems to indicate that caffein has a direct effect on the muscle tissue, and that this effect is fairly rapid in appearance. The physiology of absorption also explains the fact that the presence of food substance in the stomach retards and reduces the caffein influence. The dependence of the amount of the caffein influence on the body weight of the individual has already been explained in terms of the amount of the substance ingested per unit of tissue affected.

One of the most interesting facts shown by these experiments is the complete absence of any traces of secondary depression or of any sort of secondary reaction consequent upon the stimulation which is so strikingly present in many of the tests. Rivers' conclusion, already referred to, that "caffein increases the capacity for both muscular and mental work, ... without there being any evidence, with moderate doses, of reaction leading to diminished capacity for work," is thoroughly confirmed by the results of all the present experiments. This result is quite in contrast with the secondary reaction said to follow stimulation by such a drug as strychnine. It must be said that our present knowledge concerning the precise mode of action of drugs on nervous tissue is very inadequate. That the increased capacity for work is produced is clearly demonstrated. That this result is a genuine drug effect, and not merely the effect of excitement, interest, sensory stimulation, expectation or suggestion, the carefully controlled tests here reported prove beyond any possible doubt. But whether this increased capacity comes from a new supply of energy introduced or rendered available by the drug action, or whether energy already available comes to be employed more effectively, or whether the inhibition of secondary afferent impulses is eliminated, or whether fatigue sensations are weakened and the individual's standard of performance thereby raised, no one seems to know. The interpretation is obscure but the facts are plain.

Schematic summary of all results

St. = *Stimulation.*   0 = *No effect.*   Ret. = *Retardation*

Process	Tests	Primary Effect			Secondary Reaction	Action Time, Hours	Duration in Hours
		Small Doses	Medium Doses	Large Doses			
Motor speed	1. Tapping	St.	St.	St.	None	.75–1.5	2–4
Coordination	2. Three-hole	St.	0	Ret.	None	1–1.5	3–4
	3. Typewriting						
	(*a*) Speed	St.	0	Ret.	None	Results show only in
	(*b*) Errors . . . . .Fewer for all doses.				None	total days' work.
Association	4. Color-naming	St.	St.	St.	None	2–2.5	3–4
	5. Opposites	St.	St.	St.	None	2.5–3	Next day
	6. Calculation	St.	St.	St.	None	2.5	Next day
Choice	7. Discrimination-reaction time . . . . .Ret.		0	St.	None	2–4	Next day
	8. Cancellation . . . . Ret.		?	St.	None	3–5	No data
	9. S-W illusion 0		0	0			
General	10. Steadiness . . . .?		Unsteadiness		None	1–3	3–4
	11. Sleep quality . . . . . . ⎫ Individual differences depending on body					2?	
	12. Sleep quantity . . . . . . ⎬ weight and condition of						
	13. General health . . . . ⎭ administration.						

The widespread consumption of caffeinic beverages under circumstances in which and by individuals for whom the use of other drugs is stringently prohibited or decried seems to be justified by the results of experiment. But it should be emphasized that the results of the investigation here reported bear only on the more or less immediate effects of caffein on performance. It is true that the investigation as a whole covered a period of 40 days, and that in the intensive experiment the effect of single doses was traced for a period of 3 days. But the results can not be carried over bodily to the question of the continuous use of the drug. One can only assume that if the constant use of caffein in moderate amounts would prove deleterious, some indication of such effect would have shown itself in the careful study of performance in tests covering a wide range of mental and motor processes, a wide range of doses and of individuals, and of time and conditions of administration. Nor can any-

thing be said, on the basis of these results, concerning the physiological or neurological effect of caffein, except in so far as integrity of structure can be inferred from unimpaired function or performance.

It should be further pointed out that the quantitative results of this investigation of the influence of caffein in its pure form can not be directly compared with the action of its citrated form, which is only half caffein, the remainder being citric acid which itself has a demonstrable action on nerve and muscle tissue. Much the same thing is true of the action of tea, coffee, and other caffeinic beverages, which contain a variety of other substances which may be supposed to enhance or neutralize or otherwise modify the effect of the caffein content.[1] Many of the results commonly attributed to these beverages undoubtedly come, in so far as they can be demonstrated at all under controlled conditions, from these non-caffein ingredients.

Note

1 The average cupful of hot tea (black, 5 fluid ounces) contains about 1.5 gr. of caffein. About the same amount is present in the average after-dinner cup of black coffee (2 fluid ounces). An average glass of cold green tea (8 ounces exclusive of ice) contains about 2 grains, while an average cupful of coffee with hot milk (5 ounces, three fifths coffee and the rest milk) contains about 2.5 grains of caffein.

Coca-Cola, Caffeine, and Mental Deficiency: Harry Hollingworth and the Chattanooga Trial of 1911

Ludy T. Benjamin, Jr., Anne M. Rogers, and Angela Rosenbaum

On 20 October 1909, agents of the United States Government stopped a truck outside of Chattanooga, Tennessee, and under federal authority over interstate commerce, seized its freight. The contraband consisted of forty barrels and twenty kegs of Coca-Cola syrup on its way from the headquarters plant in Atlanta, Georgia, to the principal bottling plant in Chattanooga. The seizure was directed from Washington, D.C., under the recently passed Federal Food and Drug Act (1906), commonly known as the Pure Food and Drug Act. In the lawsuit that was to follow, the Coca-Cola Company would be charged with marketing and selling an adulterated beverage that was injurious to health because it contained a deleterious ingredient, namely, caffeine.

In early 1911 the Coca-Cola Company was preparing its defense for the upcoming trial in Chattanooga, only several months away, when Hobart Amory Hare, a noted physician, toxicologist, medical textbook author on the faculty of Jefferson Medical College in Philadelphia, and head of Coca-Cola's team of scientific experts, realized that they had almost no evidence on the behavioral effects of caffeine on human beings. He proposed that a psychologist be hired to conduct the needed research and asked a friend, Dickinson Miller, who taught philosophy and psychology at Columbia University, for a recommendation. Miller suggested Columbia's eminent psychologist, James McKeen Cattell, who declined.

Others may have been approached subsequent to Cattell, but eventually the offer fell to Harry Levi Hollingworth (1880–1956), a young instructor at Barnard College who had completed his doctorate in psychology with Cattell two years earlier. Hollingworth accepted this questionable assignment because, as he described it, he "had as yet no sanctity to preserve."[1] Writing in 1940 in an unpublished autobiography he recalled this decision:

> Here was a clear case where results of scientific importance might accrue to an investigation that would have to be financed by private interests. No experiments on such a scale as seemed necessary for conclusive results had ever been staged in the history of experimental psychology. . . .
>
> With me there was a double motive at work. I needed money, and here was a chance to accept employment at work for which I had been trained, with not only the cost of the investigation met but with a very satisfactory retaining fee and stipend for my own time and services. I believed I could conscientiously conduct such an investigation, without prejudice to the results, and secure information of a valuable scientific character as well as answer the practical questions raised by the sponsor of the study.[2]

As 1911 began, Harry Hollingworth certainly needed money. He was in his second year of teaching at Barnard earning an annual salary of $1,000, the same salary he had received the previous year.[3] Like many new faculty, especially those living in Manhattan, his standard of living was meager and he looked for ways to ameliorate that situation. He had married his college classmate from Nebraska, Leta Stetter, in 1908. She had hoped to teach as she had done for the past two years in Nebraska, and thus provide a much-

L. T. Benjamin, Jr., A. M. Rogers, & A. Rosenbaum (1991). Coca-Cola, caffeine, and mental deficiency: Harry Hollingworth and the Chattanooga trial of 1911. *Journal of the History of the Behavioral Sciences*, 27, 42–55. Copyright 1991 John Wiley and Sons, Inc. Reprinted by permission of the publisher.

needed second income. However, New York City barred married women from teaching.

Leta Hollingworth, who had graduated first in her class at the University of Nebraska, hoped to pursue graduate work but they lacked the money to do so.[4] Borrowing from their families was an impossibility because both families had less than modest incomes. So Leta kept house, shopped, cooked, sewed her own clothes and some of her husband's, and wrote short stories that she was unsuccessful in selling to magazines. Harry worked extra jobs, such as proctoring exams for fifty cents an hour, and for a while, he taught in the night school of Columbia University until the administration discovered that he was on the payroll twice and made him resign his evening faculty job. He also had begun to give workshops on the psychology of advertising to members of the Men's Advertising League of New York City.[5] Thus extra funds accumulated. Yet just when there seemed enough for Leta Hollingworth to begin graduate study, a family need in Nebraska would arise that would exhaust all of their savings. Referring to their desire for Leta to pursue her own intellectual pursuits, Harry wrote, ". . . it did not yet appear how soon, if ever, it was going to be her turn to get her feet on the glory road."[6]

The offer from Coca-Cola proved to be a windfall for the Hollingworths. The exact sum of the contract is not known although it must have been a substantial amount. It funded Harry as director of the studies and Leta as assistant director, and according to Harry, assured all of Leta's graduate school expenses.[7]

Despite his desperate need of money in 1911, Harry Hollingworth was nevertheless cautious about undertaking this research for Coca-Cola. He was clearly aware of the stigma attached to applied work, and the "unclean" nature of those efforts had been made apparent in reactions from colleagues to his earlier work on the psychology of advertising with the New York City business community.[8] However, the hesitancy in the case of this research was more than just its applied nature; there was concern about scientific integrity raised by a large company spending a lot of money for research it hoped would be favorable to its legal and commercial needs.

According to Hollingworth, he sought to minimize that concern in his contractual arrangement with the Coca-Cola Company. The contract specified that Hollingworth would be allowed to publish the results of his studies regardless of their outcome. Further, Coca-Cola was not to use the results of the research in its advertising, nor was there to be any mention of Hollingworth's name or that of Columbia University in any promotion of Coca-Cola.[9] Still, he was aware that the questions surrounding integrity would not go away. In the preface to his published report of the research he wrote:

> The writer is well aware of a popular tendency to discredit the results of investigations financed by commercial firms, especially if such concerns are likely to be either directly or indirectly interested in the outcome of the experiments. He is also aware of a similar human impulse at once to attribute interpretive bias to the investigator whose labors are supported and made possible by the financial aid of a business corporation, and hence do not represent a vicarious sacrifice of time and effort on his own part.[10]

He hoped to reduce the potential for claims of bias in the research by instituting a series of experimental controls, including blind and double-blind conditions.

Harvey Wiley and the Fight for Pure Food

The urgent necessity of Hollingworth's research and the Coca-Cola trial had come about largely because of the efforts of one man, a sixty-five-year-old chemist and long-time federal government bureaucrat – Harvey Washington Wiley (1844–1930).[11] In 1911 he was serving as Chief of the Bureau of Chemistry for the U.S. Department of Agriculture. He had gone to Washington in 1883 to join the bureau as a chemist, leaving a joint position as professor at Purdue University and chief chemist for the state of Indiana.

A trip to Germany in 1878 interested Wiley in the chemistry of food, specifically the adulteration of food. His first published report in that field, in 1881, concerned the adulteration of syrups with glucose.[12] From his post in Washington, Wiley assumed the leadership of a national effort to establish a federal law that would protect consumers from foods that were mislabeled, falsely advertised, and most important, adulterated with substances that were injurious to health. With the fervor and zeal of his strict religious upbringing, he stumped the country for the needed legislation – "every rostrum [became] a pulpit for the gospel of pure food."[13]

Wiley became a powerful figure in the federal government gathering much support from an admiring public who viewed him as their protector in Washington. He also enjoyed strong support from sections of agriculture and the food industry. However, he also had opponents, some of whom opposed him on business grounds and others who felt he had ceased being a scientist in his passion for pure foods.[14] Nevertheless, his efforts were finally rewarded on 30 June 1906 when Theodore Roosevelt signed the Pure Food and Drug Act. The bill was the result of more than twenty years of campaigning by Wiley and others, and it passed, not surprisingly, with considerable opposition. Its detractors often referred to the new law as "pure foolishness."[15]

Some of Wiley's opponents believed that his pursuit of the Coca-Cola Company was revenge against the South from whence had come the largest Congressional opposition to the passage of the pure food act. By 1910, Coca-Cola was sold in every state and territory and was, arguably, the most successful industry in the post-Reconstruction South. Thus it was a very visible target.[16] However, there seems little evidence to support a motive of vengeance. Instead, Wiley's actions can be more plausibly traced to a longstanding distaste for caffeine and his belief that it poisoned the body. As a twenty-year-old member of the Indiana Volunteers, his Civil War diary contains the following passage: "Passed outside the lines today and exchanged coffee for milk. [I am] in much better condition since I quit drinking coffee. . . ."[17]

As early as 1902, Wiley had testified before Congress that caffeine was a poison and a habit-forming drug.[18] Although he was not a proponent of coffee or tea, he was willing to tolerate public consumption of those beverages because the caffeine was a natural part of those drinks. However, caffeine was an additive in Coca-Cola which made it a beverage adulterated with a harmful ingredient. Moreover, he objected to Coca-Cola because, unlike coffee or tea, it was marketed and sold to children. He conducted investigations of Coca-Cola consumption that convinced him that there were Coca-Cola addicts. For Wiley, Coca-Cola was a serious health threat to the American public and the new law made it possible, he thought, to eradicate such products.

Wiley wanted to bring the Coca-Cola Company to court in early 1907, shortly after the Pure Food and Drug Act became law. However, he was blocked by Secretary of Agriculture James Wilson who ordered him to cease his investigations of Coca-Cola. When, in 1909, an Atlanta newspaper editor threatened to publish a story that Wilson was protecting Coca-Cola, Wilson withdrew his order. Wiley began working with the Justice Department to plan the seizure and subsequent case.[19]

The two principal charges in the suit against Coca-Cola were that it was mislabeled because it contained negligible or nonexistent quantities of either coca or cola and, of greatest significance, that it contained an *added* ingredient, caffeine, that was injurious to health. Wiley's principal objection to caffeine was its function as a stimulant. He wrote:

> . . . stimulation means increased exertion. . . . All increased energy implies increased consumption of tissue and fuel. Fatigue is nature's danger signal, to show that muscles, brain, nerves, et cetera, need rest and recreation. Any drug that strikes down the danger signal without removing the danger must of necessity be a threat. The thing to do when one is tired is to rest, to sleep, and to take real food. The thing not to do is to take a drug that makes one forget he is tired.[20]

Wiley was particularly incensed by Coca-Cola's advertisements touting the stimulant properties of the beverage. One claimed that the drink could be used to "invigorate the fatigued body and quicken the tired brain." Another said it "relieves mental and physical exhaustion." Although marketed largely as a beverage, and not a drug, advertising often conveyed the latter in proclaiming Coca-Cola as "the ideal brain tonic."[21]

Harry Hollingworth's Caffeine Studies

Hollingworth was not the first psychologist to investigate the behavioral effects of caffeine; however, the earlier research was inadequate on one or two grounds: (a) the studies concentrated largely on motor responses with little or no attention to cognitive processes, and (b) the studies did not use appropriate experimental controls.[22] The Coca-Cola Company believed it had adequate data about the effects of caffeine on human physiology; instead, it was looking for evidence of caffeine's effects on mental functioning. Specifically, was there any mental deficiency associated with its use, at least in terms of the quantities of caffeine that might be consumed by a drinker of Coca-Cola?

When Hollingworth was contacted to conduct the research, the trial date in Chattanooga was a little more than two months away. Thus the time pressures were considerable. Yet Hollingworth planned an extensive series of studies to run for approximately forty days, employing a scope of testing and a sophistication of methodology that had not been seen before in applied psychology. It is not surprising that Hollingworth was an excellent student of experimental method given that his graduate school mentors were Cattell, Edward L. Thorndike, and Robert S. Woodworth.

Clearly Cattell had some influence on the Hollingworth research, either directly or indirectly. The research design called for ten different major tests and a score of minor ones. Many of these were tests that had been recommended by Cattell for mental measurement.[23] Some were motor tests that measured speed, steadiness, and coordination. But most of the tests involved mental measurements in tasks of perception, association, attention, judgment, and discrimination, for example, color naming, identifying word opposites, mental calculations, and discrimination reaction times. These tests were selected to measure mental processes alone and in combination with other mental and motor processes.

Some tests combined several cognitive processes at once, for example, the cancellation test that combined attention and discrimination. In this test, subjects were given a sheet of paper with twenty rows of numbers, fifty numbers in each row. All digits from 0 to 9 were represented an equal number of times in a random order. The subjects were instructed to cross out all 7s on the page, beginning the task in the upper left hand corner of the page and proceeding systematically down the columns from that point. Thus it was possible to measure the accuracy of performance over time as well as the speed of the task. This test was selected largely because of its use as a measure of mental fatigue, and Hollingworth used it at varying intervals following caffeine administra-

tion to determine the period of effectiveness of the drug.[24]

The laboratory for this study was a six-room Manhattan apartment, rented specifically for this research. The kitchen was used to prepare the dosages, and several rooms were equipped with some of the specialized apparatus used in the testing. Sixteen subjects were selected, ten men and six women, ranging in age from nineteen to thirty-nine. They were selected to be a cross-section of the age group that made up most of Coca-Cola's consumers. Further, they were selected because of their normal caffeine consumption habits, and were classified as abstainers, occasional users, moderate users, and regular users.

Subjects were paid for their participation in the research and had to sign an agreement listing nine conditions to which they would adhere throughout the course of the study. These included prohibitions against any caffeine or alcohol usage during the study, except that administered as part of the research. A physician was hired to take periodic measurements on the subjects during the course of the study. All subjects kept daily records on their level of alertness, other measures of general health, and on the amount and placement of their sleep.

The research actually involved three separate studies. The first, and longest, began on 3 February 1911 and lasted four weeks. Subjects went through all the principal tests five times per day. The first testing began at 7:45 each morning and the last began at 5:30 in the afternoon. With Harry at his daily routine at Barnard, Leta Hollingworth was in charge of the research. Five different experimental stations existed in the apartment, each staffed by a different experimenter. Subject groups rotated among the experimental stations in a testing period until all five had been completed. Each testing station required about an hour to complete and all testing orders were counterbalanced over the course of the studies. Between testing periods, subjects relaxed, read, sewed, or worked in a room in the apartment reserved for those purposes.

For the first week no subjects were given caffeine. Instead, they received daily capsules of milk-sugar solution as a placebo. This period allowed for adaptation to the testing routine and collection of baseline data on the various tests.

For most subjects, caffeine doses began in the second week. At that time, subjects were divided into four groups, one of which was a milk-sugar placebo group. The three experimental groups all received caffeine of differing dosages, at different times of the day, and sometimes caffeine days were alternated with placebo days.

The study was a classic double-blind experiment. Experimenters working with the subjects did not know whether the subject had been given caffeine or the placebo. And because the substances were swallowed in capsule form, thus preventing taste, subjects were also unaware of what they were receiving. Dosage rates extended over a reasonable range on either side of the amount of caffeine a moderate drinker of Coca-Cola might consume in a day.

The second study was an intensive experiment of three days duration. This study sought specifically to determine the time course of the drug's action. All subjects were fed lunch and supper in the laboratory-apartment to control the diet. Dosage rates differed and placebos were used again. Each of the principal tests was run fifteen times on each subject, across a range of post-drug intervals. Four groups were used again, one of which took its caffeine in a mixture of soda fountain syrup and carbonated water.

The third study lasted seven days and administered differing caffeine dosages in specially prepared Coca-Cola syrup that was decaffeinated. Again, subjects and experimenters were blind as to whether the drinks did or did not contain caffeine. This study was designed to test the effects of caffeine when taken with food, namely, the sugar content of Coca-Cola and to compare the effects of the carbonated beverage with and without caffeine.

The subjects were usually gone by 6:30 each evening, yet the work for the experimenters continued. The studies were generating an enormous amount of data and Hollingworth understood that to have any results ready for the trial, it would be necessary to spend evenings analyzing the data. For that task he drew on the help of several graduate students – John Dashiell, Albert T. Poffenberger, and Edward K. Strong, Jr. – who spent their evenings together in the laboratory-apartment, generating curves, graphs, and tables. By the conclusion of the studies, more than 64,000 separate measurements had been recorded.

Because of Hollingworth's "catastrophobia," each night he and a colleague made a duplicate set of the day's data which would then be housed in a separate location.

The Trial in Chattanooga

The trial, which began on 16 March 1911, was already underway when Hollingworth completed the analyses of his studies. It was a major media event in Chattanooga, not only because of a company so visible as Coca-Cola being the defendant in the suit, but also because of the presence of Harvey Wiley. Wiley, age sixty-five and a life-long bachelor, was married only a few days prior to the start of the trial. His wife accompanied him to Chattanooga for their honeymoon and according to Wiley, "attended all the sessions of the court and also took great interest in the proceedings."[25] (One wonders if she had any other choice.)

Wiley had wanted to have the trial in Washington, D.C., instead of Chattanooga where the sentiment would be favorable to Coca-Cola, but he was overruled by officials in the Department of Agriculture. Upon his arrival in Chattanooga he learned, to his dismay, that the Hotel Patten, where he and his wife were staying, was owned by the Coca-Cola Company.

An impressive force had been assembled to try the government's case. There were three attorneys and a host of expert witnesses from science and medicine. Of course the Coca-Cola Company had the financial resources to respond in kind. Wiley would later complain that Coca-Cola had outbid the government for the services of some of its expert witnesses. Attorneys for both sides sat on opposite sides of the courtroom with their scientific and medical experts behind them. Occasionally one of the experts would suggest a question to be asked of one of the witnesses. The trial began with the government presenting its case. Its witnesses:

> . . . swore to the dangers of caffeine, saying it disguised fatigue and led to exhaustion, overstimulated the heart, overworked the kidneys, brought addiction, nervous debility, sometimes – though rarely – death. . . . Animal experiments with rabbits, mice, frogs, guinea pigs, and dogs, phar-

macologists testified, demonstrated the debilitating, even the lethal, potential of caffeine.[26]

The proceedings were not without moments of humor. One physician, testifying for the government, described how caffeine had produced congestion in the cerebral arteries of his rabbits. When asked, in cross examination, how he had killed his animals, he admitted that he had hit them on the head with a stick.[27]

Not surprisingly, Coca-Cola's witnesses presented a very different picture of caffeine in their testimony. They acknowledged that caffeine could be harmful if consumed in large doses; however, they argued that even a frequent drinker of Coca-Cola could not consume anywhere near the quantity of caffeine that could be considered harmful. Testimony focused on the benefits of caffeine as a mild stimulant that allowed individuals to avoid muscular or mental fatigue. Coca-Cola's experts could find no evidence of depression, either muscular or mental, once the effects of the caffeine wore off. Nor was there any evidence that caffeine was habit forming.

Based on the transcript of the trial, most of the research presented on both sides appears to be poor science.[28] That was particularly true of the medical research which tended to be anecdotal – physicians reporting on observations of their patients or on their own experiences with coffee or Coca-Cola. Even among the scientists in physiology, chemistry, and pharmacology the research was frequently flawed in design or interpretation or both, for example, few subjects, inadequate controls, qualitative measurements where quantification was possible, interpreting significant differences where none likely existed, excessive caffeine doses, and confounding of caffeine with other drugs. That Hollingworth's research was an exception is evident in the trial transcript, and it was evident to the reporters who were in court each day.[29]

Hollingworth testified on 27 March 1911 as the trial began its third week. He was the ninth scientific witness called by Coca-Cola's attorneys. Armed with pieces of scientific apparatus he had brought with him from New York and numerous charts, his testimony occupied most of the morning. It was noticeably more quantitative than the testimony of earlier witnesses, a fact cited in most newspaper accounts of the trial. The Chattanooga *Daily Times* which had covered each day of the trial with a front-page story, paid high tribute to Hollingworth (even if they did misspell his name): "His testimony was by far the most interesting and technical of any yet introduced. Cross-examination failed to shake any of his deductions."[30]

Hollingworth's testimony described caffeine as a mild stimulant whose effect on motor performance was rapid and transient, whereas the effect on cognitive performance appeared more slowly but was more persistent. Of particular importance, given the fatigue arguments of Wiley, was that Hollingworth found no evidence of secondary fatigue or depression as a result of the caffeine at any dosage in his studies. He argued that the enhanced performance produced by the caffeine was a genuine drug effect and not due to some other cause such as arousal, expectation, interest, suggestion, or sensory stimulation. He noted that his studies did not address the physiological mechanisms underlying this effect.

But whether this increased capacity comes from a new supply of energy introduced or rendered available by the drug action, or whether energy already available comes to be employed more effectively, or whether the inhibition of secondary afferent impulses is eliminated, or whether fatigue sensations are weakened and the individual's standard of performance thereby raised, no one seems to know.[31]

In his testimony, Hollingworth concluded that there was no evidence in his studies that caffeine produced any deleterious effects in mental or motor performance. He believed that if caffeine was harmful, surely that would have been demonstrated given the wide array of tests, dosages, subjects, and times and conditions of drug administration used in his studies. The only negative results he reported had to do with some subjects' ratings of poorer sleep quality following days when they had received the larger caffeine dosages.[32] No doubt the Coca-Cola Company must have been pleased with those conclusions.

The trial lasted another week beyond Hollingworth's testimony but it never reached the jury decision stage.[33] Once all of the testimony had been presented, Coca-Cola's attorneys introduced a motion to dismiss the case, arguing that the case was based on caffeine being an added ingredient, but the Coca-Cola Company contended that caffeine was one of several ingredients *inherent* in Coca-Cola. Why that motion was not made earlier in the trial is a mystery, because it was a claim that Coca-Cola made from the beginning in challenging the government's case. Judge Edward T. Sanford's ruling on the motion came as a shock to the government attorneys and Wiley, and likely to Coca-Cola's attorneys as well. In his twenty-five-page opinion on the meaning of the word "added" in the Pure Food Act, Judge Sanford stated:

> The conclusion is to my mind unavoidable that by the use of this language Congress intended to provide that a compound article of food thus known, labeled, and sold under its own distinctive name, should be assimilated to a natural product and not be deemed to be adulterated whatever the character of its ingredients . . . the caffeine contained in the article Coca-Cola is one of its regular, habitual, and essential constituents, and that without its presence, that is, if it were de-caffeinized, so to speak, the product would lack one of its essential elements and fail to produce upon the consumer a characteristic if not the most characteristic effect which is obtained from its use. In short Coca-Cola without caffeine would not be "Coca-Cola" as it is known to the public.[34]

In concluding his statement, Sanford declared the government's case invalid and directed the jury to return a verdict in favor of the claimant, the Coca-Cola Company. Thus the key question, whether or not caffeine was a substance injurious to health, was never decided by the jury.

The Battle Continues

The Coca-Cola Company, having endured the adverse publicity of the past years, began an advertising and consumer relations blitz touting the "vindication" of their product. Coca-Cola's president, Asa Griggs Candler, was the architect of this campaign. Candler, a long-time enemy of Wiley, must have relished the opportunity to strike back with the law on his side. Coca-Cola published several pamphlets to distribute

their message to consumers and retailers. These bore such titles as "The Truth about Coca-Cola" and "The Truth, the Whole Truth, and Nothing but the Truth about Coca-Cola."[35] These pamphlets cited the research of the authorities that testified on behalf of Coca-Cola at the trial. But Hollingworth's research was rarely mentioned, perhaps due to his agreement with the company about use of his research in advertising. When his research did appear, it was a reprinted excerpt of the newspaper coverage of the trial.[36]

While this advertising campaign was ongoing, the government attorneys were preparing for an appeal filed before the United States Circuit Court of Appeals in Cincinnati. Wiley was involved in the initiation of the appeal, but resigned from the bureau in early 1912 because of political issues he was unable to resolve to his satisfaction.[37] However, he continued his fight for pure food, including his crusade to eliminate caffeine in Coca-Cola. Prior to his resignation he had arranged to assume a position with *Good Housekeeping* magazine, which he did immediately. As director of the Good Housekeeping Bureau of Food, Sanitation, and Health, his duties chiefly entailed writing a monthly column. In these he warned about the dangers of bleached flour, white rice, and alum in baking powder. Among his strongest attacks were those directed at Coca-Cola, for example, one that objected vociferously to Coca-Cola's use of the label "soft drink." He argued that "no beverage which has added to it any stimulating or stupefying drug is properly classed under the term 'soft drinks'."[38] Thus he continued his public claim of the noxious nature of caffeine.

Three years passed before the Appeals Court in Cincinnati reached a decision. And when they did, they upheld the lower court decision. The Coca-Cola Company, elated once more, produced a new pamphlet entitled, "Truth, Justice, and Coca-Cola," whose cover pictured the scales of justice over the trademark for the company. Its opening page read:

> On Saturday, June 13, 1914, the Court of Appeals rendered its verdict in favor of Coca-Cola settling the case forever and completely vindicating Coca-Cola. This means that Coca-Cola emerges with a clean bill of health – in effect the highest

and final court decides that Coca-Cola is just exactly what we have always claimed – a wholesome, harmless, and non-habit forming beverage. And note this – this case was not decided on eloquence of counsel, or on petty technicalities. No arguments were made before jury, no play to sympathies or emotions was made, because it was the judges themselves who settled the case by a cold, critical review of the Chattanooga trial . . . The victory is absolutely one of cold justice – law and the right.[39]

The pamphlet also listed the witnesses to testify for both sides in the Chattanooga trial. Wiley is listed for the government and after his name it says in italics "who, however, failed to testify." Hollingworth is the *only* one of the Coca-Cola witnesses not listed, again, presumably because of his prior agreement with the company.

The pamphlet is clearly not very truthful. The Appeals Court did not rule on the safety of Coca-Cola as a beverage, rather it supported Judge Sanford's decision that the federal suit alleged something that was not true, that is, it upheld the opinion that caffeine was not an added ingredient. The author of the pamphlet should have known better than to say that anything is settled forever, and should have been better educated about the upper level of the judicial system of the United States. Because the U.S. Department of Justice immediately appealed the case to the Supreme Court.

Wiley, from his post at *Good Housekeeping*, was not about to let this new pamphlet of "truth" pass without comment. In a 1914 column in the magazine, he argued correctly about the meaning of the two court rulings and warned again about the dangers of Coca-Cola. The following passage is indicative of his crusading appeal:

A bright-eyed small boy of ten was turned over to me by his mother, the other day, for a few plain words as to why he had better drink lemonade and grape juice instead of Coca-Cola. I told him the story, without exaggeration; just what was in it, and why caffeine in either coffee or Coca-Cola, was not good for a growing boy. His eyes grew steadily larger, and at the end he said with great earnestness: "But why do they let them make it? The signs all say 'Delicious, Refreshing'." Why indeed?[40]

The issue that had been "settled forever" was unsettled in 1916 in a Supreme Court decision written by Justice Charles E. Hughes that stated caffeine *was* an added ingredient within the meaning of the Pure Food and Drugs Act. The case was remanded to the district court in Chattanooga to be retried on the question of whether or not the beverage contained a substance that was injurious to health. However, before the case could come to trial again, Coca-Cola changed its formula, reducing the caffeine content by half.[41] Thus at the trial, the Coca-Cola Company entered a plea of *nolo contendere*, arguing that a trial based on the seized syrup – the famous forty barrels and twenty kegs – would not be appropriate because the decision would be based on a formula that was no longer used. The judge agreed and dismissed the charges, although Coca-Cola was required to pay all court costs, which it did.[42]

The Legacy of the Caffeine Studies for Hollingworth

Harry Hollingworth published the caffeine research funded by the Coca-Cola Company in April 1912 as a 166-page monograph in Robert Woodworth's series, *Archives of Psychology*.[43] It was the first of twenty-five books that he would write in his career, most of them in the field of applied psychology. Given the controversy over caffeine, whose flames Wiley continued to fan, it is not surprising that the book got a lot of attention, particularly in the medical and pharmacological communities. No behavioral studies of such comprehensiveness, in terms of independent and dependent variables, had ever been conducted.

Reviews of the book appeared in many of the medical, pharmacological, and psychological journals which offered high praise not only for the valuable findings but also for the sophistication of the experimental design. The caffeine research on human beings, prior to Hollingworth's work, consisted largely of demonstrations of its effectiveness as a stimulant in ergographic studies or studies of reaction time. Thus the wealth of cognitive tests in Hollingworth's research added substantially to the knowledge of caffeine effects.[44] One medical journal reviewing the caffeine monograph commented:

> The careful description of methods, the presentation of a mass of entirely new data, and the obviously frank, if not actually objective, discussion of the data make this paper a very important contribution to the pharmacology of caffeine.[45]

An editorial in the *Journal of the American Medical Association* praised the studies for their rigor and argued that such thoroughness was the only way to provide "an adequate basis for correct conclusions as to the possible dangers of the use of caffeine-containing beverages."[46] One arrogant review in the *New York Medical Journal* lauded the accomplishments and conclusions of the research but cautioned "... it must be remembered that the author is a psychologist and that his experiments should be taken only from the psychological point of view."[47]

In the years that followed, Hollingworth's caffeine monograph was cited frequently in the pharmacological literature. As interest in psychopharmacology grew, it was cited in the newer literature on caffeine, and in other articles it was portrayed as a model of good research. It is still cited in current literature, mostly in pharmacological journals.[48]

The research seems to have had little impact on psychology during its time, largely because of psychology's disinterest in drug effects. The psychology textbooks of the 1910s and 1920s rarely cited Hollingworth's monograph. When it did appear, it was either in a discussion of experimental issues (mostly control) in which it was included as an example of rigorous research, or it was part of a discussion of drug effects on behavior. Nearly thirty years after conducting the studies, Hollingworth wrote:

> I have always been glad that we took on this project, which in the beginning appeared to all concerned to be a somewhat dubious undertaking. It did yield results of scientific value and they have stood the test of time and of such repetition as has been accorded them. . . . The investigation, and its report, did I believe its bit to break down some of the taboos then prevalent and to encourage cooperative investigation in which science provides the insight and technique and industry offers the problems and the means.[49]

Hollingworth's assertion that the caffeine studies helped to build the bridge between academic psychology and industry is difficult to document. Clearly such cooperative ventures in psychology increased in frequency, and the stigma associated with industry-sponsored research diminished over time. The quality of the caffeine research was generally acknowledged in the scientific community of psychology, and certainly Hollingworth's reputation as a scientist grew, earning him the presidency of the American Psychological Association in 1927 and membership in the Society of Experimental Psychologists. And maybe it increased the acceptability of such applied research.

The greatest impact of the caffeine research was on Harry Hollingworth himself. It erased the deficit line that had become an annual fixture in the Hollingworth family budget. And it showed him how he could supplement his modest faculty salary. In his autobiography he says there were two dominating "goads" in his life: one was intellectual hunger and the other was poverty. In the beginning the Hollingworths struggled to be able to afford food and decent clothing. But as those needs were met, Harry longed for the ability to "participate in life": traveling throughout the world and enjoying the many cultural opportunities in New York City.[50] The funds from the caffeine investigation, which permitted him and his wife to spend much of their summer of 1911 in Europe, provided a taste of life that drew him into a profitable career as an applied psychologist.[51]

In assessing Hollingworth's life, the caffeine research is arguably the most significant event in his career. As an immediate outcome, it provided the financial means for Leta Hollingworth's graduate education. For Harry it was a vision of his future in psychology and a means to a comfortable life. It marked an auspicious beginning to a career of substantial achievement. Thus it is a significant chapter in his life, if not, in fact, in the history of industrial psychology.

Notes

1 Harry L. Hollingworth, "Memories of the Early Development of the Psychology of Advertising," *Psychological Bulletin* 35 (1938): 308.

2 H. L. Hollingworth, "Years at Columbia," unpublished autobiography written in 1940. Collection of the Nebraska State Historical Society, Lincoln, Nebraska, p. 65.

3 Salary page showing Hollingworth's Barnard salaries from 1909–1946. In Hollingworth Papers, Archives of the History of American Psychology, University of Akron, Akron, Ohio.

4 For biographical material on Leta S. Hollingworth (1886–1939) see H. L. Hollingworth, *Leta Stetter Hollingworth: A Biography* (Lincoln: University of Nebraska Press, 1943). Reissued by Anker Publishing Company, Boston, Mass., 1990. See also the special issue of *Roeper Review* (1990, vol. 12) that contains twenty-one articles on the life and work of Leta Hollingworth.

5 H. L. Hollingworth, "Years at Columbia," pp. 56–58.

6 Ibid., p. 53.

7 Ibid., p. 96. A letter from Leta Hollingworth to Anna Stetter Fischer (Leta's cousin) dated 28 April 1911 states "We did a big experiment for the Coca-Cola Company and made quite a neat little 'wad' of money." Copy in possession of Ludy T. Benjamin, Jr.; original in family papers in Garland, Nebraska.

8 See H. L. Hollingworth, "Memories of the Early Development of the Psychology of Advertising."

9 H. L. Hollingworth, "Years at Columbia," p. 66. No copy of the contract has been located, either in the Hollingworth Papers at the Archives of the History of American Psychology or in the Coca-Cola Archives in Atlanta.

10 H. L. Hollingworth, "The Influence of Caffein on Mental and Motor Efficiency," *Archives of Psychology* 22 (April 1912): iii.

11 For biographical information on Wiley see Oscar E. Anderson, Jr., *The Health of a Nation: A Biography of Harvey Wiley* (Chicago: University of Chicago Press, 1958); Harvey W. Wiley, *An Autobiography* (Indianapolis: Bobbs-Merrill, 1930); and Maurice Natenberg, *The Legacy of Doctor Wiley* (Chicago: Regent House, 1957).

12 Harvey W. Wiley, "The Adulteration of Syrups in Indiana," report to the Indiana Department of Agriculture, 1881. See Chapter 2 of Anderson, *The Health of a Nation*. Wiley achieved his federal government post, in part, because of his expertise in sugar at a time when the government was seeking to improve sugar production, thus reducing reliance on foreign imports. See William L. Fox,

"Harvey W. Wiley's Search for American Sugar Self-sufficiency," *Agricultural History* 54 (1980): 516–526.

13 James Harvey Young, "Three Southern Food and Drug Cases," *The Journal of Southern History* 49 (1983): 4.

14 See "Review of the Wiley Investigation," *The American Food Journal* (15 November 1911): 1–4; "Dr. Wiley's Resignation," *Scientific American* (30 March 1912): 36; "Dr. Wiley, A Zealot," *The Medical Herald* 31 (1912): 187–188.

15 For an excellent history of the law see James H. Young, *Pure Food: Securing the Federal Food and Drugs Act of 1906* (Princeton, N.J.: Princeton University Press, 1989). Wiley's version of the law's history and its aftermath is presented in his book, *The History of a Crime Against the Food Law* (privately printed in 1929 and reprinted in 1976 by Arno Press, New York). The lengthy subtitle of the book is descriptive of Wiley's dissatisfaction with the subsequent enforcement and interpretation of the law – "The Amazing Story of the National Food and Drugs Law Intended to Protect the Health of the People, Perverted to Protect Adulteration of Food and Drugs." In 1956, on the fiftieth anniversary of the Pure Food and Drugs Act, the United States Postal Service issued a three-cent commemorative postage stamp featuring Wiley's picture.

16 Young, "Three Southern Food and Drug Cases," pp. 8–9. The success of soft drinks in America at the time of the seizure is indicated by the existence of 4,916 bottling plants and annual sales of $43 million in 1910. See John J. Riley, *A History of the American Soft Drink Industry: 1807–1957* (New York: Arno Press, 1972; originally published by the American Bottlers of Carbonated Beverages in 1958).

17 27 June 1864 entry in Wiley's Civil War diary. Wiley Papers, Box 213, Manuscript Division, Library of Congress, Washington, D.C. (hereafter "Wiley Papers").

18 In speeches, Wiley regularly linked caffeine with other habit-forming drugs such as opium and cocaine, and he often indicated that he viewed caffeine as the most serious public health hazard. In a 1909 lecture he stated, "It seems to me that the traffic in cocaine and opium and their products may be easily controlled because they are not produced in any quantity in the United States, nor are they generally purchased by the people. On the other hand, the beverages containing caffeine are universally employed, almost in every family. . . ." From "Abstract of Remarks Given before the Temperance Conference of the International Reform

Bureau," Washington, D.C., 16 and 17 December 1909. Wiley Papers.

19 H. W. Wiley, *Autobiography*, pp. 261–262. This incident marked Coca-Cola's third clash with the federal government since the company was founded in 1886. The first trouble resulted from the small amount of cocaine in the beverage, and that was eliminated by changing the manufacturing process in 1898. The second difficulty stemmed from exaggerated reports of its alcoholic content in 1907, a time of campaigns to establish prohibition. The U.S. Army was concerned enough to ban Coca-Cola sales on all of its bases. But the alcohol content proved to be a negligible trace. The Army ban was lifted after a few months, and the alcohol furor largely disappeared. See Young, "Three Southern Food and Drug Cases," pp. 5–8.

20 H. W. Wiley, "The Coca-Cola Controversy", *Good Housekeeping* 55 (1912): 392.

21 These slogans were used in advertisements from 1898 to 1911. From the Archives of the Coca-Cola Company, Atlanta, Georgia (Hereafter, "Coca-Cola Archives"). For a collection of older Coca-Cola advertisements, see Pat Watters, *Coca-Cola: An Illustrated History* (Garden City, N.Y.: Doubleday, 1978). Psychologist John B. Watson may have believed Coca-Cola's claim as "the ideal brain tonic." Recalling his senior year at Furman University in 1898, Watson wrote, "I was the only man who passed the final Greek exam. I did it only because I went to my room at two o'clock the afternoon before the exam, took with me one quart of Coca-Cola syrup, and sat in my chair and crammed until time for the exam next day." From John B. Watson, "Autobiography," in *A History of Psychology in Autobiography*, ed. Carl Murchison (Worcester, Mass.: Clark University Press, 1936), vol. 3, pp. 271–272.

22 The notable exception was a study on the effects of caffeine on muscular and mental fatigue performed by British psychologist W. H. R. Rivers. Although the study employed good controls, it suffered in terms of generalizability using only two subjects, three dependent variables, and a short time course. W. H. R. Rivers, *The Influence of Alcohol and Other Drugs on Fatigue* (London: Edward Arnold, 1908), pp. 22–49.

23 See Michael M. Sokal, ed., *Psychological Testing and American Society, 1890–1930* (New Brunswick, N.J.: Rutgers University Press, 1987).

24 H. L. Hollingworth, "The Influence of Caffein," pp. 121–131.

25 Wiley, *Autobiography*, p. 282. Anna Kelton Wiley kept a diary during the course of the trial. In it she gives an account of the people she and her husband met on the train to Chattanooga. They included Judge Edward T. Sanford, who would preside in the

trial, and John W. Mallett, a professor emeritus of chemistry from the University of Virginia and Confederate Army veteran who was one of Coca-Cola's star witnesses. The other diary entries on the trial consist of daily newspaper clippings. See "Account of the Coca-Cola Trial," Wiley Papers.

26 Young, "Three Southern Food and Drug Cases," p. 13.

27 Hollingworth, "Years at Columbia," p. 70.

28 Transcript for "The United States vs. Forty Barrels and Twenty Kegs Coca-Cola," in the National Archives, Atlanta Regional Archives Branch, Atlanta, Georgia, Record Group No. 21, Box 121.

29 The quality of his research was recognized by Hollingworth who wrote, somewhat immodestly, in his autobiography, "And how different were our carefully controlled experimental findings from much of the anecdotal and misguided testimony that appeared on both sides," "Years at Columbia," p. 70.

30 "Coca-Cola Compared to Other Drinks," *The Daily Times* (Chattanooga) (28 March 1911), p. 1. Wiley may not have been as impressed with Hollingworth's research or perhaps he did not like the conclusions drawn from the studies. Whatever the reason, Wiley did not include Hollingworth's research in a summary he wrote of the evidence for and against caffeine. See "The Effects of Caffein Upon the Human Organism," June 1915, Wiley Papers.

31 H. L. Hollingworth, "The Influence of Caffein," p. 165.

32 See Hollingworth's testimony in the trial transcript, National Archives, Atlanta Regional Archives Branch, pp. 1097–1119. See also H. L. Hollingworth, "The Influence of Caffein."

33 Harvey Wiley did not testify in the trial and he was soundly criticized in the press for failing to do so. Wiley said he decided not to testify because he would have been disqualified as an expert witness because he had no actual experience in caffeine research. See Anderson, *The Health of a Nation*, p. 237. The critics were especially upset that government funds had been used to send Wiley to Chattanooga explicitly as an expert witness. See letter from H. L. Harris to G. C. Morehead, 18 October 1911, Wiley Papers.

34 Chattanooga trial transcript, National Archives, Atlanta Regional Branch, pp. 3180 and 3185.

35 Copies of the pamphlets are in the Coca-Cola Archives.

36 In published accounts of the trial, Hollingworth's research was often prominently featured. See, for example, "Coca-Cola Litigation Ends with Defeat for the Government," *The American Food Journal* (15 April 1911): 1–8. The Coca-Cola Company

cited Hollingworth's research in four places in a thirty-two-page document it prepared in 1912 for the Committee of the House of Representatives on Interstate and Foreign Commerce. That document was written in response to two House bills that would amend the Pure Food Act by adding caffeine to the list of substances deemed "habit forming" and "deleterious." Hollingworth's research was cited as "proving" that caffeine was neither. See "Statement on Behalf of the Coca-Cola Company in Regard the Caffeine Contents of Coca-Cola." Coca-Cola Archives.

37 See Anderson, *The Health of a Nation*, pp. 248–253. Editorial responses to Wiley's resignation were mixed, but most journals and magazines felt that the American public had lost an important ally and protector. See *The Literary Digest* (23 March 1912): 578; *Journal of the American Medical Association* (23 March 1912): 129; *The Pacific Pharmacist* (April 1912): 327–329.

38 H. W. Wiley, "Soft Drinks and Dope," *Good Housekeeping* 55 (1912): 244. See also H. W. Wiley, "The Coca-Cola Controversy," *Good Housekeeping* 55 (April 1912): 386–394.

39 "Truth, Justice, and Coca-Cola," published by the Coca-Cola Company in 1914. Coca-Cola Archives.

40 H. W. Wiley, "Coca-Cola and the Circuit Court of Appeals," *Good Housekeeping* 59 (1914): 495–497.

41 Although the Coca-Cola attorneys testified to the reduction in caffeine in the manufacture of Coca-Cola, Wiley doubted the truth of the company's claim. He wrote to the U.S.D.A. Bureau of Chemistry asking for its data on the caffeine content of Cola-Cola taken over a ten-year span of assessing the beverage. But the bureau would not release the information to Wiley, prompting a lengthy letter of complaint to President Calvin Coolidge on 3 June 1925. Wiley Papers.

42 Coca-Cola's expenses for the three trials totaled more than $85,000. See Charles H. Candler, *Asa*

Griggs Candler (Atlanta: Emory University Press, 1950), pp. 147–152.

43 See H. L. Hollingworth, "The Influence of Caffein." Hollingworth's initial presentation of the data (other than the court testimony) was at a meeting of the College of Physicians of Philadelphia on 23 October 1911. That address, which bore the same title as the 1912 monograph, was published in *The Therapeutic Gazette* (15 January 1912): 1–16. Subsequently he used additional analyses of the caffeine data to publish three other articles: on quality and amount of sleep, *American Journal of Psychology* 23 (1912): 89–100; on typewriting performance, *Psychological Review* 19 (1912): 66–73; and on a comparison with alcohol, *The Therapeutic Gazette* (15 February 1921): 1–10.

44 See Vivian A. C. Henmon's review of the monograph in *Journal of Philosophy, Psychology, and Scientific Methods* 10 (1913): 681–682.

45 *The Post Graduate: A Monthly Journal of Medicine, Surgery, and Medical Education* (July 1912): 155.

46 "The Influence of Caffeine on Mental and Motor Efficiency and on the Circulation," *Journal of the American Medical Association* 58 (1912): 784–785.

47 "The Toxicity of Caffeine," *New York Medical Journal* (May 1912): 1052.

48 A search of the 1983–1988 annuals of the *Science Citation Index and Social Science Citation Index* yielded twenty-two citations of Hollingworth's 1912 monograph.

49 H. L. Hollingworth, "Years at Columbia," p. 72.

50 Ibid., p. 48.

51 In his career, Hollingworth accepted many consulting jobs from a wide variety of companies. Income from this work and his book royalties made him moderately wealthy. Evidence of that is the scholarship he established at Columbia University in memory of his wife with a cash gift of $51,000 in 1944. Hollingworth Papers.

Chapter 7

Psychoanalysis

As Clark University in Worcester, Massachusetts, approached its twentieth anniversary, its president, G. Stanley Hall, was busy planning an academic gathering that would prove to be the most memorable meeting in the history of American psychology (see Cromer & Anderson, 1970; Evans & Koelsch, 1985; Rosenzweig, 1994). Hall was planning a program of international speakers for this anniversary celebration, so he began with an invitation to Wilhelm Wundt. Likely Wundt was amused that an American believed that a twentieth anniversary was worthy of such an elaborate celebration. Time had a much different meaning in Europe. Wundt declined the invitation, saying that he was obligated to speak at a celebration at his own university, its 500th anniversary, having been founded in 1409!

A later invitation went to a 53-year-old physician in Vienna, Sigmund Freud (1856–1939). Freud too declined, but when Hall rescheduled the dates of the celebration from summer to fall and increased the size of the honorarium, Freud agreed to speak at the conference. He wrote to his disciple Carl Jung (1875–1961) to tell him of the invitation. In his letter, he added an exclamation point in parentheses after the mention of the twentieth anniversary, indicating his surprise that the Americans felt 20 years of existence was worth such a celebration. Even so, Freud was clearly excited about the invitation. He wrote to Jung: "I must admit that this has thrilled me more than anything else that has happened in the last few years . . . and that I have been thinking of nothing else" (McGuire, 1974, p. 210).

Eventually Jung received an invitation to speak as well, and he and Freud made plans to cross the Atlantic together. They sailed from Germany on August 21, 1909, arriving in New York City on August 29. The following day an American disciple, Abraham A. Brill, took them on a tour of the city. They visited Central Park and Chinatown in the morning and spent the afternoon at Coney Island. The next morning they toured the Metropolitan Museum of Art, a visit that Freud had looked forward to with great anticipation, principally because of the Greek antiquities in the museum's collection. Freud was a serious collector of Greek, Egyptian, and Etruscan antiquities.

The next day Freud was taken to see his first movie. We do not know what he saw, but according to Freud it involved "plenty of wild chasing." His reaction was described as "quietly amused" (Jones, 1955, p. 56). By this time Freud and Jung were suffering from their American diet. Jung, in a letter to his wife, complained that they had diarrhea and bad stomach aches. Freud even believed he might be having an attack of appendicitis. They fasted for a day in an effort to alleviate some of the discomfort. After touring New York City, Freud and Jung journeyed to Worcester, Massachusetts, arriving on September 5, where they were invited to stay in Hall's home. Freud's first lecture was scheduled two days later.

The quality of the speakers and the audience at the five-day conference was impressive. The only American psychologist invited to speak was E. B. Titchener, who used the opportunity to review the past decade of experimental psychology in America, noting the progress made in structural psychology and casting doubt on what was being accumulated from the functional approach (see Titchener, 1910b). James McKeen Cattell was there. William Stern, the inventor of the intelligence quotient, was in attendance. William James showed up for one day and stayed at Hall's home with Freud and Jung. James was quite ill at that time; in fact he would die within a matter of months.

Freud delivered five lectures, one on each day of the conference. He had debated whether to give them in English or German and decided on the latter. He would later write them out in English for Hall to publish in the *American Journal of Psychology* in 1910. Freud reasoned correctly that his audience likely knew little about psychoanalysis, either as a theory of normality or abnormality or as a method of treatment. Thus he decided to use the five lectures to cover the basics of both theory and method. He began his first lecture with a description of one of the cornerstone cases of psychoanalysis, the case of a young woman known by the code name of *Anna O.* Anna O. was actually a patient of Josef Breuer (1842–1925), a Viennese physician whom Freud much admired. Breuer and Freud had discussed the case on many occasions and had written about it in their book, *Studies on Hysteria* (Breuer & Freud, 1895). In his lecture, Freud described her as follows:

> Dr. Breuer's patient was a girl of twenty-one, of a high degree of intelligence. She had developed in the course of her two years' illness a series of physical and mental disturbances which well deserved to be taken seriously. She had a severe paralysis of both right extremities, with anesthesia, and at times the same affection of the members of the left side of the body, disturbance of eye movements, and much impairment of vision; difficulty in maintaining the position of the head, an intense Tussis nervosa [uncontrollable cough], nausea when she attempted to take nourishment, and at one time for several weeks a loss of the power to drink, in spite of tormenting thirst. Her power of speech diminished, and this progressed so far that she could neither speak nor understand her mother tongue; and finally, she was subject to states of "absence," of confusion, delirium, alteration of her whole personality. (Freud, 1910, p. 184)

Breuer had treated Anna during the period 1880–1882, at one time seeing her every day for a year. The hysterical symptoms described here were, according to Breuer, eliminated one by one until Anna was totally cured. The cure had been brought about by having Anna relive the experiences that led to her symptoms, either by talking about them naturally or while in a hypnotic state. For example, she noted that her aversion to drinking water was similar to an aversion she had experienced as a child when she saw a dog drinking water from a glass. According to Breuer, once she had discussed this earlier incident, the drinking aversion disappeared. Breuer referred to this curative method as *catharsis*, that is, the symptoms were reduced or eliminated through the release of the patient's pent-up anxiety. (The cure may not have happened as described by Breuer – see Ellenberger, 1972, for his discovery of new data that cast a very different light on this classic psychoanalytic case.) Freud, who was beginning his private practice, was especially interested in this case because of the promise of the method of catharsis in treating hysteria.

In addition to Breuer, Freud was greatly influenced by the famous French physician Jean-Martin Charcot (1825–1893), arguably the leading authority in Europe on the treatment of hysteria. Freud studied in Paris with Charcot in 1885–1886. Using non-hysterical patients, Charcot was able to demonstrate that, under hypnosis, they could be made to exhibit the convincing physical symptoms of hysteria. That meant that conditions of the body could definitely be altered by conditions of the mind, an important realization for Freud's growing interest in psychiatry. Charcot's other principal influence on Freud was the result of a casual remark suggesting that sexual problems were the underlying cause of hysteria. That remark would figure prominently in Freud's theory and guide his treatments. His emphasis on sex as a causative agent of paramount importance in neuroses eventually led to the dissolution of his friendship with Breuer (Sulloway, 1979).

In developing his method of therapy, Freud would abandon hypnosis, a technique that had figured prominently in the work of both Breuer and Charcot. He found that some patients were very difficult to hypnotize and that, in fact, he was able to get valuable insights into a patient's behavior simply by having the patient talk spontaneously about anything that came to mind, a technique he called *free association*. The free associations of Freud's patients were often shocking to him, as they frequently described sexual seductions by their parents, usually the father, when they were very young. Freud decided that sexual abuse of children by their parents was much more common than anyone had imagined. But then he had an insight that was to alter radically his interpretation of those events. He reasoned that the stories of sexual seduction revealed by his patients were, for the most part, just that – stories! They were fantasies of desired but not actual encounters. This *seduction theory* and Freud's reason for changing his mind on this issue has been a source of much controversy, and especially so more recently, stimulated in part by increased reporting of sexually abused children, including reports generated through the controversial technique known as recovered memory therapy (Esterson, 1993, 1998; Fancher, 1973; Masson, 1984; Triplett, 2004).

Freud's emphasis on sex as an etiologic agent was not altered by this new interpretation. It made him even more aware of the powerful role of unconscious processes as determinants of behavior. He understood that, for his patients, fantasy and reality were not easily distinguished. When reality was too difficult to face, the mind would create its own version of that reality, which Freud called *psychic reality*. The chief goal of psychoanalysis was to expose the psychic reality for the distortion that it was and help the patient understand and accept the actual reality. These insights led to the development of Freud's view of personality, as well as to the refinement of his therapeutic technique of psychoanalysis, ideas that were refined more fully in what Freud and many historians regard as his most important book, *The Interpretation of Dreams* (1900). One of the repressed wishes first discussed in this famous book was the Oedipus complex, an idea that generated considerable controversy.

The impetus for this book was Freud's own self-analysis, which he began in 1896. Realizing that he could not use the technique of free association for such an analysis, he began to make a record of his dreams for that task. A year earlier, Freud had begun to argue for the significance of *dreams as wish fulfillments*. He regarded that insight as so important that he recorded the exact date of its occurrence. He wrote: "In this House on July 24, 1895, the Secret of Dreams was revealed to Dr. Sigmund Freud" (E. Freud, 1960, p. 240). He understood dreams as the "royal road to the unconscious" and he had used dream analysis with his patients.

Freud's masterpiece on dreams was followed by *The Psychopathology of Everyday Life* (1901), a book that illustrated how slips of the tongue (Freudian slips), simple mistakes, and temporary losses of memory were actually revelations of unconscious conflicts. These everyday "errors" could give important insights into a person's personality. Four years later Freud published *Three Essays on the Theory of Sexuality* (1905), a book that further defined his ideas on psychoanalysis as a theory of personality, with particular emphasis on his growing realization of the nature of infantile sexuality.

When Freud received his invitation from Hall to speak at the Clark conference, none of these three books was available in English translation. His book on dreams had not even been reviewed in any American publications. He did get some publicity, however, principally in articles and reviews in the *Journal of Abnormal Psychology* edited by Morton Prince (1854–1929). It is likely that Hall had read some of Freud's books; from his correspondence we know that he had read at least some of the 1905 book on sexuality. Hall had dealt with the concept of adolescent sexuality in his two-volume work on adolescence, a part of the book that had caused discomfort in more prudish readers. Some of Hall's colleagues felt he was making a huge mistake in inviting Freud to the conference, giving such a stage to a man who was not regarded as a scientist and whose ideas were so controversial. No doubt Hall knew that Freud's presence would provide publicity for his conference, and he worked hard with the Boston and the local press to market Freud as a star. Likely Freud's potential star quality played a role in the invitation, but there is also no denying that Hall found Freud's ideas intriguing and wanted the opportunity to measure Freud in person.

The Readings

The first of the readings is Freud's first lecture at the Clark conference, taken from the version he published in 1910. Freud did not write out his lectures in advance, so the published version in Hall's journal in 1910 was based on his recollection of what he said at the conference. As noted earlier, the bulk of this first lecture was about Breuer's treatment of Anna O., and more broadly the treatment of hysteria in general. If you are interested in reading the other four Clark lectures you can find them in Freud, 1910 or Rosenzweig, 1994.

The second reading is by historian of psychology Gail Hornstein, whose historical works read like the best of mystery novels. She begins her article as follows:

> Freud and Jung were having dinner in Bremen. It was the evening before they set sail for the Clark conference, the occasion of Freud's only visit to America. Jung started talking about certain mummies in the lead cellars of the city. Freud became visibly disturbed. "Why are you so concerned about these corpses?" he asked several times. Jung went on talking. Suddenly, without warning, Freud fell to the floor in a faint. When he recovered he accused Jung of harboring death wishes against him. But it was not Jung who wanted Freud dead. Had Freud only known what American psychologists were about to do to psychoanalysis, he might never have gotten up off the floor. (Hornstein, 1992, p. 254)

Hornstein's article looks at the reception of Freud's ideas in the scientific community of psychology versus the general public. After his visit, psychology largely ignored Freud's ideas. But they spread rapidly as popular psychology with the American public, capturing the public's imagination, and being seen as the one true psychology. Hornstein's fascinating account describes this war of ideas and how it played out in America between 1909 and 1960.

The final reading is by historian of psychology Raymond Fancher (2000), an authority on Freud and the history of psychoanalysis. It provides, as the title of the article suggests, a series of snapshots of reactions to Freud in America from 1899 to 1999. Fancher's entertaining account reinforces the points made in Hornstein's article with examples of psychologists' reactions to Freud and his ideas.

When Freud made his one and only trip to America, he was surely impressed with the attention and adulation he received at the Clark conference. That feeling had begun on the boat trip over from Europe when he noticed one of the ship's stewards reading a copy of his book, *The Psychopathology of Everyday Life*. At the ceremony at which he received an honorary doctorate from Clark University, Freud was visibly moved. He thanked Hall for what he termed the "first official recognition of our endeavors" (Jones, 1955, p. 57). Freud felt he received recognition in America that was denied him in Europe. He told his biographer, "As I stepped on to the platform at Worcester to deliver my *Five Lectures Upon Psycho-Analysis* it seemed like the recognition of some incredible daydream; psychoanalysis was no longer a product of delusion; it had become a valuable part of reality" (Jones, 1955, p. 59).

There is no doubt that Freud could ever have imagined the impact his ideas would have in America. This chapter tells the story of Freud's historic visit and its dramatic aftermath for him, psychoanalysis, and American psychology.

The Origin and Development of Psychoanalysis
Sigmund Freud

First Lecture

Ladies and Gentlemen: It is a new and somewhat embarrassing experience for me to appear as lecturer before students of the New World. I assume that I owe this honor to the association of my name with the theme of psychoanalysis, and consequently it is of psychoanalysis that I shall aim to speak. I shall attempt to give you in very brief form an historical survey of the origin and further development of this new method of research and cure.

Granted that it is a merit to have created psychoanalysis, it is not my merit. I was a student, busy with the passing of my last examinations, when another physician of Vienna, Dr. Joseph Breuer, made the first application of this method to the case of an hysterical girl (1880–82). We must now examine the history of this case and its treatment, which can be found in detail in "Studien über Hysterie," later published by Dr. Breuer and myself.

But first one word. I have noticed, with considerable satisfaction, that the majority of my hearers do not belong to the medical profession. Now do not fear that a medical education is necessary to follow what I shall have to say. We shall now accompany the doctors a little way, but soon we shall take leave of them and follow Dr. Breuer on a way which is quite his own.

Dr. Breuer's patient was a girl of twenty-one, of a high degree of intelligence. She had developed in the course of her two years' illness a series of physical and mental disturbances which well deserved to be taken seriously. She had a severe paralysis of both right extremities, with anasthe-

sia, and at times the same affection of the members of the left side of the body; disturbance of eye-movements, and much impairment of vision; difficulty in maintaining the position of the head, an intense *Tussis nervosa*, nausea when she attempted to take nourishment, and at one time for several weeks a loss of the power to drink, in spite of tormenting thirst. Her power of speech was also diminished, and this progressed so far that she could neither speak nor understand her mother tongue; and, finally, she was subject to states of "absence," of confusion, delirium, alteration of her whole personality. These states will later claim our attention.

When one hears of such a case, one does not need to be a physician to incline to the opinion that we are concerned here with a serious injury, probably of the brain, for which there is little hope of cure and which will probably lead to the early death of the patient. The doctors will tell us, however, that in one type of case with just as unfavorable symptoms, another, far more favorable, opinion is justified. When one finds such a series of symptoms in the case of a young girl, whose vital organs (heart, kidneys), are shown by objective tests to be normal, but who has suffered from strong emotional disturbances, and when the symptoms differ in certain finer characteristics from what one might logically expect, in a case like this the doctors are not too much disturbed. They consider that there is present no organic lesion of the brain, but that enigmatical state, known since the time of the Greek physicians as hysteria, which can simulate a whole series of symptoms of various diseases. They consider in such a case that the life of the patient is not in danger and that a restoration to health will probably come about of itself. The differentiation of such an hysteria from a severe organic lesion is not always easy. But we do not need to know how a differential diagnosis of this kind is made; you may be sure that the case of Breuer's

First of the five lectures given at Clark University in September 1909. All five were published in the *American Journal of Psychology*, 1910, *21*, 181–218. This first lecture appeared on pages 181–190.

patient was such that no skillful physician could fail to diagnose an hysteria. We may also add a word here from the history of the case. The illness first appeared while the patient was caring for her father, whom she tenderly loved, during the severe illness which led to his death, a task which she was compelled to abandon because she herself fell ill.

So far it has seemed best to go with the doctors, but we shall soon part company with them. You must not think that the outlook of a patient with regard to medical aid is essentially bettered when the diagnosis points to hysteria rather than to organic disease of the brain. Against the serious brain diseases medical skill is in most cases powerless, but also in the case of hysterical affections the doctor can do nothing. He must leave it to benign nature, when and how his hopeful prognosis will be realized. Accordingly, with the recognition of the disease as hysteria, little is changed in the situation of the patient, but there is a great change in the attitude of the doctor. We can observe that he acts quite differently toward hystericals than toward patients suffering from organic diseases. He will not bring the same interest to the former as to the latter, since their suffering is much less serious and yet seems to set up the claim to be valued just as seriously.

But there is another motive in this action. The physician, who through his studies has learned so much that is hidden from the laity, can realize in his thought the causes and alterations of the brain disorders in patients suffering from apoplexy or dementia, a representation which must be right up to a certain point, for by it he is enabled to understand the nature of each symptom. But before the details of hysterical symptoms, all his knowledge, his anatomical-physiological and pathological education, desert him. He cannot understand hysteria. He is in the same position before it is as the layman. And that is not agreeable to any one, who is in the habit of setting such a high valuation upon his knowledge. Hystericals, accordingly, tend to lose his sympathy; he considers them persons who overstep the laws of his science, as the orthodox regard heretics; he ascribes to them all possible evils, blames them for exaggeration and intentional deceit, "simulation," and he punishes them by withdrawing his interest.

Now Dr. Breuer did not deserve this reproach in this case; he gave his patient sympathy and interest, although at first he did not understand how to help her. Probably this was easier for him on account of those superior qualities of the patient's mind and character, to which he bears witness in his account of the case.

His sympathetic observation soon found the means which made the first help possible. It had been noticed that the patient, in her states of "absence," of psychic alteration, usually mumbled over several words to herself. These seemed to spring from associations with which her thoughts were busy. The doctor, who was able to get these words, put her in a sort of hypnosis and repeated them to her over and over, in order to bring up any associations that they might have. The patient yielded to his suggestion and reproduced for him those psychic creations which controlled her thoughts during her "absences," and which betrayed themselves in these single spoken words. These were fancies, deeply sad, often poetically beautiful, day dreams, we might call them, which commonly took as their starting point the situation of a girl beside the sick-bed of her father. Whenever she had related a number of such fancies, she was, as it were, freed and restored to her normal mental life. This state of health would last for several hours, and then give place on the next day to a new "absence," which was removed in the same way by relating the newly-created fancies. It was impossible not to get the impression that the psychic alteration which was expressed in the "absence" was a consequence of the excitations originating from these intensely emotional fancy-images. The patient herself, who at this time of her illness strangely enough understood and spoke only English, gave this new kind of treatment the name "talking cure," or jokingly designated it as "chimney sweeping."

The doctor soon hit upon the fact that through such cleansing of the soul more could be accomplished than a temporary removal of the constantly recurring mental "clouds." Symptoms of the disease would disappear when in hypnosis the patient could be made to remember the situation and the associative connections under which they first appeared, provided free vent was given to the emotions which they aroused. "There was in the summer a time of intense heat, and the patient had suffered very much from thirst; for, without any apparent reason, she had suddenly become unable to drink. She would take a glass of water in her hand, but as soon as it touched her lips she would push it away as though suffering from hydrophobia. Obviously for these few seconds she was in her absent state. She ate only fruit, melons and the like, in order to relieve this tormenting thirst. When this had been going on about six weeks, she was talking one day in hypnosis about her English governess, whom she disliked, and finally told, with every sign of disgust, how she had come into the room of the governess, and how that lady's little dog, that she abhorred, had drunk out of a glass. Out of respect for the conventions the patient had remained silent. Now, after she had given energetic expression to her restrained anger, she asked for a drink, drank a large quantity of water without trouble, and woke from hypnosis with the glass at her lips. The symptom thereupon vanished permanently."

Permit me to dwell for a moment on this experience. No one had ever cured an hysterical symptom by such means before, or had come so near understanding its cause. This would be a pregnant discovery if the expectation could be confirmed that still other, perhaps the majority of symptoms, originated in this way and could be removed by the same method. Breuer spared no pains to convince himself of this and investigated the pathogenesis of the other more serious symptoms in a more orderly way. Such was indeed the case; almost all the symptoms originated in exactly this way, as remnants, as precipitates, if you like, of affectively-toned experiences, which for that reason we later called "psychic traumata." The nature of the symptoms became clear through their relation to the scene which caused them. They were, to use the technical term, "determined" (*determiniert*) by the scene whose memory traces they embodied, and so could no longer be described as arbitrary or enigmatical functions of the neurosis.

Only one variation from what might be expected must be mentioned. It was not always a single experience which occasioned the symptom, but usually several, perhaps many similar, repeated traumata co-operated in this effect. It was necessary to repeat the whole series of pathogenic memories in chronological sequence, and

of course in reverse order, the last first and the first last. It was quite impossible to reach the first and often most essential trauma directly, without first clearing away those coming later.

You will of course want to hear me speak of other examples of the causation of hysterical symptoms beside this of inability to drink on account of the disgust caused by the dog drinking from the glass. I must, however, if I hold to my programme, limit myself to very few examples. Breuer relates, for instance, that his patient's visual disturbances could be traced back to external causes, in the following way. "The patient, with tears in her eyes, was sitting by the sick-bed when her father suddenly asked her what time it was. She could not see distinctly, strained her eyes to see, brought the watch near her eyes so that the dial seemed very large (macropia and strabismus conv.), or else she tried hard to suppress her tears, so that the sick man might not see them."

All the pathogenic impressions sprang from the time when she shared in the care of her sick father. "Once she was watching at night in the greatest anxiety for the patient, who was in a high fever, and in suspense, for a surgeon was expected from Vienna, to operate on the patient. Her mother had gone out for a little while, and Anna sat by the sick-bed, her right arm hanging over the back of her chair. She fell into a revery and saw a black snake emerge, as it were, from the wall and approach the sick man as though to bite him. (It is very probable that several snakes had actually been seen in the meadow behind the house, that she had already been frightened by them, and that these former experiences furnished the material for the hallucination.) She tried to drive off the creature, but was as though paralyzed. Her right arm, which was hanging over the back of the chair, had "gone to sleep," become anasthetic and paretic, and as she was looking at it, the fingers changed into little snakes with deaths-heads. (The nails.) Probably she attempted to drive away the snake with her paralyzed right hand, and so the anasthesia and paralysis of this member formed associations with the snake hallucination. When this had vanished, she tried in her anguish to speak, but could not. She could not express herself in any language, until finally she thought of the words of an English nursery song, and thereafter she could think and speak only in this language." When the memory of this scene was revived in hypnosis the paralysis of the right arm, which had existed since the beginning of the illness, was cured and the treatment ended.

When, a number of years later, I began to use Breuer's researches and treatment on my own patients, my experiences completely coincided with his. In the case of a woman of about forty, there was a tic, a peculiar smacking noise which manifested itself whenever she was laboring under any excitement, without any obvious cause. It had its origin in two experiences which had this common element, that she attempted to make no noise, but that by a sort of counter-will this noise broke the stillness. On the first occasion, she had finally after much trouble put her sick child to sleep, and she tried to be very quiet so as not to awaken it. On the second occasion, during a ride with both her children in a thunderstorm the horses took fright, and she carefully avoided any noise for fear of frightening them still more. I give this example instead of many others which are cited in the "Studien über Hysterie."

Ladies and gentlemen, if you will permit me to generalize, as is indispensable in so brief a presentation, we may express our results up to this point in the formula: *Our hysterical patients suffer from reminiscences.* Their symptoms are the remnants and the memory symbols of certain (traumatic) experiences.

A comparison with other memory symbols from other sources will perhaps enable us better to understand this symbolism. The memorials and monuments with which we adorn our great cities, are also such memory symbols. If you walk through London you will find before one of the greatest railway stations of the city a richly decorated Gothic pillar – "Charing Cross." One of the old Plantagenet kings, in the thirteenth century, caused the body of his beloved queen Eleanor to be borne to Westminster, and had Gothic crosses erected at each of the stations where the coffin was set down. Charing Cross is the last of these monuments, which preserve the memory of this sad journey. In another part of the city, you will see a high pillar of more modern construction, which is merely called "the monument." This is in memory of the great fire which broke out in the neighborhood in the year 1666, and destroyed a great part of the city. These monuments are memory symbols like the hysterical symptoms; so

far the comparison seems justified. But what would you say to a Londoner who to-day stood sadly before the monument to the funeral of Queen Eleanor, instead of going about his business with the haste engendered by modern industrial conditions, or rejoicing with the young queen of his own heart? Or to another, who before the "Monument" bemoaned the burning of his loved native city, which long since has arisen again so much more splendid than before?

Now hystericals and all neurotics behave like these two unpractical Londoners, not only in that they remember the painful experiences of the distant past, but because they are still strongly affected by them. They cannot escape from the past and neglect present reality in its favor. This fixation of the mental life on the pathogenic traumata is an essential, and practically a most significant characteristic of the neurosis. I will willingly concede the objection which you are probably formulating, as you think over the history of Breuer's patient. All her traumata originated at the time when she was caring for her sick father, and her symptoms could only be regarded as memory symbols of his sickness and death. They corresponded to mourning, and a fixation on thoughts of the dead so short a time after death is certainly not pathological, but rather corresponds to normal emotional behavior. I concede this: there is nothing abnormal in the fixation of feeling on the trauma shown by Breuer's patient. But in other cases, like that of the tic that I have mentioned, the occasions for which lay ten and fifteen years back, the characteristic of this abnormal clinging to the past is very clear, and Breuer's patient would probably have developed it, if she had not come under the "cathartic treatment" such a short time after the traumatic experiences and the beginning of the disease.

We have so far only explained the relation of the hysterical symptoms to the life history of the patient; now by considering two further moments which Breuer observed, we may get a hint as to the processes of the beginning of the illness and those of the cure. With regard to the first, it is especially to be noted that Breuer's patient in almost all pathogenic situations had to suppress a strong excitement, instead of giving vent to it by appropriate words and deeds. In the little experience with her governess' dog, she suppressed, through regard for the conventions, all manifestations of her very intense disgust. While she was seated by her father's sick bed, she was careful to betray nothing of her anxiety and her painful depression to the patient. When, later, she reproduced the same scene before the physician, the emotion which she had suppressed on the occurrence of the scene burst out with especial strength, as though it had been pent up all along. The symptom which had been caused by that scene reached its greatest intensity while the doctor was striving to revive the memory of the scene, and vanished after it had been fully laid bare. On the other hand, experience shows that if the patient is reproducing the traumatic scene to the physician, the process has no curative effect if, by some peculiar chance, there is no development of emotion. It is apparently these emotional processes upon which the illness of the patient and the restoration to health are dependent. We feel justified in regarding "emotion" as a quantity which may become increased, derived and displaced. So we are forced to the conclusion that the patient fell ill because the emotion developed in the pathogenic situation was prevented from escaping normally, and that the essence of the sickness lies in the fact that these "imprisoned" (*dingeklemmt*) emotions undergo a series of abnormal changes. In part they are preserved as a lasting charge and as a source of constant disturbance in psychical life; in part they undergo a change into unusual bodily innervations and inhibitions, which present themselves as the physical symptoms of the case. We have coined the name "hysterical conversion" for the latter process. Part of our mental energy is, under normal conditions, conducted off by way of physical innervation and gives what we call "the expression of emotions." Hysterical conversion exaggerates this part of the course of a mental process which is emotionally colored; it corresponds to a far more intense emotional expression, which finds outlet by new paths. If a stream flows in two channels, an overflow of one will take place as soon as the current in the other meets with an obstacle.

You see that we are in a fair way to arrive at a purely psychological theory of hysteria, in which we assign the first rank to the affective processes. A second observation of Breuer compels us to ascribe to the altered condition

of consciousness a great part in determining the characteristics of the disease. His patient showed many sorts of mental states, conditions of "absence," confusion and alteration of character, besides her normal state. In her normal state she was entirely ignorant of the pathogenic scenes and of their connection with her symptoms. She had forgotten those scenes, or at any rate had dissociated them from their pathogenic connection. When the patient was hypnotized, it was possible, after considerable difficulty, to recall those scenes to her memory, and by this means of recall the symptoms were removed. It would have been extremely perplexing to know how to interpret this fact, if hypnotic practice and experiments had not pointed out the way. Through the study of hypnotic phenomena, the conception, strange though it was at first, has become familiar, that in one and the same individual several mental groupings are possible, which may remain relatively independent of each other, "know nothing" of each other, and which may cause a splitting of consciousness along lines which they lay down. Cases of such a sort, known as "double personality" ("*double conscience*"), occasionally appear spontaneously. If in such a division of personality consciousness remains constantly bound up with one of the two states, this is called the *conscious* mental state, and the other the *unconscious*. In the well-known phenomena of so-called post hypnotic suggestion, in which a command given in hypnosis is later executed in the normal state as though by an imperative suggestion, we have an excellent basis for understanding how the unconscious state can influence the conscious, although the latter is ignorant of the existence of the former. In the same way it is quite possible to explain the facts in hysterical cases. Breuer came to the conclusion that the hysterical symptoms originated in such peculiar mental states, which he called "hypnoidal states." (*hypnoide Zustände.*) Experiences of an emotional nature, which occur during such hypnoidal states, easily become pathogenic, since such states do not present the conditions for a normal draining off of the emotion of the exciting processes. And as a result there arises a peculiar product of this exciting process, that is, the symptom, and this is projected like a foreign body into the normal state. The latter has, then, no conception of the significance of the hypnoidal pathogenic situation. Where a symptom arises, we also find an amnesia, a memory gap, and the filling of this gap includes the removal of the conditions under which the symptom originated.

I am afraid that this portion of my treatment will not seem very clear, but you must remember that we are dealing here with new and difficult views, which perhaps could not be made much clearer. This all goes to show that our knowledge in this field is not yet very far advanced. Breuer's idea of the hypnoidal states has, moreover, been shown to be surperfluous and a hindrance to further investigation, and has been dropped from present conceptions of psychoanalysis. Later I shall at least suggest what other influences and processes have been disclosed besides that of the hypnoidal states, to which Breuer limited the causal moment.

You have probably also felt, and rightly, that Breuer's investigations gave you only a very incomplete theory and insufficient explanation of the phenomena which we have observed. But complete theories do not fall from Heaven, and you would have had still greater reason to be distrustful, had any one offered you at the beginning of his observations a well-rounded theory, without any gaps; such a theory could only be the child of his speculations and not the fruit of an unprejudiced investigation of the facts.

The Return of the Repressed: Psychology's Problematic Relations with Psychoanalysis, 1909–1960
Gail A. Hornstein

Freud and Jung were having dinner in Bremen. It was the evening before they set sail for the Clark conference, the occasion of Freud's only visit to America. Jung started talking about certain mummies in the lead cellars of the city. Freud became visibly disturbed. "Why are you so concerned with these corpses?" he asked several times. Jung went on talking. Suddenly, without warning, Freud fell to the floor in a faint. When he recovered, he accused Jung of harboring death wishes against him. But it was not Jung who wanted Freud dead. Had Freud only known what American psychologists were about to do to psychoanalysis, he might never have gotten up off the floor.

There is no easy way to talk about psychology's relations with psychoanalysis.[1] It is a story dense with disillusionment and the shapeless anger of rejection. Each side behaved badly, and then compounded its insensitivity with disdain. Their fates bound together like Romulus and Remus, psychology and psychoanalysis struggled to find their separate spheres, only to end up pitted against one another at every turn. Too much was at stake – property lines, areas of influence, and a deeper question: Which field would ultimately dictate the ground rules for a science of the mind?

In the 1890s, when this struggle began, there was little sign that it would become another Hundred Years' War. Psychologists had just begun to apply experimental methods to some of the classic problems of metaphysics, with the hope of answering questions that had bedeviled philosophers for centuries. By systematically organizing the psychological world into a set of discrete variables, these methods brought the unruly phenomena of mind within the purview of science. It was a heady time, a time of possibility and change and the reckless felicity of the new. American psychologists raced around founding laboratories at every college that would let them, in closets, basements or wherever they could snatch a little space, setting up apparatus in their own homes if necessary. They invented new forms of measurement, odd devices, tests of all sorts. Reports of their findings poured into the journals that sprang up suddenly to fill the need. The *new psychology*, as they liked to call it, seemed destined even in its infancy to do what had been declared since Kant to be impossible – to create a truly scientific approach to mind.

Psychoanalysts thrust themselves directly into the middle of this scene, brazenly trying to supplant the new psychology at the moment of its greatest promise. At first psychologists stood aside, astonished, as the analysts, bursting with self-importance and an almost frightening zealotry, pronounced themselves the real scientists of the mind. By the time psychologists began to take this threat seriously, psychoanalysis had so captured the public imagination that even its pretensions could not be ignored.[2]

The question was how to define science. To the analysts, science had nothing to do with method, with controlling variables or counting things. What made something scientific was that it was true. Constructing a science of the mind could mean one thing – finding some way to peer through the watery murk of consciousness to the subaquean reality that lay beyond. The efforts of psychologists, with their bulky equipment and

G. A. Hornstein (1992). The return of the repressed: Psychology's problematic relations with psychoanalysis, 1909–1960. *American Psychologist, 47*, 254–263. Copyright © 1992 by the American Psychological Association. Reprinted by permission of the publisher and the author.

piles of charts and graphs, seemed superficial and largely irrelevant to this goal.[3]

For their part, psychologists initially saw psychoanalysis as just another of the "mind cures" that flashed across the American landscape in the 1890s – like Christian Science or the Emmanuel movement – a popular craze that had nothing to do with the scientific study of mind. Most psychologists who attended Freud's Clark lectures in 1909 saw his speculations about dreams and sex as a pleasant diversion, about as relevant to their work as Mrs. Eddy's epistles. The occasional articles about psychoanalysis that appeared in psychology journals before 1910 (e.g., Putnam, 1906; Scott, 1908) made it seem mildly interesting, but not essentially different from related methods like suggestion.

By 1915, readers of a publication like *The Journal of Abnormal Psychology* had an opportunity for more varied exposure to psychoanalytic ideas.[4] Books by Freud, Jung, and A. A. Brill were regularly reviewed. Articles demonstrating the therapeutic effectiveness of psychoanalytic techniques began to appear, along with some discussion of the theory itself (see, e.g., Coriat, 1910; Emerson, 1912–1913; Gordon, 1917; MacCurdy, 1913; Maeder, 1910; Putnam, 1909–1910). Criticisms, when made, were fair-minded and well within the spirit of scientific repartee. Donley (1911), for example, suggested that anxiety neurosis might have other causes beyond those considered by Freud. Bellamy (1915a) argued that dreams fulfill fears or states of anger just as often as they represent wishes. Taylor (1911) noted that there were cases of neurosis in which patients recovered without having had their childhood or sexual life dissected. Even critics with a broader focus expressed little ire. Wells (1913) was concerned about "looseness in the formulation of psychoanalytic theories" (p. 227). Solomon (1916) argued that the term *sexual* was used inconsistently by analytic writers. The psychiatrist Morton Prince (1910) expressed the common view that psychoanalysts "fit the facts to the universal concepts which dominate the school" (p. 349).

There were occasional writers who became exasperated and called psychoanalysis "weird" (Donley, 1911), "esoteric" (Carrington, 1914), or "grotesque" (Bellamy, 1915a), its assumptions "fantastic" or "sheer nonsense" (Humphrey, 1920b), but these imprecations were unusual in the early years. The sexual nature of psychoanalytic interpretation was a problem for some; Bellamy (1915b), for example, in reviewing a book by Coriat, made plain his relief that "there is not a word or sentence in this book that a precise maiden lady need hesitate to read to her Sunday school class or at a pink tea" (p. 434). On the whole, however, psychologists were initially so supportive of psychoanalysis that when Roback reviewed Dunlap's (1920) *Mysticism, Freudianism and Scientific Psychology*, he felt he had to defend its critical tone on grounds of balance: "Freud has had so many warm advocates of his views in this country and so few systematic critics among the psychologists that Dunlap's discussion is both timely and important" (Roback, 1921, p. 406).

These positive attitudes might well have resulted from more than psychologists' open-mindedness. Analysts, ever worried about their public image, left little to chance. Soon after the Clark conference they embarked on a systematic campaign to win Americans to their cause. A. A. Brill, the founder of the New York Psychoanalytic Society, was charged with disseminating information about psychoanalysis in that city; Ernest Jones, Freud's scrappy lieutenant, took the rest of the country for himself (Burnham, 1967, pp. 134–137). Psychologists were among the major recipients of Jones's educational largess; by 1916, they had been treated to 20 of his articles, abstracts, reviews, and comments in the *Journal of Abnormal Psychology* alone. Most of these pieces were patient expositions of psychoanalytic concepts, designed to lead the uninitiated to a correct understanding of the theory. But Jones also maintained a vigilant watch over what psychologists were writing about psychoanalysis, and shot back a tart riposte whenever he encountered an "erroneous" statement (see also Tannenbaum, 1916, 1917).

Neither Jones nor his colleagues gave serious attention to the careful criticisms that psychologists leveled against psychoanalysis in the early years. Acutely aware of the tenuous status of their own new field, psychologists found this highly disconcerting. After all, they were constantly obliged to defend their science against attacks from philosophy and biology; what gave analysts the right not only to ignore legitimate criticism but to patronize their opponents? Who knows what might have happened had analysts been more responsive; what did happen was that psychologists sharpened their pencils and began to fight.

The first skirmish actually occurred as early as 1916, when the Princeton philosopher Warner Fite reviewed Jung's *Psychology of the Unconscious* for *The Nation* (Fite, 1916). His surprisingly nasty tone incited a riot of response from psychologists. In her letter to the editor, Christine Ladd-Franklin, the eminent experimentalist, characterized psychoanalysis as a product of the "undeveloped . . . German mind" (hardly a compliment in 1916), and concluded ominously that "unless means can speedily be found to prevent its spread . . . the prognosis for civilization is unfavorable" (Ladd-Franklin, 1916, p. 374). R. S. Woodworth of Columbia (1916), a bit more circumspect, called psychoanalysis an "uncanny religion" (probably not the psychologist's highest accolade) that led "even apparently sane individuals" to absurd associations and nonsensical conclusions. In a telling illustration, he showed how the words *Freudian principles* led to a train of thought that revealed his own "deep-seated wish . . . for a career of unbridled lust" (p. 396).

Woodworth went on to publish an extensive critique of "Freudism" in the 1917 volume of the *Journal of Abnormal Psychology*. Adopting the peevish tone that soon became commonplace in these sorts of articles, he complained that analysts disregarded psychological research, contemptuously dismissed it as superficial, and treated psychologists "shabbily" (Woodworth, 1917, p. 175). What most annoyed Woodworth was the analysts' slippery dodge, their way of attributing any criticism of psychoanalysis to unconscious resistance on the part of the critic.

Other writers echoed these complaints, often with less poignancy and considerably more pique than Woodworth. But what soon emerged as the real irritant for psychologists was the analysts' insistence, at times moralistic, at times snide, that only those who had themselves undergone a personal psychoanalysis were qualified to evaluate the theory. To an experimental psychology whose raison d'etre was to differentiate itself from religion, this talk of initiation rites and secret knowledge was anathema. Such a rule also conveniently disenfranchised just about every psychologist from serving as a potential critic; even those Americans who sought analysis had

a hard time finding it in this country before 1920. Of course the real issue here was not who had been analyzed and who had not (a good thing, since Freud and his closest colleagues would have had to disqualify themselves); what was at stake was the fundamental question of subjectivity in science.

For experimental psychologists, being scientific meant creating distance. It meant opening up a space, a "no man's land," between themselves and the things they studied, a place whose boundary could be patrolled so that needs or desires or feelings could never infiltrate the work itself. Every aspect of the experimental situation was bent toward this goal – the "blind subjects," the mechanized recording devices, the quantified measures, and statistically represented results (Danziger, 1990; Hornstein, 1988; Morawski, 1988). What united experimental psychologists more than anything else was a distrust of personal experience, a sense that feelings in particular were dangerous and had to be held carefully in check lest they flood in and destroy the very foundations of the work. They were willing to make a number of sacrifices to protect psychology from this threat, including a radical narrowing of the field to include only phenomena that could be studied "objectively."

Having gone to these lengths, psychologists found it profoundly disquieting to have analysts claim that being psychoanalyzed was what made someone a credible scientist. This implied that science was subjective, that is was ultimately about personal experience rather than rigorous method. Even worse, it suggested that the unconscious was so powerful a part of mind that its force had to be experienced directly, in one's own life, in order to understand the psychology of others.

Such a view could not go unchallenged. "Voodooism," Watson (1927, p. 502) called it. "A delusion," echoed Jastrow (1932, p. 285). The very idea of an unconscious conjured up the chaos and irrationality that psychologists had banded together to escape. If analysts wanted to plunge into that nightmare world and call it science, so be it, but they could not be allowed to drag everyone else down with them.

The technique of free association came in for particular scorn (Heidbreder, 1933). It struck psychologists as an elaborate subterfuge, a way for analysts to appear not to influence patients when of course they did. Interpretation, they argued, was nothing but a new name for suggestion; that patients were gullible enough to mistake it for truth was hardly proof of its scientific status. Analysts were "free," all right – free to define as evidence whatever would meet their needs, free to label any challenge "resistance," free to pretend that they were doing nothing of the sort.

Heidbreder (1933), in her typically fair-minded way, struggled to make these practices sound reasonable. But even she could muster only this faint defense: Just because "psychoanalysts offer a different kind of evidence from that accepted by science . . . does not mean that they offer *no* evidence" (p. 402). To most psychologists, calling an analyst's retrospective musings about events that occurred in the secrecy of the consulting room evidence was an insult to science. Even first-year students knew that the cardinal rule of scientific proof was publicly verifiable data. Knight Dunlap (1920, p. 8) put it bluntly: "psychoanalysis attempts to creep in wearing the uniform of science, and to strangle it from the inside."[5]

By the mid-1920s, psychologists seem to have decided that the best way to defend science was simply to do it. Critiques of psychoanalysis began to be displaced in the literature by enthusiastic works like *Great Experiments in Psychology* (Garrett, 1930). Any remaining aggressive tendencies were easily absorbed by the interminable debates over behaviorism and Gestalt psychology.[6] Psychologists did not need psychoanalysis, and it surely did not need them.

Or so it seemed, until one day in the fall of 1934 when the rumor got out that Edwin Garrigues Boring, the self-acknowledged dean of experimental psychology, had entered analytic treatment. To preserve his reputation, he told colleagues that he was studying the relation between the two fields; actually, he was depressed, frightened, and unable to work. The strange saga of Boring's analysis gives a glimpse into psychologists' continuing ambivalence about psychoanalysis.

Boring chose as his analyst the emigré Berliner, Hanns Sachs, who had been a member of Freud's inner circle and was therefore above reproach. Despite his depression, Boring embarked on the analysis with customary gusto,

quickly absorbing the daily analytic sessions into the swirl of his 80-hour work week.

Boring struggled to make the analysis a success. He missed no sessions. He wept. He threw things. He made enough of a financial sacrifice to demonstrate the seriousness of his commitment. He discussed his childhood, explored his dreams, and scrutinized the motivations for his actions. Then, at the end of 10 months, he ran out of money, time, and desire. He had completed 168 sessions, for which he had paid $1,680, more than a fifth of his yearly salary. But his efforts brought little relief:

[A]ll that happened was that the analysis petered out in an uneventful session on June 21st and my analyst went abroad! . . . I was distraught. I had tried a last resource, and it had failed. Yet, unwilling to accept so bitter a conclusion, I found myself seizing on the analyst's casual statement that I ought to wait a month. I waited anxiously, hoping for a new personality by July 21st. None came. Finally I sought out my psychologist-friends who believe in psychoanalysis, and we sat in conference discussing this sad immutability of my personality – on August 21st, as I suddenly realized. Their advice was patience, the less haste the more speed; wait at least until December 21st, they urged. So I waited. . . . And finally I ceased to expect a miracle. (Boring, 1940, pp. 9–10)[7]

How could a man like Boring, whose name was practically synonymous with hard-nosed experimentation, have such childlike faith in psychoanalysis? He actually seemed to expect that he would wake up a new man, that "a light from heaven" would change him "from Saul to Paul" (p. 9). There are certainly no hints of these hopes in his published writings. In the first edition of his classic *History of Experimental Psychology* (Boring, 1929), published just five years before the analysis, there were only four brief mentions of Freud in almost 700 pages. Psychoanalysis did not even appear in the index of *Psychology: A Factual Textbook*, the text Boring published with Langfeld and Weld in 1935, the same year he saw Sachs.

Yet in his own life, Boring kept searching for some sign that the analysis might have worked. Five years passed. Still no light. In 1940, he tried a new strategy. He proposed to the *Journal of*

Abnormal and Social Psychology that it locate other well-known psychologists who had been analyzed, solicit reports of their experiences, and publish them in a special issue. Perhaps they would reveal something that he had missed. Leaving nothing to chance, Boring even persuaded Sachs to write a companion piece to his own account, evaluating the analysis from the analyst's perspective.

Psychologists turned out to be surprisingly excited by the prospect of reading about their colleagues' adventures on the couch. The American Psychological Association even reprinted the articles and sold them as a set, exhausting the entire edition within a few months. Boring, ever hopeful, titled his piece "Was This Analysis a Success?" Sachs (1940) replied with a tactful "no." Wistful and perplexed by the whole experience, Boring struggled to come to terms with his sense of loss: "There is so much about this personality of mine that would be better if different, so much that analysis might have done and did not!" (Boring, 1940, p. 10). Yet he refrained from attacking psychoanalysis directly. His colleagues, however, knew where to lay the blame for their own failed attempts. Carney Landis of Columbia parodied his experience with a statistical analysis of how much time he had allocated to each of eight topics during free association. To Landis, analysts were scientific illiterates who did little but mouth received dogma in order to make themselves rich. Hinting that his "neurosis" was created by the analysis itself, Landis (1940) concluded his tirade by warning that psychoanalysis was safe only when used by experimental psychologists to produce psychopathic phenomena in the laboratory.

The editor of the *Journal of Abnormal and Social Psychology*, apparently concerned about the lack of balance in these articles, invited the eminent analyst Franz Alexander to contribute a rejoinder. Instead of critiquing the other papers, Alexander (1940) made a parable of his own life. Like his readers, he had spent his youth as a devotee of laboratory science. When he first tried to read Freud's work, he found its "vague and ambiguous mental excursions . . . equal almost to physical pain" (p. 312). He turned to psychoanalysis only when the evidence in support of it became undeniable. This meant sacrificing his promising academic career, enduring the

opprobrium of his colleagues, and being forced from home by his irate philosopher father, who considered psychoanalysis a "spiritual gutter." But for Alexander, there was no choice – having committed himself to empiricism, he had to adopt whatever view had the most evidence, regardless of how distasteful it might be on other grounds. Of course, in he end, his quest for truth was vindicated when his father, near death, gave up his own lifelong belief in the superiority of natural science to express the fervent wish that "psychoanalysis will enthrone again real understanding in place of fumbling – the rule of thought in place of that of the gadget" (p. 314).

Alexander's inspiring tale fell on closed ears. Distrusting subjectivity in all its forms, psychologists put little stock in personal testimony, even that of fellow scientists. This series of articles clearly had less to do with evaluating psychoanalysis than it did with assuaging the anxiety of its contributors, many of whom were worried, like Boring, that their analyses had failed. What they needed was reassurance. But the tangible benefits of this kind of therapy are always elusive. Recall Janet Malcolm's (1984) sardonic comment: "The crowning paradox of psychoanalysis is the near-uselessness of its insights. To 'make the unconscious conscious' . . . is to pour water into a sieve. The moisture that remains on the surface of the mesh is the benefit of analysis" (p. 25). Ultimately, these articles were exercises in self-persuasion, attempts by the contributors to convince themselves that psychoanalysis was too ridiculous or too ineffectual to be taken seriously. If they managed in the process to warn off colleagues who might have been tempted to try the thing themselves, so much the better.

By the early 1940s, the situation had reached a critical stage. Psychoanalysis was becoming so popular that it threatened to eclipse psychology entirely. Journalists seemed oblivious to the differences between the two fields, and exasperated psychologists often found their discipline being portrayed as if it were nothing but a branch of psychoanalytic inquiry. This was especially galling because most psychologists assumed that psychoanalytic claims were not even true. But how could they prove this? The critiques of the early years had not worked. Attacking psychoanalysis from the couch had simply allowed Alexander to make psychologists look foolish. There had to be a better way.

The solution turned out to be so obvious that it is hard to believe it took until the mid-1940s to appear. Psychologists would set themselves the job of determining through carefully controlled experiments which, if any, psychoanalytic concepts were valid. This reinstated psychologists as arbiters of the mental world, able to make the final judgment about what would and would not count as psychological knowledge. It allowed them to evaluate psychoanalysis, rather than be overshadowed or absorbed by it. Most important, it restored the objective criterion of the experiment as the basis for making claims and settling disputes, undermining the analysts' attempts to substitute a new, subjective standard for psychological truth.

Psychologists took to their new role with a vengeance. Every conceivable psychoanalytic concept was put to the test, in hundreds of studies whose creativity was matched only by the uselessness of their findings. Mowrer (1940) demonstrated that regression and reaction formation could be produced in rats. Blum and Miller (1952) found that children who were categorized as having an "oral character" ate significantly more ice cream than did other children. Scodel (1957) showed that "high-dependency" men did not manifest the predicted preference of women with large breasts. Schwartz (1956) found more castration anxiety among men than women, with homosexual men scoring the highest of all. Sarnoff and Corwin (1959) reported that "high castration anxious" men showed a greater increase in fear of death than did "low anxious" men after being exposed to photographs of nude women. And Friedman (1952) found that when children were shown a picture of a father and a child near some stairs, more girls than boys fantasized that the father would mount the stairs and enter the room.

Topics like oedipal relations and anal personality had their aficionados, but it was *perceptual defense* that really captured the imagination of psychological researchers. Their hypothesis was a simple one: If the mind did defend against forbidden material, then words with disturbing or salacious associations should be recalled less easily than more neutral stimuli. Fresh-faced graduate students spent hours making certain

that items like *whore* and *bugger* were matched in length and salience with their sexless counterparts. Controversies erupted left and right: Were taboo words difficult to recognize just because they were not used very frequently? Wiener's (1955) famous "pussy–balls" study dispatched that idea by demonstrating that the context, not the words themselves, made certain stimuli threatening. But was exposure to a list of scatological words really analogous to the sort of trauma that necessitated repression? Blum (1954) addressed that problem with a new methodology based on the Blacky Pictures, a set of cartoon images of a dog depicted in various psychoanalytically relevant poses (licking his genitals, observing his parents having sex, defecating outside their kennel). When studies with Blacky were found to support the earlier word-item findings, repression gained the sort of empirical reality that only psychologists could give it.

By the 1950s, research on psychoanalysis had become so popular that psychologists were drowning in it. No one could possibly read all the studies that were being published, much less keep track of their results.[8] A new cottage industry was born of this need, with workers who did nothing but summarize and evaluate these studies. Robert Sears had been the first such laborer, commissioned in 1943 by the Social Science Research Council to write an objective review of the scientific literature on psychoanalytic theory. Sears' approach, used by all subsequent evaluators, was straightforward: Having first divided the literature into topic categories (fixation, sexuality, object choice), he then counted how many studies in each area supported Freud's claims. The larger the number, the more scientific the claim. Taken together, these individual scores were supposed to provide an answer to the overall question of whether psychoanalytic theory was valid.

Sears (1943) hedged, saying that some of it was, and some of it was not. Such caution soon vanished. The self-appointed judges whose reports appeared up through the early 1970s placed themselves squarely on one side of the debate or the other. Evaluation studies quickly became as difficult to sort out as research on psychoanalysis itself, and much less fun to read (see, for example, Fisher & Greenberg, 1977; Kline, 1972). Each report took a tone yet more strident than the last, and the original goal of providing an objective review was lost entirely. This was nowhere more evident than in Eysenck and Wilson's (1973) polemic. Every shred of evidence seeming to support psychoanalysis was scrutinized for methodological flaws, whereas studies opposing the theory were flaunted as examples of good science.

No one especially cared that the evaluation literature was becoming debased. It made little difference what the findings were; as long as psychoanalytic phenomena were made subservient to empirical test, empiricism was vindicated.[9] That much of this research supported Freud's theory was an irony appreciated by few. It was the act of doing these studies, of piling them up and sorting them out and arguing about them that was important, not what they revealed about psychoanalysis. Some psychologists found these activities so salubrious that they recommended them even to analysts. As Albert Ellis (1950) cheerfully noted, "sociologists, who but a decade or two ago were mostly concerned with pure theory, now frequently design and execute crucial experiments which enable them to support or discredit hypotheses. There is no basic reason why psychoanalysts cannot do likewise" (p. 190).

Analysts were in no position to point out that the content of these psychological studies had only the dimmest relation to Freud's theory. "Every country creates the psychoanalysis it [unconsciously] needs," said Kurzweil (1989, p. 1), and disciplines surely do the same. Research on psychoanalysis was invigorating because it gave psychologists a sense of mastery: They had ventured onto the battlefield of the unconscious and returned, triumphant, with a set of dependent variables. Some psychologists even managed to convince themselves that the danger had been exaggerated all along, that they had really been in control. They scoffed that psychoanalysis had never been much more than an inflated way of talking about conditioning, one of psychology's oldest topics. By the time Dollard and Miller (1950) actually began translating every psychoanalytic concept into its learning theory equivalent, their efforts were almost redundant.

These behaviorist reworkings of Freud, although often clumsy, did signal a new strategy in dealing with psychoanalysis – co-optation. More satisfying than silence, with none of the pitfalls of criticism, the appropriation of psychoanalytic concepts into mainstream psychology seemed an ideal compromise. Like the Christianizing of paganism, the dangerous parts were still there somewhere, but in such diluted form as to pose no real threat.[10]

Watson had tried to move in this direction as early as the 1920s. By relabeling the *unconscious* as the *unverbalized*, he could sweep most psychoanalytic phenomena into the neat piles of behaviorist theory. Emotions became sets of habits; neurosis was conditioning; therapy, unconditioning. Watson never denied the reality of Freud's findings; he simply cast them in his own terms (e.g., when he warned [1928, p. 80] that sexual frustration made mothers want to kiss rather than shake hands with their children). At times, Watson even took to calling himself an analyst, as if, like some ancient warrior, he could magically disarm his enemy by assuming his name.[11]

Other behaviorists continued where Watson left off. Humphrey (1920a), following Holt's (1915) earlier lead, dissolved wishes into conditioned reflexes. Keller and Schoenfeld (1950) laid claim to such psychoanalytic staples as the slip of the tongue (yet another reflex) and the oedipal complex (a consequence of early conditioning). But it was Skinner who took the task of appropriating Freud most seriously. In *Science and Human Behavior* (1953), he systematically redefined each of the defense mechanisms in operant terms (*repression*: a "response which is successful in avoiding the conditioned aversive stimulation generated by punishment," p. 292; *reaction formation*: "an extension of a technique of self-control in which the environment is altered so that it becomes less likely to generate punished behavior," p. 365). By the end of the book, even symbols and dreams had taken on the veneer of conditioned responses. Artful as these efforts were, they did not really solve the problem. Freud was still there. His new operant outfit gave him a natty American look, but there was no mistaking that sardonic smile. As long as psychoanalytic concepts remained identifiable as such, they were potential rivals to psychology's own constructs.

Help with this problem came from an unlikely source – introductory textbook writers. Typically dismissed as nothing but purveyors of pabulum for college students, these authors, many of them prominent psychologists, played a major role in advancing the co-optation of psychoanalytic theory. This is not so surprising. As Morawski (1992) shows, introductory texts exist in a liminal space, neither popular nor professional, yet somehow both. They function simultaneously as translators of standard doctrine and contributors to it. Because new texts constantly supplant older ones, they become disciplinary artifacts, frozen moments of taken-for-granted knowledge, X rays of the uncontroversial.

Textbook writers took advantage of their role by assimilating psychoanalytic concepts into mainstream psychology without mentioning their origins. An early example was Walter Hunter's 1923 text, *General Psychology*, in which the various defense mechanisms were stripped of any connection to the unconscious, much the way bagels now appear in the frozen-food sections of Peoria supermarkets. Other writers soon adopted this practice, sometimes using the term *adjustment mechanisms* to expunge any remaining whiff of psychodynamics (Guthrie & Edwards, 1949; Kimble, 1956).

These appropriations took place amidst a general silence in these texts about psychoanalytic theory itself. Many writers ignored the topic entirely: Robinson and Robinson's 665-page *Readings in General Psychology* (1923) included the contributions of every conceivable psychologist, even Helen Keller and the Lord Archbishop of York, but had nothing by Freud or any other psychoanalyst (the section titled "Dreams as a Vehicle of Wish Fulfillment" was written by Watson). Readers of well-known texts like Seashore's (1923) *Introduction to Psychology* or Warren and Carmichael's (1930) *Elements of Human Psychology* would never have known that psychoanalysis existed. Even as late as 1958, a classic like Hebb's *Textbook of Psychology* barely mentioned the topic. When Freud did make an appearance, it was more likely to be in the section on punishment or motivation – topics dear to the heart of experimentalists – than in expected places like the chapter on abnormality.

Of course some textbook writers did discuss psychoanalysis in more depth, but few besides Hilgard (1953) did so sympathetically.[12] Kimble (1956) went to the trouble of including a special section in his introduction warning readers not to make the common error of confusing psychology with psychoanalysis. It was not that Freud

had no value: Kimble called his work "one of the great milestones in the history of human thought" with "insights [that] have never been equaled" (pp. 369–370). Psychoanalysis just happened to be "entirely literary and not worth discussion" in a scientific text (p. 370).

In 1956, Gardner Murphy was asked to determine the extent of Freud's impact on the various subfields of psychology. He likened the overall effect to the erosion of the rocky coastline in Maine, but admitted that some areas had remained untouched by the psychoanalytic current. His results, on a numerical scale, of course, constitute what one might call an *index of introgression*, ranging from 0, Freud never had a chance, to 6, he made it all the way in. Here are Murphy's ratings: intelligence and physiological = 0; comparative, learning, thinking, perception, and vocational = 1; memory, drive and emotion, child and adolescent = 2; social and industrial = 3; imagination = 4; abnormal = 5; personality and clinical = 6.

What is surprising about these results is that there are any high scores at all. How could a discipline that had spent 50 years protecting its chastity end up seduced by a ladykiller like Freud? Of course the problem was really only with the clinicians, but there were thousands of them, and more every year (Gilgen, 1982; Kelly, 1947). When the American Psychological Association surveyed a sample of its members in 1954, asking who had influenced them to enter the field, Freud, of all people, got the greatest number of mentions (Clark, 1957, pp. 17–18). True, by that time, 37% of APA members were clinicians (p. 116), but how had that happened? Why were so many psychologists fleeing the laboratory?

Perhaps it was just the money. Or the effects of the war. But what if this exodus had a more ominous meaning?

Repression is a perverse process. It appears to efface the offending material, but this is an illusion – the contents of the unconscious are indestructible. Repressed material, like radioactive waste, lies there in leaky canisters, never losing potency, eternally dangerous. What is worse, it actively presses for expression, constantly threatening to erupt into consciousness. No one can control these forces; the best we can do is try to deflect them. It is a sign of health if we can accomplish this with a few judiciously used defenses. We know we're in trouble when we have to resort to the rigidity of symptoms.

Experimentalists took a calculated risk in trying to create a psychology in which subjective phenomena were banned from study. They knew that this would be difficult, that it would require erecting a set of defenses (the experimental method and all its appurtenances) and being vigilant about their use. But subjectivity creeps through every crevice and finds its way around even the strongest barricade. In the early years, this threat was manageable and psychology was willing to tolerate some narrowing of its operations in exchange for the reduction of anxiety its defenses allowed. Psychoanalysis tore this fragile equilibrium to pieces. By embracing subjectivity – sometimes even reveling in it – while still proclaiming itself a science, psychoanalysis forced psychology to define itself in ever more positivist terms. This was no ordinary battle over intellectual turf. It was more like a nightmare, in which psychologists watched, horrified, as the very phenomena they had sought to banish now returned to haunt them. They did what they could to contain the threat, but each new tactic only made things worse. Co-opting analytic concepts proved to be especially disastrous because it let the banned phenomena inside psychology itself. Even in scientific disguise, they were still dangerous, like a well-dressed hitchhiker who pulls a knife after getting into the car. With the threat now internal as well as external, experimental psychology was forced to harden itself still further. What had once been science became scientism, the neurotic symptom of a frightened discipline.

In retrospect, we might say that this was all to the good. The psychology that emerged from these wrenching experiences was stronger and more resilient, able to tolerate a degree of diversity among its members that would once have been unthinkable. The past 30 years have been a time of exponential growth, as older areas like learning have reorganized and newer ones like clinical have matured. The "cognitive revolution" that brought the mind back to psychology transformed even the most hard-core behaviorist, and terms like *self-perception* are now bandied about the laboratory as if they had been there all along. The rigid experimentalism of the 1940s now seems vaguely embarrassing, one of those right-

eous crusades of adolescence that pales before the complex realities of middle age.

There were many reasons for these changes, and certainly the threat from psychoanalysis was only one of a host of factors pushing psychology toward greater flexibility. But, as Burnham (1978) has argued, psychoanalysis did represent an extreme position against which more conservative disciplines like psychology and psychiatry had to define themselves. The willingness of analysts to occupy the radical frontiers of subjectivity gave psychologists room to maneuver, to create a middle ground in which previously excluded phenomena could enter without threatening the scientific standards psychologists had fought so hard to establish.

Equally important were the changes in psychoanalysis itself. During the period from 1940 to 1960, internecine warfare reached new heights among American analysts. The purges in the New York Psychoanalytic Institute were only the most visible sign that the field had become increasingly intolerant of dissent, and the huge influx of candidates after the war accelerated this slide toward conformity and conservatism (Hale, 1978; Jacoby, 1983). Psychoanalysis in 1950 was fundamentally different from what it had been in 1920, and its new mainstream mentality made it far easier for psychologists to accept.

The Second World War also played a significant role in these dynamics. Psychologists made substantive contributions to the diagnosis and treatment of war-related disturbances, as well as to myriad other problems from personnel selection to instrument design. These efforts enhanced the reputation of professional psychology and stimulated a massive increase in funding for psychological research. The war also brought to America European refugee psychologists, many of whom saw psychoanalytic ideas as part of the psychological canon. Psychologists began to spend less time worrying about whether analysts were eroding the fragile boundary between legitimate and popular psychology (Morawski & Hornstein, 1991) and took advantage of opportunities to get some favorable press of their own.[13]

American psychology has always been distinguished by an uncanny ability to adapt itself to cultural trends as quickly as they emerge. Once it became clear that the public found psychoanalysis irresistible, psychologists found ways of accommodating to it. Instead of concentrating all their efforts on criticism, they identified those parts of the theory that were potentially useful to their own ends and incorporated them. As psychoanalysis became less threatening, psychologists were able to notice that the two fields actually shared many of the same basic assumptions: a commitment to psychic determinism, a belief in the cardinal importance of childhood experience, and an optimistic outlook about the possibility of change.

It has been only 70 years since James McKeen Cattell rose from his seat at the annual meeting of the American Psychological Association to castigate a colleague for having mentioned Freud's name at a gathering of scientists (Dallenbach, 1955, p. 523). Today that same APA celebrates the success of its lawsuit against the psychoanalytic establishment, a suit which gave psychologists the right to become bona fide candidates at the analytic institute of their choice (Buie, 1988). As the moribund institutes prepare to be enlivened by a rush of eager psychologists, perhaps it is not too much to suggest that psychology itself has benefited from having had the psychoanalytic wolf at its door.

Notes

1 The standard reference on this whole topic is Shakow and Rapaport (1964). Their study remains invaluable as a thoughtful, systematic review of much of what psychologists have had to say about psychoanalysis. However, because their goal was to document Freud's influence on American psychology, they focused more on positive effects than on negative ones. My goal is to characterize psychologists' attitudes toward psychoanalysis. Many psychologists saw psychoanalysis as a threat and not as a positive influence, and thus my version of the story is inevitably more conflicted than Shakow and Rapaport's.

2 A discussion of the popular reception of psychoanalysis in America is beyond the scope of this article. See Hale (1971, 1978) and Burnham (1968, 1978, 1979, 1987) for detailed treatments of this issue.

3 Psychologists were not alone in having to struggle with competing definitions of science. Kuklick's (1980) analysis of boundary maintenance in sociology offers a general model for understanding how each of the social sciences resolved this dilemma.

4 Of all major psychology journals of the period, the *Journal of Abnormal Psychology* was the one with the greatest number of articles relevant to psychoanalysis (both pro and con). Not all were written by psychologists, but they were clearly intended for this audience. G. Stanley Hall published the text of Freud's, Jung's, and Ferenczi's Clark lectures in his *American Journal of Psychology* in 1910, but from then on that journal concentrated primarily on reviews of the psychoanalytic literature (both German and English) and carried very few original articles by psychologists.

5 With characteristic irony, Dunlap (1920) concluded that psychoanalysis might ultimately prove beneficial to psychology: "Just as Christian Science has tremendously accelerated the progress of Scientific Medicine, so Psychoanalysis, by compelling psychology to put its house in order, will eventually help in the development of the Scientific Psychology it aims to thrust aside" (p. 9).

6 See, for example, a classic work like *Psychologies of 1925* (Murchison, 1926), which allots four chapters to behaviorism, three to Gestalt, and even three to the dying gasps of structuralism, but none to psychoanalysis.

7 Among those Boring consulted was his colleague Henry Murray, who advised him to let Sachs have it "right between his eyes. . . . give him the works – don't omit a single grievance, not one." (H. Murray to E. G. Boring [n.d., August 1935?], Box 43, Folder 919, E. G. Boring Papers, Harvard University Archives quoted by permission). There is no evidence that Boring took this advice: He and Sachs maintained a cordial relationship for some time thereafter, dining together at the Harvard Club and exchanging papers and letters on professional topics.

8 Fisher and Greenberg's (1977) review includes more than 400 studies from the 1940s and 1950s alone. By the mid-1970s, there were at least 1,000 more.

9 Hilgard (1952) was the only evaluator who seemed willing to grant this point. He chastised psychologists for doing experiments that "give merely trivial illustrations of what psychoanalysts have demonstrated . . . in clinical work," and argued that although "such illustrations may be useful as propaganda," they "do not really do much for science." In his view, psychoanalytic research "ought to *advance* our understanding, not merely *confirm* or *deny* the theories that someone [else] has stated" (p. 43).

10 Precisely the same thing was done with Gestalt psychology. At first, the philosophic assumptions of the theory were seen as a challenge to American (behaviorist) psychology, and Gestalt was explicitly opposed. Then the dangerous aspects were simply stripped away, making it appear as if the principles of organization were empirical observations that had arisen out of nowhere. A contemporary student of perceptual psychology would have no idea that these principles were originally formulated in opposition to behaviorist thought.

11 "I venture to predict that 20 years from now an analyst using Freudian concepts and Freudian terminology will be placed upon the same plane as a phrenologist. *And yet analysis based upon behavioristic principles is here to stay and is a necessary profession in society – to be placed upon a par with internal medicine and surgery*" (Watson, 1925, p. 243). The comparison of psychoanalysis to phrenology was a favorite among psychologists; Dallenbach (1955) later wrote an entire article on this theme.

12 Buys (1976) has argued that it was only in the 1970s that positive portrayals of psychoanalysis became common in introductory texts. See also Herma, Kris, & Shor (1943), whose study focused on how Freud's theory of dreams was presented in such texts. They found such a high degree of criticism that they were forced to make separate tallies for *ridicule, rejection on moral grounds,* and *sheer denial.*

13 See, for example, Gengerelli's (1957) rhetorical romp in the *Saturday Review*, which painted psychologists as tireless laborers in the "scientific vineyard" and analysts as "muddle-headed, sob-sisters" (p. 11) who are the cause of every social ill from delinquency to early marriage.

References

Alexander, F. (1940). A jury trial of psychoanalysis. *Journal of Abnormal and Social Psychology, 35,* 305–323.

Bellamy, R. (1915a). An act of everyday life treated as a pretended dream and reinterpreted by psychoanalysis. *Journal of Abnormal Psychology, 10,* 32–45.

Bellamy, R. (1915b). Review of Coriat's *The meaning of dreams. Journal of Abnormal Psychology, 10,* 433–434.

Blum, G. S. (1954). An experimental reunion of psychoanalytic theory with perceptual vigilance and defense. *Journal of Abnormal and Social Psychology, 49,* 94–98.

Blum, G. S., & Miller, D. R. (1952). Exploring the psychoanalytic theory of the "oral character." *Journal of Personality, 20,* 287–304.

Boring, E. G. (1929). *A history of experimental psychology.* New York: Century.

Boring, E. G. (1940). Was this analysis a success? *Journal of Abnormal and Social Psychology, 35,* 4–10.

Boring, E. G., Langfeld, H. S., & Weld, H. P. (1935). *Psychology: A factual textbook.* New York: Wiley.

Buie, J. (1988). Psychoanalytic group bolstered by legal win. *APA Monitor, 19,* 21.

Burnham, J. C. (1967). *Psychoanalysis and American medicine, 1894–1918.* New York: International Universities Press.

Burnham, J. C. (1968). The new psychology: From narcissism to social control. In J. Braeman, R. H. Bremner, & D. Brody (Eds.), *Change and continuity in twentieth-century America: The 1920s* (pp. 351–398). Columbus: Ohio State University Press.

Burnham, J. C. (1978). The influence of psychoanalysis upon American culture. In J. M. Quen & E. T. Carlson (Eds.), *American psychoanalysis: Origins and development* (pp. 52–72). New York: Brunner/Mazel.

Burnham, J. C. (1979). From avant-garde to specialism: Psychoanalysis in America. *Journal of the History of the Behavioral Sciences, 15,* 128–134.

Burnham, J. C. (1987). *How superstition won and science lost: Popularizing science and health in the United States.* New Brunswick, NJ: Rutgers University Press.

Buys, C. J. (1976). Freud in introductory psychology texts. *Teaching of Psychology, 3,* 160–167.

Carrington, H. (1914). Freudian psychology and psychical research. *Journal of Abnormal Psychology, 9,* 411–416.

Clark, K. E. (1957). *America's psychologists: A survey of a growing profession.* Washington, DC: American Psychological Association.

Coriat, I. H. (1910). The psycho-analysis of a case of sensory automatism. *Journal of Abnormal Psychology, 5,* 93–99.

Dallenbach, K. M. (1955). Phrenology versus psychoanalysis. *American Journal of Psychology, 68,* 511–525.

Danziger, K. (1990). *Constructing the subject: Historical origins of psychological research.* New York: Cambridge University Press.

Dollard, J., & Miller, N. E. (1950). *Personality and psychotherapy.* New York: McGraw-Hill.

Donley, J. E. (1911). Freud's anxiety neurosis. *Journal of Abnormal Psychology, 6,* 126–134.

Dunlap, K. (1920). *Mysticism, Freudianism and scientific psychology.* St. Louis, MO: Mosby.

Ellis, A. (1950). An introduction to the principles of scientific psychoanalysis. *Genetic Psychology Monographs, 41,* 147–212.

Emerson, L. E. (1912–1913). A psychoanalytic study of a severe case of hysteria. *Journal of Abnormal Psychology, 7,* 385–406; *8,* 44–56, 180–207.

Eysenck, H. J., & Wilson, G. D. (1973). *The experimental study of Freudian theories.* London: Methuen.

Fisher, S., & Greenberg, R. P. (1977). *The scientific credibility of Freud's theories and therapy.* New York: Basic Books.

Fite, W. (1916). Psycho-analysis and sex-psychology. *The Nation, 103,* 127–129.

Friedman, S. M. (1952). An empirical study of the castration and Oedipus complexes. *Genetic Psychology Monographs, 46,* 61–130.

Garrett, H. E. (1930). *Great experiments in psychology.* New York: Century.

Gengerelli, J. A. (1957, March 23). The limitations of psychoanalysis: Dogma or discipline? *The Saturday Review,* pp. 9–11, 40.

Gilgen, A. R. (1982). *American psychology since World War II: A profile of the discipline.* Westport, CT: Greenwood Press.

Gordon, A. (1917). Obsessive hallucinations and psychoanalysis. *Journal of Abnormal Psychology, 12,* 423–430.

Guthrie, E. R., & Edwards, A. L. (1949). *Psychology: A first course in human behavior.* New York: Harper.

Hale, N. G. (1971). *Freud and the Americans: The beginnings of psychoanalysis in the United States, 1876–1917.* New York: Oxford University Press.

Hale, N. G. (1978). From Berggasse XIX to Central Park West: The Americanization of psychoanalysis, 1919–1940. *Journal of the History of the Behavioral Sciences, 14,* 299–315.

Heidbreder, E. (1933). *Seven psychologies.* Englewood Cliffs, NJ: Prentice-Hall.

Hebb, D. O. (1958). *A textbook of psychology.* Philadelphia: W. B. Saunders.

Herma, H., Kris, E., & Shor, J. (1943). Freud's theory of the dream in American textbooks. *Journal of Abnormal and Social Psychology, 38,* 319–334.

Hilgard, E. R. (1952). Experimental approaches to psychoanalysis. In E. Pumpian-Mindlin (Ed.), *Psychoanalysis as science* (pp. 3–45). New York: Basic Books.

Hilgard, E. R. (1953). *Introduction to psychology.* New York: Harcourt, Brace.

Holt, E. B. (1915). *The Freudian wish and its place in ethics.* New York: Holt.

Hornstein, G. A. (1988). Quantifying psychological phenomena: Debates, dilemmas, and implications. In J. G. Morawski (Ed.), *The rise of experimental psychology* (pp. 1–34). New Haven, CT: Yale University Press.

Humphrey, G. (1920a). The conditioned reflex and the Freudian wish. *Journal of Abnormal Psychology, 14,* 388–392.

Humphrey, G. (1920b). Education and Freudianism. *Journal of Abnormal Psychology, 15,* 350–386.

Hunter, W. (1923). *General psychology.* (Rev. edn.). Chicago: University of Chicago Press.

Jacoby, R. (1983). *The repression of psychoanalysis: Otto Fenichel and the political Freudians.* New York: Basic Books.

Jastrow, J. (1932). *The house that Freud built.* New York: Chilton.

Keller, F., & Schoenfeld, W. (1950). *Principles of psychology: A systematic text in the science of behavior.* New York: Appleton-Century-Crofts.

Kelly, E. L. (1947). Clinical psychology. In W. Dennis et al. (Eds.), *Current trends in psychology* (pp. 75–108). Pittsburgh, PA: University of Pittsburgh Press.

Kimble, G. A. (1956). *Principles of general psychology.* New York: Ronald Press.

Kline, P. (1972). *Fact and fantasy in Freudian theory.* London: Methuen.

Kuklick, H. (1980). Boundary maintenance in American sociology: Limitations to academic "professionalization." *Journal of the History of the Behavioral Sciences, 16,* 201–219.

Kurzweil, E. (1989). *The Freudians: A comparative perspective.* New Haven, CT: Yale University Press.

Ladd-Franklin, C. (1916). Letter to the editor. *The Nation, 103,* 373–374.

Landis, C. (1940). Psychoanalytic phenomena. *Journal of Abnormal and Social Psychology. 35,* 17–28.

MacCurdy, J. T. (1913). The productions in a manic-like state illustrating Freudian mechanisms. *Journal of Abnormal Psychology, 8,* 361–375.

Maeder, A. (1910). Psycho-analysis in a case of melancholic depression. *Journal of Abnormal Psychology, 5,* 130–131.

Malcolm, J. (1984). *In the Freud archives.* New York: Knopf.

Morawski, J. G. (1988). Introduction. In J. G. Morawski (Ed.), *The rise of experimentation in American psychology* (pp. vii–xvii). New Haven, CT: Yale University Press.

Morawski, J. G. (1992). There is more to our history of giving: The place of introductory textbooks in American psychology. *American Psychologist, 47,* 161–169.

Morawski, J. G., & Hornstein, G. A. (1991). Quandary of the quacks: The struggle for expert knowledge in American psychology, 1890–1940. In D. van Keuren & J. Brown (Eds.), *The estate of social knowledge* (pp. 106–133). Baltimore: Johns Hopkins University Press.

Mowrer, O. H. (1940). An experimental analogue of "regression" with incidental observations on "reaction-formation." *Journal of Abnormal and Social Psychology*, 35, 56–87.

Murchison, C. (1926). *Psychologies of 1925*. Worcester, MA: Clark University Press.

Murphy, G. (1956). The current impact of Freud upon psychology. *American Psychologist*, 11, 663–672.

Prince, M. (1910). The mechanism and interpretation of dreams – A reply to Dr. Jones. *Journal of Abnormal Psychology*, 5, 337–353.

Putnam, J. J. (1906). Recent experiences in the study and treatment of hysteria at the Massachusetts General Hospital with remarks on Freud's method of treatment by "psycho-analysis." *Journal of Abnormal Psychology*, 1, 26–41.

Putnam, J. J. (1909–1910). Personal impressions of Sigmund Freud and his work, with special reference to his recent lectures at Clark University. *Journal of Abnormal Psychology*, 4, 293–310, 372–379.

Roback, A. A. (1921). Review of Dunlap's *Mysticism, Freudianism and scientific psychology*. *Journal of Abnormal and Social Psychology*, 16, 406–408.

Robinson, E. S., & Robinson, F. R. (1923). *Readings in general psychology*. Chicago: University of Chicago Press.

Sachs, H. (1940). Was this analysis a success?: Comment. *Journal of Abnormal and Social Psychology*, 35, 11–16.

Sarnoff, I., & Corwin, S. M. (1959). Castration anxiety and the fear of death. *Journal of Personality*, 27, 374–385.

Schwartz, B. J. (1956). An empirical test of two Freudian hypotheses concerning castration anxiety. *Journal of Personality*, 24, 318–327.

Scodel, A. (1957). Heterosexual somatic preference and fantasy dependency. *Journal of Consulting Psychology*, 21, 371–374.

Scott, W. D. (1908). An interpretation of the psychoanalytic method in psychotherapy with a report of a case so treated. *Journal of Abnormal Psychology*, 3, 371–379.

Sears, R. R. (1943). *Survey of objective studies of psychoanalytic concepts*. New York: Social Science Research Council.

Seashore, C. E. (1923). *Introduction to psychology*. New York: Macmillan.

Shakow, D., & Rapaport, D. (1964). *The influence of Freud on American psychology*. New York: International Universities Press.

Skinner, B. F. (1953). *Science and human behavior*. New York: Macmillan.

Solomon, M. (1916). Critical review of the conception of sexuality assumed by the Freudian school. *Journal of Abnormal Psychology*, 11, 59–60.

Tannenbaum, S. A. (1916). Letter to the editor. *The Nation*, 103, 218–219.

Tannenbaum, S. A. (1917). Some current misconceptions of psychoanalysis. *Journal of Abnormal Psychology*, 12, 390–422.

Taylor, E. W. (1911). Possibilities of a modified psychoanalysis. *Journal of Abnormal Psychology*, 6, 449–455.

Warren, H. C., & Carmichael, L. (1930). *Elements of human psychology* (Rev. edn.), Boston: Houghton Mifflin.

Watson, J. B. (1925). *Behaviorism*. New York: Norton.

Watson, J. B. (1927). The myth of the unconscious. *Harpers*, 155, 502–508.

Watson, J. B. (1928). *Psychological care of the infant and child*. New York: Norton.

Wells, F. L. (1913). On formulation in psychoanalysis. *Journal of Abnormal Psychology*, 8, 217–227.

Wiener, M. (1955). Word frequency or motivation in perceptual defense. *Journal of Abnormal and Social Psychology*, 51, 214–218.

Woodworth, R. S. (1916). Letter to the editor. *The Nation*, 103, 396.

Woodworth, R. S. (1917). Some criticisms of the Freudian psychology. *Journal of Abnormal Psychology*, 12, 174–194.

Snapshots of Freud in America, 1899–1999
Raymond E. Fancher

When Sigmund Freud received the first printed copies of his new book *Die Traumdeutung* (*The Interpretation of Dreams*) in the autumn of 1899, he was pleased to see that his publisher Franz Deuticke had postdated the title page into the new century (Freud, 1900). The product of many years' work, this book not only developed Freud's hypothesis that dreams represent the symbolic gratification of unconscious wishes but also presented a general model of the mind, constituting the foundation of a new theory he called psychoanalysis. The intensely ambitious Freud hoped that this work would secure his fame in the new century.

Obviously, those hopes were realized – and nowhere more fully than in the United States of America. There is a certain irony in this fact, for Freud spent almost his entire life in Europe, published his major work in German, and was personally less than enthusiastic about American culture – once telling his biographer that "America is a mistake; a gigantic mistake, it is true, but none the less a mistake" (Jones, 1955, p. 60). The story of Freud's reception and recognition in the United States is a fascinating one, involving many figures and institutions from the early history of the American Psychological Association (APA), that has been well told by historians such as Burnham (1967, 1978, 1979), Evans and Koelsch (1985), Hale (1971, 1995), Hornstein (1992), Rosenzweig (1994), Shakow and Rapaport (1968), and Taylor (1988). This article presents just a few representative snapshots derived from this work, mainly depicting Freud in America at some key points in the first half of the century.

American Psychologist, 2000, *55*(9), 1025–1028. Copyright 2000 by the American Psychological Association, Inc. Reprinted by permission of the publisher and author.

In late 1899, the 43-year-old Freud was already reasonably well known in Europe, with more than 70 publications to his name. His work on organic brain damage and cerebral palsy was highly esteemed, and his joint publications on hysteria with his older friend Josef Breuer had been treated with respect if not complete acceptance. His papers promoting the role of sexuality in hysterical pathogenesis aroused controversy, but still he had no trouble getting this work published. Following its publication, *Die Traumdeutung* did not become an immediate bestseller, but it nevertheless received respectful reviews in many European periodicals (Decker, 1977).

In the United States, however, the book received no reviews at all, and Freud's name was barely known. His earlier work had been mentioned occasionally in the medical literature (Burnham, 1967) but only once in a psychology journal, when William James contributed a one-paragraph abstract of Freud and Breuer's "Preliminary Communication on the Psychical Mechanism of Hysterical Phenomena" to the 1894 *Psychological Review*. Although calling the work an "important paper" by "distinguished Viennese neurologists," James also dismissed it as "an independent corroboration of [Pierre] Janet's views" (James, 1894, p. 199). Breuer and Freud's (1895) much more extensive book *Studien über Hysterie* (*Studies on Hysteria*) was not reviewed in America. Thus, to the extent that Freud was known at all to American psychologists at the dawn of the new century, it was as a junior collaborator of Josef Breuer's, on work considered secondary to that of Pierre Janet (Taylor, 1988, p. 458).

Freud's first independent recognition came during the early 1900s when a group of Boston-area doctors led by Morton Prince and James Jackson Putnam began experimenting with his psychotherapeutic techniques for hysteria. In 1906, Prince established the *Journal of Abnormal*

Psychology to deal with such subjects and invited Freud to write a paper for the first issue (Jones, 1955, p. 28). Freud declined, but Putnam (1906) contributed "Recent Experiences in the Study and Treatment of Hysteria at the Massachusetts General Hospital, With Remarks on Freud's Method of Treatment by 'Psycho-Analysis'." Here was the first extended article on psychoanalytic therapy in the English language. In the meantime, Freud had published the original German versions of *The Psychopathology of Everyday Life* in 1901 (Freud, 1901) and *Three Essays on the Theory of Sexuality* in 1905 (Freud, 1905). The second issue of the *Journal of Abnormal Psychology* carried a three-page review of *The Psychopathology of Everyday Life* (Sidis, 1906) – the first American review of a major Freudian work.

The *Three Essays* (Freud, 1905), with their controversial emphasis on childhood sexuality, now struck a resonant chord with G. Stanley Hall, one of the most powerful figures in American psychology. Hall had established *The American Journal of Psychology* in 1887, had been the founding president of the APA in 1892, and had been president of the leading American producer of Ph.D.s in psychology, Clark University in Worcester, Massachusetts, since 1889. In 1904, Hall had brought the previously obscure term adolescence to public notice with his book *Adolescence: Its Psychology and Its Relation to Physiology, Anthropology, Sociology, Sex, Crime, Religion and Education* (Hall, 1904). With interests in children's development and their sexuality, Hall saw Freud as a potential ally. Also hoping to scoop the Boston psychotherapists, with whom he felt some rivalry, Hall invited Freud to visit Clark and deliver a series of lectures on psychoanalysis as part of the university's 20th anniversary celebration in 1909. After some negotiations in which his fee was increased and he was offered an honorary degree, Freud accepted (Evans & Koelsch, 1985; and Rosenzweig, 1994, provide the fascinating details). Thus, in September of 1909, he made his one and only visit to America. His lectures, delivered in German on five consecutive days after being extemporaneously planned on walks just before, told the story of how he had arrived at the main points of his theory and technique.

Although 29 distinguished lecturers from several different fields participated in the Clark celebration, Hall worked hard to promote Freud as a star. He ensured that Freud's lectures received full press coverage and ghostwrote an appreciative article that appeared in *The Nation* (Evans & Koelsch, 1985, p. 946). Freud's name now appeared for the first time in the American popular press. More consequentially, Hall persuaded Freud to recreate his lectures in writing; these were promptly translated and published in the *American Journal of Psychology* under the title "The Origin and Development of Psychoanalysis" (Freud, 1910). This vivid and lucid account remains today among the best of Freud's popular introductions to the field he created.

The success of this publication created an appetite for English translations of Freud's other major works, and *The Interpretation of Dreams* (Freud, 1913) appeared in 1913, followed by *The Psychopathology of Everyday Life* (Freud, 1914) in 1914. Following World War I, translations of *A General Introduction to Psychoanalysis* (Freud, 1920) came out in 1920 and of *Beyond the Pleasure Principle* (Freud, 1922a) and *Group Psychology and the Analysis of the Ego* (Freud, 1922b) in 1922. The accessibility of these works helped make Freud's name a veritable household word in the United States, and in October of 1924, he made his first appearance on the cover of *Time* magazine. Even his dream theory had become common currency, as illustrated by a popular song that warned, "Don't tell me what you dream'd last night/For I've been reading Freud!" (Burnham, 1979, p. 129).

This ascension to popular acclaim did not occur without protest from the country's experimental psychologists. Hornstein's (1992) insightful analysis of psychology's "problematic relations with psychoanalysis" (p. 254) noted that the radical subjectivity inherent in psychoanalytic practice grossly violated the canons of objectivity the psychologists had so assiduously cultivated. Even at the Clark conference, Freud had anticipated criticism on that score and, when introduced to his fellow participant Edward Bradford Titchener, had said, "Oh, you are the opponent" (Evans & Koelsch, 1985, p. 944). In his second lecture, Freud pointedly noted that his own theory, in contrast to Janet's, had arisen in real-life, clinical settings, completely independent of the psychological laboratory.

At first, psychologists reacted to Freud's popularity with dismissal or contempt. Robert

Woodworth (1917) denigrated Freud's "rough and ready" methods and "one-sided and exaggerated" conclusions (p. 174). More acerbically, Knight Dunlap (1920) lumped together psychoanalysis, philosophical mysticism, and spiritualism as constituting a "siren trinity" that waged "an assault on the very life of the biological sciences"; unlike its partners in the trinity, however, psychoanalysis attempted to "creep in wearing the uniform of science, and to strangle it from the inside" (p. 8). John B. Watson and Rosalie Rayner (1920) took a sarcastic swipe at Freud in their famous case report of Albert, the 11-month-old infant they conditioned to fear a white rat. After describing how Albert's fear had generalized to other furry objects and admitting that they had not deconditioned the response, they speculated:

> The Freudians twenty years from now . . . when they come to analyze Albert's fear of a seal skin coat . . . will probably tease from him a dream which upon their analysis will show that Albert at three years of age attempted to play with the pubic hair of the mother and was scolded violently for it. (p. 14)

At the 1923 APA Convention, one hapless participant aroused James McKeen Cattell's ire by mentioning Freud's name in a discussion. Cattell "arose and, after expressing astonishment and painful surprise that a member of the Association should be so wanting in wisdom as to introduce Freud's name at a scientific meeting, castigated him for his folly, as only Cattell could do" (Dallenbach, 1955, p. 523). Elsewhere, Cattell (1926) described Freud as someone "who lives in the fairyland of dreams among the ogres of perverted sex" (p. 5).

Consistent with these attitudes, most psychology textbooks of the 1920s and early 1930s paid little or no attention to psychoanalysis (Hornstein, 1992). Yet this blindness clearly ran against the tide of American popular opinion and culture. As Freud gained ever more visibility, psychology and psychoanalysis became increasingly confounded in the public mind. Just before his death in 1939, Freud made a second appearance on *Time's* cover. Labelled an "Intellectual Provocateur," he was the subject of one of the longest articles the magazine had published to that date (Gerow, 1988, pp. 18–19).

The next stage in the psychologists' response was anticipated by a series of experiments by Saul Rosenzweig in the early 1930s, demonstrating that incompleted tasks interpreted as failures were prone to being forgotten – an apparent experimental confirmation of the repression of negative events. Freud himself was not overly impressed by this and wrote Rosenzweig, "I cannot put much value on these confirmations because the wealth of reliable observations on which [psychoanalytic] assertions rest make them independent of experimental verification. Still, it can do no harm" (Shakow & Rapaport, 1968, p. 129). Despite Freud's condescension, Rosenzweig's study showed that psychoanalytic concepts could in fact be approached in the laboratory. This suggested a strategy that, Hornstein (1992) noted, was so obvious that it was surprising it took so long to develop. Instead of ignoring psychoanalysis, psychologists would design controlled experiments to determine the validity of psychoanalytic propositions – a strategy that promised to reinstate psychologists "as arbiters of the mental world, able to make the final judgement about what would and would not count as psychological knowledge" (Hornstein, 1992, p. 258). Research by American psychologists on psychoanalysis now became a veritable growth industry, with literally hundreds of articles on the subject published in the 1940s and 1950s.

Freud's influence and visibility in America has continued unabated throughout the second half of the 20th century, both within and without the psychological community. He remains at or near the top of all citation indexes in psychology, and in 1979, following a survey indicating that approximately 10% of the APA membership were interested or involved in the subject, a Division of Psychoanalysis was created (Meisels & Lane, 1996); with more than 3,500 members, Division 39 is currently the sixth largest of the APA's 51 divisions. Also during this period, the U.S. Library of Congress became the repository of a massive Freud collection that now comprises more than 50,000 items, including Freud's own personal papers, donated by his daughter Anna in 1970 (Billington, 1998, pp. ix–x).

It is perhaps needless to say that Freud has also continued to be the object of bitter and highly publicized criticism – charged by a group of revisionist historians with assorted sins such as being an intellectual coward (Masson, 1984), a faulty logician (Grünbaum, 1984), a cryptobiologist (Sulloway, 1992), and a personal as well as a scientific fraud (Crews, 1995). When the Library of Congress planned a major exhibition of its Freud collection in the mid-1990s, the revisionists complained it was to be too celebratory and succeeded in getting some representation of their views in the exhibit and companion book that finally materialized in 1998 with the title *Freud: Conflict and Culture* (Roth, 1998). Still unsatisfied, Crews (1998) published his own selection of critical articles intended to reveal psychoanalysis as "a mistake that grew into an imposture" (p. ix). Nonetheless, Freud has had his tempered defenders among historians (e.g., Forrester, 1997; Robinson, 1993), and on March 29, 1999 – just months short of a century after the publication of *Die Traumdeutung* – he made a third appearance on the cover of *Time*. Demonstrating as well as anything that his hopes of 1899 had been amply realized, the illustration shows him analyzing Albert Einstein under a banner reading "The Century's Greatest Minds."

References

Billington, J. H. (1998). Foreword. In M. S. Roth (Ed.), *Freud: Conflict and culture* (pp. ix–x). New York: Knopf.

Breuer, J., & Freud, S. (1895). *Studien über Hysterie* [Studies on hysteria]. Leipzig, Germany: Franz Deuticke.

Burnham, J. C. (1967). *Psychoanalysis and American medicine: 1894–1918. Medicine, science, and culture.* New York: International Universities Press.

Burnham, J. C. (1978). The influence of psychoanalysis upon American culture. In J. M. Quen & E. T. Carlson (Eds.), *American psychoanalysis: Origins and development* (pp. 55–72). New York: Brunner/Mazel.

Burnham, J. C. (1979). From avant-garde to specialism: Psychoanalysis in America. *Journal of the History of the Behavioral Sciences, 15,* 128–134.

Cattell, J. M. (1926). Some psychological experiments. *Science, 63,* 5.

Crews, F. (1995). *The memory wars: Freud's legacy in dispute.* New York: New York Review of Books.

Crews, F. (1998). *Unauthorized Freud: Doubters confront a legend.* New York: Viking Press.

Dallenbach, K. M. (1955). Phrenology versus psychoanalysis. *American Journal of Psychology, 68,* 511–525.

Decker, H. (1977). *Freud in Germany: Revolution and reaction in science, 1893–1907.* New York: International Universities Press.

Dunlap, K. (1920). *Mysticism, Freudianism and scientific psychology.* St. Louis, MO: Mosby.

Evans, R. B., & Koelsch, W. A. (1985). Psychoanalysis arrives in America: The 1909 psychology conference at Clark University. *American Psychologist, 40,* 942–948.

Forrester, J. (1997). *Dispatches from the Freud wars: Psychoanalysis and its passions.* Cambridge, MA: Harvard University Press.

Freud, S. (1900). *Die Traumdeutung* [The interpretation of dreams]. Leipzig, Germany: Franz Deuticke.

Freud, S. (1901). *Zur Psychopathologie des Alltagslebens* [The psychopathology of everyday life]. Berlin, Germany: S. Karger.

Freud, S. (1905). *Drei Abhandlungen zur Sexualtheorie* [Three essays on the theory of sexuality]. Leipzig, Germany: Franz Deuticke.

Freud, S. (1910). The origin and development of psychoanalysis. *American Journal of Psychology, 21,* 181–218.

Freud, S. (1913). *The interpretation of dreams* (A. A. Brill, Trans.). New York: Macmillan.

Freud, S. (1914). *The psychopathology of everyday life* (A. A. Brill, Trans.). New York: Macmillan.

Freud, S. (1920). *A general introduction to psychoanalysis* (G. S. Hall, Trans.). New York: Boni & Liveright.

Freud, S. (1922a). *Beyond the pleasure principle* (C. Hubback, Trans.). London: International Psycho-Analytical Press.

Freud, S. (1922b). *Group psychology and the analysis of the ego* (J. Strachey, Trans.). London: International Psycho-Analytical Press.

Gerow, J. R. (Ed.). (1988). Psychology 1923–1988 [Special issue]. *Time.*

Grünbaum, A. (1984). *The foundations of psychoanalysis: A philosophical critique.* Berkeley: University of California Press.

Hale, N. G. (1971). *Freud and the Americans: The beginnings of psychoanalysis in the United States, 1876–1917.* New York: Oxford University Press.

Hale, N. G. (1995). *The rise and crisis of psychoanalysis in the United States: Freud and the Americans.* New York: Oxford University Press.

Hall, G. S. (1904). *Adolescence: Its psychology and its relation to physiology, anthropology, sociology, sex, crime, religion and education.* New York: Appleton.

Hornstein, G. A. (1992). The return of the repressed: Psychology's problematic relations with psychoanalysis, 1909–1960. *American Psychologist, 47*, 254–263.

James, W. (1894). Abstract of Breuer and Freud. *Psychological Review, 1*, 199.

Jones, E. (1955). *The life and work of Sigmund Freud* (Vol. 2). New York: Basic Books.

Masson, J. (1984). *The assault on truth: Freud's suppression of the seduction theory.* New York: Farrar, Straus & Giroux.

Meisels, M., & Lane, R. C. (1996). A history of Division 39 (Psychoanalysis). In D. Dewsbury (Ed.), *Unification through division: Histories of the divisions of the American Psychological Association.* Washington, DC: American Psychological Association.

Putnam, J. J. (1906). Recent experiences in the study and treatment of hysteria at the Massachusetts General Hospital, with remarks on Freud's method of treatment by "psycho-analysis." *Journal of Abnormal Psychology, 1*, 26–41.

Robinson, P. (1993). *Freud and his critics.* Berkeley: University of California Press.

Rosenzweig, S. (1994). *The historic expedition to America (1909): Freud, Jung, and Hall the king-maker, with G. Stanley Hall as host and William James as guest.* St. Louis, MO: Rana House.

Roth, M. S. (Ed.). (1998). *Freud: Conflict and culture.* New York: Knopf.

Shakow, D., & Rapaport, D. (1968). *The influence of Freud on American psychology.* New York: Meridian Books.

Sidis, B. (1906). Review of Freud. *Journal of Abnormal Psychology, 1*, 101–103.

Sulloway, F. (1992). *Freud: Biologist of the mind.* Cambridge, MA: Harvard University Press.

Taylor, E. (1988). On the first use of "psychoanalysis" at the Massachusetts General Hospital, 1903 to 1905. *Journal of the History of Medicine and Allied Sciences, 43*, 447–471.

Watson, J. B., & Rayner, R. (1920). Conditioned emotional reactions. *Journal of Experimental Psychology, 3*, 1–14.

Woodworth, R. S. (1917). Some criticisms of the Freudian psychology. *Journal of Abnormal Psychology, 12*, 174–194.

Chapter 8

Behaviorism and Neobehaviorism

Although less than a decade old in 1900, the University of Chicago was a university on the move, largely due to the efforts of its founding president, William Rainey Harper, who raided the established universities (especially G. Stanley Hall's Clark University) in search of their best faculty talent. Chicago was an exciting place to be at the turn of the century. The biology department included Jacques Loeb (1859–1924), an authority on animal behavior, and Henry H. Donaldson (1857–1938), an internationally known authority on the human brain. The philosophy department included John Dewey (1859–1952), who would become, arguably, America's most important philosopher, and James Rowland Angell, who headed the psychology program.

In 1900, John Broadus Watson (1878–1958) arrived at the University of Chicago from his home in rural South Carolina where he had completed his undergraduate and master's degree work at Furman University. He had planned to pursue a doctorate in philosophy, but lost interest in Dewey's classes. In Angell, though, he found the new psychology more to his liking. He took classes from Loeb and Donaldson as well, with Angell and Donaldson eventually directing his doctoral dissertation research. Watson's research was a comparative psychological investigation using infant rats of varying ages to study the relationship between neurological development and behavioral complexity. By 1903, the university had granted authority for a degree in psychology, separate from philosophy, and the first psychology doctorate was awarded to Watson in that year. His dissertation was entitled "Animal education: The psychical development of the white rat" (see Dewsbury, 1990).

Watson had several job offers upon graduation, but elected to stay at Chicago when Angell offered him an assistant professor position in psychology. There he continued his animal research until he was offered a full professor position at Johns Hopkins University in 1908.

According to his autobiography, Watson's dissatisfaction with the prevailing psychology of his day began in 1904 when he was at Chicago (Watson, 1936). Influenced by his physiological training, he searched for ways to make his own science more objective. More and more he was troubled by the mentalism of a psychology defined as the study of consciousness. He had grave doubts about the validity of the method of introspection, preferring, instead, the more controlled stimulus-response conditions of his laboratory studies with rats. He doubted that psychology would ever succeed as a science unless it shifted its focus of study from mental events to measurable and observable behaviors.

In 1912, Watson received an invitation from James McKeen Cattell to deliver a series of lectures at Columbia University beginning in February 1913. His initial lecture was entitled "Psychology as the behaviorist views it," and it no doubt irritated members of his audience. He began:

> Psychology as the behaviorist views it is a purely objective experimental branch of natural science. Its theoretical goal is the prediction and control of behavior. Introspection forms no essential part of its methods, nor is the scientific value of its data dependent upon the readiness with which they lend themselves to interpretation in terms of consciousness. (Watson, 1913, p. 158)

In his talk he rebuked not only the structuralists but also the functionalists among whom he had trained. He claimed that he could not distinguish between them, that both were mired in a mentalism that thwarted objective science. In continuing his attack he said:

> I do not wish unduly to criticize psychology. It has failed signally, I believe, during the fifty-odd years of its existence as an experimental discipline to make its place in the world as a natural science. . . . The time seems to have come when psychology must discard all reference to consciousness; when it need no longer delude itself into thinking that it is making mental states the object of observation. (Watson, 1913, p. 163)

Needless to say, those were exceptionally harsh words from this brash young man who had received his doctorate only 10 years earlier. But he did not soften his attack on the status quo. Psychology, he said, had failed, completely! Fifty years of work had amounted to very little. Psychologists were deluding themselves, thinking that they could actually study consciousness! Some psychologists referred to Watson's lecture as "the day psychology lost its mind."

Watson published his talk a few months later in the journal *Psychological Review*, a journal that he edited. That article is typically referred to as the "behaviorist manifesto," and it is the first reading in this chapter. It is one of the principal reasons that Watson is regarded as the founder of *behaviorism* as a new approach to the science of psychology, a new school that was to replace structuralism and functionalism.

The intellectual roots of behaviorism pre-date Watson, and they extend beyond the boundaries of psychology into allied fields of physiology, medicine, and sociology. But behaviorism as a movement in psychology belongs to Watson. Some historians, for example, John Burnham (1968), have argued against labeling Watson the founder of behaviorism. Burnham prefers to view Watson's role in behaviorism as that of "charismatic leader." Yet that label does not seem to do justice to Watson's role, if it implies that in 1913 the philosophical tenets of behaviorism were already in place in any centralized formulation. Watson's contribution was that he crystallized those scattered ideas into a systematic formulation that was *new*. In Burnham's (1968) words, "Watson combined these elements into a synthesis, the whole of which was greater than its parts" (p. 145). If anyone deserves the label of founder of behavioral psychology, it is John B. Watson. The impact of his words, although not immediate, has been profound in the history of modern psychology.

For Watson, psychology was to be the science of behavior, not mental states. Processes that were not directly observable would have no place in a behavioral psychology. Not only was the subject matter of psychology to be changed, but so were its methods. He called for more objective forms of observation, with and without the use of scientific instruments. He approved of the reaction time studies of Wundt, and the experimental methods Hermann Ebbinghaus used to study memory. He accepted the use of some psychological tests as long as they were not mental tests. He particularly favored the conditioned reflex method of Pavlov, which he used in his most famous study, the *conditioning of fear* in a human infant (see Harris, 1979; Watson & Rayner, 1920).

Watson followed the publication of his manifesto with his first book, *Behavior: An Introduction to Comparative Psychology* (1914), in which he lauded the value of animal research in psychology and elaborated on his views about a wholly behavioral psychology. By the time his next book appeared, *Psychology from the Standpoint of a Behaviorist* (1919), he had shifted his research to human infants, including the classic study of little Albert, who was conditioned to fear a white rat. It was one of the few studies Watson would publish from this new line of work. In the fall of 1920 he was fired from his university position because of an extramarital affair with a graduate student and the scandalous divorce that followed (see Benjamin, Whitaker, Ramsey, & Zeve, 2007: Buckley, 1989).

Watson would never return to a university position and instead began a new and very successful career in business working for two of the leading advertising agencies in New York City (see Buckley, 1989; Coon, 1994). But the seeds he planted would create a philosophy that dominated American psychology for half a century.

Recall Watson's second sentence from his behaviorist manifesto, that the theoretical goal of psychology is the *prediction and control* of behavior. Experimental psychologists in the 1930s would adopt that as a guiding principle, seeking to provide a psychological science that was more lawful, one in which cause and effect could be determined. Several behaviorisms developed during this time under the label *neobehaviorism*. These alternative behaviorisms had much in common. They used animal models to generalize to human behavior. They sought to develop theories to account for human behavior, especially the processes of learning (an influence of functionalism and Darwinian evolution). They provided *operational definitions* for their key constructs, that is, they defined their constructs in terms of the operations used to measure them (for example, hunger could be defined as the number of hours of food deprivation or a specified percentage of reduction in normal body weight). And, as noted above, they accepted the goals of prediction and control as a defining part of their work. Three key neobehaviorists emerged in the 1930s: Edward C. Tolman, Clark L. Hull, and B. F. Skinner.

Edward Tolman (1886–1959) published his most important book in 1932, entitled *Purposive Behavior in Animals and Men*. For Tolman, behavior was, in a word, *purposive*. And the purposiveness of behavior is determined by cognition. How does a behaviorist justify such obviously mentalistic terms? Tolman (1932) wrote:

> Behavior as behavior, that is, as molar, *is* purposive and *is* cognitive . . . it must nonetheless be emphasized that purposes and cognitions which are thus immediately, immanently, in behavior are wholly objective as to definition. They are defined by characters and relationships which we observe out there in behavior. (p. 5)

Tolman argued that, with experience, an organism builds up expectancies about the environment, and these expectancies are one of the determinants of responding. In essence, organisms learn what leads to what. Tolman objected to Watson's limited stimulus-response framework. His theory recognized the existence of *intervening variables* – processes within the organism that intervene between stimuli and responses. Cognitions were examples of those intervening variables and were scientifically respectable so long as they could be tied to observable referents, that is "out there in behavior." Tolman was a brilliant investigator whose cleverly designed studies demonstrated the critical role of cognitions in explaining varied behavioral outcomes (see, for example, Tolman, 1948).

Tolman's chief theoretical rival was Clark Hull (1884–1952), who published most of his early work in a series of articles in the journal *Psychological Review* in the 1930s (see Amsel & Rashotte, 1984). The integration and extension of that work appeared in Hull's 1943 book, *Principles of Behavior*. It was the most frequently cited book in its time, principally because of the large volume of experimental work that it spawned.

Hull created a grand, mathematical theory of behavior, focused especially on the processes of learning and motivation. He wrote:

> I came to the definite conclusion around 1930 that psychology is a true natural science; that its primary laws are expressible quantitatively by means of a moderate number of ordinary equations; that all the complex behavior of single individuals will ultimately be derivable as secondary laws . . . (Hull, 1952, p. 155)

It would be difficult, if not impossible, to find another psychologist who had more faith in the lawfulness of human behavior than Hull!

To test the validity of his theory he used what is called the *hypothetico-deductive method*. He began by stating a series of postulates from which one could derive testable hypotheses. The hypotheses would be tested and then the postulate would be confirmed or, if the evidence were contrary to what would be predicted, then the postulate would have to be modified.

Reinforcement was a key construct in Hull's theory, and it was said to operate by means of *drive reduction*. Drives represented bodily needs such as hunger, thirst, or sleep. When drives were activated, behaviors were initiated, some of which would lead to the reduction of those drives. Those particular behaviors would then be reinforced and would be more likely to occur in future cases when that drive was activated. Reinforcement was key to the strength of learning, or what Hull called *habit strength*. According to Hull, habit strength increased as a direct result of the number of reinforcements experienced. That is, repeated reinforcements increased the strength of association between a particular stimulus and response.

These are just a few of the many constructs in Hull's elaborate theory of behavior. The explicit nature of Hull's theory, including its mathematical form, meant that it was capable of generating many testable hypotheses, which is, in fact, what good scientific theories are supposed to do. Indeed, it is possible that Hull's theory was tested like no other theory in the history of psychology. Eventually the theory proved lacking in many areas; Hull's view of the lawfulness of human behavior seemed to be overly optimistic. Or more likely the problem was that the complexity of human behavior is such that it could not be explained by the few primary and secondary laws of Hull's theory. Although Hull's views no longer have a position of importance in psychology, historians acknowledge his important role in demanding a place for scientific theory in psychology, and his extraordinary effort to create such a comprehensive behavioral theory.

B. F. Skinner (1904–1990) was about 20 years younger than Tolman and Hull yet he published the core of his theory of behavior in the 1930s as well – *The Behavior of Organisms* (1938). Whereas Hull and Tolman were major figures in American psychology from the 1930s through the 1950s, Skinner's fame occurred largely in the 1960s and beyond, partly due to the application of his ideas to education and clinical psychology, especially behavior modification. Skinner's psychology was very different from that of his neobehaviorist colleagues. First he argued against the need for a deductive theory in psychology, which both Tolman and Hull offered. Skinner claimed to be atheoretical, but it can be argued that he had a theory, one that was inductive rather than deductive. Skinner was an animal researcher, like Hull and Tolman, yet his studies tended to use only a single animal or maybe two, instead of the groups of animals typical in the research of the others.

If Watson had been looking to anoint one of these three researchers as the heir apparent to his behavioral throne, there seems little doubt that Skinner would have been his choice. Throughout his entire career he advocated a psychology that was to be void of all mentalistic terms. Skinner saw no need for explanations of behavior that appealed to inner events. He had no regard for cognitive psychology and believed that it was an albatross around psychology's neck that seriously hindered its success as a science (see Skinner, 1990). Further, there is no psychologist in history whose system of psychology was as successful as Skinner's in terms of prediction and control of behavior.

In his 1938 book, Skinner proposed a new form of conditioning that would be called *operant conditioning*. Whereas most studies of learning emphasized stimulus–response (S–R) relationships, for example, in the way in which classical (Pavlovian) conditioning described how a stimulus elicited a response, Skinner's conditioning was a form of R–S learning. Skinner was not very interested in the eliciting stimulus. Instead, he focused on how consequences affected behavior. That is, he was interested in the stimulus events that *followed* a behavior. Manipulating those events – the consequences – allowed the psychologist to control behavioral rates. Behavior was thus the result of *consequences*, events that followed particular responses. These events were typically *reinforcers* and *punishers*. The former increased behavioral rates, the latter decreased them. Over the years he plumbed the depths of conditions of reinforcement and punishment, gaining understanding of these powerful shapers of human behavior. He provided significant findings on shaping, acquisition, extinction, discrimination, generalization, schedules of reinforcement, reinforcement delay, punishment, negative versus positive reinforcement, partial reinforcement effect, chaining, persistence, and too many phenomena to list. He achieved a consistency of results that had not been seen before, demonstrating the considerable explanatory power of his constructs and his psychological system.

The Readings

There are four readings in this chapter: two focus on John Watson and two on B. F. Skinner. The initial selection is Watson's behaviorist manifesto. It is, perhaps, the single most important article in the history of psychology. It is the document that started the behaviorist revolution. Or is it? How was this article received? It certainly should have angered psychologists far and wide in the structuralist and functionalist camps. Titchener, in particular, should have been incensed at some of the things Watson wrote about studying consciousness and about use of the method of introspection. The second reading in this chapter seeks to address the reception of this historic article.

The second reading is by historian of psychology Franz Samelson, who asks the very simple question: What happened after Watson published his 1913 article? Did anyone notice? Did anyone care? Did it spark a behavioral revolution? Was Watson hailed as a savior of psychology or a villain? Samelson's search for the answers is a model for lessons in historiography and an exemplar of excellent historical research. We will not give away the answer here. You will have to read the article.

The third reading is an excerpt from B. F. Skinner's 1938 book, *The Behavior of Organisms*. This brief excerpt deals with Type S (classical) conditioning and Type R (operant) conditioning and a comparison of the two in terms of acquisition and extinction. When this book was published readers would have been familiar with classical conditioning, but likely not with operant conditioning. Skinner explains that he intends to shift the focus on behavior in psychology from behaviors that are elicited (for example, reflexes) to behaviors that are emitted. In doing that, he shifted attention from the antecedents of behavior to an understanding of the consequences of behavior and how manipulations of those consequences could be used to control and predict behavior. In a few short years after this book was published, Skinner would understand how his manipulations of consequences could lead to a powerful behavioral technology (see Capshew, 1993; Skinner, 1983).

The final reading in this chapter is by historian of psychology Alexandra Rutherford, an authority on the psychology of B. F. Skinner. Among the readings in this book, it is one of the best examples of interpreting the reception of psychological work in a broad cultural context. Skinner has long been a controversial character. His best-selling book, *Beyond Freedom and Dignity* (1971), landed him on the cover of *Time* magazine and made him the frequent subject of television talk shows and newspaper columns. He was alternately described as a visionary with a plan to save the world and as a dictator who wanted to control it. In this article, Rutherford (2003) examines the portrayals of Skinner and his work in the popular media from the 1940s through the 1970s. She notes that any "historical analysis of Skinner and his work must take into account the cultural, social, and political milieu of mid-twentieth-century America" (p. 1). And that she accomplishes very well. Like Samelson's article in this chapter, this one too is filled with important lessons in historiography, especially the importance of external history.

Psychology as the Behaviorist Views It
John B. Watson

Psychology as the behaviorist views it is a purely objective experimental branch of natural science. Its theoretical goal is the prediction and control of behavior. Introspection forms no essential part of its methods, nor is the scientific value of its data dependent upon the readiness with which they lend themselves to interpretation in terms of consciousness. The behaviorist, in his efforts to get a unitary scheme of animal response, recognizes no dividing line between man and brute. The behavior of man, with all of its refinement and complexity, forms only a part of the behaviorist's total scheme of investigation.

It has been maintained by its followers generally that psychology is a study of the science of the phenomena of consciousness. It has taken as its problem, on the one hand, the analysis of complex mental states (or processes) into simple elementary constituents, and on the other the construction of complex states when the elementary constituents are given. The world of physical objects (stimuli, including here anything which may excite activity in a receptor), which forms the total phenomena of the natural scientist, is looked upon merely as means to an end. That end is the production of mental states that may be "inspected" or "observed." The psychological object of observation in the case of an emotion, for example, is the mental state itself. The problem in emotion is the determination of the number and kind of elementary constituents present, their loci, intensity, order of appearance, etc. It is agreed that introspection is the method *par excellence* by means of which mental states may be manipulated for purposes of psychology. On this assumption, behavior data (including

Adapted from J. B. Watson (1913). Psychology as the behaviorist views it. *Psychological Review, 20,* 158–177.

under this term everything which goes under the name of comparative psychology) have no value *per se*. They possess significance only in so far as they may throw light upon conscious states. Such data must have at least an analogical or indirect reference to belong to the realm of psychology.

Indeed, at times, one finds psychologists who are sceptical of even this analogical reference. Such scepticism is often shown by the question which is put to the student of behavior, "what is the bearing of animal work upon human psychology?" I used to have to study over this question. Indeed it always embarrassed me somewhat. I was interested in my own work and felt that it was important, and yet I could not trace any close connection between it and psychology as my questioner understood psychology. I hope that such a confession will clear the atmosphere to such an extent that we will no longer have to work under false pretences. We must frankly admit that the facts so important to us which we have been able to glean from extended work upon the senses of animals by the behavior method have contributed only in a fragmentary way to the general theory of human sense organ processes, nor have they suggested new points of experimental attack. The enormous number of experiments which we have carried out upon learning have likewise contributed little to human psychology. It seems reasonably clear that some kind of compromise must be effected: either psychology must change its viewpoint so as to take in facts of behavior, whether or not they have bearings upon the problems of "consciousness"; or else behavior must stand alone as a wholly separate and independent science. Should human psychologists fail to look with favor upon our overtures and refuse to modify their position, the behaviorists will be driven to using human beings as subjects and to employ methods of investigation which are exactly comparable to those now employed in the animal work.

Any other hypothesis than that which admits the independent value of behavior material, regardless of any bearing such material may have upon consciousness, will inevitably force us to the absurd position of attempting to *construct* the conscious content of the animal whose behavior we have been studying. On this view, after having determined our animal's ability to learn, the simplicity or complexity of its methods of learning, the effect of past habit upon present response, the range of stimuli to which it ordinarily responds, the widened range to which it can respond under experimental conditions, – in more general terms, its various problems and its various ways of solving them, – we should still feel that the task is unfinished and that the results are worthless, until we can interpret them by analogy in the light of consciousness. Although we have solved our problem we feel uneasy and unrestful because of our definition of psychology we feel forced to say something about the possible mental processes of our animal. We say that, having no eyes, its stream of consciousness cannot contain brightness and color sensations as we know them, – having no taste buds this stream can contain no sensations of sweet, sour, salt and bitter. But on the other hand, since it does respond to thermal, tactual and organic stimuli, its conscious content must be made up largely of these sensations; and we usually add, to protect ourselves against the reproach of being anthropomorphic, "if it has any consciousness." Surely this doctrine which calls for an analogical interpretation of all behavior data may be shown to be false: the position that the standing of an observation upon behavior is determined by its fruitfulness in yielding results which are interpretable only in the narrow realm of (really human) consciousness.

This emphasis upon analogy in psychology has led the behaviorist somewhat afield. Not being willing to throw off the yoke of consciousness he feels impelled to make a place in the scheme of behavior where the rise of consciousness can be determined. This point has been a shifting one. A few years ago certain animals were supposed to possess "associative memory," while certain others were supposed to lack it. One meets this search for the origin of consciousness under a good many disguises. Some of our texts state

that consciousness arises at the moment when reflex and instinctive activities fail properly to conserve the organism. A perfectly adjusted organism would be lacking in consciousness. On the other hand whenever we find the presence of diffuse activity which results in habit formation, we are justified in assuming consciousness. I must confess that these arguments had weight with me when I began the study of behavior. I fear that a good many of us are still viewing behavior problems with something like this in mind. More than one student in behavior has attempted to frame criteria of the psychic – to devise a set of objective, structural and functional criteria which, when applied in the particular instance, will enable us to decide whether such and such responses are positively conscious, merely indicative of consciousness, or whether they are purely "physiological." Such problems as these can no longer satisfy behavior men. It would be better to give up the province altogether and admit frankly that the study of the behavior of animals has no justification, than to admit that our search is of such a "will o' the wisp" character. One can assume either the presence or the absence of consciousness anywhere in the phylogenetic scale without affecting the problems of behavior by one jot or one tittle; and without influencing in any way the mode of experimental attack upon them. On the other hand, I cannot for one moment assume that the paramecium responds to light; that the rat learns a problem more quickly by working at the task five times a day than once a day, or that the human child exhibits plateaux in his learning curves. These are questions which vitally concern behavior and which must be decided by direct observation under experimental conditions.

This attempt to reason by analogy from human conscious processes to the conscious processes in animals, and *vice versa*: to make consciousness, as the human being knows it, the center of reference of all behavior, forces us into a situation similar to that which existed in biology in Darwin's time. The whole Darwinian movement was judged by the bearing it had upon the origin and development of the human race. Expeditions were undertaken to collect material which would establish the position that the rise of the human race was a perfectly natural phenomenon and not an act of special creation. Variations were carefully sought along with the evidence for the heaping up effect and the weeding out effect of selection; for in these and the other Darwinian mechanisms were to be found factors sufficiently complex to account for the origin and race differentiation of man. The wealth of material collected at this time was considered valuable largely in so far as it tended to develop the concept of evolution in man. It is strange that this situation should have remained the dominant one in biology for so many years. The moment Zoölogy undertook the experimental study of evolution and descent, the situation immediately changed. Men ceased to be the center of reference. I doubt if any experimental biologist today, unless actually engaged in the problem of race differentiation in man, tries to interpret his findings in terms of human evolution, or even refers to it in his thinking. He gathers his data from the study of many species of plants and animals and tries to work out the laws of inheritance in the particular type upon which he is conducting experiments. Naturally, he follows the progress of the work upon race differentiation in man and in the descent of man, but he looks upon these as special topics, equal in importance with his own yet ones in which his interests will never be vitally engaged. It is not fair to say that all of his work is directed toward human evolution or that it must be interpreted in terms of human evolution. He does not have to dismiss certain of his facts on the inheritance of coat color in mice because, forsooth, they have little bearing upon the differentiation of the *genus homo* into separate races, or upon the descent of the *genus homo* from some more primitive stock.

In psychology we are still in that stage of development where we feel that we must select our material. We have a general place of discard for processes, which we anathematize so far as their value for psychology is concerned by saying, "this is a reflex": "that is a purely physiological fact which has nothing to do with psychology." We are not interested (as psychologists) in getting all of the processes of adjustment which the animal as a whole employs, and in finding how these various responses are associated, and how they fall apart, thus working out a systematic scheme for the prediction and control of response in general. Unless our observed facts are indicative of consciousness, we have no use for them, and unless our apparatus and method are

designed to throw such facts into relief, they are thought of in just as disparaging a way. I shall always remember the remark one distinguished psychologist made as he looked over the color apparatus designed for testing the responses of animals to monochromatic light in the attic at Johns Hopkins. It was this: "And they call this psychology!"

I do not wish unduly to criticize psychology. It has failed signally, I believe, during the fifty-odd years of its existence as an experimental discipline to make its place in the world as an undisputed natural science. Psychology, as it is generally thought of, has something esoteric in its methods. If you fail to reproduce my findings, it is not due to some fault in your apparatus or in the control of your stimulus, but it is due to the fact that your introspection is untrained. The attack is made upon the observer and not upon the experimental setting. In physics and in chemistry the attack is made upon the experimental conditions. The apparatus was not sensitive enough, impure chemicals were used, etc. In these sciences a better technique will give reproducible results. Psychology is otherwise. If you can't observe 3–9 states of clearness in attention, your introspection is poor. If, on the other hand, a feeling seems reasonably clear to you, your introspection is again faulty. You are seeing too much. Feelings are never clear.

The time seems to have come when psychology must discard all reference to consciousness; when it need no longer delude itself into thinking that it is making mental states the object of observation. We have become so enmeshed in speculative questions concerning the elements of mind, the nature of conscious content (for example, imageless thought, attitudes, and Bewusseinslage, etc.) that I, as an experimental student, feel that something is wrong with our premises and the types of problems which develop from them. There is no longer any guarantee that we all mean the same thing when we use the terms now current in psychology. Take the case of sensation. A sensation is defined in terms of its attributes. One psychologist will state with readiness that the attributes of a visual sensation are *quality, extension, duration*, and *intensity*. Another will add *clearness*. Still another that of *order*. I doubt if any one psychologist can draw up a set of statements describing what he means by sensation which will be agreed to by three other psychologists of different training. Turn for a moment to the question of the number of isolable sensations. Is there an extremely large number of color sensations – or only four, red, green, yellow and blue? Again, yellow, while psychologically simple, can be obtained by superimposing red and green spectral rays upon the same diffusing surface! If, on the other hand, we say that every just noticeable difference in the spectrum is a simple sensation, and that every just noticeable increase in the white value of a given color gives simple sensations, we are forced to admit that the number is so large and the conditions for obtaining them so complex that the concept of sensation is unusable, either for the purpose of analysis or that of synthesis. Titchener, who has fought the most valiant fight in this country for a psychology based upon introspection, feels that these differences of opinion as to the number of sensations and their attributes, as to whether there are relations (in the sense of elements) and on the many others which seem to be fundamental in every attempt at analysis, are perfectly natural in the present undeveloped state of psychology. While it is admitted that every growing science is full of unanswered questions, surely only those who are wedded to the system as we now have it, who have fought and suffered for it, can confidently believe that there will ever be any greater uniformity than there is now in the answers we have to such questions. I firmly believe that two hundred years from now, unless the introspective method is discarded, psychology will still be divided on the question as to whether auditory sensations have the quality of "extension," whether intensity is an attribute which can be applied to color, whether there is a difference in "texture" between image and sensation and upon many hundreds of others of like character.

The condition in regard to other mental processes is just as chaotic. Can image type be experimentally tested and verified? Are recondite thought processes dependent mechanically upon imagery at all? Are psychologists agreed upon what feeling is? One states that feelings are attitudes. Another finds them to be groups of organic sensations possessing a certain solidarity. Still another and larger group finds them to be new elements correlative with and ranking equally with sensations.

My psychological quarrel is not with the systematic and structural psychologist alone. The last fifteen years have seen the growth of what is called functional psychology. This type of psychology decries the use of elements in the static sense of the structuralists. It throws emphasis upon the biological significance of conscious processes instead of upon the analysis of conscious states into introspectively isolable elements. I have done my best to understand the difference between functional psychology and structural psychology. Instead of clarity, confusion grows upon me. The terms sensation, perception, affection, emotion, volition are used as much by the functionalist as by the structuralist. The addition of the word "process" ("mental act as a whole," and like terms are frequently met) after each serves in some way to remove the corpse of "content" and to leave "function" in its stead. Surely if these concepts are elusive when looked at from a content standpoint, they are still more deceptive when viewed from the angle of function, and especially so when function is obtained by the introspection method. It is rather interesting that no functional psychologist has carefully distinguished between "perception" (and this is true of the other psychological terms as well) as employed by the systematist, and "perceptual process" as used in functional psychology. It seems illogical and hardly fair to criticize the psychology which the systematist gives us, and then to utilize his terms without carefully showing the changes in meaning which are to be attached to them. I was greatly surprised some time ago when I opened Pillsbury's book and saw psychology defined as the "science of behavior." A still more recent text states that psychology is the "science of mental behavior." When I saw these promising statements I thought, now surely we will have texts based upon different lines. After a few pages the science of behavior is dropped and one finds the conventional treatment of sensation, perception, imagery, etc., along with certain shifts in emphasis and additional facts which serve to give the author's personal imprint.

One of the difficulties in the way of a consistent functional psychology is the parallelistic hypothesis. If the functionalist attempts to express his formulations in terms which make mental states really appear to function, to play some active rôle in the world of adjustment, he almost inevitably lapses into terms which are connotative of interaction. When taxed with this he replies that it is more convenient to do so and that he does it to avoid the circumlocution and clumsiness which are inherent in any thorough-going parallelism. As a matter of fact I believe the functionalist actually thinks in terms of interaction and resorts to parallelism only when forced to give expression to his views. I feel that *behaviorism* is the only consistent and logical functionalism. In it one avoids both the Scylla of parallelism and the Charybdis of interaction. Those time-honored relics of philosophical speculation need trouble the student of behavior as little as they trouble the student of physics. The consideration of the mind-body problem affects neither the type of problem selected nor the formulation of the solution of that problem. I can state my position here no better than by saying that I should like to bring my students up in the same ignorance of such hypotheses as one finds among the students of other branches of science.

This leads me to the point where I should like to make the argument constructive. I believe we can write a psychology, define it as Pillsbury, and never go back upon our definition: never use the terms consciousness, mental states, mind, content, introspectively verifiable, imagery, and the like. I believe that we can do it in a few years without running into the absurd terminology of Beer, Bethe, Von Uexküll, Nuel, and that of the so-called objective schools generally. It can be done in terms of stimulus and response, in terms of habit formation, habit integrations and the like. Furthermore, I believe that it is really worth while to make this attempt now.

The psychology which I should attempt to build up would take as a starting point, first, the observable facts that organisms, man and animal alike, do adjust themselves to their environment by means of hereditary and habit equipments. These adjustments may be very adequate or they may be so inadequate that the organism barely maintains its existence; secondly, that certain stimuli lead the organisms to make the responses. In a system of psychology completely worked out, given the response the stimuli can be predicted; given the stimuli the response can be predicted. Such a set of statements is crass and raw in the

extreme, as all such generalizations must be. Yet they are hardly more raw and less realizable than the ones which appear in the psychology texts of the day. I possibly might illustrate my point better by choosing an everyday problem which anyone is likely to meet in the course of his work. Some time ago I was called upon to make a study of certain species of birds. Until I went to Tortugas I had never seen these birds alive. When I reached there I found the animals doing certain things: some of the acts seemed to work peculiarly well in such an environment, while others seemed to be unsuited to their type of life. I first studied the responses of the group as a whole and later those of individuals. In order to understand more thoroughly the relation between what was habit and what was hereditary in these responses, I took the young birds and reared them. In this way I was able to study the order of appearance of hereditary adjustments and their complexity, and later the beginnings of habit formation. My efforts in determining the stimuli which called forth such adjustments were crude indeed. Consequently my attempts to control behavior and to produce responses at will did not meet with much success. Their food and water, sex and other social relations, light and temperature conditions were all beyond control in a field study. I did find it possible to control their reactions in a measure by using the nest and egg (or young) as stimuli. It is not necessary in this paper to develop further how such a study should be carried out and how work of this kind must be supplemented by carefully controlled laboratory experiments. Had I been called upon to examine the natives of some of the Australian tribes, I should have gone about my task in the same way. I should have found the problem more difficult: the types of responses called forth by physical stimuli would have been more varied, and the number of effective stimuli larger. I should have had to determine the social setting of their lives in a far more careful way. These savages would be more influenced by the responses of each other than was the case with the birds. Furthermore, habits would have been more complex and the influences of past habits upon the present responses would have appeared more clearly. Finally, if I had been called upon to work out the psychology of the educated European, my problem would have required several lifetimes. But in the one I have at my disposal I should have followed the same general line of attack. In the main, my desire in all such work is to gain an accurate knowledge of adjustments and the stimuli calling them forth. My final reason for this is to learn general and particular methods by which I may control behavior. My goal is not "the description and explanation of states of consciousness as such," nor that of obtaining such proficiency in mental gymnastics that I can immediately lay hold of a state of consciousness and say, "this, as a whole, consists of gray sensation number 350, of such and such extent, occurring in conjunction with the sensation of cold of a certain intensity; one of pressure of a certain intensity and extent," and so on *ad infinitum*. If psychology would follow the plan I suggest, the educator, the physician, the jurist and the business man could utilize our data in a practical way, as soon as we are able, experimentally, to obtain them. Those who have occasion to apply psychological principles practically would find no need to complain as they do at the present time. Ask any physician or jurist today whether scientific psychology plays a practical part in his daily routine and you will hear him deny that the psychology of the laboratories finds a place in his scheme of work. I think the criticism is extremely just. . . .

In concluding, I suppose I must confess to a deep bias on these questions. I have devoted nearly twelve years to experimentation on animals. It is natural that such a one should drift into a theoretical position which is in harmony with his experimental work. Possibly I have put up a straw man and have been fighting that. There may be no absolute lack of harmony between the position outlined here and that of functional psychology. I am inclined to think, however, that the two positions cannot be easily harmonized. Certainly the position I advocate is weak enough at present and can be attacked from many standpoints. Yet when all this is admitted I still feel that the considerations which I have urged should have a wide influence upon the type of psychology which is to be developed in the future. What we need to do is to start work upon psychology, making *behavior,* not *consciousness,* the objective point of our attack. Certainly there are enough problems in the control of behavior to keep us all working many lifetimes without ever allowing us time to think of consciousness *an sich*. Once launched in the undertaking, we will find ourselves in a short time as far divorced from an introspective psychology as the psychology of the present time is divorced from faculty psychology.

Struggle for Scientific Authority: The Reception of Watson's Behaviorism, 1913–1920

Franz Samelson

If retrospectively the appearance of Watson's manifesto was a major historical event, primary sources do not quite reflect it as such. Except for Howard C. Warren's reference to the fact that he had repeatedly urged Watson to publish his position paper, none of the autobiographies of prominent psychologists of the period have marked it as a red letter day. In fact, the dean of psychology's historians, E. G. Boring, in an extended reminiscence of his professional life history, did not find it necessary to recall any encounter with Watson or Watson's ideas, even though his own orientation changed from Titchnerian structuralism to a (behavioral) "physicalism."[1]

Initial Responses: Three Themes and Some Hostility

To be sure, the contemporary literature did not ignore Watson's paper completely; neither did it give his challenge singular prominence. A summary of the events of 1913 in psychology, written by Langfeld for the *American Year Book*, started out by dealing with two other "important discussions" before mentioning the "behaviorist movement"; even then it cited Maurice Parmelee's new book *The Science of Human Behavior* rather than Watson's work. The discussion of Watson's paper came only in the second section, entitled "Psychological Method," and treated it mainly as another attack on introspection. A

second overview of the preceding year, the summary on "General Problems: Mind and Body" in the January 1914 *Psychological Bulletin* did open with the question whether psychology was purely a study of behavior, or of mental states and processes, or both; commenting that the behaviorists especially were attracting attention in the debate, it then quoted half a page from Watson's paper before going on, noncommittally, to other views on the issue.[2]

Beyond such summaries we find that, in an address on the "Study of Human Behavior" for a June 1913 Eugenics Conference, Robert M. Yerkes had begun to use the term "behaviorist" (apparently coined in late 1912 independently by both Watson and James R. Angell);[3] but his references were to three recent books: Parmelee's work mentioned above, Max Meyer's book on *The Fundamental Laws of Human Behavior*, and William McDougall's *Introduction to Social Psychology*, not to Watson's paper (with which he was familiar).[4] Apart from some footnote references added on to papers written before the appearance of Watson's article, the first direct response in print came in a short article by Mary W. Calkins, entitled "Psychology and the Behaviorist."[5] Critical of Watson's "vigorous" paper, she expressed her "radical disagreement with [its] main thesis" of the uselessness of introspection, questioned his supporting arguments, and insisted that certain kinds of psychological processes could be studied only by introspection. However, she also expressed much sympathy with the "important truth embedded" in Watson's criticism of the "undue abstractness" of the present psychology as the "study of mental state." Instead, psychology needed to be concerned with "problems of life." The study of behavior by objective methods was indeed important, as long as "behavior" was understood

Adapted from F. Samelson (1981). Struggle for scientific authority: The reception of Watson's behaviorism, 1913–1920. *Journal of the History of the Behavioral Sciences, 17*, 399–425. Copyright © 1981 by Wiley-Blackwell. Adapted and reprinted by permission of the publisher and the author.

not merely as "mechanical," but meant the study of "self related to environment."[6]

Here we have the emergence of three themes which in one form or another came to predominate in the published reactions to Watson for some time: (1) although Calkins conceded some problems with the method of introspection and granted the legitimacy of objective procedures, she nevertheless maintained the usefulness of introspection as one of the methods of psychology (what we might call the "don't throw out the baby with the bath" argument); (2) she expressed a strong desire to expand the subject matter of psychological study to a concern with real people in the real world (the "relevance" argument, as we might call it today); and (3) accepting the notion of behavior, but questioning Watson's narrow definition of the term, she attempted to redirect Watson's thrust toward her own goal, a special "self psychology" version of a functionalist approach (the "cooptation" theme). It is tempting to argue, by the way, that, taking psychology as a whole, Mary Calkin's view was more nearly prophetic of what psychology would become half a century later than was Watson's narrower position, even though his slogan of the "study of behavior" eventually carried the day.

The other direct, and quite enthusiastic, response to Watson came from Fred L. Wells, perhaps best described as a hybrid experimentalist-clinician working at McLean Hospital for the Insane. Once in the context of a review of Parmelee's book, and again in a summary review of "Dynamic Psychology" for the *Psychological Bulletin*, he put himself into Watson's corner, lauding Watson's "well-aimed blow at the autistic method in psychology. . . ."[7] and quoting with obvious relish some of his attacks on the "pure" psychologists and their lack of concern with human life. "Experimental psychology . . . dodges . . . the more actual and vital questions . . . [and retreats] into a burrow of trivial inquiries . . . ," Wells complained.[8] Yet he, like Calkins (and Angell before them, in an APA address on "Behavior as a Psychological Category," delivered about the time Watson was preparing his paper for publication), argued that at least for practical purposes some use of introspection was unavoidable. Furthermore, the crucial issue to be settled was the meaning of "behavior"; in order to be useful it

could not be restricted to activities describable in physical or physiological terms, but had to include "*mental*[!] behavior."[9]

A very brief comment in a review of "Criminology and Delinquency" by Jean Weidensall (who as a student had known Watson at Chicago and was, like Wells, working in a nonacademic setting) concludes the list of references to Watson in the *Psychological Bulletin* of 1913: Though Watson's paper seemed a bit radical, she felt that "in truth [it was outlining] the psychology we shall find most useful."[10]

There were also three brief items in the *Journal of Philosophy, Psychology*, and *Scientific Method*. In the last paragraph of a short paper on the definition of Comparative Psychology, Yerkes protested strongly against Watson's attempt to "throw overboard . . . the method of self-observation" and to usurp the science of psychology for the study of behavior, although he supported wholeheartedly the integration of behavior methods into psychology. Angell put in a brief demurrer against Watson's claim, that Angell's research on imagery had justified the dismissal of the image from psychology. And finally philosopher Henry R. Marshall, in a paper asking, "Is Psychology Evaporating?" briefly referred to Thorndike, Watson, and the objective science of behavior which was, in his view, legitimate; but it was not psychology.[11]

In late December 1913 the American Psychological Association held its annual convention at Yale University (which hosted the American Philosophical Association at the same time). APA president H. C. Warren gave an address on "The Mental and the Physical." Rejecting any solution of the metaphysical mind-body problem as premature, he went on to argue for the adoption of a double-aspect view as a working hypothesis. This position required a redefinition of psychology to embrace both inner and outer aspects of experience and made it the "science of the relations between the individual and his environment, [to] be studied either objectively as behavior, or introspectively as events of consciousness."[12]

A page-long summary of Warren's address in the proceedings did not refer to Watson at all. The paper itself contained a number of references to Watson and his position; yet it was clearly not a response to him, but to a problematic which had been debated by psychologists for some time. Warren agreed with Watson that the hope for the future might lie in the study of behavior, since it revealed "dynamic aspects" more than did introspection. But he could not accept an autocratic decree prohibiting introspective study; introspection had produced many results of scientific worth; Watson's critique was too "destructive."[13] In summary, Warren's argument, while different in the specifics, was basically the same as Calkins': don't throw out the baby of introspection, but accept behavior for the sake of "dynamics," and fashion a "double-aspect" compromise instead of splitting psychology into two different disciplines.

At the same convention, a joint session with the philosophers on the "standpoint of psychology" heard, among others, John Dewey and Hugo Münsterberg refer favorably but briefly to behaviorism. Wishing behaviorism well, Dewey expressed both fear and hope – fear, if "behavior" meant just the mechanics of the nervous system; hope, if it included the "attitudes and responses towards others which cannot be located under the skin. . . . " Münsterberg, in an exposition of his scheme of two psychologies, one "causal" and the other "teleological," expressed the opinion that behaviorism might be successful in an applied psychology derived from the causal approach. In the discussion, Knight Dunlap raised some questions about "delimiting the behaviorist's field. . . . " Earlier that year, Dunlap had presented a talk at Johns Hopkins, in which he distanced himself sharply from Watson and protested against the latter's "extreme doctrine" likely to produce opposition to more moderate innovations.[14]

The earliest recorded reference to Watson's manifesto apparently occurred in a discussion of "four recent tendencies" in psychology, presented by G. Stanley Hall at a Mental Hygiene Conference in April 1913. After introspection and psychoanalysis, "a rich, rank, seething mass of new facts and new ideas, sure to revolutionize. . . . " psychology, Hall mentioned behaviorism briefly and in rather neutral fashion, obviously quoting or paraphrasing Watson's major thesis. From there he proceeded to an extended discussion of the last tendency, Pavlov's "amazing" work on salivary conditioning, which had barely touched American psychology as yet.[15]

The seventy-year old Hall still had his ear to the ground.

The only indication of a "violent reaction" and "furor"[16] caused by Watson's polemic is found in a short notice reporting on the meeting of the Experimental Psychologists (largely the inner, Titchenerian circle of the academic discipline), held at Wesleyan University in April 1913. It appears that a "lively discussion" on the introspection and behaviorism developed in one of the sessions. Introspection had been hotly debated – without Watson – at a meeting two years earlier, with Titchener on one side and Dodge and Holt on the other.[17] This time, "the hostility to an identification of psychology with "behaviorism" was surprisingly unanimous. . . . "[18] That is unfortunately all we know about the meeting.

Concerning the other meeting, the year-end APA convention, Melvin E. Haggerty's report remarked that "in spirit [it] had a decidedly behavioristic tendency. More than half the papers either championed the behavioristic point of view in one or another form or [used] behavioristic methods [in their experiments]. A considerable part of the time the word itself was in the air."[19] Here at last is an indication of an apparently broad-based and positive response to Watson. Yet when we look for specifics (beyond the comments by Dewey, Münsterberg, and Warren), we cannot find, either in the titles or in the texts of the paper abstracts for the convention, any mention of Watson or behaviorism; at least for the modern reader, it turns out to be rather difficult to see which of these papers (with one or two exceptions) were supposed by Haggerty to champion the behaviorist point of view. (Judged by subsequent comments, Haggerty himself sympathized with behaviorism, but he also called Watson's refusal to consider introspective knowledge "the merest folly.")[20] And a different report on the convention, by APA secretary Walter V. Bingham, failed to notice any wave of behaviorism. It only remarked, with some relief, that in spite of the presence of the philosophers at the convention the paper sessions had not produced an inordinate number of philosophical or theoretical papers; instead, it had been a well-balanced program (and, we might add, apparently without major surprises).[21] We shall meet this problem again: after discovering a tantalizing reference to the popularity of behaviorism among a certain group of persons, if we ask just who was involved and how it was expressed, we find the concrete evidence to be very elusive.

A Behavioristic Underground?

On this note ends our account of the recorded responses to Watson in the first year.[22] They were not overwhelming either in their frequency or their intensity, and furthermore came mainly from authors already in favor of some changes before Watson's appeal. Criticism of introspection was not new; neither was the use of objective methods or the advocacy of the study of behavior, as references to other authors like Meyer, Parmelee, and Thorndike indicate. (As Wells had expressed it, Watson had produced an "unusually concrete statement of a central idea that has always claimed certain adherents among us. . . . "[23])

Was there a behaviorist revolution in the year 1913? The terms "behaviorist" and "behaviorism" had been accepted into professional language; there certainly was some awareness and, on occasion, lively discussion of Watson's contribution to the ongoing debate about the methods and objects of the science. In print, a few direct but mixed reactions agreed with some aspects of Watson's challenge with some enthusiasm while firmly rejecting others. But no reminiscence has described memories of a dramatic encounter with the manifesto; we have not found any contemporary evidence for the conversion of a single individual to Watson's position. While he may have issued a call to revolution, as yet we have seen no clear signs of a mass uprising. But scientific revolutions may take a bit more time. Or perhaps there was a behaviorist "movement," though it was underground, below the printed surface.[24]

Unfortunately, a laborious search of various archival collections has failed to be of much help. Indeed, I have not yet turned up a single letter from the year 1913 containing reactions to Watson's Columbia presentation or its printed version. The only contemporary references came from Watson himself. Sending some reprints of his paper to Yerkes, Watson commented: "I understand that [Yale's Roswell P.] Angier thinks I am crazy. I should not be surprised if this was the general consensus of opinion." (This estimate seems not far off the mark at least in terms of the consensus among the experimentalists, meeting at Wesleyan the following month.) While unfortunately Yerkes's reply is not preserved, Watson's next letter referred to some differences of opinion. At a later date, when the rift between Watson and Yerkes was widening, Yerkes implied that he had held back sharp criticism of the manifesto at the time.[25] And in another place, Watson indicated that James M. Cattell had scolded him for being "too radical."[26]

I have located very few additional pre-war comments (there are more later on) related to behaviorism in various archives: a very positive though brief one by Gilbert V. Hamilton, and two years later a rather solemn declaration by Margaret F. Washburn that she thought "JBW an enemy to psychology." In addition, there is the exchange of critical comments between Titchener, Angell, and Yerkes, reported earlier by Cedric A. Larson and John J. Sullivan.[27]

There are probably three reasons for this disappointing outcome of an extensive archival search. The most obvious one is that the relevant source material may be lost. Still, some of the surviving collections might have been expected to contain references to the allegedly revolutionary events. Thus a second reason, I would suggest, is that – at least by that time – the function of academic correspondence had shifted. It was no longer a scholarly discussion and sharing of views between colleagues about the substantive issues of their field (assuming gratuitously that it had been so in earlier times); it was rather (with some exceptions) a somewhat hurried bureaucratic exchange, dealing mainly with concrete administrative-political problems: jobs, students, technical details of research and publishing activities, arrangements for meetings, etc., topped off by a bit of gossip and brief personal news. The typewriter had come to the office, but not yet the secretary; letters were usually typed, but mostly by their authors (and therefore without copies). In short, writing letters had become a chore. The discussion of substantive psychological issues may have been displaced to oral exchanges at formal meetings and informal visits; major statements on psychological issues were put into print.

And yet, I believe there is a third reason for this lack of references to behaviorism. Watson had said some strongly provocative and offensive things; but criticism of important aspects of the discipline and/or proposals for new directions had appeared before and after 1913, as they have on and off throughout the history of psychology. Usually, they are taken notice of, if coming from authors with some visibility, and may even produce a bit of a stir; some new terms may become fashionable; but then business goes on as usual for the vast majority of psychologists. Their activities are determined by other forces than verbal appeals – as any good behaviorist would know. After all, Watson's initial statement had not contained many concrete suggestions, except for the prohibition on introspective procedures. His main point had been a call for reconceptualization. We shall return to this issue later.

Two additional events occurring at year's end must be mentioned. Watson was elected president of the Southern Society for Philosophy and Psychology; he also became editor of the new *Journal of Experimental Psychology*, started by Warren upon Watson's suggestion.[28] But whether these honors were bestowed on him because of his call to arms or in spite of it (i.e. were based on his reputation as an outstanding young scientist acquired before 1913) is impossible to tell. We can only note that any hostility felt by the establishment was either not intense or not powerful enough to prevent these nominations. . . .

If, on the assumption that publication lag or other reasons delayed the response to Watson's historic paper, we search the psychology journals for the following year in order to find evidence of the full impact, we are in for another disappointment. Apart from registering some of the events and talks of 1913 already described, the *Psychological Bulletin* mentioned Watson or behaviorism hardly at all. . . . Langfeld's survey of the year 1914 in the *American Year Book* noticed no major changes; he reported a continued discussion of the fundamental problem of psychology: the relation of the mental and the physical world, with references to Warren, Holt, Münsterberg, and Prince. Mention of behaviorism remained relegated to the Methods section, according to which "discussion still center[ed] about the question of introspection *versus* behaviorism . . . "; although Watson was still maintaining his radical view,

"many psychologists believe in the combination of these two methods . . . "[29]

By 1915, Watson's first book, *Behavior: An Introduction to Comparative Psychology*, had been published. The introductory chapter had reprinted his 1913 papers with only minor changes; the main text had fleshed out Watson's behaviorist program a bit more in a discussion of instincts, reflexes, and habit development in animal psychology. A short description of the book's content by Langfeld and three special reviews by Carr, Thorndike and Herrick, and Haggerty were quite favorable overall; the longer ones criticized some details and all rejected Watson's more extreme theoretical statements, especially the ban on introspection.[30] In a 1910 APA paper and in the introduction to the 1911 edition of *Animal Intelligence*, Thorndike had argued strongly for the importance of objective studies of behavior. Now he expressed his regret that Watson had not added a chapter on *human* psychology to show that recognized psychologists had, for thirty years, carried out behavioral studies of humans. Watson should have corrected the impression that human psychology had been exclusively an introspective affair. But even Thorndike found it unwise to ignore the special form of observation of themselves humans were capable of; it might "well play some part in science."[31]

Apart from the reviews, few references to Watson or his book can be found in the 1915 *Psychological Bulletin*. In the *Psychological Review* of 1915, Watson's name does not seem to have appeared even once (except on the masthead, as the journal's editor). Only one passing reference to the "behaviorist standpoint" could be located[32] while five of the six issues of the journal contained at least one article dealing with imageless thought, images, or imagery of one sort or another. The 1915 volume of the *Journal of Philosophy, Psychology, and Scientific Method* included a protest by Walter Hunter against Watson's misinterpretation of Hunter's delayed reaction experiment, and a few articles on the issues of consciousness and behavior, with both positive and critical references to Watson.[33] . . .

At year's end of 1916, the twenty-fifth anniversary of the APA and of the *Philosophical Review* elicited a number of papers by renowned psychologists discussing the past, present, and future of their science. In general, these papers treated behaviorism as only one trend among many and dealt with it briefly. Margaret Washburn defended introspection against Watson's attacks. Joseph Jastrow mentioned behaviorism in passing. Pillsbury pointed to the disagreement between Watson and Yerkes regarding animal consciousness. Cattell, while strongly urging the replacement of introspective studies of the mind by experiments on "behavior and conduct," was more concerned with other issues, especially the economics of research support. Dewey's address on the future of social psychology applauded behaviorism as a promising trend, which could – in a twist surprising to modern readers – in combination with McDougall's work on instincts lead to an understanding of the social emergence of mind – not strictly a Watsonian position. Finally G. Stanley Hall, little concerned with theoretical quibbles, speculated in the grand manner about the role of psychology in the cataclysm looming on the horizon: the war, which was soon to disrupt the lives of many psychologists.[34]

The events of the war years did not silence the behaviorism debate completely. And even before that time Watson had expanded his position in his presidential address on the conditioned reflex, begun his observational studies of human infants, and written an early version of the first chapter for his new book on behaviorism.[35] However, the narration of events will conclude with three more indications of Watson's influence, or lack thereof. In 1915, Dunlap's efforts had initiated the formation of an APA Committee on Terminology, charged with producing some agreed-upon definitions of crucial psychological terms. The first installment of this work was published in the 1918 *Psychological Bulletin*. But Watson's position was not represented in these definitions. With the exception of one subcategory, which accepted "behavior" as the "reaction of an organism to the environment" but expressly restricted it to biological usage, all relevant definitions, e.g., of "psychobiological," led back to others containing the words "mental" or "conscious."[36]

The omission of behavioristic views was apparently no accident. The papers of Mary Calkins, one of the committee members, contain a preprint of the committee report, dated September 1917, and bearing some handwritten corrections. Instead of the twenty-eight definitions published in the *Psychological Bulletin*, this document listed twenty-nine items. Number 29 was: "Behaviorism. Identification of *psychology* with the science of *behavior*." But this definition had been crossed out in ink.[37] The subsequently published version did not include the term behaviorism.

Unfortunately, no correspondence is attached to this preprint. Thus it remains uncertain whether the elimination of Watson's slogan was a bit of skullduggery on the part of one or more committee members, or whether it reflected the result of a mail survey of sixty psychologists in the fall of 1917. Still, in either case this "smoking gun" supports the argument that, five years after his manifesto, any inroads Watson had made in psychology did not lead very far into its center. Even an updated version of the committee's work published in 1922, defining eight varieties of psychology, did not include behaviorism among them. The one closest to it, "Objective Psychology," described in an added note as a "synonym for *Behavior Psychology*," was defined as "concerned with *mental*[!] *phenomena* expressed in the *behavior* of the organism to the exclusion of *introspective data*."[38] . . .

This rather detailed (though not exhaustive) account of recorded reactions to Watson stands in definite contrast to some retrospective histories which claim or at least imply that Watson's behaviorism, supported by an anonymous Zeitgeist, quickly swept the field. . . .

In Search of Explanations

Obviously, this is not the whole story. For instance, although the Terminology Committee of the APA had failed to print a definition of Behaviorism in 1918, the *Encyclopedia Americana* carried a two-page article on "Behavior and Behaviorism" in the same year.[39] Although Watson's 1914 book was never reviewed by *Science*, in spite of Watson's anxious inquiries, Edwin B. Holt had recommended it to his readers as a "valiant and clear-headed volume."[40] And though it turned out to be difficult to identify many probehaviorists in the contemporary records, later sources do indicate that behaviorism had, in the teens, an impact on a number of mainly younger people besides Weiss and Hunter: Karl S. Lashley, Harold C. Bingham, Melvin E. Haggerty, John F. Dashiell, and a group of Harvard students, among them Floyd H. and Gordon W. Allport, Richard M. Elliott, and Edward C. Tolman. (However, at Harvard the influence had come less from Watson than from Holt, who was teaching a "red-hot behaviorism" at the time,[41] and from Ralph B. Perry.)

Neither is this the end of the story of the behaviorist revolution, only of its first phase. But it is high time to ask what all the details reported so far add up to. Perhaps the general drift of this account has not really come as a surprise to the reader. Though I had initially expected a rather different course of events, once I started to think about it I found the emerging story not too surprising either. Nevertheless, it may present difficulties for some traditional explanations: If there was a Zeitgeist, it seems that so far he (or she) communicated mainly like God to Moses, on a one-to-one basis. If the fact that Watson's program was a strictly American product had any influence on its acceptance, so far we have not seen any direct or even indirect reference to it. Fred Wells, Watson's first vocal supporter, was anything but parochial; his writings were sprinkled generously with German, French, and Latin quotes.

Another popular explanation has to do with the acceptance of behaviorism because it was so practical. Although this argument touches on what I believe to be a crucial aspect (and though we have found mostly favorable responses to what was called the "relevance" theme), it puts some complex issues too simply. For instance, the (American) *Journal of Applied Psychology* did not begin publication until 1917; the similarly titled German *Zeitschrift für Angewandte Psychologie* had first appeared in 1907. An "*Institut für Angewandte Psychologie*" had been established in Berlin in 1906, almost a decade before the start of an applied psychology program at Carnegie Institute of Technology. (And the *Journal of Educational Psychology*, appearing in 1910, had been preceded by a decade by the *Zeitschrift für Pädagogische Psychologie und Experimentelle Pädagogik*.) When Titchener had warned, in 1909, against the undesirable developments toward applied psychology, his specific references were to five German psychologists (and one Frenchman: Binet).[42] While such a list may in part reflect Titchener's European orientation, it should also

help to scuttle the myth that applied psychology was "ganz amerikanisch," and that the impractical German professors were preoccupied with nothing but abstruse and esoteric speculations of a philosophical nature. Applied psychology had its roots at least as much in Europe as in America. Furthermore, as the European example shows clearly, an applied psychology does not have to be behavioristic at all (unless, of course, we view it through behaviorist eyes).

Another myth should also be laid to rest: that behaviorism developed out of animal psychology because the situation there forced the researcher into a behavioristic stance. As others[43] have pointed out before, this does not seem altogether true. At least some of the major figures in the small group of American animal psychologists did not feel at all compelled by their subject matter to adopt this position. Washburn and Yerkes both rejected Watsonian behaviorism (though Yerkes claimed that in his early days around 1900 he had been a pre-Watsonian Watsonian behaviorist).[44] Carr belongs in this category, too. In fact, in the early twenties we find more philosophers than animal psychologists among those taking a behaviorist stance; the psychologists in this group (Holt, Tolman, Edwin R. Guthrie, and a bit later Clark L. Hull) were more likely to turn to animal work after their conversion than to move in the reverse direction.

Abandoning such obviously post hoc explanations as, at the very least, overstatements, we should look at a different version of explanation, which is not new but in our days has been formulated in Kuhnian terms.[45] It goes like this: Around 1912 the "imageless thought" controversy laid bare an "anomaly" which the existing science could not deal with; this produced a "crisis" which led to the abandonment of the old "paradigm" and the acceptance of a better one, which could account for the anomaly. But this version, too, is at least a gross oversimplification; it seems to fit neither the facts nor Kuhn's theory. The imageless thought controversy was indeed a problem, but one among at least several; only retrospective historians and polemicists have made it into a "crisis." In his original paper, Watson referred to it only in one sentence in a footnote, in which he listed other problems of introspective psychology.[46] Robert S. Woodworth, not a bad scientist, was trying to solve the problem two years later; he did not see it as an anomaly creating a crisis.[47] And Titchener, in my view quite properly, replied to Watson's claims about the failure of introspection that in many scientific areas the results of observations did not always agree; it was reasonable to allow some time to work out the apparent contradictions. After all, his kind of introspection had been introduced less than ten years before, and not fifty, as Watson had asserted.[48] (We might add that after a turn to behavioral methods, the results obtained by different experimenters have not always agreed either.) And when we look carefully at Kuhn's argument, we find that anomalies are always around in science. Only rarely do they touch off crises and revolutions.

A (slow) perceptual shift and a missing paradigm-exemplar

I am impressed by the applicability of one of Kuhn's ideas: the change in the way of seeing things involved in paradigm change. Such a shift did occur in, I believe, a fundamental way. It is most visible in the manner psychologists described their methods of observation. In the earlier phase we find again and again the statement that the introspective method constitutes direct and immediate contact with the subject matter, while what we now mean by objective observation was then only an indirect or mediate one.[49] After the revolution, the meanings are reversed: objective observation is the direct contact, while information obtained through introspection, if not altogether impossible or irrelevant, is at best indirect, a tenuous base for fragile inferences from questionable verbal reports. I think this is more than a manner of speaking; it reflects a real change in the way psychologists experienced, or had been trained to experience, their reality. For most psychologists, however, this shift did not seem to occur suddenly, as an "aha" experience with a reversible figure; it took a long time to develop – even if for us, immersed as we are in post-Watson "behavior" language, it is hard to look upon the earlier construction as anything but patently contrived and transparent. But this shift is what Watson, having made it himself, demanded from others. To accept the addition of objective observations and performance measures was not so difficult for many psychologists (as we have

heard), because they had said or done so even before Watson.[50] But he rejected such a mixture of methods, such a compromise; he was asking for the reversal in the definition of what was real – this made him appear so radical, and made it difficult for others to follow him.

Besides the crisis-inducing anomaly, another element of Kuhn's theory seems to be missing: the new paradigm. Many people have, in my view, misread Kuhn (helped along by his ambiguities) and assimilated his concept of paradigm to other, more familiar ideas: theories, conceptual systems, viewpoints. But such an understanding turns Kuhn's argument into an old story. What may be novel in Kuhn was his emphasis on the role of the paradigm-exemplar, the specific case of the successful solution of a (crucial) problem, which becomes a relatively concrete model-example for the solution of other problems.[51] But where was Watson's paradigm-exemplar? It was not there.

Should one not cite the conditioned reflex and Pavlov's salivating dogs? Our textbooks often seem to portray the development of modern psychology as an historical chain, from Darwin to Pavlov to Watson, and on to Hull and Skinner. But this compact story is not entirely true. While eventually coming to play the role of paradigm-exemplar (a count of the textbooks reprinting the original line drawing of Pavlov's dog is overdue), the conditioned reflex entered only slowly and in stages into Watson's thinking and did not gain its dominant role until the mid-twenties. Even then, a close look shows the surprising fact that the actual experimental data underlying the diagram, the concrete observations made, were almost nonexistent, as far as Watson and American psychology in general were concerned. After all, Pavlov's dogs lived in a faraway country. Knowledge of them came only through indirect channels, in translations and third-hand reports; some of these reports were imprecise, obscure, or clearly wrong.[52] Did nobody try to replicate the work?

Watson's APA address describing his own and Lashley's observations on motor conditioning was actually based only on pilot studies, which had raised at least as many questions as they had answered. The literature contains no final report of Lashley's elaborate studies of salivary conditioning; a close reading of his progress reports seems to indicate that he gave up the effort because it had failed. (Hilgard and Marquis's classic on conditioning drew a similar conclusion.) As for Watson, he once mentioned briefly an attempt to develop an experimental analogue to reactions to lightning and thunder, by exposing infants to a strong light followed by a loud sound.[53] Subsequently, Watson never referred to this experiment again – had it been a failure too?

The only concrete observation Watson produced (in 1920) was the famous case of "Albert and the rat." But while this case did come to serve as a powerful exemplar, it was not a very solid data-base which could carry a whole theory. It was, after all, an experiment with a sample of one; it also involved some fairly problematic procedures.[54] Some years later, Elsie O. Bregman tried to replicate Watson's experiment in a more systematic manner. As Hilgard and Marquis summed up: "Later experiments have been unsuccessful in duplicating it. . . . The process is not as simple as the story of Albert suggests."[55]

But surely, there must have been other American conditioning studies. Not really. The first bona fide American conditioning experiment with humans was not reported until 1922, by Hulsey Cason; and he did not feel compelled to accept a Watsonian interpretation. The mass of conditioning experiments did not appear until after the translation of Pavlov's work had become available to American psychologists in 1927 and 1928. All Watson had was Little Albert. Yet while he presented a beautiful example of an idea, if one had already accepted this idea, he did not provide solid scientific evidence to a skeptical observer. The actual paradigm-exemplar, as a way of doing things, did not produce the paradigm shift at all; the exemplar came after the formula had been developed, and even then it was more like a diagram than a way of actually doing things.[56]

Here we may have put a finger on one of the places where Watson was hurting, on one of the facts at least partly responsible for the slow rate of conversion of his fellow scientists. What was it, after all, that Watson had to offer them? He had used some strong words in attacking their psychology and had exploited some of their troubles; he had proposed some intriguing ideas. But in spite of his insistence on a new, harder science, objective observations, etc., when it came to

experimental data he had very few (apart from his animal studies) to justify his attempt to usurp scientific authority.

Watson's 1913 research program, loose as it was, seems to have been plagued by false leads or experimental failures. The two concrete proposals of 1913, the identification of thinking with subvocal movements and his explanation of affection, in good Freudian fashion, in terms of activity of the sex glands, had been proffered without any empirical evidence. (The two major specifics radical behaviorism eventually became identified with, environmentalism and the conditioned response, did not become central to Watson's system until ten years later.)

Apparently, Watson spent some time trying to collect data on laryngeal movements, but eventually gave up.[57] His first attack on conditioning (still within a limited theoretical context) also seems to have ended with an impasse, and with a shift to observational work on infants. By 1920, not one concrete experimental problem of human psychology had been solved convincingly by Watson and had provided him with a Kuhnian paradigm.

Yet he was addressing professionals who had been trained in the use of introspective methods, and were so training others; who had believed all along that what they were doing was indeed real science, since it involved laboratories, observations, measurements, controlled conditions, etc. Watson was asking these professionals to throw their tools overboard as not scientific, to declare all the hard-won generalizations that filled their textbooks and their lectures to be artifacts of bad methods. This was too much to ask, as we heard one psychologist after another assert in their reaction to Watson. Though obviously they had not yet solved all the difficult problems of mental phenomena, nevertheless they were the professional experts on the mind, on the inner experience of man. All of a sudden they should forswear their claim to this expertise, surrender their scientific authority?

In recent years we have heard some calls for radical changes in psychology or in its specialities. Their reception, with responses ranging from hostility to indifference – even though there are at least *some* anomalies around in our science – should let us empathize with the feelings of the established psychologists of Watson's time. What did Watson have to offer them in return for their renunciation? He promoted a different version of science which, so it seemed to them, would make them lose their professional identity and turn them into either biologists or physiologists. Why should they risk such an exchange?

A new goal for psychology

After all, Watson's call for a revolution in psychology had been largely programmatic. His main thrust had aimed at a redefinition of scientific standards and a redirection of psychology. Put simply, this redefinition proceeded on three different levels: First was the change in *method*: the call for objective procedures and the elimination of "unscientific" introspection. This argument, having the most direct impact on the workday of psychologists, drew the largest share of public responses. While the emphasis on objective methods, already widely used and advocated, met with a good deal of sympathy, the total proscription of introspection ran into strong resistance, if only for the intolerant tone of its imposition (even from those not using introspection in their own work, like Thorndike and Yerkes).

The second level concerned the *subject matter* of psychology, changing it from mental contents and/or processes to movement and behavior, with its attendant peripheralism, rejection of central processes, and associated metaphysical connotations. This issue, too, met with considerable debate. Its acceptance required fundamental figure-ground reversal which was not easy to accomplish and took its time in coming about, although the expansion of the field to problems of "real life" had widespread support in the growing discipline.

I would like to propose, however, that the crucial argument occurred at a third level and dealt with the *goal* for psychology. According to Watson, this goal was to be the "prediction and control of behavior." Here Watson proposed something radical and new for psychology. All textbooks before him had defined psychology's aim in a different way, as description and/or explanation of mental phenomena, their understanding (on occasion including self-understanding, even self-improvement), etc.: the traditional goals of academic science.

Where Watson obtained his formula about prediction and control is not quite clear. Initially I assumed that he had taken a cliché from the natural sciences which he was trying to emulate, but a somewhat cursory search complicated this answer. Most sources I found (discussions of philosophy of science and encyclopedia definitions of "science")[58] did not define science in terms of prediction and control, mentioned prediction only in passing, and were more concerned with the problem raised by positivism: the banishment of causes, description versus explanation. However, the biologist Jacques Loeb had on several occasions described the goal of modern biology as the "control of life-phenomena" and in 1912 even referred to two outcomes, control or quantitative prediction. Watson, who had studied with Loeb at Chicago, may well have derived his novel definition of the goal of psychology from Loeb's ideas.[59] Of course some psychologists had, if only in passing, spoken of control before Watson: William James had once talked about "practical prediction and control" as the aim of all sciences, and about the demand on psychologists from all kinds of managers for "practical rules" for the "control of states of mind."[60] Cattell's famous St. Louis address had eagerly anticipated the "application of systematized knowledge to the control of human nature," to the "control of ourselves and our fellow men."[61] Thorndike had mentioned "control [of man's] acts" in a 1911 essay defining psychology as the study of behavior.[62] Yerkes's 1911 textbook contained, as sixth and final part, a rather abstract discussion of foresight and the control of mental events.[63] And finally, in England William McDougall had published a little book, in which he stated as psychology's aim: "to increase our understanding of, and our power of guidance and control over, the behaviour of men and animals."[64] (Watson knew McDougall's earlier books.)

Still I believe that Watson's treatment of the issue constituted a quantum jump. Only with him did control become a fundamental idea, part of the textbook definition; and it came right at the start, appearing in the second sentence of his 1913 paper (and at least four more times in fourteen pages): The "theoretical goal [of psychology] is the prediction and control of behavior," Why did Watson use this phrase? Why "theoretical goal" why not "practical" goal, or just "the" goal? Did theoretical mean hypothetical, ideal – a goal unreachable in practice? I do not think that this is what Watson tried to say.

Before Watson, the aims of psychology had been seen in terms of the category of pure science, as contrasted to either applied science or art. Of course, most psychologists have had their dreams of glory, in which their science would affect the real world and solve some of its problems. Even defenders of an ascetic science, like Titchener, believed that scientific knowledge would eventually produce its practical fruit and thus justify science to the impure, though true scientists ignored the question of application. But James's brief remark concerned the pressures from the *outside* for practical rules, presumably *derived* from theoretical knowledge. The quote from Cattell referred to the *application* of systematized knowledge. And Yerkes ended his discussion by saying: "Control is the outcome, albeit not the avowed goal, of scientific research. . . . Psychology is *not* the science of mental control."[65] It merely would make it possible. In other words, traditionally the issue was seen as involving two steps: first, the acquisition of knowledge as the task of science, and then its application to practical affairs. What was debatable, and debated, was the desirability, the timing, and the division of labor in such application. Watson saw the issue differently, his phrase "theoretical goal" shows him reshuffling the traditional categories;[66] prediction and control were no longer indirect or second-stage outcomes, but had become the direct focus and criterion of theory development. I think this notion was radically new (for psychology) and provided the fulcrum for the reorientation of psychology in subsequent decades, so that today any psychology major will state what is self-evident to him: that the goal of (behavioristic as well as cognitive) psychology is the prediction and control of behavior.

It is interesting, and somewhat puzzling, that the early reactions to Watson, the more intensive debate over behaviorism in the early twenties, and more recent analyses of Watson's contribution were largely silent on this point.[67] Only Titchener's rebuttal focused on the behaviorist's goal, in his accusation that Watson was trying to create a technology rather than a science. Thorndike's and Carr's reviews of Watson's *Comparative* book, which reprinted the 1913 papers, reacted in passing to this point; yet both seem to have misunderstood it. In part, I believe, the Janus-face of the term *control* is responsible for the lack of discussion. Control could mean control of conditions, precision in experimentation, elimination of unwanted influence; but that was a commonplace. Or it could mean what Watson clearly intended, at least much of the time (he also used a more abstract formula about predicting stimuli from responses and responses from stimuli), and spelled out later: *social control*, i.e., manipulation of human beings for the benefit of society.[68] But the experimental psychologist failed to confront this aspect of behaviorism in their theoretical debate and eventually defined the issue away.

Yet others did get the message. The first text in applied psychology – while not strictly Watsonian – opened on a distinctly behavioristic note. It introduced the ideas of prediction and control, and explained that the change in emphasis from consciousness to behavior may have been due in part to theoretical difficulties (as with imageless thought); but it was also due to the demands of practical life.[69] About the same time, John Dewey's address on the need for social psychology linked behaviorism with the development of a social psychology in the service of social control. Reviewing the applications of psychology to industry in 1920, Henry Link cited the Gilbreths, involved in time and motion work in industry, as the "ideal behaviorists" and concluded: "Watson's work is, in fact, the conscious methodology which practically all recent literature in industrial psychology has more or less explicitly *implied*."[70] Soon after, W. V. Bingham, head of the applied psychology unit at Carnegie Tech, was to complain about this accidental (and to him unfortunate) identification of behaviorism with applied psychology, which made his attempt to separate an applied science from the pure science of psychology more difficult. And Floyd Allport described social psychology as becoming "the study of the social behavior of the individual . . . [needed] for study and control of the socially significant aspects of individual response." He also wrote in his lecture notes: "Responsibilities incident to human control. Practical psychology is essentially behavioristic in method."[71]

Conclusion

Such beginnings are part of a larger and complex pattern of developments in the twenties, which is discussed elsewhere.[72] So far, it appears that a less than monolithic mainstream of experimental psychology, debating issues of method and concepts, resisted Watson's advances for a long time, assimilating them gradually in the form of the more abstract S-R formula. Yet in the meantime others, inside and outside psychology, more immediately concerned with problems of social control and helped along by the exigencies and opportunities of World War I, were finding Watson's arguments a convenient or inspiring rationale. Even if they may not have accepted all of his theoretical ideas, Watson had given the discipline a strong push in the direction of technological science.

Certainly, Watson had not singlehandedly transformed psychology. Too many of the specifics of his argument had not been original with him – although the common practice of briefly quoting one or another author's use of "behavioral" definitions of psychology before l913,[73] in order to demolish Watson's claim to priority, misses the mark. It overlooks the fact that Watson had already in 1907 declared that the "science of behavior" was "thoroughly established."[74] It is true enough that at this time he did not yet apply it to all of psychology; nonetheless, the phrase had been abroad long before 1913. What counted were its corollaries.

But while using ideas from others, as well as appealing to their dissatisfactions with the status quo, Watson had sharpened the arguments into a revolutionary weapon. Provoking a good deal of resistance with his rhetoric, he also discovered the price to be paid for his shift, in 1913, from a strategy of succession to, in Pierre Bourdieu's terms, a high-risk strategy of subversion of established scientific authority.[75] When the shift finally paid off, others reaped the benefits. Watson was no longer a part of the professional community, when eventually the reestablished monopoly of scientific authority had accepted prediction and control as the criterion of positive science and declared only outward manifestations, "behavior," to be legitimate scientific data. Anything mental had become unobservable, and at best problematic inference if not a superstition pure and simple.

In a sense, the present research effort turned out to be a failure. Looking for the sources of behaviorism's powerful appeal to American psychologists, we found more often criticisms or partial acceptance. Did we look in the wrong place? What I had not realized at the outset was that the victory of behaviorism took so much longer in coming about. And at least this scientific revolution did not involve simply conceptual transformations and conversions, but something Kuhn has not talked about – a power struggle in a discipline, affected by events without. Like the other social sciences,[76] the young profession of psychology grew up facing a predicament, in its dependence on a larger clientele, on the one hand, and its desire for autonomy and academic status, on the other – as reflected in the rhetorics of relevance and purity. Eventually, psychology adopted Watson's ingenious solution combining the appeals of hardheaded science, pragmatic usefulness, and ideological liberation.

Notes

(1) Howard C. Warren, (Autobiography), in *A History of Psychology in Autobiography*, vol. 1, ed. Carl Murchison (Worcester Mass.: Clark University Press, 1930), p. 462. See also John B. Watson "Psychology as the Behaviorist Views It," *Psychological Review 20* (1913): 158–177. Walter B. Pillsbury recalled, in his autobiography, that he had read Watson's paper while in Germany. However, his only concern was Watson's misinterpretation of a comment Pillsbury had made about Watson's animal lab. See Pillsbury, *A History of Psychology*

in *Autobiography*, vol. 2 (1932), p. 285. Finally, John F. Dashiell's autobiography mentions Watson's "prompt appeal" without giving any specifics (although Dashiell attended Columbia University at the time of Watson's presentation); nor do his early writings show much of a behavioristic influence. Dashiell, (Autobiography), in *A History of Psychology in Autobiography*, vol. 5 (1967), pp. 117–118; and "Spirit and Matter: A Philosophical Tradition," *Journal of Philosophy, Psychology, and Scientific Method* 14 (1917): 66–

74. E. G. Boring, *Psychologist at Large* (New York: Basic Books, 1961).

(2) H. S. Langfeld, "Psychology," in *The American Year Book, 1913*, ed. Francis G. Wickware (New York: Appleton, 1914), p. 704; Maurice Parmelee, *The Science of Human Behavior* (New York: Macmillan, 1913); Walter T. Marvin, "General Problems; Mind and Body," *Psychological Bulletin* 11 (1914): 1–7.

(3) Robert M. Yerkes, "The Study of Human Behavior," *Science* 39 (1914): 625–633; James R. Angell, "Behavior as a Category of Psychology," *Psychological Review* 20 (1913): 225–270, pp. 261, 264; for the origin of the term see also Howard C. Warren, "Terminology," *Psychological Bulletin* 11 (1914): 10–11.

(4) Max F. Meyer, *The Fundamental Laws of Human Behavior* (Boston: Badger, 1911); William McDougall, *An Introduction to Social Psychology* (London: Methuen, 1908).

(5) Angell, "Behavior as a Category"; Fredrick J. E. Woodbridge, "The Belief in Sensations," *Journal of Philosophy, Psychology, and Scientific Method* 10 (1913): 599–608; Mary W. Calkins, "Psychology and the Behaviorist," *Psychological Bulletin* 10 (1913): 288–291.

(6) Calkins, "Psychology," p. 289.

(7) Fredrick L. Wells, "Special Reviews" and "Dynamic Psychology," *Psychological Bulletin* 10 (1913): 280–281 and 434–440, p. 434.

(8) Wells, "Special Reviews," p. 281.

(9) James R. Angell, "Behavior as a Psychological Category," (abstract), *Psychological Bulletin* 10 (1913): 48–49; Wells, "Special Reviews," p. 281.

(10) Jean Weidensall, "Criminology and Delinquency," *Psychological Bulletin* 10 (1913): 229–237, p. 232.

(11) Robert M. Yerkes, "Comparative Psychology: A Question of Definitions," *Journal of Philosophy, Psychology, and Scientific Method* 10 (1913): 580–582, p. 581; James R. Angell, "Professor Watson and the Image," *Journal of Philosophy, Psychology, and Scientific Method* 10 (1913): 609; Henry R. Marshall, "Is Psychology Evaporating?" *Journal of Philosophy, Psychology, and Scientific Method* 10 (1913): 710–716.

(12) Howard C. Warren, "The Mental and the Physical," *Psychological Bulletin* 11 (1914): 35–36 (abstract), and *Psychological Review* 21 (1914): 79–100, p. 100.

(13) Ibid., pp. 97, 95.

(14) John Dewey, "Psychological Doctrine and Philosophical Teaching," *Journal of Philosophy, Psychology, and Scientific Method* 11 (1914): 505–511, p. 511; Harold C. Brown, "The Thirteenth Annual Meeting of the American Philosophical Association," *Journal of Philosophy, Psychology, and Scientific Method* 11 (1914): 57–67, p. 65; Knight Dunlap, "Images and Ideas," *Johns Hopkins University Circular* 33 (1914): 25–41.

(15) G. Stanley Hall, "Food and Mind," Mental Hygiene Conference, Boston, 4 April 1913 (typed ms.), p. 3, Box 29, G. Stanley Hall Papers, Clark University Archives. (I am indebted to David E. Leary for making this item available to me.)

(16) John C. Burnham, "On the Origins of Behaviorism," *Journal of the History of the Behavioral Sciences* 4 (1968): 143–151.

(17) E. G. Boring, "The Society of Experimental Psychologists; 1904–1938," *American Journal of Psychology* 51 (1938): 410–423.

(18) "Notes and News," *Psychological Bulletin* 10 (1913): 211–212; see also Samuel W. Fernberger, "Convention of Experimental Psychologists," *American Journal of Psychology* 24 (1913): 445; and for a retrospective account in almost the same words, Boring, "The Society," p. 414.

(19) Melvin E. Haggerty, "The Twenty-second Annual Meeting of the American Psychological Association," *Journal of Philosophy, Psychology, and Scientific Method* 11 (1914): 85–109, p. 86.

(20) Melvin E. Haggerty, "The Relation of Psychology and Pedagogy," *Psychological Bulletin* 13 (1916): 55–56, and "Reviews and Abstracts of the Literature," *Journal of Philosophy, Psychology, and Scientific Method* 13 (1916): 470–472, p. 472.

(21) Walter V. Bingham, "Proceedings of the Twenty-second Annual Meeting of the American Psychological Association," *Psychological Bulletin* 11 (1914): 29–35, p. 29.

(22) This account is not exhaustive. For instance, a summary of Watson's manifesto by J. R. Tuttle appeared in the *Philosophical Review* 22 (1913): 674; "Notes and News," *Journal of Educational Psychology* 4 (1913): 180, reported briefly on Watson's Columbia address.

(23) F. L. Wells, "Dynamic Psychology," p. 434.

(24) Howard C. Warren's autobiography (p. 462) recounted two decades later that, although he could not accept Watson's position, "the younger psychologists hailed Watson as a second Moses." Yet specifics supporting and detailing this dramatic image are hard to find in the contemporary record. In "The Origins of Behaviorism," (1979 Ph.D. dissertation) John O'Donnell discusses at length what he calls Watson's "silent majority" which, however, was not a group converted by the manifesto (as Warren had it), but which had been interested in applied psychology, and thus had been behavioristic, before 1913. But even if there was such a majority for behaviorism, the very fact that its members are hard to track down in the record (even O'Donnell gives us only a few names)

indicates their marginal role in the development of the academic discipline, its publications, and its training of students. Finally, O'Donnell's argument, in which applied interests are equated with behaviorism, seems problematical to me; at the very least it proceeds at a more global level of analysis than does the present paper.

(25) J. B. Watson to R. M. Yerkes, 26 March 1913; R. M. Yerkes to J. B. Watson, 16 May 1916, Robert M. Yerkes Papers, Historical Library, Yale Medical Library, New Haven, Conn.

(26) John B. Watson, "Image and Affection in Behavior," *Journal of Philosophy, Psychology, and Scientific Method* 10 (1913): 421–428.

(27) Gilbert V. Hamilton to R. M. Yerkes, 22 December 1914. (Hamilton was a former Yerkes student with an M.D. degree, involved in animal research at the time); Margaret F. Washburn to R. M. Yerkes, 26 May 1916, Yerkes Papers. Cedric A. Larson and John J. Sullivan, "Watson's Relation to Titchener," *Journal of the History of the Behavioral Sciences* 1 (1965): 338–354.

(28) "Notes and News," *Psychological Bulletin* 11 (1914): 28, 79.

(29) H. S. Langfeld, "Psychology," in *American Year Book, 1914* (New York: Appleton, 1915), 674.

(30) John B. Watson, *Behavior: An Introduction to Comparative Psychology* (New York: Holt, 1914); H. S. Langfeld, "Text-books and General Treatises," *Psychological Bulletin* 12 (1915): 30–37; Harvey A. Carr, "Special Reviews," *Psychological Bulletin* 12 (1915): 308–312; Edward L. Thorndike and C. Judson Herrick, "Watson's 'Behavior'," *Journal of Animal Behavior* 5 (1915): 462–470; M. E. Haggerty, "Reviews and Abstracts of Literature," *Journal of Philosophy, Psychology, and Scientific Method* 13 (1916): 470–472.

(31) E. L. Thorndike, "The Study of Consciousness and the Study of Behavior," (abstract), *Psychological Bulletin* 8 (1911): 39; Thorndike, *Animal Intelligence* (New York: Macmillan, 1911); Thorndike and Herrick, "Watson's 'Behavior'," p. 464.

(32) George A. Coe, "A Proposed Classification of Mental Functions," *Psychological Review* 22 (1915): 87–98, p. 91.

(33) Walter S. Hunter, "A Reply to Some Criticisms of the Delayed Reaction," *Journal of Philosophy, Psychology, and Scientific Method* 12 (1915): 38–41; Edwin B. Holt, "Response and Cognition," *Journal of Philosophy, Psychology, and Scientific Method* 12 (1915): 38–41; Edwin B. Holt, "Response and Cognition," *Journal of Philosophy, Psychology, and Scientific Method* 12 (1915): 365–373 and 393–409; C. Judson Herrick, "Introspection as a Biological Method," *Journal of Philosophy, Psychology, and Scientific Method* 12 (1915): 543–551.

(34) Margaret F. Washburn, "Some Thoughts on the Last Quarter Century in Psychology," *Philosophical Review* 26 (1917): 46–55; Joseph Jastrow, "Varieties of Psychological Experience," *Psychological Review* 24 (1917): 249–265; Walter B. Pillsbury, "The New Developments in Psychology in the Past Quarter Century," *Philosophical Review* 26 (1917): 56–59; James M. Cattell, "Our Psychological Association and Research," *Science* 45 (1917): 275–284; John Dewey, "The Need for Social Psychology," *Psychological Review* 24 (1917): 266–277; G. Stanley Hall, "Practical Relations between Psychology and the War," *Journal of Applied Psychology* 1 (1917): 9–16.

(35) John B. Watson, "The Place of the Conditioned Reflex in Psychology," *Psychological Bulletin* 23 (1916): 89–117. Apparently this address did not produce much of a reaction. See H. S. Langfeld to H. Münsterberg, 1 January 1916, Hugo Münsterberg Papers, Boston Public Library; Watson, "An Attempted Formulation of the Scope of Behavior Psychology," *Psychological Review* 24 (1917): 329–352; Watson and John J. B. Morgan, "Emotional Reactions and Psychological Experimentation," *American Journal of Psychology* 28 (1917): 163–174.

(36) Howard C. Warren, Mary W. Calkins, Knight Dunlap, H. N. Gardiner, and C. A. Ruckmich, "Definitions and Delimitations of Psychological Terms," *Psychological Bulletin* 15 (1918): 89–95, p. 94.

(37) Preprint located in 3P, Mary Whiton Calkins Unprocessed Papers, Wellesley College Archives, Wellesley, Mass.

(38) Warren et al., "Definitions, II," *Psychological Bulletin* 19 (1922): 230–235, p. 231.

(39) Walter B. Pillsbury, "Behavior and Behaviorism," *Encyclopedia Americana* (New York: Encyclopedia Americana Corporation, 1918); 446–448.

(40) See J. B. Watson to J. M. Cattell, 15 January 1915, Cattell Papers, and J. B. Watson to R. M. Yerkes, 27 March 1916, Yerkes Papers; Holt, "Response and Cognition," p. 409n.

(41) Gardner Murphy to Robert S. Woodworth, n.d. (in reply to Woodworth's letter dated 27 October 1932), Robert S. Woodworth Papers, Library of Congress.

(42) E. B. Titchener, "The Past Decade in Experimental Psychology," *American Journal of Psychology* 21 (1910): 404–422.

(43) David Bakan, "Behaviorism and American Urbanization," *Journal of the History of the Behavioral Sciences* 2 (1966): 5–28.

(44) R. M. Yerkes, "Behaviorism and Genetic Psychology," *Journal of Philosphy, Psychology, and Scientific Method* 14 (1917): 154–161, p. 161.

(45) Thomas S. Kuhn, *The Structure of Scientific Revolutions* (Chicago: University of Chicago Press, 1962).

(46) Watson, "Psychology," p. 163n.

(47) Robert S. Woodworth, "A Revision of Imageless Thought," *Psychological Review* 22 (1915): 1–27.

(48) Edward B. Titchener, "On 'Psychology as the Behaviorist Views It,' " *Proceedings of the American Philosophical Society* 53 (1914): 1–17, p. 8. See also Kurt Danziger, "The History of Introspection Reconsidered," *Journal of the History of the Behavioral Sciences* 16 (1980): 241–262.

(49) E. g., James R. Angell, *Psychology*, 3rd edn. (New York: Holt, 1906), p. 4; Harvey A. Carr, *Psychology* (New York: Longmans Green, 1926), p. 7.

(50) See Danziger, "History of Introspection," pp. 257–258.

(51) Franz Samelson, "Paradigms, Labels, and Historical Analysis," *American Psychologist* 28 (1973): 1141–1143. See also Brian D. Mackenzie, *Behaviorism and the Limits of Scientific Method* (London: Routledge & Kegan Paul, 1977).

(52) Karl S. Lashley, "Recent Literature of a General Nature on Animal Behavior," *Psychological Bulletin* 11 (1914): 269–277, p 272.

(53) Watson, "The Place of the Conditioned-Reflex"; Karl S. Lashley, "The Human Salivary Reflex and Its Use in Psychology," *Psychological Review* 23 (1916): 445–464; Lashley, "Reflex Secretions of the Human Parotid Gland," *Journal of Experimental Psychology*, 1 (1916): 461–495; Ernest R. Hilgard and Donald G. Marquis, *Conditioning and Learning* (New York: Appleton-Century, 1940), p. 13. Watson and Morgan, "Emotional Reactions," p. 171.

(54) J. B. Watson and Rosalie Rayner. "Conditioned Emotional Reactions," *Journal of Experimental Psychology* 3 (1920): 1–14; J. B. Watson and R. R. Watson, "Studies in Infant Psychology," *Scientific Monthly* 13 (1921): 493–515. For a more detailed discussion, see Franz Samelson, "John B. Watson's Little Albert, Cyril Burt's Twins, and the Need for a Critical Science," *American Psychologist* 35 (1980): 619–625.

(55) Elsie O. Bregman, "An Attempt to Modify the Emotional Attitudes of Infants by the Conditioned Response Technique," *Journal of Genetic Psychology* 45 (1934): 169–198; Hilgard and Marquis, *Conditioning and Learning*, pp. 293, 294.

(56) Hulsey Cason, "The Conditioned Pupillary Reaction," *Journal of Experimental Psychology* 5 (1922): 108–146; Ivan P. Pavlov, *Conditioned Reflexes*, trans. G. V. Anrep (London: Oxford University Press, 1927); Pavlov, *Lectures on Conditioned Reflexes*, trans. W. Horsley Gantt (New York:

International Publishers, 1928). Two earlier American conditioning studies do not qualify for inclusion, for different technical reasons: Ignatius A. Hamel, "A Study and Analysis of the Conditioned Reflex," *Psychological Monographs* 27 (1919): No. 1; Florence Mateer, *Child Behavior* (Boston: Badger 1918). Of course, others had started to *talk* about conditioning (F. L. Wells, "Von Bechterew and Uebertragung," *Journal of Philosophy, Psychology, and Scientific Method* 13 [1916]: 354–356; William H. Burnham, "Mental Hygiene and the Conditioned Reflex," *Pedagogical Seminary* 24 [1917]: 449–488), but that only proves my point. Cf. Hilgard and Marquis, *Conditioning and Learning*, on this issue although their emphasis is different.

(57) J. B. Watson to R. M. Yerkes, 22 October 1915 and 17 February 1916, Yerkes Papers.

(58) For instance, Karl Pearson, *The Grammar of Science*, 2nd edn. (London: Black, 1900).

(59) Jacques Loeb, *Comparative Physiology of the Brain and Comparative Psychology* (New York: Putnam, 1907), p. 287; Loeb, *The Mechanistic Conception of Life* (Chicago: University of Chicago Press, 1912), pp. 3, 196. Philip J. Pauly's recent work on Loeb comes independently to similar conclusions; see his "Jacques Loeb and the Control of Life," unpublished Ph.D. dissertation, Johns Hopkins University, 1980. Of course, in at least a loose sense these ideas go back to Auguste Comte and beyond.

(60) William James, "A Plea for Psychology as a 'Natural Science'," *Philosophical Review* 1 (1892): 146–153, p. 148 (I am indebted to John O'Donnell for this reference).

(61) James M. Cattell, "The Concepts and Methods of Psychology," *Popular Science Monthly* 66 (1904): 176–186, pp. 185, 186.

(62) Thorndike, *Animal Intelligence*, p. 15.

(63) Robert M. Yerkes, *Introduction to Psychology* (New York: Holt, 1911).

(64) William McDougall, *Psychology: The Study of Behavior* (London: Butterworth, 1912), p. 21.

(65) Yerkes, *Introduction to Psychology*, p. 416 (italics added). Thorndike had said: "Science seeks to know the world; the arts, to control it." *The Elements of Psychology* (New York: Seiler, 1905), p. 324.

(66) See Watson's argument that "applied psychology" was a misnomer; "Psychology," p. 169.

(67) Gustav Bergman, "The Contribution of John B. Watson," *Psychological Review* 63 (1956): 265–276; Herrnstein, Introduction to Watson's *Behavior;* Mackenzie, *Behaviorism;* not so John C. Burnham, whose repeated references to the "social control" theme helped to direct my attention to this issue.

See also Lucille C. Birnbaum, *Behaviorism: John Broadus Watson and American Social Thought*, unpublished Ph.D. dissertation (Berkeley: University of California, 1965).

(68) John B. Watson, "An Attempted Formulation of the Scope of Behavior Psychology," *Psychological Review* 24 (1917): 329–352 and *Psychology from the Standpoint of a Behaviorist* (Philadelphia: Lippincott, 1919); p. 2. See also Paul T. Young to J. B. Watson, 27 May 1917, P. T. Young Papers.

(69) Harry L. Hollingworth and Albert T. Poffenberger, *Applied Psychology* (New York: Appleton, 1917), pp. 5, 6.

(70) Dewey, "The Need for Social Psychology"; Henry C. Link, "The Application of Psychology to Industry," *Psychological Bulletin* 17 (1920): 335–346, pp. 341, 345 (italics added).

(71) Walter V. Bingham, "On the Possibility of an Applied Psychology," *Psychological Review* 30 (1923): 289–305; Floyd H. Allport, "Social Psychology," *Psychological Bulletin* 17 (1920): 85–94, p. 85; F. H. Allport, Lecture Notes, "Psychology 35;

Industrial and Vocational Psychology," (typed, 1923?), Box 3, Walter V. Bingham Papers, University Archives, Carnegie-Mellon University, Pittsburgh, Penn.

(72) Franz Samelson, "Early Behaviorism, Pt. 3. The Stalemate of the Twenties," Paper presented at the 12th annual meeting of Cheiron, Bowdoin College, Brunswick, ME, June 1980; See also F. Samelson, "Putting Psychology on the Map," *Psychology in Social Context*, pp. 101–168.

(73) For instance, O'Donnell, "Origins," p. 537.

(74) John B. Watson, "Comparative Psychology," *Psychological Bulletin* 4 (1907): 208.

(75) Pierre Bourdieu, "The Specificity of the Scientific Field and the Social Conditions of the Progress of Reason," *Social Science Information* 14 no. 6 (1975): 19–47.

(76) Cf. Dorothy Ross, "The Development of the Social Sciences," in *The Organization of Knowledge in Modern America, 1860–1920*, ed. Alexandra Oleson and John Voss (Baltimore: Johns Hopkins University Press, 1979), pp. 107–138.

A System of Behavior
B. F. Skinner

A Definition of Behavior

It is necessary to begin with a definition. Behavior is only part of the total activity of an organism, and some formal delimitation is called for. The field might be defined historically by appeal to an established interest. As distinct from the other activities of the organism, the phenomena of behavior are held together by a common conspicuousness. Behavior is what an organism is *doing* – or more accurately what it is observed by another organism to be doing. But to say that a given sample of activity falls within the field of behavior simply because it normally comes under observation would misrepresent the significance of this property. It is more to the point to say that behavior is that part of the functioning of an organism which is engaged in acting upon or having commerce with the outside world. The peculiar properties which make behavior a unitary and unique subject matter follow from this definition. It is only because the receptors of other organisms are the most sensitive parts of the outside world that the appeal to an established interest in what an organism is doing is successful.

By behavior, then, I mean simply the movement of an organism or of its parts in a frame of reference provided by the organism itself or by various external objects or fields of force. It is convenient to speak of this as the action of the organism upon the outside world, and it is often desirable to deal with an effect rather than with the movement itself, as in the case of the production of sounds. . . .

From B. F. Skinner (1938). *The behavior of organisms.* New York: Appleton-Century-Crofts, pp. 6, 18–26. Copyright © 1938 by B. F. Skinner. Adapted and reprinted by permission of the B. F. Skinner Foundation.

Type S and Type R Conditioning

In the course of this book I shall attempt to show that a large body of material not usually considered in this light may be expressed with dynamic laws which differ from the classical examples only in the nature of the operations. The most important instances are conditioning and extinction (with their subsidiary processes of discrimination), drive, and emotion, which I propose to formulate in terms of changes in reflex strength. One type of conditioning and its corresponding extinction may be described here.

The Law of Conditioning of Type S. The approximately simultaneous presentation of two stimuli, one of which (the "reinforcing" stimulus) belongs to a reflex existing at the moment at some strength, may produce an increase in the strength of a third reflex composed of the response of the reinforcing reflex and the other stimulus.

The Law of Extinction of Type S. If the reflex strengthened through conditioning of Type S is elicited without presentation of the reinforcing stimulus, its strength decreases.

These laws refer to the Pavlovian type of conditioned reflex. . . . I wish to point out here simply that the observed data are merely changes in the strength of a reflex. As such they have no dimensions which distinguish them from changes in strength taking place during fatigue, facilitation, inhibition, or, as I shall show later, changes in drive, emotion, and so on. The process of conditioning is distinguished by what is done to the organism to induce the change; in other words, it is defined by the operation of the simultaneous presentation of the reinforcing stimulus and another stimulus. The type is called Type S to distinguish it from conditioning of Type R (see below) in which the reinforcing stimulus is contingent upon a response.

Before indicating how other divisions of the field of behavior may be formulated in terms of reflex strength, it will be necessary to consider another kind of behavior, which I have not yet mentioned. The remaining dynamic laws will then be taken up in connection with both kinds at once.

Operant Behavior

With the discovery of the stimulus and the collection of a large number of specific relationships of stimulus and response, it came to be assumed by many writers that all behavior would be accounted for in this way as soon as the appropriate stimuli could be identified. Many elaborate attempts have been made to establish the plausibility of this assumption, but they have not, I believe, proved convincing. There is a large body of behavior that does not seem to be *elicited*, in the sense in which a cinder in the eye elicits closure of the lid, although it may eventually stand in a different kind of relation to external stimuli. The original "spontaneous" activity of the organism is chiefly of this sort, as is the greater part of the conditioned behavior of the adult organism, as I hope to show later. Merely to assert that there *must* be eliciting stimuli is an unsatisfactory appeal to ignorance. The brightest hope of establishing the generality of the eliciting stimulus was provided by Pavlov's demonstration that part of the behavior of the adult organism could be shown to be under the control of stimuli which had *acquired* their power to elicit. But a formulation of this process will show that in every case the response to the conditioned stimulus must first be elicited by an unconditioned stimulus. I do not believe that the "stimulus" leading to the elaborate responses of singing a song or of painting a picture can be regarded as the mere substitute for a stimulus or a group of stimuli which originally elicited these responses or their component parts.

Most of the pressure behind the search of eliciting stimuli has been derived from a fear of "spontaneity" and its implication of freedom. When spontaneity cannot be avoided, the attempt is made to define it in terms of unknown stimuli. Thus, Bethe says that the term "has long been used to describe behavior for which the stimuli are not known and I see no reason why the word should be stricken from a scientific vocabulary." But an event may occur without any observed antecedent event and still be dealt with adequately in a descriptive science. I do not mean that there are no originating forces in spontaneous behavior but simply that they are not located in the environment. We are not in a position to see them, and we have no need to. This kind of behavior might be said to be *emitted* by the organism, and there are appropriate techniques for dealing with it in that form. One important independent variable is time. In making use of it I am simply recognizing that the observed datum is the appearance of a given identifiable sample of behavior at some more or less orderly rate. The use of a rate is perhaps the outstanding characteristic of the general method to be outlined in the following pages, where we shall be concerned very largely with behavior of this sort.

The attempt to force behavior into the simple stimulus-response formula has delayed the adequate treatment of that large part of behavior which cannot be shown to be under the control of eliciting stimuli. It will be highly important to recognize the existence of this separate field in the present work. Differences between the two kinds of behavior will accumulate throughout the book, and I shall not argue the distinction here at any length. The kind of behavior that is correlated with specific eliciting stimuli may be called *respondent* behavior and a given correlation a *respondent*. The term is intended to carry the sense of a relation to a prior event. Such behavior as is not under this kind of control I shall call *operant* and any specific example *an operant*. The term refers to a posterior event, to be noted shortly. The term reflex will be used to include both respondent and operant even though in its original meaning it applied to respondents only. A single term for both is convenient because both are topographical units of behavior and because an operant may and usually does acquire a relation to prior stimulation. In general, the notion of a reflex is to be emptied of any connotation of the active "push" of the stimulus. The terms refer here to correlated entities, and to nothing more. All implications of dynamism and all metaphorical and figurative definitions should be avoided as far as possible.

An operant is an identifiable part of behavior of which it may be said, not that no stimulus can be found that will elicit it (there may be a respondent the response of which has the same topography), but that no correlated stimulus can be detected upon occasions when it is observed to occur. It is studied as an event appearing spontaneously with a given frequency. It has no static laws comparable with those of a respondent since in the absence of a stimulus the concepts of threshold, latency, after-discharge, and the *R/S* ratio are meaningless. Instead, appeal must be made to frequency of occurrence in order to establish the notion of strength. The strength of an operant is proportional to its frequency of occurrence, and the dynamic laws describe the changes in the rate of occurrence that are brought about by various operations performed upon the organism.

Other Dynamic Laws

Three of the operations already described in relation to respondent behavior involve the elicitation of the reflex and hence are inapplicable to operants. They are the refractory phase, fatigue, and conditioning of Type S. The refractory phase has a curious parallel in the rate itself, as I shall note later, and a phenomenon comparable with fatigue may also appear in an operant. The conditioning of an operant differs from that of a respondent by involving the correlation of a reinforcing stimulus with a *response*. For this reason the process may be referred to as of Type R. Its two laws are as follows.

The Law of Conditioning of Type R. If the occurrence of an operant is followed by presentation of a reinforcing stimulus, the strength is increased.

The Law of Extinction of Type R. If the occurrence of an operant already strengthened through conditioning is not followed by the reinforcing stimulus, the strength is decreased.

The conditioning is here again a matter of a change in strength. The strength cannot begin at zero since at least one unconditioned response must occur to permit establishment of the relation with a reinforcing stimulus. Unlike conditioning of Type S the process has the effect of determining the form of the response, which is provided for in advance by the conditions of the correlation with a reinforcing stimulus or by the way in which the response must operate upon the environment to produce a reinforcement. . . .

It is only rarely possible to define an operant topographically (so that successive instances may be counted) without the sharper delineation of properties that is given by the act of conditioning. This dependence upon the posterior reinforcing stimulus gives the term operant its significance. In a respondent the response is the result of something previously done to the organism. This is true even for conditioned respondents because the operation of the simultaneous presentation of two stimuli precedes, or at least is independent of, the occurrence of the response. The operant, on the other hand, becomes significant for behavior and takes on an identifiable form when it acts upon the environment in such a way that a reinforcing stimulus is produced. The operant-respondent distinction goes beyond that between Types S and R because it applies to unconditioned behavior as well; but where both apply, they coincide exactly. Conditioning of Type R is impossible in a respondent because the correlation of the reinforcing stimulus with a response implies a correlation with its eliciting stimulus. It has already been noted that conditioning of Type S is impossible in operant behavior because of the absence of an eliciting stimulus.

An operant may come to have a relation to a stimulus which seems to resemble the relation between the stimulus and response in a respondent. The case arises when prior stimulation is correlated with the reinforcement of the operant. The stimulus may be said to set the occasion upon which a response will be reinforced, and therefore (through establishment of a discrimination) upon which it will occur; but it does not elicit the response. The distinction will be emphasized later.

One kind of operation that affects the strength of reflexes (both operant and respondent) falls within the traditional field of drive or motivation. It would be pointless to review here the various ways in which the field has been formulated. In a description of behavior in terms of the present system the subject presents itself simply as a class of dynamic changes in strength. For example, suppose that we are observing an organism in the presence of a bit of food. A certain sequence of progressive, manipulative and ingestive reflexes will be evoked. The early stages of this sequence are operants, the later stages are respondents. At any given time the strengths may be measured either by observing the rate of occurrence in the case of the former or by exploring the static properties in the case of the latter. The problem of drive arises because the values so obtained vary between wide extremes. At one time the chain may be repeatedly evoked at a high rate, while at another no response may be forthcoming during a considerable period of time. In the vernacular we should say that the organism eats only when it is hungry. What we observe is that the strengths of these reflexes vary, and we must set about finding the operations of which they are a function. This is not difficult. Most important of all are the operations of feeding and fasting. By allowing a hungry organism, such as a rat, to eat bits of food placed before it, it is possible to show an orderly decline in the strength of this group of reflexes. Eventually a very low strength is reached and eating ceases. By allowing a certain time to elapse before food is again available it may be shown that the strength has risen to a value at which responses will occur. The same may be said of the later members of the chain, the strengths of which (as respondents) must be measured in terms of the static properties. Thus, the amount of saliva secreted in response to a gustatory stimulus may be a similar function of feeding and fasting. A complete account of the strengths of this particular group of reflexes may be given in terms of this operation, other factors being held constant. There are other operations to be taken into account, however, which affect the same group, such as deprivation of water, illness, and so on.

In another important group of changes in reflex strength the chief operation with which the changes are correlated is the presentation of what may be called "emotional" stimuli – stimuli which typically elicit changes of this sort. They may be either unconditioned (for example, an electric shock) or conditioned according to Type S where the reinforcing stimulus has been emotional (for example, a tone which has preceded a shock). Other operations which induce an emotional change in strength are the restraint of a response, the interruption of a chain of reflexes through the removal of a reinforcing stimulus (see later), the administration of certain drugs, and so on. The resulting change in behavior is again in the strength of reflexes. . . .

The operations characterizing drive and emotion differ from the others listed in that they effect concurrent changes in *groups* of reflexes. The operation of feeding, for example, brings about changes in all the operants that have been reinforced with food and in all the conditioned and unconditioned respondents concerned with ingestion. Moreover, a single operation is not unique in its effect. There is more than one way of changing the strength of the group of reflexes varying with ingestion or with an emotional stimulus. In addition to the formulation of the effect upon a single reflex, we must deal also with *the* drive or *the* emotion as the "state" of a group of reflexes. This is done by introducing a hypothetical middle term between the operation and the resulting observed change. "Hunger," "fear," and so on, are terms of this sort. The operation of feeding is said to affect the hunger and the hunger in turn the strength of the reflex. The notion of an intermediate state is valuable when (a) more than one reflex is affected by the operation, and (b) when several operations have the same effect. Its utility may perhaps be made clear with the following schemes. When an operation is unique in its effect and applies to a single reflex, it may be represented as follows:

Operation I — (   ) — Strength of Reflex I,

where no middle term is needed. When there are several operations having the same effect and affecting several reflexes, the relation may be represented as follows:

Operation I   Strength of Reflex I
Operation II ⟩ "State" ⟨ Strength of Reflex II
Operation III   Strength of Reflex III

In the present system hypothetical middle terms ("states") will be used in the cases of drive and emotion, but no other properties will be assigned to them. A dynamic law always refers to the change in strength of a single reflex as a function of a single operation, and the intermediate term is actually unnecessary in its expression.

An observation of the state of a reflex at any given time is limited to its strength. Since the data are changes in strength and therefore the same in all dynamic laws, the system emphasizes the great importance of defining and classifying operations. The mere strength of the reflex itself is an ambiguous fact. It is impossible to tell from a momentary observation of strength whether its value is due especially to an operation of drive, conditioning, or emotion. Suppose, for example, that we have been working with an operant that has been reinforced with food and that at a given time we observe that the organism does not respond (i.e., that the strength is low). *From the state of the reflex itself*, it is impossible to distinguish between the following cases. (1) The organism is hungry and unafraid, but the response has been extinguished. (2) The response is conditioned and the organism is hungry but afraid. (3) The response is conditioned, and the organism is unafraid but not hungry. (4) The response is conditioned, but the organism is both not hungry and afraid. (5) The organism is hungry, but it is afraid, and the response has been extinguished. (6) The organism is not afraid, but it is not hungry and the response has been extinguished. (7) The response has been extinguished, and the organism is afraid but not hungry. We can decide among these possibilities by referring to other behavior. If we present the stimulus of an *unconditioned* reflex varying with hunger and fear (say, if we present food), the question of conditioning is eliminated. If the organism eats, the first case listed above is proved. If it does not eat, the possibilities are then as follows. (1) The organism is

hungry but afraid. (2) It is unafraid but not hungry. (3) It is both not hungry and afraid. If we then test another reflex, the strength of which decreases in a state of fear but which does not vary with hunger, and find it strong, the organism is not afraid and must therefore not be hungry.

The strength of a reflex at any given time is a function of all the operations that affect it. The principal task of a science of behavior is to isolate their separate effects and to establish their functional relationships with the strength.

The development of dynamic laws enables us to consider behavior which does not invariably occur under a given set of circumstances as, nevertheless, reflex (i.e., as lawful). The early classical examples of the reflex were those of which the lawfulness was obvious. It was obvious because the number of variables involved was limited. A flexion reflex could be described very early because it was controlled by a stimulus and was not to any considerable extent a function of the operations of drive, emotion, or conditioning, which cause the greatest variability in strength. The discovery of conditioning of Type S brought under the principle of the reflex a number of activities the lawfulness of which was not evident until the conditioning operation was controlled. Operants, as predictable entities, are naturally isolated last of all because they are not controlled through stimuli and are subject to many operations. They are not *obviously* lawful. But with a rigorous control of all relevant operations the kind of necessity that naturally characterizes simple reflexes is seen to apply to behavior generally. I offer the experimental material described later in this book in support of this statement.

B. F. Skinner's Technology of Behavior in American Life: From Consumer Culture to Counterculture
Alexandra Rutherford

American academics and intellectuals have, over the years, rendered extensive critiques of B. F. Skinner and his work, excoriating both his theory and his technology of behavior (e.g., Chomsky, 1959; Krutch, 1954; Szasz, 1975). Writers for the popular press and lay readers have also identified Skinner as a figure worthy of intense social debate (see Dinsmoor, 1992; Rutherford, 2000). Recently, Bjork has suggested in his biography of Skinner that the heated criticism he has evoked "is culturally and intellectually significant, for such generally negative opinion suggests that Skinner – regardless of the truth or error of his position – has touched something that . . . is worth knowing about American values, or more concretely, the American predicament" (Bjork, 1996, p. 36). Thus, a complete historical analysis of Skinner and his work must take into account the cultural, social, and political milieu of mid-twentieth-century America.

In this paper, I explore some of the relationships between popular portrayals of Skinner and American social values from the 1940s to the 1970s. Specifically, I explore how popular coverage of Skinner's work was influenced by a complex host of cultural factors, as well as some enduring features of the American predicament. Although Bjork (1996) has suggested that public opinion of Skinner's work has been generally *negative*, I argue that public opinion (or in this case, popular portrayals) was more highly nuanced than is typically acknowledged. These nuances can be understood, at least in part, by examining the complexity of the American cultural landscape in which Skinner's work was produced and received.

Journal of History of the Behavioral Sciences, 2003, *39*(1), 1–23. Reprinted by permission of Wiley-Blackwell.

While others have written about the effect of social and political factors on Skinner's work itself (e.g., Bjork, 1993, 1996; Capshew, 1996), and on the development of behaviorism in American culture (e.g., Bakan, 1966, 1998), in this paper I analyze the effect of these factors on the *popular* reception of Skinner using popular press coverage and responses from readers as a window on his public image. From the baby tender to teaching machines to *Beyond Freedom and Dignity*, Skinner's work was part of the popular – as well as the academic – culture of mid-twentieth-century America. Thus, presentations of his work have been highly context dependent, that is, they have ranged widely depending on the particular social discourses in which they were embedded. In no instance has the popular reception of Skinner's work been either straightforward or clear-cut. Because so many aspects of his work fell at the crossroads of conflicting American social values, presenting him simply as a maligned behaviorist or as a controversial social scientist significantly obscures the complexity of his relationship with American culture.

B. F. Skinner and "Better Living" in 1950s America

One of Skinner's first major contributions to the popular press was an article in the *Ladies Home Journal* entitled "Baby in a Box," a catchy title chosen by the editors to replace Skinner's original title, "Baby Care Can Be Modernized" (Skinner, 1945). In this article, Skinner introduced a new invention he called the baby tender (later, the air crib). Designed on the eve of the birth of his second daughter, the baby tender was Skinner's solution to his wife Eve's concerns about the drudgery associated with the tasks of child rearing. Briefly, the baby tender was intended to be a replacement for the ordinary crib. It consisted of an enclosed, humidity and temperature-controlled space in which the baby could sleep comfortably, unencumbered by clothes and blankets. The tender had a Plexiglas front, which allowed the baby an unobstructed view of the surrounding environment. Among the advantages of the new crib were less laundry for the parents, as well as less exposure to noise and germs and more mobility for the baby (for more details see Benjamin & Nielsen-Gammon, 1999; Skinner, 1979).

Reactions to the baby tender were mixed. This diversity of opinion was reflective of several ongoing cultural debates of 1950s America, such as the proper role for technology in the life of the modern family, and appropriate parenting methods – among others. In this section, I contextualize coverage of the baby tender by connecting it to these public debates and areas of ongoing social concern.

The "New Look" in 1950s parenting

Cultural historians have described distinct trends in entertainment, fashion, design, and architecture during the late 1940s and early 1950s that were collectively termed the "New Look" (e.g., Jackson, 1998; Steele, 1997). The "New Look," a reaction against the frugality, efficiency, and austerity of the war years, expressed the postwar optimism and ebullience of a new era of peace and increasing economic abundance. It emphasized appearance and glamour – the "outsides of things" (Marling, 1994, p. 14) – how things looked, not necessarily how they worked. The adage "form follows function" was replaced by "form is function," as designers embraced the idea that how something looked was just as important as what it did. After the economic hardship of the 1930s and the turbulence of World War II, Americans seemed ready to enjoy themselves again – to attend to the comfort and aesthetic of their surroundings (for cultural histories of the 1950s, see Foreman, 1997; Hart, 1982; Miller & Nowak, 1975a).

In addition to the aesthetic of the "New Look," a palpable trend towards better living also characterized the late 1940s and 1950s. Bird (1999) has argued that the "better living campaign" was initiated by businesses as early as the mid-1930s, to counteract Franklin Delano Roosevelt's anti-corporate, New Deal agenda. This better living campaign focused on claims of "new," "more," and "better" as business attempted to reclaim the public's confidence and its consumer market, and to capitalize on the public optimism created by Roosevelt's dynamic leadership. Better living meant increased consumption. At the same time, major technological innovations, such as the automobile, the television, and the airplane, were assimilated into the changing patterns of American life. Bjork (1996, p. 46) has noted that in this period "Skinner's America . . . not only accepted the automobile, the airplane, and the electrification of cities as progressive modernization; it assumed as a matter of course that humans could control their environment through the efforts of inventors and industrial scientists."

Skinner's invention of the baby tender occurred in this era of growing public emphasis on better living, the cultural aesthetic of the "New Look," and the growing popularity of household technology. The widespread adoption of this technology resulted both in better living and increased control of domestic space. Advances in household technology also served a politically symbolic function. The 1959 Kitchen Debate between Richard Nixon and Nikita Khrushchev was held in the RCA Whirlpool "miracle kitchen" created for the American Exhibition in Moscow. The appliances, including "mechanical maid" that would wash the floor and then put itself away, sent a strong message about American national identity. Marling (1994) has written:

> In the 1950s, the United States bought fully three-fourths of all the appliances produced in the world. Along with cars and Levittowns . . . they stood for something fundamental to the postwar understanding of national identity: a sense of freedom, of effortless ease, of technological mastery, modernity, and access to conveniences formerly reserved for the very rich. (p. 255)

Inasmuch as the labor-saving function of the baby tender matched the ethos of better living through household technology, reflected an emphasis on the "outsides of things" (that is, the baby's environment), and itself embodied mastery of this environment, one might have expected fairly positive popular coverage of the baby tender in this period. In fact, a number of encouraging articles appeared in the popular press after the announcement of the baby tender in the pages of the *Ladies Home Journal* (e.g., "Baby box," 1947; "Boxes for babies," 1947; "Box-reared babies," 1954; "Heated, air-conditioned baby box," 1948; "How a tech professor raises his youngsters," 1954; Schur, 1946). By and large, these articles were enthusiastic about the tender and highlighted its advantages over traditional cribs.

For example, "Boxes for Babies," an article appearing in 1947 in *Life* magazine, pictured one infant, alert and content in his tender, with the caption "John Gray Jr. plays happily in his box. Like Debby Skinner he has never had a cold or a stomach upset, is smarter than the average child" (p. 73). Although acknowledging concerns about lack of contact comfort for children in the tender, the article nevertheless concluded that "the Skinner boxes have proved successful thus far and will be put on the market commercially next year" (p. 73).[1]

"Box-Reared Babies," appearing in *Time* magazine in 1954, informed readers that aptly named Roy and Ray Hope, a pair of Six-year-old "bright-eyed twins" had spent "the first 18 months of their lives in a Skinner baby box" (p. 66). These "disarmingly normal" young boys were presented as pictures of physical and psychological health. The mother of the twins expressed her enthusiasm about the device, reporting that "the box is a boon to mothers because it cuts down on laundry and bathing" (p. 66). Similar sentiments were expressed in a *New Yorker* article: "Skinner is the inventor of the mechanical baby tender, counted on to revolutionize the rearing of children and enormously diminish parental strain" ("Baby box," 1947, pp. 19–20). This article concluded with an optimistic assessment of the "excellent results" achieved thus far with the tender.

These and other largely upbeat portrayals in the popular press of this period certainly indicate that the public image of the baby tender benefited from the better living campaign of the 1950s. Skinner wrote that he received hundreds of letters requesting instructions on how to build a tender, and that, by and large, the results seemed to have been highly satisfactory. He aptly expressed the mood of the times when he wrote: "It is quite in

the spirit of the 'world of the future' to make favorable conditions available everywhere through simple mechanical means" (Skinner, 1945, p. 136).

Another popular development in this period no doubt affected response to Skinner's invention. Although some have cited the baby tender's similarity to an experimental Skinner box (and even to a coffin) as a liability to its public image,[2] the fact remains that many of these early assessments ignored these unfortunate parallels. Perhaps the popularity and appeal of another type of box mitigated critical assessment of the baby tender in this period. As Americans became economically secure and advances in technology streamlined the work-place, the question of how to spend now-ample leisure time loomed large on the cultural horizon. It was during this period that television – entertainment in a box – became a national phenomenon (for accounts of the impact of television on 1950s culture, see Miller & Nowak, 1975b; Newcomb, 1997; Spigel, 1992).

The growing leisure class now spent large portions of their free time glued to the antics of Lucille Ball and Desi Arnaz, or absorbed in *Howdy Doody, Disneyland*, or *Father Knows Best*. In 1952, the TV-tray table first appeared in national advertising, attesting to the fact that even dinner could not lure people away from their television sets. The problem of what to eat in front of the TV was quickly solved when Swanson's introduced the first TV dinner in October of 1953, making the square meal a snap for 1950s housewives and working women (Marling, 1994). Dinner-in-a-box became the natural companion to entertainment-in-a-box.

In 1957, a group of architects at the Massachusetts Institute of Technology designed the "Monsanto House of the Future" for Disneyland (Marling, 1994). Perched on some rocks overlooking a pond at the country's most famous theme park, the Monsanto House was in fact a life-sized, stylized, TV set. The lady of the house could be seen peering out of her picture window "screen," which in appearance was not unlike the Plexiglas front of the Skinners' baby tender. Life inside a box, for many Americans, was associated with the glamorous, exciting, and invariably blissful lives of their favorite television characters.[3]

So, despite some early misgivings, and later criticisms, of the mechanical baby tender, many articles in this period were positive and optimistic about the potential of the new device. It had become a matter of social respectability to keep up with the numerous technological innovations transforming the home. As Spigel (1992) has written, "in the postwar years it appeared that tomorrow had arrived . . . living without an array of machines meant that you were anachronistic, unable to keep pace with tomorrow" (p. 46).

Finally, in what may have been a more subtle but nonetheless pervasive cultural attitude of postwar, 1950s America, the emphasis of the "New Look," the focus on the "outsides of things," provided a much-needed antidote to almost two decades of deprivation and political unrest. Americans visited Disneyland, embarked on home improvement projects,[4] and watched their television sets. Skinner's emphasis on creating a better environment for the baby, and his concentration (both technologically and philosophically), on the "outsides of things," was closely aligned with this aspect of the popular mindset.[5]

Mechanical mothers invade the nursery

While many readers of Skinner's 1945 article praised the baby tender for its labor-saving potential, other readers censured the device. Specifically, they argued that raising a child in the baby tender was a sign of parental (especially maternal) neglect, and that it would cause significant physical and emotional problems in the child. Many critics noted the potential lack of contact comfort available to children brought up in temperature-controlled boxes (e.g., McKean, 1945). In a letter to Skinner upon receipt of his *Ladies Home Journal* article, the editor of the magazine expressed concern about whether parents would be able to hear children crying in the box and then respond to them accordingly. She also asked whether the reduction in the number of baths would not cut into the time mothers would spend having fun with their babies (Page, 1945). Somewhat later, rumors developed concerning the fate of Skinner's daughter Deborah, the first baby-in-a-box, suggesting that she had become psychotic, or perhaps even killed herself as a result of being raised in the tender. Julie Skinner Vargas has reported that she still hears stories about her father "raising his kids in boxes like rats" (Vargas, 2000).

In 1945, Dr. Benjamin Spock published *Baby and Child Care*, which inspired renewed social debate on the issue of permissiveness in child rearing, and influenced thousands of parents eagerly looking for expert advice on parenting. Spock's treatise debunked much of the extant behaviorist literature that had generally advocated a firm and somewhat detached approach to "bringing up baby." In 1928, John B. Watson's *Psychological Care of Infant and Child* had exhorted parents to treat their offspring like small adults; to desist from the coddling that, in Watson's view, protracted the child's dependence and immaturity. In contrast, Spock recommended that parents be more affectionate, warm, and available to their children. Unfortunately for Skinner, the image of the baby box seemed incongruent with this more permissive and affectionate approach to child rearing. Although Skinner repeatedly emphasized that the child would remain in the tender no longer than in a traditional crib (i.e., only while sleeping), and that parents would have more quality time to spend with their infants when much of their work was reduced, many parents nonetheless rejected the tender in the belief that it would inhibit important parent-child interactions.

The 1950s also witnessed a rise in the influence of psychoanalytic ideas on popular culture, including popular writing, theatre, television, and cinema (see Hale, 1995; Walker, 1993). As part of this influence, theories emphasizing the importance of very early infancy and infant attachment on subsequent development (specifically, the appropriate care and ministrations of the mother) became widely accepted. This undoubtedly exacerbated cultural anxiety about the baby tender, fuelling the belief that a child with a deficient early attachment would face serious and lifelong mental health problems. In the late 1950s, psychologist Harry Harlow's work on the importance of contact comfort in the attachment of infant monkeys was also publicized (see Harrison, 1958), further substantiating the public's conviction about the importance of parental warmth and availability, both of which seemed thwarted by the tender.

Finally, the shifting roles of the mother and housewife preoccupied the national psyche. In the 1950s, women were often faced with specific contradictory messages and social expectations.

As Spigel has explained, "Although middle- and working-class women had been encouraged by popular media to enter traditionally male occupations during the war, they were now told to return to their homes where they could have babies and make color-coordinated meals" (Spigel, 1992, p. 41). Confusingly, in addition to the expectation that working women would retreat subserviently to their domestic spaces and resume their roles as wives and mothers, the emphasis on material consumption brought an added financial burden that was often eased only by having women work outside the home. Thus, middle-class women in post-World War II America were thrust into a maelstrom of often contradictory cultural expectations.

Popular representations of the baby tender reflected this set of cultural anxieties about the proper roles of women, both at work and at home. Was the mother of a box-raised child shirking her primary role as caregiver and housewife? One anonymous writer to Skinner remarked of the tender, "It is the most ridiculous, crazy invention ever heard of. Caging this baby up like an animal, just to relieve the Mother of a little more work" (Anonymous, 1945). Or was she simply streamlining her domestic responsibilities in order to do more and do it better? Unlike other household technologies, such as the dishwasher, that promised to streamline mundane tasks, the baby tender affected the most sacrosanct of domestic tasks – parenting. The 1950s was an era inundated with "robot nurses" and "mechanical mothers" – from the television screen to the baby box.

Teaching by Machine: The Promise and Peril of the Automated Classroom

Although the baby tender was Skinner's first widely publicized invention, he was perhaps better known for the teaching machine (for a discussion of Skinner as social inventor, see Bjork, 1996). Throughout the late 1950s and early 1960s, Skinner's efforts to develop teaching machines and programmed instruction received extensive coverage in the popular press. Skinner's interest in designing a machine that could teach began with a visit to his daughter's fourth-grade math class, where he quickly saw how the principles of operant analysis could be used to make teaching more effective, and learning more successful (Skinner, 1983; for histories of the teaching machine see Benjamin, 1988; Vargas & Vargas, 1996).

The teaching machine quickly became one of the focal points of a widespread educational technology movement that received its fullest expression in the early-to-mid 1960s (see, for example, Boroff, 1963; Cuban, 1986; "What's happening in education?," 1967). Throughout the 1950s, film, television, and other audiovisual devices made their way into classrooms across the country.[6] In 1953, the first educational television network was established (Packer, 1963). A decade later, there were 62 educational television stations serving the students of the United States (Boroff, 1963). In Hagerstown, Maryland, 18,000 children in forty-eight public schools received some instruction by television by the late 1950s as part of a project supported by the Ford Fund for the Advancement of Education (Seligman, 1958). Indeed, the Ford Fund poured millions of dollars into the education industry in this period, responding in part to a perceived teacher shortage, and to the need to improve educational practices for students across widely ranging ability levels.

A number of articles in the mid-1950s announced Skinner's work with the machines (see, for example, "Mechanical teacher," 1954; "Miracle gadget," 1954; "Teaching by machine," 1954; Ubell, 1954). These articles were undoubtedly written in response to Skinner's first public demonstration of a machine for teaching spelling and arithmetic at a conference entitled "Current Trends in Psychology" held at the University of Pittsburgh in the spring of 1954 (Skinner, 1954). A few years later, in the early 1960s, Skinner's teaching machines and programmed instruction were proclaimed by some to be the most radical of the new educational technologies. It was anticipated that the machines and the programs fed into them would completely change the face of education, and society. *Time* magazine reported that programmed learning "promises the first real innovation in teaching since the invention of movable type in the 15th century. . . . Conceivably, programing might change school design and the entire social structure of U.S. youth" ("Programed learning," 1961, p. 36). *Fortune* magazine similarly enthused that programmed instruction "could, in the next decade or two, revolutionize education. . . . Conceivably it could upset the whole social structure of American youth" (Boehm, 1960, p. 176).

The revolutionary potential of programmed teaching was also noted by a writer for *Science Digest:* "A few months ago, thousands of school children from coast to coast were quietly subjected to what may turn out to be the greatest educational revolution in history. They began the first large-scale experiment in learning, not from human teachers, but from teaching machines" (Gilmore, 1961, p. 77).

In 1961, testifying to the perceived importance and potential impact of the new technology, the American Psychological Association (APA), the American Educational Research Foundation, and the Department of Audiovisual Instruction, collaborated to issue a statement on self-instructional materials and devices. It was noted that: "The use of self-instructional programed [sic] learning materials in teaching machines and similar devices represents a potential contribution of great importance to American education" (APA, 1961, p. 512). The statement presented guidelines for the use of the materials, as well as suggestions on how to select and evaluate instructional programs.

Obviously, there was widespread hope that the implementation of programmed instruction would greatly improve education at the elementary, secondary, and postsecondary levels. This hope extended to other forms of educational technology as well. But while many were enthusiastic and optimistic about teaching machines, the next "revolution in education" was not regarded enthusiastically by all. To what set of national concerns can this opposition be connected?

Benjamin (1988) has considered this question and has ruled out several areas of possible contention, such as high cost and low efficacy. He showed that the machines were usually quite inexpensive (although the programs were more so), and that numerous studies touted widely in the popular press demonstrated their effectiveness, not only in boosting grades, but also in improving morale and increasing motivation (e.g., Bell, 1961). Despite early concerns about lack of programs for the machines (e.g., Terte,

1961), Benjamin reported that by the late 1960s, there were thousands of available programs covering a wide range of subjects. He suggested instead that cultural inertia, resistance to technology, or "simply old-fashioned resistance to change" (p. 711) contributed to the machine's failure to thrive. He also noted the general failure of educational technologies (the teaching machine among them) that appear to invalidate the student-teacher bond – a bond that has traditionally been seen as an essential ingredient in the learning process.

Some further considerations can be added to Benjamin's analysis. The appearance of computers in the late 1960s may have made the hardware of the teaching machine obsolete and redirected energy away from its development towards more sophisticated machines. Cognitive and information-processing theories were also changing the way researchers modeled thought processes and thus learning, rendering Skinner's behavioral theories less fashionable. However, the development of computers in and of itself cannot explain why the technique of programmed learning was all but abandoned. Certainly if the technique were deemed revolutionary, and the public wholeheartedly accepted the benefits of programmed instruction, then interest in writing computer programs using the technique should have been high. Julie Skinner Vargas has remarked that as the popularity of teaching machines began to increase, program writing was taken on by people with little or no training, resulting in extremely dull programs that didn't work (Vargas, 2000). Geiser (1976) noted similarly (and colorfully) that in the hands of inexpert programmers, "some of the programs had all the inherent interest of three-day-old dead fish" (p. 105).

I would suggest that apprehension about the teaching machine was also rooted in the growing cultural unease towards what Theodore Roszak, in the late 1960s, termed "the technocracy" (Roszak, 1998/1968). Popular articles in the early 1960s, besides noting the revolutionary potential of programmed instruction, also repeatedly reported the public's concern about the dehumanization of education through machine technology. Teachers and parents were especially sensitive to this issue. Boehm, writing for *Fortune* magazine in 1960, noted these concerns: "Others argue that the new method 'dehumanizes' education by breaking the personal bond between teacher and student. But what bothers most opponents is that programs seem to them basically more appropriate to an animal psychology laboratory than to a school" (Boehm, 1960, p. 177).

The social anomie of the late 1950s, with the subsequent rise of the counterculture and the development of the humanistic movement, clearly signaled an increasingly pervasive social apprehension about dehumanization, alienation, conformity, and loss of agency (Herman, 1992). In essence, the public's specific concerns about the teaching machine revealed an important and significant fact about the nature of the historical moment in which the machines were introduced. An invention that could be perceived as a mechanical antidote to human inefficiency, along with Skinner's emphasis on using the machines not to "teach" in the traditional sense, but to bring the student's behavior under the control of the environment, may have met resistance in any period. However, the likelihood of the public embracing programmed instruction was perhaps particularly low at the precise historical moment in which it appeared. The teaching machine, perhaps more than any other educational technology, came to epitomize the type of automated mass society to which participants in the counterculture movement were so vehemently opposed.

Specifically, popular articles about programmed instruction touched on themes of control, alienation, and conformity, even though the objective benefits of the technique were acknowledged and even praised. Some of these reactions highlighted the public's ambivalence toward achieving better educational results through the more rigid control of human behavior. For example, a reporter for *Popular Mechanics* remarked on his own sense of unease about the programs:

> One question in particular kept nagging at me as I talked with the people who are propagating machine teaching. The problem was articulated by teaching-machine expert Hugh Anderson, who told me, "My wife was going through a programming sequence the other day in which the word 'response' was sought repeatedly as the correct terminology. . . . She wanted to say

'answer' instead. She resisted for a while, but soon she was automatically supplying the correct word so she could move on to the next point. Thus the programming had already shaped her behavior pattern." (Bell, 1961, p. 157)

Skinner made no secret of the fact that programmed material was designed to shape verbal behavior, rather than "teach" in any traditional sense of the word (i.e., to impart knowledge or skills). In his 1958 article for *Science*, for example, he wrote: "Teaching spelling is mainly a process of shaping complex forms of behavior" (Skinner, 1958, p. 971), and in his 1961 *Scientific American* article, "Knowing how to read means exhibiting a behavioral repertory of great complexity" (Skinner, 1961, p. 98).

Popular writers picked up on this nuance, and often compared Skinner's technique (referred to as linear programming) with the multiple-choice branching method developed and advocated by Norman Crowder. Crowder, a psychologist employed by the United States Industries Western Design Division in Santa Barbara, California, devised a teaching method in which large chunks of information were presented to the student, who was then tested with a multiple-choice question. If the student responded correctly, he/she would proceed. If not, the machine would branch to another frame that would give more details, explain why the response was incorrect, and then test again. It was acknowledged that Skinner's method, unlike Crowder's, was one of "conditioning" a response. One reporter for *Time* referred to Skinner's method as "Orwellian" ("Programed learning," 1961, p. 38).

The question of who would control the types of behaviors and responses that would be elicited (or conditioned) inevitably emerged. A writer for *Parents' Magazine*, began her article: "I'd been reading educational journals which questioned many aspects of automated instruction, not to mention newspaper warnings about robots taking over classrooms. . . . Was the dehumanized Brave New World really with us, I wondered. Is it 1984 already?" (Kreig, 1961, p. 45). Later, she quoted a "leading authority" on audio-visual instruction who noted, "Teaching machine programming is a social problem. . . . He who controls the programming heartland controls the educational system" (p. 80).

Clearly, mass automated instruction based on the principles of operant conditioning was perceived as potentially powerful. This led directly to concerns about control. Not only was the public uncertain about the desirability of controlling individual student behavior, they were also alarmed by the notion that the whole educational system might come under some kind of centralized authority, more powerful than any individual teacher in a conventional classroom. As Anthony Oettinger of Harvard University noted in an article for *Today's Health*, "To understand the seriousness of the problem, one need only picture the use a Hitler or a Stalin could have made of a national educational information pool" ("The critics speak," 1967, p. 56).

Issues of freedom and control were in the forefront of the American psyche as the 1960s unfolded. Programmed instruction, more than any other educational technology, was premised on the control of student behavior. Its behavioristic underpinnings were obvious. As Curti (1980) has noted, "[M]uch that was done in applying behavioral theory seemed to limit experience or to control it in questionable ways. This seemed evident in programmed instruction, teaching machines, and in time, the management . . . of youths by behavior modification techniques" (p. 400).

Parents were also worried about the potential for social alienation through the use of machine teaching. One parent at the Collegiate School for Boys in New York City, the site of one of the first experimental trials of the teaching machine, remarked, "If they're just going to stick our boys behind machines, they might as well be in classes of 50 or even a 100 instead of a dozen" (as cited in Kreig, 1961, p. 76). William Ferry, president of the center for the Study of Democratic Institutions, wrote that the teaching machine trend was responsible for the adoption of the "totally wrong notion that an educational system is like a factory for producing steel plate or buttons. . . . The central claim is efficiency. Mass education, it is said, requires mass production. The result is already discernible, and may be called technication" ("The critics speak," 1967, p. 56). Luce (1960), in an article for the *Saturday Evening Post*, reported one parent's reaction to the idea of machine teaching: "A machine teach my child?

Not on your life! A child needs human warmth" (p. 102).

Conformity in thinking was also cited as a potential problem of programmed instruction. Kreig (1961) noted, "What will happen to the nurturing of creativity, imagination, and the intangibles of learning? Will reliance on programs discourage independent thinking and result in stultifying conformity among students and teachers alike?" (p. 80). It was especially in the mid-to-late 1960s that the values of conformity and passive acceptance of authority were seriously questioned. Some felt that programmed instruction discouraged the development of the capacity to question, think critically, and consider multiple answers to a particular problem. A writer for *Fortune* magazine wrote, "[T]he rigidity of structure that seems to be inherent in programed [*sic*] instruction may imply to students that there is indeed only one approach, one answer; yet what the students may need to learn most is that some questions may have more than one answer or no answer at all" (Silberman, 1966, p. 198). This writer also noted, "If programing [*sic*] is used too extensively, moreover, it may prevent the development of intuitive and creative thinking or destroy such thinking when it appears" (p. 198).

A writer for *Harper's Magazine*, himself a developer of programmed texts for Harper & Row Publishers, reported the opinion held by some critics that the learning offered by programmed instruction actually helped no one but the programmer. The student, according to these critics, was reduced to giving "some final response that the programmer considers advantageous" (Bender, 1965, p. 52).

As the 1960s progressed, more popular writers addressed the need to consider values, purpose, and meaning in education. In January of 1967, *Saturday Review* published a series of articles in a section entitled "Changing Directions in American Education." One writer noted, "In a society that feeds on a rapidly advancing and sophisticated technology, the failure to have clear and forceful purposes and viable ends could be disastrous. We could become the creators of a technological order in which our ends would be defined and established by the instruments that were fashioned to serve us rather than by considerations of human value" (McMurrin, 1967, p. 40).

This apprehension about the creation of a technological order was likely increased by corporate America's annexation of the new technology. From 1962 to 1966, as big business picked up on the profit potential of the largely untapped educational industry, a number of electronics companies bought or merged with publishing houses that made educational films, designed tests, programmed instructional materials, and produced other small educational instruments (Ridgeway, 1966; Silberman, 1966). For example, in 1964, IBM merged with Science Research Associates; in 1965 Xerox purchased American Education Publications; and in the same year General Electric acquired Time Inc.'s General Learning Corporation (Silberman, 1966). Simultaneously, sizeable segments of the American population, especially its youth, expressed increasing dissatisfaction with a society that seemed increasingly corporatized and technocratic in its orientation. That programmed instruction, along with other educational technologies, had been co-opted into this technocracy was not overlooked.

As educational technologies were increasingly co-opted into the technocracy, and as society at large became increasingly concerned with the reclamation of humanistic values expressed so forcefully by the counterculture movement, the possibility of mass educational reform through programmed instruction dwindled considerably. In the age of encounter groups, Esalen, and authenticity, automated education meted out by large corporations had to fight not only "old-fashioned resistance to change," but also the tide of anti-technocratic sentiment that washed over society in the late 1960s.

Thus, although the promise of programmed instruction and the mechanized classroom seemed immense, serious concerns about the perils of the approach also prevailed. Themes of control, conformity, and social alienation became attached to the teaching machine. The machine came to embody the very trends that were anathematized by the hippies and the flower children of the counterculture movement. As one critic remarked, "University students can see what is happening to them, and complain, and demonstrate. For this reason alone it would seem likely that technication will make its slowest inroads in the colleges and universities" (Ferry, as cited in "The critics speak," 1967, p. 57).

Beyond Freedom and Dignity: Behavioral Technology in the Age of Aquarius

Although many aspects of Skinner's work had attracted significant popular attention by the late 1960s, the apogee of his public recognition came with the publication of *Beyond Freedom and Dignity (BFD)* in 1971. Reaction to the book was immediate, extensive, and vehement. Many readers likened Skinner to a Hitler or a Stalin. Described as despotic and tyrannical, Skinner was anathematized as an enemy of freedom and democracy. Many popular writers opined that his views were dehumanizing and fascistic. What was the nature of the cultural and historical moment that contributed to such virulent criticism of Skinner? Why did *BFD* shoot to the top of the *New York Times* bestseller list, and why did Skinner become one of the most sought-after interviewees on major radio and television networks for weeks and months thereafter?

Clearly, the 1960s witnessed a societal shift toward humanism (Maslow, 1969; Rogers, 1961), anti-institutionalism (Laing, 1967), and the rejection of many traditional social values, including the adherence to civility, order, and control (Cmiel, 1994, Zinn, 1968). Many intellectuals and reformers of this era targeted science and technology as primary culprits in the development of the "dehumanized social order" that had emerged from the 1950s (Mumford, 1970; Roszak, 1998/1968). They advocated no less than the complete rejection of the scientific worldview. As Roszak wrote in 1968:

What is it that has allowed so many of our men of science, our scholars, our most sophisticated political leaders, even our boldest would-be revolutionaries to make their peace with the technocracy . . . ? It is that technocratic assumptions about the nature of man, society, and nature have warped their experience at the source, and so have become the buried premises from which intellect and ethical judgment proceed. . . . In order, then, to root out those distortive assumptions, nothing less is required than the subversion of the scientific worldview. . . . In its place, there must be a new culture in which the non-intellective capacities of the personality . . .

become the arbiters of the good, the true, and the beautiful. (Roszak, 1998/1968, pp. 50–51)

Skinner's vision for cultural reform and the values guiding *BFD* collided with the antitechnocratic and anti-intellectual atmosphere of the early 1970s. Thus, 1971 was a *particularly* inauspicious historical moment for the appearance of the book. Coupled with this heightened antitechnocratic sentiment was the intense backlash against governmental control and authority that accompanied opposition to America's involvement in the Vietnam War. Thus, instead of slipping unnoticed onto the shelves of a few academics, *BFD* attracted widespread interest and incited vocal criticism. It focused attention on Skinner, not only as a scientist and psychologist, but as an individual, and catalyzed debate among intellectuals and lay readers alike. However, I would suggest that this analysis is incomplete. After all, as Thomas Szasz noted in the aftermath of the furor over *BED*: "Physicalism, biologism, reductionism, scientism – all have had much more eloquent spokesmen than Skinner. Why all the fuss about him, then?" (Szasz, 1975, p. 28). What is worth exploring is why *Skinner*, and not any number of other potential spokespersons, attracted such widespread popular attention.

To help answer Szasz's question, I suggest that one of the reasons for "all the fuss about him" was that while Skinner's work struck several highly sensitive cultural nerves in the early 1970s, it was another strain in his writing – namely his promise of a better world – that also ensured a wide audience. Awarded the title "Humanist of the Year" in 1972 by the American Humanist Association, Skinner's commitment to social change resonated with the utopian ideals that fuelled the counterculture movement and united behaviorists and humanists alike. As Leonard Krasner has written, "A major characteristic of the postwar period shared by both the humanist and the behaviorist was the desire to create a better world, a desire shared by many other professionals, politicians, and ordinary citizens of the time" (Krasner, 1978. p. 800). Ironically, the people who were most actively looking for and trying to create this better world were likely also the people most opposed to the philosophical underpinnings of Skinner's technology of behavior. In *BFD*, Skinner expressed

a philosophical outlook that clashed with many of the specific values upheld by participants in the counterculture movement (e.g., student radicals, liberals, humanists), but both were seeking alternatives to a way of life viewed as increasingly untenable.

The war on freedom and dignity

At the forefront of the American psyche throughout the late 1960s and early 1970s was the war in Vietnam. In 1961, President John F. Kennedy expressed the fervor and hyperbole of the upcoming decade when he stated: "We shall pay any price, bear any burden, meet any hardship, support any friend, oppose any foe, in order to assure the survival and success of liberty" (as cited in Farber, 1994, p. 2). Although Americans were subsequently told that their involvement in the Vietnam War was required to defend freedom and democracy throughout the world, many soon came to believe that this so-called defense of freedom was itself an illusion. Public trust in the authority of the American government eroded, and governmental control of individual behavior (chiefly in the form of the draft) was vehemently protested. In this atmosphere of disillusionment, Skinner's authoritative call for more control met a particularly cold public reception.

As news reports of the atrocities perpetrated both by South Vietnamese and American soldiers unfolded, it also became clear that the war depended on the ability of all concerned to grossly dehumanize thousands of the war's victims. Paul Potter, president of a newly organized group called Students for a Democratic Society, remarked in his 1965 speech before the organization's first antiwar rally in Washington, DC, "[B]ut the war goes on; the freedom to conduct that war depends on the dehumanization not only of Vietnamese people but of Americans as well..." (Potter, 1965, as cited in Bloom & Breines, 1995).

With the Vietnam War, the heinous consequences of dehumanization were on prominent display before the American people. In this context, Skinner's message that human beings were objects became increasingly distasteful. Even though Skinner himself opposed American involvement in Vietnam (Vargas, 2000, *personal communication*), and he argued that behaviorism treated the human object as exceedingly subtle and complex (see Skinner, 1971b), his objectification of human life was nonetheless intolerable to many members of his popular audience.

In addition to the backlash against authority and control provoked by opposition to the Vietnam War, as civil unrest mounted in the United States many Americans felt that their government was waging war against its own citizens in a frightening display of strong-arm tactics and militaristic authority. Again, Skinner's call for more control fell on unreceptive ears. One reader, identifying himself simply as a "worker" from San Francisco, wrote:

> It should be clear by now that the "liberty and justice" of this country consist largely of political harassment. In Oakland last month, a man was maced and beaten for arousing suspicion by walking around the block. . . . Enter B. F. Skinner, the true cop in cool clothing, bearing his brand-new streamlined model of Utopia. The Pentagon will love it: "You can show us how to guarantee we won't have no more hippie commie faggot radicals? Suppose we make you Secret Cultural Designer #1! All under cover, of course." (Grapevine, 1971)

Although liberals and radicals were more sympathetic than their conservative counterparts towards socialism and communism, anticommunist sentiment ran high in many circles. For conservatives, the defense of democracy was not only inherently important, it was necessary to stop the pernicious threat of communist expansion. Skinner's insistence that we are not free struck at the very heart of conservative America's vulnerability. Films such as *One Flew over the Cuckoo's Nest* (1975) and *A Clockwork Orange* (1971) portrayed the frightening consequences of restricting the right to self-determination and individual freedom of expression, exactly the principles undermined in Skinner's treatise. This concern was reflected in the public's interpretation that Skinner's technology of behavior would result in a system akin to Hitler's National Socialism, or Stalin's Marxist regime. One reader wrote, "It is to be hoped that Dr. Skinner's work, coming at the fortieth anniversary of Hitler's rise to power, is not an indication that he plans to run in the 1972 elections. . . . Here's hoping that Dr. Skinner

will be recognized soon as visibly insane . . . " (Ewing, 1971).

Skinner versus the "New Left"
and the "Third Force"

Although perceived by some as a communist sympathizer, Skinner did not become a hero of the growing New Left. For them, it was his perceived antihumanism that made him a threat. One of the documents that ushered in the 1960s was the Port Huron Statement, written in 1960 and published in 1962 by the Students for a Democratic Society (SDS). It was regarded as the manifesto of the growing student movement and the New Left. This group's desire for social change was clearly expressed in the questions posed in the statement's opening section on values: "[W]hat is really important? Can we live in a different and better way? If we wanted to change society how would we do it?" (cited in Bloom & Breines, 1995, p. 65).

Ironically, these were the very same questions that had led Skinner to write *Walden Two* in the aftermath of World War II, and that energized his message in *BFD*. Skinner and the student radicals of the 1960s, however, differed quite dramatically in how they answered these questions. Skinner advocated more social control, hippies advocated less. The counterculture focused attention on the inner self, while Skinner sought to excise traditional notions of selfhood and replace them with an externalized self. He wrote: "A self is a repertoire of behavior appropriate to a given set of contingencies. . . . The picture which emerges from a scientific analysis is not of a body with a person inside, but of a body which *is* [italics in original] a person in the sense that it displays a complex repertoire of behavior (Skinner, 1971a, p. 199).

A student at Keystone Junior College wrote to Skinner in 1968: "I would like to know your educated opinion about the hippie movement of today" (Ford, 1968). Skinner replied, "I believe the hippie philosophy emphasizes doing little or nothing for society. It seems to me that the hippie culture does not take its ultimate consequences into account, and that it could not survive except as a parasite" (Skinner, 1968).

Student radicals, humanists, and other proponents of the New Left were committed to a conceptualization of the human being as a self-determining, active, and creative agent. They looked to "inner" man to help solve some of the problems that the dehumanization of the social order seemed to have created. Contrast this with Skinner's outlook in *BFD*: "Autonomous man is a device used to explain what we cannot explain in any other way. . . . Science does not dehumanize man, it de-homunculizes him, and it must do so if it is to prevent the abolition of the human species. To man qua man we readily say good riddance" (Skinner, 1971a, pp. 200–201). One cannot help but forgive some of Skinner's lay readers for not quite appreciating the difference between dehumanizing and de-homunculizing, and accusing him of presenting a sterile, objectified "outer" man. Critics also objected to Skinner's emphasis on determinism, and accused him of contributing to the erosion of the values that the counterculture was hoping to reclaim to create a more meaningful life. As one disillusioned reader wrote, "It is indeed sad, when in our world today where both young and old alike are becoming drug-crazed and dropping out because they see life as meaningless, that someone like B. F. Skinner . . . comes along and tells us that life is even more meaningless than we think . . . (Dye, 1971).

Skinner's focus on the environment as the agent of control, and his eschewal of the importance of inner life was thus completely at odds with the spirit of the times. Skinner's own field, the discipline of psychology, was itself witnessing the arrival of a "third force" – the humanistic psychology movement. This movement, which both arose out of and influenced the cultural undercurrent of the times, took up the attack on behaviorism (for an account of the opposing views of Skinner and prominent humanistic psychologist Carl Rogers, see Rogers & Skinner, 1956). One spokesperson, in a call to arms for humanistic psychologists, wrote: "Let us become the active conscience of the psychological fraternity . . . condemning each and every dehumanizing, depersonalizing and demoralizing force that would move us further down the road to the Brave New World and the technocratic society – that social laboratory of the behaviorist's dreams and the humanist's nightmares" (Matson, 1971, p. 11).

The Esalen Institute in Big Sur, California was established in 1962 as a center for some of the early activities of humanistic psychologists and other participants in the human capacity, or human potential, movement.[7] By 1970, this movement was attracting its own press (see, for example, "Coast group spearheads a movement," 1967; Fiske, 1970; Reinhold, 1970). The activities at Esalen included encounter groups, body awareness classes, sensitivity training, Gestalt therapy, and improvisational dance. All were designed to facilitate awareness of participants' inner lives in the "here and now."

The emphasis on feeling and consciousness (and altered states of consciousness, see T. Leary, 1968; Watts, 1962) was not restricted to the activities of the Institute. Members of many other segments of American society were turning to alternative experiences, intentional communities, and other experiments in living to reclaim a sense of inner purpose and meaning. At the same time that many were striving to "get in touch" with their inner selves, Skinner wrote:

> Physics did not advance by looking more closely at the jubilance of a falling body, or biology by looking at the nature of vital spirits, and we do not need to try to discover what personalities, states of mind, feelings, traits of character, plans, purposes, intentions, or the other perquisites of autonomous man really are in order to get on with a scientific analysis of behavior. (Skinner, 1971a, p. 15)

In addition to eliminating the importance of inner life in an explanation of behavior, Skinner's work offended some readers because of its strident intellectualism – its constant appeal to the world of scientific scholarship, facts, and experiments. Part of the student unrest that fuelled revolt on college campuses involved a growing disdain for the perceived authority, establishment-mindedness, and stultification of the academic elite:

> If student movements for change are still rarities on the campus scene, what is commonplace there? The real campus, the familiar campus, is a place of . . . commitment to business-as-usual, getting ahead, playing it cool. . . . Rules are accepted as "inevitable," bureaucracy as "just circumstances," irrelevance as "scholarship" . . . . But neglected generally is real intellectual status, the personal cultivation of the mind.

(The Port Huron Statement, as cited in Bloom &
Breines, 1995. p. 69)

Many found *BFD* hard to take because a
Harvard professor, rallying the results from ivory
tower experiments, felt free to pronounce so
forcefully on what was right for society. As one
reader put it: "BFD was the biggest bunch of
scholarly garbage I've ever read. After attending
three different colleges, both as an undergraduate
and graduate, I've been exposed to a great deal of
it, but Dr. Skinner's work beats it all" (Dye, 1971).
Another reader wrote: "Must be wonderful to
have a lot of 'education' – seems that you guys
with all the book-learning always come up with
the wrong answers. . . . That's the trouble with
you bastards. You get so damn educated you
simply miss the entire point (of life). I feel terribly
sorry for you" (Pfui, 1971).[8]

A final shift in the sociocultural ethos was
marked by the abrupt end, during the period of
the counterculture movement, of the era of technological enthusiasm that had predominated in
American society since the late 1800s (see Hughes,
1989). This enthusiasm, although on the wane
after the bombing of Hiroshima and Nagasaki
(see Boyer, 1985), was further dampened by the
public's awareness of the devastation of Vietnam
through the use of military technology. In this
period, Rachel Carson's *Silent Spring* (1962),
Reich's *The Greening of America* (1970), and Barry
Commoner's *Science and Survival* (1966) and
The Closing Circle (1971), implored readers to
acknowledge the environmental crises created by
large-scale technological systems designed to
accelerate material wealth and the domination
of the natural world. As Hughes (1989) put it,
"Thoughtful Americans could no longer glibly
associate technology with incandescent lamps,
Model T's, and 'better things for better living'"
(p. 444). The technofervor of the l950s was
over.

Even though Skinner acknowledged the role
of physical technologies in creating many contemporary social and environmental problems,
he nonetheless held an unwavering faith in the
technological ideal of science, and in the promise
of his system of behavioral technology (see L. D.
Smith, 1992). For example, in the opening chapter
of *BFD* he wrote: "In trying to solve the terrifying
problems that face us in the world today, we natu-

rally turn to the things we do best. We play from
our strength, and our strength is science and
technology. . . . But things grow steadily worse,
and it is disheartening to find that technology
itself is increasingly at fault" (Skinner, 1971a,
p. 3).

Skinner's solution to this predicament was a
psychotechnology that would induce desirable,
prosocial, culture-sustaining behavior. These
culture-sustaining behaviors themselves involved
technology, such as encouraging the use of con-
traception to curb population growth, or practicing new methods of medicine or agriculture.
Despite Skinner's emphasis, especially in *Walden
Two*, on the use of small-scale technology to
promote a sustainable culture, his message in
BFD was not in line with the antitechnocratic
sentiment of the era. In fact, in suggesting that
we bring human behavior within the purview
of the technological world order, Skinner was
striking at the very heart of antitechnocratic
anxiety – the subversion of all personal control,
including the control of one's own behavior – by
technology.

An Unlikely Utopia: Walden Two and the Intentional Communities Movement

Although Skinner himself never attempted a systematic application of behavioral principles to
the design of culture, and although the political
ethos of the late 1960s and early 1970s certainly
predisposed negative reaction to many of his
ideas, the utopian and melioristic spirit of Skinner's writing was responsible for a completely
different kind of reaction in this period. This
reaction came from individuals and groups who
were trying to find alternatives to the lifestyle
of mainstream society, and who discerned the
melioristic strain in Skinner's work. These individuals gravitated towards Skinner's utopian
novel *Walden Two* (1948),[9] and selected it as the
blueprint for this alternative. As one individual
wrote, in reflecting on her reaction to the novel
and its protagonist. Frazier:

> To comprehend what the B. F. Skinner novel
> *Walden Two* meant to me in the early years, you
> have to understand that I was in love, Not with
> anyone I knew, all just flawed humans, but with
> Frazier. . . . I was also in love with Frazier's

creation. I longed to spend my life at Walden Two. . . . It had everything I wanted. (Kinkade, 1999, p. 49)

These words, written by one of the founders of a *Walden Two*-inspired intentional community, express the passion and fervor that Skinner's novel inspired for many readers in the late 1960s and 1970s. It is true that *Walden Two* was frequently decried as antihumanistic, and that Skinner's version of the good life was often perceived as sterile, regimented, and dull (see Rutherford, 2000). It is also clear that many believed that the science of human behavior as applied to culture would result in a dystopian Brave New World. Despite these powerful objections, however, reaction to *Walden Two* was not uniformly negative. Coinciding with the growth of the communities movement in the late 1960s and throughout the 1970s came a growing interest in Skinner's novel. For example, one reader wrote to Skinner, "Is there such a place as 'Walden Two?' I feel like I have been looking for it all my life" (S. Skinner, 1979). Another reader, already committed to cooperative living, wrote: "I'm an Aldous Huxley fan and a humanist and therefore an automatic critic of anything smaking [*sic*] of psychological manipulation, but I must say that I have reversed my original opinion of Walden Two since the breaking up of our commune makes many of your suggestions painfully meaningful" (C. Smith, 1968).

One precocious and independent-minded 14-year-old writing to Skinner noted the widespread negative reaction to the novel, but declared his allegiance to the *Walden Two* model in the following words: "Young as I may be (although this may be a reason) I appear to be the only one of the others I know who read your book (my two brothers, my teacher, and a friend) who does not believe the Walden society would 'belittle man' or 'turn us into robots.' In fact I suppose I could and would become a member of such a utopia as soon as I was of age" (Burkan, 1968).

In an era characterized by a growing disillusionment with the status quo and dissatisfaction with the values and mores of mainstream society, communal living appealed to many as a potential solution to personal and ideological crises. For some of these people, *Walden Two* offered the specific blueprint for such an alternative. One

reader wrote to Skinner, "I have been running away from what I do not like, but there has not seemed to be any place worth running to. I have just finished reading *Walden Two*, and . . . it seems to me that there *is* [italics in original] a place worth running to with all alacrity" (Morgan, 1966).

Thus, Skinner's vision did appeal to a significant number of pioneering would-be communitarians in the late 1960s. In 1965, one such group made an initial attempt at communal living à la Walden Two by purchasing a dilapidated house in Washington D.C., which they named Walden House. This group would subsequently band together with a group called Walden Pool from Atlanta, Georgia, to found Twin Oaks, a Walden Two-inspired intentional community in the lush countryside of rural Virginia (for accounts of Twin Oaks and its development, see Kinkade, 1973, 1994, 1999; Komar 1983). In 1974, a group of behaviorally oriented psychologists and educators set up a community called Los Horcones in Hermosillo, Mexico, to systematically apply Skinnerian principles to their own lives and to the design of culture (for information about Los Horcones, see Comunidad Los Horcones, 1982, 1989).

In sum, the sociopolitical and cultural landscape of the late 1960s was complex and historically unique. Skinner's desire to create a new and better world resonated with many of the utopian ideals of the counterculture, but his means and ends were almost completely at odds with the ideology guiding the movement. For his commitment to social meliorism he was considered a humanist by some. Others felt he embodied the most dangerous antihumanism since Hitler. Why all the fuss about Skinner? Perhaps in an era when many were desperately seeking value and purpose in their lives, Skinner's message was at once unbearably tantalizing and devastatingly empty. One reader expressed his disillusionment this way:

As a sophomore student at UC Santa Barbara in 1967, I can remember reading Walden II and being extremely impressed by the ideas set forth therein. It seemed to me that someone had finally outlined in a coherant [*sic*] and unemotional way most of the major flaws in our contemporary socio/economic situation. . . .

However, later, while a student at UC Berkeley in Psychology, I realized that Skinner had failed to provide the single most essential ingredient for a realistic attempt at change. This ingredient was a practical outline and guide to the techniques necessary to the promotion of his amoral ideas in a moralistically oriented culture. (Miller, 1971)

Skinner's refusal to address the importance of values in the implementation of his technology of behavior was consistent with his scientific outlook and background. He viewed the science of behavior as itself value-free: "A science of behavior does not contain within itself any means of controlling the use to which its contributions will be put" (Skinner, 1953, p. 437). He believed that decisions about which behaviors and thus which ways of life should be reinforced would be made by the environment, in much the same way physical characteristics were selected by the environment through the process of natural selection. Specifically those behaviors that ensured the survival of the culture would be selected – although he cautioned that, "The principle of survival does not permit us to argue that the status quo must be good because it is here now" (Skinner, 1953, p. 432). However, he also advocated taking direct control of the present environment in order to produce these culture-sustaining behaviors. Science, in the form of direct and dispassionate observation of past behavior, could serve as our guide in deciding which behaviors would lead to survival. But in both posing and answering the question "Who will control?" Skinner was evasive. In one answer to this self-posed question, he stated: "The answer requires the kind of prediction which cannot be made with any certainty because of the extremely complex circumstances to be taken into account. In the long run, however, the most effective control from the point of view of survival will probably be based upon the most reliable estimates of the survival value of cultural practices" (Skinner, 1953, p. 446).

Although Skinner was frustratingly unwilling to tackle the question of exactly how to implement his technology of behavior, including what value system it would support, several groups found inspiration in his writings and undertook just such an implementation. Although many

readers reacted to Skinner's work in this period with hostility and contempt, others were attracted to it for the alternatives it presented. Thus, it collided with one set of American social values emphasizing self-determination and free will, but appealed to another set emphasizing self-improvement, social meliorism, and utopianism. In part, Skinner's relevance to both of these enduring features of the American predicament accounted for his rapid ascendance to the status of public intellectual in this period.

Conclusion: The Social Construction of Behaviorism

From the foregoing, it is clear that an undifferentiated acceptance of Skinner's public image as maligned behaviorist significantly obscures the complexity of his relationship with psychology's public. From the 1940s to the 1970s, the intricate topography of the American cultural and political landscape determined how Skinner's work was constructed by popular audiences. Due to the contradictions and debates inherent in much of the social discourse of this period, Skinner appeared in a broad array of guises – from educational revolutionary, to utopian, to scientific despot and totalitarian.

Here, I have suggested that diverse reactions to the baby tender were embedded in a cultural milieu that simultaneously *praised* household technology as symbolic of the good life of 1950s America and *denounced* mechanized mothering under the influence of contemporaneous psychoanalytic and popular literature on child rearing. Reactions to the teaching machine were affected by similar contradictions. The machine represented the best in American technological innovation, promising a revolution in education that could not fail to appeal to progressives and technological enthusiasts alike, while simultaneously resonating with the growing sense of alienation, conformity, and general social anomie of the late 1950s. Popular articles and personal reactions to both devices reflected these diverse sentiments.

With the publication of *BFD*, popular reaction to Skinner became even more vociferous. The unique nature of the cultural and historical moment greeting *BFD*, which encompassed both rejection of the existing social order and a fervent desire for alternatives, created a spotlight for Skinner. He seized the popular imagination in the early 1970s, not because he supplied the right (or at least socially acceptable) answers, but because he asked the right questions. For many, Skinner's proposed solutions to society's pressing social problems were unpalatable, but still he held out hope for a new and radically different social order. Despite widespread condemnation, there were those among the hippies and the flower children who discerned an appealing strain of utopianism and social meliorism in Skinner's work. Thus, although decried as a Nazi by some, others adopted Skinner as the inspiration for alternative social practices and built humanist, egalitarian communities based on his principles.

Through all of these examples, it is clear that the American cultural milieu exerted a multifaceted and complex influence on the popular interpretation and reception of Skinner's work. Popular reaction to Skinner was not based on the public's perception of the "truth or error" of his position, nor even on the potential usefulness of his technologies. Science writers and readers used neither positivist nor technological ideals of science to guide popular interpretations of Skinner's psychology. As Cooter and Pumfrey have pointed out, "'Successfully popularized' natural knowledge may take on very different meanings within popular culture from those intended by its popularizers" (Cooter & Pumfrey, 1994, p. 249). Understanding and interpreting these meanings can help clarify the process and products of psychology's popularization and help reveal the relationships between professional and popular conceptualizations of psychology. Ultimately, this analysis may help elucidate the successes and failures of the discipline's social impact.

Finally, it should be noted that the very nature of Skinner's work was influenced by the characteristics of the society in which it was produced. As Leary (1987) has noted, the theories of contemporary psychology have appealed to the American public precisely because the theories draw on metaphors already in common usage (e.g., efficiency, productivity, etc.). As he puts it, the stories of modern psychology "make use of familiar cultural categories" (Leary, 1987, p. 329). Skinner's development as a scientist and his appeal to a technology of behavior were deeply rooted in progressivist values and in the American technological imperative. His work drew on several of the cultural categories that have organized American social thought throughout the twentieth century. As a public intellectual, Skinner was both a product of the American context and a challenger of some of its most prized ideals.

Notes

1 John Gray Sr., an engineer, had built his own baby tender for John Jr. Several years later, after Skinner had made several unsuccessful attempts to commercially manufacture the device, he and Gray struck up a collaboration that resulted in the Aircrib Corporation. The company made a few well-constructed models before Gray's untimely death. Julie Vargas, who raised both of her daughters in an air crib, reported that she still gets about one inquiry a month from people interested in building their own tenders (Vargas, 2000).

2 Skinner (1979) noted that the use of the title "Baby in a Box" probably did little to help the image of the baby tender. He reported an observation made by one of his colleagues: "The only time that human beings are subject to boxes is when they are dead" (Skinner, 1979, p. 305). He also noted the unavoidable similarity between the baby box and the "Skinner box," an experimental chamber used to test operant principles with animals.

3 Incidentally, in this period Americans witnessed the advent of another enclosed, climate-controlled space. Southdale, the first fully enclosed suburban shopping mall, opened in Minneapolis, Minnesota in 1956 (Marling, 1994).

4 During the 1950s, businessmen and other 9-to-5ers were dabbling in home improvement as never before. A 1951 article by Skinner, entitled "How to Teach Animals," demonstrated that the family pet was not left out of the do-it-yourself trend: "Since nearly everyone at some time or another has tried, or wished he knew how, to train a dog, cat, or some other animal, perhaps the most useful way to explain the learning process is to describe some simple

experiments which the reader can perform himself"
(Skinner, 1951).

5 This focus on the "outsides of things" extended to
automobile design. The 1950s witnessed the rise of
the engineered "cycle of artificial obsolescence" in
which car manufacturers preyed on the public's
desire to own the newest and flashiest cars. Each year,
despite few changes in fundamental design, cars
would take on a new look, often sporting fancy grill
work, fins, and other cosmetic flourishes (see
Gartman, 1994, for a social history of the automobile
in America).

6 In fact, one of the first televised educational courses
for college credit on the West Coast debuted on
January 15, 1952. It was a course in child psychology,
produced and presented by Mary Cover Jones and
her husband Harold Ellis Jones at the University of
California, Berkeley (Reiss, 1990).

7 Skinner, in fact, gave talks at the Esalen Institute on
two occasions in the late 1960s. One, delivered on
September 18, 1967, was entitled "The Scope of the

Human Potential." For an account of his experiences
there, see Skinner, 1983, pp. 275–276. Despite the
philosophical differences between his orientation
and that of many participants in the human potential movement, Skinner was on good terms with
many of the people who established the Esalen Institute. After the publication of *BFD*, Michael Murphy,
one of the founders of Esalen, wrote to Skinner
offering him accommodation at the Institute as a
sort of sanctuary or retreat. He wrote, "If you ever
feel like a retreat in Big Sur, we have a house there
away from the madding crowd in which you could
hide out for a while. I would enjoy seeing you"
(Murphy, 1973).

8 It seems probable that this letter, written by
"McDermott X. Pfui," was written under a pseud-
onym to phonetically express the author's attitude
toward Skinner and his work.

9 Although *Walden Two* was written in 1945 and published in 1948, it received most of its popular attention when it was republished in paperback in 1962.

References

American Psychological Association (1961). Self-
instructional materials and devices. *American Psychologist, 16,* 512.

Anonymous (1945, September 30). Letter to B. F.
Skinner (Skinner papers). Cambridge, MA: Harvard
Archives.

Baby box. (1947, July 19). New Yorker, 19–20.

Bakan, D. (1966). Behaviorism and American urbanization. *Journal of the History of the Behavioral Sciences, 2,* 5–28.

Bakan, D. (1998). American culture and psychology. In
R. W. Rieber and K. Salzinger (Eds.), *Psychology:
Theoretical-historical perspectives* (pp. 217–226).
Washington, DC: APA.

Bell, J. N. (1961, October). Will robots teach your children? *Popular Mechanics,* 153–157, 246.

Bender, E. (1965, January). The other kind of teaching.
Harper's Magazine, 48–55.

Benjamin, L. T. (1988). A history of teaching machines.
American Psychologist, 43, 703–712.

Benjamin, L. T., & Nielsen-Gammon, E. (1999). B. F.
Skinner and psychotechnology. The case of the heir
conditioner. *Review of General Psychology, 3,* 155–
167.

Bird, W. L. (1999). *"Better living": Advertising, media,
and the new vocabulary of business leadership, 1935–
1955.* Evanston, IL: Northwestern University Press.

Bjork, D. W. (1993). *B. F. Skinner: A life.* New York:
Basicbooks.

Bjork, D. W. (1996). B. F. Skinner and the American
tradition: The scientist as social inventor. In L. D.
Smith and W. R. Woodward (Eds.), *B. F. Skinner and
behaviorism in American culture.* Cranbury, NJ:
Associated University Presses.

Bloom, A., & Breines, W. (1995). *"Takin' it to the streets":
A sixties reader.* New York: Oxford University
Press.

Boehm, G. A. (1960, October). Can people be taught
like pigeons? *Fortune,* 176–179, 259–260, 265–266.

Boroff, D. (1963, February). Education comes of age.
Parents' Magazine, 38, 74, 116, 118, 120.

Boxes for babies. (1947, November 3). *Life,* 73–74.

Box-reared babies: Skinner baby-box (1954, February
22). *Time,* 66.

Boyer, P. (1994). *By the bomb's early light: American
thought and culture at the dawn of the atomic age.*
Chapel Hill, NC: The University of North Carolina
Press.

Burkan, B. (1968, June 28). Letter to B. F. Skinner
(Skinner papers). Cambridge, MA: Harvard University Archives.

Capshew, J. H. (1996). Engineering behavior: Project
pigeon, World War II, and the conditioning of B. F.
Skinner. In L. D. Smith and W. R. Woodward (Eds.),
B. F. Skinner and behaviorism in American culture.
Cranbury, NJ: Associated University Press.

Chomsky, N. (1959). [Review of the book *Verbal behavior*]. *Language, 35,* 26–58.

Cmiel, K. (1994). The politics of civility. In D. Farber (Ed.), *The sixties: From memory to history*. Chapel Hill, NC: The University of North Carolina Press.

Coast group spearheads a movement seeking clue to human feelings (1967, October 8) *New York Times*, p. 55.

Comunidad Los Horcones (1982). Pilot Walden Two experiments: Beginnings of a planned society. *Behaviorists for Social Action Journal, 3*, 25–29.

Comunidad Los Horcones (1989). Walden two and social change: The application of behavior analysis to cultural design. *Behavior Analysis and Social Action, 7*, 35–41.

Cooter, R., & Pumfrey, S. (1994). Separate spheres and public places: Reflections on the history of science popularization and science in popular culture. *History of Science, 32*, 237–265.

The critics speak – Teaching machines: What's ahead? (1967, September). *Today's Health*, 56–57.

Cuban, L. (1986). *Teachers and machines: The classroom use of technology since 1920*. New York: Teachers' College Press.

Curti, M. (1980). *Human nature in American thought: A history*. Madison, WI: University of Wisconsin Press.

Dinsmoor, J. A. (1992). Setting the record straight: The social views of B. F. Skinner. *American Psychologist, 47*, 1454–1463.

Dye, B. (1971, September 8). Unpublished letter to the editor of *Psychology Today* (Skinner papers). Cambridge, MA: Harvard University Archives.

Ewing, C. (1971, August 16). Unpublished letter to the editor of *Psychology Today* (Skinner papers). Cambridge, MA: Harvard University Archives.

Farber, D. (Ed.) (1994). *The sixties: From memory to history*. Chapel Hill, NC: The University of North Carolina Press.

Fiske, E. B. (1970, September 5). Commune built by "Republican types." *New York Times*, p. 23.

Ford, A. L. (1968). Letter to B. F. Skinner (Skinner papers). Cambridge, MA: Harvard University Archives.

Foreman, J. (Ed.) (1997). *The other fifties: Interrogating midcentury American icons*. Urbana, IL: University of Illinois Press.

Gartman, D. (1994). *Auto opium: A social history of American automobile design*. New York: Routledge.

Geiser, R. L. (1976). *Behavior mod and the managed society*. Boston: Beacon Press.

Gilmore, K. (1961, February). Teaching machines – Blessing or curse? *Science Digest*, 76–80.

Grapevine, D. J. (1971, July 25). Unpublished letter to the editor of *Psychology Today*. (Skinner papers). Cambridge, MA: Harvard University Archives.

Hale, N. G. (1995). The "golden-age" of popularization, 1945–1965. In N. G. Hale, *The rise and crisis of psy-choanalysis in the United States*. New York: Oxford University Press.

Harrison, E. (1958, September 1). Baby monkeys trained to love mother made of block of wood. *New York Times*, p. 15.

Hart, J. (1982). *When the going was good: American life in the fifties*. New York: Crown Publishers.

Heated, air-conditioned 'baby box' aids mothers (1948, March 17). *Indianapolis News*.

Herman, E. (1992). Being and doing: Humanistic psychology and the spirit of the 1960s. In B. L. Tischler (Ed.). *Sights on the sixties*. New Brunswick, NJ: Rutgers University Press.

How a tech professor raises his youngsters in a "baby box" (1954, March 7). *Boston Sunday Globe*.

Hughes, T. P. (1989). *American genesis: A century of invention and technological enthusiasm, 1870–1970*. New York: Viking.

Jackson, L. (1998). *The New Look: Design in the fifties*. New York: Thames and Hudson.

Kinkade, K. (1973). *A Walden two experiment*. New York: Quill.

Kinkade, K. (1994). *Is it utopia yet?* Louisa, VA: Twin Oaks Publishing.

Kinkade, K. (1999, Summer). But can he design community? *Communities: A Journal of Cooperative Living, 103*, 49–52.

Komar, I. (1983). *Living the dream: A documentary study of the Twin Oaks community*. Norwood, PA: Norwood Editions.

Krasner, L. (1978, September). The future and the past in the behaviorism-humanism dialogue. *American Psychologist*, 799–804.

Kreig, M. B. (1961, February). What about teaching machines? *Parents' Magazine*, 44–45, 76, 78, 80.

Krutch, J. W. (1954). *The measure of man: On freedom, human values, survival and the modern temper*. New York: Grosset & Dunlap.

Laing, R. D. (1967). *The politics of experience*. New York: Pantheon Books.

Leary, D. E. (1987). Telling likely stories: The rhetoric of the New Psychology, 1880–1920. *Journal of the History of the Behavioral Sciences, 23*, 315–331.

Leary, T. (1968). *The politics of ecstasy*. New York: Putnam.

Luce, G. G. (1960, September 24). Can machines replace teachers? *Saturday Evening Post*, 36–37, 102, 104–106.

Marling, K. A. (1994). *As seen on TV: The visual culture of everyday life in the 1950s*. Cambridge, MA: Harvard University Press.

Maslow, A. H. (1969). *Toward a psychology of being*, 2nd edn. New York: D. Van Nostrand.

Matson, F. W. (1971, March/April). Humanistic theory: The third revolution in psychology. *The Humanist 31*, 7–11.

McKean, N. (1945, September 29). Letter to B. F. Skinner (Skinner papers). Cambridge, MA: Harvard Archives.

McMurrin, S. M. (1967, January 14). What tasks for the schools? *Saturday Review*, 40–43.

Mechanical teacher aids 3-Rs. (1954, June 29). *Boston Globe*.

Miller, D. T., & Nowak, M. (1975a). *The fifties: The way we really were*. Garden City, NY: Doubleday.

Miller, D. T., & Nowak, M. (1975b). TV's the thing. In D. T. Miller and M. Nowak, *The fifties: The way we really were* (pp. 343–374). Garden City, NY: Doubleday.

Miller, M. S. (1971, August 5). Letter to the editor of *Psychology Today* (Skinner papers). Cambridge, MA: Harvard University Archives.

Miracle gadget makes boys like arithmetic. (1954, June 29). *Boston Herald*, pp. 1, 3.

Morgan, S. (1966, March 20). Letter to B. F. Skinner (Skinner papers). Cambridge, MA: Harvard University Archives.

Mumford, L. (1970). *The pentagon of power*. New York: Harcourt Brace Jovanovich.

Murphy, M. (1973, September 26). Letter to B. F. Skinner (Skinner papers). Cambridge, MA: Harvard University Archives.

Newcomb, H. (1997). The opening of America: Meaningful difference in 1950s television. In J. Freeman (Ed.), *The other fifties: Interrogating mid-century American icons*. Chicago: University of Illinois Press.

Packer, R. E. (1963, May). Tomorrow: Automated schools. *Science Digest*, 34–38.

Page, M. L. (1945, June). Letter to B. F. Skinner (Skinner papers). Cambridge, MA: Harvard University Archives.

Pfui, M. X. (1971). Letter to B. F. Skinner (Skinner papers). Cambridge: Harvard University Archives.

Programed learning (1961, March 24). *Time*, 36, 38.

Reinhold, R. (1970, September 4). Humanistic psychology shows its force. *New York Times*, p. 13.

Reiss, B. K. (1990). *A biography of Mary Cover Jones*. Unpublished doctoral dissertation. The Wright Institute, Los Angeles, CA.

Ridgeway, J. (1966, June 4). Computer-tutor. *The New Republic*, 19–22.

Rogers, C. R. (1961). *On becoming a person*. Boston: Houghton-Mifflin Company.

Rogers, C. R., & Skinner, B. F. (1956). Some issues concerning the control of human behavior. *Science, 124*, 1057–1066.

Roszak, T. (1998). *The making of a counterculture: Reflections on the technocratic society and its youthful opposition* (Original work published 1968). Berkeley: University of California Press.

Rutherford, A. (2000). Radical behaviorism and psychology's public: B. F. Skinner in the popular press, 1934–1990. *History of Psychology, 3*, 371–395.

Schur, C. (1946, March 4). Mechanical baby-tender saves mother time. *Toronto Star*.

Seligman, D. (1958, October). The low productivity of the education industry. *Fortune*, 135–138. 195–196.

Silberman, C. E. (1966, August). Technology is knocking at the schoolhouse door. *Fortune*, 120–125, 198, 203–205.

Skinner, B. F. (1945, October). Baby in a box – Introducing the mechanical baby tender. *Ladies Home Journal, 62*, 30–31, 135–136, 138.

Skinner, B. F. (1948). *Walden two*. New York: Macmillan.

Skinner, B. F. (1951, December). How to teach animals. *Scientific American*, 26–29.

Skinner, B. F. (1953). *Science and human behavior*. New York: The Free Press.

Skinner, B. F. (1954). The science of learning and the art of teaching. *The Harvard Educational Review, 24*, 86–97.

Skinner, B. F. (1958, October 24). Teaching machines. *Science, 128*, 969–977.

Skinner, B. F. (1961, November). Teaching machines. *Scientific American*, 90–102.

Skinner, B. F. (1968, August 8). Letter to L. Ford (Skinner papers). Cambridge, MA: Harvard University Archives.

Skinner, B. F. (1971a). *Beyond freedom and dignity*. New York: Knopf.

Skinner, B. F. (1971b, May/June). Humanistic behaviorism. *The Humanist, 31*, 35.

Skinner, B. F. (1979). *The shaping of a behaviorist*. New York: Knopf.

Skinner, B. F. (1983). *A matter of consequences*. New York: Knopf.

Skinner, S. (1979, August 4). Letter to B. F. Skinner (Skinner papers). Cambridge, MA: Harvard University Archives.

Smith, C. (1968, May 24). Letter to B. F. Skinner (Skinner papers). Cambridge, MA: Harvard University Archives.

Smith, L. D. (1992). On prediction and control: B. F. Skinner and the technological ideal of science. *American Psychologist, 47*, 216–223.

Spigel, L. (1992). *Make room for TV: Television and the family ideal in postwar America*. Chicago: The University of Chicago Press.

Steele, V. (1997). *Fifty years of fashion: New Look to now*. New Haven, CT: Yale University Press.

Szasz, T. (1975). A critique of Skinner's behaviorism. *The Humanist, 35*, 28–31.

Teaching by machine (1954, July 17). *Science News Letter*, p. 38.

Terte, R. H. (1961, March 2). Tight rein urged on robot teacher. *New York Times*, p. 24.

Ubell, E. (1954, June 29). Machine teaches kids arithmetic painlessly. *New York Herald Tribune.*

Vargas, J. S. (2000, March 3). Interview with author. Morgantown, WV.

Vargas, E. A., & Vargas, J. S. (1996). B. F. Skinner and the origins of programmed instruction. In L. D. Smith and W. R. Woodward (Eds.), *B. F. Skinner and behaviorism in American culture.* Cranbury, NJ. Associated University Presses.

Walker, J. (1993). *Couching resistance: Women, film, and psychoanalytic psychiatry.* Minneapolis, MN: University of Minnesota Press.

Watts, A. (1962). *The joyous cosmology: Adventures in the chemistry of consciousness.* New York: Pantheon.

What's happening in education? (1967, September). *Today's Health*, 47–55.

Zinn, H. (1968). *Disobedience and democracy.* New York: Random House.

Chapter 9

The New Profession of Psychology

At the beginning of the twentieth century, psychology was still an academic discipline, meaning that most psychologists worked as college professors. Some of those were involved in applied endeavors as ways to supplement their income, the way Harry Hollingworth did throughout his career. But there were relatively few psychologists who worked in settings beyond the universities. Most of those who did were women because the academic jobs were largely closed to them except for positions in women's colleges such as Vassar or Wellesley. Grace Fernald (1879–1950) and Augusta Bronner (1881–1966) worked at the Juvenile Psychopathic Institute in Chicago, a site for research, diagnosis, and treatment of youths who had run afoul of the law. Leta Hollingworth worked for the City of New York at its Clearinghouse for Mental Defectives, doing interviews and administering intelligence tests to aid in proper referrals of individuals brought to the agency. Marion Bills (1880–1970) worked for the Aetna Life Insurance Company in Hartford, Connecticut, for 30 years, overseeing personnel selection and doing sales research. Elsie Bregman (1896–1969), a student of Cattell's, served as personnel officer at Macy's Department Store in New York City where, in the mental testing tradition of her mentor, she developed a battery of tests for employees.

Some male psychologists also held full-time applied jobs. One was J. E. Wallace Wallin (1876–1969), who worked as a school psychologist in St. Louis and other locations. Another was Henry Herbert Goddard (1866–1957), who was director of research at the Vineland Training School for Feebleminded Boys and Girls in New Jersey. It was Goddard who learned of Alfred Binet's (1857–1911) intelligence test when he was on a research trip to Europe. Goddard would transform and translate the test for use in English, publishing his version of the Binet intelligence test in 1908 (see Zenderland, 1998).

Recall that, in 1917, Leta Hollingworth and J. E. Wallace Wallin had organized the American Association of Clinical Psychologists. The label "clinical psychologist" had a different meaning in 1917 than it does today. It was more of a generic label, often used synonymously with the term consulting psychologist, to indicate a psychologist who worked in a clinical or testing or advisory role. By 1917, many of these clinical psychologists were involved with psychological assessment of children or adults, and typically that meant intellectual assessment using the Binet test. Lewis Terman (1877–

1956), a psychologist at Stanford University, had revised the Binet scale in 1916, publishing a version of the test that would dominate the field of intelligence testing for decades, a test known as the *Stanford–Binet Intelligence Test* (Terman, 1916).

As evidence of the growing faith in the abilities of these practicing psychologists, two states passed laws in 1917 permitting judges to commit individuals to mental hospitals based on the expert testimony of clinical psychologists and without corroboration from medical experts. That was a major achievement for the fledgling practice of clinical psychology, and one that was vociferously opposed by the medical profession.

In 1917 the United States declared war on Germany and thus entered the Great War raging in Europe. The United States army sought the services of psychologists for two principal duties: to assess the intellectual functioning of military recruits and to assess soldiers and recruits with respect to job placement in the services. We have already mentioned the job that Walter Dill Scott did with regard to selection tests for the army, a program, you may recall, that tested more than 3.5 million individuals by the war's end. The other activity was headed by Robert M. Yerkes (1876–1956), who assembled a group of psychologists to develop group measures of intelligence. The tests had to be developed quickly, in a matter of months. Two tests emerged, known as the *Army Alpha* and the *Army Beta*. The latter was a test that could be given to individuals who were illiterate or for whom English was not their first language. These tests were used to assess nearly 2 million military personnel and recruits (Samelson, 1977; von Mayrhauser, 1989).

Not only did the war extend psychology's involvement in psychological testing, both in intellectual assessment and personnel selection instruments, but it also involved psychologists in the army hospitals, principally with assessment and treatment of what would have been termed "shell shock" victims (post-traumatic stress disorder or PTSD in today's language). The first personality tests developed by psychologists were constructed in World War I, intended to screen out soldiers who might be susceptible to shell shock. Those tests proved useless for that purpose, but other personality tests would prove more successful, including the projective personality tests of the 1920s and later (for example, the *Rorschach Inkblot Test*).

Urbanization in the twentieth century brought new problems to American society. Especially prominent was a rise in juvenile delinquency. With new waves of immigrants coming to America after World War I, that problem became even more salient with continued growth of the cities, poverty of many of the immigrants, and the social and cultural problems of being in a new country, often not speaking the dominant language. In a nationwide effort aimed at prevention of delinquency, the first child guidance clinic was established in 1921. By 1927 there were more than 100 such clinics, and more than 200 by the 1940s. Typically these clinics were headed by a psychiatrist, assisted by a clinical psychologist and one or more social workers. Thus the number of positions for applied psychologists continued to grow.

Since 1917, applied psychologists had petitioned the American Psychological Association (APA) to create a special division for clinical/consulting psychologists. Yet the APA was reluctant to do this, arguing that the by-laws of the association stated that its sole purpose was to advance psychology as a science. The APA permitted a clinical section for a few years but the arrangement never proved very satisfactory. In 1930 the Association for Consulting Psychologists (ACP) was formed as an organization to house psychologists who worked in applied settings, for example, clinics, businesses, schools. The group published the first code of ethics for practicing psychologists in

1933, something that consulting psychologists had been requesting from the APA for more than 15 years. The ACP also founded the first journal for professional psychologists, the *Journal of Consulting Psychology*, begun in 1937. Despite these considerable accomplishments, the ACP was mostly a New York-based organization that was never able to generate a national membership base. In 1938 it gave way to a new organization, the American Association for Applied Psychology (AAAP), which took over the ACP journal as its own publication. The AAAP began with an initial membership of about 400 psychologists in four divisions: clinical, consulting, educational, and industrial. This organization promoted the interests of professional psychologists well. Likely it would have continued as an independent organization for many years, but the emergency situation of World War II called for its merger with the APA in order to ensure high-quality training of clinical psychologists. That merger took place in 1945, creating a new American Psychological Association with a divisional structure borrowed from AAAP and a promise to the professional psychologists to pay more attention to the issues that concerned them. The new APA changed its by-laws to indicate that it was to advance psychology as a science and as a profession (Benjamin, 1997).

If there is any single event that was most responsible for the modern profession of psychology it was World War II. With the war coming to a close, some in the federal government were busy making plans to deal with the healthcare needs of the returning veterans. The planning had actually begun in 1942 when the government directed the Veterans Administration (VA) and the United States Public Health Service (USPHS) to greatly expand the pool of mental health professionals. The need was going to be critical at the war's end, and there simply weren't nearly enough psychiatrists available to meet the need, nor could many more be trained given the size of medical school enrollments and the number of medical students choosing psychiatry as their specialty. So where could they find these mental health professionals? Answer: clinical psychology.

The reason for the government's insistence on the merger of AAAP and APA was that one body represented those who practiced as clinical psychologists and the other body represented the university faculty who educated psychologists. Obviously those two groups needed to work together for the common good.

The VA and USPHS worked with the newly organized APA to (a) develop doctoral programs in clinical psychology, and (b) identify programs of acceptable quality. The former goal led the APA to work with university psychology departments to improve the extant clinical psychology training programs and to encourage departments not engaged in clinical training to initiate such programs. The latter goal led to the creation of the APA's accreditation program that began accrediting doctoral training programs in clinical psychology in 1946. The USPHS promised federal funds to psychology departments training clinical psychologists and the VA promised funding for practicum and internship training for clinical psychology doctoral students. As it turned out, the federal government was accurate in its forecast of a great need for mental health services for veterans. On April 1, 1946, a few months after the end of World War II, there were 74,000 patients being cared for by the VA. Of that number, 44,000 (nearly 60 percent!) were classified as neuropsychiatric patients (Miller, 1946).

The government was concerned about the quality of graduate training, which is why the VA and APA had worked together to establish the accreditation program that the APA would administer to assure some minimal level of quality in clinical programs. Medical schools had a standardized curriculum followed by all accredited medical schools, and the government looked to psychology to function in a similar way. But psychology doctoral programs, which had been around since the 1880s, had never agreed to any standard curriculum for the doctoral degree in psychology (Benjamin, 2001). Thus the idea of creating such a uniform model, even if it was just for clinical psychologists and not for the rest of psychologists, was a difficult sell to academic psychologists, who were not keen on outsiders telling them how to structure their curriculum. With funds provided by the newly formed National Institute of Mental Health (NIMH), psychologists were urged to find a common training model (Baker & Benjamin, 2005).

Working with NIMH and the VA, the APA invited 73 people to a two-week conference in August 1949 in Boulder, Colorado, to attempt to create a framework for a grand educational experiment. They were asked to examine the then present methods of training psychologists for clinical work, to assess the current and future needs for psychological services, and to recommend a model, if possible, that would offer some level of standardization for how clinical psychologists were trained across diverse psychology departments. Academic departments had enjoyed more than 60 years of independent development; how could there possibly be any hope of consensus?

The agenda was full and the issues complex. The participants discussed such issues as the core curriculum; clinical specialties; private practice; master's-level psychologists; postdoctoral training; undergraduate student access to clinical courses; standards for agencies beyond the university that offered practicum and internship work; student characteristics for selection; financial aid for clinical students; training in ethics; the relationship of clinical psychology to other fields such as medicine, social work, and vocational guidance; licensing and certification; accreditation of programs; federal government involvement with clinical training; training of clinical faculty; placement of the internship (predoctoral or postdoctoral, in the university or outside); society's needs for clinical services; training in psychotherapy and other clinical skills; and training for research. Clearly the task was immense!

The meeting schedule for the two weeks was grueling. If there were any in the group who had looked forward to a summer vacation in the Rocky Mountains, they were quickly disabused of such fantasy. The published papers as well as the private papers and correspondence tell of a dedication to the task that is laudable. In the end the group accomplished what they had come to Boulder to do. They reached consensus on a large number of resolutions, endorsing a model for clinical psychology that called for extensive training in research and practice. Thus was born the scientist-practitioner, or Boulder model, a model that is very evident today in professional training. It is a model that has been much praised, much maligned, and, according to some, rarely if ever tried.

Psychologists had acquitted themselves well in World War II. Whereas their work had mostly been limited to psychological testing in World War I, their roles in the second war spanned the gamut of wartime activities: design of aircraft instrument panels, bomb sights, and other instrumentation; development of training protocols; contributing to the plans for the occupation of Germany and Japan after the war; intelligence work; military recruitment; propaganda; attitude studies; job selection; and testing prisoners of war. After the war, applied psychology benefited enormously, with the two greatest beneficiaries being clinical psychology and industrial psychology. But other fields prospered as well, such as counseling psychology, whose practitioners began being hired by the VA in 1952, the same year that the APA began accrediting doctoral programs in counseling psychology.

The growth of professional psychology in the last half of the twentieth century would be substantial. For example, by the 1970s, psychologists were the major deliverers of psychotherapy, something that had been virtually the sole practice of psychiatrists prior to World War II. (The fight to achieve that status, where clinical and counseling psychologists could practice independently, where they could be reimbursed for their services from insurance companies as part of healthcare coverage, where they would have hospital privileges, and now, in some states, prescription privileges for psychotropic medications, is a book in itself.) In addition to the older professional specialties, namely clinical, school, industrial-organizational, and counseling psychology, new professional specialties began to develop, including forensic psychology, health psychology, and sport psychology (see Benjamin & Baker, 2004). Although the profession of psychology is ever changing, the prospects for psychologists to serve in the public sector continue to look good. This is perhaps most evident in the field of healthcare, where psychology has a huge role to play in reducing deaths from the major killers, namely heart disease, cancer, and stroke, all of which have lifestyle variables as part of their etiology. For that reason, health psychology is the fastest growing of the professional specialties.

The Readings

The profession of psychology consists of many practitioner specialties, the largest of which is clinical psychology. The readings selected here focus exclusively on clinical psychology and more so on what is arguably one of the most significant events in the history of psychology, the Boulder conference of 1949 that produced the training model that is still used today by most doctoral programs in clinical, counseling, and school psychology. There are five readings, although three of them are very brief.

The first reading is chapter 3 from the Boulder Report, which was published in 1950 (Raimy, 1950). The chapter is entitled "Professional Training in the Light of a Changing Science and Society." It acknowledges that this model training program is being established in the midst of significant changes in the science of psychology and within a post-war American society. It discusses concerns about validation of the instruments used in assessment (such as personality tests) and about therapeutic techniques. It comments on the dangers of a training model that is too uniform. It stresses a need to keep abreast of societal needs to have a clinical profession that will serve the public good. This chapter will give you a feeling for the compromise, caution, and courage that were manifested at this historic conference.

The second reading is by the editor of this book and by historian of psychology David Baker. Baker is the Director of the Archives of the History of American Psychology at the University of Akron (discussed in Chapter 1). This article describes the events in the second half of the 1940s that led to the Boulder conference. It provides a detailed description of the conference in terms of its structure, its goals, and its accomplishments. Emphasis is placed especially on the preparatory work of David Shakow (1901–1981), whose life-long interest in understanding and treating psychological disorders and whose diligent pursuit of clinical psychology as an established mental health profession provided much of the impetus for the growth of clinical psychology in the 1940s (see Cautin, 2006). In fact, Shakow's 1947 committee report, which recommended a graduate training program in clinical psychology, was the structural backbone of the Boulder Report. Its importance is evidenced by its inclusion as a 35-page appendix in the published report of the Boulder conference, the only topical appendix in the report (Committee on Training in Clinical Psychology, 1947).

The final three readings are brief commentaries, published in 2000, and written by three very distinguished clinical psychologists: George Albee, Peter Nathan, and George Stricker. Each has written about the Boulder model with the hindsight of 50 years. The comments are insightful and provocative. They raise important questions about the intent of the Boulder architects, the willingness of traditional academic departments to train for clinical service, the nature of the Boulder model in professional schools, the adoption of a medical model for clinical psychology, and the flexibility of scientist-practitioner training. Was the Boulder model a failure from the beginning? Was it tried and found wanting? Was it not tried? These commentaries speak to all of those questions and more. We expect you will find them to be fascinating reading.

Professional Training in the Light of a Changing Science and Society
Victor Raimy

Participants at the [Boulder] Conference were acutely aware that the formulation of training policies is a task that requires analysis of the needs of many segments of society as well as analysis of the over-all public need itself. In addition to the various clinical and age groups for whom the services of clinical psychologists are intended – such as behavior problem children, the aging, and the mentally disturbed – there also must be considered the professional needs of the graduate students undergoing training and of the members of allied professions. Furthermore, the events of the past decade that had brought such marked changes to clinical psychology served to emphasize the fact that the policies of today might well be out of date by tomorrow.

In one sense, the decision to train students broadly in clinical psychology so that their training will include clinical practice with all age groups, and in addition to train them in general psychology and in research methods, represents in itself something of a safeguard against the intensive cultivation of a small area of contemporary social need that might rapidly become insignificant as society and the allied professions undergo changes. For this reason, one of the most frequent comments at the Boulder Conference was that training in clinical psychology should be broadly professional in the doctoral program, leaving most specialization to post-doctoral experience.

The previous chapter discussed the views of the Conference in regard to the relation between clinical psychology and the needs of society. The

From V. C. Raimy (Ed.) (1950). *Training in clinical psychology* (pp. 24–33). Englewood Cliffs, NJ: Prentice Hall. Reprinted by permission.

next section of the present chapter discusses the very likely possibility that changes will take place within clinical psychology. The final section of this chapter is devoted to various methods for insuring that when changes occur, in either social need or psychology itself, these changes will be recognized and incorporated into training programs.

The Validity of Present Assumptions in Clinical Psychology

Early in the Conference it was felt that some attention should be given to a survey of participants' opinions on the validity of current techniques in clinical psychology. Two extreme viewpoints are most likely to be elicited by such a survey: condemnation of the techniques as being poor, and therefore invalid; or acclamation of them as having demonstrated their usefulness, and as therefore being valid. Accepting either of the extreme viewpoints is probably a matter of individual optimism or pessimism motivated by the purposes one has in mind in making definitive statements. As in any other effort to reach an inclusive generalization, marked inaccuracies are very likely to become intermingled with adequate statements. The validity of the techniques of clinical psychology obviously can be considered only in terms of particular techniques used for specified purposes. Final decisions on the "validity" of a tool or a technique depend ultimately upon objective evidence. Yet at some point in the process, subjective opinions have demonstrable value, if only to chart the next logical steps in finding out how "good" one's present tools may be.

This was the spirit behind the discussions relating to the validity of present techniques in clinical psychology. That our techniques have considerable value must be regarded as an unstated accompaniment to the remainder of this chapter. The Conference would not have been called if this assumption were untenable. Since, however, a discussion of the validity and usefulness of techniques in an admittedly developing field is inevitably oriented toward finding weaknesses and places for desirable improvements, it is only to be expected that unflattering evaluations are likely to predominate. Furthermore, in the field of clinical psychology we have special reasons to be concerned with the validity of the assumptions underlying the techniques in daily use. All the mental health professions are in a similar position of being forced to use whatever techniques *seem* to be effective, since human welfare does not permit the considerable periods of time necessary to evaluate thoroughly those methods devised for diagnosis or treatment in the mental health area. Nor should it be overlooked that research in human personality represents one of the most difficult areas of scientific endeavor, as gauged by the present rash of untested theory in psychology, clinical psychology, psychiatry, and social work.

The urgent needs for service have sometimes forced the psychological worker to use inadequately tested tools and techniques. The war and postwar requests for service faced the clinical psychologist with many new demands for which he was only partially equipped. Since no other discipline seemed to be any better equipped for certain types of work in this field, the clinical psychologist usually accepted the responsibility of trying to do what he was asked.

The following report from a special committee appointed to consider the "validity of present assumptions" furnishes some of the tenor of discussions on this topic.

> Social needs, demands for service, and our own desire to serve effectively have compelled us to engage in programs of action before their validity could be adequately demonstrated. We have, perforce, used tools in need of sharpening, and relied on intuition in lieu of data. We have accepted assumptions, sometimes uncritically, sometimes skeptically, and sometimes for the time being only or as "best available knowledge."

> We are assuming, most broadly perhaps, that we are of service. We are assuming that we do know something about human behavior and its betterment, that our instruments and techniques are relevant and effective, that our training procedures enhance the competence and sensitivity of our successors, and that new knowledge of importance emerges from our research. We believe that many of these and other assumptions can be validated.

> We accept assumptions of this order without apology. While we believe in what we are doing, we also accept the responsibilities it entails. At the same time we accept an obligation to evaluate our work and ourselves. We accept it as an obligation in some sense peculiar to clinical psychology, implicit in our role of clinician among scientists and scientist among clinicians.

> Examining the validation task before us, this Conference finds encouragement in the progress we have made through the years – but it is chiefly impressed by the work that is still to be done.

> We recognize the difficulties inherent in bringing scientific methods to bear upon living people, particularly upon the scientist himself, in validating method and criterion against each other simultaneously, and in measuring status in the midst of change and change from uncertain base lines of status. We recognize subtle conflicts between the therapeutic attitude and impartial objectivity. We are, nonetheless, determined, as a profession, to face the validation issue squarely. We challenge ourselves to make our predictions more explicit, and to subject them to rigorous verification tests, to deal with the socially significant, tangible problems of concern to the lay community, to fit theory to facts, methodology to function.

A summary of the Conference's attitudes toward the validity of our present techniques was approved, without a dissenting vote, in the form of the following resolution:

> While the clinical psychologist has faith in the value of his service efforts, he is increasingly concerned with the improvement of the scientific status of his profession through meeting the needs for validation in the following areas.
>
> (1) Personality theories
> (2) Research methodology and validity criteria
> (3) Training procedures

(4) The clinical psychologist himself as a participant observer and professional practitioner

(5) The instruments and technique used in clinical practice.

Personality Theory. Although some participants may have come to the Conference prepared to do battle for or against certain specific techniques, the discussion during the opening days revealed such unanimity of opinion about the primary task of the clinical psychologist that what had been thought of as major battles turned out to be minor skirmishes. The discussion of technique validity pointed to one rather simple fact: only when there is general agreement on the major principles of personality organization will the problem of evaluating techniques designed to assess personality manifestations or to change personality functioning be much nearer solution. Without an underlying theoretical framework, the evaluation of a particular technique becomes an almost hopeless task of trying to decide whether one observer's opinion is any better than that of another. Observable data, in the form of objective behavior or even verbal report, form the only basis for progress in scientific psychology. Deciding what observable data to select for analysis constitutes the great contribution to be made by personality theory.

The Criterion. As in many previous meetings and in countless published articles, the problem of finding suitable criteria against which test or treatment results can be gauged was a major topic of lament. One sub-group reported, "The unavailability of good criterion indices and measurements constitutes a major obstacle to the validation of our techniques and theories. Ratings, clinical diagnoses, and the like, which commonly serve as criteria, leave much to be desired. Behavioral events seem to hold the greatest promise as dependable and meaningful criteria." This statement was obviously directed against the acceptance of "expert judgment" as a criterion for deciding whether, for example, a group of subjects actually were particular kinds of schizophrenics, whether particular patients under treatment had actually improved, and so forth. Who is mentally healthy and who is not mentally healthy also seems to be a problem in urgent need of solution.

Economics and Cooperative Research. Throughout every discussion of research in clinical psychology arose an insistent complaint over the sheer expense of assembling sufficient personnel, subjects, and time to make a thorough study of a given problem. Fragmented research seems to be uncomfortably characteristic of our present literature. New techniques or hypotheses spring into existence with impressive supporting theory or significant differences between groups, only to shrink into question marks after the passage of a number of years. Such developments are undoubtedly characteristic of scientific progress, but need not always be tasted to the dregs.

One possible solution is to encourage particular individuals to devote their lives to small areas in the hope that time will substitute for numbers; but many of the problems of psychology and psychiatry should not wait a lifetime for solution, although many undoubtedly will. Another solution, which has received much support in the physical sciences (atomic development) and the biological sciences (cancer research), lies in the possibility of cooperative investigation on a national or regional scale. Clinical psychology and psychiatry are badly in need of many extended investigations into the validity of their constructs in personality theory and the usefulness of their diagnostic and therapeutic techniques.

Unanimously, therefore, the Conference approved the following resolution:

This Conference approves national planning and cooperative group research among universities and other institutions on the evaluation of clinical techniques and personality constructs. Such investigations can often be carried on most effectively by large-scale carefully integrated program planning.

Implementation of this resolution must, of necessity, wait upon the efforts of individuals or small groups to provide significant and convincing research programs that can be widely endorsed and for which financial support can be secured. Since large-scale cooperative investigations seem at present to represent one of the most effective methods for securing badly needed research data, this resolution in reality presents a challenge to individuals in the research field to devise plans that will call forth the necessary support. The implication for training is obvious. Universities should rather encourage students to consider the possibilities of cooperative research than insist upon the creative insights of the individual psychologist as the only method for conducting research investigations.

In summary, it seems that the Conference was quite willing to go on record as believing that our tools and techniques are badly in need of validation despite the fact that they serve some useful purposes at the present time. In the field of psychotherapy, validation of present techniques and development of more effective ones constitute two of the most pressing problems. It may well be that research designed to clarify principles of personality organization will be more effective for providing solutions to present problems of technique than will research in any other area.

Diversity versus Uniformity

It has been previously pointed out that the Conference deliberately decided to emphasize the importance of broad, fundamental training in the doctoral program as one means of insuring that clinical psychologists will have an opportunity to develop a professional *field* rather than a narrow specialty. An emphasis upon diversity can also help to prevent the professional stagnation that may result from a highly uniform training program so set in a particular orientation that the profession remains unresponsive to new or changed social and professional needs.

This interest in diversity does not mean that the Conference failed to reach any agreement on a basic minimum of training in clinical psychology. The following resolution was prepared to express the view of the Conference in this respect:

The graduate education of all clinical psychologists should involve thorough and intensive work in four areas:

(1) General psychology, which includes such subjects as systematic, experimental, and social psychology
(2) Clinical psychology and mental hygiene, which include broad training in theory, method, and techniques

(3) Field work with a variety of clinical problems at different levels of responsibility
(4) Research and methods of investigation.

Beyond these core areas, each department should provide additional education in accordance with its distinctive facilities and objectives. The resources of each university should be so integrated and used as to provide that diversity of methods and objectives which will insure the continued possibility of experimentation with new methods of education to the end that quality and vitality are not sacrificed for uniformity.

Such a policy of encouraging diversity of training might well be undetermined or blocked by accrediting bodies that insist upon uniformity as a short-sighted means of achieving immediate goals at the expense of more important, long-range objectives. Although the accrediting body for clinical training programs has itself been urging a policy of diversity, the Conference thought that future committees might change their thinking in this respect. Realizing that a policy of diversity should be fostered at all levels in order to insure its acceptance, the Conference adopted the following resolution, which was forwarded to the American Psychological Association at its Denver meeting in September, 1949:

We urge the creation of a committee with broad powers to examine and review educational philosophy, methods, and standards beyond those serving as the foundation for accreditation in any one field of applied psychology, and with the power to review accreditation policies and practices. (Further discussion of accreditation will be found in Chapter 15.)

The Pros and Cons of Uniform Training Programs. Although the Conference endorsed a policy of diversity in training programs, it also agreed upon a minimum core of common training. The following advantages and disadvantages of *a* uniform educational program were considered.

In some ways, highly uniform training provides protection to the public in that the title "clinical psychologist" then comes to have a very definite meaning. Such protection may be illusory, however, in view of the fact that insistence upon uniformity may sacrifice the advantages to the public that may be gained more effectively by keeping the profession constantly aware of long-range objectives than by trying to satisfy immediate goals. Furthermore, employing agencies and institutions are well aware that most professional training attracts students with widely divergent goals and backgrounds so that selection of professional employees becomes a matter of selecting individuals with particular qualifications rather than of selecting employees because of the titles they bear. The inclusion of a common core of training should help to identify broadly those persons who have been trained as "clinical psychologists"; but not all clinical psychologists will have identical interests and competencies, any more than all lawyers are alike because they have the same degree and have passed similar examinations.

A highly uniform training would also make for easier relationships between clinical psychologists and members of allied professions, with whom clinical psychologists are in constant contact. Here again, the same counter-arguments seem to be valid. No one expects all persons called psychiatrists or psychiatric social workers to bear the same stamp. Differences in interest and area of activity are positive assets in those professions. Different persons with the same title cover broad fields of work in improving mental health, from children to the aged, and from minor maladjustments to serious psychoses. It was felt that the needs of the other professions will best be served if clinical psychology likewise supports a policy that trains persons for many types of clinical psychology rather than for one narrow specialty.

One of the most regrettable aspects of diversified training programs lies in the difficulty that arises when a student transfers from one institution to another. Time is almost inevitably lost in such transfers. Since, however, the number of transfers is very small, and likely to become even smaller as admission to clinical training programs becomes more difficult to obtain, little action was taken on this problem. There are sometimes distinct advantages to students in being able to transfer from one university to another in order to study with staff members known for a particular specialty. Such cross-fertilization has been encouraged in the past. Its advantages may still be utilized in some instances by having students attend other universities for a semester or even a full year without transferring for completion of the degree.

Mention should also be made of two further points that were influential in the thinking of Conference participants. First, in its present stage of development, training in clinical psychology cannot afford to become crystallized. Second, a too uniform development is often conducive to compliance in the accepting of educational goals and methods, rather than to the use of individual initiative in the working out of more desirable programs.

In summary, the Conference felt that training programs for clinical psychologists must reflect the changing needs of society as well as the theoretical and technical changes taking place within the profession of psychology and its related fields. It was agreed that in view of the wide gaps in our present knowledge, the validation of our working assumptions is a task of the utmost importance. In addition to research carried out by individuals, group or cooperative research would help in arriving more quickly at answers to pressing problems of human welfare. In order to keep the profession sensitive to changes in society and in psychology, diversified university training programs should be encouraged, although a basic core of general and clinical psychology will be necessary to provide a certain amount of uniform background.

The Affirmation of the Scientist–Practitioner: A Look Back at Boulder

David B. Baker and Ludy T. Benjamin, Jr.

The science of psychology has responsibilities in the matter which cannot be evaded. The need for applied psychological work is great and unless psychology can provide adequately trained personnel, other disciplines, which recognize both the need and responsibilities, will take over the function of which are more properly the province of the psychologist. (Shakow, 1942, pp. 277–278)

It seems hard to imagine that 50 years ago professional psychology was in its infancy. The demand for professional psychologists increased dramatically after World War II, and the realization that demand greatly exceeded supply resulted in a flurry of activity among psychologists, government agencies, and institutions of higher education. The synthesis of this was the Boulder Conference on Graduate Education in Clinical Psychology (referred to throughout as the "Boulder conference") held in Boulder, Colorado, from August 20 through September 3, 1949. A publication of the proceedings appeared in 1950 (Raimy, 1950).

The legacy of the Boulder conference is lasting. The mention of Boulder creates an instantaneous association with the scientist–practitioner model of training in professional psychology. Indeed, one outcome of the Boulder conference was a strong endorsement of the belief that the professional psychologist could and should be both researcher and practitioner. Psychologists have grown accustomed to this linkage, and for better or worse, the scientist–practitioner has become an axis around which

American Psychologist, 2000, 55(2), 241–247. Copyright 2000 by the American Psychological Association, Inc. Reprinted by permission of the publisher and author.

many decisions, judgments, arguments, and philosophies of training revolve (for a review, see Freedheim, 1992).

The Boulder conference was an ambitious undertaking. The debate over the scientist–practitioner model was one of the many substantive issues addressed by the 73 conferees during an intensive two weeks of self-evaluation of the then current values, beliefs, and practices in training for professional psychology. A look back at Boulder is instructive for many reasons. Among others, it highlights the contributions and motivations of those who were crucial in shaping professional psychology and reveals how those actions were shaped by the historical period in which they occurred.

Preludes to Boulder

Concerns about the training of professional psychologists had been voiced for decades before the Boulder conference (see Routh, 2000, this issue). The 1940s saw unprecedented attention to the issue, and in the span of a decade, the professional psychologist was engineered and produced in a way that has stayed more or less constant for half a century. As historical shorthand, it is often tempting to point to an individual as representative of a time, an event, or a movement. Many times such a designation can do a disservice as it may dismiss relevant information, context, and achievement. In a few other cases, the contributions of a single individual are of such magnitude that the designation is appropriate. It could be argued that this is true of the work of David Shakow (1901–1981), a psychologist whose contributions to he formal development of the Boulder model were substantial.

Shakow's 1941 American Association for Applied Psychology (AAAP) report

In 1941, David Shakow, chief psychologist at the Worcester State Hospital, was a member of the Committee on the Training of Clinical Psychologists that had been appointed by the AAAP. A. T. Poffenberger, who had attempted to set up a training program for clinical psychologists at Teachers College, Columbia University, in the 1930s (Morrow 1946), served as chair. In addition to Shakow and Poffenberger, the committee included Henry Murray, C. M. Louttit, Elaine Kinder, Joseph Zubin, Edgar Doll, Carl Rogers, Robert Yerkes, H. S. Liddell, Donald Lindsley. Donald Marquis, Carney Landis, Ward Halstead, Carlyle Jacobsen, J. Q. Holsopple and F. Heiser (Poffenberger, 1941). Shakow set much of the agenda for the initial meeting by providing a list of topics for discussion and providing a list of relevant references for reading.

The committee met for a day-long conference on May 3, 1941, at the New York Psychiatric Institute. Following the meeting, Shakow prepared a draft of a training document and asked Lindsley to distribute it to the committee members for reaction (Shakow, 1941). Shakow outlined a four-year PhD program in which the first year was given to establishing a systematic foundation in psychology and medical science needed for clinical work, the second year for psychometric and therapeutic principles and practices, a third year for internship experience, and the fourth year for completion of the dissertation (Shakow, 1942). Reaction to the report was largely favorable, although a few members, including Robert Yerkes, encouraged Shakow to adopt a broader perspective of professional psychology training to include such areas as "industrial psychology, educational psychology, [and] social-consulting" (Yerkes, 1941). Shakow (1942) responded,

> In presenting this program of training of the clinical psychologist, it is recognized that the training is weighted in the direction of psychopathology, especially as it is represented in the psychiatric hospital. This is in part deliberate, in part due to the background and experience of the writer. With relatively few changes, however, the general scheme is adaptable to other clinical fields and even to the educational and industrial fields. (p. 76)

By August of 1941, Shakow's report had been endorsed by the committee and forwarded to the AAAP by Poffenberger, who recommended that the AAAP appoint a committee to design a program for the professional training of clinical psychologists.

The Penn State conference

At the annual meeting of the AAAP in Evanston, Illinois, in August of 1941, Poffenberger's recommendation was accepted and the Committee on Training in Clinical (Applied) Psychology was formed with Bruce V. Moore of The Pennsylvania State University (Penn State) serving as chair. There was continued concern that Shakow's plan failed to adequately incorporate a range of applied areas. As Moore noted,

> This committee, which was originally authorized at the Evanston meeting in 1941, was continued at the New York meeting with instructions to expand its study to include all fields of application of psychology and make whatever reorganization of its membership would be necessary to expedite this expanded field of responsibility. (AAAP, 1943, p. 23)

The reorganization included the formation of three subcommittees: Educational Institutions, Health and Welfare Institutions (of which Shakow was a member), and Business and Industry.

On June 22, 1942, the Institute on Professional Training for Clinical Psychologists met at Penn State. The conference bulletin (*The Pennsylvania State College Bulletin*, 1942) described the purposes:

> To provide for a conference of all psychologists interested in the professional preparation of psychologists, to provide an opportunity for the Committee on Training in Professional (Clinical) [Applied] Psychology of the American Association for Applied Psychology, to hold meetings and have hearings of other psychologists interested in professional training, and to provide an advanced symposium of lectures and seminars for graduate students preparing for professional work in clinical psychology.

Representatives of each of the three subcommittees presented papers related to their areas of interest and expertise. The outcome was an abbreviated outline of a training program (AAAP, 1943) largely along the lines of what Shakow had presented a year earlier to the AAAP.

The 1945 clinical training report

World War II saw the mobilization of psychologists in service to the war effort, which among other things included the integration of AAAP with the American Psychological Association (APA) in 1944. As part of this reorganization, AAAP's Committee on Training in Professional (Applied) Psychology and APA's Committee on Graduate and Professional Training merged and appointed the Subcommittee on Graduate Internship Training. The new subcommittee was chaired by Shakow and included many familiar names in clinical psychology training, including Robert Brotemarkle, Edgar Doll, Elaine Kinder, Bruce Moore, and Stevenson Smith (Morrow, 1946). The committee met at the Vineland Training School (where Doll was director of research) from October 12 to 14, 1944. The result of that meeting was the report "Graduate Internship Training in Psychology," which appeared in the *Journal of Consulting Psychology* in 1945 (Shakow et al., 1945).

The title of the report is somewhat misleading as it contained considerable discussion of an entire training program in clinical psychology, not only internship training. In discussing the current state of affairs the report noted,

> The scope of activity permitted the clinical psychologist has generally been quite limited. To explain this situation, the suggestion has frequently been advanced that it was primarily due to the poor preparation of its practitioners and the low standards in the field generally. Whether this is so or not, certainly any real broadening of its scope can come only through the institution of sound professional instruction and standards. (Shakow et al., 1945, p. 244)

The committee was intent on elevating the status of clinical psychology:

> We believe that there is general concurrence in our opinion that few clinical psychologists, as

they are at present prepared, can, at the end of their instruction period cope adequately with the problems with which they are faced. It is the purpose of this report to present a program which should go far towards remedying the situation for the future. (Shakow et al., 1945, p. 246)

The report's discussion of professionalizing clinical psychology supported the doctoral standard and gave rise to consideration of alternatives to the traditional PhD:

> It is doubtful if anything less than a doctor's degree would be satisfactory for the practice of clinical psychology. Some question might be raised as to the kind of doctor's degree to be awarded. Although there are some reasons to adhere to the Ph.D. degree, the arguments for a truly professional degree, for example, a Ps.D. are many, and should be given careful consideration. (Shakow et al., 1945, p. 265)

The report, although a committee document, clearly carried the signature of David Shakow. By now there had been enough iterations of Shakow's triadic concept of diagnosis, therapy, and research to make it a permanent feature of the training landscape.

The Committee on Training in Clinical Psychology (CTCP)

The ever-increasing recognition of the need for professional psychologists in the public sector led the United States Public Health Service (USPHS) and the Veterans Administration (VA) to appropriate funds for training of professional psychologists (for an extended discussion, see Miller, 1946; Moore, 1992; Sears, 1947). The programs offered by these agencies were tremendous in scope and cost and were positioned to make professional psychology a dominant force in graduate education and within the newly reorganized APA. In 1947, the VA and the USPHS requested APA's assistance to detail how more professional psychologists could be trained. The CTCP was authorized to include a representative of general psychology, a department head, and a university administrator. APA President Carl Rogers asked Shakow to chair the committee, and by June of 1947, the remainder of the committee was constituted to include Ernest Hilgard, E. Lowell Kelly, Bertha Luckey, Nevitt Sanford, and Laurance Shaffer. The task of the committee, which seemed enormous, was to (a) formulate a recommended program for training in clinical psychology; (b) formulate standards for institutions giving training in clinical psychology, including both universities and internship and other practice facilities; (c) study and visit institutions giving instruction in clinical psychology and make a detailed report on each institution; and (d) maintain liaisons with other bodies concerned with these problems, including the committees of the American Orthopsychiatric Association, the National Committee for Mental Hygiene, and others (APA, 1947, p. 539).

The committee was asked to have a report on a recommended training program by the September meeting of the APA. Concerned with the limited time available, Shakow (1947) sent each member a copy of the 1945 report "Graduate Internship Training in Psychology" (Shakow et al., 1945). As before, Shakow asked committee members to critique the report, and as before, the committee was largely unanimous in its support of the document. The CTCP report was submitted and endorsed at the 1947 meeting of the APA in Detroit and published in the *American Psychologist* in December 1947 (APA, 1947). Known as the "Shakow Report," it would become the central working document of the Boulder conference. It was the most comprehensive statement of training for clinical psychology ever written, offering detailed recommendations on achieving competence in diagnosis, therapy, and research.

The task of visiting and evaluating institutions giving instruction in clinical psychology was begun in February 1948 and resulted in two published reports on doctoral training facilities (APA, 1948, 1949). By 1949, the committee had accredited 43 doctoral training programs at 41 universities. At these universities, clinical psychology students represented nearly half of the doctoral students in psychology, with an estimated 175 receiving the doctoral degree in clinical psychology in 1949 (APA, 1949).

The committee applauded the efforts of these programs, but some serious concerns were raised. It was noted that clinical techniques were empha-

sized at the expense of instruction in theory and research methodology, prompting a call for more rigorous testing of basic assumptions in theory, practice, and teaching. The committee also believed that the scope of clinical psychology was too narrow. Although the focus on psychiatric hospitals and severely disturbed populations was justified as a response to social need, it was also noted that clinical psychology should be prepared to apply its skills to other social needs as they arose. Psychotherapy was also a pressing concern, and the committee advocated supervised experience throughout the training years, not just during internship or postdoctoral years.

Finally, the committee addressed the issue of students entering private practice:

> Most all departments are opposed in principle to the private practice of clinical psychology. The Committee, as such, takes no stand on the question, though it is our consensus that the problems and responsibilities of clinical practice are so complex that, in our present state of knowledge, private practice by the single, independent psychologist offers much less value either to the client or to the psychologist than does the team or group approach in association with competent members of other professions. (APA, 1949, p. 340)

The Boulder Conference

By 1949, clinical psychology had a prescribed program of doctoral training, standards for accreditation of doctoral programs, accredited doctoral training programs and internships, growing ranks of students with strong government support, and a ready supply of employment opportunities. Relations with other mental health professions were cordial, as there were plenty of needs and jobs to be filled.

The USPHS was pleased with the progress of the CTCP but had concerns that the rapid expansion of professional psychology left little time for interaction and communication between VA hospitals, mental health centers, and university departments. What was termed "wide variation in practice and thinking" (Raimy, 1950, p. 8) led the USPHS to join forces with the APA to support conferences to formulate principles and procedures for the training of clinical psychologists.

At a joint meeting of the USPHS and the CTCP on September 5, 1948, the suggestion of a six-week summer institute to discuss problems in clinical training was made. The institute would be financed by the USPHS with a training grant of $40,000 and would be sponsored by the APA.

On January 8 and 9, 1949, a planning meeting was held in Chicago. Members of the CTCP, the representatives of the APA board of directors, and Carlyle Jacobsen and John Eberhart of the USPHS met under the chairmanship of David Shakow to discuss the summer institute ("Report of the Planning Committee," 1949). Over the two-day meeting, major details of the institute were worked out. Among other things, a name had to be selected, and after some discussion there was agreement on the Boulder Conference on Graduate Education in Clinical Psychology. An executive planning committee, chaired by E. Lowell Kelly, that would oversee the conference was appointed to include two members of the CTCP, two representatives of the clinical directors group, one member from the departmental chairmen group, and two ex-officio members, one to represent the USPHS and the other an administrative officer ("Minutes of the Planning Committee", 1949).

Conference participants were to be selected from a number of sources. All the members of the CTCP would participate. The largest group would be composed of a representative from each of the university training programs evaluated during the 1948–1949 site visits. Universities were also to be represented by a number of department chairs of general and experimental programs. One person would represent internship centers from a hospital, clinic, and school program. A representative from the VA would be invited, as well as a psychiatrist, social worker, and psychiatric nurse as representatives of their respective disciplines. It was estimated that there would be some 60–65 participants. An invitation had been made to hold the meeting at the University of Colorado at Boulder, thus making it convenient for the participants to attend the annual meeting of the APA scheduled in Denver.

Victor Raimy, director of the clinical training program at the University of Colorado at Boulder, became the administrative assistant to the executive planning committee and did considerable work on the logistics of the conference. Kelly convened the executive planning committee in Chicago on April 30 and May 1, 1949. The committee expressed the hope that the Boulder meeting would improve communication between individuals and institutions interested in the development of professional psychology, provide a new feeling of unity in psychology, and serve as a model for future training conferences ("Minutes of the Executive Planning "Committee," 1949).

On Saturday, August 20, 1949, 73 participants from across the United States and one from Canada, representing a diverse mix of individuals and institutions, arrived in Boulder and settled into Regents Hall or various motels and cottages in the Boulder area (see Benjamin & Baker, 2000, this issue, for a list of participants and their affiliations). The conference opened with welcoming addresses by the vice president of the University of Colorado at Boulder and Karl Muenzinger, chair of the psychology department. Kelly provided an overview of the conference, and Robert Felix, of the USPHS, gave an address on the role of psychology in meeting the mental health needs of the nation. The agenda for the next 15 days consisted largely of intensive consideration of 18 key discussion points that addressed the issues germane to the development of a profession: needs and function, training, ethics, relations with other professions, certification and licensure, and so on. Each day participants were divided into four groups, each with a chair and a reporter. All groups considered the same topic during a morning session. In the afternoon, everyone would be assembled together to review and summarize the reports of each of the morning groups. The final days of the meeting gave considerable attention to clarifying the most significant issues relating to policy. Issues on which a consensus could be reached were framed as resolutions and endorsed by the conference. By the end of the conference, approximately 70 resolutions had been adopted.

1950: The published proceedings

The most complete report of what occurred during the Boulder conference can be found in *Training in Clinical Psychology*, edited by Victor

Raimy (1950). Essentially, each chapter covered one of the topic areas addressed by the conference. The report's appendix contained a reprint of Shakow's 1947 report on training in clinical psychology.

The conference had to serve many masters, one of which was its main benefactor, the USPHS. A resolution that served the needs of the USPHS also served as an opening for the introduction of the scientist–practitioner model, which was the embodiment of Shakow's trinity of diagnosis, therapy, and research:

The basic needs of our society for the services of clinical psychology are of two major kinds:

a. Professional services to:
   (1) Individuals through corrective and remedial work as well as diagnostic and therapeutic practices
   (2) Groups and social institutions needing positive mental hygiene programs in the interest of better community health
   (3) Students in training, members of other professions, and the public through systematic education and the general dissemination of information
b. Research contributions designed to:
   (1) Develop better understanding of human behavior
   (2) Improve the accuracy and reliability of diagnostic procedures
   (3) Develop more efficient methods of treatment
   (4) Develop methods of promoting mental hygiene and preventing maladjustment. (Raimy 1950, pp. 20–21)

The other master that had to be served was a vocal segment of the academic community that was scornful of the professional psychologist and doubtful about whether such a psychologist could also be a researcher:

There was much honest doubt whether all graduate students could be trained in both areas [research and practice]. Such doubts and questionings continued, for many, throughout most of the Conference. At the end, however, the original chasm seemed to have largely disappeared, and recognition of the importance of including research training in the preparation of all clinical psychologists was generally accepted. (Raimy, 1950, p. 23)

In a prophetic note it was offered that "The decision of the Conference to recommend the training of the clinical psychologist for research and practice, with equal emphasis on both, is likely to chart major policies in training institutions for some time to come" (p. 79).

A number of themes ran throughout the report, some unique to the conference, others common in the reports of the decade leading up to Boulder. The interests of the USPHS in prevention were echoed throughout Boulder, and a philosophy of understanding normal persons in the context of the environment in which they lived was often repeated. Together with earlier protests about Shakow's emphasis on the hospital-based training, a consensus emerged:

The majority of the Conference was clearly in favor of encouraging the broad development of clinical psychology along the lines that extend the field of practice from the frankly psychotic or mentally ill to the relatively normal clientele who need information, vocational counseling, and remedial work. Specialization in any of these less clearly-defined branches has now become an open issue that must be faced sooner or later. (Raimy, 1950, p. 113)

Looking back, it is easy to see that in 1949 the concept of clinical psychology included what would today be called counseling psychology. The comparison was not lost on the conferees who voted to support a recommendation that

The American Psychological Association and its appropriate division should study the common and diverse problems and concepts in the fields of clinical psychology and counseling and guidance with a view to immediate interfield enrichment of knowledge and methods. Consideration should also be given to the possibility of eventual amalgamation of these two fields. (Raimy, 1950, p. 148)

Such agreement was more elusive in the case of personnel and school psychology.

The market for mental health professionals was strong, and the perceived economic threat from professional psychologists was not high, making more collegial relations with allied disciplines possible. The conferees addressed issues of relationships with allied disciplines (psychiatry, nursing, social work, and school, counseling, and personnel psychology), and the tone was clearly cooperative. This pleased the USPHS, which was far less concerned about professional rivalries and jealousies and much more concerned with developing a sound national mental health policy.

There were calls for better advising of students and improved mentoring in teaching, practice, and research. Discussion was given to the type of personality and the traits best suited for training. Rigidity, social prejudice, frequent changes in courses of study, and an excessive concern for helping others were mentioned as undesirable, and conferees agreed that more research on selection was desirable. The issue of diversity in the selection of doctoral students was debated, and with what was termed "minor exception" the conference affirmed that "Graduate students in clinical psychology should be selected solely on the basis of reasonably determined aptitudes for education and practice in the profession, without regards for economic status, race, creed, or sex" (Raimy, 1950, p. 122). The resolution was an ideal; the realities of the times were that prejudice and discrimination did occur.

The question of control was frequently addressed. In contrast to today, where the pursuit of large federal grants is akin to the search for the Holy Grail, 50 years ago there was fear of meddlesome purse strings attached to federal dollars. The conference went to great lengths to assert that the substantial financial support of the USPHS and the VA was not synonymous with government control. This concern was expressed through a unanimous resolution that read,

> Despite the deep-seated and recurrent fear on the part of the universities, domination by the Federal Government through financial coercion appears up to this point to be at a minimum. Federal agencies are to be commended for their sincere efforts to avoid coercion or domination of educational programs. (Raimy, 1950, p. 162)

Control was also in question as the conferees struggled with accreditation. Many feared that accreditation of clinical psychology training programs would lead to blanket evaluations of departments based solely on the merits of their clinical programs. This fear was justified given that clinical psychology training was relatively new with few experienced programs and even fewer experienced faulty. A larger concern was that accreditation would bring with it a demand for a uniform curriculum, thus denying individual departments the freedom to structure degree programs as they wished. It appeared to some that the CTCP held too much power in its role to develop and evaluate training programs. In response to this, the conference adopted a resolution stating that "the APA [should] consider the possible advantages of separating the two functions of establishing objectives and standards for training in psychology, on the one hand, and accreditation, on the other" (Raimy, 1950, p. 177).

Summary and Conclusions

In the aftermath of World War II, several influences were paramount in forcing academic psychology to recognize, albeit reluctantly, the coming professionalization of psychology. The federal government, wishing to avoid a repeat of blunders following World War I that led to significant dissatisfaction among veterans, took proactive steps to ensure that mental health needs of the new veterans would be met. The USPHS and the VA were mandated to expand significantly the pool of mental health practitioners, a direction that led not only to the funding of the Boulder conference but also to the development of APA's accreditation program, funded practica and internship arrangements with the VA and the USPHS grants to academic departments for clinical training.

The GI Bill, amended to include payment for graduate education, created tremendous interest in graduate programs in psychology. As a result, psychology programs were inundated with funded applicants, most of whom were interested in the application of psychology to clinical and other applied fields.

Graduate psychology departments were mixed in their views of this "blessing." The reality of a separate curriculum for professional training in psychology was a bitter pill for some academic psychologists to swallow. Graduate departments feared that control of their programs would be taken over by external forces and that they would lose their right to determine their own curriculum. Further, they feared the domination of clinical training within their own departments and the effects of such educational emphasis on their traditional experimental programs.

The Boulder conference brought together these disparate needs and concerns, although one can argue about how well some points of view were represented with respect to others. It was a time of high anticipation and fear. The conference could easily have ended in failure, with such diverse interests being unable to reach any consensus. There are many letters in the correspondence of committee members that suggest disagreements serious enough to prevent the development of any single model of training. Instead, by most yardsticks that one could apply, the conference succeeded, perhaps beyond the dreams of many of those in attendance who were most invested in a model for professional training.

In evaluating the legacy of Boulder, several points are apparent. First, the conference succeeded because 73 individuals were able to agree to some 70 resolutions in 15 days, creating the scientist–practitioner model of professional training. Such consensus was arguably a remark-able achievement. The endorsement of the model by academic units followed with little evident resistance, although it is clear that some Boulder-model programs were developed that bore little resemblance to the model's insistence on significant training in both research and practice. Second, as a response to social and political needs, the conference was clearly a success. The cooperation of the APA, the USPHS, and the VA benefited all three entities. Clinical psychology was given the financial support and backing to advance it as a profession, and the federal government was able to begin the process of securing the personnel needed to address the mental health needs of the nation.

The architects of Boulder were clear that their vision of training for professional psychology should be viewed as dynamic and experimental rather than fixed and prescribed. Certainly there are several variants of professional training extant today, yet the overwhelming majority of currently accredited programs in psychology label themselves as "Boulder-model" programs or "scientist–practitioner" programs. Still, new national conferences on professional training in psychology occur with some regularity as participants seek to resolve many of the same concerns debated by those at Boulder. The grand experiment goes on.

References

American Association for Applied Psychology, Committee on Training in Clinical (Applied) Psychology (B. V. Moore, Chair). (1943). Proposed program of professional training in clinical psychology. *Journal of Consulting Psychology, 7*, 23–26.

American Psychological Association, Committee on Training in Clinical Psychology. (1947). Recommended graduate training program in clinical psychology. *American Psychologist, 2*, 539–558.

American Psychological Association, Committee on Training in Clinical Psychology. (1948). Training facilities: 1948. *American Psychologist, 3*, 317–318.

American Psychological Association, Committee on Training in Clinical Psychology. (1949). Doctoral training programs in clinical psychology: 1949. *American Psychologist, 4*, 331–341.

Benjamin, L. T., Jr., & Baker, D. B. (2000). Fifty years of Boulder: Introduction to the special section. *American Psychologist, 55*, 233–236.

Freedheim, D. K. (Ed.). (1992). *History of psychotherapy: A century of change.* Washington, DC: American Psychological Association.

Miller, J. G. (1946). Clinical psychology in the Veterans Administration. *American Psychologist, 1*, 181–189.

Minutes of the Executive Planning Committee on the Boulder Conference on Graduate Education of Clinical Psychologists. (1949). (Shakow Papers, M1383). Archives of the History of American Psychology, University of Akron, Akron, OH.

Moore, D. L. (1992). The Veterans Administration and the training program in psychology. In D. K. Freedheim (Ed.), *History of psychotherapy: A century of change* (pp. 776–800). Washington, DC: American Psychological Association.

Morrow, W. R. (1946). The development of psychological internship training. *Journal of Consulting Psychology, 10*, 65–183.

The Pennsylvania State College Bulletin, 36. (1942, June 11). Institute on Professional Training for Clinical Psychologists. (Shakow Papers, M1330). Archives of the History of American Psychology, University of Akron, Akron, OH.

Poffenberger, A. T. (1941, August 9). Letter to C. M. Louttit. (Shakow Papers, M1506). Archives of the History of American Psychology, University of Akron, Akron, OH.

Raimy, V. C. (Ed.). (1950). *Training in clinical psychology.* Englewood Cliffs, NJ: Prentice Hall.

Report of the Planning Committee on the Boulder Conference on Graduate Education of Clinical Psychologists. (1949). (Shakow Papers, M1383). Archives of the History of American Psychology, University of Akron, Akron, Ohio.

Routh, D. K. (2000). Clinical psychology training: A history of ideas and practice prior to 1946. *American Psychologist, 55,* 236–241.

Sears, R. R. (1947). Clinical training facilities: 1947. A report from the Committee on Graduate and Professional Training. *American Psychologist, 2,* 199–205.

Shakow D. (1941, June 9). Letter to D. Lindsley. (Shakow Papers, M1506). Archives of the History of American Psychology, University of Akron, Akron, OH.

Shakow D. (1942). The training of the clinical psychologist. *Journal of Consulting Psychology, 6,* 277–288.

Shakow, D. (1947, June 25). Letter to Committee on Training in Clinical Psychology. (Shakow Papers, M1502). Archives of the History of American Psychology, University of Akron, Akron, OH.

Shakow, D., Brotemarkle, R. A., Doll, E. A., Kinder, E. F., Moore, B. V. & Smith, S. (1945). Graduate internship training in psychology: Report by the Subcommittee on Graduate Internship Training to the Committees on Graduate and Professional Training of the American Psychological Association and the American Association for Applied Psychology. *Journal of Consulting Psychology, 9,* 243–266.

Yerkes, R. (1941, July 7). Letter to D. Lindsley. (Shakow Papers, M1506). Archives of the History of American Psychology, University of Akron, Akron, OH.

The Boulder Model's Fatal Flaw
George W. Albee

The Boulder model contained a fatal flaw that has distorted and damaged the development of clinical psychology ever since. The flaw was *not* the insistence on scientific training for clinicians. It was the uncritical acceptance of the medical model, the organic explanation of mental disorders, with psychiatric hegemony, medical concepts, and language. More than anyone else, it was David Shakow, a respected clinician and scientist, who influenced the new field's training and orientation in the medical direction. Doing research at Worcester State Hospital, he accepted the concept of "mental disease" largely because there was no alternative for him. For years, he argued that clinical psychologists should be trained in the "best" places, psychiatric centers (Albee, 1969).

Psychology departments, after World War II, accepted uncritically and ignorantly the temptation to help train clinical graduate students in the mushrooming Veterans Administration (VA) mental health clinics, in VA hospitals, and in state hospitals. University hospitals were especially favored. Psychologists were needed to provide "psychiatric services," especially for the vast number of veterans needing interventions for mental and emotional disorders (Albee, 1998). By placing psychology graduate students in psychiatric settings for training and service, psychologists lost their students to the invalid, ideologically tattered, often incompetent psychiatric worldview. Psychologists violated, again out of ignorance and inexperience, the fundamental criterion for professional training: Train students in your own house, otherwise you are an ancillary profession (Albee, 1964).

American Psychologist, 2000, 55(2), 247–248. Copyright 2000 by the American Psychological Association, Inc. Reprinted by permission of the publisher.

Psychologists made another major error when they tried to educate clinical psychologists in university graduate schools, where psychology was not in control of its own budget and had no experience in professional preparation to control its own destiny. Professionals must be trained in separate professional schools. I was one of the first to argue for separate professional schools of psychology in universities, with separate psychological centers where psychologists spoke their own language (Albee, 1964). After nearly 20 years of the Boulder model, many psychologists had developed a strong opposition to the domination of clinical psychology by psychiatry and psychiatric models. These psychologists urged psychology to establish its own training-service centers where psychological learning models were presented, and the psychological model of mentoring was the norm (Albee, 1964). It was not to be. Clinical psychologists had learned to treat their "patients" in private offices and to collect from third-party payers who required only a medical–psychiatric diagnosis for reimbursement. Things might have been different with the choice of a national training committee chair steeped in learning theory and education rather than in hospital psychiatry. The course of psychological history would have been completely different. Psychology passed up a learning model more appropriate for its intervention (Albee, 1975).

There are major political differences between a medical/organic/brain-defect model to explain mental disorders and a social-learning, stress-related model. The former is supported by the ruling class because it does not require social change and major readjustments to the status quo. The social model, on the other hand, seeks to end or to reduce poverty with all its associated stresses, as well as discrimination, exploitation, and prejudices as other major sources of stress leading to emotional problems. By aligning itself with the conservative view of causation, clinical psychology has joined the forces that perpetuate social injustice.

Psychologists are now stuck in a blind alley blocked by a for-profit health care system, a corporate world where the only concern is for the bottom line. Psychotherapy is effective, but it is too expensive to be profitable to the corporate health system, so psychotherapy is not supported. Drug therapies, developed by the giant pharmaceutical companies, are in, and clinical psychology, long ago locked into the organic/medical model, has little choice but to go along. Now to survive psychologists must strive to obtain prescription privileges, an effort that further supports the organic/brain-disease model. Psychologists have sold their souls to the devil: the disease model of mental disorders (Albee, 1998).

References

Albee, G. W. (1964). President's message: A decaration of independence for psychology [Unnumbered centerfold]. *Ohio Psychologist*, No. 4.

Albee, G. W. (1969). Who shall be served? My argument with David Shakow. *Professional Psychology: Research and Practice*, *1*, 4–7.

Albee, G. W. (1975). About Dr. Shakow. *The Clinical Psychologist*, *29*, 1.

Albee, G. W. (1998). Fifty years of clinical psychology: Selling our soul to the devil. *Applied and Preventive Psychology*, *7*, 189–194.

The Boulder Model: A Dream Deferred – Or Lost?
Peter E. Nathan

Over the past few years, a number of psychologists have written and spoken a good deal about empirically supported treatments. I have been among them (e.g., Nathan, 1996, 1998, 1999; Nathan & Gorman, 1998; Nathan, Stuart, & Dolan, in press). As a consequence, I have become very familiar with the rhetoric, pro and con, relating to what has turned out to be a surprisingly controversial issue, even among Boulder model psychologists. However, I acquired a new perspective on the issue recently when my brother, who is not a psychologist but is bright and learned nonetheless, responded to something I had written on the topic by asking me, simply, what all the fuss was about. Isn't it obvious, he said, that health professionals use the best science they can to guide them in their choice of interventions? Don't psychologists prefer treatments that research has shown are likely to be effective over those without empirical support?

Contrary to what we have told ourselves through the years about the primacy of the Boulder model for clinical training and practice, few clinicians undertake research or, for that matter, even read about it. The infrequency with which clinical practitioners utilize clinical research, an issue ever since Hans Eysenck (1952) published his initial evaluation of the effects of psychotherapy almost 50 years ago, continues to be a disappointment and an embarrassment to the discipline. David Barlow said very well almost 20 years ago what could also be said today:

At present, clinical research has little or no influence on clinical practice. This state of affairs

American Psychologist, 2000, *55*(2), 250–252. Copyright 2000 by the American Psychological Association, Inc. Reprinted by permission of the publisher and author.

should be particularly distressing to a discipline whose goal over the last 30 years has been to produce professionals who would integrate the methods of science with clinical practice to produce new knowledge. (Barlow, 1981, p. 147)

The low utilization of clinical research findings by practitioners received renewed attention in the 1990s with the publication of practice guidelines and lists of empirically supported treatments. The most influential of these were produced by the American Psychiatric Association (e.g., 1993, 1994, 1995, 1996, 1997) and the Division of Clinical Psychology of the American Psychological Association (Division 12 Task Force, 1995, 1996, 1998). Although to many these documents simply spell out in appropriate detail the interventions all clinicians should be expected to know and be prepared to use, to others they are extremely troubling. They are troubling to some because they have the potential to interfere with practice and disenfranchise clinicians whose interventions have received little or no empirical support. They trouble others because despite marked advances over the past several decades in psychotherapy outcome methodology, the science that underlies empirically supported treatments, that methodology is still evolving. Whereas guild-based concerns about practice guidelines can generally be deflected, others are not so easy to dismiss, especially when they are expressed by respected colleagues who have devoted many years to the study of psychotherapy outcomes. For example, we must listen when Sol Garfield (1996) concludes, on the basis of his assessment of the science on which the report depends, that the language of the 1995 Division 12 Task Force report is overly strong and its recommendations are premature.

Nonetheless, even while I wish that the science underlying empirically supported treatments was a bit more mature, I am convinced it is strong enough to justify the key claims made for it. Accordingly, I believe that we can no longer justify choosing to endorse or not to endorse empirically supported treatments and practice guidelines, despite their evolving status (Beutler, 1998; Persons & Silberschatz, 1998). It is clear to me that even if we choose to reject empirically supported treatments and practice guidelines, they will not disappear. Rejecting them will simply mean that we have opted not to participate in their certain further development. The major consequence of that decision will be to give to another profession primary responsibility for the processes by which we choose our interventions, just as our diagnoses have been largely shaped by a psychiatric nomenclature first published by the American Psychiatric Association in 1952.

It seems obvious to me that clinical psychology must finally do more than pay lip service to the Boulder model; the stakes for doing so are higher now than they have ever been. It is time to call upon the impressive psychotherapy research findings for which we are largely responsible to determine our own professional future. Allow me to reiterate: The choice is not between empirically supported treatments and practice guidelines or the old days. It is between empirically supported treatments and practice guidelines developed by and for psychology or empirically supported treatments and practice guidelines developed by and for psychiatry. To me, the choice is clear.

References

American Psychiatric Association. (1952). *Diagnostic and statistical manual of mental disorders.* Washington, DC: American Psychiatric Association.

American Psychiatric Association. (1993). Practice guideline for the treatment of major depressive disorder in adults. *American Journal of Psychiatry, 150*(4, Suppl.), 1–26.

American Psychiatric Association. (1994). Practice guideline for the treatment of patients with bipolar disorder. *American Journal of Psychiatry, 151*(12, Suppl.), 1–36.

American Psychiatric Association. (1995). Practice guideline for the treatment of patients with substance use disorders: Alcohol, cocaine, opioids. *American Journal of Psychiatry, 152*(11, Suppl.), 1–59.

American Psychiatric Association. (1996). Practice guideline for the treatment of patients with nicotine dependence. *American Journal of Psychiatry, 153*(10, Suppl.), 1–31.

American Psychiatric Association. (1997). Practice guideline for the treatment of patients with schizophrenia. *American Journal of Psychiatry, 154*(4, Suppl.), 1–63.

Barlow, D. H. (1981). On the relation of clinical research to clinical practice: Current issues. *Journal of Consulting and Clinical Psychology, 49,* 147–155.

Beutler, L. E. (1998). Identifying empirically supported treatments: What if we didn't? *Journal of Consulting and Clinical Psychology, 66,* 113–120.

Division 12 Task Force. (1995). Training in and dissemination of empirically validated psychological treatments: Report and recommendations. *Clinical Psychologist, 48,* 3–23.

Division 12 Task Force. (1996). An update on empirically validated therapies. *Clinical Psychologist, 49,* 5–18.

Division 12 Task Force. (1998). Update on empirically validated therapies: II. *Clinical Psychologist, 51,* 3–16.

Eysenck, H. J. (1952). The effects of psychotherapy: An evaluation. *Journal of Consulting Psychology, 16,* 319–324.

Garfield, S. L. (1996). Some problems associated with "validated" forms of psychotherapy. *Clinical Psychology: Science and Practice, 3,* 218–229.

Nathan, P. E. (1996, August). *American Psychological Foundation Rosalee G. Weiss Lecture: Treatments that work – and what convinces us they do.* Lecture presented at the 104th Annual Convention of the American Psychological Association, Toronto, Ontario, Canada.

Nathan, P. E. (1998). Practice guidelines: Not yet ideal. *American Psychologist, 53,* 290–299.

Nathan, P. E. (1999). *Distinguished Professional Contributions to Knowledge award address: And the dodo bird asked, "What about studies of psychotherapy effectiveness?"* Award address presented at the 107th Annual Convention of the American Psychological Association, Boston, MA.

Nathan P. E., & Gorman, J. M. (1998). *A Guide to treatments that work.* New York: Oxford University Press.

Nathan, P. E., Stuart, S., & Dolan, S. L. (in press). Research on psychotherapy efficacy and effectiveness: Between Scylla and Charybdis? *Psychological Bulletin.*

Persons, J. B., & Silberschatz, G. (1998). Are results of randomized controlled trials useful to psychotherapists? *Journal of Consulting and Clinical Psychology, 66,* 126–135.

The Scientist–Practitioner Model: Gandhi Was Right Again
George Stricker

Several years ago, I had lunch with a psychologist from Sweden. He asked me if it was true that most clinical psychologists in the United States had PhDs, and when I said that it was, he remarked about how wonderful it was that science was so intimately involved with practice in this country. I told him about David Shakow, who had the same illusion.

The scientist–practitioner model is the single most important statement of training philosophy in clinical psychology. Virtually every program either has adopted this model or has developed an alternative model in reaction to it. The model is as basic to training in clinical psychology as the Bill of Rights is to the foundation of our government. And yet, gentle reader, please sit down and try to write the first 10 amendments to the Constitution and see how far short you come. Then ask yourself when you last read the report written by Shakow (Committee on Training in Clinical Psychology, 1947) that forms the basis of the scientist–practitioner model or the report of the conference at Boulder that gave the model its name (Raimy, 1950). These works truly are classics, and Mark Twain defined a classic as a book that people praise but do not read. I suspect that there are very few trainers who actually have read those seminal documents, although most have clear opinions about their strengths and weaknesses. I must confess that I had not read them until I was preparing a chapter that required specific knowledge, despite having been engaged in training for decades before then, and that I was pleasantly surprised by what I found.

American Psychologist, 2000, *55*(2), 253–254. Copyright 2000 by the American Psychological Association, Inc. Reprinted by permission of the publisher and author.

The excuse of ignorance did not apply to the people who set up training programs in the immediate post-Boulder years, as many of these were the people who had attended the conference and developed the model. Nonetheless, of the 83 accredited training programs that existed one decade after the conference, only one (Adelphi University) did not subscribe to the scientist–practitioner model as it had been distorted in that first decade. I say distorted because the students of that decade, in the main, sought jobs in the clinical arena, as was their probable intention when they chose graduate studies in clinical psychology, and they found themselves unhappy and woefully unprepared. Some stated that their success was despite, rather than because of, their graduate training (Garfield & Kurtz, 1976). They rebelled against the SCIENTIST–practitioner model that was the basis of their training, and a subsequent series of conferences first questioned (at Chicago; Hoch, Ross, & Winder, 1966) and then challenged (at Vail, Colorado; Korman, 1976) the Boulder blueprint. This was followed by the professional-school movement (Stricker & Cummings, 1992), which at its best embodies the intention of the scientist–practitioner model and at its worst expresses a scientist–PRACTITIONER or pure practitioner model.

What can be guessed about the intention of the conferees at Boulder, without considering the operationalization that followed and distorted the model? The model endorsed a thousand-flowers approach to training, specifically arguing against the conformity that followed the issuance of the report. The model's creators expected that some programs would emphasize one end of the continuum at the expense of the other but did not expect a bimodal distribution of programs that left little room in the center for programs that truly valued both scientific and practitioner approaches. The model specifically recommended the adoption of standards of clinical competence for students, the active engagement in clinical practice by faculty members in clinical psychology, and the use of the predoctoral internship as an extension of graduate training rather than as a "repair shop" for omissions in the clinical curriculum.

Where, if anywhere, do such Boulder-model programs exist? Primarily they exist in the better professional schools, where faculty members do practice. In these schools, students receive extensive training in practice skills and are held accountable for clinical competence, and they also develop a scientific attitude toward their approach to clinical practice. This attitude often is not expressed through the sole and rigid use of experimentally validated approaches, although these certainly should be known and used where appropriate, but rather through the application of available scientific knowledge and the adoption of the attitudes of skepticism, curiosity, and inquiry about practice that typify a good scientist. This is the local clinical scientist model (Stricker & Trierweiler, 1995; Trierweiler & Stricker, 1998), and to my mind, it comes closer to the intent of the scientist–practitioner model than some of the more vaunted university science exemplars that downplay the needs of practice, or some of the professional school exemplars that train technicians rather than true professionals.

It is reported that Gandhi was once asked what he thought about Western civilization and that he replied he thought it was a good idea and somebody should try it. Similarly, my feeling about the scientist–practitioner model is that it is a good idea and that more programs should try it as it was originally described.

References

Committee on Training in Clinical Psychology. (1947). Recommended graduate training program in clinical psychology. *American Psychologist, 2*, 539–558.

Garfield, S. L., & Kurtz, R. (1976). Clinical psychologists in the 1970s. *American Psychologist, 31*, 1–9.

Hoch, E. L., Ross, A. O., & Winder, C. L. (Eds.). (1966) *Professional preparation of clinical psychologists.* Washington, DC: American Psychological Association.

Korman, M. (Ed.). (1976). *Levels and patterns of professional training in psychology.* Washington, DC: American Psychological Association.

Raimy, V. (Ed.). (1950). *Training in clinical psychology.* New York: Prentice Hall.

Stricker, G., & Cummings, N. A. (1992). The professional school movement. In D. K. Freedheim (Ed.), *History of psychotherapy: A century of change* (pp. 801–828). Washington, DC: American Psychological Association.

Stricker, G., & Trierweiler, S. J. (1995). The local clinical scientist: A bridge between science and practice. *American Psychologist, 50*, 995–1002.

Trierweiler, S. J., & Stricker, G. (1998). *The scientific practice of professional psychology.* New York: Plenum.

Chapter 10

A Psychology of Social Change:
Race and Gender

As noted in the previous chapter, when the American Psychological Association (APA) was founded in 1892, its sole objective, according to its by-laws, was to advance psychology as a science. That statement of objectives remained unchanged until the merger of the APA and the American Association for Applied Psychology (AAAP) in 1945. The new by-laws read: "The objects of the American Psychological Association shall be to advance psychology as a science, as a profession, and as a means of promoting human welfare" (Wolfle, 1946, p. 3). Those two additions recognized significant roles for psychologists in the application of psychological science.

To *advance psychology as a profession* acknowledged the growing importance of applied psychology, and was the by-law change needed to accommodate the interests of the members of the AAAP. To *advance psychology as a means of promoting human welfare* described a third role for psychologists, one that included psychologists in research as well as those in practice. That by-law addition came about because of the work of another organization founded in the 1930s, the Society for the Psychological Study of Social Issues (SPSSI).

Early in the twentieth century, American psychologists had seen their research and theories used in the debates over social issues such as child labor, coeducation, immigration, and prohibition. Some of these early psychologists actually initiated research programs specifically aimed at social issues, for example Leta Hollingworth, who investigated the assertions of the biological and psychological inferiority of women (recall the discussion by Stephanie Shields of Hollingworth's work in Chapter 5). Her work occurred at a time in American history when women were struggling to gain the right to vote, a right eventually achieved in 1920 by the nineteenth amendment to the United States Constitution.

Psychological research on social issues was not widespread before the 1930s, nor was it popular in the community of academic psychologists. Applying psychology to social problems was stigmatized in the same way that all applied psychology was viewed as less important than the "pure" research of the laboratory. There were many in psychology who felt that application was not the role of the psychologist, that psychologists were to remain true to research, allowing the application to be done by lawyers, educators, politicians, physicians, and so forth. To be a scientist meant a life engaged in the pursuit of truth, a kind of holy crusade. This attitude was expressed quite well by sociologist Albion Small, who wrote that "The prime duty of everyone connected with our graduate schools is daily to renew the vow of allegiance to research ideals . . . The first commandment with promise for graduate schools is: Remember the research ideal, to keep it holy!" (Storr, 1973, pp. 48–49). For those who agreed with Small, applied psychology was bad enough; applied psychology aimed at social issues was even worse. And yet there was a growing awareness among American psychologists that the science of psychology was important for improving human welfare, and they were interested in engaging in that kind of work. A twist of fate in American history was soon to give them their chance.

The good times of the 1920s in America came to an end at the close of that decade with the crash of the stock market signaling the beginning of the Great Depression. In contrast to the public euphoria of the 1920s, the 1930s brought social problems to the awareness of many: unemployment, hunger, racism, labor–management disputes, poverty, and impending war.

In the midst of the Great Depression, a new psychological organization was formed. An extremely controversial organization, its founding represented an act of courage, because there were many psychologists who saw the society as a communist or socialist organization; indeed, the FBI established a file on the organization in the 1930s (see Harris, 1980). The organization was named the Society for the Psychological Study of Social Issues (SPSSI), and it continues today as one of the more than 50 divisions of the APA.

The beginnings of SPSSI can be traced to 1935, when psychologists Ross Stagner (1909–1997) and Isadore Krechevsky (later David Krech, 1909–1977) talked about common frustrations such as the avoidance of political questions by psychologists and the lack of opportunity for psychology to contribute solutions to the social ills of the day (Stagner, 1986). They also were frustrated by the problems of unemployment faced by new psychologists, a problem exacerbated by the influx of European psychologists fleeing the Nazi regime. It has been suggested that some of the SPSSI organizers hoped to manufacture jobs for psychologists by creating a social agenda for behavioral research (see Finison, 1976, 1979).

The discussions between Stagner and Krechevsky led to a plan of action to organize psychologists with similar interests. In February of 1936, Krechevsky wrote to a small number of psychologists he felt might be kindred spirits. Sixteen, in addition to Stagner and Krechevsky, agreed to be part of an organizing committee, including social psychologist Gordon Allport (who would, in 1954, publish an important book on the psychology of prejudice) and learning theorist Edward C. Tolman (whose work was discussed in Chapter 8). Acting as secretary, Krechevsky mailed a letter to several hundred members of the APA, describing the plans for the new organization and asking for indications of interest. He wrote: "In general, we wish to establish an organization of accredited psychologists to promote specific research projects on *contemporary* psychological problems; to collect, analyze, and disseminate data on the psychological consequences of our present economic, political and cultural crisis; to encourage the participation of psychologists *as psychologists* in the activities of the day" (Benjamin, 2006, p. 189). Most replies supported the goals of the new society, but several were quite critical, such as the one from Colgate University's G. H. Estabrooks, who wrote: "With reference to your mimeographed sheets concerning participation of psychologists in the contemporary political world, allow me to register my hearty dissent with approximately everything contained therein" (Benjamin, 2006, p. 193).

The initial organizing meeting of SPSSI was held in September of 1936 in conjunction with the annual meeting of the APA, and more than 100 people attended. Following this meeting another letter was sent to the nearly 2,000 members of the APA explaining the two goals of the new society as follows:

> One is to encourage research upon those psychological problems most vitally related to modern social, economic and political policies. The second is to help the public and its representatives to understand and to use in the formation of social policies, contributions from the scientific investigation of human behavior. (Krech & Cartwright, 1956, p. 471)

Over 330 psychologists accepted the invitation to join SPSSI as charter members, including Kurt Lewin (1890–1947), whose program of "action research" on social issues, so clearly consistent with SPSSI's goals, would define the field of social psychology for more than three decades. In the years that followed, SPSSI encouraged research on social issues and even founded its own journal, *The Journal of Social Issues*, to publish such research. It supported the application of psychological knowledge to a multitude of social problems such as divorce, war, pornography, drug addiction, violence, racism, and sexism. The last two of those subjects are the focus of this chapter.

Racism

When the science of psychology emerged in the late nineteenth century, the Western world already was clear on the question of the comparative worth of the races. In his classic book, *Hereditary Genius*, Francis Galton (1869) had, via his own observations during a trip to Africa, determined that the "black race" was substantially inferior to the "white race" on a number of intellectual and behavioral dimensions. Those comments merely confirmed what almost all of white Europe already believed to be the truth. By the time that psychology laboratories were being founded in America, the "race question" had already been answered there as well. Psychologists, almost exclusively white, believed, like most white Americans, that blacks, Hispanics, and Native Americans were inferior to whites. This conclusion was not based on any research. In fact, the idea of doing research to discover if there were differences among the races would have been considered incredibly absurd. The differences among races were so patently obvious to whites that to have subjected them to scientific investigation would clearly have been a waste of time (see Duckitt, 1992). So for whites, the race "question" had already been answered. What remained was how to deal with the inferior races, the so-called "race problem."

The race question, although "answered," would not stay answered. There were dissenters, growing in number in the twentieth century, who questioned the agreed-upon conclusion. Among them were William James, who spoke and wrote about racial injustice in America (Plous, 1994) and E. B. Titchener (Beardsley, 1973). Some psychologists felt that scientific data were needed to show these nonbelievers the nature of their folly.

Perhaps the first research to be conducted in race psychology was an 1895 study of reaction time published in the *Psychological Review* by R. M. Bache. The data were actually collected, at Bache's suggestion, by Lightner Witmer in his psychology laboratory at the University of Pennsylvania. Witmer tested the reaction times of 12 whites,

11 blacks, and 11 Native Americans to auditory, visual, and tactile stimuli, and found that Native Americans had the fastest reaction times in all three conditions, followed by blacks, and then by the whites. Thus whites had the *slowest* reaction times. Clearly those data did not fit with a notion of white superiority. However, for Bache they did. He reasoned that the faster reaction times for Native Americans and blacks indicated that their minds operated automatically and reflexively as opposed to the contemplative nature of white minds. Thus the slower reaction times were, after all, indicative of the mental superiority of whites. This was one of many examples where problematic data were "reinterpreted" to maintain existing beliefs.

In the first couple of decades of the twentieth century, a number of prominent American psychologists offered their views on the nature of African Americans. G. Stanley Hall referred to black Americans as primitive people whose mental development approximated that of a white adolescent, and, for Native Americans, that of a child (Hall, 1905; Muschinske, 1977). Columbia University's Robert S. Woodworth (1916) and Stanford University's Lewis Terman (1916), the creator of the *Stanford–Binet Intelligence Test*, also wrote about the mental inferiority of black Americans. Had you been reading the American psychology journals at this time you would have encountered a number of articles that testified to the inferiority of blacks (see, for example, Bruner, 1912).

With the emphasis on mental tests, and particularly intelligence tests, in the 1910s and 1920s, a number of studies reported race differences that supported beliefs in white superiority. But in the 1930s those views began to be altered dramatically, partly because many Americans looked at racial issues in the new light cast by Adolf Hitler's notions of racial superiority. By the 1940s many American psychologists had abandoned their belief in inherent racial differences and were arguing instead that the differences were the result of prejudice and bias in American society or within the psychological studies themselves (Samelson, 1978).

Sexism

We have already addressed the topic of sexism in Chapter 5 in the article by Stephanie Shields (1975) that discussed the changing views of the sexes in the light of Darwinism, functionalism, and the psychological science that grew out of those influences. In that article Shields discussed the work of both Helen Thompson Woolley (1874–1947) and Leta S. Hollingworth (1886–1939). You will have the opportunity to read from their work in this chapter.

When Woolley and Hollingworth were young women they faced a host of prejudices because of their gender, prejudices that severely limited the opportunities women enjoyed in American society. Common beliefs asserted that women were both biologically and psychologically inferior to men. Men were believed to be more intelligent, more emotionally stable, and more competent. Women were seen as fragile creatures for whom difficult physical or mental efforts could seriously compromise their health. They were believed to be victims of their hormonal cycle, rendered "semi-invalids" during menstruation in terms of physical, mental, and emotional functioning (see Shields, 2007). Realize that, when American democracy was established in 1776, women were denied the most basic of democratic rights, the right to vote. And they were denied that vote for nearly 150 years! Why were women excluded from the vote? Among the reasons often given were that women could not reason sufficiently to decide among important issues or political candidates, that women would make voting decisions based on emotion and not reason, and that politics simply was not a subject in which women should be interested.

In the nineteenth century, women were often denied opportunities for higher education, especially graduate education (see Scarborough & Furumoto, 1987). Some individuals, such as G. Stanley Hall, believed that women should be educated in fields such as home-making and child care but should not be allowed to pursue a curriculum, for example, in math or science or engineering, which was believed to be far beyond their abilities. We have already discussed the fact that women PhDs found the doors of colleges and universities closed to them for jobs, except jobs in women's colleges, and they were able to take those jobs only if they were single. Leta Hollingworth, who had graduated valedictorian of her college class at the University of Nebraska in 1906 and had taught three years in the public schools of Nebraska, found that she could not get a teaching job in New York City in 1909 after marrying Harry Hollingworth. She was barred from teaching by law because of her marital status. Such laws were based on the belief that if women were married, that *was* their job, that is, to be a wife and ultimately a mother.

Woolley (as doctoral student Helen Thompson) was perhaps the first to bring the science of psychology to bear on the questions of *sex differences*. She was James Angell's student at the University of Chicago and, according to the preface to her dissertation, he encouraged her to pursue her interests in this area. She completed her degree in 1900, and her dissertation was published as a book (Thompson, 1903). Her dissertation was groundbreaking in subjecting males and females to a battery of motor and mental tests. She found that men were better on most tests of motor ability, but not all. Women did better on some of the coordination tasks, had better memory performance, and demonstrated more acute senses. Men showed more creativity. In looking at the role of emotion as a factor in performance, she found no differences between the sexes. Overall she reported that she found more similarities in performance between the sexes than differences, and that the differences, when obtained, tended to be small. Her results were mostly ignored or discounted by the male establishment in psychology at the time, but the door had been cracked open. And it wouldn't be possible to close it again.

Hollingworth began her work about a decade later in the midst of renewed fervor in the women's suffrage movement to get voting rights for women. She used the money from the caffeine studies for the Coca-Cola Company to fund her doctoral studies at Columbia University, where she worked with Edward L. Thorndike. Hollingworth focused on two issues initially. Her dissertation work (Hollingworth, 1914a) examined the *effects of the menstrual cycle* on mental and motor performance. She tested a sample of women over three months (with men as control subjects) and found no differences that corresponded with any part of the hormonal cycle.

The second area of Hollingworth's early research focused on the variability hypothesis (a concern that Helen Woolley had addressed as well). The *variability hypothesis*, as Shields (1975) explained, stated that men were more variable than women, that all women were mostly the same, whereas men would differ enormously in their talents and defects. That meant that the tails of the distributions for men would always exceed those for women in both directions. So if intelligence was the concern, there would be more male geniuses, but also more males at the bottom of the distribution. If the issue was morality, the most moral individuals would be men, but they would also be the most immoral as well. Woolley's data did not support this hypothesis; nor did the studies of Hollingworth (1913, 1914b). These studies and others eventually led, over many years, to the demise of the variability hypothesis (see Shields, 1982).

To this point we have provided the briefest of overviews of early ideas on racism and sexism. The readings that follow are intended to provide some of the rest of the story.

The Readings

The five selections in this chapter address the application of psychological science to the social issues of racism and sexism. The first selection is one of the most historic documents in psychology. It is the social science brief that was submitted to the United States Supreme Court in the case of *Brown v. Board of Education* (1954). The brief was written by three psychologists, all members of SPSSI – Kenneth B. Clark, Isidor Chein, and Stuart W. Cook – working with the attorneys for the National Association for the Advancement of Colored People (NAACP). The document was a summary of the extant behavioral and social science evidence that showed the harm created by involuntary segregation. Psychological studies from that summary document were cited in the Supreme Court decision that overturned segregation in schools, a decision that many legal scholars and historians regard as the most historic court decision of the twentieth century (Patterson, 2001).

Kenneth B. Clark (1914–2005) completed his baccalaureate and master's degrees at Howard University before going to Columbia University for his doctorate, which he received in 1940. At Columbia, Clark was most influenced by social psychologist Otto Klineberg (1899–1992) whose 1935 book, *Race Differences*, concluded that "there is no adequate proof of fundamental race differences in mentality, and that those differences which are found are in all probability due to culture and the social environment" (p. vii).

While a graduate student at Columbia, Clark collaborated on a series of studies initiated by Mamie Phipps (1917–1983, then a graduate student at Howard University, who would later marry Kenneth Clark) on racial identification in black pre-school children. These studies investigated self-awareness and self-esteem in black children and were published jointly by the Clarks in the 1930s and 1940s. When they completed these studies the Clarks could never have imagined how important they would prove to be.

The lead attorney for Brown, the plaintiff in *Brown v. Board*, was Thurgood Marshall (1908–1993), later a distinguished Supreme Court justice, who was employed by the Legal Defense Fund of the NAACP. SPSSI was active in helping Marshall with the testimony, and Kenneth Clark and several other prominent SPSSI members testified before the courts for the plaintiff. The research of the Clarks was among the scientific works cited in the decision as demonstrating the harmful effects of segregation (see Guthrie, 1998; Kluger, 1975). It was not only a great victory for all Americans who opposed school segregation, but it was an important accomplishment for the science of psychology as well, because it marked the first time that psychological research had ever been cited in a Supreme Court decision. And it was a dream come true for the members of SPSSI to see one of their goals realized, to have psychological research impact national social policy.

The second reading is by historian Ben Keppel (2002) and is entitled "Kenneth B. Clark in the Patterns of American Culture." It focuses on three of Clark's books, published in the 1950s, 1960s, and 1970s, and how they shaped Clark's growing pessimism about racial equality in America. It discusses the legacy of *Brown v. Board* and the place of the doll studies in American culture and the civil rights movements. Most poignantly, Keppel argues that the real message of Clark's research and writing on the tragic outcomes of racial prejudice and discrimination and the cultural messages of *Brown v. Board* has been lost in contemporary American society.

The final three readings concern the psychology of women. The first of these selections is by Helen Thompson (Woolley). The excerpt includes two chapters from her book, *The Mental Traits of Sex* (1903) – the introductory chapter and the conclusion to the book. This material includes the rationale for her study, the design of the study including the tests employed, and her interpretation and discussion of her data. In reading this, remember that you are reading about the first psychological research undertaken to answer some of the questions about alleged differences between the sexes.

The next reading is by Leta Hollingworth and is, perhaps, one of the most intriguing articles that she wrote. The article is entitled "Social Devices for Impelling Women to Bear and Rear Children." Before reading this article you might want to reread the section on "maternal instinct" in the Shields (1975) article in Chapter 5. There was no field known as evolutionary psychology in Hollingworth's day, but had there been, her article would have been required reading for those interested in that subject. Hollingworth discusses the validity of the concept of maternal instinct in light of the social controls in place that were designed to encourage (maybe even force) women to bear and rear children. She discusses controls found in common beliefs, art, education, law, and public opinion, and asks what would happen to birth rates without these social forces. It is a provocative article that is illustrative of the beginnings of a feminist approach to psychological science.

The final reading is a fitting conclusion to the earlier readings and an excellent summary of the issues faced by women who chose to pursue graduate education or to seek professional employment. This article is by historian of psychology Katharine S. Milar (2000), the leading scholar on the work of Helen Woolley (see Milar, 1999, 2004). It speaks to the courage and advocacy of the first generation of American women psychologists who sought to make the path easier for the women who would follow them. This article will introduce you to others of the early feminist ranks of scientific psychology, including Kate Gordon (1878–1963) and Christine Ladd-Franklin (1847–1930).

IN THE

Supreme Court of the United States

October Term, 1952

No. 8

Oliver Brown, Mrs. Richard Lawton, Mrs. Sadie
Emmanuel, *et al.*, Appellants,

vs.

Board of Education of Topeka, Shawnee County,
Kansas, *et al.*

No. 101

Harry Briggs, Jr., *et al.*, Appellants,

vs.

R. W. Elliott, Chairman, J. D. Carson, *et al.*, Members
of Board of Trustees of School District No. 22, Clarendon
County, S. C., *et al.*

No. 191

Dorothy E. Davis, Bertha M. Davis and Inez D. Davis, etc., *et al.*,
Appellants

vs.

County School Board of Prince Edward County, Virginia, *et al.*

APPENDIX TO APPELLANTS' BRIEFS

**The Effects of Segregation and the Consequences of
Desegregation: A Social Science Statement**

This brief, written by psychologists Kenneth B. Clark, Isidor Chein, and Stuart W. Cook, was filed with the
Supreme Court in the *Brown v. Board* case on September 22, 1952.

The problem of the segregation of racial and ethnic groups constitutes one of the major problems facing the American people today. It seems desirable, therefore, to summarize the contributions which contemporary social science can make toward its resolution. There are, of course, moral and legal issues involved with respect to which the signers of the present statement cannot speak with any special authority and which must be taken into account in the solution of the problem. There are, however, also factual issues involved with respect to which certain conclusions seem to be justified on the basis of the available scientific evidence. It is with these issues only that this paper is concerned. Some of the issues have to do with the consequences of segregation, some with the problems of changing from segregated to unsegregated practices. These two groups of issues will be dealt with in separate sections below. It is necessary, first, however, to define and delimit the problem to be discussed.

Definitions

For purposes of the present statement, *segregation* refers to that restriction of opportunities for different types of associations between the members of one racial, religious, national or geographic origin, or linguistic group and those of other groups, which results from or is supported by the action of any official body or agency representing some branch of government. We are not here concerned with such segregation as arises from the free movements of individuals which are neither enforced nor supported by official bodies, nor with the segregation of criminals or of individuals with communicable diseases which aims at protecting society from those who might harm it.

Where the action takes place in a social milieu in which the groups involved do not enjoy equal social status, the group that is of lesser social status will be referred to as the *segregated* group.

In dealing with the question of the effects of segregation, it must be recognized that these effects do not take place in a vacuum, but in a social context. The segregation of Negroes and of other groups in the United States takes place in a social milieu in which "race" prejudice and discrimination exist. It is questionable in the view of some students of the problem whether it is possible to have segregation without substantial discrimination, Myrdal[1] states: "Segregation . . . is financially possible and, indeed, a device of economy only as it is combined with substantial discrimination" (p. 629). The indebtedness of segregation in such a context makes it difficult to disentangle the effects of segregation per se from the effects of the context. Similarly, it is difficult to disentangle the effects of segregation from the effects of a pattern of social disorganization commonly associated with it and reflected in high disease and mortality rates, crime and delinquency, poor housing, disrupted family life and general substandard living conditions. We shall, however, return to this problem after consideration of the observable effects of the total social complex in which segregation is a major component.

At the recent Mid-century White House Conference on Children and Youth, a fact-finding report on the effects of prejudice, discrimination and segregation on the personality development of children was prepared as a basis for some of the deliberations.[2] This report brought together the available social science and psychological studies which were related to the problem of how racial and religious prejudices influenced the development of a healthy personality. It highlighted the fact that segregation, prejudices and discriminations, and their social concomitants potentially damage the personality of all children – the children of the majority group in a somewhat different way than the more obviously damaged children of the minority group.

The report indicates that as minority group children learn the inferior status to which they are assigned – as they observe the fact that they are almost always segregated and kept apart from others who are treated with more respect by the society as a whole – they often react with feelings of inferiority and a sense of personal humiliation. Many of them become confused about their own personal worth. On the one hand, like all other human beings they require a sense of personal dignity; on the other hand, almost nowhere in the larger society do they find their own dignity as human beings respected by others. Under these conditions, the minority group child is thrown into a conflict with regard to his feelings about himself and his group. He wonders whether his group and he himself are worthy of no more respect than they receive. This conflict and confusion leads to self-hatred and rejection of his own group.

The report goes on to point out that these children must find ways with which to cope with this conflict. Not every child, of course, reacts with the same patterns of behavior. The particular pattern depends upon many interrelated factors, among which are: the stability and quality of his family relations; the social and economic class to which he belongs; the cultural and educational background of his parents; the particular minority group to which he belongs; his personal characteristics, intelligence, special talents, and personality pattern.

Some children, usually of the lower socio-economic classes, may react by overt aggressions and hostility directed toward their own group or members of the dominant group.[3] Anti-social and delinquent behavior may often be interpreted as reactions to these racial frustrations. These reactions are self-destructive in that the larger society not only punishes those who commit them, but often interprets such aggressive and anti-social behavior as justification for continuing prejudice and segregation.

Middle class and upper class minority group children are likely to react to their racial frustrations and conflicts by withdrawal and submissive behavior. Or, they may react with compensatory and rigid conformity to the prevailing middle class values and standards and an aggressive determination to succeed in these terms in spite of the handicap of their minority status.

The report indicates that minority group children of all social and economic classes often react with a generally defeatist attitude and a lowering of personal ambitions. This, for example, is reflected in a lowering of pupil morale and a depression of the educational aspiration level among minority group children in segregated schools. In producing such effects, segregated schools impair the ability of the child to profit from the educational opportunities provided him.

Many minority group children of all classes also tend to be hypersensitive and anxious about their relations with the larger society. They tend to see hostility and rejection even in those areas where these might not actually exist.

The report concludes that while the range of individual differences among members of a rejected minority group is as wide as among other peoples, the evidence suggests that all of these children are unnecessarily encumbered in some ways by segregation and its concomitants.

With reference to the impact of segregation and its concomitants on children of the majority group, the report indicates that the effects are somewhat more obscure. Those children who learn the prejudices of our society are also being taught to gain personal status in an unrealistic and non-adaptive way. When comparing themselves to members of the minority group, they are not required to evaluate themselves in terms of the more basic standards of actual personal ability and achievement. The culture permits and, at times, encourages them to direct their feelings of hostility and aggression against whole groups of people the members of which are perceived as weaker than themselves. They often develop patterns of guilt feelings, rationalizations and other mechanisms which they must use in an attempt to protect themselves from recognizing the essential injustice of their unrealistic fears and hatreds of minority groups.[4]

The report indicates further that confusion, conflict, moral cynicism, and disrespect for authority may arise in majority group children as a consequence of being taught the moral, religious and democratic principles of the brotherhood of man and the importance of justice and fair play by the same persons and institutions who, in their support of racial segregation and related practices, seem to be acting in a prejudiced and discriminatory manner. Some individuals may attempt to resolve this conflict by intensifying their hostility toward the minority group. Others may react by guilt feelings which are not necessarily reflected in more humane attitudes toward the minority group. Still others react by developing an unwholesome, rigid, and uncritical idealization of all authority figures – their parents, strong political and economic leaders. As described in *The Authoritarian Personality*,[5] they despise the weak, while they obsequiously and unquestioningly conform to the demands of the strong whom they also, paradoxically, subconsciously hate.

With respect to the setting in which these difficulties develop, the report emphasized the role of the home, the school, and other social institutions. Studies[6] have shown that from the earliest school years children are not only aware of the status differences among different groups in the society but begin to react with the patterns described above.

Conclusions similar to those reached by the Mid-century White House Conference Report have been stated by other social scientists who have concerned themselves with this problem. The following are some examples of these conclusions:

Segregation imposes upon individuals a distorted sense of social reality.[7]

Segregation leads to a blockage in the communications and interaction between the two groups. Such blockages tend to increase mutual suspicion, distrust and hostility.[8]

Segregation not only perpetuates rigid stereotypes and reinforces negative attitudes toward members of the other group, but also leads to the development of a social climate within which violent outbreaks of racial tensions are likely to occur.[9]

We return now to the question, deferred earlier, of what it is about the total society complex of which segregation is one feature that produces the effects described above – or, more precisely, to the question of whether we can justifiably conclude that, as only one feature of a complex social setting, segregation is in fact a significantly contributing factor to these effects.

To answer this question, it is necessary to bring to bear the general fund of psychological and sociological knowledge concerning the role of various environmental influences in producing feelings of inferiority, confusions in personal roles, various types of basic personality structures and the various forms of personal and social disorganization.

On the basis of this general fund of knowledge, it seems likely that feelings of inferiority and doubts about personal worth are attributable to living in an underprivileged environment only insofar as the latter is itself perceived as an indicator of low social status and as a symbol of inferiority. In other words, one of the important determinants in producing such feelings is the awareness of social status difference. While there are many other factors that serve as reminders of the differences in social status, there can be little

doubt that the fact of enforced segregation is a major factor.[10]

This seems to be true for the following reasons among others: (1) because enforced segregation results from the decision of the majority group without the consent of the segregated and is commonly so perceived; and (2) because historically segregation patterns in the United States were developed on the assumption of the inferiority of the segregated.

In addition, enforced segregation gives official recognition and sanction to these other factors of the social complex, and thereby enhances the effects of the latter in creating the awareness of social status differences and feelings of inferiority.[11] The child who, for example, is compelled to attend a segregated school may be able to cope with ordinary expressions of prejudice by regarding the prejudiced person as evil or misguided; but he cannot readily cope with symbols of authority, the full force of the authority of the State – the school or the school board, in this instance – in the same manner. Given both the ordinary expression of prejudice and the school's policy of segregation, the former takes on greater force and seemingly becomes an official expression of the latter.

Not all of the psychological traits which are commonly observed in the social complex under discussion can be related so directly to the awareness of status differences – which in turn is, as we have already noted, materially contributed to by the practices of segregation. Thus, the low level of aspiration and defeatism so commonly observed in segregated groups is undoubtedly related to the level of self-evaluation; but it is also, in some measure, related among other things to one's expectations with regard to opportunities for achievement and, having achieved, to the opportunities for making use of these achievements. Similarly, the hypersensitivity and anxiety displayed by many minority group children about their relations with the larger society probably reflects their awareness of status differences; but it may also be influenced by the relative absence of opportunities for equal status contact which would provide correctives for prevailing unrealistic stereotypes.

The preceding view is consistent with the opinion stated by a large majority (90%) of social scientists who replied to a questionnaire concerning the probable effects of enforced segregation under conditions of equal facilities. This opinion was that, regardless of the facilities which are provided, enforced segregation is psychologically detrimental to the members of the segregated group.[12]

Similar considerations apply to the question of what features of the social complex of which segregation is a part contribute to the development of the traits which have been observed in majority group members. Some of these are probably quite closely related to the awareness of status differences, to which, as has already been pointed out, segregation makes a material contribution. Others have a more complicated relationship to the total social setting. Thus, the acquisition of an unrealistic basis for self-evaluation as a consequence of majority group membership probably reflects fairly closely the awareness of status differences. On the other hand, unrealistic fears and hatreds of minority groups, as in the case of the converse phenomenon among minority group members, are probably significantly influenced as well by the lack of opportunities for equal status contact.

With reference to the probable effects of segregation under conditions of equal facilities on majority group members, many of the social scientists who responded to the poll in the survey cited above felt that the evidence is less convincing than with regard to the probable effects of such segregation on minority group members, and the effects are possibly less widespread. Nonetheless, more than 80% stated it as their opinion that the effects of such segregation are psychologically detrimental to the majority group members.[13]

It may be noted that many of these social scientists supported their opinions on the effects of segregation on both majority and minority groups by reference to one or another or to several of the following four lines of published and unpublished evidence.[14] First, studies of children throw light on the relative priority of the awareness of status differentials and related factors as compared to the awareness of differences in facilities. On this basis, it is possible to infer some of the consequences of segregation as distinct from the influence of inequalities of facilities. Second, clinical studies and depth interviews throw light on the genetic sources and causal sequences of

various patterns of psychological reaction; and, again, certain inferences are possible with respect to the effects of segregation per se. Third, there actually are some relevant but relatively rare instances of segregation with equal or even superior facilities, as in the cases of certain Indian reservations. Fourth, since there are inequalities of facilities in racially and ethnically homogeneous groups, it is possible to infer the kinds of effects attributable to such inequalities in the absence of effects of segregation and, by a kind of subtraction to estimate the effects of segregation per se in situations where one finds both segregation and unequal facilities.

Segregation is at present a social reality. Questions may be raised, therefore, as to what are the likely consequences of desegregation.

One such question asks whether the inclusion of an intellectually inferior group may jeopardize the education of the more intelligent group by lowering educational standards or damage the less intelligent group by placing it in a situation where it is at a marked competitive disadvantage. Behind this question is the assumption, which is examined below, that the presently segregated groups actually are inferior intellectually.

The available scientific evidence indicates that much, perhaps all, of the observable differences among various racial and national groups may be adequately explained in terms of environmental differences.[15] It has been found, for instance, that the differences between the average intelligence test scores of Negro and white children decrease, and the overlap of the distributions increases, proportionately to the number of years that the Negro children have lived in the North.[16] Related studies have shown that this change cannot be explained by the hypothesis of selective migration.[17] It seems clear, therefore, that fears based on the assumption of innate racial differences in intelligence are not well founded.

It may also be noted in passing that the argument regarding the intellectual inferiority of one group as compared to another is, as applied to schools, essentially an argument for homogeneous groupings of children by intelligence rather than by race. Since even those who believe that there are innate differences between Negroes and whites in America in average intelligence grant that considerable overlap between the two groups exists, it would follow that it may be expedient to group together the superior whites and Negroes, the average whites and Negroes, and so on. Actually, many educators have come to doubt the wisdom of class groupings made homogeneous solely on the basis of intelligence.[18] Those who are opposed to such homogeneous grouping believe that this type of segregation, too, appears to create generalized feelings of inferiority in the child who attends a below average class, leads to undesirable emotional consequences in the education of the gifted child, and reduces learning opportunities which result from the interaction of individuals with varied gifts.

A second problem that comes up in an evaluation of the possible consequences of desegregation involves the question of whether segregation prevents or stimulates interracial tension and conflict and the corollary question of whether desegregation has one or the other effect.

The most direct evidence available on this problem comes from observations and systematic study of instances in which desegregation has occurred. Comprehensive reviews of such instances[19] clearly establish the fact that desegregation has been carried out successfully in a variety of situations although outbreaks of violence had been commonly predicted. Extensive desegregation has taken place without major incidents in the armed services in both Northern and Southern installations and involving officers and enlisted men from all parts of the country, including the South.[20] Similar changes have been noted in housing[21] and industry.[22] During the last war, many factories both in the North and South hired Negroes on a non-segregated, non-discriminatory basis. While a few strikes occurred, refusal by management and unions to yield quelled all strikes within a few days.[23]

Relevant to this general problem is a comprehensive study of urban race riots which found that race riots occurred in segregated neighborhoods, whereas there was no violence in sections of the city where the two races lived, worked and attended school together.[24]

Under certain circumstances desegregation not only proceeds without major difficulties, but has been observed to lead to the emergence of more favorable attitudes and friendlier relations between races. Relevant studies may be cited with respect to housing,[25] employment,[26] the armed services[27] and merchant marine,[28] recreation agency,[29] and general community life.[30]

Much depends, however, on the circumstances under which members of previously segregated groups first come in contact with others in unsegregated situations. Available evidence suggests, first, that there is less likelihood of unfriendly relations when the change is simultaneously introduced into all units of a social institution to which it is applicable – e.g., all of the schools in a school system or all of the shops in a given factory.[31] When factories introduced Negroes in only some shops but not in others the prejudiced workers tended to classify the desegregated shops as inferior, "Negro work." Such objections were not raised when complete integration was introduced.

The available evidence also suggests the importance of consistent and firm enforcement of the new policy by those in authority.[32] It indicates also the importance of such factors as: the absence of competition for a limited number of facilities or benefits;[33] the possibility of contacts which permit individuals to learn about one another as individuals;[34] and the possibility of equivalence of positions and functions among all of the participants within the unsegregated situation.[35] These conditions can generally be satisfied in a number of situations, as in the armed services, public housing developments, and public schools.

The problem with which we have here attempted to deal is admittedly on the frontiers of scientific knowledge. Inevitably, there must be some differences of opinion among us concerning the conclusiveness of certain items of evidence, and concerning the particular choice of words and placement of emphasis in the preceding statement. We are nonetheless in agreement that this statement is substantially correct and justified by the evidence, and the differences among us, if any, are of a relatively minor order and would not materially influence the preceding conclusions.

Floyd H. Allport
Gordon W. Allport
Charlotte Babcock
Viola W. Bernard
Jerome S. Bruner
Hadley Cantril

Isidor Chein	*Robert K. Merton*
Kenneth B. Clark	*Gardner Murphy*
Mamie P. Clark	*Theodore M. Newcomb*
Stuart W. Cook	*Robert Redfield*
Bingham Dai	*Ira DeA. Reid*
Allison Davis	*Arnold M. Rose*
Else Frenkel-Brunswik	*Gerhart Saenger*
Noel P. Gist	*R. Nevitt Sanford*
Daniel Katz	*S. Stanfield Sargent*
Otto Klineberg	*M. Brewster Smith*
David Krech	*Samuel A. Stouffer*
Alfred McClung Lee	*Wellman Warner*
R. M. MacIver	*Robin M. Williams*

Notes

1 Myrdal, G., *An American Dilemma*, 1944.

2 Clark, K. B., *Effect of Prejudice and Discrimination on Personality Development*, Fact Finding Report Mid-century White House Conference on Children and Youth, Children's Bureau, Federal Security Agency, 1950 (mimeographed).

3 Brenman, M., The Relationship Between Minority Group Identification in A Group of Urban Middle Class Negro Girls, *J. Soc. Psychol.*, 1940, 11, 171–197; Brenman, M., Minority Group Membership and Religious, Psychosexual and Social Patterns in A Group of Middle-Class Negro Girls, *J. Soc. Psychol.*, 1940, 12, 179–196; Brenman, M., Urban Lower-Class Negro Girls, *Psychiatry*, 1943, 6, 307–324; Davis, A., The Socialization of the American Negro Child and Adolescent, *J. Negro Educ.*, 1939, 8, 264–275.

4 Adorno, T. W.; Frenkel-Brunswik, E.; Levinson, D. J.: Sanford, R. N., *The Authoritarian Personality*, 1951.

5 Adorno, T. W.; Frenkel-Brunswik, E.; Levinson, D. J.: Sanford, R. N., *The Authoritarian Personality*, 1951.

6 Clark, K. B. & Clark, M. P., Emotional Factors in Racial Identification and Preference in Negro Children, *J. Negro Educ.*, 1950, 19, 341–350; Clark, K. B. & Clark, M. P., Racial Identification and Preference in Negro Children, *Readings in Social Psychology*, Ed. by Newcomb & Hartley, 1947; Radke, M.; Trager, H.; Davis, H., Social Perceptions and Attitudes of Children, *Genetic Psychol. Monog.*, 1949, 40, 327–447; Radke, M.; Trager, H.; Children's Perceptions of the Social Role of Negroes and Whites, *J. Psychol.*, 1950, 29, 3–33.

7 Reid, Ira, What Segregated Areas Mean; Brameld, T., Educational Cost, *Discrimination and National Welfare*, Ed. by MacIver R. M., 1949.

8 Frazier, E., *The Negro in the United States*, 1949; Krech, D. & Crutchfield, R. S., *Theory and Problems of Social Psychology*, 1948; Newcomb, T., *Social Psychology*, 1950.

9 Lee, A. McClung and Humphrey, N. D., *Race Riot*, 1943.

10 Frazier, E., *The Negro in the United States*, 1949; Myrdal, G., *An American Dilemma*, 1944.

11 Reid, Ira, What Segregated Areas Mean, *Discrimination and National Welfare*, Ed. by MacIver, R. M., 1949.

12 Deutscher, M. and Chein, I. The Psychological Effects of Enforced Segregation: A Survey of Social Science Opinion, *J. Psychol.*, 1948, 26, 259–287.

13 Deutscher, M. and Chein, I., The Psychological Effects of Enforced Segregation: A Survey of Social Science Opinion, *J. Psychol.*, 1948, 26, 259–287.

14 Chein, I., What Are the Psychological Effects of Segregation Under Conditions of Equal Facilities?, *International J. Opinion and Attitude Res.*, 1949, 2, 229–234.

15 Klineberg, O., *Characteristics of American Negro*, 1945; Klineberg, O., *Race Differences*, 1936.

16 Klineberg, O., *Negro Intelligence and Selective Migration*, 1935.

17 Klineberg, O., *Negro Intelligence and Selective Migration*, 1935.

18 Brooks, J. J., Interage Grouping on Trial-Continuous Learning, *Bulletin #87, Association for Childhood Education*, 1951; Lane, R. H., Teacher in Modern Elementary School, 1941; Educational Policies Commission of the National Education Association and the American Association of School Administration Report in *Education For All Americans*, published by the N. E. A. 1948.

19 Delano, W., Grade School Segregation: The Latest Attack on Racial Discrimination, *Yale Law Journal*,

1952, 61, 5, 730–744; Rose, A., The Influence of Legislation on Prejudice; Chapter 53 in *Race Prejudice and Discrimination*, Ed. by Rose, A., 1951; Rose, A., *Studies in Reduction of Prejudice*, Amer. Council on Race Relations, 1948.

20 Kenworthy, E. W., The Case Against Army Segregation, *Annals of the American Academy of Political and Social Science*, 1951, 275, 27–33; Nelson, Lt. D. D., *The Integration of the Negro in the U. S. Navy*, 1951; Opinions About Negro Infantry Platoons in White Companies in Several Divisions, *Information and Education Division, U. S. War Department, Report No. B-157*, 1945.

21 Conover, R. D., *Race Relations at Codornices Village, Berkeley-Albany, California: A Report of the Attempt to Break Down the Segregated Pattern on A Directly Managed Housing Project*, Housing and Home Finance Agency, Public Housing Administration, Region I, December 1947 (mimeographed); Deutsch, M. and Collins, M. E., *Interracial Housing, A Psychological Study of A Social Experiment*, 1951; Rutledge, E., *Integration of Racial Minorities in Public Housing Projects: A Guide for Local Housing Authorities on How to Do It*, Public Housing Administration, New York Field Office (mimeographed).

22 Minard, R. D., The Pattern of Race Relationships in the Pocahontas Coal Field, *J. Social Issues*, 1952, 8, 29–44; Southall, S. E., *Industry's Unfinished Business*, 1951; Weaver, G. L-P, *Negro Labor, A National Problem*, 1941.

23 Southall, S. E., *Industry's Unfinished Business*, 1951; Weaver, G. L-P, *Negro Labor, A National Problem*, 1941.

24 Lee, A. McClung and Humphrey, N. D., *Race Riot*, 1943; Lee, A. McClung, Race Riots Aren't Necessary, *Public Affairs Pamphlet*, 1945.

25 Deutsch, M. and Collins, M. E., *Interracial Housing, A Psychological Study of A Social Experiment*, 1951; Merton, R. K.; West, P. S.; Jahoda, M., *Social Fictions and Social Facts: The Dynamics of Race Relations in Hilltown*, Bureau of Applied Social Research Columbia, Univ., 1949 (mimeographed); Rutledge, E., *Integration of Racial Minorities in Public Housing Projects; A Guide for Local Housing Authorities on How To Do It*, Public Housing Administration, New York Field Office (mimeographed); Wilner, D. M.; Walkley, R. P.; and Cook, S. W., Intergroup Contact and Ethnic Attitudes in Public Housing Projects, *J. Social Issues*, 1952, 8, 45–69.

26 Harding, J., and Hogrefe, R., Attitudes of White Department Store Employees Toward Negro Co-workers, *J. Social Issues*, 1952, 8, 19–28; Southall, S. E., *Industry's Unfinished Business*, 1951; Weaver, G. L-P., *Negro Labor, A National Problem*, 1941.

27 Kenworthy, E. W., The Case Against Army Segregation, *Annals of the American Academy of Political and Social Science*, 1951, 275, 27–33; Nelson, Lt. D. D., *The Integration of the Negro in the U. S. Navy*, 1951; Stouffer, S., et al., *The American Soldier*, Vol. I, Chap. 19. A Note on Negro Troops in Combat, 1949; Watson, G., *Action for Unity*, 1947; Opinions About Negro Infantry Platoons in White Companies in Several Divisions, *Information and Education Division, U. S. War Department, Report No. B-157*, 1945.

28 Brophy, I. N., The Luxury of Anti-Negro Prejudice, *Public Opinion Quarterly*, 1946, 9, 456–466 (Integration in Merchant Marine); Watson, G., *Action for Unity*, 1947.

29 Williams, D. H., *The Effects of an Interracial Project Upon the Attitudes of Negro and White Girls Within the Young Women's Christian Association*, Unpublished M. A. thesis, Columbia University, 1934.

30 Dean, J. P., *Situational Factors in Intergroup Relations: A Research Progress Report*. Paper Presented to American Sociological Society, 12/28/49 (mimeographed); Irish, D. P., Reactions of Residents of Boulder, Colorado, to the Introduction of Japanese Into the Community, *J. Social Issues*, 1952, 8, 10–17.

31 Minard, R. D., The Pattern of Race Relationships in the Pocahontas Coal Field, *J. Social Issues*, 1952, 8, 29–44; Rutledge, E., *Integration of Racial Minorities in Public Housing Projects; A Guide for Local Housing Authorities on How to Do It*, Public Housing Administration, New York Field Office (mimeographed).

32 Deutsch, M. and Collins, M. E., *Interracial Housing, A Psychological Study of A Social Experiment*, 1951; Feldman, H., The Technique of Introducing Negroes Into the Plant, *Personnel*, 1942, 19, 461–466; Rutledge, E., *Integration of Racial Minorities in Public Housing Projects; A Guide for Local Housing Authorities on How to Do It*, Public Housing Administration, New York Field Office (mimeographed); Southall, S. E., *Industry's Unfinished Business*, 1951; Watson, G., *Action for Unity*, 1947.

33 Lee, A. McClung and Humphrey, N. D., *Race Riot*, 1943; Williams, R., Jr., *The Reduction of Intergroup Tensions*, Social Science Research Council, New York, 1947; Windner, A. E., *White Attitudes Towards Negro-White Interaction In An Area of Changing Racial Composition*. Paper Delivered at the Sixtieth Annual Meeting of the American Psychological Association, Washington, September 1952.

34 Wilner, D. M.; Walkley, R. P.; and Cook, S. W., Intergroup Contact and Ethnic Attitudes in Public Housing Projects, *J. Social Issues*, 1952, 8, 45–69.

35 Allport, G. W., and Kramer, B., Some Roots of Prejudice, *J. Psychol.*, 1946, 22, 9–39; Watson, J., Some Social and Psychological Situations Related to Change in Attitude, *Human Relations*, 1950, 3, 1.

References

Adorno, T. W., Frenkel-Brunswik, E., Levinson, D. J., & Sanford, R. N. (1951). *The Authoritarian Personality.*

Allport, G. W., & Kramer, B. (1946). Some Roots of Prejudice, *J. Psychol., 22,* 9–39.

Bauer, C. (1951). Social Questions in Housing and Community Planning, *J. of Social Issues, VII,* 1–34.

Brameld, T. (1949). Educational Costs. *Discrimination and National Welfare,* Ed. by MacIver, R. M.

Brenman, M. (1940). The Relationship Between Minority Group Identification in A Group of Urban Middle Class Negro Girls, *J. Soc. Psychol., 11,* 171–197.

Brenman, M. (1940). Minority Group Membership and Religious, Psychosexual and Social Patterns In A Group of Middle-Class Negro Girls. *J. Soc. Psychol., 12,* 179–196.

Brenman, M. (1943). Urban Lower-Class Negro Girls. *Psychiatry, 6,* 307–324.

Brooks, J. J. (1951). Interage Grouping on Trial, Continuous Learning. *Bulletin #87 of the Association for Childhood Education.*

Brophy, I. N. (1946). The Luxury of Anti-Negro Prejudice. *Public Opinion Quarterly, 9,* 456–466 (Integration in Merchant Marine).

Chein, I. (1949). What Are the Psychological Effects of Segregation Under Conditions of Equal Facilities? *International J. Opinion & Attitude Res., 2,* 229–234.

Clark, K. B. (1950). Effect of Prejudice and Discrimination on Personality Development, *Fact Finding Report Mid-Century White House Conference on Children and Youth,* Children's Bureau-Federal Security Agency (mimeographed).

Clark, K. B., & Clark, M. P. (1950). Emotional Factors in Racial Identification and Preference in Negro Children, *J. Negro Educ., 19,* 341–350.

Clark, K. B., & Clark, M. P. (1947). Racial Identification and Preference in Negro Children. *Readings in Social Psychology,* Ed. by Newcomb & Hartley.

Conover, R. D. (1947). *Race Relations at Codornices Village, Berkeley-Albany, California: A Report of the Attempt to Break Down the Segregated Pattern On A Directly Managed Housing Project,* Housing and Home Finance Agency, Public Housing Administration, Region I (mimeographed).

Davis, A. (1939). The Socialization of the American Negro Child and Adolescent, *J. Negro Educ., 8,* 264–275.

Dean, J. P. (1949). *Situational Factors in Intergroup Relations: A Research Progress Report,* paper presented to American Sociological Society, Dec. 28 (mimeographed).

Delano, W. (1952). Grade School Segregation: The Latest Attack on Racial Discrimination, *Yale Law Journal, 61,* 730–744.

Deutscher, M., & Chein, I. (1948). The Psychological Effects of Enforced Segregation: A Survey of Social Science Opinion, *J. Psychol., 26,* 259–287.

Deutscher, M., & Collins, M. E. (1951). *Interracial Housing, A Psychological Study of A Social Experiment.*

Feldman, H. (1942). The Technique of Introducing Negroes Into the Plant, *Personnel, 19,* 461–466.

Frazier, E. (1949). *The Negro In the United States.*

Harding, J., & Hogrefe, R. (1952). Attitudes of White Department Store Employees Toward Negro Co-workers, *J. Social Issues, 8,* 19–28.

Irish, D. P. (1952). Reactions of Residents of Boulder, Colorado to the Introduction of Japanese Into the Community, *J. Social Issues, 8,* 10–17.

Kenworthy, E. W. (1951). The Case Against Army Segregation, *Annals of the American Academy of Political and Social Science, 275,* 27–33.

Klineberg, O. (1945). *Characteristics of American Negro.*

Klineberg, O. (1935). *Negro Intelligence and Selective Migration.*

Klineberg, O. (1935). *Race Differences.*

Krech, D., & Crutchfield, R. S. (1948). *Theory and Problems of Social Psychology.*

Lane, R. H. (1941). *Teacher in Modern Elementary School.*

Lee, A. McClung, & Humphrey, N. D. (1943). *Race Riot.*

Lee, A. McClung. (1945). Race Riot Aren't Necessary, *Public Affairs Pamphlet.*

Merton, R. K., West, P. S., & Jahoda, M. (1949). *Social Fictions and Social Facts: The dynamics of Race Relations in Hilltown,* Bureau of Applied Social Research, Columbia University (mimeographed).

Minard, R. D. (1952). The Pattern of Race Relationships in the Pocahontas Coal Field, *J. Social Issues, 8,* 29–44.

Myrdal, G. (1944). *An American Dilemma.*

Newcomb, T. (1950). *Social Psychology.*

Nelson, Lt. D. D. (1951). *The Integration of the Negro in the U. S. Navy.*

Rackow, F. (1951). Combatting Discrimination in Employment. *Bulletin #5, N. Y. State School of Industrial and Labor Relations,* Cornell Univ.

Radke, M., Trager, H., & Davis, H. (1949). Social Perceptions and Attitudes of Children. *Genetic Psychol, Monog., 40,* 327–447.

Radke, M., & Trager, H. (1950). Children's Perceptions of the Social Role of Negroes and Whites. *J. Psychol., 29,* 3–33.

Reid, Ira. (1949). What Segregated Areas Mean. *Discrimination and National Welfare*, Ed. by MacIver, R. M.

Rose, A. (1951). The Influence of Legislation on Prejudice, Chapter 53 in *Race Prejudice and Discrimination*, Ed. by Rose, A.

Rose, A. (1948). *Studies in Reduction of Prejudice*, Amer. Council on Race Relations.

Rutledge, E. *Integration of Racial Minorities in Public Housing Projects; A Guide for Local Housing Authorities on How to Do It*. Public Housing Administration, New York Field Office (mimeographed).

Saenger, G., & Gilbert, E. (1950). Customer Reactions to the Integration of Negro Sales Personnel, *International Journal of Attitude and Opinion Research*, *4, 1*, 57–76.

Saenger, G., & Gordon, N. S. (1950). The Influence of Discrimination on Minority Group Members in its Relation to Attempts to Combat Discrimination. *J. Soc. Psychol., 31*.

Southall, S. E. (1951). *Industry's Unfinished Business*.

Stouffer, S. et al. (1949). *The American Soldier*, Vol. I, Chap. 19, A Note on Negro Troops in Combat.

Watson, G. (1947). *Action for Unity*.

Watson, J. (1950). Some Social and Psychological Situations Related to Change in Attitude. *Human Relations, 3*, 1.

Weaver, G. L-P. (1941). *Negro Labor, A National Problem*.

Williams, D. H. (1934). *The Effects of an Interracial Project Upon the Attitudes of Negro and White Girls Within the Young Women's Christian Association*, Unpublished M. A. thesis, Columbia University.

Williams, R., Jr. (1947). *The Reduction of Intergroup Tensions*, Social Science Research Council.

Wilner, D. M., Walkley, R. P., & Cook, S. W. Intergroup Contact and Ethnic Attitudes in Public Housing Projects. *J. Social Issues, 8*, 45–69.

Windner, A, E. (1952). *White Attitudes Towards Negro-White Interaction in an Area of Changing Racial Composition*, Paper delivered at the Sixtieth Annual Meeting of The American Psychological Association, Washington, September.

Opinions about Negro Infantry Platoons in White Companies in Several Divisions, *Information and Education Division, U. S. War Department, Report No. B-157*, 1945.

Educational Policies Commission of the National Education Association and the American Association of School Administration Report in, *Education For All Americans* published by the N. E. A. 1948.

Kenneth B. Clark in the Patterns of American Culture
Ben Keppel

Kenneth B. Clark is perhaps best remembered – in psychology and beyond – as the social scientist whose psychological research was cited by the U.S. Supreme Court in footnote 11 of *Brown v. Board of Education* in 1954. In the many retellings of the Court's invalidation of legal segregation in the nearly half a century since that historic decision, the "doll studies" that Clark and his wife Mamie Phipps Clark conducted have become symbolic of the leading role played by psychologists in bringing about peaceful and constructive social change (see Lal, 2002, this issue). What this popular understanding obscures are some crucial details. The Supreme Court did not cite the doll studies themselves; what it did cite was a summary written by Kenneth Clark of psychological theories about the "effect of prejudice and discrimination on personality development" (Clark, 1989b, p. 164). As *Brown* grew in importance as an historical event, the story of Clark and the footnote became legendary as students, scholars, and journalists discovered the doll studies while they sought to determine why Kenneth Clark was important to *Brown*.

Although Clark's career properly began in the 1930s and extended well into the 1980s, I focus here on its most broadly public chapter, which opened with the publication of Clark's *Prejudice and Your Child* in 1955 and began its last phase nearly 20 years later with the appearance of a collection of essays, *Pathos of Power* (Clark, 1974), in 1974. In the period covered here, Clark sought to bring certain well-established social scientific conclusions to a general audience and to present an innovative and original interpretation of America's racial crisis. In choosing to become a

American Psychologist, 2002, *57*(1), 29–37. Copyright 2002 by the American Psychological Association, Inc. Reprinted by permission of the publisher and author.

scientist advocating social change, Clark joined a distinguished tradition, one centered at Columbia University, where he earned his doctorate in 1940. Over the course of the 20th century, this tradition became essential to the grounding of American social science as a legitimate influence in policy making and social thought. When Clark was debunking the tenets of scientific racism, for example, he was continuing important work begun in the 1920s and 1930s by many scholars, including psychologist Otto Klineberg, anthropologist Franz Boas, and sociologists E. Franklin Frazier and Charles S. Johnson. In designing the projective methods that constituted the doll studies, Kenneth and Mamie Phipps Clark built on the formative research of psychologists Kurt Lewin, Ruth Horowitz, and others. When Clark demanded that Americans examine their culture and themselves more critically, he was carrying forward an argument made earlier by Boas and his students Ruth Benedict and Margaret Mead, political economist Gunnar Myrdal, and historian W. E. B. Du Bois. In his conviction that the majorities that sanctioned the structuring of their societies to treat some groups with contempt were also victims of social pathology (the least understood theme of his work), Clark drew on analyses advanced by the theorists of the Frankfurt School.

Clark has a cultural significance that goes beyond his importance within psychology; he was speaking not only as a scientist but also as a Black intellectual whose words would be given greater visibility by the mainstream media, which were seeking authentic interpreters of the "Black experience" during the civil rights years. As a result, Clark became, like many other accomplished African Americans of that era, a "participant-symbol" of racial progress in the United States (Keppel, 1995, p. 3). In the midst of profound and wrenching change, such participant-symbols find themselves in unstable cultural territory, where their words and actions must coexist and even become densely mixed with the necessarily selective symbolic represen- tations of them by others. The results of this process are such things as magazine articles, interviews, and, in Clark's highly unusual case, even movies in which the person is presented as a specific embodiment of a general idea: in this case, that of integration. Some symbols are cau- tionary: The widely broadcast ideological travails of Paul Robeson, for example, were a warning that African Americans advocating racial equality at home must not stray from cold war orthodoxy on foreign policy.

Although Clark was by no means the most famous participant-symbol of his time (in com- parison, say, with actor Sidney Poitier or social activist Martin Luther King, Jr.), he did nonethe- less become, by the 1960s, a living symbol to the press of the supposed alliance between progres- sive social science and the federal judiciary in bringing integration to American society. (Inter- estingly enough, integration is a word that does not appear anywhere in the text of the *Brown* decision.) The preceding generation of Black scholars who came to professional maturity during the 1920s and 1930s faced many burdens and pressures – but being a participant-symbol was not one of them because the American estab- lishment was not generally interested in them or what they had to say.

The Patterns of American Culture, 1944–1974

The first step toward understanding Clark's effort to address the general public is to appreciate some of the patterns that defined American culture in the generation after the end of World War II. Among the most significant changes in these patterns is the fact that the second world war had thrust the United States onto the global stage as the preeminent democratic power in an ideological contest with the Soviet Union. As Myrdal (1944) had predicted in *An American Dilemma*:

> The main international implication [of America's preeminence] is . . . that America, for its international prestige and power, and future security, needs to demonstrate to the world that American Negroes can be satisfactorily inte- grated into its democracy. . . . Statesmen will need to take cognizance of the changed geopo- litical situation . . . and carry out important adaptions of the American way of life to new necessities. A main adaption is bound to be a redefinition of the Negro's status in American democracy. (p. 1016)

The new cultural and political dynamics identi- fied by Myrdal were magnified by the cold war with the Soviet Union, which added an element of ideological immediacy to American efforts to project an image of democracy and pluralism to the world. In addition, beginning in the 1950s, the new medium of television would broadcast throughout the world images that illustrated the contrast between the nation's rhetoric of racial inclusion and the reality of the American practice of racial segregation.

The United States' new position of power and leadership also had important consequences for the social sciences as changes in educational pat- terns took hold. Most notably, the social sciences increased in size as the G.I. Bill and expanded defense spending enlarged the entire American higher education establishment. In turn, as mil- lions more Americans attended college, the audi- ence for general works by social scientists became far larger than had been the case for the works of an earlier generation of researchers. It was in this context, for example, that successive waves of undergraduate students were introduced to the Clarks' work (Clark & Clark, 1947) in Newcomb and Hartley's (1947) *Readings in Social Psychol- ogy*. In addition, one must note what Ellen Herman (1995) has identified as "the romance of American psychology," that is, the attraction of experts to the idea that psychological explana- tions have a unique power to illuminate the dynamics of human affairs.

Finally, among the many salutary conse- quences of the civil rights movement was the changed relationship of Black intellectuals to the American general public. In the first half of the 20th century, African American social scien- tists writing about race found little demand for their words from the nations' mainstream media and still less interest from anything other than a small fragment of the American public. The civil rights movement changed that cultural calculus, as actor and political activist Ossie Davis observed in 1965, in his eulogy of Malcolm X:

> Protocol and common sense require that Negroes stand back and let the White man speak up for us, defend us, and lead us from behind the scene in our fight. This is the essence of Negro politics. But Malcolm said to hell with that. (quoted in X, 1999, p. 464)

One of the victories that African Americans won for themselves in the 1950s and 1960s was a greater freedom of speech with regard to how they could address the White public than they had ever been previously permitted in American culture. All of these factors taken together help to explain not only the incendiary rhetoric of the Black power movement but also why, during the 1960s, the most important social scientist to reach the public on the subject of race was a Black man named Kenneth B. Clark.

The emergence of Clark as a recognized public intellectual did not happen instantaneously with the citation of his name and work beside that of Myrdal by the Supreme Court in 1954. It was a process that proceeded along two lines that were irretrievably enmeshed: Clark's own production of books for audiences beyond psychology's disciplinary journals and the increasing attention of the mass media to issues of race and politics. As important as *Brown* was in the 1950s, it took nearly 10 years for most of the press and the attentive public to explicitly recognize and publicize the connection between social science – which would come to be symbolized by Clark – and that decision (see Benjamin & Crouse, 2002, this issue). As Randall Kennedy, a professor at Harvard Law School, noted recently during a discussion of that decision, "If *Brown v. Board of Education* had meant as much [in 1954] as we now think it means, one would not have engaged in a year-long boycott [in Montgomery]" ("Brown v. Board of Education," 2000). Indeed, if one returns to and examines the general press coverage of *Brown* in the weekly magazines of 1954, one finds no quotations from Clark and no profiles of the 40-year-old psychology professor whose work had been cited by the nation's court of last appeal in its desegregation decision. *Brown* was not the

beginning, but it was certainly a beginning: Only as crises that centered on the desegregation of schools and other institutions mounted did *Brown* mature from being a potent sign of promise into a more fully elaborated symbol in a more protracted process that historians have generally referred to as a second Reconstruction.

When the racial crisis reached one of its defining moments in the spring of 1963, members of the media, scrambling to get up to speed on the origins of the civil rights movement (which many came to identify incorrectly as beginning with *Brown*), discovered Clark. Clark, of course, was not absent from the written record immediately surrounding *Brown*; he is simply not to be found as a voice featured in the broad public space that he would occupy 10 years later during a time of more visible racial crisis. A close reading of *The New York Times* provides skeletal documentation of his contribution in the decade after *Brown* to the largely unsuccessful efforts to desegregate New York City schools at a time when the project of Northern desegregation went largely unacknowledged in the press. It is true that specialists in psychology knew of his involvement, along with that of psychologist David Krech and others. In short, Clark, before the early 1960s, was primarily an expert well known to other experts.

With the outlines of the cultural setting in which Clark worked in place, I now turn to a consideration of the psychologist's own efforts to persuade Americans of the damage caused by racism. After *Brown*, Clark began his journey to reach those outside of the academy with the publication in 1955 of *Prejudice and Your Child* (Clark, 1955), a simply written summary of psychological research on the relationship between prejudice and personality development. It was, Clark stated, an explicit effort to give to the American public "the same type of objective information that was available to the justices of the United States Supreme Court" when it rendered its decision in *Brown* (Clark, 1989b, p. 13). *Prejudice and Your Child* was Clark's optimistic beginning of what he hoped would be a fruitful dialogue between social science and the American public. As I discuss in the next section, Clark would become far more pessimistic about whether such a discussion would be possible, as is evidenced in *Dark Ghetto* (Clark, 1965) and *Pathos of Power* (Clark, 1974).

Clark Speaks to the Public

The nation's past and the nation's future: Prejudice and Your Child

The key message Clark conveyed to the audience of parents whom he sought to reach with *Prejudice and Your Child* (Clark, 1955) was that "social scientists are now convinced that children learn prejudice in the course of observing and being influenced by the existence of patterns in the culture in which they live" (Clark, 1989b, p. 17) and that the "normal American environment" provided no "opportunity to learn any new attitude except one that stereotypes individuals of a different race" (Clark, 1989b, p. 127). One of Clark's most daring statements was to suggest forcefully that a normal environment could also be one filled with antisocial and antidemocratic symbols and attitudes to which parents might be so adjusted that they failed to notice their presence, even as their children were encountering them. Clark (1989b) argued that

> racial symbols are so prevalent in the American scene that all normal children eventually perceive them. They observe segregated residential areas, segregated and often inferior schools for Negro children, segregated recreational facilities, and, in some areas of the country, segregated transportation. They see Negroes often only in domestic service or in other menial occupations. Such observations contribute to the young child's attitude toward those individuals whom the society consistently labels as "inferior." (p. 128)

These words may well strike contemporary readers as unremarkable; however, it is critical that it be kept in mind when they were written. The 1950s were not only the decade in which the civil rights movement gained force but also a period characterized by extreme intolerance of dissent and suspicion of those who questioned any aspect of the social arrangements that were held to constitute the status quo.

On the other hand, some of Clark's other conclusions might disturb or even offend contemporary readers, such as the following: "If society says it is better to be White, not only White people but Negroes come to believe it. And a child may try to escape the trap of inferiority by denying the fact of his own race"

(Clark, 1989b, p. 37). The reader of today might find the preceding statement to be wrong because it does not take into account the ways that human beings have of surviving and preserving themselves in circumstances designed to humiliate them. Because Clark wanted to make certain that Americans understood that the patterns of prejudice woven into American culture that had long gone unchallenged contained destructive consequences, he chose to focus on these negative effects in *Prejudice and Your Child*. That Clark did not highlight positive responses in coping with the nation's racial dynamic was due to his belief in the mid-1950s of how necessary it was that his fellow citizens be sensitized to the real harm caused by prejudice and hate. His approach makes sense if one remembers the tired axiom that every American learns as a schoolchild: "Sticks and stones may break my bones, but words will never hurt me." *Prejudice and Your Child* instead argued that certain words, said long enough and loud enough, are stronger than any stone.

Clark's discussion of the doll studies is a case in point. Above and beyond his recitation of statistics of the children's responses to various questions, Clark gives descriptions of how individual children reacted when probed about their choices of which dolls – brown or white – they liked best, or looked most like them, and so forth. One vivid example from his Northern sample is of "one little girl who had shown a "clear preference for the white doll and who described the brown doll as ugly and dirty" (Clark, 1989b, p. 45). When the investigator responded by noting the fact that the child herself was brown, she "broke into a torrent of tears" (Clark, 1989b, p. 45). Other African American children in the Northern sample "looked at the investigator with terror or hostility" (Clark, 1989b, p. 45). In contrast, children from the South, a majority of whom preferred the brown doll, did so by saying, "This one. It's a nigger. I'm a nigger" (Clark, 1989b, p. 45). Their matter-of-fact identification of themselves as "niggers" led Clark to the conclusion that they were far more damaged than African American children in the North, who, because of the distress they exhibited, seemed healthier in that they were displaying discomfort with the complicated and harsh reality of racial mores rather than resignation. This is why he stated that although such findings could be read as suggesting that "Northern children suffer more personality damage from racial prejudice and discrimination than Southern Negro children," this possibility was "not only superficial but incorrect" (Clark, 1989b, p. 45). According to Clark, these findings confirmed instead that "rigid racial segregation and isolation" had caused Southern Black children to accept "as normal the fact of [their] inferior social status. . . . Such an acceptance," Clark continued, "is not symptomatic of a healthy personality" (Clark, 1989b, p. 45).

In *Prejudice and Your Child* (Clark, 1955, 1989b), Clark did not restrict himself to a discussion of the psychological consequences of American racism for Black children. As the doll studies have become better known in popular culture, Clark's arguments concerning how prejudice affects the children of the White majority have been largely overlooked. Clark was as concerned with the psychological damage done to White people by segregation as with that done to African Americans; in *Prejudice and Your Child*, he devoted an entire chapter to "The White Child and Prejudice." Clark contended that White children become deeply disturbed by the conflict between what Myrdal (1944) had called "the American creed" (p. xliii) of equality and fair play and the practice of racial segregation:

Just as the Negro child is required to use and adjust to various techniques for the protection of his self-esteem, so must the White child fall back on various techniques of adjustment in his attempt to cope with his profound moral conflict, which soon becomes a personal one. Some children react by a rigid repression or a refusal to recognize the contradiction of the democratic creed inherent in racial prejudice. Others fall back upon partial or temporary repression of one or more of the contradictory ideas. Others begin to accept the rationalizations or excuses that their parents or other adults offer in the attempt to resolve this moral conflict. The uncritical acceptance of the superiority of one's own group and the related assumption of the "inferiority" of the rejected group may be considered one way of dealing with the basic problem. Some of these children may develop intense guilt feelings; others may become more hostile and more rigid in their stereotyped ideas in order to protect themselves from recognizing

the moral confusion in which they are placed. (Clark, 1989b, pp. 78–79)

Although possessing considerable value for explaining the massive resistance of the White majority in the South to school desegregation during the 1950s, this analysis should not have merely historical significance. Such an interpretation may well have continued relevance today, in understanding the mind of Timothy McVeigh, for example, or the psychological states of the young students who attempted to kill their peers at Columbine and a host of other predominantly White schools.

It would take 10 years for *Prejudice and Your Child* to find a steady readership, but this is not to say that its themes failed to evoke a public response (Keppel, 1995). What proved to be more effective as a conduit for disseminating the psychological interpretations contained in *Prejudice and Your Child* was the discourse generated by the civil rights movement; even people who knew nothing of the Clarks' projective research were exposed to their message about the psychological damage inflicted on children by a society that consistently valued white over black. Rhetoric strikingly similar to that of Clark appeared in such works as *Why We Can't Wait* (M. L. King, 1964), Martin Luther King, Jr.'s account of the racial crisis in Birmingham, Alabama. In this account, King offered personal testimony of the pain he felt as a parent at having to explain to his six-year-old daughter why a local amusement park was closed to "colored children." He recounted that it was then that he witnessed "ominous clouds of inferiority begin to form in her little mental sky," the effect of prejudice on his child being that her developing personality began to be "distorted" by "an unconscious bitterness toward White people" (M. L. King, 1964, p. 81).

There are other manifestations of this line of psychological analysis in postwar popular culture as well. For example, the opening scene from the 1967 film comedy *The President's Analyst* (Rubin & Flicker, 1967) also portrays the childhood moment when a grade-schooler's decisions about how to deal with prejudice affect personality development. In that film, James Coburn plays Sydney Schaffer, a Park Avenue psychoanalyst about to be recruited to treat the President of the United States. Don Masters (played by Godfrey Cambridge), an agent for the Central Enquiries Agency, is coming for his weekly appointment, having just murdered an Albanian double agent on New York's Seventh Avenue. The African American Agent Masters is troubled by a recurring dream about his second day in kindergarten, "the day I found out about niggers." He recalls that as his younger self approached the schoolyard, he observed a group of White children shouting the following words with glee:

> "Run, run, here comes the nigger, run, run, here comes the nigger!" . . . I looked around and I didn't see any nigger, but if they wanted to play, so did I; so I started laughing and running and yelling, "Here comes the nigger!" . . . Suddenly there was my big brother and I ran up to him and started yelling, "Run, run, here comes the nigger!" . . . Then he did something even worse – he told me what a nigger was and that I was it. (Rubin & Flicker, 1967)

At hearing this news, Masters recalled, "A hate flashed in me and I started to hate my brother; I hated him and I hit him. I hated me and hit him." The opening scene is punctuated by Schaffer's acerbic observation that growing up to become a secret agent with a license to kill "is a great solution to the hostility problem" (Rubin & Flicker, 1967).

The President's Analyst not only portrays a child discovering racism and the effect of this fact on his personality exactly when the Clarks' research said he would but also touches on the violent reactions to that discovery that the Clarks had observed in their research. Frank public discussions of childhood lessons about racism such as King's parable and this Hollywood film's opening frames indicate that the operational assumptions underlying the Clark studies had become part of the conventional wisdom of a society struggling to come to terms with the effects of racial stereotyping. Other elaborations of this theme include such celebrated products as Harper Lee's (1960) novel *To Kill a Mockingbird*, published in 1960 (and itself made into an Academy Award–winning motion picture in 1962 [Pakula & Mulligan, 1962]), which covers some of the same territory from a somewhat different angle. The popularity of Atticus Finch as a role model of courageous and compassionate parenthood causes one to miss the more significant dimension of the story: It chronicles how White children learn about their role in a segregated social system. Those formative lessons haunt them for years (Lee, 1960).

In *Prejudice and Your Child* (Clark, 1955), Clark seized the moment and began to speak as a psychologist for society. If his push to recruit a new generation of parents to consider aspects of childhood experience that had rarely been addressed before in such a straightforward way did not receive the immediate response he had hoped for, its arguments nevertheless did eventually begin to gain acceptance. Because Beacon Press published an expanded version of *Prejudice and Your Child* (Clark, 1963) in 1963, it might be supposed that a happy convergence of audience and author had occurred. Yet it is noteworthy that *Prejudice and Your Child*'s optimism that significant social change could be accomplished if individuals were simply provided with the right information by social scientists would prove to be anomalous for Clark when put beside his later books. Clark's first words to his readers in *Prejudice and Your Child* paid tribute to the fact that "ours is a child-centered society" (Clark, 1963, p. 3) in which many parents defended segregation "in the belief that they are protecting their children" (Clark, 1963, p. 4). Clark sought to reach the public beyond the specialized academic class out of his strong belief that "if parents understood that, far from protecting their children, acts of this type distort and damage the core of their children's personalities, they would not act this way" (Clark, 1963, p. 4). The prospects for cleansing the nation of racial prejudice were strong because desegregation was already underway in the armed forces, higher education, and professional sports (Clark, 1963, p. 131). Americans, Clark stated, were now equipped to "wage a dramatic and successful war against racial prejudice and its effects upon human beings" (Clark, 1963, p. 139). By the opening years of the next decade, Clark would view the situation quite differently.

Toward pessimism: Dark Ghetto

The tone of *Dark Ghetto* (Clark, 1965) was far bleaker in its assessment of the willingness and the ability of Americans to confront their own racism. Much of this change in attitude occurred, I strongly suspect, in reaction not only to well-publicized events such as the abuse of the Little Rock Nine by a White mob in the fall of 1957 but also to inaction in Clark's own New York City on the issue of school desegregation. Strong evidence for this conclusion is provided by Clark's comments to a panel brought together in early 1964 by *Commentary*, then a leading journal of the New York left:

> Negro Americans will have ... to learn ... how to deal with a curious and insidious adversary – much more insidious than the outright bigot. ... The public schools in New York City are not headed by bigots, they're not headed by people who say outwardly, "I believe that Negroes are inferior. ... " But the fact is that these schools are woefully inferior. ... They are not getting better, the evidence is that they are getting worse and worse. And the people who are directly responsible for this are self-identified liberals. (quoted in Podhoretz, 1964, p. 39)

Clark had been no mere armchair observer of these trends. By the early 1960s, he had come to see American race problems as the product of deep systemic flaws. For a sense of how much more somber and, indeed, angry he had become, consider the following passage, written at least one year before the Black power phase of the civil rights movement made references to internal colonialism fashionable:

> Ghettoes are the consequence of the imposition of external power and the institutionalization of powerlessness. In this respect they are in fact social, political, educational, and – above all – economic colonies. Those confined within ghetto walls are subject peoples. They are victims of the greed, cruelty, insensitivity, guilt and fear of their masters. (Clark, 1964, p. xi)

This argument became a core theme in *Dark Ghetto*. It also became central to the articulation of the political program of the Black power movement. In the most important founding text of that movement, Stokely Carmichael and Charles V. Hamilton's *Black Power* (1967), Clark's formulation of the ghetto as a domestic colony opened the book's first chapter as its epigraph, followed

by other quotations from *Dark Ghetto* elaborating on the colonial analogy. Obviously, Clark served an important function for these theorists because they could point to him as a member of the social science establishment to legitimate their indictment of American society.

The single most dominant feature of *Dark Ghetto* (Clark, 1965), however, was not Clark's use of the neocolonialist metaphor but his insistence on a framework emphasizing pathology. "The dark ghetto is institutionalized pathology; it is chronic, self-perpetuating pathology; and it is the futile attempt by those in power to confine that pathology so as to prevent the spread of its contagion to the 'larger community'" (Clark, 1989a, p. 27). *Dark Ghetto* has a complicated place in the history of American social thought. In his insistence that the ghetto is "institutionalized pathology," Clark was working within a tradition that sought to reach the conscience of White society by emphasizing the damage to African Americans for which it bore responsibility. At the same time, Clark's challenge to the idea that the educational difficulties of African Americans in "ghetto schools" (Clark, 1989a, p. 117) resulted in "cultural deprivation" (Clark, 1989a, p. 126) associated him with a new generation of scholars, heavily influenced by the civil rights movement, who attacked the widespread assumption that the poor were trapped in a self-perpetuating "culture of poverty" (Valentine, 1968, pp. 78–82).

In 1935, Otto Klineberg published two studies (Klineberg, 1935a, 1935b) that argued convincingly that a hostile social environment, rather than inferior genetics, explained gaps in performance between African Americans and Whites on standardized tests. One generation later, the belief in the inherent inferiority of certain groups was, Clark feared, back in a new scholarly packaging. Clark was alarmed that theorists positing the cultural deprivation of the poor were now applying a static concept of culture to make the same inherently racist argument all over again: that the causes of poverty lay not in a sick society but in the presumed character flaws, and perhaps even the inferior genes, of its victims (Clark, 1974, p. 128).

Whether the students were held to be culturally or racially inferior, this form of argument led to "identical practical educational consequences" (Clark, 1989a, p. 147). For Clark, cultural deprivation theory was "primarily an alibi for educational neglect" (Clark, 1989a, p. 127). Theories of deprivation, he argued, "contribute to the perpetuation of inferior education for lower class children. Each [theory] intensifies racial and class cleavages in the schools and therefore perpetuates and extends such cleavages in society" (Clark, 1989a, p. 127). As a result, "public schools and public education are not instruments in facilitating social mobility, but very effective instruments in widening socioeconomic and racial cleavages in our society and in imposing caste and class rigidities" (Clark, 1989a, p. 127).

Clark's discussion of the nature of the ghetto was based not only on his canvassing of census records – which he included in the book – and other quantitative research but on even more familiar ground: his own memories of a Harlem childhood. In *Prejudice and Your Child* (Clark, 1955), Clark had not disclosed information about his own life – the relevance, for example, of his own experiences of racism to his research on racism. In *Dark Ghetto* (Clark, 1965), however, he grounded the validity of his harsh words in the fact that

> more than forty years of my life have been lived in Harlem. . . . In a very real sense, therefore, *Dark Ghetto* is a summation of my personal and lifelong experiences and observations as a prisoner within the ghetto long before I was aware that I was really a prisoner. (Clark, 1989a, p. xxix)

Clark (1989a) wrote these words because he saw himself as what he termed an "involved observer" (p. xxx) in the Harlem story. He was frustrated that

> to my knowledge, there is . . . nothing in the vast literature of social science and nothing in the practical or field training of students in social science to prepare them for the realities and complexities of this type of involvement in a real, dynamic, turbulent, and at times seemingly chaotic community. (Clark, 1989a, p. xxix)

In writing *Dark Ghetto*, Clark questioned one of the verities of social science: the value and attainability of objectivity. He could not deny – and would not deny – that how he saw Harlem was rooted in his formative experiences as a resident of that community. He sought to use that fact to deepen his own understanding of the ghetto and that of his readers as well.

Clark's last book, *Pathos of Power* (Clark, 1974), completed his departure from an earlier optimism about the capacity of American society and its social scientists to go beyond tokenism in creating a truly inclusive society. Clark's special concern here was with those forms of social power that thwarted change (see Pickren & Tomes, 2002, this issue). As Clark looked back, he saw that, for a comparatively brief moment, social scientists wishing to challenge specific long-standing patterns in American culture had received the nation's attention, but they and their fellow citizens had failed to understand the depth of American racism (Clark, 1974, p. 100). As the political mood hardened against increasing efforts to desegregate public education, the center of gravity changed, and Clark stated that social scientists once again had become "agents of those who are in political power . . . whose main responsibility [is] to explain or apologize for the actions of those who wield political and economic power" (Clark, 1974, p. 129). It was time, Clark believed, for social scientists to turn their analytical focus back on themselves and the "status hierarchy" that afforded them positions of privilege, "rather than merely to study some system 'out there'" (Clark, 1974, p. 71). It is hard to see how a social science so contaminated by its interaction with power could serve the constructive public role that Clark had seen for it 20 years earlier.

Because *Dark Ghetto* (Clark, 1965) had been published in the midst of so much other controversy on race issues – most especially about how White America was to interpret the Watts riots of 1965 – its author became a much sought-after voice, and it is in this period that Clark emerged as a public figure of national stature. His presence as a participant-symbol was not limited to the writing of books: In the late spring of 1963, he also hosted one of the first television programs to introduce Americans to the contrasting ideas of Martin Luther King, Jr., Malcolm X, and James Baldwin (K. B. King, 1988). In that program, titled "The Negro and the Promise of American

Life," Clark took part in an active dialogue with each of the participants about the challenges facing the nation. At that time, he was also one of a small group of African Americans brought together by entertainer Harry Belafonte to educate Attorney General Robert Kennedy about racial issues (Kepple, 1995, p. 136). In 1968, the much-quoted report of the Kerner Commission used part of Clark's testimony before the commission as its entire conclusion (Kerner Commission, 1968). The Kerner Commission (officially, the President's Commission on Civil Disorders) had been appointed by President Lyndon B. Johnson to investigate the causes of the urban riots that had occurred every summer since 1964. In his words to the commission, Clark expressed doubt that anything would happen as a result of its work. He reminded them that each of the preceding riots in the 20th century had been followed by reports and by the "same analysis, the same recommendations, and the same inaction" (quoted in Koppel, 1992, p. 7).

Patterns of Recognition and Remembrance

Since the 1990s, Americans have been looking backward to the high points in their long journey to the end of the cold war. They have rediscovered the "greatest generation" of Americans who fought World War II, they have increased their fascination with the Kennedy-era Camelot, and they have arrived at a more complex appreciation of the Vietnam War. As part of this retrospective process, the civil rights movement has also been rediscovered. One example of this is the use of Kenneth Clark's words to the Kerner Commission by journalist Ted Koppel to end a broadcast of *Nightline* (Koppel, 1992) on the topic of the Los Angeles race riots of 1992. These riots had been provoked by the not guilty verdict rendered in the case of police officers who had been videotaped beating an African American motorist. By reaching back to the last great moment of national reflection on race and then transporting Clark's words into the present, Koppel showed that Clark, although retired and out of the public spotlight, remained a symbol of the spirit of the 1960s on into the 1990s. One cannot know how Koppel or his staff came across Clark's testimony, but the

fact that Clark came to mind is an example of the current mood of cultural retrospection.

Among the many results of this retrospection is that Clark's image as a significant figure is seen more clearly and sharply than it was in 1950s. The story of Clark and the doll studies was first retold to the general public in Richard Kluger's popular history of the *Brown* decree, *Simple Justice* (Kluger, 1975). Nearly 20 years later, Clark's role as the doll man was prominently featured in two television films, *Separate But Equal* (Stevens, 1991) and an adaptation of *Simple Justice* (McGreevery & Head, 1993). These retellings reflect the fact that, for all its controversy, *Brown* has become one of a small cluster of moments now seen as symbolically central to America's collective narrative of coming of age as a great nation after World War II. As part of this retroactive celebration, the Clark doll studies have been reenacted in popular culture in a way that they never were – and perhaps never could have been – in the years during and immediately after the civil rights movement.

The commemoration of the doll studies in popular culture exposes two important ironies. First, the doll studies have reached their widest public audience at the same time that the academic community is reaching a new consensus emphasizing their limitations. Consider the conclusions offered recently by two historians of American social science and social policy, James T. Patterson and Daryl Michael Scott. Patterson (2001) has suggested that

> scholar activists like Kenneth Clark may have been wrong to maintain that school segregation deeply damaged the self-esteem of young Black people. After all, the student leaders of the civil rights movement did not *seem* passive or unsure of themselves. (p. 131)

Scott (1996) has gone much further and argued that the reliance of liberal social scientists on "damage imagery" (Scott, 1996, p. xi) to elicit White support for social reform has backfired; when the political atmosphere grew more conservative, that same imagery was appropriated by conservatives to argue against further social change. Secondly, as Americans in the 1990s viewed reenactments of a victory in *Brown*, they were living in a nation that, in the words of Gary Orfield (1996), was "sleepwalking back to *Plessy* [*v. Ferguson*]" (p. 331), the 1896 Supreme Court decision that enunciated the doctrine of "separate but equal." "The political victory of the Right," Orfield argued, "has almost ended intelligent discussion of integration, probably the only viable alternative for successfully organizing the multicultural society emerging in the United States" (p. 333).

Kenneth Clark's role as the leading social science expert for the National Association for the Advancement of Colored People (NAACP) in *Brown* has been reenacted in two recent television films. The first, *Separate but Equal* (Stevens, 1991) focuses primarily on the South Carolina chapter of the litigation. Clark appears in two 7-minute segments: In the first, he is shown administering the doll studies to two African American children and encountering the responses I cited earlier from *Prejudice and Your Child* (Clark, 1995). The second segment shows Clark testifying in court about the "evil and warping effect" (Stevens, 1991) of segregation on African Americans.

The second recounting of *Brown* for television is *Simple Justice* (McGreevey & Head, 1993), based on Richard Kluger's (1975) book. The doll studies frame the entire cinematic narrative of this film. The four dolls of the Clark research are the very first thing shown – the images against which the film's title is projected. As the opening credits roll, the image of the dolls is supplemented by pictures of children in classrooms and with their families. Early in the film, Charles H. Houston is shown telling Thurgood Marshall about a scene he had recently witnessed involving his young son, Beau. Father and son were in a drug store not far from their Washington, DC, home when young Beau climbed on a soda-fountain stool so that he could order an ice cream soda. Seeing this, the druggist yelled, "Get down from there, you little nigger!" "I saw the hurt and fear in his eyes," Houston tells Marshall. "And what could I do? Nothin'!" The scene ends with Houston asking Marshall to "look after my boy."

More than 30 minutes of this two-and-a-half-hour film are devoted to elaborating the place of social science in *Brown*. In fact, the second hour opens with an extended discussion of the role of social scientists. NAACP attorney William Coleman is shown arguing that the organization will be "laughed out of court" for relying on "social science voodoo." Marshall ends the argument by showing Coleman a newspaper ad for Fred Palmer's Skin Whitener and saying that it is important to show "real damage to real children." The Clarendon County doll tests appear in this version as well and, as in *Separate but Equal*, replay the muted reactions of Southern children first described by Clark in *Prejudice and Your Child* (Clark, 1995).

As salutary as these motion picture moments are as efforts to educate the public, it is important to inquire into the contrast they present between national admiration of *Brown* and the movement of American social policy away from *Brown's* goals. In addition, this celebration of Clark as the doll man is but a partial picture; to see only that aspect of his research prevents the public from learning what Clark has to tell them about the pathology caused in White people when they become participants in discriminating against others.

Conclusion

Clark's effort to change the "patterns of culture" (Benedict, 1934) was not without precedent; he was indeed part of a long tradition embedded within the development of modern social science in the United States. However, as an African American pioneer in a society trying to come to terms with its own past and present racism, Clark became a participant-symbol and entered territory reached by few of his peers in social science before or after. In the generation since the peak of the civil rights movement, Clark and the doll studies that he conducted with his wife, Mamie Phipps Clark, have become nearly legendary. Ironically, this celebration comes at a time when the nation is moving further and further away from the vision and values expressed in *Brown* and in the public work of Kenneth B. Clark.

References

Benedict, R. (1934). *Patterns of culture.* Boston: Houghton Mifflin.

Benjamin, L. T., Jr., & Crouse, E. M. (2002). The American Psychological Association's response to *Brown v. Board of Education*: The case of Kenneth B. Clark. *American Psychologist, 57,* 38–50.

Brown v. Board of Education, 347 U.S. 483 (1954).

Brown v. Board of Education [Television series episode] (2000). In *America and the courts.* Washington, DC: National Cable Satellite Corporation.

Carmichael, S., & Hamilton, C. V. (1967). *Black power: The politics of liberation.* New York: Random House.

Clark, K. B. (1955). *Prejudice and your child* (1st edn.). Boston: Beacon Press.

Clark, K. B. (1963). *Prejudice and your child* (2nd edn.). Boston: Beacon Press.

Clark, K. B. (1964). *Harlem Youth Opportunities Unlimited: Youth in the ghetto – A study of the consequences of powerlessness and a blueprint for change.* New York: Harlem Youth Opportunities Unlimited.

Clark, K. B. (1965). *Dark ghetto: Dilemmas of social power* (1st edn.). New York: Harper & Row.

Clark, K. B. (1974). *Pathos of power.* New York: Harper & Row.

Clark, K. B. (1989a). *Dark ghetto: Dilemmas of social power* (2nd edn.). Middletown, CT: Wesleyan University Press.

Clark, K. B. (1989b). *Prejudice and your child* (3rd edn.). Middletown, CT: Wesleyan University Press.

Clark, K. B., & Clark, M. P. (1947). Racial identification and preference in Negro children. In T. M. Newcomb & E. L. Hartley (Eds.), *Readings in social psychology* (pp. 169–178). New York: Holt.

Herman, E. (1995). *The romance of American psychology: Political culture in the age of experts, 1940–1970.* Berkeley: University of California Press.

Keppel, B. (1995). *The work of democracy: Ralph Bunche, Kenneth B. Clark, Lorraine Hansberry, and the cultural politics of race.* Cambridge, MA: Harvard University Press.

Kerner Commission. (1968). *Report of the President's Commission on Civil Disorders.* New York: Dutton.

King, K. B. (1988). *Martin, Malcolm, and Baldwin: The interviews with Kenneth B. Clark.* Middletown, CT: Wesleyan University Press.

King, M. L., Jr. (1964). *Why we can't wait.* New York: Harper & Row.

Klineberg, O. (1935a). *Negro intelligence and selective migration.* New York: Columbia University Press.

Klineberg, O. (1935b). *Race differences.* New York: Harper.

Kluger, R. (1975). *Simple justice: The history of Brown v. Board of Education and Black America's struggle for equality.* New York: Vintage.

Koppel, T. (1992). *The L. A. riots and a view of history* [Transcript of *Nightline* television broadcast]. New York: American Broadcasting Company.

Lal, S. (2002). Giving children security: Mamie Phipps Clark and the racialization of child psychology. *American Psychologist, 57,* 20–28.

Lee, H. (1960). *To kill a mockingbird.* New York: Lippincott.

McGreevey, J. (Writer), & Head, H. (Director). (1993). Simple justice [Television series episode]. In Y. K. Brandt (Producer) & A. Kirkland (Executive Producer), *The American Experience.* Boston: WGBH.

Myrdal, G. (1994). *An American dilemma: The Negro problem in American democracy.* New York: Harper.

Newcomb, T. M., & Hartley, E. L. (Eds.). (1947). *Readings in social psychology.* New York: Holt.

Orfield, G. (1996). Toward an integrated future: New directions for courts, educators, civil rights groups, and scholars. In G. Orfield & S. Eaton (Eds.), *Dismantling desegregation: The quiet reversal of Brown v. Board of Education* (pp. 331–361). New York: New Press.

Pakula, A. J. (Producer), & Mulligan, R. (Director). (1962). *To kill a mockingbird* [Motion picture]. United States: Universal-International Pictures.

Patterson, J. T. (2001). *Brown v. Board of Education: A civil rights milestone and its troubled legacy.* New York: Oxford University Press.

Pickren, W. E., & Tomes, H. (2002). The legacy of Kenneth B. Clark to the APA: The Board of Social and Ethical Responsibility for Psychology. *American Psychologist, 57,* 51–59.

Podhoretz, N. (1964, March). Liberalism and the Negro. *Commentary, 39,* 25–42.

Rubin, S. (Producer), & Flicker, T. J. (Writer/Director). (1967). *The president's analyst* [Motion picture]. United States: Paramount Pictures.

Scott, D. M. (1996). *Contempt and pity: Social policy and the image of the damaged Black psyche.* Chapel Hill: University of North Carolina Press.

Stevens, G., Jr. (Executive Producer/Writer/Director). (1991). *Separate but equal* [Motion picture]. United States: Republic Pictures.

Valentine, C. A. (1968). *Culture and poverty: Critique and counterproposals.* Chicago: University of Chicago Press.

X, M. (1999). *The autobiography of Malcolm X.* New York: Ballantine.

The Mental Traits of Sex
Helen Bradford Thompson [Woolley]

Chapter I Introduction

The object of the present monograph is to furnish some accurate information on the much-discussed question of the psychology of the sexes. The main part of it consists in the report of a series of experiments carried on in the psychological laboratory of the University of Chicago during the years 1898–99 and 1899–1900. To have an adequate setting, such a study should be prefaced by a review of the historical aspects of the problem, a critical summary of the large mass of argumentative literature on the subject, and a discussion of the facts of anatomy and physiology which are supposed to have a bearing on the psychology of sex. The mass of material to be dealt with is far too great, however, to be satisfactorily treated within the necessary limits of the present work. It has therefore been necessary to restrict this monograph to a report of the experimental work which forms the real contribution to the field, a review of previous experimental work bearing on the subject, and a brief discussion of the results.

The present research is the first attempt to obtain a complete and systematic statement of the psychological likenesses and differences of the sexes by the experimental method. Needless to say, the goal has not been reached within the limits of such an investigation. All that has been done is to gather together some evidence bearing on the problem, which is trustworthy so far as it goes. Previous experimental work has been in the form of detached experiments on some single sense or intellectual process. Usually the experiments have not been made for the purpose of a comparison of the sexes, but have been performed with some other interest in view, and have been incidentally formulated with reference to sex. Much of the material is the experimental work on school children done under the influence of the child-study movement. The only previous attempt to sum up the experimental evidence on the subject is that by Havelock Ellis (23),* in his book *Man and Woman*, published in 1894. The work contains no original investigation.

In making a series of tests for comparative purposes, the first prerequisite is to obtain material that is really comparable. It has been shown that the simple sensory processes vary with age and with social condition (11, 20, 51, 54, 63, 64, 65, 67). No one would question that this statement is true for the intellectual processes also. In order to make a trustworthy investigation of the variations due to sex alone, therefore, it is essential to secure as material for experimentation, individuals of both sexes who are near the same age, who have the same social status, and who have been subjected to like training and social surroundings. The complete fulfilment of these conditions, even in the most democratic community, is impossible. The social atmosphere of the sexes is different from the earliest childhood to maturity. Probably the nearest approach among adults to the ideal requirement is afforded by the undergraduate students of a coeducational university. For most of them the obtaining of an education has been the one serious business of life. They have had at least the similarity of training and surroundings incident to school life. Most of those in a western university have received their preparatory education in coeducational schools.

From H. B. Thompson (1903). *The mental traits of sex* (pp. 1–7, 169–182). Chicago: University of Chicago Press.

* The numbers which appear in parentheses throughout the text refer to the reference list at the end of the chapter.

The individuals who furnished the basis for the present study were students of the University of Chicago. They were all juniors, seniors, or students in the first year of their graduate work. The original intention was to limit the ages to the period from twenty to twenty-five years. Owing to the difficulty of obtaining a sufficient number of subjects within these limits, a few individuals of nineteen years, and a few over twenty-five were admitted. The subjects were obtained by requesting members of the classes in introductory psychology and ethics to serve. They were told nothing about the object of the tests except that they were for the purpose of determining psychological norms. The series of questions on age, health, and nationality, reported in chap. viii, shows that in all these respects the men and women tested were closely comparable.

Two methods may be followed in planning a series of tests designed to yield material for the comparison of groups or classes. It is possible either to make rapid and more or less superficial measurements on a large number of individuals, depending on numbers to counterbalance the errors of single tests, or to make careful and accurate observations of a smaller number of persons. The ideal procedure would unquestionably be to make careful measurements of a large number of individuals, but since the amount of time available for any problem is limited, the practical question to be decided is – Given a limited amount of time, which of the two modes of procedure mentioned is more likely to yield valuable results? Accuracy of measurement seemed an indispensable requirement for such a study as the present one. Any reliable determination of a threshold or a discriminative sensibility requires a somewhat extended series of experiments. With subjects untrained in psychological experiments – as most of these were – it is essential to take a large enough series of measurements to give some assurance that the results represent a characteristic reaction, and not haphazard answers. In so simple a test as that of dermal two-point discriminations the first few judgments are very likely to be little more than guesses. In a series of rapid tests like those employed at Columbia University (82) the subject is given only five stimulations with the æsthesiometer. The points are kept a fixed distance apart and the subject is given both one- and two-point stimulations in his series of five. It seems improbable that the results of such a test on unpracticed subjects mean anything more than random answers. The Columbia experiments on a large number of students failed to reveal any difference of sex in the fineness of two-point discriminations, while the present accurate measurement of fifty subjects shows a clear difference.

The series of tests employed in this investigation required from fifteen to twenty hours of time from each subject. The hours were arranged from one sitting to the next according to the convenience of the subject. It was not possible to have the hours for any one test constant for all subjects, since the schedules varied so widely. No attempt was made to keep the order of experiments rigidly the same for all. Convenience and economy of time necessarily determined the order to a great extent. In general, however, the simple sensory and motor tests were given in the early part of the series, and the intellectual tests in the latter part. The questions on personality usually came last. The taste and smell experiments had to be scattered through most of the periods, since only a few at a time could be performed without fatigue. The entire series was applied to fifty subjects, twenty-five men and twenty-five women.

The experiments fell into seven groups, dealing respectively with motor ability, skin and muscle senses, taste and smell, hearing, vision, intellectual faculties, and affective processes. One chapter of this monograph is devoted to each group. A list of the experiments under each group will be found at the beginning of each chapter. At the end of each chapter there is a comparison of results with those of other investigators, and a general summary. The numbers in parentheses used in the summaries of other experimental work and throughout the text, refer to the bibliography at the end of the volume. The bibliography pretends to completeness only in its enumeration of the experimental researches bearing on the problem, and even here there are doubtless omissions, although it is hoped that all the important papers are mentioned. Whenever for the sake of brevity a dogmatic statement is made to the effect that there are no data on a certain point, or only such data as are quoted, the qualification, *so far as the author knows*, is to be understood.

The report of each experiment includes a description of the apparatus used, a statement of the method, and a formulation of the results. Since the value of experimental work, and the possibility of comparing one set of results with another depend so largely upon the method, the greatest pains has been taken to secure uniformity, and to describe the method in full in each case. The experiments were all performed by the author, with the exception of a part of the reaction-time tests, which had to be repeated because of a source of error in the apparatus. For these the author is indebted to Dr. W. C. Gore and Mr. H. J. Pearce, of the Graduate School of the University of Chicago.

A few words in general on the methods employed may not be out of place, in spite of the fact that each is described in full in connection with the test. The guiding principle in selecting the method was the desire to make the directions to the subject as clear and simple as possible and at the same time secure the greatest possible accuracy of result. In all the tests on discriminative sensibility this double end seemed best secured by requiring a simple judgment of comparison (i.e., lighter or heavier, more or less cold, etc.) between two stimuli. The subject was told nothing of a standard stimulus, and the order of the standard and stimulus of comparison was varied. The difference in intensity between the standard and the stimulus of comparison was varied until the point was found at which three-fourths of the judgments were correct. In the threshold tests of taste and smell, tasteless and odorless preparations were used to control the threshold illusions. The greatest care was taken to avoid suggestion of all sorts in all the tests. The descriptions of method have been made explicit at the risk of their being perhaps somewhat tedious and needlessly detailed.

The results of the experiments have been presented graphically wherever possible. In all the curves, the dotted line is for women and the unbroken line for men. The ordinates always represent the number of subjects. In no case have the results been averaged. Wherever graphic representation was impracticable, they have been grouped. The purpose of the research was norms, not averages.

Chapter IX Conclusion

In the previous chapters the separate divisions of conscious processes, motor ability, the various sensory fields, intellectual faculties, and the affective processes have been considered single with reference to their comparative development in men and women. We may now bring together the results obtained from the various fields, and ascertain whether or not any broad generalizations with reference to the psychological norms of men and women which can be regarded as of fundamental importance have been reached.

It has been found that motor ability in most of its forms is better developed in men than in women. In strength, rapidity of movement, and rate of fatigue, they have a very decided advantage, and in precision of movement a slight advantage. These four forms of superiority are probably all expressions of one and the same fact – the greater muscular strength of men. In the formation of a new co-ordination women are superior to men. The greater muscular strength of men is a universally accepted fact. There has been more or less dispute as to which sex displays greater manual dexterity. According to the present results, manual dexterity which consists in the ability to make very delicate and minutely controlled movements is slightly greater in men; that which consists in the ability to co-ordinate movements rapidly to unforeseen stimuli is clearly greater in women.

There have been two opposing views on the general subject of the sensibility of the sexes; one assigning the keener senses to men, and the other to women. They have been based either on inadequate experiment in a few fields of sensibility or on general theoretical considerations. The present investigation of the total field of sensibility has resulted in the following conclusions regarding thresholds and discriminative sensibility:

Thresholds. – Women have lower thresholds in the recognition of two points on the skin; in touch; in sweet, salt, sour, and bitter taste; in smell; in color; and in pain through pressure. Men and women are alike in respect to the upper and lower limits of pitch. Men have a lower threshold in the perception of light.

Discriminative sensibility. – Women have finer discrimination in pitch and in color. Men and women have equal discrimination in temperature, in odor, and in passive pressure. Men have finer discrimination in lifted weights; in sweet, sour, and bitter taste; in shades of gray; probably in areas on the skin (the test on this subject does not warrant certainty); and in visual areas.

The number of cases in which the advantage is on the side of the women is greater than the number of cases in which it is on the side of the men. The thresholds are on the whole lower in women; discriminative sensibility is on the whole better in men. Those sensory judgments into which sensations of movement enter directly, such as the discrimination of lifted weights and of visual lines and areas are somewhat better in men. All these differences, however, are slight.

As for the intellectual faculties, women are decidedly superior to men in memory, and possibly more rapid in associative thinking. Men are probably superior in ingenuity. In general information and intellectual interests there is no difference characteristic of sex.

The data on the life of feeling indicate that there is little, if any, sexual difference in the degree of domination by emotion, and that social consciousness is more prominent in men and religious consciousness in women.

Let us now turn to the question how well or how ill these results accord with the prevailing biological view of the mental differences between the sexes.

It is perhaps not fair to speak of a prevailing view in a question regarding which dispute is so rife; but the view which seems to command the adherence of most scientists at present is that advanced by Geddes and Thomson (29). It is worked out in some detail on the psychological side by Fouillée (25); Brooks (10) and Patrick (68) represent the same tendency. The view is not altogether free from contradictions, nor entirely satisfactory in so far as it pretends to be a theory of the evolution of sex. Leaving these points aside, its general tenets are that the differentiation between the sexes in the course of evolution has been in the direction of a sort of division of labor, the male assuming the processes of nutrition and the female those of reproduction, which has made women more anabolic and men more catabolic in physiological structure. This difference is displayed in its most elementary form by the two sexual cells. The female is large and immobile. It represents stored nutrition. The male cell is small

and agile. It represents expenditure of energy. From these fundamental characteristics the social and psychological differences can be deduced. The female represents the conservation of the species – the preservation of past gains made by the race. Her characteristics are continuity, patience, and stability. Her mental life is dominated by integration. She is skilled in particular ideas and in the application of generalizations already obtained, but not in abstraction or the formation of new concepts. Since woman is receptive, she possesses keener senses and more intense reflexes than man. Her tendency to accumulate nutrition brings about a greater development of the viscera, and, since emotions are reflex waves from the viscera, woman is more emotional than man. The male, on the other hand, represents the introduction of new elements. Males are more variable than female throughout the animal kingdom. Everywhere we find the male sex adventurous and inventive. Its variety of ideas and sentiments is greater. Its activities are characterized everywhere by impulsiveness and intensity, rather than by patience and continuity. Men are more capable of intense and prolonged concentration of attention than women. They are less influenced by feeling than women. They have greater powers of abstraction and generalization.

It is evident that, on the surface at least, the results at which we have arrived accord very well with this theory. Men did prove in our experiments to have better-developed motor ability and more ingenuity. Women did have somewhat keener senses and better memory. The assertion that the influence of emotion is greater in the life of women found no confirmation. Their greater tendency toward religious faith, however, and the greater number of superstitions among them, point toward their conservative nature – their function of preserving established beliefs and institutions.

But before we accept the theory advanced as the correct interpretation of the facts, it would be well to examine a little more closely the evidence on which it rests, and consider whether or not there is any other possible interpretation with equal claims to a hearing.

In the first place, this theory, in so far as its deductions about mental characteristics are derived as necessary conclusions from the nature of the genital cells, seems to rest on somewhat far-fetched analogies only. The sets of characteristics deduced for the sexes may be correct, but the method of defying them is not very convincing, nor is the set of characteristics derived for each sex entirely consistent. Women are said to represent concentration, patience, and stability in emotional life. One might logically conclude that prolonged concentration of attention and unbiased generalization would be their intellectual characteristics. But these are the very characteristics assigned to men. Women, though more stable in their emotions, are more influenced by them, and, although they represent patience and concentration, they are incapable of prolonged efforts of attention. Men, whose activity is essentially intermittent, and whose emotions are greater in variety and more unstable, are characterized by prolonged strains of attention and unbiased judgment. It may be true, but the proof for it does not appeal to one as very cogent. In fact, after reading the several expositions of this theory, one is left with a strong impression that, if the authors' views as to the mental differences of sex had been different, they might as easily have derived a very different set of characteristics. There is truth as well as humor in Lourbet's (52, chap. vi) suggestion that, if the nature of the genital cells were reversed, it would be a little easier for this school of evolutionists to derive the characteristics of sex with which they finally come out. In that case, the female cell, smaller and more agile than the male, would represent woman with her smaller size, her excitable nervous system, and her incapacity for sustained effort of attention; while the male cell, large, calm, and self-contained, would image the size and strength, the impartial reason, and the easy concentration of attention of men.

The fact which is put forward to prove the greater natural ingenuity and inventiveness of man is his greater variability. Lombroso, without more ado, asserts that the male is everywhere, and in all respects, more variable than the female, and that this fact alone is sufficient to prove his greater creative ability. The doctrine has been unquestioningly adopted by all the advocates of this theory. It is called upon to explain the occurrence of more individuals of unusual mental capacity, both above and below the norm, as well as to account for the greater versatility and inventiveness of the male mind.

Unfortunately for the theory, the latest researches on the question of variability have failed to sustain it. Pearson (69) subjects the previous methods of measuring variability to criticism, and finds them very faulty. He insists that pathological variations are not a fair test of average variability in the sexes, because many diseases have a tendency to attack one sex rather than the other. The true measure of the variability which must be regarded as important in evolution is, he says, the amount of normal variation found in organs or characteristics not of a secondary sexual character. The variation, however, of any organ must be judged by its relative departure from its mean, not, as has formerly been done, by its absolute variation, or by its variation relatively to some other organ. Taking all the available physical measurements of human beings as a basis for his calculation, Pearson finds the total trend of his observations to be toward a somewhat greater tendency to variation in women than in men. He concludes that "the principle that man is more variable than woman must be put aside as a pseudoscientific superstition until it has been demonstrated in a more scientific manner than has hitherto been attempted."

While it may still prove true that men are intellectually more variable than women, it cannot be deduced directly from the universally greater variability of man. The fact is often held to be proved from the greater prevalence of both genius and imbecility among men, but, as Pearson points out, these are both forms of abnormal variation. It is perfectly conceivable that the class which presented the greatest number of abnormalities in a character might not be the class which displayed the widest normal variations of that character.

But even though it could be shown that men are intellectually more variable than women, it is still difficult to see why this would give a basis for the statement that inventiveness and ability to arrive at new generalizations are characteristic of the male mind as opposed to the female. It would, if true, lead us to expect a greater number of intellectually inferior and of intellectually superior individuals belonging to the male sex. In so far as great originality is characteristic of exceptional mental ability, it would lead us to expect that the greatest discoveries and inventions should come from these exceptional individuals. But that is not at all the same thing as saying that original-ity and inventiveness are characteristic of the male mind as a whole, in opposition to the female mind, as a whole. This statement assumes not merely greater variability of mind in general, but the presence of a variation in a given direction.

The biological theory of psychological differ-ences of sex is not in a condition to compel assent. While it is true, therefore, that the present inves-tigation tends to support the theory, it is just as true that the uncertain basis of the theory itself leaves room for other explanations of the facts, if there are other satisfactory ways of explaining them.

In considering the question whether or not there is any other explanation for the facts in the case, it is important to remember that the make-up of any adult individual cannot be attributed entirely to inherited tendency. The old question of the relative importance of heredity and envi-ronment in the final outcome of the individual must be taken into consideration. Although the timeworn controversy is far from satisfactory settlement, the results of recent observation on individual development have tended to empha-size more and more the extreme importance of environment. The sociological experiments in which very young children from the criminal classes have been placed in good surroundings, with no knowledge of their antecedents, have shown that such children usually develop into good members of society. The entire practical movement of sociology is based on the firm con-viction that an individual is very vitally molded by his surroundings, and that even slight modi-fications may produce important changes in character.

The suggestion that the observed psychologi-cal differences of sex may be due to difference in environment has often been met with derision, but it seems at least worthy of unbiased consid-eration. The fact that very genuine and important differences of environment do exist can be denied only by the most superficial observer. Even in our own country, where boys and girls are allowed to go to the same schools and to play together to some extent, the social atmosphere is different, from the cradle. Different toys are given them, different occupations and games are taught them, different ideals of conduct are held up before them. The question for the moment is not at all

whether or not these differences in education are right and proper and necessary, but merely whether or not, as a matter of fact, they exist, and, if so, what effect they have on the individuals who are subjected to them.

The difference in physical training is very evident. Boys are encouraged in all forms of exer-cise and in out-of-door life, while girls are restricted in physical exercise at a very early age. Only a few forms of exercise are considered lady-like. Rough games and violent exercise of all sorts are discouraged. Girls are kept in the house and taught household occupations. The development of physical strength is not held up to girls as an ideal, while it is made one of the chief ambitions of boys.

While it is improbable that *all* the difference of the sexes with regard to physical strength can be attributed to persistent difference in training, it is certain that a large part of the difference is explicable on this ground. The great strength of savage women and the rapid increase in strength in civilized women, wherever systematic physical training has been introduced, both show the importance of this factor. When we consider other forms of motor ability than mere muscular force, such as quickness of reaction and accuracy of co-ordination, it seems very probable that mere differences of physical training are ample to account for these differences of sex. While it seems to be true that slower rates of movement and decreased accuracy of co-ordination do result from greatly inferior physical strength it is not true that the correlation is quantitatively a close one. Even with wide differences in muscular force, the difference in motor ability is compara-tively slight. Where the differences in strength are slight, we have no reason to expect differences in motor ability on that ground.

When we consider the other important respect in which men are supposed to be superior to women – ingenuity or inventiveness – we find equally important differences in social surround-ings which would tend to bring about this result, Boys are encouraged to individuality. They are trained to be independent in thought and action. This is the ideal of manliness held up before them. They are expected to understand the use of tools and machinery, and encouraged to experi-ment and make things for themselves. Girls are taught obedience, dependence, and deference.

They are made to feel that too much independence of opinion or action is a drawback to them – not becoming or womanly. A boy is made to feel that his success in life, his place in the world, will depend upon his ability to go ahead with his chosen occupation on his own responsibility, and to accomplish something new and valuable. No such social spur is applied to girls. Royce (73) in his article on the psychology of invention says:

> Only heredity can account for the very wide differences between clever men and stupid men, or explain why men of genius exist at all. But the minor and still important inventiveness of the men of talent, the men of the second grade, is somehow due to a social stimulation which sets their habits varying in different directions. And this stimulation is of the type which abounds in periods of individualism. . . . For once more, the primary character of the social influences to which we are exposed is that, within limits, they set us to imitating models; they tend to make us creatures of social routine, slaves of the mob, or obedient servants of the world about us. . . . Inventions thus seem to be the results of the encouragement of individuality.

If one applies these words to the question of the relative inventiveness of the sexes, and realizes the wide differences in social influence which still exist even in a community where women have more freedom and more education than anywhere else in the world, it seems rash to assume that the observed difference in inventiveness represents a genuine and fundamental sexual difference of mind. The fact that the difference revealed by experiment is so slight in men and women whose educations have been as nearly alike as those of students in a co-educational university, tends to throw further doubt on the fundamental importance of this distinction. The very brief period in which women have been given any systematic education, or any freedom of choice in occupation, makes it impossible to decide the question on the basis of previous achievement.

The same social influences which have tended to retard the development of motor ability and of inventiveness in women would tend to develop keenness of sense and the more reproductive mental processes, such as memory. The question is largely one of the distribution of attention. A large part of a boy's attention goes toward his activities – the learning of new movements, the manipulating of tools, the making of contrivances of various sorts. A girl's less active existence must be filled with some other sort of conscious process. The only possibility is that sensory and perceptual processes should be more prominent. In some cases the special training of girls tends directly toward the development of a special sense. This is notably true in color, and perhaps has some influence in taste. On the more purely intellectual level, it is only natural that in the absence of a sufficient social spur toward originality and inventiveness, they should depend more upon memory for their supply of ideas. It is easier for any individual to learn some one else's ideas than to think out his own. Every teacher has to struggle against the tendency to memorize merely, and to endeavor in every way to stimulate original thought and help pupils to form the habit of doing their own thinking. It is no great matter for surprise that in the absence of social stimulus toward originality of thought, women should have tended, from inertia, to stay in the realm of reproductive thinking.

It will probably be said that this view of the case puts the cart before the horse – that the training and social surroundings of the sexes are different because their natural characteristics are different. It will be said that a boy is encouraged to activity because he is naturally active – that he is given tools instead of a doll because he is naturally more interested in tools than in dolls. But there are many indications that these very interests are socially stimulated, A small boy with an older sister and no brothers is very sure to display an ambition to have dolls. It is in most cases quenched early by ridicule, but it is evident that a boy must be taught what occupations are suited to boys. The sorrows of a small girl with brothers because she is not allowed to run and race with the boys and take part in their sports and games have frequently been recounted. If it were really a fundamental difference of instincts and characteristics which determined the difference of training to which the sexes are subjected, it would not be necessary to spend so much effort in making boys and girls follow the lines of conduct proper to their sex. The more probable interpretation of the facts is that the necessities of social organization have in the past brought about a division of labor between the sexes, the usefulness of which is evident. Social ideals have been developed in connection with this economic necessity, and still persist.

This is not the place to discuss the question whether or not the conditions of social organization still demand the same division of labor, and make the preservation of the traditional ideals for the sexes necessary to the good of society. If such is the case, there is no doubt that the present state of affairs will persist. There are, as everyone must recognize, signs of a radical change in the social ideals of sex. The point to be emphasized as the outcome of this study is that, according to our present light, the psychological differences of sex seem to be largely due, not to difference of average capacity, nor to difference in type of mental activity, but to differences in the social influences brought to bear on the developing individual from early infancy to adult years. The question of the future development of the intellectual life of women is one of social necessities and ideals, rather than of the inborn psychological characteristic of sex.

References

10 Brooks, W. K. (1896). Woman from the standpoint of a naturalist. *Forum, 22*, 286.

11 Bryan, W. L. (1892). On the development of voluntary motor ability. *American Journal of Psychology, 5*, 123.

20 Dehn, W. (1894). *Vergleichende Prüfung über den Haut-und Geschmach-Sinn bei Männer und Frauen verschiedener Stände.* Dorpat.

23 Ebbinghaus, H. (1897). Über eine neue Methode zur Prüfung geistiger Fähigkeiten und ihre Anwendung bein Schulkinder. *Zeitschrift für Psychologie und Physiologie, 8*, 401.

25 Fouillée, A. (1895). *Tempérament et caractère selon les individus, les sexes et les races.* Paris.

29 Geddes, P., & Thomson, A. (1889). *The evolution of sex.* London.

51 Lombroso, C. (1893). *La donna delinquente, la prostituta e la donna normale.* Turin & Rome.

52 Lourbet, J. (1896). *La femme devant la science contemporaine.* Paris.

54 MacDonald, A. (1895). Sensibility to pain by pressure in the hands of individuals of different classes, sexes, and nationalities. *American Journal of Psychology, 9*, 621. See also *Psychological Review, 11*, 156.

63 Ottolenghi, S. (1889). Il gusto nei criminali in rapporto coi normali. *Arch. di Psichiat., 10.*

64 Ottolenghi, S. (1888). L'olfatto nei criminali. *Arch. di Psichiat., 9*, 495.

65 Ottolenghi, S. (1895). La sensibilité et l'âge. *Arch. ital. de biol., 24*, 139.

67 Ottolenghi, S. (1898). La sensibilità e la condizione sociale. *Arch. di Psichiat., 19*, 101.

68 Patrick, G. T. W. (1895). The psychology of woman. *Popular Science Monthly, 47*, 209.

69 Pearson, K. (1897). *Variation in man and woman,* Vol. 1. London. See chapter 8.

73 Royce, J. (1898). The psychology of invention. *Psychological Review, 5*, 113.

82 Wissler, C. (1901). The correlation of mental and physical tests. *Monograph Supplement of the Psychological Review,* No. 16.

Social Devices for Impelling Women to Bear and Rear Children
Leta S. Hollingworth

Again, the breeding function of the family would be better discharged if public opinion and religion conspired, as they have until recently, to crush the aspirations of woman for a life of her own. But the gain would not be worth the price.–E. A. Ross, Social Control (1904)

In this quotation from Ross we have suggested to us an exceedingly important and interesting phase of social control, namely, the control by those in social power over those individuals who alone can bring forth the human young, and thus perpetuate society. It is necessary that at the very outset of this discussion we should consent to clear our minds of the sentimental conception of motherhood and to look at facts. Sumner[1] states these facts as well as they have ever been stated, in his consideration of the natural burdens of society. He says:

> Children add to the weight of the struggle for existence of their parents. The relation of parent to child is one of sacrifice. The interests of parents and children are antagonistic. The fact that there are or may be compensations does not affect the primary relation between the two. It may well be believed that, if procreation had not been put under the dominion of a great passion, it would have been caused to cease by the burdens it entails.

This is especially true in the case of the mothers.

The fact is that child-bearing is in many respects analogous to the work of soldiers: it is necessary for tribal or national existence; it means

great sacrifice of personal advantage; it involves danger and suffering, and, in a certain percentage of cases, the actual loss of life. Thus we should expect that there would be a continuous social effort to insure the group-interest in respect to population, just as there is a continuous social effort to insure the defense of the nation in time of war. It is clear, indeed, that the social devices employed to get children born, and to get soldiers slain, are in many respects similar.

But once the young are brought into the world they still must be reared, if society's ends are to be served, and here again the need for and exercise of social control may be seen. Since the period of helpless infancy is very prolonged in the human species, and since the care of infants is an onerous and exacting labor, it would be natural for all persons not biologically attached to infants to use all possible devices for fastening the whole burden of infant-tending upon those who are so attached. We should expect this to happen, and we shall see, in fact, that there has been consistent social effort to establish as a norm the woman whose vocational proclivities are completely and "naturally" satisfied by child-bearing and child-rearing, with the related domestic activities.

There is, to be sure, a strong and fervid insistence on the "maternal instinct," which is popularly supposed to characterize all women equally, and to furnish them with an all-consuming desire for parenthood, regardless of the personal pain, sacrifice, and disadvantage involved. In the absence of all verifiable data, however, it is only common-sense to guard against accepting as a fact of human nature a doctrine which we might well expect to find in use as a means of social control. Since we possess no scientific data at all on this phase of human psychology, the most reasonable assumption is that if it were possible

Appeared originally in *American Journal of Sociology*, 1916, *22*, 19–29.

to obtain a quantitative measurement of maternal instinct, we should find this trait distributed among women, just as we have found all other traits distributed which have yielded to quantitative measurement. It is most reasonable to assume that we should obtain a curve of distribution, varying from an extreme where individuals have a zero or negative interest in caring for infants, through a mode where there is a moderate amount of impulse to such duties, to an extreme where the only vocational or personal interest lies in maternal activities.

The facts, shorn of sentiment, then, are: (1) The bearing and rearing of children is necessary for tribal or national existence and aggrandizement. (2) The bearing and rearing of children is painful, dangerous to life, and involves long years of exacting labor and self-sacrifice. (3) There is no verifiable evidence to show that a maternal instinct exists in women of such all-consuming strength and fervor as to impel them voluntarily to seek the pain, danger, and exacting labor involved in maintaining a high birth rate.

We should expect, therefore, that those in control of society would invent and employ devices for impelling women to maintain a birth rate sufficient to insure enough increase in the population to offset the wastage of war and disease. It is the purpose of this paper to cite specific illustrations to show just how the various social institutions have been brought to bear on women to this end. Ross has classified the means which society takes and has taken to secure order, and insure that individuals will act in such a way as to promote the interests of the group, *as those interests are conceived by those who form "the radiant points of social control."* These means, according to the analysis of Ross, are public opinion, law, belief, social suggestion, education, custom, social religion, personal ideals.... (the type), art, personality, enlightenment, illusion, and social valuation. Let us see how some of these means have been applied in the control of women.

Personal Ideals (the Type)

The first means of control to which I wish to call attention in the present connection is that which Ross calls "personal ideals." It is pointed out that "a developed society presents itself as a system of unlike individuals, strenuously pursuing their personal ends." Now, for each person there is a "certain zone of requirement," and since "altruism is quite incompetent to hold each unswervingly to the particular activities and forbearances belonging to his place in the social system," the development of such allegiance must be –

> effected by means of types or patterns, which society induces its members to adopt as their guiding ideals.... To this end are elaborated various patterns of conduct and of character, which may be termed social types. These types may become in the course of time personal ideals, each for that category of persons for which it is intended.

For women, obviously enough, the first and most primitive "zone of requirement" is and has been to produce and rear families large enough to admit of national warfare being carried on, and of colonization.

Thus has been evolved the social type of the "womanly woman," "the normal woman," the chief criterion of normality being a willingness to engage enthusiastically in maternal and allied activities. All those classes and professions which form "the radiant points of social control" unite upon this criterion. Men of science announce it with calm assurance (though failing to say on what kind or amount of scientific data they base their remarks). For instance, McDougall[2] writes:

> The highest stage is reached by those species in which each female produces at birth but one or two young, and protects them so efficiently that most of the young born reach maturity; the maintenance of the species thus becomes in the main the work of the parental instinct. In such species the protection and cherishing of the young is the constant and all-absorbing occupation of the mother, to which she devotes all her energies, and in the course of which she will at anytime undergo privation, pain, and death. The instinct (maternal instinct) becomes more powerful than any other, and can override any other, even fear itself.

Professor Jastrow[3] writes:

> ... *charm* is the technique of the maiden, and *sacrifice* the passion of the mother. One set of feminine interests expresses more distinctly the issues of courtship and attraction; the other of qualities of motherhood and devotion.

The medical profession insistently proclaims desire for numerous children as the criterion of normality for women, scornfully branding those so ill-advised as to deny such desires as "abnormal." As one example among thousands of such attempts at social control let me quote the following, which appeared in a New York newspaper on November 29, 1915:

> Only abnormal women want no babies. Trenchant criticism of modern life was made by Dr. Max G. Schlapp, internationally known as a neurologist. Dr. Schlapp addressed his remarks to the congregation of the Park Avenue M. E. Church. He said, "The birth rate is falling off. Rich people are the ones who have no children, and the poor have the greatest number of offspring. Any woman who does not desire offspring is abnormal. We have a large number, particularly among the women, who do not want children. Our social society is becoming intensely unstable."

And this from the *New York Times*, September 5, 1915: "Normally woman lives through her children; man lives through his work." Scores of such implicit attempts to determine and present the type or norm meet us on every hand. This norm has the sanction of authority, being announced by men of greatest prestige in the community. No one wishes to be regarded by her fellow-creatures as "abnormal" or "decayed." The stream of suggestions playing from all points inevitably has its influence, so that it is or was, until recently, well-nigh impossible to find a married woman who would admit any conflicting interests equal or paramount to the interest of caring for children. There is a universal refusal to admit that the maternal instinct, like every other trait of human nature, might be distributed according to the probability curve.

Public Opinion

Let us turn next to public opinion as a means of control over women in relation to the birth rate. In speaking of public opinion Ross says:

> Haman is at the mercy of Mordecai. Rarely can one regard his deed as fair when others find it foul, or count himself a hero when the world deems him a wretch ... For the mass of men the blame and the praise of the community are the very lords of life.

If we inquire now what are the organs or media of expression of public opinion we shall see how it is brought to bear on women. The newspapers are perhaps the chief agents, in modern times, in the formation of public opinion, and their colunms abound in interviews with the eminent, deploring the decay of the population. Magazines print articles based on statistics of depopulation, appealing to the patriotism of women. In the year just passed fifty-five articles on the birth rate have chanced to come to the notice of the present writer. Fifty-four were written by men, including editors, statesmen, educators, ex-presidents, etc. Only one was written by a woman. The following quotation is illustrative of the trend of all of them:

> M. Emil Reymond has made this melancholy announcement in the Senate: "We are living in an age when women have pronounced upon themselves a judgment that is dangerous in the highest degree to the development of the population. ... We have the right to do what we will with the life that is in us, say they."
>
> Thus the desire for the development of interests and aptitudes other than the maternal is stigmatized as "dangerous," "melancholy," "degrading," "abnormal," "indicative of decay." On the other hand, excessive maternity receives many cheap but effective rewards. For example, the Jesuit priests hold special meetings to laud maternity. The German Kaiser announces that he will now be godfather to seventh, eighth, and ninth sons, even if daughters intervene. The ex-President has written a letter of congratulation to the mother of nine.

Law

Since its beginning as a human institution law has been a powerful instrument for the control of women. The subjection of women was originally an irrational consequence of sex differences in reproductive function. It was not *intended* by either men or women, but simply resulted from the natural physiological handicaps of women, and the attempts of humanity to adapt itself to physiological nature through the crude methods of trial and error. When law was formulated, this subjection was defined, and thus furthered. It would take too long to cite all the legal provisions that contribute, indirectly, to keep women from developing individualistic interests and capacities. Among the most important indirect forces in law which affect women to keep them child-bearers and child-rearers only are those provisions that tend to restrain them from possessing and controlling property, such provisions have made of women a comparatively possessionless class, and have thus deprived them of the fundamentals of power. While affirming the essential nature of woman to be satisfied with maternity and with maternal duties only, society has always taken every precaution to close the avenues to ways of escape therefrom.

Two legal provisions which bear directly on women to compel them to keep up the birth rate may be mentioned here. The first of these is the provision whereby sterility in the wife may be made a cause of divorce. This would be a powerful inducement to women who loved their husbands to bear children if they could. The second provision is that which forbids the communication of the data of science in the matter of the means of birth control. The American laws are very drastic on this point. Recently in New York City a man was sentenced to prison for violating this law.

The more advanced democratic nations have ceased to practice military conscription, they no longer conscript their men to bear arms, depending on the volunteer army. But they conscript their women to bear children by legally prohibiting the publication or communication of the knowledge which would make child-bearing voluntary.

Child-rearing is also legally insured by those provisions which forbid and punish abortion, infanticide, and infant desertion. There could be no better proof of the insufficiency of maternal instinct as a guaranty of population than the drastic laws which we have against birth control, abortion, infanticide, and infant desertion.

Belief

Belief, "which controls the hidden portions of life," has been used powerfully in the interests of population. Orthodox women, for example, regard family limitation as a sin, punishable in the hereafter. Few explicit exhortations concerning the birth rate are discoverable in the various "Words" of God. The belief that family limitation will be punished in the hereafter seems to have been evolved mainly by priests out of the slender materials of a few quotations from Holy Writ, such as "God said unto them, 'Multiply and replenish the earth,'" and from the scriptural allusion to children as the gifts of God. Being gifts from God, it follows that they may not be refused except at the peril of incurring God's displeasure.

Education

The education of women has always, until the end of the nineteenth century, been limited to such matters as would become a creature who could and should have no aspirations for a life of her own. We find the proper education for girls outlined in the writings of such educators as Rousseau, Fénelon, St. Jerome, and in Godey's *Lady's Book*. Not only have the "social guardians" used education as a negative means of control, by failing to provide any real enlightenment for women, but education has been made a positive instrument for control. This was accomplished by drilling into the young and unformed mind, while yet it was too immature to reason independently, such facts and notions as would give the girl a conception of herself only as future wife and mother. Rousseau, for instance, demanded freedom and individual liberty of development for everybody except Sophia, who was to be deliberately trained up as a means to an end. In the latter half of the nineteenth century when the hard battle for the real enlightenment of women was being fought, one of the most frequently recurring objections to admitting women to knowledge was that "the population would suffer," "the essential nature of woman would be changed," "the family would decay," and "the birth rate would fall." Those in control of society yielded up the old prescribed education of women only after a stubborn struggle, realizing that with the passing of the old training an important means of social control was slipping out of their bands.

Art

A very long paper might be written to describe the various uses to which art has been put in holding up the ideal of motherhood; The mother, with children at her breast, is the favorite theme of artists. The galleries of Europe are hung full of Madonnas of every age and degree. Poetry abounds in allusions to the sacredness and charm of motherhood, depicting the yearning of the adult for his mother's knee. Fiction is replete with happy and adoring mothers. Thousands of songs are written and sung concerning the ideal relation which exists between mother and child. In pursuing the mother-child theme through art one would not be led to suspect that society finds it necessary to make laws against contraconception, infanticide, abortion, and infant desertion. Art holds up to view only the compensations of motherhood, leaving the other half of the theme in obscurity, and thus acting as a subtle ally of population.

Illusion

This is the last of Ross's categories to which I wish to refer. Ross says:

> In the taming of men there must be provided coil after coil to entangle the unruly one. Mankind must use snares as well as leading-strings, will-o-the-wisps as well as lanterns. The truth by all means, if it will promote obedience, but in any case obedience! We shall examine not creeds

now, but the films, veils, hidden mirrors, and half lights by which men are duped as to that which lies nearest them, their own experience. This time we shall see men led captive, not by dogmas concerning a world beyond experience, but by artfully fostered misconceptions of the pains, satisfactions, and values lying under their very noses.

One of the most effective ways of creating the desired illusion about any matter is by concealing and tabooing the mention of all the painful and disagreeable circumstances connected with it. Thus there is a very stern social taboo on conversation about the processes of birth. The utmost care is taken to conceal the agonies and risks of child-birth from the young. Announcement is rarely made of the true cause of deaths from child-birth. The statistics of maternal mortality have been neglected by departments of health, and the few compilations which have been made have not achieved any wide publicity or popular discussion. Says Katharine Anthony, in her recent book on *Feminism in Germany and Scandinavia* (1915):

> There is no evidence that the death rate of women from child-birth has caused the governing classes many sleepless nights.

Anthony gives some statistics from Prussia (where the figures have been calculated), showing that

> between 1891 and 1900 11 per cent of the deaths of all women between the age of twenty-five and forty years occurred in child-birth. . . . During forty years of peace Germany lost 400,000 mothers' lives, that is, ten times what she lost in soldiers' lives in the campaign of 1870 and 1871.

Such facts would be of wide public interest, especially to women, yet there is no tendency at all to spread them broadcast or to make propaganda of them. Public attention is constantly being called to the statistics of infant mortality, but the statistics of maternal mortality are neglected and suppressed.

The pains, the dangers, and risks of child-bearing are tabooed as subjects of conversation. The drudgery, the monotonous labor and other

disagreeable features of child-rearing are minimized by "the social guardians." On the other
hand, the joys and compensations of motherhood are magnified and presented to consciousness on every hand. Thus the tendency is to create
an illusion whereby motherhood will appear to
consist of compensations only and thus come
to be desired by those for whom the illusion is
intended.

There is one further class of devices for
controlling women that does not seem to fit any
of the categories mentioned by Ross. I refer to
threats of evil consequence to those who refrain
from child-bearing. This class of social devices I
shall call "*bugaboos.*" Medical men have done
much to help population (and at the same time
to increase obstetrical practice!) by inventing
bugaboos. For example, it is frequently stated by
medical men, and is quite generally believed by
women, that if first child-birth is delayed until the
age of thirty years the pains and dangers of the
process will be very gravely increased, and that
therefore women will find it advantageous to
begin bearing children early in life. It is added
that the younger the woman begins to bear the
less suffering will be experienced. One looks in
vain, however, for any objective evidence that
such is the case. The statements appear to be
founded on no array of facts whatever, and until
they are so founded they lie under the suspicion
of being merely devices for social control.

One also reads that women who bear children
live longer on the average than those who do not,
which is taken to mean that child-bearing has a
favorable influence on longevity. It may well be
that women who bear many children live longer
than those who do not, but the only implication
probably is that those women who could not
endure the strain of repeated births died young,
and thus naturally did not have many children.
The facts may indeed be as above stated, and yet
child-bearing may be distinctly prejudicial to
longevity.

A third bugaboo is that if a child is reared
alone, without brothers and sisters, he will grow
up selfish, egoistic, and an undesirable citizen.
Figures are, however, so far lacking to show the
disastrous consequences of being an only child.

From these brief instances it seems very
clear that "the social guardians" have not really
believed that maternal instinct is alone a suffi-

cient guaranty of population. They have made
use of all possible social devices to insure not only
child-bearing, but child-rearing. Belief, law,
public opinion, illusion, education, art, and bugaboos have all been used to re-enforce maternal
instinct. We shall never know just how much
maternal instinct alone will do for population
until all the forces and influences exemplified
above have become inoperative. As soon as
women become fully conscious of the fact that
they have been and are controlled by these devices
the latter will become useless, and we shall get a
truer measure of maternal feeling.

One who learns why society is urging him into
the straight and narrow way will resist its pressure. One who sees clearly how he is controlled
will thenceforth be emancipated. To betray the
secrets of ascendancy is to forearm the individual
in his struggle with society.

The time is coming, and is indeed almost at
hand, when all the most intelligent women of the
community, who are the most desirable child-
bearers, will become conscious of the methods of
social control. The type of normality will be questioned; the laws will be repealed and changed;
enlightenment will prevail; belief will be seen to
rest upon dogmas; illusion will fade away and
give place to clearness of view; the bugaboos will
lose their power to frighten. How will "the social
guardians" induce women to bear a surplus population when all these cheap, effective methods
no longer work?

The natural desire for children may, and probably will, always guarantee a stationary population, even if child-bearing should become a
voluntary matter. But if a surplus population is
desired for national aggrandizement, it would
seem that there will remain but one effective
social device whereby this can be secured, namely,
adequate compensation, either in money or in
fame. If it were possible to become rich or famous
by bearing numerous fine children, many a
woman would no doubt be eager to bring up
eight or ten, though if acting at the dictation of
maternal instinct only, she would have brought
up but one or two. When the cheap devices no
longer work, we shall expect expensive devices to
replace them, if the same result is still desired by
the governors of society.

If these matters could be clearly raised to consciousness, so that this aspect of human life could

be managed rationally, instead of irrationally as at present, the social gain would be enormous – assuming always that the increased happiness and usefulness of women would, in general, be regarded as social gain.

Notes

1 W. G. Sumner, *Folkways*, 1906.
2 W. McDougall, *Social Psychology*, 1908.

3 J. Jastrow, *Character and Temperament*, 1915.

The First Generation of Women Psychologists and the Psychology of Women
Katharine S. Milar

Between the beginning and the end of the 19th century, enormous gains were made in the education of women. Under the leadership of pioneers such as Emma Willard and Mary Lyon, first a rigorous secondary education and then a collegiate-level education became available to women. With the founding of Vassar College in 1865, full four-year collegiate education for women was finally accomplished more than 200 years after both Harvard University and the College of William and Mary had begun offering college degrees to men (Rossiter, 1982; Solomon, 1985). Although the justification for the higher education of women was embedded in the notion of *republican motherhood* – that is, better educated women would be better wives and mothers and raise better sons for the republic – the women who pursued this new college education had other ideas, and, as graduate education began to become available, many of them began very quickly to aspire to advanced degrees (Rossiter, 1982).

At about the same time these major advances in women's education were occurring, psychology was becoming established as an academic discipline. Recruiting and training more psychologists was an important part of establishing the academic credentials of the new science. Between 1892 and 1904, over 100 psychology doctorates were awarded, and for the five-year period between 1898 and 1903, psychology ranked fourth among the sciences in doctorate production (Camfield, 1973; Napoli, 1981). Some of these new doctors of philosophy were women; in fact, psychology was among the most hospitable

of the sciences in opening graduate study to women (Rossiter, 1982). Elizabeth Scarborough and Laurel Furumoto (1987) have suggested that the admission of women to graduate programs in psychology was an advantage for the discipline because women could "swell the numbers and generate studies that would establish the legitimacy of the new science" (p. 136). The picture was not entirely rosy: A number of women who pursued graduate study in psychology were not awarded the degree, among them Mary Whiton Calkins and Lillien Jane Martin. However, women with and without the formal doctoral degree were nevertheless admitted to the professional ranks through election to membership in the American Psychological Association (APA). Eight women were elected by 1900; the first to be elected were Calkins and Christine Ladd-Franklin in 1893, the year after the founding of the association (Scarborough, 1992).

Furumoto and Scarborough have sketched the collective portrait of this "first generation" of American women psychologists (Furumoto & Scarborough, 1986; Scarborough & Furumoto 1987). They identified 25 women who had entered the field by 1906, as evidenced either through their listing as psychologists in the first edition of *American Men of Science* (Cattell, 1906) or through their election to membership in APA. Because the collective biography and a number of beautifully detailed individual sketches of these women have been provided by these authors (e.g., Furumoto, 1980, 1992; Goodman, 1980), to avoid repetition I instead examine the way in which some members of this cohort exerted their personal and professional influence in addressing the question of the psychological characteristics and proper social and professional roles of women.

By the time APA was founded in 1892, some 20 psychology laboratories were operating, but

American Psychologist, 2000, 55(6), 616–619. Copyright 2000 by the American Psychological Association, Inc. Reprinted by permission of the publisher and author.

the emphasis of the American model differed somewhat from the German laboratories' emphasis on the normal human adult male mind. As Sokal (1992) has asserted, "From the start . . . this science [of American psychology] was functionally oriented and deeply concerned with development – especially with individual differences" (p. 46). The study of individual differences logically included the question of sex differences.

In one of the earliest comparisons of sex differences, Joseph Jastrow (1891) examined "the unconscious and natural mental processes" (p. 559) of his students at the University of Wisconsin by having them write a list of 100 words as rapidly as possible. His report that women produced lists with much less variety than those of men was consistent with views of the period that men were the more variable sex in both physical and mental characteristics. Greater variability was viewed as a positive trait, because it was seen as the mechanism for evolutionary progress (see Shields, 1975, for discussion). Jastrow's findings were challenged by Mary Whiton Calkins (1896; Nevers & Calkins, 1895), whose sample of Wellesley women showed no such lack of originality in word production. Calkins criticized Jastrow and sexologist Havelock Ellis, suggesting that their attempts to characterize a "masculine and feminine intellect . . . [seemed] futile and impossible because of our entire inability to eliminate the effect of environment" (Calkins, 1896, p. 430).

Helen Bradford Thompson was the first psychologist to undertake an extensive and systematic experimental examination of the psychological characteristics of the sexes. Her dissertation, completed at the University of Chicago in 1900 and later published as *The Mental Traits of Sex* (1903), was an analysis of the performance of 25 women and 25 men on tests of motor ability, sensations, intellect, and affect. Careful, detailed analysis of the results led to her conclusion that,

The psychological differences of sex seem to be largely due, not to difference of average capacity, nor to difference in type of mental activity, but to differences in the social influences brought to bear on the developing individual from early infancy to adult years. (Thompson, 1903, p. 182)

Her later review of the literature on sex differences written under her married name, Helen Thompson Woolley, was sharply critical of authors such as Havelock Ellis, asserting.

There is perhaps no field aspiring to be scientific where flagrant personal bias, logic martyred in the cause of supporting a prejudice, unfounded assertions, and even sentimental rot and drivel, have run riot to such an extent as here. (Woolley, 1910, p. 340)

Despite the publication of Thompson's research and the increasing numbers of women attending college, the debate about the advisability of higher education for women had not been quieted. Psychologists were called on to join in the debate. The aspiration of the founders to establish the scientific and professional status of their fledgling discipline generated an interest in proving psychology's practical value as well (Camfield, 1973; Sokal, 1992). Beginning in 1896, much of early clinical practice was directed at children with learning problems (Fagan, 1992; Witmer, 1907/1996). The exploration of individual adjustment to education led naturally to the question of whether education needed to be different for men and women either because of inherent intellectual differences or because different education was needed for differing social roles.

One psychologist who argued that the differing biological roles of women and men demanded segregated education was G. Stanley Hall. In his book *Adolescence* (1904/1937), Hall proffered the view that appropriate roles for women were those of wives and mothers. The notion promoted in 1873 by Edward Clarke, that higher education for women would jeopardize their reproductive capacity and threaten the future of the species, was wholeheartedly endorsed by Hall, who became one of the leaders of an anticoeducation movement in the 1900s (Diehl, 1986).

Hall used data gathered by psychologist Millicent Shinn (who had earned her doctorate of philosophy at the University of California, Berkeley, in 1898) on marriage rates of college-educated women to bolster his claim that higher education was hazardous for the female sex. In summarizing Shinn's report on the substantially lower marriage rates of members of the Association of Collegiate Alumnae (ACA), Hall accurately reported some of her data but not the qualifications she placed on that data nor her conclusions. In asking why the marriage figures were lower for college-educated women, Shinn first pointed to the youthfulness of the women in the sample: Nearly 50% were recent graduates still in their 20s. Many alumnae were resident teachers in girls' schools, an occupation Shinn characterized as second only to the life of a nun as a cause for celibacy. Beyond this, she provided two additional reasons: The college-educated woman had higher standards for a marriage partner and, because she had the training necessary to support herself, was under less pressure to accept a partner who did not meet those standards. Shinn also admitted, "I have no doubt that . . . many men dislike intellectual women, – whether because such women are really disagreeable or because men's taste is at fault, I shall not try to determine" (Shinn, 1895, p. 948).

Hall's vision of appropriate education for women incorporated not only evolutionary biology and psychology but also religion:

> Biological psychology already dreams of a new philosophy of sex which places the wife and mother at the heart of a new world and makes her the object of a new religion and almost of a new worship. (Hall, 1904/1937, p. 562)

Kate Gordon (who had earned her doctorate of philosophy at the University of Chicago in 1903) scoffed at Hall's notions of making women religious objects in a speech given in 1905: "This attitude toward women did very well in the Middle Ages, but, to tell the truth, the modern woman is made a little bit ill by the incense" (Gordon, 1905, p. 790). Gordon characterized Hall's work as too "bizarre" to be literature and too "uncritical in method" to be considered science (p. 790).

Gordon separated what she termed the social question, "Should a woman's school and college training be in any sense a matrimonial education?" and the psychological question, "When pursuing the same subject that a man is, must she be taught by a different method?" (Gordon, 1905, p. 790). Basing her argument in part on Helen Bradford Thompson's dissertation research, which Hall had dismissed as "feministic," Gordon repudiated the idea that men and women required different methods of instruction:

> There is an old superstition that women's minds work by feeling and men's by reason. Surely it is time to give that up. Does a woman solve the binomial theorem by feeling, or a quadratic equation by intuition? Does [a man] appreciate a sonnet by logical deduction? (p. 793)

To Hall's and others' claim that coeducation would coarsen women and make men effeminate, Gordon responded that if they were fit to marry each other, they were certainly fit to go to school together (Gordon, 1905, p. 794).

On the question of designing a woman's education for marriage, Gordon argued that because marriage was only one of many possible occupations for a woman, to educate her only for a domestic career would unfairly limit her freedom of choice. Further, a woman's "social equality with men is conditioned by her ability to do the same work, and this ability is largely dependent upon her having the same school and college training which a man has" (Gordon, 1905, p. 793).

Kate Gordon's argument for social and educational equality for men and women would have been heartily endorsed by fellow psychologist Christine Ladd-Franklin, who had been engaged for some time in promoting the entry of more women into the professorial ranks. In 1878, Ladd-Franklin applied for admission to graduate study at Johns Hopkins University and was admitted as a special student. Her work at Hopkins was sufficiently distinguished to merit the award of a stipend in 1879 that was renewed yearly thereafter, but the stipend was recorded only in a note to avoid setting any precedent with regard to the admission of women (Furumoto, 1992; Hurvich, 1971). She completed work for the degree in 1882, but because of the university's policy she did not receive her doctorate until 1926, when it was finally awarded to the 79-year-old psychologist as part of the celebration of the 50th anniversary of the university (Rossiter, 1982).

Perhaps partly in response to her experience, Ladd-Franklin was one of the prime movers behind the ACA's establishment of a European fellowship to provide American college women with an opportunity to spend a postgraduate year studying in Europe. The fellowship was designed to give women the opportunity to do postgraduate research that would lead to their being hired to teach at the college level – and not just at women's colleges but at men's colleges and coeducational institutions. Ladd-Franklin argued that increasing the numbers of women teaching at the college level would have an important psychological effect, improving the status and salaries of women teaching at the lower levels: "As long as women are thought to be not worthy of being college professors, it will be impossible for them to receive equal pay with men in the secondary schools" (Ladd-Franklin, 1890, p. 4).

By 1904, Ladd-Franklin was pressing the ACA to establish special endowed professorships for women. She noted that the doctoral degree or an equivalent course of study was now being required for college professorships, and that although women were earning the degree, they were not being hired for academic positions "in proportion to their attainments" (Ladd-Franklin, 1904, p. 54). Her argument was valid. Comparison of the first generation of women psychologists with their male counterparts showed that 65% of the men but only 50% of the women had professorial rank. All of the women who held professorial rank were single and were teaching predominantly in women's colleges. Among this cohort, only Lillien Jane Martin held the position of full professor at a coeducational institution: She was promoted to that rank at Stanford University in 1911 (Furumoto & Scarborough, 1986).

In 1907, Ladd-Franklin successfully secured the funds for what became known as the Berliner Fellowship of the ACA. The recipient received a salary to pursue her research at the college or university of her choice. The university only had to permit her to give a series of lectures during the year she was in residence. Ladd-Franklin assumed that once women had demonstrated their ability to give lectures to coeducational classrooms, the universities would want to retain them and hire other qualified women:

All we ask for our sex is that positions in colleges to which women are admitted as students should be filled . . . by the brilliant and the distinguished among existing Doctors of Philosophy without regard to sex, or with very little regard to sex – with the understanding that whenever the

woman applicant for the position is distinctly superior to the man she shall have the position. (Ladd-Franklin, 1908, p. 144)

Ladd-Franklin herself held the title of lecturer at Columbia University, but it was an unpaid position. In a 1917 letter to a colleague she resentfully reported that she had never refused a salary, but "lacking a better option, had offered to lecture for nothing" (cited in Furumoto, 1992, p. 180).

Despite such fellowships and the activism of women like Gordon and Ladd-Franklin, women who found academic employment were segregated primarily to women's colleges and to the lower academic ranks. Married women, like Ladd-Franklin, were doubly disadvantaged: Women's colleges would hire only single women. In a 1897 letter to Ladd-Franklin, Helen Ridgely wrote that a woman "ought to be taught that she cannot serve two masters, that if she chooses the higher path of learning and wants to do herself and her sex justice, she must forgo matrimony" (cited in Scarborough & Furumoto, 1987, p. 71). This dilemma faced Ethel Puffer, who had graduated from Smith College in 1891 and completed her doctoral work with Hugo Münsterberg at Harvard in 1898, supported by an ACA American fellowship. Like Johns Hopkins, Harvard did not grant degrees to women, but Puffer accepted a Radcliffe doctorate in 1902; Mary Whiton Calkins, who completed her doctoral work at Harvard in 1895, declined the Radcliffe degree (Furumoto, 1980). When Puffer married Benjamin Howes in 1908, she forfeited her chance for an academic position at Barnard, and she struggled the rest of her life with the marriage–career dilemma. She found making time for scholarship while managing a home a difficult task. Puffer Howes wrote later that it was not only the job discrimination but the lack of "the possibility of mental concentration, of long-sustained intensive application, of freedom from irrelevant cares and interruptions" that marriage brought to the woman professional and that prevented her from achieving career success (Howes, 1922, p. 446). Her attempt in the 1920s to establish programs for women to help them manage marriage, motherhood, and professional activities did not succeed (Scarborough & Furumoto, 1987).

Psychology's first generation of women professionals made its presence felt in a number of ways. These women conducted research that challenged prevailing notions of sex differences in psychological characteristics. They used their knowledge as women and as psychologists to press for equal educational and professional opportunities for women. Professional careers for psychologists were almost exclusively found in academia until after World War I. Despite their efforts, women psychologists continued to experience difficulty in obtaining academic positions except in women's colleges. For this reason, as the 20th century marched onward, more and more women were to move into the burgeoning area of applied psychology, which was to have consequences for both their status within the profession and the status of some applied areas of the profession (Furumoto, 1987; Napoli, 1981).

References

Calkins, M. W. (1896). Community of ideas of men and women. *Psychological Review, 3*, 426–430.

Camfield, T. M. (1973). The professionalization of American psychology, 1870–1917. *Journal of the History of the Behavioral Sciences, 9*, 66–75.

Cattell, J. M. (Ed.). (1906). *American men of science: A biographical directory.* New York: Science Press.

Diehl, L. A. (1986). The paradox of G. Stanley Hall: Foe of coeducation and educator of women. *American Psychologist, 41*, 868–878.

Fagan, T. K. (1992). Compulsory schooling, child study, clinical psychology, and special education: Origins of school psychology. *American Psychologist, 47*, 236–243.

Furumoto, L. (1980). Mary Whiton Calkins (1863–1930). *Psychology of Women Quarterly, 5*, 55–68.

Furumoto, L. (1987). On the margins: Women and the professionalization of psychology in the United States, 1890–1940. In M. G. Ash & W. R. Woodward (Eds.), *Psychology in twentieth-century thought and society* (pp. 93–113). Cambridge, England: Cambridge University Press.

Furumoto, L. (1992). Joining separate spheres – Christine Ladd-Franklin, woman – scientist (1847–1930). *American Psychologist, 47*, 175–182.

Furumoto, L., & Scarborough, E. (1986). Placing women in the history of psychology. *American Psychologist, 41*, 35–42.

Goodman, E. S. (1980). Margaret F. Washburn (1871–1939): First woman Ph.D. in psychology. *Psychology of Women Quarterly, 5*, 69–80.

Gordon, K. (1905). Wherein should the education of a woman differ from that of a man. *School Review, 13*, 789–794.

Hall, G. S. (1937). *Adolescence* (Vol. 2). New York: Appleton-Century-Crofts. (Original work published 1904).

Howes, E. P. (1922, April). "Accepting the universe." *Atlantic Monthly, 129*, 444–453.

Hurvich, D. J. (1971). Christine Ladd-Franklin. In E. T. James, J. W. James, & P. S. Boyer (Eds.), *Notable American women, 1607–1950* (Vol. 2, pp. 354–356). New York: Belknap Press.

Jastrow, J. (1891). A study in mental statistics. *The New Review, 5*, 559–568.

Ladd-Franklin, C. (1890). The usefulness of fellowships. *Publications of the Association of Collegiate Alumnae Series II*(31), 1–4.

Ladd-Franklin, C. (1904, February). Endowed professorships for women. *Publications of the Association of Collegiate Alumnae, Series III*(a), 53–61.

Ladd-Franklin, C. (1908, February). Report of the committee on the endowment of fellowships. *Publications of the Association of Collegiate Alumnae, Series III*(17), 143–146.

Napoli, D. S. (1981). *Architects of adjustment: The history of the psychological profession in the United States.* Port Washington, NY: Kennikat Press.

Nevers, C. C., & Calkins, M. W. (1895). Wellesley College psychological studies: Dr. Jastrow on community of ideas of men and women. *Psychological Review, 2*, 363–367.

Rossiter, M. (1982). *Women scientists in America: Struggles and stategies to 1940.* Baltimore: Johns Hopkins University Press.

Scarborough, E. (1992). Women in the American Psychological Association. In R. B. Evans, V. S. Sexton, & T. C. Cadwallader (Eds.), *The American Psychological Association: A historical perspective* (pp. 303–325). Washington, DC: American Psychological Association.

Scarborough, E., & Furumoto, L. (1987). *Untold lives: The first generation of American women psychologists.* New York: Columbia University Press.

Shields, S. A. (1975). Functionalism, Darwinism, and the psychology of women. *American Psychologist, 30*, 739–754.

Shinn, M. W. (1895). The marriage rate of college women. *Century Magazine, 28*, 946–948.

Sokal, M. M. (1992). Origins and early years of the American Psychological Association: 1890 to 1906. In R. B. Evans, V. S. Sexton, & T. C. Cadwallader (Eds.), *The American Psychological Association: A historical perspective* (pp. 43–71). Washington, DC: American Psychological Association.

Solomon, B. (1985). *In the company of educated women.* New Haven, CT: Yale University Press.

Thompson, H. B. (1903). *The mental traits of sex.* Chicago: University of Chicago Press.

Witmer, L. (1996). Clinical psychology. *American Psychologist, 51,* 248–251. (Original work published 1907)

Woolley, H. T. (1910). A review of recent literature on the psychology of sex. *Psychological Bulletin, 7,* 335–342.

Chapter 11

Cognitive Psychology

When John Watson delivered his behaviorist manifesto in New York City in February 1913, it was his intention to bury the psychology of James and Titchener and anyone else who believed psychology was about the mind. Recall his quite clear directive: "The time seems to have come when psychology must discard all reference to consciousness, when it need no longer delude itself into thinking that it is making mental states the object of observation" (Watson, 1913, p. 164). For Titchener, psychology was all about mental states – sensations, images, feelings. And for James too, there was no doubt about where he stood. After 12 years of work on his magnum opus, his *Principles of Psychology* began with the following line: "Psychology is the Science of Mental Life" (1890, Vol. 1, p. 1). You have read in Chapter 8, especially in the article by Franz Samelson (1981), that the banishment of the mind was slow in coming but eventually behaviorism won the battle. In truth, the investigation of cognitive processes, for example sensation and perception, did not disappear. But they no longer dominated as they had in the psychologies of Wundt and Titchener. American psychology's definition had changed from consciousness to behavior, and it would remain so until the 1960s (see Leahey, 1992b). The words "consciousness" and "mind" largely dropped from the vocabularies of psychologists eager to talk the talk of the new order. But it was more than just talk; it was a belief that a focus on behavior would ensure psychology's success as a science.

Cognitive psychology today includes all those areas that involve cognitive or mental processes. It includes, for example, sensation, perception, attention, learning, memory, thinking, problem solving, language, emotion, and dreaming. All of those topics existed in the beginning of the science of psychology. Sensation and perception dominated Wundt's laboratories, with over half of the studies at Leipzig concerning those subjects. But Wundt's laboratory also investigated attention, memory, thinking, and emotion. As scientific psychology spread rapidly to other German universities, the emphases were on mental states as well. Hermann Ebbinghaus (1850–1909), of the University of Berlin, did studies on memory in the 1880s whose findings were so robust that they are still cited in textbooks today. His colleague Georg Elias Müller (1850–1934) also worked on memory in his laboratory at the University of Göttingen, as well as on studies of color vision, learning, and attention. Oswald Külpe (1862–1915), who studied with Wundt and G. E. Müller, began his own laboratory work at the University of Würzburg in 1894, where he did groundbreaking work on thinking.

Much other work in Germany, Austria, France, Italy, the United Kingdom, and the United States could be cited to illustrate that the beginnings of psychological science were concerned with the investigation of mental states. It is important to make this point to underscore that the rise of cognitive psychology in the 1960s was a rebirth of the field and not a beginning. Indeed, the rebirth was essentially an American phenomenon because behaviorism did not have a very great impact beyond the borders of the United States. For example, cognitive psychology remained a mainstay of psychology in Canada and the United Kingdom throughout the period of behaviorism's dominance.

One of the other precursors to the rebirth of American cognitive psychology was *Gestalt psychology*, imported from Germany in the 1920s and 1930s. Gestalt psychology emerged in Germany in opposition to the psychologies there that were seen as atomistic, looking for the primary elements of consciousness. The starting point for Gestalt psychology is typically given as 1912, the year in which Max Wertheimer (1880–1943) published his classic article on the *phi phenomenon*, a form of apparent movement. In producing this phenomenon, two black lines were stroboscopically presented against a white background. The first line was vertical, the second horizontal, and the two were positioned so that if they were seen simultaneously they would form a right angle. The first line would appear briefly and then disappear, followed by the appearance of the second line. The position of the lines was held constant, as was their time of exposure. Only the temporal interval between the offset of the first line and the onset of the second line was varied. When the interval was approximately 30 milliseconds, the observer reported that the lines appeared and disappeared simultaneously. Yet if the interval was increased to 60 milliseconds, the observer reported seeing movement; that is, the observer saw a single line moving from the vertical position to the horizontal position, rather than two separate lines appearing in succession (Wertheimer, 1912).

This form of apparent movement was not new to the scientific world. What was new was Wertheimer's interpretation of it. He viewed it as a conscious experience that was not reducible to its component elements. Not only was it impossible to make such a reduction by even the most deliberate of introspections, but the seen movement could not be readily explained by describing the appearance and disappearance of the two static lines. There was something more to the experience than was evident in those line stimuli (see O'Neill & Landauer, 1966). This awareness is indicated in the Gestalt maxim that "the whole is different from the sum of its parts"; that is, there is a quality of experience that is often independent of the collection of stimulus elements that make up that experience.

The phi phenomenon was illustrative of a central tenet in Gestalt psychology which was its adherence to phenomenology, meaning that experience was to be studied exactly as it occurred, in meaningful wholes, and not broken down in an artificial analysis. Yes, it might be possible to identify elements of the wholes of consciousness, but studies of those elements might not tell the investigator anything useful about the experience itself. Thus Gestalt psychologists would have been especially critical of Titchener's structural psychology.

Most Americans knew nothing of Gestalt psychology until 1922, when Kurt Koffka (1886–1941) published an article in the journal *Psychological Bulletin* entitled "Perception: An introduction to Gestalt-theorie." A few years later, in 1925 and 1926, a series of four articles on Gestalt psychology appeared in the *American Journal of Psychology*, adding greatly to the exposure of this European psychology in America. Because of the Koffka article, many American psychologists assumed that Gestalt psychology was about perception. But it was much broader than that, extending its theory to learning, thinking, problem solving, and memory (Ash, 1995).

In the 1930s, Gestalt psychology arrived in America in person. Koffka was already in the United States at Smith College in the 1920s. But the other Gestaltists arrived in the 1930s, fleeing Nazi Germany. Max Wertheimer came in 1933, taking a position at the New School for Social Research in New York City. Wolfgang Köhler (1887–1967), who held the most prestigious psychology position in Germany as director of the Psychological Institute at the University of Berlin, arrived in 1935, taking a faculty position at Swarthmore College. Koffka and Köhler had been part of Gestalt's founding triumvirate, with Wertheimer as the key figure. A fourth major figure in this group was Kurt Lewin (1890–1947) who, like Wertheimer, had come to America in 1933, fleeing the Nazis. He taught briefly at Cornell University and then at the University of Iowa and Massachusetts Institute of Technology. Lewin's influence was clearly the greatest of the four, as he virtually created the field of experimental social psychology and had a hand in training many of the leading social psychologists in the second half of the twentieth century.

The Gestalt psychologists had no choice but to leave Germany. Most of them were Jewish, and they almost certainly would have died in the Nazi death camps had they not escaped when they did (for information on this part of Gestalt psychology history, see Benjamin, 2006; Henle, 1978; King & Wertheimer, 2005; Mandler & Mandler, 1969). But, when they arrived in behaviorist America, their theory ran counter to the philosophies and methods of mainstream psychology. Behaviorism was a stimulus–response psychology that the Gestaltists would have seen as reductionistic compared to their holistic approach. The behaviorists were strongly on the side of nurture in the nature–nurture arguments, whereas the Gestalt psychologists were nativists, for example, in arguing for inborn perceptual organizing tendencies. Historian Michael Sokal (1984) has distinguished between Gestalt psychology and Gestalt theory, noting that the Americans were open to many Gestalt ideas, that is, parts of their psychology, but were opposed to embracing Gestalt theory as an organizing framework. Although Gestalt psychologists did not achieve the success they had enjoyed in Germany, they did influence American psychology in important ways, including providing a cognitive psychology in opposition to a dominant and often extreme behaviorism. Many Gestalt ideas remain today a part of contemporary psychology, and their importance has been reasserted in the rebirth of American cognitive psychology. That rebirth, as noted already, we have dated to the 1960s. But putting a precise date on it is not easy. There are key events in the 1950s that could be identified as origins.

The rebirth of cognitive psychology in the face of a dominant philosophy of behaviorism occurred because experimental psychologists were finding behaviorism incapable of explaining psychological functioning. Behaviorism was supposed to rid psychology of unscientific approaches, and in doing so it had created the psychology of the empty organism, not allowing any speculation about what went on in mental life. Pick up almost any introductory psychology textbook today and look at the definition of psychology. It is likely to state: "psychology is the scientific study of behavior and mental processes." Realize that, for approximately 50 years, the words "mental processes" could not be uttered, and could not appear in those texts. Contemporary introductory psychology textbooks typically have a chapter on states of consciousness. That chapter did not exist in the textbooks of the 1950s, nor in most of those of the 1960s.

The American psychologists who broke ranks with behaviorism were trained in behaviorism. They grew up on that philosophy but ultimately found it wanting. Theories and experiments that ignored mental processes were proving to be woefully inadequate. The dramatic changes of the 1950s would alter a number of fields, including psychology. Most notable among these changes was the computer. Computer metaphors found a home in psychology with models of input, output, storage, information processing, and languages. Linguists were studying the psychology of language and offering insights into complex behavior that psychologists had been ignoring. Artificial intelligence developed in the 1950s, and psychologists were involved in these efforts to create computers that could think (see Simon, 1991). Psychologist Ulric Neisser (b. 1928), who wrote perhaps the defining book on cognitive psychology in the 1960s, summarized the rationale for a cognitive psychology: "The basic reason for studying cognitive processes has become as clear as the reason for studying anything else: because they are there . . . Cognitive processes surely exist, so it can hardly be unscientific to study them" (Neisser, 1967, p. 5).

Today, experimental psychology is dominated by an approach that might best be termed cognitive-behaviorist, recognizing an amalgamation of the objective science of behaviorism and the needs of a science of the mind. Modern cognitive psychologists have called for a multidisciplinary approach, borrowing what they need from computer science, linguistics, economics, communication science, information theory, social psychology, and neuroscience. Part of the success of cognitive psychology has been the development of new methods to study mental processes. Not everyone became a convert. B. F. Skinner was defiant to the end of his life, arguing that cognitive psychologists were engaged in creating a fictional account of behavior that would set back the true science of psychology. Perhaps time will prove him correct; however, most psychologists are not betting on it. Most contemporary psychologists have grown up in a time when it was okay to utter the word "mind" in a scientific context. They have grown up in a psychology that eschews traditional boundaries, recognizing instead the need for collaboration with scholars in numerous fields who have talents and methodologies to bring to the study of behavior and mental processes. These changes are signs of the continuing evolution of psychology as a science, a historical path not dissimilar to other sciences.

The Readings

There are three readings in this chapter – two primary sources and one secondary source reading. The first selection is by Max Wertheimer. It is an overview of Gestalt theory as given in a lecture before the Kant Society in Berlin in 1924. Wertheimer begins the lecture with his view of the sterility and irrelevance of the experimental psychology of his time. He asks his audience:

> What happens when a problem is solved, when one suddenly "sees the point"? Common as this experience is, we seek in vain for it in the textbooks of psychology. Of things arid, poor, and inessential there is an abundance, but that which really matters is missing. (Wertheimer, 1938, p. 1)

The focus of this article is on the notion of wholes and the value of a scientific approach that is not reductionistic. Wertheimer notes that most sciences, including psychology, persist in the belief that the one true approach is to break phenomena down into their component elements, isolate these elements, then discover how they fit together, perhaps in a lawful way. But he argues that there is an artificial quality to such an atomistic approach, and the result may be to miss the very essence of what one is trying to study. The holistic approach that he describes in this article is meant to producer a richer, more meaningful psychology.

The second reading is an excerpt taken from Frederic Bartlett's book, *Remembering: A Study in Experimental and Social Psychology* (1932). It is considered one of the two or three most important books in the history of cognitive psychology. Although this book was published in 1932, its impact on American cognitive psychology would not take place until the 1960s. It was in this book that Bartlett (1886–1969) introduced the concept of *schema*, cognitive frameworks that organize past experiences related to particular concepts. Bartlett's book described his innovative studies of memory that led to the discovery that the mind is involved as much in constructing as in reconstructing. Thus memory isn't just about recalling exactly what happened but involves the operation of schema to choose what information is processed, how it is interpreted, how it is recalled, and how it is used. In this reading Bartlett discusses the nature of schema and their adaptive role in cognitive functioning, the nature of constructive memory, and finally his own theory of memory. Neisser's 1967 book on cognitive psychology was very much in debt to Bartlett's earlier book (Bruce & Winograd, 1998; Roediger, 2000).

The final reading is by George Mandler, a cognitive psychologist who has published important articles on the history of psychology. In this article he takes a look at his own field, primarily on the subject of memory, and examines the failures of behaviorism that led to the rebirth of cognitive psychology. Mandler (2002) argues that the seeds of behaviorism's failure were sown in Watson's own behaviorist manifesto. The article is an excellent description of the evolution of cognitive psychology from the Gestalt work in Germany through the other European contributions to the developments in American psychology. In this historical review, Mandler also addresses the question of whether there was a cognitive revolution.

Gestalt Theory
Max Wertheimer

What is Gestalt theory and what does it intend? Gestalt theory was the outcome of concrete investigations in psychology, logic, and epistemology. The prevailing situation at the time of its origin may be briefly sketched as follows. We go from the world of everyday events to that of science, and not unnaturally assume that in making this transition we shall gain a deeper and more precise understanding of essentials. The transition should mark an advance. And yet, though one may have learned a great deal, one is poorer than before. It is the same in psychology. Here too we find science intent upon a systematic collection of data, yet often excluding through that very activity precisely that which is most vivid and real in the living phenomena it studies. Somehow the thing that matters has eluded us.

What happens when a problem is solved, when one suddenly "sees the point"? Common as this experience is, we seek in vain for it in the textbooks of psychology. Of things arid, poor, and inessential there is an abundance, but that which really matters is missing. Instead we are told of formation of concepts, of abstraction and generalization, of class concepts and judgments, perhaps of associations, creative phantasy, intuitions, talents – anything but an answer to our original problem. And what are these last words but names for the problem? Where are the penetrating answers? Psychology is replete with terms of great potentiality – personality, essence, intuition, and the rest. But when one seeks to grasp their concrete content, such terms fail.

This is the situation and it is characteristic of modern science that the same problem should appear everywhere. Several attempts have been made to remedy the matter. One was a frank

defeatism preaching the severance of science and life: there are regions which are inaccessible to science. Other theories established a sharp distinction between the natural and moral sciences: the exactitude and precision of chemistry and physics are characteristic of natural science, but "scientific" accuracy has no place in a study of the mind and its ways. This must be renounced in favour of other categories.

Without pausing for further examples, let us consider rather a question naturally underlying the whole discussion: Is "science" really the kind of thing we have implied? The word science has often suggested a certain outlook, certain fundamental assumptions, certain procedures and attitudes – but do these imply that this is the only possibility of scientific method? Perhaps science already embodies methods leading in an entirely different direction, methods which have been continually stifled by the seemingly necessary, dominant ones. It is conceivable, for instance, that a host of facts and problems have been concealed rather than illuminated by the prevailing scientific tradition. Even though the traditional methods of science are undoubtedly adequate in many cases, there may be others where they lead us astray. Perhaps something in the very nature of the traditional outlook may have led its exponents at times to ignore precisely that which is truly essential.

Gestalt theory will not be satisfied with sham solutions suggested by a simple dichotomy of science and life. Instead, Gestalt theory is resolved to penetrate the problem itself by examining the fundamental assumptions of science. It has long seemed obvious – and is, in fact, the characteristic tone of European science – that "science" means breaking up complexes into their component elements. Isolate the elements, discover their laws, then reassemble them, and the problem is solved. All wholes are reduced to pieces and piecewise relations between pieces.

From M. Wertheimer (1938). Gestalt theory. In W. D. Ellis (Ed.), *Source book of Gestalt psychology* (pp. 1–11) New York: Harcourt, Brace. [A lecture before the Kant Society in Berlin in 1924]. Reprinted with permission.

The fundamental "formula" of Gestalt theory might be expressed in this way. There are wholes, the behaviour of which is not determined by that of their individual elements, but where the part-processes are themselves determined by the intrinsic nature of the whole. It is the hope of Gestalt theory to determine the nature of such wholes.

With a formula such as this one might close, for Gestalt theory is neither more nor less than this. It is not interested in puzzling out philosophic questions which such a formula might suggest.

Gestalt theory has to do with concrete research; it is not only an outcome but a device: not only a theory about results but a means toward further discoveries. This is not merely the proposal of one or more problems but an attempt to see what is really taking place in science. This problem cannot be solved by listing possibilities for systematization, classification, and arrangement. If it is to be attacked at all, we must be guided by the spirit of the new method and by the concrete nature of the things themselves which we are studying, and set ourselves to penetrate to that which is really given by nature.

There is another difficulty that may be illustrated by the following example. Suppose a mathematician shows you a proposition and you begin to "classify" it. This proposition, you say, is of such and such type, belongs in this or that historical category, and so on. Is that how the mathematician works?

"Why, you haven't grasped the thing at all," the mathematician will exclaim. "See here, this formula is not an independent, closed fact that can be dealt with for itself alone. You must see its dynamic functional relationship to the whole from which it was lifted or you will never understand it."

What holds for the mathematical formula applies also to the "formula" of Gestalt theory. The attempt of Gestalt theory to disclose the functional meaning of its own formula is no less strict than is the mathematician's. The attempt to explain Gestalt theory in a short essay is the more difficult because of the terms which are used: part, whole, intrinsic determination. All of them have in the past been the topic of endless discussions where each disputant has understood them differently. And even worse has been the cata-loguing attitude adopted toward them. What they lacked has been actual research. Like many another "philosophic" problem they have been withheld from contact with reality and scientific work.

About all I can hope for in so short a discussion is to suggest a few of the problems which at present occupy the attention of Gestalt theory and something of the way they are being attacked.

To repeat: the problem has not merely to do with scientific work – it is a fundamental problem of our times. Gestalt theory is not something suddenly and unexpectedly dropped upon us from above; it is, rather, a palpable convergence of problems ranging throughout the sciences and the various philosophic standpoints of modern times.

Let us take, for example, an event in the history of psychology.

One turned from a living experience to science and asked what it had to say about this experience, and one found an assortment of elements, sensational images, feelings, acts of will and laws governing these elements – and was told, "Take your choice, reconstruct from them the experience you had." Such procedure led to difficulties in concrete psychological research and to the emergence of problems which defied solution by traditional analytic methods. Historically the most important impulse came from v. Ehrenfels, who raised the following problem. Psychology had said that experience is a compound of elements: we hear a melody and then, upon hearing it again, memory enables us to recognize it. But what is it that enables us to recognize the melody when it is played in a new key? The sum of the elements is different, yet the melody is the same; indeed, one is often not even aware that a transposition has been made.

When in retrospect we consider the prevailing situation we are struck by two aspects of v. Ehrenfels's thesis; on the one hand one is surprised at the essentially summative character of his theory, on the other one admires his courage in propounding and defending his proposition. Strictly interpreted, v. Ehrenfels's position was this: I play a familiar melody of six tones and employ six new tones, yet you recognize the melody despite the change. There must be a something more than the sum of six tones, viz. a seventh something, which is the form-quality, the Gestaltqualität, of the original six. It is this seventh factor or element which enabled you to recognize the melody despite its transposition. However strange this view may seem, it shares with many another subsequently abandoned hypothesis the honour of having clearly seen and emphasized a fundamental problem.

But other explanations were also proposed. One maintained that in addition to the six tones there were intervals – relations – and that these were what remained constant. In other words we are asked to assume not only elements but "relations-between-elements" as additional components of the total complex. But this view failed to account for the phenomenon because in some cases the relations too may be altered without destroying the original melody.

Another type of explanation, also designed to bolster the elementaristic hypothesis, was that to this total of six or more tones there come certain "higher processes" which operate upon the given material to "produce" unity.

This was the situation until Gestalt theory raised the radical question: Is it really true that when I hear a melody I have a sum of individual tones (pieces) which constitute the primary foundation of my experience? Is not perhaps the reverse of this true? What I really have, what I hear of each individual note, what I experience at each place in the melody is apart which is itself determined by the character of the whole. What is given me by the melody does not arise (through the agency of any auxiliary factor) as a secondary process from the sum of the pieces as such. Instead, what takes place in each single part already depends upon what the whole is. The flesh and blood of a tone depends from the start upon its role in the melody: a b as leading tone to c is something radically different from the b as tonic. It belongs to the flesh and blood of the things given in experience, how, in what role, in what function they are in their whole.

Let us leave the melody example and turn to another field. Take the case of threshold phenomena. It has long been held that a certain stimulus necessarily produces a certain sensation. Thus, when two stimuli are sufficiently different, the sensations also will be different. Psychology is filled with careful inquiries regarding threshold phenomena. To account for the difficulties constantly being encountered it was assumed that these phenomena must be influenced by higher mental functions, judgments, illusions, attention, etc. And this continued until the radical question was raised: Is it really true that a specific stimulus always gives rise to the same sensation? Perhaps the prevailing whole-conditions will themselves determine the effect of stimulation? This kind of formulation leads to experimentation, and experiments show, for example, that when I see two colours the sensations I have are determined by the whole-conditions of the entire stimulus situation. Thus, also, the same local physical stimulus pattern can give rise to either a unitary and homogeneous figure, or to an articulated figure with different parts, all depending upon the whole-conditions which may favour either unity or articulation. Obviously the task, then, is to investigate these "whole-conditions" and discover what influences they exert upon experience.

Advancing another step we come to the question whether perhaps any part depends upon the particular whole in which it occurs. Experiments, largely on vision, have answered this question in the affirmative. Among other things they demand that the traditional theory of visual contrast be replaced by a theory which takes account of whole-part conditions.

Our next point is that my field comprises also my Ego. There is not from the beginning an Ego over-against others, but the genesis of an Ego offers one of the most fascinating problems, the solution of which seems to lie in Gestalt principles. However, once constituted, the Ego is a functional part of the total field. Proceeding as before we may therefore ask: What happens to the Ego as a part of the field? Is the resulting behaviour the piecewise sort of thing associationism, experience theory, and the like, would have us believe? Experimental results contradict this interpretation and again we often find that the laws of whole-processes operative in such a field tend toward a "meaningful" behaviour of its parts.

This field is not a summation of sense data and no description of it which considers such separate pieces to be primary will be correct. If it were, then for children, primitive peoples and animals experience would be nothing but piece-sensations. The next most developed creatures would have, in addition to independent sensations, something higher, and so on. But this whole picture is the opposite of what actual inquiry has disclosed. We have learned to recognize the "sensations" of our textbooks as products of a late culture utterly different from the experiences of more primitive stages. Who experiences the sensation of a specific red in that sense? What the man of the streets, children, or primitive men normally react to is something coloured but at the same time exciting, gay, strong, or affecting – not "sensations."

The programme to treat the organism as a part in a larger field necessitates the reformulation of the problem as to the relation between organism and environment. The stimulus-sensation connection must be replaced by a connection between alteration in the field conditions, the vital situation, and the total reaction of the organism by a change in its attitude, striving, and feeling.

There is, however, another step to be considered. A man is not only a part of his field, he is also one among other men. When a group of people work together it rarely occurs, and then only under very special conditions, that they constitute a mere-sum of independent Egos. Instead the common enterprise often becomes their mutual concern and each works as a meaningfully functioning part of the whole. Consider a group of South Sea Islanders engaged in some community occupation, or a group of children playing together. Only under very special circumstances does an "I" stand out alone. Then the balance which obtained during harmonious and systematic occupation may be upset and give way to a surrogate (under certain conditions, pathological) new balance.

Further discussion of this point would carry us into the work of social and cultural science which cannot be followed here. Instead let us consider certain other illustrations. What was said above of stimulus and sensation is applicable to physiology and the biological sciences no less than to psychology. It has been tried, for example, by postulating sums of more and more special apparatus, to account for meaningful or, as it is often called, purposive behaviour. Once more we find meaninglessly combined reflexes taken for granted although it is probable that even with minute organisms it is not true that a piece-stimulus automatically bring about its corresponding piece-effect.

Opposing this view is vitalism which, however, as it appears to Gestalt theory, also errs in its efforts to solve the problem, for it, too, begins with the assumption that natural occurrences are themselves essentially blind and haphazard – and adds a mystical something over and above them which imposes order. Vitalism fails to inquire of physical events whether a genuine order might not already prevail amongst them. And yet nature does exhibit numerous instances of physical wholes in which part events are determined by the inner structure of the whole.

These brief references to biology will suffice to remind us that whole-phenomena are not "merely" psychological, but appear in other sciences as well. Obviously, therefore, the problem is not solved by separating off various provinces of science and classifying whole-phenomena as something peculiar to psychology.

The fundamental question can be very simply stated: Are the parts of a given whole determined by the inner structure of that whole, or are the events such that, as independent, piecemeal, fortuitous and blind the total activity is a sum of the part-activities? Human beings can, of course, devise a kind of physics of their own – e.g. a sequence of machines – exemplifying the latter half of our question, but this does not signify that all natural phenomena are of this type. Here is a place where Gestalt theory is least easily understood and this because of the great number of prejudices about nature which have accumulated during the centuries. Nature is thought of as something essentially blind in its laws, where whatever takes place in the whole is purely a sum of individual occurrences. This view was the natural result of the struggle which physics has always had to purge itself of teleology. To-day it can be seen that we are obliged to traverse other routes than those suggested by this kind of purposivism.

Let us proceed another step and ask: How does all this stand with regard to the problem of body and mind? What does my knowledge of another's mental experiences amount to and how do I obtain it? There are, of course, old and established dogmas on these points: The mental and physical are wholly heterogeneous: There obtains between them an absolute dichotomy. (From this point of departure philosophers have drawn an array of metaphysical deductions so as to attribute all the good qualities to mind while reserving for nature the odious.) As regards the second question, my discerning mental phenomena in others is traditionally explained as inference by analogy. Strictly interpreted the principle here is that something mental is meaninglessly coupled with something physical. I observe the physical and infer the mental from it more or less according to the following scheme: I see someone press a button on the wall and infer that he wants the light to go on. There may be couplings of this sort. However, many scientists have been disturbed by this dualism and have tried to save themselves by recourse to very curious hypotheses. Indeed, the ordinary person would violently refuse to believe that when he sees his companion startled, frightened, or angry he is seeing only certain physical occurrences which themselves have nothing to do (in their inner nature) with the mental, being only superficially coupled with it: you have frequently seen this and this combined . . . etc. There have been many attempts to surmount this problem. One speaks, for example, of intuition and says there can be no other possibility, for I see my companion's fear. It is not true, argue the intuitionists, that I see only the bare bodily activities meaninglessly coupled with other and invisible activities. However inadmissible it may otherwise be, an intuition theory does have at least this in its favour, it shows a suspicion that the traditional procedure might be successfully reversed. But the word intuition is at best only a naming of that which we must strive to lay hold of.

This and other hypotheses, apprehended as they now are, will not advance scientific pursuit, for science demands fruitful penetration, not mere cataloguing and systematization. But the question is, How does the matter really stand? Looking more closely we find a third assumption, namely that a process such as fear is a matter of consciousness. Is this true? Suppose you see a person who is kindly or benevolent. Does anyone suppose that this person is feeling mawkish? No one could possibly believe that. The characteristic feature of such behaviour has very little to do with consciousness. It has been one of the easiest contrivances of philosophy to identify a man's real behaviour and the direction of his mind with his consciousness. Parenthetically, in the opinion of many people the distinction between idealism and materialism implies that between the noble and the ignoble. Yet does one really mean by this to contrast consciousness with the blithesome budding of trees? Indeed, what is there so repugnant about the materialistic and mechanical? What is so attractive about the idealistic? Does it come from the material qualities of the connected pieces? Broadly speaking most psychological theories and textbooks, despite their continued emphasis upon consciousness, are far more "materialistic", arid, and spiritless than a living tree – which probably has no consciousness at all. The point is not what the material pieces are, but what kind of whole it is. Proceeding in terms of specific problems one soon realizes how many bodily activities there are which give no hint of a separation between body and mind. Imagine a dance, a dance full of grace and joy. What is the situation in such a dance? Do we have a summation of physical limb movements and a psychical consciousness? No. Obviously this answer does not solve the problem; we have to start anew – and it seems to me that a proper and fruitful point of attack has been discovered. One finds many processes which, in their dynamical form, are identical regardless of variations in the material character of their elements. When a man is timid, afraid or energetic, happy or sad, it can often be shown that the course of his physical processes is Gestalt-identical with the course pursued by the mental processes.

Again I can only indicate the direction of thought. I have touched on the question of body and mind merely to show that the problem we are discussing also has its philosophic aspects. To strengthen the import of the foregoing suggestions let us consider the fields of epistemology and logic. For centuries the assumption has prevailed that our world is essentially a summation of elements. For Hume and largely also for Kant the world is like a bundle of fragments, and the dogma of meaningless summations continues to play its part. As for logic, it supplies: concepts, which when rigorously viewed are but sums of properties; classes, which upon closer inspection prove to be mere catchalls; syllogisms, devised by arbitrarily lumping together any two propositions having the character that . . . etc. When one considers what a concept is in living thought, what it really means to grasp a conclusion; when one considers what the crucial thing is about a mathematical proof and the concrete interrelationships it involves, one sees that the categories of traditional logic have accomplished nothing in this direction.

It is our task to inquire, whether a logic is possible which is not piecemeal. Indeed the same question arises in mathematics also. Is it necessary that all mathematics be established upon a piecewise basis? What sort of mathematical system would it be in which this were not the case? There have been attempts to answer the latter question but almost always they have fallen back in the end upon the old procedures. This fate has overtaken many, for the result of training in piecewise thinking is extraordinarily tenacious. It is not enough and certainly does not constitute a solution of the principal problem if one shows that the atoms of mathematics are both piecemeal and at the same time evince something of the opposite character. The problem has been scientifically grasped only when an attack specifically designed to yield positive results has been launched. Just how this attack is to be made seems to many mathematicians a colossal problem, but perhaps the quantum theory will force the mathematicians to attack it.

This brings us to the close of an attempt to present a view of the problem as illustrated by its specific appearances in various fields. In concluding I may suggest a certain unification of these illustrations somewhat as follows. I consider the situation from the point of view of a theory of aggregates and say: How should a world be where science, concepts, inquiry, investigation, and comprehension of inner unities were impossible? The answer is obvious. This world would be a manifold of disparate pieces. Secondly, what kind of world would there have to be in which a piecewise science would apply? The answer is again quite simple, for here one needs only a system of recurrent couplings that are blind and piecewise in character, whereupon everything is available for a pursuit of the traditional piecewise methods of logic, mathematics, and science generally in so far as these presuppose this kind of world. But there is a third kind of aggregate which has been but cursorily investigated. These are the aggregates in which a manifold is not compounded from adjacently situated pieces but rather such that a term at its place in that aggregate is determined by the whole-laws of the aggregate itself.

Pictorially: suppose the world were a vast plateau upon which were many musicians. I walk about listening and watching the players. First suppose that the world is a meaningless plurality. Everyone does as he will, each for himself. What happens together when I hear ten players might be the basis for my guessing as to what they all are doing, but this is merely a matter of chance and probability much as in the kinetics of gas molecules. – A second possibility would be that each time one musician played *C*, another played *F* so and so many seconds later. I work out a theory of blind couplings but the playing as a whole remains meaningless. This is what many people think physics does, but the real work of physics belies this. – The third possibility is, say, a Beethoven symphony where it would be possible for one to select one part of the whole and work from that towards an idea of the structural principle motivating and determining the whole. Here the fundamental laws are not those of fortuitous pieces, but concern the very character of the event.

A Theory of Remembering
Frederic C. Bartlett

1. The Method of Approach

The most persistent problems of recall all concern the ways in which past experiences and past reactions are utilised when anything is remembered. From a general point of view it looks as if the simplest explanation available is to suppose that when any specific event occurs, some trace, or some group of traces, is made and stored up in the organism or in the mind. Later, an immediate stimulus re-excites the trace, or group of traces, and, provided a further assumption is made to the effect that the trace somehow carries with it a temporal sign, the re-excitement appears to be equivalent to recall. There is, of course, no direct evidence for such traces, but the assumption at first sight seems to be a very simple one, and so it has commonly been made.

Yet there are obvious difficulties. The traces are generally supposed to be of individual and specific events. Hence, every normal individual must carry about with him an incalculable number of individual traces. Since these are all stored in a single organism, they are in fact bound to be related one to another, and this gives to recall its inevitably associative character; but all the time each trace retains its essential individuality, and remembering, in the ideal case, is simple re-excitation, or pure reproduction.

Now we have seen that a study of the actual facts of perceiving and recognising suggests strongly that, in all relatively simple cases of determination by past experiences and reactions, the past operates as an organised mass rather than as a group of elements each of which retains its specific character. If we are to treat remembering as a biological function, it looks as if a sound rule of method would compel us to approach its problems through a study of these relatively less complex cases of determination of present reactions by the past. At any rate, this is the line of approach to which the argument of the preceding chapter has committed us, for it was there indicated that very probably the outstanding characteristics of remembering all follow from a change of attitude towards those masses of organised past experiences and reactions which function in all high-level mental processes.

If this be admitted, there is an exceedingly interesting way of approach to the problems of recall along a line of studies which would often, no doubt, be called neurological rather than psychological, and this I propose to explore. During many years Sir Henry Head carried out systematic observations on the nature and functions of afferent sensibility, that is to say, of those sensations which are set up by the stimulation of peripheral nerves. He was particularly interested in the functions and character of the sensations which can be aroused by the stimulation of nerve endings in the skin and the underlying tissues, and in those which are initiated by the contraction and relaxation of muscles. He wished to find out exactly what part is played by the cortex in interpreting and relating these sensations, or the nerve impulses of which the sensations may be regarded as a sign. One of the most important and interesting of these groups of impulses consists of those which underlie the recognition of bodily posture and of passive movement.

Every day each normal individual carries out a large number of perfectly well-adapted and co-ordinated movements. Whenever these are arranged in a series, each successive movement is made as if it were under the control and direction of the preceding movements in the same series.

From F. C. Bartlett (1932). *Remembering: A study in experimental and social psychology*. Cambridge: Cambridge University Press.

Yet, as a rule, the adaptive mechanisms of the body do not demand any definite awareness, so far as change of posture or change of movement is concerned. In every skilled bodily performance, for example, a large number of movements are made in succession, and every movement is carried out as if the position reached by the moving limbs in the last preceding stage were somehow recorded and still functioning, though the particular preceding movement itself is past and over. This obvious fact has given rise to many speculations concerning the ways in which the movements which are past nevertheless still retain their regulative functions.

Munk, the physiologist, writing in 1890, said that they did this because the brain must be regarded as a storehouse of images of movement, and he was unreflectingly followed by a great many other writers. It is supposed that a preceding movement produces a cortical image, or trace, which, being somehow re-excited at the moment of the next succeeding movement, controls the latter.

Head showed definitely and finally that this cannot be the explanation. For images may persist perfectly when all appreciation of relative movement carried out in this unwitting manner is totally lost. A patient with a certain cortical lesion may be able to image accurately the position of his outstretched arm and hand on the counterpane of a bed. He can equally image his arm and hand in any of the possible positions which it might occupy. Now let him close his eyes and let the hand be picked up and the hand and arm moved. He may be able to localise the spot touched on the skin surface perfectly well, but he refers it to the position in which the hand was, because he has entirely lost the capacity to relate serial movements. Images may be intact; appreciation of relative movement lost. Conversely, as everybody knows, appreciation of movement may be as perfect as ever it can be without any appearance of images. It is futile to say that in these cases the images are so slight, or so fleeting, that we do not notice them. The truth is that with all the effort in the world we cannot notice them; and since the evidence for their absence is similar in source and character to that cited for their presence on other occasions, it is most unjustifiable to accept the latter and to reject the former.

Accordingly, Head justly discarded the notion of individual images, or traces, and proposed in its place a different solution—one which is certainly speculative, offers difficulties of its own, and has never yet been properly worked out; but one which seems to me to have great advantages when we are dealing with these somewhat elementary instances of the persistent effects of past reactions. I believe, also, that it points the way to a satisfactory solution of the phenomena of remembering in the full sense.

At this point I must quote Head's own words: "Every recognisable (postural) change enters into consciousness already charged with its relation to something that has gone before, just as on a taximeter the distance is presented to us already transformed into shillings and pence. So the final product of the tests for the appreciation of posture, or of passive movement, rises into consciousness as a measured postural change.

For this combined standard, against which all subsequent changes of posture are measured before they enter consciousness, we propose the word 'schema'. By means of perpetual alterations in position we are always building up a postural model of ourselves which constantly changes. Every new posture of movement is recorded on this plastic schema, and the activity of the cortex brings every fresh group of sensations evoked by altered posture into relation with it. Immediate postural recognition follows as soon as the relation is complete."

And again: "The sensory cortex is the storehouse of past impressions. They may rise into consciousness as images, but more often, as in the case of special impressions, remain outside central consciousness. Here they form organised models of ourselves which may be called schemata. Such schemata modify the impressions produced by incoming sensory impulses in such a way that the final sensations of position or of locality rise into consciousness charged with a relation to something that has gone before."

Although I am going to utilise these notions in developing a theory of remembering, I must claim the prerogative of a psychologist of objecting to the terminology of another writer. There are several points in the brief descriptions I have quoted that seem to me to present difficulty.

First, Head gives away far too much to earlier investigators when he speaks of the cortex as "a storehouse of past impressions". All that his experiments show is that certain processes cannot be carried out unless the brain is playing its normal part. But equally those very reactions could be cut out by injuries to peripheral nerves or to muscular functions. One might almost as well say that because nobody who is suffering from a raging toothache could calmly recite "Oh, my love's like a red, red rose", the teeth are a repository of lyric poetry. In any case, a storehouse is a place where things are put in the hope that they may be found again when they are wanted exactly as they were when first stored away. The schemata are, we are told, living, constantly developing, affected by every bit of incoming sensational experience of a given kind. The storehouse notion is as far removed from this as it well could be.

Secondly, Head constantly uses the perplexing phrase "rising into consciousness". It may be the case that in exceptional circumstances an unwitting alteration of position is actually known as a "measured" postural change. But this is not the rule. Every day, many times over, we make accurate motor adjustments in which, if Head is right, the schemata are active, without any awareness at all, so far as the measure of the changing postures is concerned.

Thirdly, and perhaps most important, I strongly dislike the term "schema". It is at once too definite and too sketchy. The word is already widely used in controversial psychological writing to refer generally to any rather vaguely outlined theory. It suggests some persistent, but fragmentary, "form of arrangement", and it does not indicate what is very essential to the whole notion, that the organised mass results of past changes of position and posture are actively doing something all the time; are, so to speak, carried along with us, complete, though developing, from moment to moment. Yet it is certainly very difficult to think of any better single descriptive word to cover the facts involved. It would probably be best to speak of "active, developing patterns"; but the word "pattern", too, being now very widely and variously employed, has its own difficulties; and it, like "schema", suggests a greater articulation of detail than is normally found. I think probably the term "organised setting" approximates most closely and clearly to the notion required. I shall, however, continue to use the

term "schema" when it seems best to do so, but I will attempt to define its application more narrowly.

"Schema" refers to an active organisation of past reactions, or of past experiences, which must always be supposed to be operating in any well-adapted organic response. That is, whenever there is any order or regularity of behaviour, a particular response is possible only because it is related to other similar responses which have been serially organised, yet which operate, not simply as individual members coming one after another, but as a unitary mass. Determination by schemata is the most fundamental of all the ways in which we can, be influenced by reactions and experiences which occurred some time in the past. All incoming impulses of a certain kind, or mode, go together to build up an active, organised setting: visual, auditory, various types of cutaneous impulses and the like, at a relatively low level; all the experiences connected by a common interest: in sport, in literature, history, art, science, philosophy and so on, on a higher level. There is not the slightest reason, however, to suppose that each set of incoming impulses, each new group of experiences persists as an isolated member of some passive patchwork. They have to be regarded as constituents of living, momentary settings belonging to the organism, or to whatever parts of the organism are concerned in making response of a given kind, and not as a number of individual events somehow strung together and stored within the organism. [. . .]

3. The Constructive Character of Remembering

We must, then, consider what does actually happen more often than not when we say that we remember. The first notion to get rid of is that memory is primarily or literally reduplicative, or reproductive. In a world of constantly changing environment, literal recall is extraordinarily unimportant. It is with remembering as it is with the stroke in a skilled game. We may fancy that we are repeating a series of movements learned a long time before from a text-book or from a teacher. But motion study shows that in fact we build up the stroke afresh on a basis of the immediately preceding balance of postures and the momentary needs of the game. Every time we make it, it has its own characteristics.

The long series of experiments which I have described were directed to the observation of normal processes of remembering. I discarded nonsense material because, among other difficulties, its use almost always weights the evidence in favour of mere rote recapitulation, and for the most part I used exactly the type of material that we have to deal with in daily life. In the many thousands of cases of remembering which I collected, a considerable number of which I have recorded here, literal recall was very rare. With few exceptions, the significance of which I will discuss shortly, re-excitement of individual traces did not look to be in the least what was happening. Consider particularly the case in which a subject was remembering a story which he heard, say, five years previously, in comparison with the case in which he was given certain outline materials and constructs what he calls a new story. I have tried the latter experiment repeatedly, and not only the actual form and content of the results, but what is of more significance for the moment, the attitudes of the subject in these two cases were strikingly similar. In both cases, it was common to find the preliminary check, the struggle to get somewhere, the varying play of doubt, hesitation, satisfaction and the like, and the eventual building up of the complete story accompanied by the more and more confident advance in a certain direction. In fact, if we consider evidence rather than presupposition, remembering appears to be far more decisively an affair of construction rather than one of mere reproduction. The difference between the two cases, if it were put in Head's terminology, seems to be that in remembering a man constructs on the basis of one "schema", whereas in what is commonly called imaging he more or less freely builds together events, incidents and experiences that have gone to the making of several different "schemata" which, for the purposes of automatic reaction, are not normally in connexion with one another. Even this difference is largely only a general one, for as has been shown again and again, condensation, elaboration and invention are common features of ordinary remembering, and those all very often involve the mingling of materials belonging originally to different "schemata".

4. A Theory of Remembering

In attempting to develop a theory of the whole matter, so far as I can see it, we must begin with an organism which has only a few sense avenues or connexion with its environment, and only a few correlated series of movements, but is devoid of all the so-called higher mental functions. To this organism Head's notions, derived from a mass of experimental observations, have the most perfect applicability. Any reaction of such an organism which has more than a mere momentary significance is determined by the activity of a "schema" in relation to some new incoming impulse set up by an immediately presented stimulus. Since its sensory equipment and the correlated movements are very limited in range, and since the mode of organisation of the "schema" follows a direct chronological sequence, circularity of reaction, the repetition over and over again of a series of reactions, is very prominent. Habits, moreover, are relatively easily formed, as is witnessed by a great amount of research of an experimental nature upon the lower animals. From the outside, all this may look like the continual re-excitement of well-established traces; but it is not. It is simply the maintenance of few "schemata", each of which has its natural and essential time order.

However, in the course of development the special sense avenues increase in number and range, and concurrently there is an increase in number and variety of reactions. With this, and a matter of vital importance, as my experiments repeatedly show, goes a great growth of social life, and the development of means of communication. Then the "schema" determined reactions of one organism are repeatedly checked, as well as constantly facilitated, by those of others. All this growth of complexity makes circularity of reaction, mere rote recapitulation and habit behaviour often both wasteful and inefficient. A new incoming impulse must become not merely a cue setting up a series of reactions all carried out in a fixed temporal order, but a stimulus which enables us to go direct to that portion of the organised setting of past responses which is most relevant to the needs of the moment.

There is one way in which an organism could learn how to do this. It may be the only way. At any rate, it is the way that has been discovered and it is continually used. An organism has somehow to acquire the capacity to turn round upon its own "schemata" and to construct them afresh. This is a crucial step in organic development. It is where and why consciousness comes in; it is what gives consciousness its most prominent function. I wish I knew exactly how it was done. On the basis of my experiments I can make one suggestion, although I do so with some hesitation. Suppose an individual to be confronted by a complex situation. This is the case with which I began the whole series of experiments, the case in which an observer is perceiving, and is saying immediately what it is that he has perceived. We saw that in this case an individual does not normally take such a situation detail by detail and meticulously build up the whole. In all ordinary instances he has an over-mastering tendency simply to get a general impression of the whole; and, on the basis of this, he constructs the probable detail. Very little of his construction is literally observed and often, as was easily demonstrated experimentally, a lot of it is distorted or wrong so far as the actual facts are concerned. But it is the sort of construction which serves to justify his general impression. Ask the observer to characterise this general impression psychologically, and the word that is always cropping up is "attitude". I have shown how this "attitude" factor came into nearly every series of experiments that was carried out. The construction that is effected is the sort of construction that would justify the observer's "attitude". Attitude names a complex psychological state or process which it is very hard to describe in more elementary psychological terms. It is, however, as I have often indicated, very largely a matter of feeling, or affect. We say that it is characterised by doubt, hesitation, surprise, astonishment, confidence, dislike, repulsion and so on. Here is the significance of the fact, often reported in the preceding pages, that when a subject is being asked to remember, very often the first thing that emerges is something of the nature of attitude. The recall is then a construction, made largely on the basis of this attitude, and its general effect is that of a justification of the attitude.

A rapid survey of the experimental results will show this factor at work in different subjects and with diverse materials and methods, in the case of every one of my experimental series. In the

Perception Series the subjects got their general impression, felt the material presented to be regular, or exciting, or familiar and so on, and built up their results by the aid of that and a little definitely observed detail. In the Imaging Series, I have recorded a number of cases where, particularly in the case of the subjects prone to personal reminiscence, an attitude developed into a concrete and detailed imaginal construction. With *The Method of Description* the affective attitude openly influenced the recall. *Repeated Reproduction* yielded many cases in which the stories or other material were first charactised as "exciting", "adventurous", "like what I read when I was a boy", labelled in some way or other, and then built up or "remembered". The instance in which *The War of the Ghosts* was constructed gradually from a little general starting-point, after a very long interval, is a brilliant, but by no means isolated, illustration of this constructive character of recall. Serial Reproduction showed the same features in the readiness with which material assumed established conventional forms, and *The Picture Sign Method* also brought out the same point repeatedly. I have attempted to observe as closely as possible the behaviour of young children when they remember. So far as it is valid to guess from this what are the processes actually going on, here also, in very many instances, there comes first an attitude and then the recall of the material in such a way as to satisfy, or fortify, the attitude. The constant rationalisation which remembering effects is a special case of the functioning of this constructive character upon which memory is largely based.

What, precisely, does the "schema" do? Together with the immediately preceding incoming impulse it renders a specific adaptive reaction possible. It is, therefore, producing an orientation of the organism towards whatever it is directed to at the moment. But that orientation must be dominated by the immediately preceding reaction or experiences. To break away from this the "schema" must become, not merely something that works the organism, but something with which the organism can work. As I will show later, its constituents may perhaps begin to be reshuffled on a basis of purely physical and physiological determinants. This method is not radical enough. So the organism discovers how to turn round upon its own "schemata", or, in other words, it becomes conscious. It may be that what then emerges is an *attitude* towards the massed effects of a series of past reactions. Remembering is a constructive justification of this attitude; and, because all that goes to the building of a "schema" has a chronological, as well as a qualitative, significance, what is remembered has its temporal mark; while the fact that it is operating with a diverse organised mass, and not with single undiversified events or units, gives to remembering its inevitable associative character. Whether or not the attitude is a genetically primitive characteristic possessing this function in recall is, of course, a speculative matter. I think it is, but nothing is served by dogmatism at this point. The experiments do, however, appear to demonstrate that, at the level of human remembering, the attitude functions in the way I have suggested.

[. . .]

7. A Summary

Remembering is not the re-excitation of innumerable fixed, lifeless and fragmentary traces. It is an imaginative reconstruction or construction, built out of the relation of our attitude towards a whole active mass of organised past reactions or experience, and to a little outstanding detail which commonly appeals in image or in language form. It is thus hardly ever really exact, even in the most rudimentary cases of rote recapitulation, and it is not at all important that it should be so. The attitude is literally an effect of the organism's capacity to turn round upon its own "schemata", and is directly a function of consciousness. The outstanding detail is the result of that valuation of items in an organised mass which begins with the functioning appetite and instinct, and goes much further with the growth of interests and ideals. Even apart from their appearance in the form of censorial images, or as language forms, some of the items of a mass may stand out by virtue of their possession of certain physical characteristics. But there is no evidence that these can

operate in determining a specific reaction, except after relatively short periods of delay. The active settings which are chiefly important at the level of human remembering are mainly "interest" settings; and, since an interest has both a definite direction and a wide range, the development of these settings involves much reorganisation of the "schemata" that follow the more primitive lines of special sense differences, of appetite and of instinct. So, since many "schemata" are built of common materials, the images and words that mark some of their salient features are in constant, but explicable, change. They, too, are a device made possible by the appearance, or discovery, of consciousness, and without them no genuine long-distance remembering would be possible.

It may be said that this theory after all does very little. It merely jumbles together innumerable traces and calls them "schemata", and then it picks out a few and calls them images. But I think this would be hardly fair criticism. All conventional theories of memory as reduplicative try to treat traces as somehow stored up like so many definite impressions, fixed and having only the capacity of being reexcited. The active settings, which are involved in the way of looking at the matter developed in the present chapter, are living and developing, are a complex expression of the life of the moment, and help to determine our daily modes of conduct. The theory brings remembering into line with imagining, an expression of the same activities; it has very different implications in regard to forgetting from those of the ordinary trace view; it gives to consciousness a definite function other than the mere fact of being aware. This last point is not entirely unimportant. There is an active school in current psychological controversy which would banish all reference to consciousness. It is common to try to refute this school by asserting vigorously that of course we know that we are conscious. But this is futile, for what they are really saying is that consciousness cannot effect anything that could not equally well be done without it. That is a position less easy to demolish. If I am right, however, they are wrong.

Origins of the Cognitive (R)evolution
George Mandler

The facts of the cognitive revolution in psychology in mid-twentieth century have been well documented (see, for example, Baars, 1986; Greenwood, 1999, and on more special issues see Murray, 1995; Newell & Simon, 1972). What follows is intended as a further elaboration of those previous presentations. The adoption of, or return to, cognitive themes occurred in other disciplines as well, for example in linguistics, but those developments are outside the scope of this presentation. Nor do I wish to treat in detail all areas of experimental psychology; I will concentrate on approaches to human memory. I wish to add the following four arguments to our general understanding of the events surrounding the cognitive resurgence: (1) Part of Watson's program prevented the success of behaviorism and contributed to its replacement. (2) The term "revolution" is probably inappropriate – there were no cataclysmic events, the change occurred slowly in different subfields over some 10 to 15 years, there was no identifiable flashpoint or leader, and there were no Jacobins. (3) The behaviorist dogmas against which the revolution occurred were essentially confined to the United States. At the same time that behaviorism reigned in the U.S. structuralist, cognitive, and functionalist psychologies were dominant in Germany, Britain, France, and even Canada. (4) Stimulus-response behaviorism was not violently displaced, rather as a cognitive approach evolved behaviorism faded because of its failure to solve basic questions about human thought and action, and memory in particular.

Journal of History of the Behavioral Sciences, 2002, 38(4), 339–353. Adapted and reprinted by permission of Wiley-Blackwell.

The Birth and Failure of American Behaviorism

The early twentieth century in the United States was marked by a turning inward, a new American consciousness.[1] In science and philosophy, the new twentieth century was marked by a pragmatic, antitheoretical preoccupation with making things work – a trend that was to find its expression in psychology in J. B. Watson's behaviorism. I add a remark of Alexis de Tocqueville's which is apposite of the behaviorist development and relates its origin to a more lasting tradition of American democracy: ". . . democratic people are always afraid of losing their way in visionary speculation. They mistrust systems; they adhere closely to facts and study facts with their own senses" (Tocqueville, 1889, p. 35).

I want to stress a part of J. B. Watson's arguments that has been neglected in the past. Watson's dismissal of the introspectionism of his predecessors is well known and documented (see, for example, Baars, 1986). I argue in addition that another part of his attack against the established psychology contained the seeds of the failure of his program. In his behaviorist manifesto of 1913, Watson, who had been doing animal experiments for some years, claimed to be "embarrassed" by the question what bearing animal work has upon human psychology and argued for the investigation of humans that is the exact same as that used for "animals." In the first paragraph of the article, he asserted: "The behaviorist, in his efforts to get a unitary scheme of animal response, recognizes no dividing line between man and brute" (Watson, 1913, p. 158). The manifesto was in part a defense of his own work, a way of making it acceptable and respectable. Watson's preoccupation with marking his place in American psychology was also noticeable in his treatment of his intellectual predecessors. He referred to "behaviorists," i.e., his colleagues in work on animal behavior, but there was no acknowledgment that animal researchers as G. J. Romanes, C. Lloyd Morgan, or Jacques Loeb are his conceptual predecessors and pathfinders.[2] He did give credit to Pillsbury for defining psychology as the "science of behavior."

Watson's continuing argument was clothed primarily in the attack on structuralism and E. B. Titchener's division of experience into the *minutiae* of human consciousness (Titchener, 1910, particularly pp. 15–30). However he expanded the argument for behaviorism on the basis of using animal experiments as the model for investigating human functioning. The following year, in his banner book (Watson, 1914), he complained even more strongly that his work on animal learning and related topics had not been used in our understanding of human psychology. Watson's unification of human and nonhuman behaviors into a single object of investigation prevented a psychology of the human and the human mind from being established, and in particular it avoided sophisticated investigations of human problem solving, memory, and language.[3] Eventually behaviorism failed, in part because it could not satisfy the need for a realistic and useful psychology of human action and thought.

Watson's goal was the prediction and control of behavior, particularly the latter when he equates all of psychology with "applied" psychology. There is the reasonable suggestion, made *inter alia*, that we need to be – as we have since learned to call it – methodological behaviorists, i.e., concerned with observables as the first order of business of our, as of any, science. Post-behaviorist psychologies did not ask for the feel or constituents of conscious experience, but rather were concerned with observable actions from which theories about internal states could be constructed.

Watson's influence was probably most pervasive in his emphasis on the stimulus–response (S–R) approach.[4] The insistence on an associative basis of all behavior was consistent with much of the empiricist tradition. The exceptions were E. C. Tolman's invocation of "cognitive maps" and Skinner's functional behaviorism. However, most behaviorists seriously attempted to follow Watson's lead in insisting on the action of stimuli in terms of their physical properties, and on defining organism response in terms of its physical parameters – the basis for a popular reference to behaviorism as the psychology of "muscle twitches." The position is of course a direct result of working with nonhuman animals, for whom it was at least difficult to postulate a "cognitive" transformation of environmental events and physical action. B. F. Skinner on the other hand used functionalist definitions of stimuli and responses as eliciting/discriminative conditions and operant behavior (Skinner, 1995). However, his initial focusing on the behavior of pigeons and rats also alienated him from research on specifically human functions, and it is likely that Chomsky's review of Skinner's "Verbal Behavior" put him beyond the pale of the burgeoning cognitive community.

One of the consequences of Watson's dicta was the switch to animal work in the mainstream of American psychology. Table 1 shows the shift over decades into animal work as well as its subsequent decline in the primary journal (*Journal of Experimental Psychology*).

Table 1 Articles in the *Journal of Experimental Psychology*

Year	No. Articles	Nonhuman Subjects, %	Editor
1917	33	0	J. B. Watson
1927	33	6	M. Bentley
1937	57	9	S. W. Fernberger
1947	50	30	F. I. Irwin
1957	67	22	A. W. Melton
1967	87	15	D. A. Grant
1977*	20	10	G. A. Kimble

* These data are for JEP's successor journal, the *Journal of Experimental Psychology: General*.

This rise and decline in animal research[5] took place independently of the interests of the editors, the majority of whom were in fact not doing research on nonhuman subjects. It also illustrates the basis of the developing unhappiness among many psychologists doing research on human memory and related topics at being shut out of the most prestigious publication outlets (see below). When human subjects were used, it was frequently for studies of eyelid conditioning and related topics in uncomplicated (noncognitive?) conditions and environments. For example, in addition to the 30% animal studies in the 1947 volume, another 14% were on conditioning.

At the theoretical level, very little of Hullian theory was applicable to complex human behavior. John Dollard and Neal Miller (1950) presented a major attempt to integrate personality theory (mostly derived from Freud) into the Hullian framework, and Charles Osgood (1950) tried to explain much of human action in terms of associationist mediation theory. The major attempt to apply Hullian principles was in the volume on a mathematico-deductive theory of rote learning (Hull et al., 1940). Apart from a somewhat naive and rigid positivism, the theory generated predictions (primarily about serial learning) that were patently at odds with existing information, the logical apparatus was clumsy, and the predictions difficult to generate. The book generated no follow-ups of any influence, nor any body of empirical research. It was irrelevant. The proposals developed few consequences, and together with the insistence that all thought processes could be reduced to implicit speech, it was generally accepted that the Hullian approach had little to offer to an understanding of human thought and action.

There is a wealth of anecdotal information about the difficulty of getting human research work into print during the behaviorist period. Much of the work was eventually reported in relatively obscure (and essentially unrefereed) journals like those of the Murchison group (e.g., *Journal of Psychology, Journal of Genetic Psychology*) and *Psychological Reports*. One example of work sidelined into secondary journals were studies on clustering (categorical and otherwise) in memory organization and related activities. W. Bousfield started these major deviations from the stimulus-response orthodoxy with

a paper in 1953, a change which C. N. Cofer recognized early on as a tie to Bartlett's work (Jenkins & Bruce, 2000). When James Jenkins and Wallace Russell pursued a related topic, they published in the *Journal of Abnormal and Social Psychology* because they believed that Arthur Melton would not accept it for the *Journal of Experimental Psychology* since it was concerned with recall rather than learning (Jenkins & Russell, 1952). A few years later, Jenkins and associates sent Melton one of their papers (the subsequently widely cited Jenkins, Mink, & Russell, 1958) and were told by Melton, scribbled across their submission letter, that "this would be of no interest to my readers."[6] Another example of behaviorist hegemony was the difficulty that K. and M. Breland had in publishing any criticisms of Skinner's position on innate dispositions (Bailey & Bailey, 1980).

As I have indicated, one of the reasons why stimulus-response behaviorism and research on human memory and thought were incompatible was the physicalism of the S–R position. The eliciting stimuli were defined in terms of their physical characteristics and, in principle, responses were either skeletal/muscular events or their equivalents in theoretical terms. Such concepts as the "pure stimulus act" and r_g – the anticipatory goal response – were theoretical notions that were to act implicitly in the same manner as observable behavior and were intended to do much of the "unconscious" work of processing information. Greenwood (1999) has discussed in detail the shortcomings of Hullian psychology with respect to representation and to conceptual processing.

Whether the cognitive revolution had a specific target is debatable because the change was one of movement to a more adaptable set of presuppositions rather than the destruction of the old ones. Research on human information processing, as the cognitive movement was called early on, moved to new or neglected areas of research (such as free recall and problem solving) rather than attacking research with non-human animals. If there was a target it was the Hull–Spence position – primarily because of its preeminence in the field as a whole and its dominance over contending behaviorist positions such as Tolman's. I would argue that it is not the case, as Amsel has argued, that the "behaviorism that cognitive scientists attack is a caricature . . . of J. B. Watson and B. F. Skinner" (Amsel, 1992, p. 67). During the 1930s and 1940s, the dominant figures of American behaviorism were Clark Hull, and eventually Kenneth Spence, and to the limited extent that the new cognitivists drew boundaries it was between them and the Hull-Spence axis. However, the latter's influence declined as behaviorism in general faded. Skinner, on the other hand, maintained some of his influence, so that in the year 2000 there were 220 literature citations for B. F. Skinner, while there were 73 for C. L. Hull and 26 for K. W. Spence.[7]

As S-R behaviorism faded, there was little in the way of Jacobin sentiments, of a radical rooting out of the previous dogmas. Certainly, a few of such sentiments found their way into print. Much was said in colloquia and in congress corridors, but the written record does not record a violent revolution. If anything qualifies as a Jacobin document it was Noam Chomsky's attack on Skinner's *Verbal Behavior* (1957), though the attack was not against the dominant Hull–Spence position (Chomsky, 1959). It might also be argued that Chomsky failed to distinguish between the stimulus-response analyses of Hull–Spence and the functionalism of Skinner.

The Limited Appeal of Behaviorism and the Seeds of Change

If it is the case, as I have implied, that behaviorism represented only an interlude in the normal flow of the development of psychological science, what was it that was interrupted and what was there to replace the behaviorist position, once it was shown to be inadequate. J. D. Greenwood (1999) has discussed one such tradition that developed out of the work of the Würzburg school, Oswald Külpe in particular, of the psychology of Otto Selz, of the work on directed thought by Ach, as well as later content and rule based psychologies.[8]

Within the United States, the 1940–1945 war created another nest of antibehaviorist developments. The war effort brought together a number of people in various projects. Of special importance to later developments was a group at MIT and Harvard, which included J. C. R. Licklider, S. S. Stevens, Ira Hirsh, Walter Rosenblith, George

A. Miller, W. R. Garner, and Clifford Morgan. Their original war work was primarily in psychoacoustics and noise research, but it extended into signal detection and related topics. With the creation of the Lincoln Laboratory at MIT in 1951, this early deviation from behaviorist dogma prepared the ground for mathematical models and the commanding influence of signal detection theory in perception as well as memory and other fields (Green & Swets, 1966). By the time the revolution started, these strands were ready to contribute to a new psychology. Similar accumulations of talent occurred in other parts of the war establishment as well as in Britain (e.g., in the influence of the military interest in vigilance phenomena on D. E. Broadbent). Finally, an important influence that was not Hullian (despite its origins at Hull's Yale) was Carl Hovland's work on concept formation, attitude change, and related phenomena (e.g., Hovland, 1952).

What about the psychology that coexisted in Europe with the behaviorism of the United States? The important aspect of European psychology of the time was that not only was Europe essentially unaffected and uninfluenced by behaviorism,[9] but also that the developments in Europe became part of the American mainstream after the decline of behaviorism. There was both a general opening up of America to European ideas and the influx of European psychologists into the United States. Interestingly, if there was little influence from the United States to Europe so was there relatively little leakage of psychological theory across European frontiers. In the nineteenth century, William James was read in Europe and Wilhelm Wundt was an international figure up to the beginning of the next century. But in the twentieth century the various national groups were relatively insulated.

In Germany – apart from the early influence or the Würzburg school – the major development in the early years of the twentieth century was the advent of Gestalt psychology. Wolfgang Köhler, Kurt Koffka, and Max Wertheimer created a psychology that was concerned with an analysis of human conscious experience and with organizing structures, concepts alien to behaviorism. Gestalt psychology introduced – without apology or embarrassment – structures that controlled experience but were themselves not amenable to observation or introspection. Gestalt psychology was the earliest European influence on U.S. psychology, primarily because the advent of National Socialism eradicated German scholarship and forced the major figures of the Gestalt movement to leave the country. Most of them arrived in a behaviorist America where they failed to have any immediate influence as they were forced to make do on the fringes of the psychological academic establishment.[10] Despite their apparent marginality in a behaviorist environment, they still had an important influence on the nascent cognitive developments (see, for example, Hochberg, 1968, and Köhler, 1959).

In francophone Europe (mainly Switzerland and France), much of the work in the early twentieth century was in developmental psychology. The major figure was Jean Piaget, whose work was available in English as early as the 1920s (Piaget, 1926). Similarly, Edouard Claparède's work with children had been translated, but not his major contribution to the problem of hypothesis formation (Claparède, 1934). Binet's work on intelligence testing was well known early on. However, there was little early interest in a theoretical developmental psychology, much of the focus was on clinical developmental problems. In particular, the interest in cognitive development did not take off until well after World War II. But there is no doubt that figures like Jean Piaget were central in that development in the United States.

The most extensive cognitive developments during the behaviorist interlude in the United States occurred in Britain. It is of particular interest since no language barrier would have prevented these ideas from being generally adopted in America – but it was not to be. The early stages in the British history of cognition (see also Collins, 2001) were set by F. C. Bartlett in the l930s, and by the brilliant Kenneth Craik who died in an accident in 1945. Craik suggested in 1943 that the mind constructs models of reality: "If the organism carries a small-scale model of external reality and its own possible actions within its head, it is able to try out various alternatives, conclude which is the best of them, react to future situations before they arise, utilize the knowledge of past events in dealing with the present and future, and in every way react to a much fuller, safer and more competent manner to emergencies which face it" (Craik, 1943, p. 57).

Craik was the first director of the Applied Psychology Unit in Cambridge which for another half century would be a leading center for cognitive psychology. He was succeeded by F. C. Bartlett and Norman Mackworth. In 1958 Donald Broadbent became the APU director. Broadbent also anticipated the American revolution with his early work on attention in the 1950s and his work on communication (Broadbent, 1958). Another important influence in Britain was George Humphrey whose two books on the history and data on thinking summarized the field and pointed to new directions (Humphrey, 1948, 1951). And, finally, mention must be made of our British–Canadian neighbors and the influence of D. O. Hebb on the postbehaviorist psychologies in the United States (Hebb, 1949).

In summary, there was an obvious plethora of nonbehaviorist ideas available in the world during the 1930s and 1940s. Some of them were heard in the U.S. but none of them was rigorously or widely followed. It was not until the late 1950s that the failure of behaviorism made room for these "foreign" notions.

The Waxing and Waning of Associationism

In the nineteenth century, experimental psychology was initially dominated by German psychology, which, in turn, had embraced British empiricism and associationism to large extent. That embrace was particularly evident in the experimental study of memory started by Hermann Ebbinghaus (1885). Ebbinghaus introduced the serial and associative learning paradigms that were to dominate the field for many decades.[11] With minor perturbations, the Ebbinghaus tradition smoothly merged into the functionalist tradition of the early twentieth century (McGeoch, 1942), and then into the behaviorist methodologies. The research was behaviorist in style, emphasizing stimulus–response connections and some concepts (such as reinforcement and stimulus generalization) imported from the Hull-Spence tradition. Thus, an often atheoretical neo-Ebbinghaus tradition survived the war and continued into the 1950s. The preoccupations of the verbal learning psychologists were focussed on associations, their nature and strengths. Was there an alternative conception?

In fact a productive movement of work on memory had subverted the dominant associationist and behaviorist themes for some time. Historically, as Greenwood (1999) has noted, it was Locke who had pointed out that the "association of ideas" did not provide a general explanation of human reasoning. In modern times, the movement was characterized by Bartlett's work with schemas and his insistence that memory was constructive not reproductive (Bartlett, 1932) and by the associationist Thorndike's experiments demonstrating that *belongingness* ("this goes with that") was a major factor in determining what was learned and retained (Thorndike, 1932, p.72). The culmination was the publication of George Katona's book on memorizing and organizing (Katona, 1940).[12] Katona spent much time in explicating, both experimentally and theoretically, basic principles of *Gestalt* psychology such as understanding, grouping, whole-relations and the function of meaning; the final message is clear: "[O]rganization is a requirement for successful memorization. It must be present in some form in all kinds of learning" (p. 249). Organization refers to the establishment or discovery of relations among constituent elements. Katona's book characterized the organizational movement. It was typical of the behaviorist interlude that, in 1941, Arthur Melton, one of its gatekeepers, dismissed Katona's book as lacking operational definitions and producing unreliable results (Melton, 1941). Not surprisingly the attempts to introduce notions of organization into American psychology were not successful.

With the onset of the "revolutionary" period, new attempts were mounted to replace associationist thinking with organizational principles, i.e., that the glue that held together memorial contents were categories and organizations of words, thoughts, and concepts rather than item to item associations (Bower, 1970; Mandler, 1967, 1977, 1979; Tulving, 1962). By 1970, organization had been reinvented and became the major direction for memory research for about ten years. The new organizational psychology was probably a significant improvement over its predecessor – advances in experimental and statistical techniques and specifications of theoretical mechanisms represented significant forward steps over the *Gestalt* notions of the earlier period.[13]

The "revolution" tended to be long and convoluted, highlighted in a series of conferences. I will discuss the ones on memory below, but memory was not the only nor was it the first field of psychology to organize conferences on the new directions. One of the most direction-giving occasions was the "Special Group on Information Theory" of the Institute of Electrical and Electronics Engineers which met at MIT in 1956 (see Baars, 1986, passim). At that meeting Noam Chomsky, George Miller, and Alan Newell and Herbert Simon presented the initial papers of a trend that would be defining in the next decade. A similar pace setter, in that case for the emergence of Artificial Intelligence and its relation to cognitive processes, was the London Symposium on the Mechanisation of Thought Processes in 1958 (Anonymous, 1959). In other areas the attention to cognitive factors developed at various times during the decades following the 1950s, as in emotion (Schachter & Singer, 1962), perception (Hochberg, 1968), and personality theory (Mischel, 1968).

I now turn to a case study of the "revolution" in the memory field, which illustrates the successive steps toward a different way of looking at a discipline. The field was called "verbal learning" under the behaviorist aegis, continuing a belief that basic learning processes (no different from those operative for nonhuman animals) were being investigated. Since "learning" – the novel association of stimuli with responses – was the basic law of psychology, all behavioral phenomena, including so-called memory processes, had to be brought under the operation of that basic law. [Note: This section has been omitted.]

Epilogue

I close with a reminder that psychology, just as many other intellectual endeavors, conforms to Hegel's view of the spiral of thought, with topics recurring repeatedly in the history of a discipline, often at a more sophisticated or developed level. The advent of connectionism has already shown a return of associationism in modern clothing. At the turn of the century we are in the midst of a preoccupation with neurophysiological reduction, a concern that psychology had previously displayed at a periodic cycle of some 40–50 years. The notion of recurring cycles is alien to a recent attempt to see the future of the "cognitive revolution" (Johnson & Erneling, 1997). The mirror that book displayed is cloudy indeed with a variety of different predictions. The most unlikely is the one presented by the keystone chapter of the book

in which Jerome Bruner endorses a postmodern view of cognitive science (Bruner, 1997), which is the one position least likely – given its postulates – to foresee any future at all. But psychology has been one of the disciplines that have essentially been unchanged by postmodern attempts (in contrast, for example, to literature and anthropology). The most likely case is that psychology will – as it has in the past – muddle along, encountering other revolutions, whether cognitive or not.

Notes

1 I have sketched the socio-political origins of American behaviorism elsewhere (Mandler, 1996, reprinted in Mandler, 1997). For a discussion of the prebehaviorist "cognitive" psychologies see Greenwood (1999) and Mandler & Mandler (1964).

2 The omission of Loeb may have been deliberate, since Watson had been warned away from him as a graduate student (Watson, 1936, p. 273).

3 Though by 1919 he was fully committed to the investigation of human emotion from a behaviorist standpoint, i.e., "that the human organism is built to react in emotional ways." (Watson, 1919, p. 223).

4 However, as Samelson's (1981) research has shown, it took some years after 1913 before one could speak of a general acceptance of behaviorism.

5 Robins, Gosling, & Craik (1999) also noted a general decline in articles on animal research during the second half of the twentieth century.

6 Personal communications from James Jenkins.

7 Courtesy of the WebofScience.

8 For a discussion of and presentation of a selection of those earlier developments, see Mandler & Mandler (1964).

9 For example, George Miller (in Baars, 1986, p. 212) reports being told after a talk at Oxford in 1963 in which he had attacked behaviorism: "[T]here are only three behaviorists in England, and none of them were here today!" In 1965, I was approached

by a senior British psychologist and asked, in all seriousness, whether anybody in America really believed any of the behaviorist credo.

10 For an account of the German immigration in psychology, see Mandler & Mandler (1968). For a specific account of the Gestalt psychologists in the U.S., see Sokal (1984).

11 Though it was Ebbinghaus who first noted that much of human memory, particularly in every day thought, was nondeliberate (Mandler, 1985) and not represented by the very experimental methods he had popularized – an important addendum and mostly and mistakenly ignored for nearly a century.

12 Murray and Bandomir (2000) have discussed insightfully Katona's indebtedness to G. E. Müller for many of his insights into problems of organization.

13 It is difficult to specify exactly when organizational variables stopped attracting both theoretical and empirical attention, but by the early 1990s the status of organization as necessary for recall and recognition was all but forgotten. Studies of the "strength" of individual items and their connection to other items regained prominence and the connectionist movement (Hinton & Anderson, 1981; Rumelhart & McClelland, 1985), a highly sophisticated replay of age-old associationist themes, became dominant, but that tale is beyond the scope of this article.

References

Amsel, A. (1992). Skinner and the cognitive revolution. *Journal of Behavior Therapy and Experimental Psychiatry, 23*(2), 67–70.

Anonymous (1959). *Mechanisation of thought processes.* (Vol. Symposium No. 10, National Physical Laboratory). London: Her Majesty's Stationery Office.

Baars, B. J. (1986). *The cognitive revolution in psychology.* New York: Guilford Press.

Bailey, R. E., & Bailey, M. B. (1980). A view from outside the Skinner box. *American Psychologist, 35,* 942–946.

Bartlett, F. C. (1932). *Remembering.* Cambridge: Cambridge University Press.

Bousfield, W. A. (1953). The occurrence of clustering in the recall of randomly arranged associates. *Journal of General Psychology, 49,* 229–240.

Bower, G. H. (1970). Organizational factors in memory. *Cognitive Psychology, 1,* 18–46.

Broadbent, D. E. (1958). *Perception and communication.* London: Pergamon Press.

Bruner, J. (1997). Will cognitive revolutions ever stop? In D. M. Johnson & C. E. Erneling (Eds.), *The future of the cognitive revolution.* New York: Oxford University Press.

Chomsky, N. (1957). *Syntactic structures.* The Hague: Mouton.

Chomsky, N. (1959). Review of B. F. Skinner's "Verbal Behavior." *Language, 35,* 26–58.

Claparède, E. (1934). *La genèse de l'hypotheses.* Geneva: Kundig.

Cofer, C. N. (1961). *Verbal learning and verbal behavior.* New York: McGraw-Hill.

Cofer, C. N. (1978). Origins of the Journal of Verbal Learning and Verbal Behavior. *Journal of Verbal Learning & Verbal Behavior, 17*(1), 113–126.

Cofer, C. N., & Musgrave, B. S. (Eds.). (1963). *Verbal behavior and learning.* New York: McGraw-Hill.

Collins, A. (2001). The psychology of memory. In G. C. Bunn, A. D. Lovie, & G. D. Richards (Eds.), *Psychology in Britain* (pp. 150–168). Leicester, UK: The British Psychological Society.

Craik, K. J. W. (1943). *The nature of explanation.* Cambridge: Cambridge University Press.

Dixon, T. R., & Horton, D. L. (Eds.). (1968). *Verbal behavior and general behavior theory.* Englewood Cliffs NJ: Prentice Hall.

Dollard, J., & Miller, N. E. (1950). *Personality and psychotherapy.* New York: McGraw-Hill.

Ebbinghaus, H. (1885). *Ueber das Gedächtnis: Untersuchungen zur experimentellen Psychologie.* Leipzig: Duncke und Humblot.

Feigenbaum, E. A. (1959). *An information processing theory of verbal learning.* (RAND Report P-1817). Santa Monica CA: RAND Corporation.

Green, D. M., & Swets, J. A. (1966). *Signal detection theory and psychophysics.* New York: Wiley.

Greenwood, J. D. (1999). Understanding the "cognitive revolution" in psychology. *Journal of the History of the Behavioral Sciences, 35*(1), 1–22.

Hebb, D. O. (1949). *The organization of behavior.* New York: Wiley.

Hinton, G. E., & Anderson, J. A. (1981). *Parallel models of associative memory.* Hillsdale NJ: Lawrence Erlbaum Associates.

Hochberg, J. (1968). In the mind's eye. In R. N. Haber (Ed.), *Contemporary theory and research in visual perception.* New York: Holt.

Hovland, C. I. (1952). A "Communication Analysis" of concept learning. *Psychological Review, 59,* 461–472.

Hull, C. L., Hovland, C. I., Ross, R. T., Hall, M., Perkins, D. T., & Fitch, F. B. (1940). *Mathematico-deductive theory of rote learning; a study in scientific methodology.* New Haven CT: Yale University Press.

Humphrey, G. (1948). *Directed thinking.* New York: Dodd Mead.

Humphrey, G. (1951). *Thinking; an introduction to its experimental psychology.* New York: John Wiley.

Jenkins, J. J. (Ed.). (1955). *Associative processes in verbal behavior: A report of the Minnesota conference.* Minneapolis MN: Department of Psychology, University of Minnesota.

Jenkins, J. J., & Bruce, D. (2000). Charles Norval Cofer (1916–1998). *American Psychologist, 55*(5), 538–539.

Jenkins, J. J., Mink, W. D., & Russell, W. A. (1958). Associative clustering as a function of verbal association strength. *Psychological Reports,* 127–136.

Jenkins, J. J., & Postman, L. J. (1957). The Minnesota conference on associative processes in verbal behavior. *American Psychologist, 12,* 499–500.

Jenkins, J. J., & Russell, W. A. (1952). Associative clustering during recall. *Journal of Abnormal & Social Psychology, 47,* 818–821.

Johnson, D. M., & Erneling, C. E. (Eds.). (1997). *The future of the cognitive revolution.* New York: Oxford University Press.

Katona, G. (1940). *Organizing and memorizing.* New York: Columbia University Press.

Köhler, W. (1959). Gestalt psychology today. *American Psychologist, 14,* 727–734.

Mandler, G. (1967). Organization and memory. In K. W. Spence & J. T. Spence (Eds.), *The psychology of learning and motivation: Advances in research and theory* (pp. 328–372). New York: Academic Press.

Mandler, G. (1977). Commentary on "Organization and memory". in G. H. Bower (Ed.), *Human memory: Basic processes* (pp. 297–308). New York: Academic Press.

Mandler, G. (1979). Organization, memory, and mental structures. In C. R. Puff (Ed.), *Memory organization and structure.* New York: Academic Press.

Mandler, G. (1985). From association to structure. *Journal of Experimental Psychology: Learning, Memory, and Cognition, 11,* 464–468.

Mandler, G. (1996). The situation of psychology: Landmarks and choicepoints. *American Journal of Psychology, 109,* 1–35.

Mandler, G. (1997). *Human nature explored.* New York: Oxford University Press.

Mandler, G., Rabinowitz, J. C., & Simon, R. A. (1981). Coordinate organization: The holistic representation of word pairs. *American Journal of Psychology, 94,* 209–222.

Mandler, J. M., & Mandler, G. (1964). *Thinking: From Association to Gestalt*. New York: Wiley (repr. Westport CT: Greenwood Press, 1981).

Mandler, J. M., & Mandler, G. (1968). The diaspora of experimental psychology: The Gestaltists and others. In D. Fleming & B. Bailyn (Eds.), *The intellectual migration: Europe and America, 1930–1960*. Cambridge MA: Charles Warren Center, Harvard University.

McGeoch, J. A. (1942). *The psychology of human learning: an introduction*. New York: Longman, Green.

Melton, A. W. (1941). Review of Katona, *Organizing and memorizing*. *American Journal of Psychology, 54*, 455–457.

Miller, G. A., Galanter, E. H., & Pribram, K. (1960). *Plans and the structure of behavior*. New York: Holt.

Mischel, W. (1968). *Personality and assessment*. New York: Wiley.

Murray, D. J. (1995). *Gestalt psychology and the cognitive revolution*. New York: Harvester Wheatsheaf.

Murray, D. J., & Bandomir, C. A. (2000). G. E. Müller (1911, 1913, 1917) on memory. *Psychologie et Histoire, 1*, 208–232. (Also available at http://Ipe.psycho.univ-paris5.fr/membres Murray.htm).

Musgrave, B. S. (1959). *Memorandum: A Few Notes on the Conference on Verbal Learning*. Verbal Learning Conference – Fall 1959, Gould House, Dobbs Ferry, NY.

Newell, A., & Simon, H. (1972). *Human problem solving*. Englewood Cliffs NJ: Prentice-Hall.

Osgood, C. E. (1953). *Method and theory in experimental psychology*. New York: Oxford University Press.

Piaget, J. (1926). *The language and thought of the child*. New York: Harcourt, Brace.

Robins, R. W., Gosling, S. D., Craik, K. H. (1999). An empirical analysis of trends in psychology. *American Psychologist, 54*(2), 117–128.

Rumelhart, D. E., & McClelland, J. L. (1985). *Parallel distributed processing: Explorations on the microstructure of cognition*. Cambridge MA: MIT Press.

Samelson, F. (1981). Struggle for scientific authority: The reception of Watson's behaviorism, 1913–1920. *Journal of the History of the Behavioral Sciences, 17*, 399–425.

Schachter, S., & Singer, J. E. (1962). Cognitive, social and physiological determinants of emotional state. *Psychological Review, 69*, 379–399.

Skinner, B. F. (1957). *Verbal behavior*. New York: Appleton-Century-Crofts.

Skinner, B. F. (1995). "The Behavior of Organisms" at fifty. In J. T. Todd & E. K. Morris (Eds.), *Modern perspectives on B. F. Skinner and contemporary behaviorism* (pp. 149–161). Westport CT: Greenwood Press.

Sokal, M. (1984). The Gestalt psychologists in behaviorist America. *American Historical Review, 89*, 1240–1263.

Thorndike, E. L. (1932). *The fundamentals of learning*. New York: Teacher's College.

Titchener, E. B. (1910). *A textbook of psychology*. New York: Macmillan.

Tocqueville, A. de (1889). *Democracy in America* (Henry Reeve, Trans.). (Vol. II). London: Longmans Green.

Tolman, E. C. (1948). Cognitive maps in rats and men. *Psychological Review, 55*, 189–208.

Tulving, E. (1962). Subjective organization in free recall of "unrelated" words. *Psychological Review, 69*, 344–354.

Watson, J. B. (1913). Psychology as the behaviorist views it. *Psychological Review, 20*, 158–177.

Watson, J. B. (1914). *Behavior: An introduction to comparative psychology*. New York: Holt.

Watson, J. B. (1919). *Psychology from the stand-point of a behaviorist*. Philadelphia: Lippincott.

Watson, J. B. (1936). John Broadus Watson. In C. Murchison (Ed.), *A history of psychology in autobiography* (Vol. 3, pp. 271–281). Worcester MA: Clark University Press.

References

Adler, H. E. (1977). Vicissitudes of Fechnerian psychophysics in America. *Annals of the New York Academy of Sciences, 291,* 21–32.

Albee, G. W. (2000). The Boulder model's fatal flaw. *American Psychologist, 55,* 247–248.

Allport, G. W. (1954). *The nature of prejudice.* Reading, MA: Addison-Wesley.

Amsel, A., & Rashotte, M. E. (1984). *Mechanisms of adaptive behavior: Clark L. Hull's theoretical papers with commentary.* New York: Columbia University Press.

Anderson, P. (1998). *The origins of postmodernity.* London: Verso.

Angell, J. R. (1907). The province of functional psychology. *Psychological Review, 14,* 61–91.

Ash, M. G. (1995). *Gestalt psychology in German culture, 1890–1967: Holism and the quest for objectivity.* New York: Cambridge University Press.

Bache, R. M. (1895). Reaction time with reference to race. *Psychological Review, 2,* 475–486.

Baker, D. B. (1988). The psychology of Lightner Witmer. *Professional School Psychology, 3,* 109–121.

Baker, D. B., & Benjamin, L. T., Jr. (2000). The affirmation of the scientist-practitioner: A look back at Boulder. *American Psychologist, 55,* 241–247.

Baker, D. B., & Benjamin, L. T., Jr. (2005). Creating a profession: The National Institute of Mental Health and the training of psychologists, 1946–1954. In W. E. Pickren & S. F. Schneider (Eds.), *Psychology and the National Institute of Mental Health: A historical analysis of science, practice, and policy* (pp. 181–207). Washington, DC: American Psychological Association.

Bartlett, F. C. (1932). *Remembering: A study in experimental and social psychology.* Cambridge: Cambridge University Press.

Baum, W. K. (1981). *Transcribing and editing oral histories.* Nashville, TN: American Association for State and Local History.

Beardsley, E. H. (1973). The American scientist as social activist: Franz Boas, Burt G. Wilder, and the cause of racial justice, 1900–1915. *Isis, 64,* 50–66.

Benjamin, L. T., Jr. (1977). The Psychological Round Table: Revolution of 1936. *American Psychologist, 32,* 542–549.

Benjamin, L. T., Jr. (1980). Research at the Archives of the History of American Psychology: A case history. In J. Brozek & L. J. Pongratz (Eds.), *Historiography of modern psychology,* (pp. 241–251). Toronto: Hogrefe.

Benjamin, L. T., Jr. (1997). The origin of psychological species: History of the beginnings of the American Psychological Association divisions. *American Psychologist, 52*, 725–732.

Benjamin, L. T., Jr. (2000). The psychology laboratory at the turn of the 20th century. *American Psychologist, 55*, 318–321.

Benjamin, L. T., Jr. (2001). American psychology's struggles with its curriculum: Should a thousand flowers bloom? *American Psychologist, 56*, 735–742.

Benjamin, L. T., Jr. (2004). Science for sale: Psychology's earliest adventures in American advertising. In J. D. Williams, W. N. Lee, & C. P. Haugtvedt (Eds.), *Diversity in advertising: Broadening the scope of research directions* (pp. 21–39). Mahwah, NJ: Lawrence Erlbaum.

Benjamin, L. T., Jr. (2006). *A history of psychology in letters* (2nd edn). Malden, MA: Blackwell.

Benjamin, L. T., Jr. (2007). *A brief history of modern psychology*. Malden, MA: Blackwell.

Benjamin, L. T., Jr., & Baker, D. B. (2004). *From séance to science: A history of the profession of psychology in America*. Belmont, CA: Wadsworth.

Benjamin, L. T., Jr., Durkin, M., Link, M., Vestal, M., & Acord, J. (1992). Wundt's American doctoral students. *American Psychologist, 47*, 123–131.

Benjamin, L. T., Jr., Rogers, A. M., & Rosenbaum, A. (1991). Coca-Cola, caffeine, and mental deficiency: Harry Hollingworth and the Chattanooga trial of 1911. *Journal of the History of the Behavioral Sciences, 27*, 42–55.

Benjamin, L. T., Jr., Whitaker, J. L., Ramsey, R. M., & Zeve, D. R. (2007). John B. Watson's alleged sex research: An appraisal of the evidence. *American Psychologist, 62*, 131–139.

Bjork, D. W. (1983). *The compromised scientist: William James in the development of American psychology*. New York: Columbia University Press.

Blumenthal, A. L. (1975). A reappraisal of Wilhelm Wundt. *American Psychologist, 30*, 1081–1088.

Boring, E. G. (1950). *A history of experimental psychology* (2nd edn). New York: Appleton-Century-Crofts.

Breuer, J., & Freud, S. (1885). *Studies on hysteria*. New York: Basic Books.

Broca, P. (1861). Remarques sur le siège de la faculté du langage articulé, suivies d'une observation d'aphémie. *Bulletin de la Société Anatomiaque de Paris, 6*, 343–357.

Brozek, J. (1975). Irons in the fire: Introduction to a symposium on archival research. *Journal of the History of the Behavioral Sciences, 11*, 15–19.

Brozek, J. (1980). The echoes of Wundt's work in the United States, 1887–1977: A quantitative citation analysis. *Psychological Research, 42*, 103–107.

Bruce, D. (2000). Review of *Constructing scientific psychology: Karl Lashley's mind-brain debates* by Nadine M. Weidman. *Isis, 91*, 824–825.

Bruce, D., & Winograd, E. (1998). Remembering Deese's 1959 articles: The Zeitgeist, sociology of science, and false memories. *Psychonomic Bulletin and Review, 5*, 615–624.

Bruner, F. G. (1912). The primitive races in America. *Psychological Bulletin, 9*, 380–390.

Buckley, K. W. (1989). *Mechanical man: John Broadus Watson and the beginnings of behaviorism*. New York: Guilford Press.

Burnham, J. C. (1968). On the origins of behaviorism. *Journal of the History of the Behavioral Sciences, 4*, 143–151.

Butterfield, H. (1931). *The Whig interpretation of history*. London: G. Bell & Sons.

Butterfield, H. (1981). *The origins of history*. New York: Basic Books.

Cadwallader, T. C. (1975). Unique value of archival research. *Journal of the History of the Behavioral Sciences, 11*, 27–33.

Cahan, E. D., & White, S. H. (1992). Proposals for a second psychology. *American Psychologist, 47*, 224–235.

Capshew, J. H. (1992). Psychologists on site: A reconnaissance of the historiography of the laboratory. *American Psychologist, 47*, 132–142.

Capshew, J. H. (1993). Engineering behavior: Project Pigeon, World War II, and the conditioning of B. F. Skinner. *Technology and Culture, 34,* 835–857.

Cardno, J. A. (1965). Victorian psychology: a biographical approach. *Journal of the History of the Behavioral Sciences, 1,* 165–177.

Carr, E. H. (1961). *What is history?* New York: Random House.

Cattell, J. McK. (1890). Mental tests and measurements. *Mind, 15,* 373–381.

Cattell, J. McK. (1893). Tests of the senses and faculties. *Educational Review, 5,* 257–265.

Cautin, R. L. (2006). David Shakow: Architect of modern clinical psychology. In D. A. Dewsbury, L. T. Benjamin, Jr., & M. Wertheimer (Eds.), *Portraits of pioneers in psychology,* (Vol. 6, pp. 207–221). Washington, DC & Mahwah, NJ: American Psychological Association & Lawrence Erlbaum.

Collingwood, R. G. (1946). *The idea of history.* London: Oxford University Press.

Commager, H. S. (1965). *The nature and the study of history.* Columbus, OH: Charles Merrill.

Committee on Training in Clinical Psychology. (1947). Recommended graduate training program in clinical psychology. *American Psychologist, 2,* 539–558.

Coon, D. J. (1994). "Not a creature of reason": The alleged impact of Watsonian behaviorism on advertising in the 1920s. In J. T. Todd & E. K. Morris (Eds.), *Modern perspectives on John B. Watson and classical behaviorism* (pp. 37–63). Westport, CT: Greenwood Press.

Cromer, W., & Anderson, P. A. (1970). Freud's visit to America: Newspaper coverage. *Journal of the History of the Behavioral Sciences, 6,* 349–353.

Daniels, R. V. (1981). *Studying history: How and why* (3rd edn). Englewood Cliffs, NJ: Prentice Hall.

Danziger, K. (1980). Wundt and the two traditions in psychology. In R. W. Rieber (Ed.), *Wilhelm Wundt and the making of a scientific psychology* (pp. 73–88). New York: Plenum Press.

Davidson, E. S., & Benjamin, L. T., Jr. (1987). A history of the child study movement in America. In J. A. Glover & R. R. Ronning (Eds.), *Historical foundations of educational psychology* (pp. 41–60). New York: Plenum Press.

Dewsbury, D. A. (1990). Early interactions between animal psychologists and animal activists and the founding of the APA Committee on Precautions in Animal Experimentation. *American Psychologist, 45,* 315–327.

Dewsbury, D. A. (2006). *Monkey farm: A history of the Yerkes Laboratories of Primate Biology, Orange Park, Florida, 1930–1965.* Lewisburg, PA: Bucknell University Press.

Duckitt, J. (1992). Psychology and prejudice: A historical analysis and integrative framework. *American Psychologist, 47,* 1182–1193.

Ellenberger, H. F. (1972). The story of "Anna O": A critical review with new data. *Journal of the History of the Behavioral Sciences, 8,* 267–279.

Esterson, A. (1993). *Seductive mirage: An exploration of the work of Sigmund Freud.* New York: Open Court.

Esterson, A. (1998). Jeffrey Masson and Freud's seduction theory: A new fable based on old myths. *History of Human Sciences, 11,* 1–21.

Evans, R. B. (1985). E. B. Titchener and American experimental psychology. In H. Carpintero & J. M. Piero (Eds.), *Psychology in its historical context* (pp. 117–125). Valencia, Spain: University of Valencia.

Evans, R. B. (1991). E. B. Titchener on scientific psychology and technology. In G. A. Kimble, M. Wertheimer, & C. L. White (Eds.), *Portraits of pioneers in psychology* (Vol. 1, pp. 89–103). Washington, DC & Hillsdale, NJ: American Psychological Association and Lawrence Erlbaum.

Evans, R. B. (2000). Psychological instruments at the turn of the century. *American Psychologist, 55,* 322–325.

Evans, R. B., & Koelsch, W. (1985). Psychoanalysis arrives in America: The 1909 psychology conference at Clark University. *American Psychologist, 40,* 942–948.

Fagan, T. K. (2000). Practicing school psychology: A turn-of-the-century perspective. *American Psychologist, 55,* 754–757.

Fancher, R. E. (1973). *Psychoanalytic psychology: The development of Freud's thought.* New York: W. W. Norton.

Fancher, R. E. (2000). Snapshots of Freud in America, 1899–1999. *American Psychologist, 55,* 1025–1028.

Fechner, G. T. (1860). *Elemente der Psychophysik* [Elements of psychophysics]. Leipzig: Breitkopf & Härtel. English translation by H. Adler published by Holt, Rinehart & Winston, 1966.

Ferguson, L. W. (1976). The Scott Company. *JSAS Catalog of Selected Documents in Psychology, 6,* 128 (Ms. 1397).

Finger, S. (1994). *Origins of neuroscience: A history of explorations into brain function.* New York: Oxford University Press.

Finison, L. J. (1976). Unemployment, politics, and the history of organized psychology. *American Psychologist, 31,* 747–755.

Finison, L. J. (1979). An aspect of the early history of the Society for the Psychological Study of Social Issues: Psychologists and labor. *Journal of the History of the Behavioral Sciences, 15,* 29–37.

Freud, E. (1960). *The letters of Sigmund Freud.* New York: Basic Books.

Freud, S. (1900). *The interpretation of dreams.* Available from Avon Books, New York, 1968.

Freud, S. (1901). *The psychopathology of everyday life.* Available from Avon Books, New York, 1965.

Freud, S. (1905). *Three essays on the theory of sexuality.* Available from Avon Books, New York, 1962.

Freud, S. (1910). The origin and development of psychoanalysis. *American Journal of Psychology, 21,* 181–218.

Furumoto, L. (1989). The new history of psychology. In I. S. Cohen (Ed.), *The G. Stanley Hall lecture series* (Vol. 9, pp. 8–34). Washington, DC: American Psychological Association.

Galton, F. (1869). *Hereditary genius.* London: Macmillan.

Garfield, E. (1964). Citation indexing: A natural science literature retrieval system for the social sciences. *American Behavioral Scientist, 7,* 58–61.

Garfield, E. (1979). *Citation indexing: Its theory and application in science, technology, and humanities.* New York: Wiley.

Gilderhus, M. T. (2007). *History and historians: A historiographical introduction* (6th edn). Upper Saddle River, NJ: Prentice Hall.

Guthrie, R. V. (1998). *Even the rat was white: A historical view of psychology* (2nd edn). Boston: Allyn & Bacon.

Hall, G. S. (1893). Child study: The basis of exact education. *Forum, 16,* 429–441.

Hall, G. S. (1904). *Adolescence: Its psychology and its relations to physiology, anthropology, sociology, sex, crime, and religion* (2 vols.). New York: D. Appleton & Co.

Hall, G. S. (1905). The Negro in Africa and America. *Pedagogical Seminary, 12,* 350–368.

Harris, B. (1979). Whatever happened to Little Albert? *American Psychologist, 34,* 151–160.

Harris, B. (1980). The FBI's files on APA and SPSSI: Description and implications. *American Psychologist, 35,* 1141–1144.

Henle, M. (1978). One man against the Nazis: Wolfgang Köhler. *American Psychologist, 33,* 939–944.

Hilgard, E. R., Leary, D. E., & McGuire, G. R. (1991). The history of psychology: A survey and critical assessment. *Annual Review of Psychology, 42,* 79–107.

Hill, M. R. (1993). *Archival strategies and techniques.* Newbury Park, CA: Sage Publications.

Hogan, J. D. (2003). G. Stanley Hall: Educator, innovator, pioneer of developmental psychology. In G. A. Kimble & M. Wertheimer (Eds.), *Portraits of pioneers in psychology* (Vol. 5, pp. 19–36). Washington, DC & Mahwah, NJ: American Psychological Association & Lawrence Erlbaum.

Hollingworth, H. L. (1912). The influence of caffein on mental and motor efficiency. *Archives of Psychology, 22.* New York: Science Press.

Hollingworth, H. L. (1913). *Advertising and selling: Principles of appeal and response.* New York: D. Appleton.

Hollingworth, L. S. (1913). The frequency of amentia as related to sex. *Medical Record, 84,* 753–756.

Hollingworth, L. S. (1914a). *Functional periodicity: An experimental study of the mental and motor abilities of women during menstruation.* New York: Teachers College, Columbia University.

Hollingworth, L. S. (1914b). Variability as related to sex differences in achievement. *American Journal of Sociology, 19,* 510–530.

Hollingworth, L. S. (1916). Social devices for impelling women to bear and rear children. *American Journal of Sociology, 22,* 19–29.

Hollingworth, L. S. (1918). Tentative suggestions for the certification of practicing psychologists. *Journal of Applied Psychology, 2,* 280–284.

Holsti, O. R. (1969). *Content analysis for the social sciences and humanities.* Reading, MA: Addison-Wesley.

Hoopes, J. (1979). *Oral history: An introduction for students.* Chapel Hill: University of North Carolina Press.

Hornstein, G. A. (1992). The return of the repressed: Psychology's problematic relations with psychoanalysis, 1909–1960. *American Psychologist, 47,* 254–263.

Hull, C. L. (1943). *Principles of behavior.* New York: Appleton-Century-Crofts.

Hull, C. L. (1952). Clark L. Hull. In E. G. Boring, H. Werner, H. S. Langfeld, & R. M. Yerkes (Eds.), *A history of psychology in autobiography* (Vol. 4, pp. 143–162). Worcester, MA: Clark University Press.

James, W. (1890). *The principles of psychology* (2 vols.). New York: Henry Holt.

Jarausch, K. H., & Hardy, K. A. (1991). *Quantitative methods for historians.* Chapel Hill: University of North Carolina Press.

Jones, E. (1955). *The life and work of Sigmund Freud.* Vol. 1. New York: Basic Books.

Keppel, B. (2002). Kenneth B. Clark in the patterns of American culture. *American Psychologist, 57,* 29–37.

King, D. B., & Wertheimer, M. (2005). *Max Wertheimer & Gestalt theory.* New Brunswick, NJ: Transaction Publishers.

Klineberg, O. (1935). *Race differences.* New York: Harper & Brothers.

Kluger, R. (1975). *Simple justice: The history of Brown v. Board of Education and Black America's struggle for equality.* New York: Random House.

Koffka, K. (1922). Perception: An introduction to Gestalt-theorie. *Psychological Bulletin, 19,* 531–585.

Krech, D., & Cartwright, D. (1956). On SPSSI's first twenty years. *American Psychologist, 11,* 470–473.

Kuna, D. P. (1976). The concept of suggestion in the early history of advertising psychology. *Journal of the History of the Behavioral Sciences, 12,* 347–353.

Lange, L. L. (2005). Sleeping beauties in psychology: Comparisons of "hits" and "missed signals" in psychological journals. *History of Psychology, 8,* 194–217.

Larsen, J. C. (Ed.). (1988). *Researcher's guide to archives and regional history sources.* Hamden, CT: Library Professional Publications.

Leahey, T. H. (1981). The mistaken mirror: On Wundt's and Titchener's psychologies. *Journal of the History of the Behavioral Sciences, 17,* 273–282.

Leahey, T. H. (1991). *A history of modern psychology.* Englewood Cliffs, NJ: Prentice Hall.

Leahey, T. H. (1992a). *A history of psychology: Main currents in psychological thought* (3rd edn). Englewood Cliffs, NJ: Prentice Hall.

Leahey, T. H. (1992b). The mythical revolutions of American psychology. *American Psychologist*, *47*, 308–318.

Leary, D. E. (1992). William James and the art of human understanding. *American Psychologist*, *47*, 152–160.

Locke, J. (1905/1690). *An essay concerning human understanding*. Chicago: Open Court Publishing Company.

Lummis, T. (1987). *Listening to history: The authenticity of oral evidence*. London: Hutchinson.

Mandler, G. (2002). Origins of the cognitive (r)evolution. *Journal of the History of the Behavioral Sciences*, *38*, 339–353.

Mandler, J. M., & Mandler, G. (1969). The diaspora of experimental psychology: The Gestaltists and others. In D. Fleming & B. Bailyn (Eds.), *The intellectual migration: Europe and America, 1930–1960* (pp. 371–419). Cambridge, MA: Belknap Press.

Masson, J. M. (1984). *The assault on truth: Freud's suppression of the seduction theory*. New York: Farrar, Straus & Giroux.

McGuire, W. (Ed.) (1974). *The Freud-Jung letters: The correspondence between Sigmund Freud and C. G. Jung*. Princeton, NJ: Princeton University Press.

McReynolds, P. (1997). *Lightner Witmer: His life and times*. Washington, DC: American Psychological Association.

Milar, K. S. (1999). "A coarse and clumsy tool": Helen Thompson Woolley and the Cincinnati Vocational Bureau. *History of Psychology*, *2*, 219–235.

Milar, K. S. (2000). The first generation of women psychologists and the psychology of women. *American Psychologist*, *55*, 616–619.

Milar, K. S. (2004). Breaking the silence: Helen Bradford Thompson Woolley. In T. C. Dalton & R. B. Evans (Eds.), *The life cycle of psychological ideas: Understanding prominence and the dynamics of intellectual change* (pp. 301–328). New York: Kluwer Academic/Plenum Publishers.

Mill, J. S. (1843). *A system of logic, ratiocinative and inductive, being a connected view of the principles of evidence, and the methods of scientific investigation* (2 vols.). London: John W. Parker.

Miller, J. G. (1946). Clinical psychology in the Veterans Administration. *American Psychologist*, *1*, 181–189.

Murphy, G., & Ballou, R. O. (Eds.). (1961). *William James on psychical research*. London: Chatto & Windus.

Muschinske, D. (1977). The nonwhite as child: G. Stanley Hall on the education of nonwhite peoples. *Journal of the History of the Behavioral Sciences*, *13*, 328–336.

Nathan, P. E. (2000). The Boulder model: A dream deferred – or lost? *American Psychologist*, *55*, 250–252.

Neisser, U. (1967). *Cognitive psychology*. New York: Appleton-Century-Crofts.

Novick, P. (1988). *That noble dream: The "objectivity question" and the American historical profession*. New York: Cambridge University Press.

O'Donnell, J. M. (1979). The clinical psychology of Lightner Witmer: A case study of institutional innovation and intellectual change. *Journal of the History of the Behavioral Sciences*, *15*, 3–17.

O'Donnell, J. M. (1985). *The origins of behaviorism: American psychology, 1870–1920*. New York: New York University Press.

O'Neill, W. M., & Landauer, A. A. (1966). The phi-phenomenon: Turning point or rallying point. *Journal of the History of the Behavioral Sciences*, *2*, 335–340.

Patterson, J. T. (2001). *Brown v. Board of Education: A civil rights milestone and its troubled legacy*. New York: Oxford University Press.

Petryszak, N. G. (1981). Tabula rasa – Its origin and implications. *Journal of the History of the Behavioral Sciences, 17,* 15–27.

Philogène, G. (Ed.). (2004). *Racial identity in context: The legacy of Kenneth B. Clark.* Washington, DC: American Psychological Association.

Pickren, W. E. (2004). Between the cup of principle and the lip of practice: Ethnic minorities and American psychology, 1966–1980. *History of Psychology, 7,* 45–64.

Plous, S. (1994). William James' other concern: Racial injustice in America. *The General Psychologist, 30,* 80–88.

Popplestone, J. A. (2004). Reinventing the past through interpretation: Reflections on the history of psychology – 35 years in the trenches. In T. C. Dalton & R. B. Evans (Eds.), *The life cycle of psychological ideas: Understanding prominence and the dynamics of intellectual change* (pp. 59–81). New York: Kluwer.

Popplestone, J. A., & McPherson, M. W. (1976). Ten years at the Archives of the History of American Psychology. *American Psychologist, 31,* 533–534.

Raimy, V. (Ed.). (1950). *Training in clinical psychology.* Englewood Cliffs, NJ: Prentice Hall.

Ritchie, D. A. (2003). *Doing oral history: A practical guide* (2nd edn). New York: Oxford University Press.

Roediger, H. L., III. (2000). Sir Frederic Charles Bartlett: Experimental and applied psychologist. In G. A. Kimble & M. Wertheimer (Eds.), *Portraits of pioneers in psychology* (Vol. 4, pp. 149–161). Washington, DC & Mahwah, NJ: American Psychological Association & Lawrence Erlbaum.

Rosenzweig, S. (1994). *The historic expedition to America (1909): Freud, Jung, and Hall the kingmaker.* St. Louis: Rana House.

Ross, D. (1972). *G. Stanley Hall: The psychologist as prophet.* Chicago: University of Chicago Press.

Rutherford, A. (2003). B. F. Skinner's technology of behavior in American life: From consumer culture to counterculture. *Journal of the History of the Behavioral Sciences, 39,* 1–23.

Samelson, F. (1977). World War I intelligence testing and the development of psychology. *Journal of the History of the Behavioral Sciences, 13,* 274–282.

Samelson, F. (1978). From "race psychology" to "studies in prejudice": Some observations of the thematic reversal in social psychology. *Journal of the History of the Behavioral Sciences, 14,* 265–278.

Samelson, F. (1981). Struggle for scientific authority: The reception of Watson's behaviorism, 1913–1920. *Journal of the History of the Behavioral Sciences, 17,* 399–425.

Scarborough (Goodman), E. (1971). Citation analysis as a tool in historical study: A case study based on F. C. Donders and mental reaction times. *Journal of the History of the Behavioral Sciences, 7,* 187–191.

Scarborough, E., & Furumoto, L. (1987). *Untold lives: The first generation of American women psychologists.* New York: Columbia University Press.

Schlesinger, A., Jr. (1963, July). The historian as artist. *Atlantic Monthly, 12,* 35–41.

Schmidgen, H. (2003). Wundt as chemist? A fresh look at his practice and theory of experimentation. *American Journal of Psychology, 116,* 469–476.

Scott, W. D. (1903). *The theory of advertising.* Boston: Small, Maynard.

Scott, W. D. (1908). *The psychology of advertising.* Boston: Small, Maynard.

Shields, S. A. (1975). Functionalism, Darwinism, and the psychology of women: A study in social myth. *American Psychologist, 30,* 739–754.

Shields, S. A. (1982). The variability hypothesis: The history of a biological model of sex differences in intelligence. *Signs: Journal of Women in Culture and Society, 7,* 769–797.

Shields, S. A. (2007). Passionate men, emotional women: Psychology constructs gender difference in the late 19th century. *History of Psychology, 10,* 92–110.

Simon, H. A. (1991). *Models of my life.* New York: Basic Books.

Simonton, D. K. (1990). *Psychology, science, & history: An introduction to historiometry*. New Haven, CT: Yale University Press.

Skinner, B. F. (1938). *The behavior of organisms*. New York: Appleton-Century-Crofts.

Skinner, B. F. (1971). *Beyond freedom and dignity*. New York: Alfred A. Knopf.

Skinner, B. F. (1983). *A matter of consequences: Part three of an autobiography*. New York: Alfred A. Knopf.

Skinner, B. F. (1990). Can psychology be a science of mind? *American Psychologist, 45*, 1206–1210.

Sokal, M. M. (1980a). *Science* and James McKeen Cattell, 1894–1945. *Science, 209*, 43–52.

Sokal, M. M. (1980b). Graduate study with Wundt: Two eyewitness accounts. In W. G. Bringmann & R. D. Tweney (Eds.), *Wundt studies* (pp. 210–225). Toronto: C. J. Hogrefe.

Sokal, M. M. (1981). *An education in psychology: James McKeen Cattell's journal and letters from Germany and England, 1880–1888*. Cambridge, MA: MIT Press.

Sokal, M. M. (1982). James McKeen Cattell and the failure of anthropometric mental testing, 1890–1901. In W. R. Woodward & M. G. Ash (Eds.), *The problematic science: Psychology in nineteenth-century thought* (pp. 322–345). New York: Praeger.

Sokal, M. M. (1984). The Gestalt psychologists in behaviorist America. *American Historical Review, 89*, 1240–1263.

Sokal, M. M. (1992). Origins and early years of the American Psychological Association, 1890–1906. *American Psychologist, 47*, 111–122.

Sokal, M. M., & Rafail, P. A. (Eds.). (1982). *A guide to manuscript collections in the history of psychology and related areas*. Millwood, NY: Kraus International Publishers.

Stagner, R. (1986). Reminiscences about the founding of SPSSI. *Journal of Social Issues, 42(1)*, 35–42.

Stocking, G. W., Jr. (1965). On the limits of "presentism" and "historicism" in the historiography of the behavioral sciences. *Journal of the History of the Behavioral Sciences, 1*, 211–218.

Storr, R. J. (1973). *The beginning of the future: A historical approach to graduate education in the arts and sciences*. New York: McGraw-Hill.

Stricker, G. (2000). The scientist–practitioner model: Gandhi was right again. *American Psychologist, 55*, 253–254.

Sulloway, F. J. (1979). *Freud: Biologist of the mind*. New York: Basic Books.

Terman, L. M. (1916). *The measurement of intelligence*. Boston: Houghton Mifflin.

Thompson, H. B. (1903). *The mental traits of sex*. Chicago: University of Chicago Press.

Titchener, E. B. (1898). The postulates of a structural psychology. *Philosophical Review, 7*, 449–465.

Titchener, E. B. (1901–1905). *Experimental psychology: A manual of laboratory practice* (4 vols.). New York: Macmillan.

Titchener, E. B. (1910a). *A textbook of psychology*. New York: Macmillan.

Titchener, E. B. (1910b). The past decade in experimental psychology. *American Journal of Psychology, 21*, 404–421.

Tolman, E. C. (1932). *Purposive behavior in animals and men*. New York: D. Appleton.

Tolman, E. C. (1948). Cognitive maps in rats and men. *Psychological Review, 55*, 189–208.

Triplett, H. (2004). The misnomer of Freud's "seduction theory." *Journal of the History of Ideas, 65*, 647–665.

Urch, G. (1992, August 9). Seeing the world through Rachel's eyes. *Chicago Tribune*, Section 6, p. 8.

Von Mayrhauser, R. T. (1989). Making intelligence functional: Walter Dill Scott and applied psychological testing in World War I. *Journal of the History of the Behavioral Sciences, 25*, 60–72.

Watson, J. B. (1913). Psychology as the behaviorist views it. *Psychological Review, 20*, 158–177.

Watson, J. B. (1914). *Behavior: An introduction to comparative psychology.* New York: Henry Holt.

Watson, J. B. (1919). *Psychology from the standpoint of a behaviorist.* Philadelphia: J. B. Lippincott.

Watson, J. B. (1936). John B. Watson. In C. Murchison (Ed.), *A history of psychology in autobiography* (Vol. 3, pp. 271–281). Worcester, MA: Clark University Press.

Watson, J. B., & Rayner, R. (1920). Conditioned emotional reactions. *Journal of Experimental Psychology, 3,* 1–14.

Wertheimer, M. (1912). Experimentelle studien über das Sehen von Bewegung. *Zeitschrift fur Psychologie, 61,* 161–265. English translation in T. Shipley (Ed.). (1961), *Classics in psychology* (pp. 1032–1089). New York: Philosophical Library.

Wertheimer, M. (1938). Gestalt theory [1924]. In W. D. Ellis (Ed.), *Source book of Gestalt psychology* (pp. 1–11). New York: Harcourt, Brace.

Winston, A. S. (Ed.). (2004). *Defining difference: Race and racism in the history of psychology.* Washington, DC: American Psychological Association.

Witmer, L. (1897). The organization of practical work in psychology. *Psychological Review, 4,* 116–117.

Witmer, L. (1907). Clinical psychology. *The Psychological Clinic, 1,* 1–9.

Wolfle, D. (1946). The reorganized American Psychological Association. *American Psychologist, 1,* 3–8.

Woodworth, R. S. (1916). Comparative psychology of races. *Psychological Bulletin, 13,* 388–397.

Woolley, H. B. T. See Thompson, H. B.

Wundt, W. (1862). *Beiträge zur theorie der Sinneswahrnehmung* [Contributions to the theory of sense perception]. Leipzig: Winter.

Wundt, W. (1874). *Grundzüge der physiologischen Psychologie* [Principles of physiological psychology]. Leipzig: Wilhelm Engelmann.

Wundt, W. (1896/1902). *Outlines of psychology.* New York: Gustav Sechert. Translation by C. H. Judd.

Zammito, J. H. (2004). *A nice derangement of epistemes: Post-positivism in the study of science from Quine to Latour.* Chicago, IL: University of Chicago.

Zenderland, L. (1998). *Measuring minds: Henry Herbert Goddard and the origins of American intelligence testing.* New York: Cambridge University Press.

Index